Theoretical-Practical Theology

Volume 4: Redemption in Christ

PET. VAN MASTRICT.
PHILOSOPH. ET· THEOL. DOCT. ET PROFESSOR,
in Academiis: Francofurt. ad Oderam, Duisburg. et Ultrajectinâ.
SYMBOL.
Ὅταν ἀφενῶς τότε δωνατόν
εἶμι.

Theoretical-Practical Theology

Volume 4: Redemption in Christ

by
Petrus van Mastricht

Todd M. Rester, Translator
Joel R. Beeke, Editor
Michael T. Spangler, Assistant Editor
and Translator

REFORMATION HERITAGE BOOKS
Grand Rapids, Michigan

Theoretical-Practical Theology, Volume 4: Redemption in Christ
© 2023 by The Dutch Reformed Translation Society

Reformation Heritage Books
3070 29th St. SE
Grand Rapids, MI 49512
616-977-0889
orders@heritagebooks.org
www.heritagebooks.org

Printed in the United States of America
26 27 28 29 30/12 11 10 9 8 7 6 5 4

Library of Congress Cataloging-in-Publication Data

Names: Mastricht, Peter van, 1630–1706, author.
Title: Theoretical-practical theology / by Petrus van Mastricht ; translated by Todd M. Rester ; edited by Joel R. Beeke.
Other titles: Theologia theoretico-practica. English
Description: Grand Rapids, Michigan : Reformation Heritage Books, 2018–
Identifiers: LCCN 2018014361 (print) | LCCN 2018028430 (ebook) ISBN 9781601785602 (epub) | ISBN 9781601785596 (v. 1 : hardcover : alk. paper)
Subjects: LCSH: Reformed Church—Doctrines—Early works to 1800.
Classification: LCC BX9422.3 (ebook) | LCC BX9422.3 .M2813 2018 (print) | DDC 230/.42—dc23
LC record available at https://lccn.loc.gov/2018014361

Contents

Part One, Continued
PROLEGOMENA AND FAITH
Book Five: **Redemption in Christ**

Chapter 1: *The Covenant of Grace*

The Exegetical Part

The Dogmatic Part

Chapter 2: *The Mediator of the Covenant of Grace*

Chapter 3: *The Names of the Mediator*

The Exegetical Part

The Dogmatic Part

The Elenctic Part

Chapter 5: *The Threefold Office of the Mediator*

Chapter 6: *The Mediator as a Prophet*

Contents

Chapter 10: *The Incarnation of the Mediator*

The Elenctic Part

The Practical Part

Chapter 11: *The Life of the Mediator*

The Exegetical Part

The Dogmatic Part

The Elenctic Part

Chapter 12: *The Death of the Mediator*

Chapter 15: *The Resurrection of the Mediator*

Chapter 18: *The Mediator's Redemption Itself*

Preface

It is our privilege to present the fourth of seven volumes of Petrus van Mastricht's *Theoretical-Practical Theology* in English. The previous volume treated God's works, in his decrees, in creation, and in providence (book 3), and then in regard to the fall of man into sin (book 4). This fourth volume opens God's great work of obtaining redemption in the Mediator, Jesus Christ (book 5). The application of that redemption (book 6), and its subject, the church (book 7), will follow in volume 5.

This volume is rich in topics worthy of introduction, many of which we will have to pass over here. For example, in 1.5.1 §XLI Mastricht touches on one aspect of the question of the republication of the covenant of works, a theme that will be considered at greater length in volume 6 (especially 1.8.3 §XLIX). In 1.5.8 §XXV, where he urges earthly kings to imitate Christ's kingship, he applies a doctrine of the relation of church and state which will be further developed in volume 5 (esp. 1.7.7 §X). In ten distinct questions in the elenctic part of 1.5.18 (§§XXIII–XXXII), he addresses antinomian errors concerning redemption, defending the length of his treatment not only from its relevance to his day, but from the tendency of those errors "to enervate all practice of godliness and Christianity" (§XXXII).

This is not to mention portions of his practical parts which are particularly rich in depth and detail: under Christ's resurrection, the road to Emmaus becomes a window into the manner in which a sinner is converted (1.5.15 §XXVII); the glory of Christ's ascension, and our duty to rejoice in it, is made more evident by comparing it to ancient Roman triumphs (1.5.16 §XIX); and that same ascension brings sweet comfort because Christ the Advocate possesses all the qualities people look for in the best of earthly lawyers (§XX). Especially noteworthy are his extended presentation of Christ's life as a model for that of the believer in all its stages, from raising infants to preparing to die well (1.5.11 §§XXXVI–XXIX), and his thirteen applications of the Mediator's death (1.5.12 §§XXIX–XLI).

There is one topic treated in this volume for which we will give a more extended introduction here, for our readers' better understanding: the nature of Christ's surety.

What is the nature of the salvation, according to the trinitarian counsel, that Jesus Christ as Mediator of the covenant of grace has accomplished and which God will apply to all elect sinners? A more important and foundational question regarding salvation could hardly be asked, but the answer must be developed and unfolded carefully. We beg readers' patience as Mastricht's fuller explanation of the application of the accomplished redemption must be extended over three volumes spanning almost 800,000 words. In part 1, book 5 (volume 4 in translation), Mastricht addresses redemption accomplished via the covenant of grace and its Mediator Jesus Christ. The covenant of grace in its definition as well as the requisite person and mediatorial work are exposited in the course of eighteen chapters here in volume four. Part 1, books 6 and 7 (volume 5), address the way redemption is applied to individuals via regeneration, union with Christ, conversion, and the several benefits that flow from it (part 1, book 6), and then the church, its ministers, sacraments, discipline, and governance (part 1, book 7). In part 1, book 8 (volume 6), Mastricht details the administration of the covenant of grace in history during the time of the patriarchs, Moses, and Christ, as well as eternity.

From the perspective of extra-Reformed debates in the period regarding the person and work of Christ, perhaps the starkest difference among those calling themselves Christians exists between the Reformed and Socinian positions. Confessionally, by way of contrast with respect to the person of Jesus Christ, Roman Catholics, Lutherans, and the Reformed, for example, do not take exception to the articles of the Nicaeno-Constantinopolitan Creed, though they do debate their meanings and implications. The Socinians, however, do take exception to the articles respecting the God-man as they do not confess a second person of the Trinity.[1] Viewed from the early creeds accepted by Roman Catholics, Lutherans, and the Reformed, the Socinians promote a form of Arianism as well as categorically deny orthodox trinitarianism.[2] Secondly, with respect to

---

1. See *Catechesis Ecclesiarum Polonicarum*, ed. J. Crell (Irenopolis [Rakow]: Fridericus Theophilus, 1659), 45–144; idem, *The Racovian Catechism of 1605*, trans. Thomas Rees (London: printed for Longman, Hurst, Rees, Orme, and Brown, 1818), sect. 4, ch. 1, pp. 52–55: "But do you not acknowledge in Christ a divine, as well as a human nature or substance? If by the terms divine nature or substance I am to understand the very essence of God, I do not acknowledge such a divine nature, for this were repugnant both to right reason and to the Holy Scriptures."

2. *The Racovian Catechism*, sect. 3, ch. 1, p. 34, "Who is this one divine Person? The Father of our Lord Jesus Christ." Cf. sect. 5, ch. 6, pp. 284–85: "Explain to me the other promise, and state what the Holy Spirit is? The Holy Spirit is a virtue or energy flowing from God to men, and

the work of Jesus Christ, in general the Roman Catholics at Trent (1545–1563) and the Lutherans in the Book of Concord (1580) received the Apostles', Nicene, and Athanasian creeds, and the Reformed heartily agree that Christ must die in the place of sinners to purchase salvation and redeem the debt of sin.[3] That is categorically denied explicitly by the Socinians in the Racovian Catechism:

> But did not Christ die also, in order, properly speaking, to purchase our salvation, and literally to pay the debt of our sins? Although Christians at this time commonly so believe yet this notion is false, erroneous, and exceedingly pernicious.[4]
>
> How is this opinion repugnant to the Scriptures? Because the Scriptures everywhere testify that God forgives men their sins freely.... But to a free forgiveness nothing is more opposite than such a satisfaction as they contend for, and the payment of an equivalent price....
>
> Let it be added that God himself has redeemed us, and given his most beloved son for us, without however paying any one anything for us; and that Christ has bought us to God in order that we might thenceforth be his servants.[5]

With these few exemplary statements, one can understand why Mastricht addresses the Socinians pointedly in every chapter of this work on the person and work of Christ to defend the confessional conclusions of the Heidelberg Catechism, the Belgic Confession, and the Canons of Dort. The Socinians erred by defect in their distortion of the biblical texts and their subversion of orthodox Christology. And as was noted in the last citation, the emphasis is placed upon the example that Christ has set and the obedience that we must render, not in salvation by Christ alone.

From the perspective of the intra-Reformed debate between the Voetians and Cocceians, the person and work of Christ as Mediator of the covenant of grace raises questions regarding the nature of Christ's *sponsio*, or surety, that is, his promise, in the eternal covenant, to procure redemption by bearing the sins of his people (on this, see especially 1.5.1 §XXXIV). Is it synergistically partial or monergistically complete? *When* is it complete? Is it conditional or

---

communicated to them, whereby he separates them from others, and consecrates them to his own service," and sect. 5, ch. 6, p. 289, "After you have explained to me what the gift of the Holy Spirit is, I wish you to inform me also, whether the Holy Spirit be a person of the Godhead? That the Holy Spirit is not a person in the Godhead you may learn from hence."

3. Cf. *The Canons and Decrees of the Sacred and Oecumenical Council of Trent*, trans. J. Waterworth (London: Dolman, 1848), Session Three, pp. 15–17; Heidelberg Catechism, Q. 22–58.

4. *The Racovian Catechism*, sect. 5, ch. 8, pp. 303–4.

5. *The Racovian Catechism*, sect. 5, ch. 8, pp. 304–5, 313.

unconditional, and if so, relative to what consideration? Given its completeness, then what of Old Testament believers prior to Christ's incarnation, life, death, resurrection, and session at the right hand of God? How is the redemption not yet accomplished to be already applied to them? And within the Old Testament, what of Old Testament believers prior to Moses but after Genesis 3:15? Do different time periods in the administration of the covenant of grace introduce different pathways and degrees of law and gospel? These are all questions that the Voetians, Cocceians, and moderating positions sought to solve. The present volume provides Mastricht's answer over eighteen chapters to the biblical questions what the Mediator must accomplish and in what way. Unlike his approach to the Socinians, Mastricht throughout his elenctic sections will address the Cocceians as *fratres* despite his sincere differences with them.

The *sponsio*, among contemporary theologians and historians studying Reformed theology, has stimulated several works exploring and evaluating the question of whether Christ was a conditional surety (*fidejussor*), the Cocceian position, wherein the Mediator takes on only the deficiencies in righteousness that the elect sinner cannot supply, or an absolute surety (*expromissor*), the Voetian position, wherein the Mediator takes on the entirety of the obligation.[6] Some have sought to arbitrate the question of whether Mastricht should be classed as a strict Voetian or a moderate one with appreciation for Cocceian dispensations of time in the economy of the covenant of grace.[7] Perhaps a better approach is to note that Mastricht structures his response to the Cocceians point for point, and while there may be engagement of their terms, frequently this is by way of clarification or rebuttal. The Cocceian theology certainly was a proximate concern in the Netherlands at the time with multiple proponents.[8] One might

---

6. J. Mark Beach, *Christ and the Covenant: Francis Turretin's Federal theology as a Defense of the Doctrine of Grace* (Göttingen: Vandenhoeck & Ruprecht, 2007); idem, "The Doctrine of the *Pactum Salutis* in the Covenant Theology of Herman Witsius," *Mid-America Journal of Theology*, 13 (2002): 101–42; Gyeongcheol Gwon, *Christ and the Old Covenant: Francis Turretin (1623–1687) on Christ's Suretyship under the Old Testament* (Göttingen: Vandenhoeck & Ruprecht, 2019); idem, "Petrus van Mastricht on Christ's Suretyship in the Old Testament" in *Petrus van Mastricht (1630–1706): Text, Context, and Interpretation*, ed. A. C. Neele (Göttingen: Vandenhoeck & Ruprecht, 2020), 71–89; Adriaan C. Neele, *Petrus van Mastricht (1630–1706): Reformed Orthodoxy Method and Piety* (Leiden: Brill, 2009), 261–62.

7. Gwon, "Petrus van Mastricht on Christ's Suretyship in the Old Testament," 76; Neele, *Petrus van Mastricht*, 68n28.

8. E.g. Wilhelmus Momma, *Disputatio Theologica de Oeconomia Temporum…sub praesidio… D. Johannis Cocceji…proponit Wilhelmus Momma* (Leiden, 1662); idem, *De Varia Conditione et Statu Ecclesiae Dei sub Triplici Oeconomia*, 2 vols. ([Amsterdam]: the widow of Joannes à Sommeren, 1673); Franciscus van Leenhof, *J. Cocceji Godtgeleertheydt verdedight en opengeleght* (Amsterdam: Johannes Janssonius van Waesberge, 1673).

observe that the Cocceians were viewed as erring by excess, for example, in the multiplication of divisions and distinctions regarding the Old Testament, such that salvation in the Old Testament was not substantially the same in the differing administrations since Genesis 3:15. In fact, some Cocceians argued that the covenant of grace started with Moses after a period of pre-Mosaic promise where sin and law were not active (cf. 1.8.1 §§XXXIV–XXXIX).

At the root of Mastricht's concern for these doctrines is the glory of God and his worship, as well as the solid progress of God's people. Without a solid understanding of the redemption we have in Christ Jesus, there is no solid joy and assurance. It is our hope that Mastricht's exposition will both challenge and comfort believers.

* * *

We give special thanks for the assistance of the several people who have helped prepare this text and its critical apparatus for publication, including Travis Fentiman and Gary and Linda den Hollander.

We commit our readers now to Mastricht's teaching, with sincere prayers that through it they "may be able to comprehend with all saints what is the breadth, and length, and depth, and height, and to know the love of Christ, which passeth knowledge" (Eph. 3:18–19).

—Joel R. Beeke
Todd M. Rester
Michael T. Spangler

Abbreviations

ANF	*Ante-Nicene Fathers*
FOTC	*Fathers of the Church*
LCL	*Loeb Classical Library*
LFC	*Library of the Fathers of the Church*
NPNF1	*Nicene and Post-Nicene Fathers*, Series I
NPNF2	*Nicene and Post-Nicene Fathers*, Series II
PG	*Patrologia Graeca*
PL	*Patrologia Latina*
ST	*Summa Theologiae*
TPT	*Theoretico-Practica Theologia*

CHAPTER ONE

The Covenant of Grace

I will put enmity between you and the woman, and between your seed and her seed: he shall crush your head, and you shall crush his heel.

—Genesis 3:15

The method and order of speaking

I. In the previous book we spoke of the apostasy of man, which occurred by the violation of the covenant of works, and of the utmost misery of the violator that resulted from it. Now follows his raising up[1] or restoration, by which he is raised from the state of sin and death to a state of grace and life. This is done in two parts: in redemption and the application of redemption. Both as it were lay claim to the covenant of grace as their norm, which has been substituted for the violated covenant of works. We will, Lord willing, handle redemption in the fifth book, and its application in the sixth book. Therefore we must first speak of the covenant of grace, next of its Mediator, or the Redeemer, and finally of redemption. We will explain the covenant of grace in the initial promise made to our first parents as sinners, immediately after the violation of the covenant of works, which occurs in Genesis 3:15.

The Exegetical Part

The text is analyzed and explained.

II. Although in these words the sentence is expressly contained wherein destruction is pronounced upon Satan the seducer, yet implicitly, not only is the promise of the restoration of the seduced present, but also all the material and essential elements of the covenant of grace (although the term and formal elements of a

---

1. Latin: *anastasia seu restitutio*; Dutch: *herstelling, waardoor hy opgebeurt en opgerigt wordt*; *anastasia*, "a raising up," or in other contexts, "resurrection": the opposite of *apostasia*, "apostasy," that is, "a falling away."

covenant are not so obvious), which we will clearly address in its own place.[2] The ancient Jews, in opposition to the modern Jews, seem at least to have acknowledged that there is a certain mystical sense present in the words, when they interpret them in that way. The Jerusalem Targum, interpreted by Paul Fagius, does so in this way: "And it will be, when the sons of the woman shall give heed to the law, and shall have kept the precepts, then they will be eager to crush your head, and they will slay you. Yet when the sons of the woman shall have abandoned the precepts of the law, and shall not keep the commandments, you will be watchful to bite them on their heels, and so harm them. Notwithstanding, there will be a *remedy* for the sons of the woman, but for you, serpent, there will be no remedy, seeing that it will come to pass that they remove the bite which was made on the heel in the *end* of days, that is, in the days of *Messiah*."[3] Nearly in the same words Rabbi Jonathan, according to the Swiss expositor, says the same thing, and slightly differently Onkelos, according to the translation found in Benito Arias Montano's *Antwerp Polyglot*.[4] Nevertheless, the words as they stand offer to us the condemning sentence of God against Satan, the seducer of the woman. Concerning this sentence are recorded:

A. The judge who condemns the seducer, and thus effectively promises deliverance to the seduced, and at the same time establishes the covenant of grace. He is included in the word אשית, "I will put," but who this is, is demonstrated in the preceding verse, ויאמר יהוה אלהים, "And Jehovah Elohim said," that is, Jehovah, one in essence, three in persons, to which words are joined a verb singular in number, so that it means that the triune God is the author of the covenant of grace, insofar as in the economy of the Trinity, the restoration of the sinner was agreed upon from eternity, and meanwhile, that the first promulgation of this covenant was accomplished through the work of that person, according to the economy,[5] through whom God speaks, that is, of the Son, who from אמר, "to say," in Aramaic is called מימרא, the Word; in the New Testament, λόγος, the Word, that is, ὁ ἐξαγγελτικός, the revealing Word,[6]

---

2. §§III–IV, below

3. On Gen. 3:17, Paul Fagius (1504–1549), *Thargum, hoc est, paraphrasis Onkeli chaldaica in sacra biblia…tomus primus* (Strasbourg: Jerg Messerschmidt, 1546), fol. [a7]r.

4. Benito Arias Montano (1527–1598), *Biblia Sacra Hebraice, Chaldaice, Graece et Latine*, 4 vols. (Antwerp: Christoph Plantin, 1569–1572), 1:9. This work is also known as the *Plantin Polyglot, Biblia Regia,* or *King's Bible.*

5. κατ' οἰκονομίαν

6. The 1749–1753 Dutch translation expands this term as: *het aankondigendt, het verkondigendt, het bekentmakendt Woordt,* that is, "the announcing, message-spreading, and expounding

as Gregory of Nazianzus calls him,[7] because he is the interpreter τῶν μεγάλων βουλημάτων τοῦ θεοῦ, of the great purposes of God, as Epiphanius says in *Panarion*, §73,[8] from the bosom of the Father, expounding mysteries (John 1:18), concerning whom Paul testifies that through him the mystery of the gospel has been revealed, which was kept secret from times eternal (Rom. 16:25; Eph. 1:9–10; 3:9; 2 Tim. 1:10). This certainly happened not only in the fullness of time, but also in the beginning of the world. This one condemned Satan (John 12:31) and declared deliverance to the woman, as the messenger of the covenant (Mal. 3:1).

B. The judgment, which is indeed a condemning one against the seducer, is a liberating one toward the seduced. For while in favor of the seduced, the one seducing is condemned, there is signified at least an inclination and benevolence toward the seduced; while to the former is proclaimed a curse, "You shall be cursed" (v. 14), to the latter at least a slender crack of blessing seems to be opened; while enmity is clearly enough placed in man against Satan, the enemy of God, it appears to be said that friendship with God will be restored; while it is said to the enemy of the woman that his head will be crushed, and all his power to harm will be taken away, is it not surely pronounced that the one seduced will be delivered? However, as a penalty to the seducer God pronounces enmity, concerning which these things must be observed:

1. The enmity as established: "I will put enmity," ואיבה אשית, "And I will put enmity." Here there is:

   a. The thing established: איבה. This the Vulgate renders *inimicitias*, "enmities," but more correctly it is "enmity," that is, one that will continue until the consummation of the ages. It denotes the most extreme and thorough opposition, πόλεμος ἄσπονδος, a war where there will be no place for either armistice or pacification (cf. Deut. 28:57; Ps. 7:5). The Septuagint translates it as ἔχθραν, the

---

Word"; cf. G. W. H. Lampe, ἐξαγγελτικός, "expressive," *Patristic Greek Lexicon* (Oxford: Oxford University Press, 1961), 489.

7. Gregory of Nazianzus (c. 329–390), *Oratio XXX (Theologica IV)*, §XX in *Patrologia Graeca (PG)*, ed. Jacques-Paul Migne (Paris, 1857–1866), 36:129–30, λόγος δὲ, ὅτι…τὸ ἐξαγγελτικόν; idem, *Fourth Theological Oration*, §XX in *Nicene and Post-Nicene Fathers*, Series II (NPNF2), ed. Philip Schaff and Henry Wace (New York: Christian Literature Co., 1890–1900; reprint Peabody, Mass.: Hendrickson, 1994), 7:316, "And he is called the Word, because…of his declaratory function."

8. Epiphanius of Salamis (d. 403), *Panarion (Adversus haereses)* in *PG* 42:428.

same as ἔχθος, hatred, and it seems it can be derived from ἔχεσθαι, to cling closely, such that it is a hatred that clings closely fixed in the soul, that is, an inveterate hatred. Moreover, there is understood not only a natural enmity between the animal serpent and man, whereby both sides strive for mutual destruction, but also, and much more, a spiritual enmity. On the one hand, this enmity speaks of a mutual contrariety and antipathy of nature, affections, and pursuits, and certainly in the seed of the woman it implies principles hostile to Satan and the works of Satan (that is, to sins), and thus regeneration, conversion, sanctification, faith, repentance, and so forth. On the other hand, it speaks of friendship and reconciliation with the Creator, insofar as not only can an enemy of Satan not but be a friend of God, from the analogy of Matthew 6:24, but also, that spirit hostile to Satan, conferred by regeneration, conversion, and sanctification, cannot flow from anywhere other than from the love of God. Accordingly, in this one enmity is included the whole business of restoration, as we will demonstrate more distinctly in its own place.[9]

b. Its establishment: "I will put," אָשִׁית. The Septuagint reads θήσω, "I will put." Piscator renders it, "I put," by an enallage of time,[10] because this enmity began soon after this sentence was delivered, namely decretively, if I may speak thus, and in an inchoate fashion, in the members, but by way of fulfillment and execution in the fullness of time. Therefore, it means that God established the work of redemption by an eternal decree, procured redemption in time, and applies it through calling, regeneration, conversion, sanctification, and so forth; and that he is the author, font, and source of it.

2. The enemies or contending parties, namely a pair of enemies considered in two ways:

a. The first way: "between you and the woman," בֵּינְךָ וּבֵין הָאִשָּׁה. Here the Septuagint translators render בֵּין as ἀνὰ μέσον, *per medium*, "by means of," but others more correctly as *inter*, "between." In these:

---

9. §§III–IV, below

10. Johann Piscator (1546–1625), *Commentarius in Genesin* (Herborn: Christopher Covinus, 1601), 72–73.

i.   The first party is the נחש, the serpent, in verse 14. What sort of serpent was it? Not only an animal, as some of the more recent Jews believe (cf. Rivet, *Exercises on Genesis*, ex. 25, and Pareus on Genesis 3:14–15),[11] because there is imposed a spiritual penalty, the curse, enmity, and crushing of the head. Nor is it only an immaterial Satan (Rev. 20:2), as it seemed to not a few fathers, such as Ambrose, Augustine, Gregory, and to other more recent contemporaries, because there is also imposed a corporeal penalty: "You shall crawl on the ground, you shall lick the dust" (v. 14). So then it is understood as both material and immaterial, and we have likewise considered this more carefully elsewhere, in book 4, chapter 1.[12]

ii. The second party: האישה, "and between this woman." The demonstrative ה denotes a certain woman, namely directly and in a restricted way, that very woman who was seduced, who is mentioned more than once in this chapter. She was thus named from *vir*, the man, because she had been taken out of man (Gen. 2:23). In that verse Pagnino translates the noun as *virissa*, which is hardly a Latin word.[13] Arias Montano has *virago*,[14] which denotes not just any woman, but a certain singular one, which the demonstrative ה clearly enough hints at, that is, (1) not the mystical woman of Revelation 12:1, as the Anabaptists believe without any reason, nor (2) only the blessed Virgin, according to the common version of the papists, approved by the Council of Trent, which by the treachery of Guido Fabricius, did violence to the original and authentic text, by replacing the masculine הוא with היא: both are grammatically inconsistent with the

---

11. André Rivet (1572–1651), *Theologicae et scholasticae exercitationes CXC in Genesin* (Leiden, 1633), 126–39; David Pareus (1548–1622), *In Genesin Mosis commentarius quo praeter accuratam textus sacri analysin atque interpretationem theoricam et practicam, controversiae et dubia fidei plurima perspicue explicantur* (Geneva: Pierre et Jacob Chouët, 1614), 539–73; idem, *Opera theologicorum exegeticorum*, 3 vols. (Geneva: Pierre Chouët, 1642–1650), 1:125–32.

12. 1.4.1 §§II.A.1, IX, XVII, esp. XXI–XXII

13. Latin translators had long attempted to match the Hebrew parallel in Genesis 2:23 for man and woman (איש and אישה), e.g. Santes Pagnino and John Calvin render them as *vir* and *virissa*, whereas Jerome's Vulgate has *vir* and *virago*. Santes Pagnino (1470–1536), *Biblia Veteris ac Novi Testamenti* (Basel: Thomas Guarinus, 1564), 2; cf. John Calvin (1509–1564), *A Commentarie of John Caluine upon the First Booke of Moses Called Genesis* (London: Thomas Tymme, 1578), 77.

14. Montano, *Biblia Sacra*, 1:6. The citation is to Montano's edition of the Vulgate.

masculine syntax[15] as well as with the subject matter, because properly speaking it was not the Virgin, or she only, who would crush the head of the serpent Satan, but immediately Eve, the only woman at this time, and mediately other women, by whose labors the Savior descended into the flesh, among whom the most proximate and eminent is the blessed Virgin.

b. The second way of considering the contenders: "between your seed and her seed." There is here:

i. The seed of the serpent: זַרְעֲךָ, "your seed," that is, of the serpent, of whom he had already spoken. זרע is employed either in its proper sense, insofar as it is in plants, trees, and flowers, insofar as likewise it is in animals, both brute and rational: namely, that stuff of generation,[16] from which each thing procreates something similar to itself; or in a metaphorical sense, and that either by metonymy, the matter for what consists of matter,[17] the subject for the adjunct, the container for the content, and thus in Haggai 1:11 the grain denotes the fields (cf. 1 Sam. 8:15), or by synecdoche and in a collective sense, posterity, descendants, and a multitude of persons from the seed, which meaning is obvious throughout the Scriptures. Again it is employed either regarding one certain individual, for example, regarding Seth (Gen. 4:25), Isaac (Gen. 15:13), Ishmael (Gen. 21:13), or preeminently regarding the Messiah, as we will see momentarily. Finally, it is used regarding children not by generation but by agreement, those who have been bound to someone, those who imitate another, and by their efforts express his character. And this sense of *seed* is taken, again, in two ways: first for the good part, regarding the adherents to the Messiah (Ps. 22:30; Isa. 53:10), and then for the bad part, regarding the adherents to Satan, partly among the devils, one of which is the chief[18] whom the rest follow, for which reason we read of Beelzebub (Matt. 12:24), and likewise "the devil and his angels" (Matt. 25:41), and partly among the impious, for which reason

---

15. The Hebrew verb connected to the pronoun in question is masculine in gender, as is the parallel pronoun suffix on the verb following that.

16. *illa generationis* ὕλη, i.e. matter, cf. Aristotle, *Physics* 1.7.

17. *materia pro materiato*

18. *Coriphaeus*

Isaiah 1:4 mentions a seed of the impious, and John 8:44 children of the devil. And this meaning of seed obtains here.

ii. The seed of the woman: וּבֵין זרעה, "and between her seed," that is, האישה, "of the woman," which, because the Septuagint translators in regard to both parties render the word by σπέρμα, and there is frequent mention of that word in the New Testament, it will be worth observing that it is used sometimes metaphorically, regarding the children of God or the regenerate (Matt. 13:38), regarding the word of God (1 Peter 1:23), regarding the posterity of Abraham, as much natural (Luke 1:55; John 8:33, 37) as spiritual (Rom. 9:8; Gal. 3:29). There are among the Reformed, and especially among the Lutherans, those who by this seed of the woman do not understand anyone except Christ alone, exclusively,[19] because throughout the Scriptures he is called the seed—the seed of Abraham (Gen. 22:18), of Isaac (Gen. 26:4), of Jacob (Gen. 28:14), of David (2 Sam. 7:12; 1 Chron. 17:11)—but especially because the apostle in Galatians 3:16 speaks of one seed, not of seeds, but ὡς ἐφ᾽ ἑνὸς, καὶ τῷ σπέρματί σου, "as of one, 'And to your seed,' which is Christ," and also because he alone crushed the head of the serpent. However, others, at least in my judgment more accurately, through that seed understand Christ with all his elect πληθυντικῶς, collectively—thus Calvin, Rivet, and Pareus, who in his *Calvinus orthodoxus* (p. 266), speaks in this way: "When Paul says that the seed of Abraham, to whom the promises were made, is Christ, he does not deny that the seed is collective, and signifies a multitude (for this is certainly assumed in the promises, 'Your seed will be as the sand of the sea,' 'I will be your God and the God of your seed,' and so forth), but asserts that, even if there may be many seeds which arose from Abraham according to the flesh, yet in the singular number, the promises are restricted to the one seed, which is Christ, that is, in the seed of Abraham are reckoned only Christ with his believing members, Jews together with Gentiles, the rest being an impure seed, and strangers to the promise, just as he says elsewhere, 'They who are the children of the flesh, those are not the

---

19. μονοπροσώπως

children of God, but those who are the children of the promise are reckoned in the seed.'"[20] Nor do the patrons of the prior opinion, after their Scriptures and reasons are brought forth, reach any further than to prove that Christ is truly that seed of the woman. Yet while we have stated here that the seed is collective, we want it to be understood in this sense, that Christ alone is the primary seed of the woman, while the elect are only the secondary seed; while Christ alone, with respect to this enmity, conquered the serpent, the elect only oppose him (1 Peter 5:9; Eph. 4:27; James 4:7); while Christ alone crushed the head of the serpent, the elect only wound it; while Christ crushed the head of the serpent for each and every one of the elect, the elect wound it only for themselves. Moreover, Christ is called the seed of the woman because he was made of a woman alone (Gal. 4:4), born of a virgin (Isa. 7:14), from which he also seems to be named שׁילה, *Shiloh*, in Genesis 49:10, which in the opinion of many comes from שׁליה (Deut. 28:57), the membrane with which the fetus in the womb is enveloped, or the *secundinae*, afterbirth, such that Shiloh is ὁ υἱὸς τῶν ὑστεραίων, "son of the afterbirth," or the seed of the woman.

3. The double enmity, or conflict of the enemies:

a. The prior conflict, of the seed of the woman against the serpent: הוא ישופך ראש, "he shall crush your head." This conflict includes:

i. The attacker: הוא, "he," or this seed of the woman. In place of this, as we have said, the papists read היא, "she."[21] It is referred to the most closely preceding word, זרעה, "her seed." It is understood, as we have observed, first and foremost as Christ, then secondarily as the elect, who in a different way contend with the serpent.

ii. The one attacked: "your," speaking of the head, that is, of the personified serpent, "with your seed."

---

20. Rom. 9:8 in David Pareus, *Calvinus orthodoxus, hoc est, doctrina orthodoxa Johannis Calvini de Sacrosancta Trinitate: et de aeterna Christi divinitate* (Neustadt: Harnisius, 1595), 263; idem (1600), 266.

21. Vulgate, Gen. 3:15, *ipsa conteret caput tuum*.

iii. The end of the conflict, or the victory: "he shall crush your head," that is, he will take your life, and all your power of harming him or his own (Heb. 2:14). Here is denoted:

 a) The crushing: יְשׁוּפְךָ, *conteret tibi,* "he shall crush you," from שׁוּף, which only occurs three times in the Scriptures, namely here, Job 9:17, and Psalm 139:11. It denotes "he crushed," "violently shattered," "ground down," "struck through." The Septuagint translators render it ἐκτρίψῃ,[22] "he will shatter," the Aramaic, "he will break in pieces," Rabbi Levi, "he will grind down."[23] The Targum of Jonathan explains it by "he will smite," the Jerusalem Targum by "he will kill," and Ibn Ezra by "he will strike through."[24] All these correspond nearly to the same thing, although not in the same mode of meaning.

 b) The thing to be crushed: "the head," רֹאשׁ. Some search here in vain for an ellipsis, so that it may be בְּרֹאשׁ, "on the head." It signifies, properly, the head, the chief member of the body; metaphorically, the highest power, excellence, and authority. At least for a serpent, its life is in the head, and thus when the head is crushed, it is dead (1 Cor. 15:54–56). Thus is signified that all power of truly harming Christ and his own will be taken away from the devil.

b. The latter conflict is in the words וְאַתָּה תְּשׁוּפֶנּוּ עָקֵב, "and you shall bruise his heel." There is here again:

 i. The attacker, וְאַתָּה, "and you," that is, the personified serpent, namely, first in your proper person (Matt. 4:1), then in your seed, in whatsoever evil persons, the Jewish common people, their nobles, the Pharisees, scribes, priests, in their prefects, Herod, Pontius Pilate, in the soldiers, as is evident through the whole history of the gospels.

 ii. The one attacked: "his," speaking of the seed of the woman, first the primary seed, his person, as the head; then the secondary

---

22. Cf. Gen. 3:15, LXX τηρήσει, and Job. 9:17, LXX, ἐκτρίψῃ.

23. *Pentateuchal Targumim: The Targums of Onkelos and Jonathan Ben Uzziel,* trans. J. W. Etheridge, 2 vols. (London: Longman, Green, Longman, and Roberts, 1862–1865), 1:166.

24. Cf. On Genesis 3:15, R. Abraham ben Meier Ibn Ezra (fl. 1165), *Ibn Ezra's Commentary on the Pentateuch: Genesis,* ed. H. N. Strickman and A. M. Silver (New York: Menorah, 1988).

seed, his members, that is, the elect, true believers, whom Satan continually has attacked and does attack (1 Peter 5:8).

iii. The end of the conflict, or the victory of a sort: "you shall tread upon his heel." There is here again:

a) The crushing, or the effort of crushing: תשופנו, *conteres ei*, "you shall crush for him." The Targum Onkelos renders this by נטר, "you will observe him," that is, "you will hold fast the memory of the injuries"; according to the Venetian edition it is זכר, "you will remember"; the Jonathan and Jerusalem Targumim have the verbs "to wound" and "to kill," as we mentioned just above.[25] Thus he has crushed him and his seed, by his temptations, persecutions, calumnies, and enmities of every kind, according to the history of the gospels.

b) The thing crushed, or to be crushed: עקב, "the heel," either "on the heel" or "following the heel." Certainly the verb form of this word denotes to wait in ambush, and to attack from ambush (Gen. 27:36; Jer. 9:4), though the noun means nothing except the heel. עקב, from the curved shape, denotes the outside part of the foot, a rather ignoble part of a person, where when a person is wounded, he derives no danger to his life. It is signified that Satan will cause Christ to suffer natural death, and that only for a brief time, for the three days, that is, of his being buried, from which wound he will be healed, in his glorious resurrection, ascension into heaven, and session at the right hand of God. Nor will he crush only him, but also his seed, the elect, with respect to their heel, by his temptations (Luke 22:31; 2 Cor. 12:2–4; 7; 1 Peter 5:8), by every kind of persecution (Job 1–2; Rev. 2:10; 12:13–17), and finally by temporal death, from which things he is called a murderer from the beginning (John 8), though at the same time, their spiritual state will remain unwounded (Rom. 8:28).

---

25. *Pentateuchal Targumim*, 1:166. The Venetian edition in question could be חמשה חומשי תורה, ed. Asher ben Jacob Parenzo (Venice, 1590).

The Dogmatic Part

God, with regard to the restitution of the sinner, inaugurated the covenant of grace. The promised restitution is proved from the text.

III. Therefore, it is evident that immediately after the fall, God not only promised restoration for miserable man, but also, in regard to that restitution, initiated the covenant of grace. We just previously pointed out the promise when we outlined the enmity put in place by God, in which most of the heads of the gospel are evident, namely that: (1) God is the author of all of our salvation. (2) He inaugurated the covenant of nature with man who was created in his image. (3) By its violation man became most miserable. (4) Nevertheless, to him he promised the Mediator, who would free them from their enemy. (5) This Mediator would be man, inasmuch as he would be the seed of the woman, who would have a heel to be bruised, as well as God, as the one who could conquer Satan. (6) And by his being crushed, that is, by his passion and death, he would abrogate all of Satan's power over himself and his own. (7) In addition, to his own, by his Spirit, he would bestow a heart hostile to Satan and his works (by regeneration, conversion to faith and repentance, and sanctification to a devotion to good works). (8) Also, after the distinction was made between the seed of the woman and the seed of the serpent, he would call the elect to faith by the voice of the gospel, and by that faith would unite them with him, and from this would communicate all saving benefits, justification, adoption, sanctification, and glorification. (9) Thus there would be a church, which would constitute the seed of the woman, as distinct from the seed of the serpent. (10) And the ministry of the Word would serve the gathering of this church, by aid of which ministry the promise made of restitution might be disclosed to the sinner, and he invited to embrace by faith, first the Mediator, then his benefits, procured by the crushing of the serpent's head.

It is demonstrated by the words of the text that the covenant of grace was erected.
IV.[26] Moreover, that in this promise are contained, if not all the formal qualities, at least the essentials of the covenant of grace, could be made evident in the following way. Among these essentials are: the author of the covenant, the covenanted parties, and the matter and form of the covenant, which all coincide in this promise, although unequally. (1) The author of the covenant of grace is God, and his pure, unadulterated grace, from which is the common phrase "my covenant," "I will make my covenant" (Gen. 17:2; Deut. 8:18)—with this agrees our protevangelium, "I will put enmity." And that there could not be here another

---

26. The 1698 Latin edition skips §IV and labels this as §V.

leading cause than his merciful good pleasure,[27] is evident from the condition of the most miserable violator, being guilty as well as dead. (2) The covenanted parties are the triune God on the one part, and the mystical Christ, that is, Christ with his own, on the other. They concur in the protevangelium, where: (a) God promises that he will establish enmity; (b) the seed of the woman, that is, Christ with his own, accepts the condition, and promises that he will crush the head of the serpent. For God could not have promised that crushing so categorically, if the seed of the woman, or the Son the Mediator, had not previously received it of his own right. (3) The matter of the covenant is the reciprocal promise, when God promises the restoration of the one fallen through the Mediator, the Mediator accepts the redemption, and his seed accepts the accepting of the Mediator, and his redemption, as well as the manner of life worthy of the Mediator and redemption. Concurring with this is the promise of the text, by which God promises enmity between the seed of the woman and the serpent; the seed of the woman promises that he will crush the head of the serpent, and in this Christ, certainly primarily, promises that he will crush it by his incarnation, life, and death; moreover, his seed or members, secondarily, promise that they in the virtue of their head will strenuously fight against Satan and his followers; and the whole mystical seed promises that it will suffer its heel to be crushed by the serpent, in temptations, afflictions, and death. (4) The form of the covenanting is the reciprocal consent of the parties, and this arises from what has been said.

The establishment of the covenant of grace is confirmed by the Scriptures and reasons.

V. Therefore it is evident through the text that in this first promise the covenant of grace is represented, and that without delay God substituted the covenant of grace for the violated covenant of works. So then: (1) there is a mention made of a new covenant, and God promises that he will erect a new covenant, either by establishing it, or by renewing it (Jer. 31:31, 35; 32:40; Heb. 8:8ff.). For (2) not without the universal and entirely hopeless destruction of the whole human race could God have chosen not to establish the covenant of grace, once the covenant of works was violated, since not inflicting death upon the violator of the covenant, or after sin giving eternal life on account of good works, or expecting perfect obedience from man dead in sins, then on account of that obedience rewarding him with eternal life, are inconsistent with his being God. Moreover, (3) out of the covenant of grace, the divine goodness, love for mankind, mercy, long-suffering, and kindness most brilliantly shines forth (Rom.

---

27. *nec aliam hic esse potuisse* προηγουμένην, *quam misericordem ejus* εὐδοκίαν

9:23). Finally, also (4) to restored sinners there is supplied from the covenant of grace a more effective stimulus to love, thankfulness, submission, reverence, and the other duties of religion.

The eternal covenant of grace, between the Father and the Son
VI. Moreover, there is a twofold covenant of grace: one eternal, the other temporal. The former was established from eternity between the Father and the Son and concerns the restoration of the elect sinner. The latter is established in time between God and the elect sinner. The former is like the prototype of the latter, the latter like its ectype. Both of these seem to be signified in Luke 22:29, καγὼ διατίθεμαι ὑμῖν καθὼς διέθετό μοι ὁ πατὴρ μοῦ, "And I establish by covenant for you, just as the Father by covenant has established for me, a kingdom." We will deal with each individually.

It is proved.
First with the eternal covenant. Certainly the term, if it occurs, is at least more rarely found, in the Scriptures as well as the fathers, and indeed the older Reformed, and yet it is evident that its substance does obtain, by more than one reason: (1) this covenant seems to be mentioned in the passage already cited, Luke 22:29, where the Savior says that a kingdom has been appointed for him by the Father by covenant. For this is the force of the word διέθετο, a paronym of which is διαθήκη, "covenant." To this end he says that a kingdom has been appointed or promised to him, that is, the mediatorial kingdom, as a reward for procuring redemption for the elect. (2) Likewise Galatians 3:17, where there is mentioned the διαθήκη προκεκυρωμένη εἰς χριστόν, the covenant already ratified in Christ, but promulgated four hundred years prior to Abraham, before the law. However, when was that covenant προκεκυρωμένη, "pre-confirmed"? Certainly from eternity, although its first promulgation was in paradise: you cannot reasonably designate a more suitable origin than eternity, when Christ was already foreknown, as is said in 1 Peter 1:20. To the same conclusion seems to point (3) Psalm 2:7, "I will tell you the decree," חֹק (decreed, that is, in the covenant), "the Lord said to me, 'You are my Son, today I have begotten you; ask of me and I will give you the nations for your inheritance.'" Here is told of a decree between the Lord, the Father, and his Son, and that also eternal, made when the Son was born, "today," that is, from eternity, and indeed, such an eternal decree that the Son could ask or stipulate from it. Nor differs from this (4) the passage Zechariah 6:12–13, "Thus said Jehovah of hosts, saying, 'Behold the man צֶמַח, the Branch, and from him shall branch forth, and he shall build the temple of the Lord, and he himself shall raise the temple of the Lord, and he himself shall bear

the glory, and shall sit and rule upon his throne, and he shall be a priest upon his throne, and the counsel of peace shall be between them both.'" Here is mentioned the counsel of peace, that is, regarding the peace and reconciliation of elect sinners, indubitably the same thing that was included in the counsel of peace, or the covenant. There are mentioned the covenanted persons, namely Jehovah and the man צמח, or the shoot. There is mentioned the duty stipulated by Jehovah of this man, "he shall build the temple of the Lord," that is the church, the house of God (1 Tim. 3:15 with Heb. 3:4; Matt. 16:18). There is mentioned the promise of reward: "And he shall bear the glory and shall sit and rule upon his throne, and he shall be a priest upon his throne" (cf. Phil. 2:9; Matt. 28:18). There is mentioned the consent of the parties, when it says that these things will certainly occur. The same also seems to be said in (5) Isaiah 53:10, where there are portrayed not only the contracting parties, namely Jehovah who crushes, and that righteous servant, or the Messiah; but also evidence of a contract, that is, the stipulation of the duty that is to be rendered by the Messiah, if he should give his own soul as an אשם, a sacrifice for sin; and the promise of reward, "he shall see his seed, he shall prolong his days, and the good pleasure of the Lord shall be prospered by his hand." Nor can anyone doubt regarding the consent of both parties. What therefore is lacking, on account of which there would not be here a covenant of grace? And (6) it is not for nothing that the Son frequently calls the Father *his* God (Ps. 22:2; 45:7; Isa. 49:4–5; John 20:17), which is the formula of the covenant of grace. Likewise, (7) that he employed the sacraments, which are seals of the covenant of grace (Rom. 4:11). To which, finally, (8) we subjoin the fact that all the essentials of the covenant of grace in the business of redemption are conspicuously identified between the Father and the Son, as we will demonstrate through its parts just below.

And it is vindicated.

The most specious thing that could be said to the contrary is in this, that since consent of the parties, through which their wills agree to the same conditions, is the form of a covenant, and such a consent between the Father and the Son could not have obtained from eternity, because to both belong one and the same will, there also cannot be allowed a covenant between them. We meet this objection by observing that just as in God the essence, one and the same in number, is as it were contracted through the characteristic properties in such a way that three persons are constituted, so also the will, which coincides with the essence, is as it were contracted in the same manner, so that to each person belongs, with the essence, his own will. This same thing is more clearly evident than the noonday sun in the internal operations of God, *ad intra*, as much in the reciprocal essential operations, by which for example, the Father knows the Son, and loves him, and the Son in turn the Father, as in the personal operations, by which the Father generates the Son, the Son proceeds through generation from the Father, and so forth. In addition, in the external operations, the same thing is observable in its own way, insofar as creation is asserted for the Father, redemption for the Son, and sanctification for the Holy Spirit.

What the eternal covenant of grace is
VII. Moreover, to us this covenant of grace is nothing but the personal and economic transaction between the Father and the Son, by which from eternity the Father required from the Son all those things which were necessary for procuring the eternal salvation of elect sinners, and promised, as if as a reward, among other things, the mediatorial glory; the Son on the other hand promised to the Father the things required, and in turn required the things promised to him, to the advantage of both parties. Each of these things in turn will be a bit more carefully explained.

It is an economic pact.
VIII. This covenant is, first, according to the nature of any covenant, a certain pact or transaction, but one that is personal and economic, such as there was also concerning the first constitution of man, among the persons of the Trinity (Gen. 1:26), and such as concerning the restitution of the same, to one more attentively observing, seems to occur between the Father and the Son in Proverbs 8:22–32, or at least in Isaiah 53:10. Moreover, what the economic operations are, we have already said in book 2, chapter 24, §§XI–XVI.

Its contracting parties
IX.[28] The contracting parties of this covenant must be truly distinct: for just as the Mediator is not a mediator of one (Gal. 3:20), so the covenant is not of a covenant of one (1 Tim. 2:5). Here the Father and the Son are such, as persons distinct not only in their modes of subsisting, from their characteristic properties, but also by this covenanting.

The Father
And certainly the Father, in this business of covenanting is such, as the Creator, who through the Son and the Holy Spirit brought forth all things (Ps. 33:6), and

---

28. The 1698 edition repeats §VIII, so section numbers are the same in Latin and English from here on.

thus as a potter (Rom. 9:21 from Jer. 18:6; Isa. 45:9), and likewise the begetter of the Son (Ps. 2:7). According to the economy he is considered as the Lord and Lawgiver, against whom we sinned (Ps. 51:4), as the Judge (Gen. 18:25), as the avenger of the law (Rom. 1:18; Nah. 1:2), and accordingly, God, not only theologically, but also economically, the one whom also, from this business, the Son frequently calls his God (Ps. 22:2; 45:7; John 20:17), who, in the order of reason,[29] as they say, first undertakes this covenant.

The Son

The Son, as the οἰκονόμος, steward, the Mediator and expromissor (1 Tim. 2:5; Heb. 7:22), our *Goel*, Redeemer (Isa. 38:14; Job 19:25), assented to the requirement of the Father (Ps. 40:7–8), pledged and promised himself for the elect sinner.

The Holy Spirit

Likewise the Holy Spirit, as the consummator of all things, through whom the Trinity executes all things, and as the emissary, consents and executes the agreements,[30] distributes his gifts among the elect as he wills (1 Cor. 12:8–9, 11), and regenerates (John 3:5; Titus 3:5; etc.).

The substance of the covenant: The Father's promises

X. The substance of the covenant, first generally, was the restoration of the elect sinner (1 Tim. 1:15), from which the Son is called Jesus (Matt. 1:21), and likewise Jesus is called "he who delivers us from the wrath to come" (1 Thess. 1:10), but specifically, there are mutual stipulations and promises. Indeed on the one hand are the actions of the Father toward the Son, and in them: (1) the promises made to the Son, namely, that (a) he would invest him with the most honored office of Mediator (Isa. 42:6–7; 49:6; Ps. 89:19–20; Matt. 2:6), and in that office, constitute him prophet, a light of the Gentiles (Isa. 42:6–7 with 50:4), high priest (Ps. 110:4), and king (Ps. 2:6–9 with Rev. 2:26–27; 19:15); (b) he would accept whatever he as Mediator offered for his own (Isa. 49:8; 42:1 with Luke 3:22), and thus he would give him the elect as his own possession (Ps. 2:7–8); (c) in the function of his mediatorial office, he would be near him by his grace, and would strengthen him by his power, against whatever difficulties he might encounter in the way (Isa. 42:5–7; Ps. 89:21–24; 2:4–6); (d) he would glorify him (Isa. 53:9–11; Ps. 110:6; Zech. 9:10), by resurrection from death (Ps. 2:7 with Acts 13:31,

---

29. *in signo rationis*
30. *pacta*

33; Ps. 16:8–10 with Acts 13:31, 33; Ps. 16:8–10 with Acts 2:25–32; 13:35–36), by assumption into heaven, as the throne of glory (Ps. 68:18), by being set at his right hand (Ps. 110:1), by being given all power in heaven and in earth (Matt. 28:18), by being given the authority of judging the living and the dead (Ps. 89:14 with John 5:22); (e) he would exceedingly exalt him, and would give him a name above every name, that to him all things that are in heaven, on earth, and within the earth should bow the knee, and acknowledge that he is Lord (Phil. 2:9–11); (f) he would raise up for him a seed (Isa. 53:10), innumerable in number (Gen. 15:5). These are the Father's promises to the Son.

The Father's requirements of the Son
(2) The duties stipulated from the Son, which generally consist in this, that he would offer all those things that would be necessary for the restoration of the elect sinner (1 Tim. 1:15). This is that will of the Father, about which Psalm 40:8 speaks (cf. John 6:39), and specifically, that (a) in the incarnation he would as it were be clothed with the flesh of those who would be restored—to this end he pierced his ears (Ps. 40:6), as Paul interprets (Heb. 10:5, 10); (b) he would willingly submit to the worst things that had to be suffered for the sake of restoring the sinner, that is, by draining that cup (Matt. 26:39); (c) he would offer his soul as a sacrifice, אשם, for sins (Isa. 53:10; Ps. 40:6–8); (d) he would generously dispense all the gifts necessary for the application or possession of the accomplished redemption in the sinners to be restored—the Holy Spirit, regeneration, conversion, faith, hope, and love—by rising again, ascending, and sitting at the right hand of the Father (Ps. 68:18 with Eph. 4:8). And these then are the acts of the Father toward the Son.

The reciprocal acts of the Son toward the Father
The acts of the Son toward the Father in this covenant, are, on the one hand, the promise by which he willingly receives to himself all the requirements of the Father (Ps. 40:6–11 with Heb. 10:5–11; Isa. 61:1–3 with Luke 4:18–21; Isa. 50:5–9), and on the other hand, the stipulation by which he seeks for himself the promised reward (Ps. 2:8, "Ask of me"), for example, the glorification of himself (John 17:4–5), the preservation of his own (v. 11), the sanctification of the same (v. 17), the glorification of the same (v. 24), and so forth. Therefore, the chief work of this covenant, at least with regard to the Son, was his solemn *sponsio*, surety, for restoring sinners, from which he is named ערב, "the one engaged" (Jer. 30:21), and ἔγγυος, "surety" (Heb. 7:22), through which he took upon himself once and for all the whole cause of restoring the sinner (Isa. 53:4, 7). And that not under a certain condition, if the sinner to be restored could not render the

things that must be rendered, but absolutely (Isa. 53:4, 7; Ps. 40:8). Thus this surety is not so much a *fidejussio*, conditional surety, as an *expromissio*, absolute surety, as will be spoken of more copiously in the next chapter.[31]

The consent of the parties of this covenant

XI. Finally, as in any covenant, especially that which exists between equals, a consent of the contracting parties is required, and that free, not extorted, and such that the things promised by it are within the power and ability of both parties. So it is also the case in this covenant, which is between equals who are entirely in possession of their own right,[32] and thus have both the authority by which they may contract *de jure*, and ability by which *de facto* they can render the things agreed. There is observed a consent of the Father and the Son on the things agreed, which consent, although we can sufficiently gather it from what has been said throughout the preceding section, Scripture also speaks of clearly enough, when: it declares that the counsel of peace was established in common by these two, the man *Zemach*, the Branch, and Jehovah (ועצת שלום תהיה בין שניהם, "And the counsel of peace shall be between them both," Zech. 6:13), which consent we have already vindicated in §VI. If you should say that this passage speaks about a future counsel, it would be easy to respond, that it speaks about a future counsel with respect to future execution, not with respect to the first establishment of this consent, unless you want to add an enallage of time, which occurs most frequently in the Scriptures, especially in continued actions, by which the future is taken for the past (Ps. 17:3). The Savior signifies the same mutual consent when he says that he came into the world to accomplish the will of the Father (John 4:34; 5:30; 6:38–40). And for this consent, that the Father was entirely free and self-determined,[33] either to save or condemn the sinner, no one can doubt; and also that the consent of the Son was equally free and self-determined, is visibly evident from Psalm 40:6, Hebrews 10:5, and John 10:11–12. For he voluntarily did whatever he promised and did for the sinner (John 10:18). Also this voluntary undertaking of the Son provided for the Father the foundation of that authoritative sending and sealing unto the mediatorial duties imposed upon the Son, which are designated throughout the Scripture (Ps. 40:6–7; Heb. 10:5; John 10:11–12), and from which he is also described as the servant of the Father (Isa. 53:11; 42:1, 6; 49:6; Zech. 13:7).

---

31. 1.5.2 §IX. Cf. esp. this chapter, §XXXIV.

32. *sui juris*

33. αὐτεξούσιον

The temporal covenant of grace. Its foundation

XII. We have seen the eternal covenant of grace; now follows the temporal, which has the eternal covenant as its idea, norm, basis, and foundation. It is elegantly spoken of in the parallelism between the first and second Adam (Rom. 5:14; 1 Cor. 15:22), that is, just as (1) the first Adam was the foundation of the legal covenant, so the second Adam exists as the foundation of the evangelical covenant. Just as (2) the first had his own natural seed, for whom he procured sin and death (Rom. 5:12), so the second has his own seed, for whom he procured righteousness and life (Rom. 5:15–17; Isa. 53:10–11; Ps. 22:30–31; 110:3; Heb. 2:13), which seed is the elect, those given to him by the Father (John 17:2, 9, 24), his sheep (John 10:15–17, 28–29), inasmuch as they are elect in Christ (Eph. 1:4–5), as if born from him, as the "Father of eternity" (Isa. 9:6), and thus his children (Heb. 2:13). Just as (3) the violation of the natural covenant implicated the first Adam himself together with his entire seed in sin and death, so religious obedience to the covenant of grace implicates the entire progeny of the elect and believing in righteousness and life (Rom. 5:18–19).

Its designation

XIII. This covenant is designated, first in the Scriptures, sometimes as the new covenant (Jer. 31:31; Heb. 8:8), which in nature as well as in time is different from the antiquated covenant of works (Heb. 8:17, 13); sometimes the law of faith (Rom. 3:27), because it stipulates faith from the elect, whereas the covenant of works is called the law of works, because it required exact obedience of the law, as the δικαίωμα τοῦ νόμου, the righteousness of the law (Rom. 8:3–4); sometimes the gospel of peace (Eph. 6:15), because it restores the peace taken away by the violation of the covenant; sometimes the gospel (Rom. 1:16), because the contents of this covenant are opened to us through the proclamation of the gospel, just as the contents of the covenant of works are opened to us through the law; sometimes the word of life (Phil. 2:16), because it alone recovered life for the sinner, whereas the violated covenant of nature is called the ministry of death and condemnation (2 Cor. 3:7, 9). Among theologians, to some it is called the evangelical covenant, whereas to them the violated covenant is called the legal covenant; others prefer it to be named the covenant of faith, because faith alone is stipulated as the condition. Most satisfying to me is the designation *the covenant of grace*, not so much because it is built upon divine grace, which obtains in the covenant of nature also, as because it is, in everything, directed by grace, such that there is nothing in it that does not breathe of every sort of grace.

The description of the temporal covenant of grace
XIV. Moreover, this temporal covenant of grace is nothing other than that gracious agreement between the triune God and the elect sinner, in which: according to the eternal covenant of grace, on account of the surety of his Son, to the elect individually he promises redemption, calling, regeneration, and the other means of salvation, absolutely, without any prerequisite condition; with respect to justification, adoption, and glorification, he stipulates from them faith, to which they bear witness by repentance and zeal for new obedience; the elect, on the other hand, promise to God the things required of them, and stipulate the things promised to them from God, to the glory of God and the Mediator.

The contracting parties
XV. Here the contracting parties are, on the one side, the triune God, who concurs in this business, not only as a party, but also as the author (Gen. 3:14–15; 17:1; 2 Sam. 23:5; Ps. 89:34; Jer. 32:40; Heb. 8:8–10), and he alone, inasmuch as he alone was wounded by the violation of the covenant of nature (Ps. 51:4), likewise he alone is suitable to devise and designate the method and laws of grace and remission, and he alone is capable to confer to them the promised benefits of the covenant. Moreover, God concurs in this covenanting under a double consideration: (1) theologically, not just as the benevolent Creator, who would establish a covenant of friendship, as he once did with the covenant of nature, but as the merciful deliverer, who would establish a covenant of reconciliation (2 Cor. 5:19). (2) Economically, insofar as the individual persons of the Trinity concur individually, and in individual modes (2 Cor. 13:14): the Father as the wounded Lord, who would reconcile the world to himself (2 Cor. 5:19); the Son as the intermediary and expromissor (Luke 22:29; John 10:28); the Holy Spirit as the consummator and executor of the covenant, who produces the stipulated duties of faith, repentance, regeneration, and conversion, and with these things supplied, applies the things promised, and as the seal, pledge, and earnest, seals them (2 Cor. 1:20–22; 1 Cor. 12:3; Eph. 1:13–14). As to the moving cause, there was properly speaking none in God, because he is in all things immovable and independent, for which reason in this matter his pure, unadulterated good pleasure is spoken of throughout (Eph. 1:5; Matt. 11:26). However, there does occur a double reason from which he does all things wisely: one with respect to God, the manifestation of the glory of his mercy (Rom. 9:23), and the other with respect to men, namely, their gracious restoration and eternal salvation (Rom. 9:23), and thus are mentioned τὰ σπλάγχνα τῶν οἰκτιρμῶν, "bowels of mercy" (Luke 1:54–55, 72–73, 77–78; Ezek. 16:4–9, 36:22, 32), just as the same reason is spoken of when it comes to the renewal of the covenant with Israel (Deut. 7:8;

10:15). Thus on the one side, God alone, by his mercy, exists as the cause of this covenant, as well as one of its parties.

And elect man

XVI. On the other side is man, but only elect man, as he is: (1) wretched, and from the violation of the prior covenant, endowed with no authority to contract, no strength to supply the stipulated conditions, and having nothing outside himself by help of which he could commend himself to God for covenanting (Titus 3:3–4; Ezek. 16:1–6); (2) foreknown by God, according to his most absolute liberty, to grace as well as to glory (Luke 22:32); (3) already included in the eternal covenant of grace, through the absolute surety of Christ (Heb. 7:22).

The substance of the covenant

XVII. The substance or matter of this covenant, first the general substance, was in the restoration of the elect sinner, and redounding from this, the manifestation of his glorious mercy; moreover, the specific substance was in the reciprocal promises and stipulations. God indeed promises here: (1) that he will deliver the elect from all misery, first of sins and then of penalties (Heb. 10:16–18; Jer. 31:31–35; Rom. 11:27; Heb. 8:8), that is, as through the disobedience of the first Adam many were made sinners and guilty of death, so through the obedience of the second Adam many are made righteous and heirs of life (Rom. 5:10, 12; cf. Ezek. 11:19–20; 36:25–27). (2) The bestowal of righteousness and life (Rom. 5:17, 21ff.), which things seem to be prefigured, first in the leading of Israel out of Egyptian slavery, and the leading of them into the land of promise (Gen. 15:13–15; Deut. 5:2–3, 6), then the leading of the Jews back from the Babylonian captivity into the Judean homeland (Jer. 24:5–7). These things include: (3) that he will redeem that elect seed by the blood of the Son, as the ransom for the sinner who would be redeemed[34] (1 Cor. 6:20; 1 Peter 1:18–19; Titus 2:14; Gal. 3:13); likewise, (4) the mediation of the Redeemer (1 Tim. 2:5); (5) the most exact satisfaction of the same Mediator for those who would be redeemed (Rom. 3:25; Eph. 5:2; Heb. 9:13–14; 10:11–15); thus (6) the reconciliation of the same, which would be procured and was procured by the satisfaction (2 Cor. 5:19–20); furthermore, (7) the application of redemption by the Holy Spirit, who convicts those who are to be redeemed of their sin (John 16:8–11), who regenerates (John 3:3, 5), makes alive (Eph. 2:5–6), renews (Titus 3:5), converts (Acts 26:18), effectually calls (Rom. 8:30), justifies (Rom. 5:1), adopts (John 1:12), sanctifies (1 Peter 1:2; 1 Cor. 6:11), and finally glorifies (Rom. 8:30), and

---

34. *peccatoris redimendi* ἀντιλύτρῳ

in addition, raises from the dead (1 Thess. 4:16–17; etc.). And by all these things, he presents himself as God to them, for all eternity (Gen. 17:2, 7; Jer. 31:33; Ps. 33:12). These are the promises of God.

The things stipulated from sinners and promised to them
XVIII. Moreover, God stipulates from the sinner who is to be restored, and the elect person also promises and pledges to God in this covenant that: (1) he, by a living faith, will receive God as his chief end, and his Son as the only Mediator (Ps. 73:25; John 1:12; 14:1, 6); (2) he will walk worthy of God, and in this covenant with God (Gen. 17:1–2; 1 Thess. 2:12; 2 Thess. 1:5, 11), and that he will in all things demonstrate to him his gratefulness for redemption, and for the benefits of this covenant (Col. 1:10–14); (3) they will be to God a people (Jer. 24:7; 30:22; Heb. 8:10), with all that they are (1 Cor. 6:19–20; 3:16–17; Rom. 12:1; 14:7–9; 2 Cor. 5:8), that they possess (2 Cor. 8:3–5; Phil. 3:7–8), and that they can either do (Phil. 1:20–21) or suffer for God (Acts 20:24; Heb. 12:4).

Together with the reciprocal stipulation of the elect
When the duties stipulated by God have been fulfilled, the elect also in turn stipulate and expect the benefits promised by God to them; in this is "the stipulation of a good conscience toward God" (1 Peter 3:21), that we may come with confidence to the throne of grace, and obtain mercy and grace (Heb. 4:16; Ps. 27:8).

The agreement of God
XIX. From what has already been said, the consent of both contracting parties to the reciprocal stipulations and promises, which is as if the form of covenants, is more than abundantly clear. On his part, God has made known this consent in all the more solemn renewals of this covenant: for example, in its first establishment (Gen. 3:15), its renewal with Noah (Gen. 6:18), with Abraham (Gen. 17:2), at Sinai with Israel (Ex. 34:10), with David (Ps. 89:3), with Israel before the Babylonian captivity (Ezek. 16:60), in the renewal promised and provided in the New Testament (Jer. 31:31; Heb. 8:7–9). And in turn, on their part, elect sinners supply this consent, frequently explicitly (Josh. 24:15–16, 21–22, 25; 2 Chron. 15:12–14; Ezra 10:3–4, 12), but most times implicitly, by supplying the things stipulated of them, as is evident in most of the renewals of the covenant of grace, for example, with Noah, Abraham, Israel, and day to day with the use of the sacraments of baptism and the Lord's Supper. Nor is it uncommon for there to be, even very frequently, a consent that is merely external, oral, and hypocritical (Ps. 78:10, 36–37; 50:16–17; Matt. 15:8), which if it is such as would not openly prove the one consenting guilty of lying, it makes him suitable for the church to

admit him to its communion, and to the privileges of the covenant that are only external and ecclesiastical (Acts 8:13, 20–21).

The covenant of grace is conditioned.

XX. And in what has been said it is apparent that, how, and to what extent the covenant of grace ought to be considered conditioned. Of course it is not conditioned: (1) such that God himself would be suspended upon faith or anything else in the establishment and offering of the covenant, or the conferral of its benefits, which all those who suspend both election and the covenant upon things foreseen desire. For Scripture constantly declares that the cause of establishing the covenant, and of admitting into it this one rather than that one, is only the good pleasure of his will (Matt. 11:26; Rom. 3:24; 4:16; 5:15–21; 9:15–16, 18; Eph. 1:4–5, 9, 11), as does right reason, which proclaims that God is independent in all things. (2) Such that any condition would be the meritorious cause of the benefits of this covenant, either from intrinsic condignity or from extrinsic agreement,[35] because the grace of this covenant, by which it differs from the covenant of works, in the constant tenor of Scripture excludes any kind of merit. (3) Such that it might be fulfilled by our own strength, because not only—and by this—is it different from the covenant of works, the condition of which was to be supplied by man's own strength, but also, through the violated covenant of works we are so dead in sins that we are unfit even for spiritual thought (2 Cor. 3:5; 1 Cor. 15:10). (4) Nor in such a way that some condition is prerequisite for acquiring each and every benefit of this covenant, because even calling, regeneration, conversion, sanctification, faith, repentance, and all those things that are accounted as means to the end of this covenant,[36] do not depend upon any condition that must be supplied by the elect, but upon the absolute good pleasure of the giver, just as with election itself (Jer. 31:33; Heb. 8:10). But rather, (5) because the rest of the benefits of this covenant—union with Christ, and flowing from it, the communion of his benefits, justification, adoption, sanctification, and glorification, that is, those things that are accounted more as an end[37]—by the establisher of this covenant are suspended upon a certain condition that must be supplied by the elect (Phil. 3:9; Gal. 2:16; John 1:12). Not to add that each and every benefit of the covenant of grace is suspended upon a condition that must be supplied by Christ (Isa. 53:10–11).

---

35. *vel ex condignitate intrinseca, vel ex pacto extrinseco*
36. *ea omnia quae habent rationem mediorum ad finem hujus foederis*
37. *ea scil. quae magis habent rationem finis*

Because it is accomplished by a mutual promise

XXI. Therefore it does not absolutely lack a condition because, according to the nature of any covenant properly speaking, it consists in a mutual promise, as its form, when: God on his part promises that he will establish enmity (Gen. 3:15), will give a seed to the Mediator (Isa. 53:10), a new heart to the elect (Jer. 32:38–39; 31:31–34); he stipulates from the Mediator that he should give himself as a sacrifice for transgression (Isa. 53:10); he stipulates from the elect that they receive him and the Mediator with a living faith (Acts 10:43; John 1:12); the Mediator, who accepts the condition, in turn promises it (Ps. 40:7–8; Heb. 10:5; Phil. 2:8); the elect likewise, once the promises made by God to them have been stipulated, promise in return their duty (Ps. 27:8; Song 2:16). Thus not even with respect to men, concerning which there is the greatest difficulty, is it entirely without any condition, as we will show more fully in the elenctic part.[38]

What the condition of the covenant of grace is

XXII. However, what the condition of the covenant of grace on the part of man is, is not defined in the same way by all. The papists prefer good works as meritorious causes, as do the Socinians, but as good works required by grace. There are those who prefer faith and repentance taken jointly, and there are several who are pleased with repentance, faith, and obedience. Most of the orthodox, with the Scriptures, most accurately admit here faith alone. At the same time, so that we may touch the matter with the most precision, it seems that there must be a distinction between a condition understood most broadly and more strictly. Most broadly understood it includes anything that is required in any way for the covenant of grace, whether: (1) antecedently, and as it were in a preparatory fashion, in which sense the hearing of the promulgated covenant, a general assent given to the divine Word, a conviction of the necessity of the covenant of grace, an effectual call to faith (prior to faith, if not in time, at least in nature), an acknowledgement and sense of one's misery, a godly desperation about oneself and all things outside the Mediator, and so forth, can be called a condition. Or, (2) concomitantly, in which manner self-denial (Luke 9:23; Phil. 3:4–12), the exercise of repentance (Mark 1:15; Acts 2:38–39), and so forth, can be taken as a condition. Or, (3) consequently, as covenantal duties, in which sense evangelical obedience (cf. Gen. 12:1–3; 15:18; 117:1–2; 9:1–15) and renewal of repentance (Deut. 30:1–9 with 29:24 to the end) can be admitted as a condition. More strictly and most properly understood, a condition denotes that by which, when it is given in man, from the divine promise, the covenant of grace is entered into.

---

38. §XXXVII

In this sense faith alone supplies the condition of the covenant of grace, for by this: (1) it is distinguished from the covenant of works (Rom. 3:27; 10:5–14); (2) it is denominated the law of faith (Rom. 3:27); and (3) its righteousness, the righteousness of faith (Rom. 10:6; Phil. 3:9; Heb. 11:7); (4) its covenanted parties are called οἱ ἐκ πίστεως, those who are of faith (Gal. 3:9).

The covenant of grace is not offered to and conferred upon each and every person.
XXIII. So then it is clear that the covenant of grace: (1) is not offered to each and every person, since each and every person is not called to faith (Ps. 147:19–20); much less (2) is it conferred upon each and every person, or established with each and every person, because by far the greatest portion of mankind is devoid of living faith (John 1:11; Matt. 20:16). Although at the same time, into the external covenant of grace (about which there will be more in its own place)[39] or into its external status, that is, into the ecclesiastical covenant, there are also admitted very many hypocrites, because they only profess the condition of the covenant of grace. Thus once under the Old Testament, the national covenant of grace was established between God and Israel, the entirety of Israel, and in it also with those whom God had not given a heart to know, and eyes to see, with all of them indiscriminately—infants, women, foreigners, cutters of wood, with those present and those absent (Deut. 29:1–2, 4, 10–11, 14–15; Ps. 81:7, 10–11; Isa. 1:3, 12). Under the New Testament the parables seem to point to the same end (Matt. 13:24–25, 47; 3:12; 2 Tim. 2:20). But at present this external and ecclesiastical covenant is not our concern.

The qualities of the covenant of grace are that it is:
1. Gracious
XXIV. And so this covenant (with respect to its properties and qualities) is: (1) most gracious (Rom. 4:16), insofar as, led by sheer grace, God (a) established the covenant, (b) gave the Mediator, (c) accepted the mediation, (d) confers the condition of the covenant, (e) through faith, gives the Mediator with all his benefits, such that for conferring these things, God not only stipulates from the elect no meritorious cause, but no cause at all. Indeed, he rests satisfied in only the condition of faith (Rom. 3:28; Gal. 2:16; Eph. 2:8).

2. Holy
It is (2) holy (Dan. 11:28, 30; Luke 1:72; Ps. 105:42–43), insofar as (a) its author is the thrice holy one (Isa. 6:3), and holiness itself (Ps. 89:35); (b) its Mediator

---

39. §XXVIII, below

is that Holy One (Acts 2:27; 13:35) whom the Father sanctified (John 10:36); (c) its parties are holy, God on the one side, the elect on the other (Heb. 3:1; 1 Peter 1:22; 2:5; Eph. 2:21; Deut. 7:6); (d) the matter or business of this covenant is holy, that is, to transfer a sinner by sanctification from the state of sin into a state of righteousness and life; and finally, (e) its condition is a holy faith (Jude 20), to walk before God in holiness and righteousness throughout all the days of our life (Luke 1:75), to perfect holiness in the fear of God (2 Cor. 7:1).

3. Ordered

It is (3) arranged or ordered in all things, ברית ערוכה בכל, a covenant ordered in all things (2 Sam. 23:5), insofar as both (a) its material components are with exceeding skill mutually subordinated and coordinated: God, from his side, promises restoration through his Son the Mediator from the state of sin and death into a state of righteousness and life, and then at length that he will be God to those who are restored; the Mediator accepts the cause of the sinner, that for his sake he will crush the head of the serpent; the person to be restored accepts the promise, accepts for himself God and the Mediator with a living faith, offers himself grateful to both, and walks as is worthy of this covenant. And (b) its formal components involve mutual consent, stipulation and restipulation, and obligation of the parties. How brilliantly here are all things arranged!

4. Firm

(4) It is firm and immovable, from the side of God, in all things solemnly preserved, שמורה (2 Sam. 23:5), from שמר, which (as Mercier observes upon Santes Pagnino's *Thesaurus*) denotes care, concern, and diligence so that nothing is omitted, lapsed, or cast off.[40] For which reason it is called incorruptible (Jer. 33:20–21), a promise sure to all the seed, βεβαία παντὶ τῷ σπέρματι (Rom. 4:16), πρᾶγμα ἀμετάθετον, an immutable thing, of God who cannot lie, confirmed by a promise and an oath (Heb. 6:17–18). This is so: (a) from the immutable nature of God (Dan. 9:4; Neh. 1:5; 9:32; 1 Kings 8:23; 2 Chron. 6:14); (b) from the most solid method of settling it, for he promised it (Gen. 17:2), he rather frequently repeated it (Deut. 7:12; Judg. 2:1; Ps. 89:34–35; 111:5), he confirmed it with covenantal solemnities, with sacrifices and splitting of livestock (Gen. 15:8–10, 17–18; Ps. 50:5; Jer. 34:18), likewise with signs and seals (Gen. 17:11; Rom. 4:11), with an oath (Heb. 6:16–18; Deut. 29:12, 14; Ps.

---

40. Jean Mercier (c. 1510–1570), commenting on Santes Pagnino, *Thesaurus linguae sanctae, sive Lexicon Hebraicum…Opera Joannis Merceri, Ant. Ceuallerij et B. Cornelij Bertrami* (Lyon: Bartholomaeus Vincentius, 1575), 3042.

89:3–4), and with the very death of the testator (Gal. 3:15 with Heb. 9:15–18); and (c) from its meticulous actual observance in all places and times, as we will specifically expand upon in its own place,[41] through all the periods of both testaments, from head to heel of the created world.

5. Eternal

So then finally, it is (5) eternal, ברית עלם, a covenant of eternity (Gen. 17:19; Isa. 24:5; 55:3; 61:8; Jer. 32:40; Ezek. 16:60), διαθήκη αἰώνιος, an eternal covenant (Heb. 13:20), that is, with respect to its substantials, although with respect to its circumstantials, or mode of administration, after the last judgment it will come to cease.

A comparison of the covenant of grace with the covenant of works:
With respect to their agreement
XXV. From what has been said, without difficulty will be made known, first the agreement, and then the difference of the two covenants, of works and of grace. The first (the agreement) is evident in (1) the author of both covenants, God (Gen. 2:16–17 with 3:15; Jer. 32:38–40; Heb. 8:8); (2) the impelling cause, the divine good pleasure (Gen. 2:16–17; 1 Cor. 4:7 with Ezek. 16:1–8; 36:22, 32); (3) the contracting parties, God and man, not an angel or brute beast (Gen. 2:16–17 with 17:2); (4) the matter and substance of the covenant, insofar as in both God promises and stipulates (Gen. 2:16–17; 3:15; Deut. 5:1–2); (5) the reciprocal consent and obligation, which is like the form of every covenant; (6) the goal, the manifestation of his glory and the communication of blessedness. Thus far the agreement.

With respect to their difference, in eight particulars: 1. Nature, 2. Impelling cause, 3. Contracting parties, 4. The matter of the covenant
XXVI. The second (namely, the difference of the two covenants) is seen in: (1) their nature, since the former was, as it were, a covenant of friendship between the Creator and the creature, whereas the latter is one of reconciliation between enemies; (2) the impelling cause,[42] which in the first was the grace of benevolence, in the second the grace of pity; (3) the covenanted parties, for in the former, the one party was God as the benevolent Creator, and the other, in Adam, the whole human race; in the latter, the one party was God as the merciful Redeemer, and the other the mystical Christ, or, in Christ, only the elect seed,

---

41. 1.8.1–4
42. *causa* προηγουμένῃ

or the seed of the woman; (4) the matter of the pact, since in the first covenant God prescribed the obedience of works, and in it, faith also in God, as his Creator (Rom. 3:27; Gal. 3:11–12), an obedience to be provided by man himself, by his own strength (Gen. 2:16–17; Gal. 3:10), in which the condition was natural, and in return he promised life as the reward for righteousness, and that after a perfect, perpetual, and personal obedience, with all repentance and remission excluded, even after the least fault;[43] yet he did not add also the strength by which that exact obedience might continue. On the contrary, in the second, so that the covenant might be established, he does not prescribe anything properly speaking for a condition except faith, and that not only in him as the Creator, but also in the Son as the Mediator (John 14:1), and to be supplied not by one's own strength, but by a strength communicated and to be communicated from the covenant, and indeed as an entirely supernatural condition, and that not as perfect in every way, but only as sincere. In turn he promises not only life of every sort, but also the strength necessary to supply the condition of the covenant; indeed, he even promises the condition itself. Additionally, after faults, he accepted repentance and promised remission; indeed, he also promised life, not as the reward of righteousness, but as the gift of grace.

5. The form of the covenant

(5) The form of the covenant, or the diverse method: (a) of revealing, for whereas (i) the first was promised and established at one and the same time (Gen. 2:16–17), the second was certainly promised throughout the Old Testament, but was established at last in the blood of the Mediator under the New Testament. Whereas (ii) the condition of the first was known by nature, the condition of the second cannot become known except by extraordinary revelation. (b) Of ratifying and establishing, for whereas the first began by a commandment of duty, a threat of death in case of disobedience, an implied promise in the case of a fulfilled condition, with two sacramental trees added, and without any Mediator, the second prescribes a condition, promises a reward, with added signs, but all these things are found in no other way than in the Mediator Jesus. (c) Of administrating, since (i) the first covenant is accomplished by a natural inscription (Rom. 2:14–15), the second by a supernatural inscription (Heb. 8:10); (ii) the first only by voice, the second by voice and Scripture simultaneously; (iii) the first dispenses the benefit of life as wages from the merit of perfect obedience, the second as a reward from the grace of faith.

---

43. ἥττημα

6. Properties

(6) Properties and perfections: (a) the first resulted only from the grace of benevolence, the second in addition from the grace of pity. (b) The first was uncertain with respect to its outcome, the second most certain and immovable. (c) The first was profitable only for a perfect person, the second for a sinner. (d) The first lasted inviolate for a short time, the second will last eternally, without any total violation. (e) The former is abolished by the latter, with respect to those who are partakers of the latter.

7. Fruits

(7) Fruits and effects: (a) the first offered communion with God as the Creator, the second presents it as with the Redeemer in the Christ. (b) The first would have elevated the perfectly just man to the dignity of a servant of God, by which he would have been a little lower than the angels (Ps. 8:5), the second elevates him to the dignity of a son, heir, joint heir, and member of Christ, by which he becomes, in his own way, a little higher than the angels. (c) The first did not exclude all boasting (Rom. 3:27), the second thoroughly excludes it (Eph. 2:9). (d) The first presupposed perseverance as a condition, the second confers the same as a benefit.

8. Ends

(8) Finally, its ends: (a) the first intended to reveal only the glory of God's dominion, liberty, wisdom, goodness, and righteousness, the second in addition the riches of his mercy, patience, and longsuffering. (b) The first displayed the glory of God in dealing with the creatures without any Mediator, the second in the Mediator, the Son (John 5:22–23).

Six consequences from the covenant of grace
XXVII. From what has been said it is clear that: (1) once the covenant of grace was established, the covenant of works was thoroughly abrogated, at least with respect to its efficacy for justifying and saving, for which reason also Christ can be called the end of the law for justification to everyone who believes (Rom. 10:4). (2) Once we faithfully have received the condition of the covenant of grace, the covenant of works immediately becomes void with respect to its force for condemning (Rom. 8:1). Accordingly, (3) the same persons cannot simultaneously be under the covenant of works and under the covenant of grace (Rom. 11:6), although they can be so successively, first under the covenant of works, and then under the covenant of grace; however, not in the reverse order. So then also, (4) the covenant of grace surpasses the covenant of works by a thousand

miles, for: (a) the covenant of works was from God as the generous Creator, the covenant of grace is from the same as the merciful Redeemer. (b) The former is from benevolence alone, the latter in addition from mercy. (c) The former was in the first Adam with a mere man, the latter in the second Adam with Christ the God-man.[44] (d) The former demanded exact and perpetual obedience from man himself, the latter the righteousness and obedience of Christ the God-man. (e) The former was founded on a perfect nature without a mediator, the latter on the most perfect grace of Christ the Mediator. (f) The former was mutable, the latter eternal. (g) The former produced a servant of God, the latter preeminently a son, heir, and joint heir with Christ. (h) The former concerned the exalting of the glory of divine wisdom, goodness, and righteousness, the latter in addition the glory of mercy and longsuffering. Therefore also, (5) it is in many ways better to be under the covenant of grace than under the covenant of works, since those who are under the former are under a curse and death, whereas those who are under the latter are under a blessing and life. Finally, from this, (6) although we all prior to the fall were greatly obligated to God from the covenant of works, yet after the fall we are a thousand times more obligated from the covenant of grace, because though in the one the infinite God did as it were descend to the finite creature, additionally in the latter he descended to the sinner, his enemy; in the former God conferred great goodness upon the creature, who certainly did not deserve any good, in the latter, every grace upon the sinner, who deserved nothing but punishment; God supplied much more for us according to the covenant of grace in the second Adam than according to the covenant of works in the first: by the former he conferred a single blessedness, by the latter, a double.

The twofold communion of the covenant of grace
XXVIII. There are three things that are part of this covenant of grace: the communion of the covenant, the promulgation of the same, and its dispensation. First is the communion or communication of the benefits of this covenant, which is twofold: for since this covenant has promise of this life, and of that which is to come (1 Tim. 4:8), just as the covenant with Abraham had the promise of the land of Canaan and other temporal benefits, and in addition the spiritual promise, "I will be your God" (Gen. 17:7–8), which can also be separated, as is evident among the Israelites, some of whom enjoyed only the temporal benefits, and others in addition the spiritual benefits, and since, moreover, the stipulated duties of the covenant of grace are received by some indeed only by an external profession of the mouth, as we have already taught (from Matt. 15:9; Ps. 78:10,

---

44. *cum Christo* θεανθρώπῳ

32–33; Matt. 7:21–22),[45] though others receive it also by an internal profession of the heart (Acts 8:37; Rom. 10:10). So then there also arises a twofold communion of the covenant of grace: one total, or as others say, internal, by which those who give assent to the stipulations of the covenant genuinely (that is, with heart and mouth), or the children of the promise (Rom. 9:8), become participants in all the promises (2 Cor. 1:20), as much the spiritual as the corporeal (1 Tim. 4:8); the other, partial or external only, by which the sons of the kingdom (Matt. 8:12) who do not receive the conditions of the covenant genuinely, but only by mouth without the heart, or only by an external profession (Matt. 7:21–22; etc.), become participants in the external ecclesiastical privileges and the temporal benefits only, just as once under the old dispensation the impious and hypocrites among the Israelites, who enjoyed only the external privileges and benefits of the church (1 Cor. 10:1–6; Ps. 115:9–11), as well as under the new, for example, Judas Iscariot (Matt. 10:1, 4), Simon the Magician (Acts 8:13), and all the temporary ones[46] (Matt. 13:3ff.), the branches in Christ that do not bear fruit (John 15:2). In this sense it is said that many are called, but few are chosen (Matt. 20:16; 22:14).

The promulgation of the covenant of grace, or the gospel
XXIX. Second is the promulgation of the covenant of grace, which forms the gospel, just as the promulgation of the covenant of works, the law. *Evangelium,* "gospel," from εὐαγγέλλω, "I announce good things," is here to us not a reward, good things to the one announcing, such as is customarily given, but the announcement of a good thing. With respect to the term, it seems to have been borrowed from the Septuagint, from Isaiah 52:7 and 61:1. Also, here to us it is neither the instrument in which the acts of this covenant are publicly written, in the way we enumerate the four Gospels, nor the gospel doctrine itself contained in these Gospels, or in the entire Holy Instrument. When these were less accurately distinguished among themselves, they presented an opportunity to adversaries for confusing the covenant of works with the covenant of grace, because they observed that in both places, as much in the Old Testament as in the New, or, as they say, as much in the law as in the gospel, is urged the exercise of good works. Accordingly in addition, in their opinion there arises a triple law—natural, Mosaic, and evangelical—and so then a triple way of obtaining eternal life, namely through the observance of the natural law under the patriarchs, the Mosaic law up to Christ, and the evangelical law to the end of

---

45. §XXIII, above
46. πρόσκαιροι

the age. The gospel, as the promulgation of the covenant of grace, includes two parts, namely, the covenant of grace, as its material part; and the promulgation, as its formal part, just as the law, as the promulgation of the covenant of nature, includes as many things: the covenant of nature, and its promulgation. From this it is easy to perceive that these two agree, namely with respect to promulgation, as likewise they differ, namely as the covenant of nature and of grace.

It is opposed to the law.

XXX. Therefore it is not promulgated by any law, namely, not by the Decalogue, inasmuch as it demands those works by the rendering of which our first parents in the state of creation would have merited eternal life for themselves, concerning which applies, "Do this, and you shall live" (Lev. 18:5; Rom. 10:5; Ezek. 20:11; Luke 10:28), as well as, "Cursed is he who will not remain in all things which are written in the book of the law, to do them" (Deut. 27:26; Gal. 3:10), by which law cannot but be understood the Decalogue. Thus to this extent, with respect to fallen man, they are mutually contrary to one another, they are mutually exclusive, such that he who is under the law cannot be under grace and the gospel, and vice versa (Rom. 4:14–15; 6:14–15; 7:1ff.; 9:31–32; 10:3; Gal. 3:5; 5:4). For this reason, the gospel, as such, does not contain the law, just as the law, as such, does not contain the gospel, although from the fact that faith is demanded by God as a condition of the covenant of grace, it is called the law of faith (Rom. 3:27), and its rendering, the work of faith (John 6:29).

The law is subordinate and serves the same.

XXXI. Nevertheless, by this it does not become the case that, under a different consideration, they in many ways are not subordinated to and serve each other. Thus the law is said to be a tutor to Christ (Gal. 3:24), and the end of the law, Christ (Rom. 10:3–4), in which respect it is denied that the law is against the promise (Gal. 3:21). The law serves the gospel: (1) when the former prescribes righteousness to man (Lev. 18:5), the latter supplies it (Rom. 8:2–3); (2) the former imposes a curse upon the sinner (Deut. 27:26), the latter removes it from him (Gal. 3:10, 13); (3) the former lays the sinner low with the threat of the curse (Ps. 51:3 with v. 8), the latter raises up the one prostrated with the promise of grace (Matt. 11:28); (4) the former displays the necessity of deliverance and a deliverer and kindles a desire for both (Rom. 7:24; Acts 2:37; 16:30), the latter satiates that desire by conferring them (Acts 2:38; 16:31); (5) the former designates the manner of living and gratitude which the latter requires (Rom. 3:31; Gal. 3:17, 19; Luke 1:74–75).

The gospel is twofold: of promise and fulfillment

XXXII. So then, among theologians the gospel has been customarily divided into the gospel of promise and of fulfillment, insofar as in the former both redemption and the Redeemer are only promised, but in the latter they are exhibited (Gal. 4:4; Heb. 1:1). For this reason the former was much more incomplete, obscure, and narrow than the latter, as we expressly show in its own place.[47] In both of these gospels, the covenant of grace is either only external, ecclesiastical, and national, in which the internal covenant is only offered, in which sense, prior to Christ, God entered into covenant with the entire Jewish nation, with each and every member of it, even the wicked, insofar as God chose only that nation from all others as a people for himself (Deut. 4:37; 7:6–7; 10:15; 14:2; Isa. 41:8–9), to which alone he would offer the spiritual benefits of the covenant of grace (Ps. 147:19–20; Rom. 9:4), and which would also receive the conditions of the covenant, at least with respect to profession (Ps. 50:16). Just as also under the New Testament, in the same sense, the ecclesiastical covenant of grace and its temporal benefits are extended to any who, at least by profession, receive the condition of the covenant of grace offered to them in the gospel, although they do not actually fulfill it. To this points the comparison of the unclean threshing floor (Matt. 3:12), and of the field planted differently in different parts (Matt. 13:3); and in particular, the temporary ones (Matt. 13:21), the sons of the kingdom who shall be cast out (Matt. 8:12), the branches in Christ that do not bear fruit (John 15:2), among whom was Judas (Matt. 10:1, 4), Simon the Magician (Acts 8:13), those who say and do not do (Matt. 7:22), in which sense it is said that many are called, but few are chosen (Matt. 20:16), as we taught just above.[48]

The dispensation of the covenant, that is, the testament

XXXIII. Third is the dispensation of the covenant of grace, which forms the testament. For a testament is nothing except a dispensation of the covenant of grace, insofar as that dispensation depends upon the death of the testator, Christ. Accordingly (just like the gospel), it implies two things, namely, the covenant of grace and its promises, and also its dispensation according to the difference of the times, but under this reckoning: insofar as that dispensation depends upon the death of the testator, from which arises the denomination *testament*. So then, the covenant of grace is also designated as a testament (Heb. 9:15–22), under which meaning come ברית and διαθήκη (Ex. 24:8 with Heb. 9:20; Gal. 3:15). For (1) it totally depends upon and is ratified by the death and blood of the

---

47. 1.8.3 §VIII
48. §XXVIII

testator (Ex. 24:8; Heb. 9:15), whether it be typical, under the Old Testament (Lev. 14:4–7; Ps. 51:7), or proper (Zech. 9:11; Heb. 10:29; 13:11–12, 20; Rom. 3:25; Matt. 26:28). (2) It acknowledges a testator, Christ the Mediator (Heb. 9:15; 12:24). (3) It confers the benefit of eternal life, not as wages, but as an inheritance, and that to the covenanted as the heirs (Rom. 8:17; Gal. 3:18; Matt. 25:34). (4) Its benefits are conferred to the covenanted not from any of their own merit, but purely from the divine establishment (Luke 22:29). And so finally in this sense, namely insofar as the testament coincides with the covenant of grace, from the first establishment of the covenant of grace, it always was and will be one, because it has acknowledged and does acknowledge only one inheritance, and one death of the testator; yet insofar as the testament does not designate the covenant of grace itself, but only its dispensation, it is acknowledged to be not one, but double, Old and New (Heb. 8:8), inasmuch as the former offers the covenant of grace that will be ratified in the future death of the testator, and the blood still to be shed, yet the latter offers the covenant ratified in the death that was accomplished and the blood that was shed. What further remains to be said about the dispensation of the covenant of grace, or about the testaments, we lay aside for its own place, namely book eight.

The Elenctic Part

1. Is the surety of the Son in the eternal covenant of grace accounted as a conditional surety or an absolute surety?

XXXIV. It is asked, first, whether the *sponsio*, surety, of the Son in the eternal covenant of grace is accounted as a *fidejussio*, conditional surety, or an *expromissio*, absolute surety.[49] The Socinians, because they deny that the *sponsor*, the

---

49. *Sponsio*, from *spondeo*, "I answer," in Roman Law referred to the binding acceptance of an obligation contract and its terms by a debtor in agreement with a creditor. Cf. Rudolf Sohm, *The Institutes: A Textbook of the History and System of Roman Private Law*, 3rd ed. (Clarendon Press: Oxford, 1907), 382–86, esp. 384, n. 3. This is an argument based on legal terms found in the *Corpus Iuris Civilis*, vol. 1 (Berlin: Weidmanns, 1889). In Roman Law, a *fidejussor* is a surety who is liable only after the original debtor defaults. It is understood that the principal debtor is bound absolutely for any debt, whereas a *fidejussor* is only conditionally bound unless specifically stipulated as absolutely bound (*Digesta*, XLVI, title I, §8.7), *Corpus Iuris Civilis*, I.739–44; cf. Sohm, 385. The term *fidejussio*, as Sohm indicates, arises from the formula in which the creditor would ask the surety, for example, "*centum quae Titius mihi debet, eadem fide tua esse jubes?*" to which the surety replies, "*fide mea esse jubeo.*" Sohm clarifies, "The effect of such a fidejussio is to make the surety a co-real debtor with the principal debtor, his co-real liability being accessory to that of the principal, i.e. he (the surety) is liable *after* (emphasis original) the principal debtor. That is the reason why the liability of the surety depends on the existence of the principal debt, and why further, the surety has the *beneficium excussionis* (sometimes called the *beneficium ordinis*)…which consists in the right to demand that the principal debtor…if 'present' (capable of being sued) and

surety himself, existed from eternity, and because they likewise assert that God, when he sent his Son, was reconciled to man, and thus was in need of no surety by which a satisfaction on behalf of man would be promised to him, but only on behalf of God, that he in time pledged to man a trust for the benefits that would be offered, if he would obey his commands; they therefore deny all idea of an eternal surety. Those brethren who follow the celebrated Cocceius, after his death, so that they might more easily hold that Old Testament believers, notwithstanding the eternal surety, were under liability until the time of the actual satisfaction, maintain that the surety was a conditional surety, through which the principal debtor remains under liability until the time of the actual payment. The rest of the Reformed hold the view that the Son, by that eternal surety, pledged payment or satisfaction absolutely, without any reservation of the rights of order and seizure[50] (which the jurists leave to their *fidejussio*), took upon himself at one and the same time the entire cause and liability of the sinner, and consequently freed those to be redeemed from all liability, although they add at the same time that this divine absolute surety must not be held so rigidly and in all things to the laws of every civil *expromissio*.

Arguments

They hold this view because: (1) from this surety comes, in the Old Testament, the appellation ערב, he who pledged (Jer. 30:21), and in the New Testament, ἔγγυος, surety (Heb. 7:22), which at least to Scapula, in his lexicon at this word,[51] is from γυῖον, hand, as if to say ἐν γυίοις, in the hands, because in an absolute surety, the creditor accepts the certificate of his debt as if into his hands; or, it is from γύης, immovable land, according to the Suda and others,[52] because the absolute surety makes the debt immovable. In the absolute surety there was as it were a certain virtual satisfaction and reconciliation, by means of which even

---

solvent, shall be sued first." In an *expromissio*, by contrast, the expromissor assumes the debt of the original debtor and becomes the principal debtor, whereas the original debtor is released from all obligation (*Digesta*, XLVI, Title 2), *Corpus Iuris Civilis*, I.744–46. This is also called a *novatio*, a new contract that changes the parties or terms. Cf. Sohm, 386–87.

50. *absque ulla reservatione beneficiorum ordinis et excussionis.* A *fidejussor* in this legal theory retained the right to refer creditors to recover a debt first from the resources of the principal debtor, and the right to demand a ranking or ordering of any other co-fidejussors before repayment was sought from himself. See references in previous note.

51. Johannes Scapula (c. 1540–1600), *Lexicon Graeco-Latinum* (Amsterdam: Joannes Blaeuw, 1652), 416.

52. For a Greek-Latin version of this Greek lexicon developed from the church fathers to the medieval period, see *Suidas, nunc primum integer latinitate donatus*, ed. Aemilius Portus (Geneva: Pierre et Jacob Chouët, 1619), 833.

those who believed before the actual satisfaction of Christ were delivered. (2) The contrary conditional surety is repugnant to all those passages of both Testaments that teach that believers had obtained forgiveness[53] of their sins before the satisfaction was made (Ps. 103:3–4; 51:title, vv. 1, 7–9; 32:5; Matt. 6:12; 9:5). (3) It is repugnant to the wisdom both of the offended God and of the interceding surety, to undertake and accept the liability of the offender on the condition that the offender cannot make satisfaction for the debt, when both are persuaded that it is impossible for the offender himself to make satisfaction. (4) It is repugnant to the salvation of Old Testament believers, for if, notwithstanding a conditional surety, they were under guilt until the actual satisfaction of the surety, by what reason could they have been admitted into heaven? Unless we want to assert that those still set under the liability of death and eternal damnation could be set for heavenly liberty, which surpasses all absurdity. (5) It colludes with the hypotheses of the papists, which from this conditional surety thrust Old Testament believers into their limbo of the fathers, from which they would be freed through the actual satisfaction of Christ. (6) It is repugnant to those passages of the Old Testament Scripture in which it is read that God had already at that time cast our sins upon the Mediator, and exacted them from him (Isa. 53:4–7 with 2 Cor. 5:19, 21), that is, virtually. But how could this happen, except on account of an absolute surety, or a satisfaction promised absolutely?

Objections

Nor do they validly object: (1) that the Mediator is called an ἔγγυος (Heb. 7:22). For that word denotes *sponsor*, surety, as the genus, with *fidejussor*, conditional surety, and *expromissor*, expromissor or absolute surety, as its species; moreover, *sponsio*, the suretyship itself, speaks of nothing but some sort of promise and stipulation, for which reason, among theologians and philologists *sponsio* and *expromissio* are often interchanged. Thus, in Matthias Martinius's *Lexicon Philologicum* ἐγγυὴ is *sponsio, expromissio,* and ἀναδοχή, a promise to undertake;[54] and in the *Lexicon* of Hesychius of Alexandria, ἔγγυος is ἀνάδοχος, one promising to undertake;[55] and ἀναδοχή in Guillaume Budé's *Commentary on the Greek Language* means *expromissio*: "Ἀναδέχεσθαι," he says, "is to promise and

---

53. ἄφεσις, as opposed to πάρεσις, the Cocceian term for the mere passing over of sins, said to belong to Old Testament believers before Christ's actual satisfaction. Cf. 1.6.6 §XXIX.

54. Matthias Martinius (1572–1630), *Lexicon philologicum praecipue etymologicum et sacrum…pars tertia* (Frankfurt am Main: Thomas Matthias Goetzen, 1655), "sponsio."

55. Hesychius, Ἡσυχίου Λεξικον *cum variis doctorum virorum notis* (Leiden: Hack, 1668), 281.

to receive to oneself, and to acknowledge as one's own, a deed or debt."[56] Indeed also, the same Budé wants ἐγγυᾶσθαι to mean to promise absolutely, in fact, the same as ἀναδέχεσθαι.[57] But even if these things are not so, let those of the opposing view teach us that ἔγγυος in the New Testament means nothing other than a conditional surety. (2) That an expromissor does not satisfy for another but for himself alone, and thus from our hypothesis the satisfaction of Christ for us is displaced. For we assert that the surety promised absolutely not for his own debt, but for ours. (3) That in this way we are delivered not through satisfaction but through absolute surety. But if that logical connection is valid, on the hypothesis of the opposing view, will not believers in the Old Testament have to be said to have been delivered, not by a satisfaction, but by a conditional surety? Yet we are not delivered by absolute surety alone, but by a satisfaction undertaken by absolute surety, and thus a satisfaction more certainly than certain to be rendered, and therefore one enveloped in the absolute surety. (4) Nor is it solidly concluded that the surety did not promise absolutely for us, and did not draw off our debt absolutely upon himself, from the fact that if he had not satisfied, the elect would be said to still be in their sins (1 Cor. 15:17), since it was impossible that the surety, as the God-man, would not render payment for what was promised absolutely, and thus also impossible that the elect would be in their sins. Finally, (5) that our sins are said to have been in the world until the payment. For they were certainly not upon the sinners, but upon the expromissor.

2. Could the Son have not undertaken, or once undertaken, have resigned the mediatorial office? A comparison of opinions. The opinion of the Reformed, with their reasons
XXXV. It is asked, second, whether the Son, when the Father required that he take upon himself the mediatorial office, could have not undertaken it, or when he had undertaken it, have removed himself from the burden of it. Episcopius and his Remonstrant Apologists, so that they may more easily hold that the liberty of choice consists in an omnimodal indifference, affirm that he could (*Apology*, ch. 17, p. 187).[58] The Reformed acknowledge both that God freely required that the Son would undertake the mediatorial office, and that the Son

---

56. Guillaume Budé (1467–1540), *Commentarii linguae Graecae* (Basel: Johann Bebel, 1530), 80.

57. Budé, *Commentarii linguae Graecae* (1530), 90.

58. Commonly attributed to Simon Episcopius (1583–1643) and the Remonstrant Brotherhood (*Remonstrantse Broederschap*), *Apologia pro confessione sive declarationes sententiae eorum, qui in Foederato Belgio vocantur Remonstrantes, super praecipuis articulis religionis Christianae* (n.p., 1630), fols. 187v–188r.

most freely undertook the same, insofar as both acted from counsel and rational complacency, from which it is said that the counsel of peace was contracted between Jehovah and the man *Zemach*, the Branch (Zech. 6:13; Ps. 40:6–8). They likewise acknowledge that both the Father and the Son, as divine persons, clearly possessed their own right, and thus the Father, considered in himself and by his own nature, could have not required, and in this respect the Son also could have not accepted the requirement, but yet to say that given the Father's requirement, the Son could have not yielded, not accepted, they consider hard and crude; and after he accepted the office, to have removed himself from the burden of it, they additionally think would be treacherous: and thus the Son could not have retreated from it. This is so because: (1) the counsel between the Father and the Son is said to be immovable (Heb. 6:17, "the immutability of his counsel," compared with Zech. 6:13), reinforced with an oath (Ps. 110:4). Then (2) because from this undertaking, he is called the servant of the Father (Isa. 42:1; 52:13; 53:11), who cannot but obey his Lord, at least *de jure*. (3) From the same undertaking, the Father made him subject to the law, as his subordinate (Gal. 4:4), he placed our sins upon him (Isa. 53:4), he by his own right exacted the same from him (Isa. 53:7), he made him to be sin for us (2 Cor. 5:21). (4) To retreat from the things agreed is treachery, which to think concerning a divine person is a horrendous blasphemy. (5) By such a refusal of the Son, the Father would have been deprived of the glory of his grace and mercy, the elect of their salvation, and the Son himself of the glory of his mediation.

Objections

At the same time they allege to the contrary: (1) that if he could not but have undertaken the office, or could not have resigned it, then he did not freely undertake it and perform it. I respond, There is presupposed something that will never be proved, that liberty consists in mere indifference, when it in fact consists in the faculty of acting from counsel, which obtained between the Father and the Son, as we have already taught.[59] (2) That Christ obeyed the Father, but not as we obey the divine law, under the threat of eternal death. I respond, The Father certainly did not impose the mediatorial office upon the Son under the threat of death, because that would have been superfluous and absurd, since the Son of God by his nature could not have sinned or disobeyed the Father; then also, from the fact that the Father did not present the office to the Son with a threat, it does not follow that the Son could have not complied with the Father when he required it, or have retreated from it once undertaken.

---

59. 1.3.9 §VI; 1.3.10 §§XVII, XXXI

3. Is there a universal covenant of grace? The opinion of the semi-Pelagians
XXXVI. It is asked, third, whether there is a universal covenant of grace, to
which each and every person is subject. The semi-Pelagians, and among them
especially the Remonstrants, so that they may more effectively protect universal grace, and predestination from things foreseen, state that God from eternity
decreed to predestine the Mediator for each and every person, that he might
redeem them by his satisfaction; thus that he wills for each and every person to
be saved through Christ, if only they themselves should will; thus in addition,
that to each and every person he offers and also confers sufficient strength, under
the condition that through the strength of their free choice they will to believe
in the Mediator and repent from their sins; and moreover, that those he foresaw
would believe, he will elect, and on the contrary those whom he foresaw to be
unwilling, he will reprobate. They state that there is a universal covenant of grace.

The opinion of the Reformed with their reasons
The Reformed on the contrary, since they deny a universal decree for saving each
and every person, as we taught in book 2 (ch. 15, §XXX), since likewise they
deny that God predestined redemption through Christ for each and every person, as we demonstrated in book 2 (ch. 17, §XXXII), since furthermore they
hold that Christ was not given for each and every person, as we will demonstrate
in its own place, in the chapter on the procurement of redemption,[60] and finally
since he could not have foreseen that this person would believe rather than that
one, state that there is not a universal covenant of grace. They do so especially
because: (1) there is a difference between the covenant of grace and the covenant
of nature in this, that the latter extends in Adam to all, whereas the covenant of
grace is only entered into with the seed of the woman as distinct from the seed
of the serpent (Gen. 3:15), with the house of Israel (Jer. 31:33), with the children
of the covenant (Acts 3:25), with the children of the promise (Rom. 9:8), and
with the heirs of the promise (Heb. 6:17): to them is said to pertain the covenant
(Rom. 9:4) and the promise (Acts 2:39), whereas the others are strangers to
the testaments of promise (Eph. 2:12). (2) In no place throughout the entirety
of Scripture is the covenant of grace extended to each and every person; in fact
on the contrary, many are excluded from it (Ps. 147:19–20; Acts 14:16). Nor do
those of the contrary opinion have anything to present for their case, except the
things that they have customarily adduced in favor of universal grace, which we
have previously struck down, in the places already cited.

---

60. 1.5.18 §XL

4. Is the covenant of grace conditioned? A comparison of opinions

XXXVII. It is asked, fourth, whether the covenant of grace is conditioned. The Pelagianizers, in order that they may suspend participation in the covenant of grace upon conditions to be fulfilled by the strength of free choice, teach that the whole covenant of grace in its entirety is conditioned. On the contrary, the Antinomians, under the pretext of elevating grace, teach that the covenant is wholly absolute. Nor are there absent from among the Reformed those who, so that they may not only more effectively avoid the traps of the Pelagianizers, but also so that the right to the things promised in the covenant of grace may not be suspended upon fulfilled conditions, state that the temporal covenant of grace is entirely absolute, yet in such a way that no one obtains salvation except by the way of faith and holiness.

The common opinion of the Reformed with their reasons

I think it is most accurate to make a distinction among the promises of the covenant of grace: those which are accounted as means to an end, such as the procurement of redemption through Christ, regeneration, conversion, the conferring of faith and of the purpose of repentance; and those such as are accounted as an end, such as justification, adoption, glorification, and so forth. With this done, it seems that it must be said that the first kind of promises of the covenant of grace are completely absolute, for it implies a manifest contradiction to stipulate from a person dead in his sins the fulfilled condition for the redemption of Christ, regeneration, and so forth. However, the promises of the second kind—justification, adoption, and so forth—are altogether conditioned, yet in such a way that the fulfilment of the conditions depends not upon the strength of free choice, but upon the absolute promises of this covenant. We have stated it in this way, because: (1) constantly in the Scriptures our justification is suspended upon faith (John 3:16; Acts 10:43), as is adoption (John 1:11–12). (2) To conceive of a covenant properly so called that does not consist of mutual promises and stipulations, in which the parties do not consent to the same conditions, is to conceive of a covenant that is not a covenant. Accordingly, (3) covenants with God are throughout Scripture read to have been made through the proposal and reception of conditions (Deut. 30:15ff.; Ex. 19:5–6, 8; 2 Chron. 15:12–13; Gen. 17:1–2; 2 Cor. 6:17–18; etc.). I would add that (4) the covenant of grace, offered indiscriminately, is not conferred to this one more than that one except upon some fulfilled condition (John 1:12; 3:16; Acts 10:43). (5) No one could be certain that he more than anyone else has been admitted into participation in the covenant, except from the fulfillment of some condition of it (Gal. 2:16). This is not to mention (6) the gravest problems which arise from the denial of any condition for the covenant of grace, such as that: (a) by this reasoning, one only of the covenanted parties will be obligated, namely God. (b) The covenant of grace could be contracted between God and man without the consent of man. (c) Those covenanted with God, by virtue of this covenant, will not be more obligated to any duty, of love, of obedience, of reverence, after the communion of this covenant has been received, than before the consummation of the same. (d) In this way the one covenanted with God could be differentiated by no extrinsic or intrinsic difference or quality from those not covenanted. (e) The neglect of faith and repentance could not separate a person from participation in the covenant. (f) Faith and repentance would not be the path to the remission of sins and eternal salvation. (g) By this rationale, the entire ministry of the Word would be in vain, because it looks to no end more than to preparing and raising up a person for receiving the condition of the covenant of grace, or to faith in Christ, and living worthy of him.

Objections

What may be objected to these things can be blunted with no trouble from what we have already observed in the dogmatic part, for example: (1) that by this reasoning, the covenant of grace would not be firm and eternal (Gen. 17:13, 19), if namely it should depend upon a condition to be humanly fulfilled. I respond, That is true, if it should depend upon a condition to be fulfilled by human strength and in an uncertain way; we do not admit this kind of condition in the covenant of grace. (2) That nothing is required from man as a condition for participation in the covenant of grace (Jer. 31–32; Heb. 8:10; John 6:45; Ezek. 36:25–26). I respond: (a) We have taught that a condition is required, and by what rationale, in its own place (from John 1:12; 3:16; Gal. 2:16; etc.), although perhaps it might not be expressed in the passages cited by the objector. But (b) it is expressed adequately enough even in those passages, when in Hebrews 8:10 is added, "And they will be to me a people," that is, by the consent of faith; in John 6:45, "That man comes to me," that is, by faith; in Ezekiel 36:28, "And you will be to me a people, and I will be God to you," that is, by reciprocal consent; although in these passages it is said that that condition will be procured by God. (3) That a condition properly speaking, in the matter of covenants, is such an action that, once fulfilled, it confers upon a person the right to a reward, which is invalid in the covenant of grace. I respond, The condition fulfilled in the covenant of grace, does not confer the right to the conditioned promises, but only their possession, which is a commonly received distinction in the business of justification. (4) That the covenant of grace is a testament, which does not imply a condition; indeed, according to the jurists it excludes all contracting and mutual consent to conditions. I respond: (a) A testament properly speaking is nothing other than a dispensation of the covenant of grace, insofar as it depends upon the death of the testator. Accordingly, a testament certainly implies the covenant of grace, as its material part, but it is not the covenant itself, but rather its dispensation, which is like the formal part of a testament. (b) Even the jurists in their testaments allow conditions, for example, "If Titius should want to marry my granddaughter, he shall be my heir."

5. Does the covenant of grace stipulate from men any good works of their own?
A comparison of opinions
XXXVIII. It is asked, fifth, whether the covenant of grace stipulates from men any good works of their own. The papists, in favor of their own condign merits,[61] state that the covenant of grace stipulates good works as meritorious causes. The Socinians, so that they may obtain that man is justified not on account of the righteousness of the satisfaction and merits of Christ, but on account of their own works, certainly not of the law, but of the gospel, that is, of the Mosaic law insofar as through Christ it has been corrected and augmented, and on account of those works not from merit but from the grace of God, state that the covenant of grace stipulates those good works. The Remonstrants, so that they may avoid the idea that man is justified on account of Christ's imputed righteousness alone, state that the covenant of grace stipulates faith, and that certainly alone, but insofar as it is effective through good works, or insofar as faith, through divine acceptilation,[62] is in place of total obedience of the law.

The opinion of the Reformed with their reasons
The Reformed, although they admit that the covenant of grace stipulates the work of faith (John 6:29) with its ingredients—knowledge, assent, trust, and special application—yet they think of this faith, not insofar as it is some work, or works, but insofar as it is this specific work, namely, the apprehension of Christ; otherwise, they state that the covenant of grace does not at all stipulate good works, because: (1) by this, even from its very denomination, as if by its species, the covenant of grace, which is promulgated in the gospel, is distinguished from the covenant of works, which is manifested in the law, because the former has the doctrine of things to be believed, the latter of things to be done (Rom. 10:5, 8–11); indeed also, from this form they are opposed to each other as contraries, in such a way that, from the affirmation of the one, the negation of the other is

---

61. *in gratiam suorum meritorum ex condigno*
62. *per acceptilationem divinam.* Cf. 1.6.6 §XXV. On *acceptilation,* see 1.5.18 §IX.

inferred, and vice versa (Rom. 3:27–28; Gal. 2:16, 21; Phil. 3:9; 2 Tim. 1:9–10). (2) The benefits of the covenant of grace, in the perpetual tenor of Scripture, are suspended upon faith alone (John 3:16ff.; Mark 16:16; Eph. 2:8; Rom. 3:28; Gal. 2:16). Thus (3) the law, from the covenant of works, is called the ministry of death, whereas the gospel is called the ministry of the Spirit and life (2 Cor. 3:7–8). Finally, (4) only the covenant of works in the law attributes a reward from works, whereas the covenant of grace in the gospel promises one without works (Rom. 4:4–6), from pure grace (Rom. 6:23). Now what they oppose to these—namely that in the New Testament (1) a doctrine of works is taught, (2) laws properly speaking are taught (Matt. 5–7), (3) threats are added against the willfully disobedient, (4) promises are suspended upon the obedience of works (Luke 17:10; Rom. 8:13; and so forth)—can be dispatched with no trouble, when their first-order falsehood has been observed and demonstrated, in which they do not distinguish the doctrine of the New Testament from the covenant of grace, and from the gospel, by which that covenant is promulgated. Compare §XXII.

6. Does the covenant of grace stipulate faith as to be supplied by one's own strength?
XXXIX. It is asked, sixth, whether the covenant of grace stipulates faith as to be supplied by one's own strength, or the natural strength of free choice. The Pelagians and the semi-Pelagians, the Socinians, Jesuits, Remonstrants, and Anabaptists, so that they may hold that the strength of free choice, from the violation of the covenant of works, was not only not extinguished in regard to spiritual goods, but was also unwounded, state not only that the entire covenant of grace is conditioned, but also that the stipulated conditions, whatever they may happen to be, whether faith and repentance, or good works, are expected from men as to be supplied by the strength of their own free will. The Reformed judge that the covenant of grace stipulates faith, not as to be supplied by one's own strength, but by the strength to be conferred from the promises of this very covenant, since: (1) in this the covenant of grace is essentially different from the covenant of works, because the former was contracted with man blessed with original righteousness (Eccl. 7:29), and thus spiritually alive, yet the latter with man dead in sins (Eph. 2:1, 3), for whom it is impossible to supply the righteousness of the law (Rom. 8:3–4), who does not subject himself to the divine law, and also cannot (Rom. 8:7), who no more can perform a good work than the Ethiopian can change his skin (Jer. 13:23). Accordingly, to him (2) through the covenant of grace itself is promised and restored the strength, the new heart and new spirit, by which he is able and willing to supply the condition of the covenant of grace (Jer. 31:33–34; 32:39–40; Heb. 8:8; Ezek. 36:26–27). (3) Faith

is expressly called the gift of God (Phil. 2:29). Nor is what they allege of any consequence, that you would stipulate conditions in vain if it should not be in the other party's power to fulfill them, because the covenant of grace itself promises and confers the power to that party. Compare book 4, chapter 4, §XXXII.

7. Was the gospel present also under the Old Testament?
A comparison of opinions
XL. It is asked, seventh, whether the gospel was present also under the Old Testament. The Pelagians, with whom the papists agree, since they assert that believers under the patriarchs were saved by the observance of the law of nature, under Moses by the observance of the Mosaic law, and under Christ by the observance of the gospel, state that the gospel was not present under the Old Testament. The Socinians, because they believe nearly the same thing as the Pelagians, and because they define the gospel as the doctrine of the commandments of Christ and spiritual promises, the remission of sins, and eternal life, and since they likewise separate believers in the Old Testament from the doctrine of Christ's satisfaction and merit as well as the faith that would receive Christ's satisfaction and merits, state that the gospel was not present under the Old Testament. The Anabaptists, since they believe nearly the same thing as the Socinians, and also confuse the gospel with the books of the New Testament, just as the law with the books of the Old Testament, likewise deny that the gospel was present under the Old Testament. The celebrated Dr. Cocceius with his followers, since they segment the entire time of the church into three periods, under the promise, the law, and the gospel, and accordingly refer the gospel to the New Testament, and likewise since they define the gospel as the doctrine and promise of the goods of the New Testament, the forgiveness[63] of sins, the removal of all guilt, although at the same time they acknowledge an eternal and universal testament which flourishes throughout all the ages of the church, and concerns the heavenly homeland to be given on account of Christ to all believers under every age, which in most things coincides with the covenant of grace, still they state, in this sense of theirs, that the gospel pertains only to the New Testament.

The opinion of the Reformed with their reasons
The rest of the Reformed, although they leave the gospel of fulfillment to only the New Testament, yet state that the gospel of promise has its origin in the protevangelium of paradise, and thus it also was present under the Old Testament, since: (1) the gospel to them is not anything except the promulgation of the covenant of

---

63. ἀφέσει. Cf. note on §XXXIV, above.

grace, just as a testament to them is not anything except the dispensation of the covenant of grace, insofar as it depends upon the death of the testator Christ, either future or present, from which to them are produced two Testaments, the Old and the New, just as we taught in the dogmatic part.[64] From which it follows, since this promulgation, and also the dispensation of the promises of the covenant of grace, also was present under the Old Testament, the covenant of grace also was present under the Old Testament. (2) The hypotheses of our adversaries' opinion (provided that you except the hypotheses of Cocceius and his followers), namely that (a) believers under the Old Testament did not have spiritual promises, of remission of sins and of eternal life, (b) they were saved apart from Christ, (c) without faith in Christ, (d) saved by their own works, that (e) the religion of the Old Testament was different in its entire essence from the religion of the New Testament, and so forth, are plainly intolerable to the Christian religion.

8. Is the covenant of grace promulgated in the Decalogue?
A comparison of opinions
XLI. It is asked, eighth, whether the covenant of grace was promulgated in the Decalogue. The famous Cameron, because he did not distinguish carefully enough between the use of the Decalogue and its nature, stated that the Decalogue was neither the covenant of works nor the covenant of grace, but a certain subservient covenant, insofar as like a pedagogue, it drove the elect to seek Christ (Gal. 3:24; Rom. 10:4–5). The celebrated Cocceius with his followers, since he stated that by its violation the covenant of works was plainly abolished, nor did anything remain except the eternal and universal testament of grace until the Israelites' making of the calf,[65] after which the Decalogue, with the adding of the twofold formula, "Do this and you will live," and, "Cursed be the one who will not remain in all things which are written in the book of the law," accepted not indeed the essence of the covenant of works, but yet the appearance of it, stated that the Decalogue is the pure, unadulterated covenant of grace.

The more received opinion of the Reformed with their reasons
On the contrary, the rest of the Reformed state that in the Decalogue there is no promulgation of the covenant of grace, but only the renewal of the covenant of works, although that renewal, at least in relation to the elect, had an evangelical use, that it would drive them to embrace Christ. This is so because: (1)

---

64. §XXXIII

65. μοσχοποιίαν *Israeliticam*

the Decalogue has nothing of Christ, nothing of faith in Christ. (2) Even if it did set forth Christ and faith in Christ, which yet we do not grant, yet it still has in addition all moral good works; accordingly we would not be justified by faith alone, because without any doubt we are justified by the observance of the covenant of grace. (3) The Decalogue has all those things (with only the positive commandment excepted, concerning not eating the forbidden fruit) which God stipulated from our first parents in the covenant of works. (4) It is also sanctioned with threats and promises, in the same way as the covenant of works. Therefore nothing prohibits saying that it properly presents the covenant of works again, although in relation to the elect, for an evangelical end and use. Nor is it any hindrance that in it mention is made of that formula which pertains to the covenant of grace, "I am your God," because entirely nothing is repugnant to urging obedience to the covenant of works by arguments and motives taken from the benefits of the covenant of grace. But we will set aside this argument for its proper place, concerning the dispensation of the covenant of grace under Moses (bk. 8, ch. 2).[66]

9. Does the covenant of grace differ from the covenant of nature only in degrees of accidental perfection? A comparison of opinions
XLII. It is asked, ninth, whether the covenant of grace differs from the covenant of nature only in degrees of accidental perfection. The papists, in favor of their monasticism, since they want in the gospel for there to be added to the law evangelical counsels or monastic vows, from which the gospel would become more perfect than the law, answer in the affirmative. The Socinians, so that they may form the gospel out of the law, and may more effectively hold that a person is justified by the observance of the laws of Christ, state that Christ did not only correct the Mosaic law, but also in individual commandments rendered it broader, and thus more perfect. The Remonstrant Apologists, so that they may show approval to the Socinians as much as they can, even while they dare not openly pass into their camp, state that Christ added at least these three things to the law: the denial of self, the bearing of the cross, and the imitation of him (Luke 9:23).

The opinion of the Reformed
The Reformed state that the covenant of grace differs from the covenant of nature in its entire essence, its entire species, just as a human being and a brute beast, and thus also in degrees of perfection, but degrees that are essential, and

---

66. 1.8.2 §§XVI–XX, LI

not only accidental, and otherwise that there belongs to both law and gospel their own perfection in their own species, insofar as both the covenant of nature, by its observance, once could confer life to man according to its formula, "Do this and you will live," and the covenant of grace now in actuality confers eternal salvation. From what has already been said, not only about the covenant of nature in book 3, chapter 12, but also from this very chapter, these things are abundantly evident.

Objections

To rout the individual hypotheses of each individual viewpoint individually does not belong to this place, especially because we have already expressly overthrown the evangelical counsels of the papists (bk. 3, ch. 11, §XII). The additions of the Socinians, by which Christ would have rendered the gospel more perfect, do not have any foundation in Matthew 5 (vv. 21–22, 27–28, etc.). For in that passage the Savior does not correct or augment the law of Moses, as is clearer than the sun from verse 45, "You shall pursue your enemy in hatred," which nowhere occurs in Moses; rather, he vindicates it from the Pharisaical glosses. Nor also do the Arminian additions appear in Matthew 16:24 and Luke 9:23, because in these passages not even the least little bit appears about the law of Moses augmented by these duties, and in addition, not only these three duties, but also all those things of the Socinians, which the Socinians advertise as additions to the law, are also obvious in the Old Testament, just as we will expressly show in its own place, on the law of Moses.[67] Those points about the testaments, their nature, number, and differences, which could be disputed here, should be brought back to here from book eight of this theology, where they will be expressly aired.[68]

The Practical Part

The covenant of grace: 1. Enraptures us in admiration.
XLIII. With respect to practice, the contemplation of the covenant of grace, first, enraptures us in pious admiration of it, from so many, so great, and such excellent mysteries that it reveals, whereas: (1) it displays the doctrine of restoration and salvation of the sinner through Christ, which is called the mystery of the gospel (Eph. 6:19), the mystery of faith (1 Tim. 3:9), the mystery of God, of the Father, and of Christ (Col. 2:2). (2) It explains the doctrine of the person and office of the Mediator of this covenant, which is called the "without doubt great mystery of godliness" (1 Tim. 3:16). (3) It discloses the union of Christ and believers in

---

67. E.g. 1.8.2 §XLVIII
68. 1.8.1 §§XXXIV–XXXVIII, VII–IX

the one seed of the woman, and in one body, as if by a certain spiritual marriage, that which is named a great mystery (Eph. 5:29–33). (4) It displays the good pleasure of God concerning calling the nations to participation in the covenant, which the apostle calls the mystery of Christ hidden from times eternal (Rom. 16:25–26). (5) It reveals to us the mystery of the divine will according to his free benevolence, which he had purposed in himself, that in the dispensation of the fullness of times he might gather together in one all things in Christ (Eph. 1:9–10). (6) It makes evident the various dispensations of this covenant, through various ecclesiastical statutes, from which ministers of the divine Word are called stewards of the mysteries of God (1 Cor. 4:1). Finally, (7) it also makes known the resurrection of the flesh, and our sudden change in a moment, which the apostle emphatically names a mystery (1 Cor. 15:51–52 with 1 Thess. 4:16–17).

The manner
Let us recount these and other so great and so numerous mysteries of the covenant of grace, in such a way that: (1) the stewards of the divine mysteries carefully teach the doctrine of the covenant of grace (1 Cor. 4:1; 2 Cor. 3:6, 14; Jer. 11:1–2; Ex. 24:7). (2) All people accurately learn of it (Heb. 8:10–11; Deut. 4:23; Jer. 11:3; Deut. 5:1–2). (3) All who long to become participants in it think on it frequently and much, meditate on it day and night (Ps. 25:14; 50:5 with 105:8).

2. It shows us various attributes of God for his glorification. Which ones
XLIV. Second, it displays the glory of: (1) the most free and absolute divine good pleasure, by which, when all equally had fallen from the covenant of works, and become liable to death and eternal condemnation, he willed to receive this one rather than that one into the covenant of grace (Matt. 11:25–26). (2) The most tender mercy and love for mankind, by which he embraces the most miserable sinner, one not only most unworthy of all grace and kindness, but also liable to all indignation and punishment, not by any common sort of grace, but also by such and so great a grace that he admitted him into the covenant, and made himself a debtor to him, gave him his only begotten Son, delivered him from desperate misery, gave him the right of eternal life and glory, and so forth (John 3:16; Rom. 5:8; cf. Deut. 5:2–3; Ezek. 34:25, 30–31; 37:26). (3) The most rigid justice (Rom. 3:25), by which on account of sin, he made his only begotten Son, who knew no sin, to be sin for us, so that in him we might be made righteousness before him (2 Cor. 5:21). (4) Infinite power, by which he reconciled to himself, restored to liberty, and made alive his own enemy, a slave of Satan, dead in sins (Eph. 2:5–6). (5) Inscrutable wisdom, by which the gospel is called the wisdom

of God (1 Cor. 1:21), the wisdom of God in a mystery, the hidden wisdom, which he predetermined before the ages, which none of the princes recognized (1 Cor. 2:6–8), and Christ is called the power and wisdom of God (1 Cor. 1:24). For what more profound wisdom can be thought of than that by which the highest justice is reconciled with the highest mercy, by which the very Son of God is substituted for the sinner, and so forth? Here surely, if anywhere, you could exclaim, "O the depth of the riches of the wisdom and knowledge of God! How unsearchable are his judgments!" (Rom. 11:33). But especially of (6) grace and love, more than that of a father, from which it is called the covenant of *grace* par excellence, at which the Savior himself is astounded: "God so loved the world!" (John 3:16), and which God himself commends (Rom. 5:8), by which in particular: (a) he established this covenant, "Behold I, even I will establish my covenant with you" (Gen. 6:17–18); (b) he gave the expromissor (Heb. 7:22), the Mediator (Heb. 8:6), the seed of the woman, he established enmity, he crushed the head of the serpent (Gen. 3:15); (c) he chose the Mediator of the covenant from eternity (Eph. 1:5–6), promised him (Luke 1:72), supplied him in the fullness of time, from which he is called the gift of God (John 4:10; Isa. 9:6); (d) in him he gives to us most great and precious promises (2 Peter 1:4; 2 Cor. 1:20); and (e) he so generously offers and conveys to us all things (Isa. 55:1; Rev. 22:17).

To what end?

The covenant of grace presents these things and many others to us, so that (1) we would acknowledge and magnify him in our heart (Luke 1:46–47), and (2) we would celebrate him in word and deed (1 Peter 2:9; 1 Cor. 6:20; etc.).

3. It commends to us the blessedness of those covenanted.

XLV. Third, the covenant of grace on the one hand commends to us the ineffable blessedness of those who are partakers of it: "Blessed is the nation whose God is the Lord" (Ps. 33:12), inasmuch as by it: (1) they are now not servants of God, which is great, nor only friends, which is greater (John 15:15), but even covenanted ones, to whom God is bound in covenant by his own grace, חסידי כרתי בריתי, "My kind ones, entering my covenant" (Ps. 50:5). (2) They have been delivered: (a) from the enmity with God (Rom. 5:10); (b) from the slavery of Satan (Heb. 2:15); (c) from the guilt of sins (Ps. 32:1); and (d) from the curse of the law (Gal. 3:13). (3) On the contrary, they have become partakers of the most great and precious promises of God (2 Peter 1:4), because in Christ, according to the covenant of grace, all the promises of God are yes and amen (2 Cor. 1:20). (4) They are made members of Christ, comprehended under the same seed of the woman, united with him who by God was made unto us wisdom, righteousness, sanctification, and redemption (1 Cor. 1:30), from whose fullness we receive grace for grace (John 1:16), in whom we are complete (Col. 2:10). In a word I will say, (5) by this covenant they receive God himself (Jer. 30:22), the most all-sufficient one (Gen. 17:1–2), that he may be to them their portion and inheritance (Ps. 16:5–6; 73:25–26), their sun and shield (Ps. 84:11), their exceeding great reward (Gen. 15:1), bound to them and to their benefit by the gracious promise of the covenant in such a way that he cannot but serve them (Jer. 31:20; Ps. 23:1ff.). In fact, (6) not only by this covenant do they receive God, but also all his attributes, so that all of them are always and everywhere brought forth to serve for their advantage (Rom. 8:30–31): for example, (a) his immutability makes it that he is always God to them (Mal. 3:6; Rom. 11:29); (b) his truthfulness, that they can always and securely rely upon his promises (Isa. 34:16); (c) his love, that all things work together for their good (Rom. 8:28, 38–39; Heb. 12:6); (d) his mercy, that all their sins are forgiven (Ps. 103:8, 10; Ex. 34:6); (e) his wisdom, that he knows how to provide for them in all things, and how to rescue them from all their adversities (2 Peter 2:9); (f) his omnipotence, that he is also able to do so (2 Thess. 1:11; Eph. 3:20).

And it declares the misery of others.
On the other hand, the covenant of grace displays to us the misery of those who are constituted outside the covenant of grace, which the apostle represents as in an outline in Ephesians 2:12, insofar as they remain liable to all the evils from which, through the covenant of grace, others are delivered, and on the contrary, deprived of all those prerogatives and benefits in which others rejoice from this covenant, as we just said.

4. It warns us that we should explore whether we are participants in the covenant of grace. The marks
XLVI. Accordingly, fourth, it warns us that we should earnestly explore whether we are under the covenant of grace, or under the covenant of works; under the curse of the law, or under the blessing of the gospel. For upon this exploration, and the certainty that arises from it, depends all our spiritual security, tranquility of soul, peace, joy, comfort, and so forth. The marks by which this may be safely and evidently known are supplied: (1) certainly and principally, by the fulfilled or unfulfilled condition of the covenant of grace, that is, true and living faith in God and the Mediator (John 1:11–12; 3:16, 36), and thus from all those things by which that faith is discerned, which are treated in their own place (bk. 2, ch.

1, §§XXIV–XLIII), and in our *Syntagma on Saving Faith* (ch. 11–13).[69] Then (2) also from the first formula of this covenant (Gen. 3:15). If namely we should detect that (a) we are of the seed of the woman, and not of the seed of the serpent, that is, if we have been united with Christ by the Spirit and by faith, for the covenant of grace is entered into with only the seed of the woman, and only in Christ are all the promises of God yes and amen (2 Cor. 1:20); outside of him there is no salvation (Acts 4:12), without him no one comes to the Father (John 14:6). If (b) we should discern an irreconcilable enmity between us and the serpent. In particular, if (i) God has established it by regeneration, conversion, and sanctification (John 3:3, 5; cf. John 8:44). If (ii) a hostile affection thrives between us and the serpent, arising from a change of our status, that is, because we have gone from being carnal to being spiritual (John 3:3, 5–6), from natural to supernatural (1 Cor. 2:14–15), from dead in sin to alive by grace (Eph. 2:1–10), from devilish, divine (John 8:44; 1 John 3:12; cf. 2 Peter 1:4). If (iii) inimical and hostile pursuits are discerned between us and the serpent, so that whereas he, for example, gives himself to lies, we give ourselves to truth (John 8:44; 1 John 3:19), whereas he behaves as the prince of darkness, we behave as children of light (Eph. 6:12 with 5:8), whereas he is an impure spirit, we are those purified by the Word and Spirit (Matt. 12:43; John 15:2; 1 Cor. 6:11), whereas he is the god of this world, we are such who, with Christ, are not of the world (2 Cor. 4:4; John 15:19). If (4) a perpetual conflict thrives between us, and the serpent and his seed (Gal. 5:17), that is, a hatred of sins (as the works of Satan) and of those sinning (1 John 3:8–9; Ps. 139:21–22), a struggle against his dominion, by which he takes us captive at his will (2 Tim. 2:26) and works in the children of disobedience (Eph. 2:2), and a zeal for striving against his temptations in the strength of Christ, and the whole armor of the Spirit (Eph. 6:12–13). If on the contrary (5) we within ourselves keep our soul friendly toward God, and his ways and people (Ps. 97:10; 1 John 5:1; Ps. 16:3–5; 139:21–22). If by all the aforementioned things (6) we endeavor earnestly in the strength of Christ to crush the head of the serpent, by denial of ourselves, crucifixion of the flesh, mortification of the old man (Luke 9:23; Gal. 5:24; Col. 3:5), by striving against our corruption until it is entirely dead. Finally, (7) from the effects and benefits of the covenant of grace, which are expressed more distinctly in the later formulas of this covenant (Jer. 31:31–34; Heb. 8:8–12): if, for example, we observe that the laws of God are written in our mind, and so forth.

---

69. Mastricht, *De fide salvifica syntagma theoretico-practicum* (Duisburg: Sas, 1671), 277–356.

5. It exhorts us that we should strive for participation in the covenant of grace.

XLVII. So then, fifth, if when the exploration has been completed we discern that we are so far still outside of the covenant of grace (Eph. 2:12), let us be stirred up to long for, and with all our strength to strive for participation in it. The motivating reasons for settling the covenant of grace will be supplied from §XLV. And the manner of settling consists in consent, by which we earnestly receive the conditions to which God promises the benefits of the covenant of grace, that is, in true and living faith (John 3:16), such that here pertain all those things by which faith is commonly begotten, which we have presented above (bk. 2, ch. 1, §§XLIV–XLVII), to which, out of desire for brevity, we will add nothing.

6. It commands keeping the covenant religiously once contracted.

XLVIII. Furthermore, sixth, if when the exploration has been completed we discern that we have already settled the covenant of grace with God, it rouses us that we would most religiously observe it inviolate (Gen. 17:9, 14; Deut. 29:9). If you should say, This covenant cannot be violated, from the divine promise (Heb. 8:9–10), I will grant it, if it is understood as concerning a total and final violation, that is, concerning a total unfaithfulness of the truly covenanted; I will deny it, if it is said concerning a partial unfaithfulness, which in any way runs against the duties of this covenant, to which end tend all the sins by which it is read to have been rather frequently violated by the Israelites (Heb. 8:9; Deut. 4:23; 29:25; 31:20; Josh. 23:16), namely: (1) idolatry, by which, either in place of the one and true God, or next to him, we receive another (Jer. 2:13, 17–18; Deut. 29:25–27); (2) profaneness and atheism, by which, either in word or in fact we do not receive any God (Ps. 14:1–2; 10:4); (3) superstition and will-worship, by which, if not by profession, at least by worship, we revere another god (Deut. 29:19–21, 25; Jer. 3:17); (4) rebellion, by which we knowingly and willingly strike against the duties of the covenanted (Jer. 44:16–17).

The duties of the covenanted

And so that we may keep the covenant of grace inviolate, it is necessary that, on the one side, we most religiously take heed of these and other sins, and on the other side, that we most religiously devote ourselves to the duties and virtues of the covenanted, that: (1) we hold God as our highest end (Ps. 33:12; 16:5–6, 8; 84:1–2); (2) Jesus as our only Mediator (Phil. 3:8–9); (3) to them before anything in this world we always and everywhere concede the prerogative (Matt. 10:37; 19:27); (4) we arrange all our affairs to their glory (1 Cor. 10:31); (5) we perform all our affairs according to their precept (Matt. 6:10).

7. It stirs us up to the renewal of the covenant.

XLIX. In addition, seventh, once the covenant of grace has been contracted, we should renew it quite frequently, after the example of Joshua (Josh. 24:14–26), and of the Israelites (2 Chron. 15:12–13): (1) with the memory of the covenant renewed (Deut. 4:23; 8:10, 14, 18–19); (2) with a holy resolve to persist in the promised duties of the covenant (Deut. 29:9; 23:23; Ps. 25:14); (3) with a religious use of the seals of the covenant, especially of the Holy Supper (Gen. 17:11; Rom. 4:11; 1 Cor. 11:25).

Motives

Because God (1) so many times, from the beginning to the end of the world, throughout so many periods, is read to have renewed this covenant, with Noah, with Abraham, Isaac, Jacob, the entirety of Israel at Sinai, with David and Solomon; and indeed he gave signs and seals to this end, that by each one the covenant might be renewed. (2) He is frequently said to remember his covenant, and not to forget it (Ex. 2:24; 6:4; Deut. 4:31), and to remember it to this end, that (3) he may keep it (Deut. 7:9; 8:18).

8. It exhorts us to turn this covenant to our use.

L. Finally, eighth, let us turn the covenant begun, observed, renewed to our own use (Deut. 29:12), first: (1) for comfort in all adversities, as much bodily as spiritual, namely because we are the covenanted ones of God (Ps. 4:3; 23:1, 4–5). Then, (2) for holiness, so that by thinking of this covenant, (a) we would be deterred from every sin, inasmuch as by it our covenant with God, though in differing degrees, is broken, and we ourselves are rendered faithless against our God (Ps. 50:17–19); (b) we would be raised up to every duty of piety, inasmuch as we have been bound to it from the covenant with God (Ps. 116:14). (3) For thankfulness, from love, grace, mercy, redemption, so many and such great benefits, by which God made himself a debtor to us in this covenant, by free obligation (Deut. 32:6–7).

CHAPTER TWO

The Mediator of the Covenant of Grace

And on account of this, he is the Mediator of the new covenant, so that by a death intervening for the redemption of the transgressions that were under the previous covenant, those who are called might receive the promised eternal inheritance.

—Hebrews 9:15

What has been said and what will be said in this chapter are connected.

I. The norm and pattern according to which God dispenses every saving grace is the covenant of grace, which we have already said. The procurer of grace, who according to the covenant of grace acquires as well as applies every benefit of grace, is the Mediator Jesus Christ, and in this book we will present his: (1) mediatorial dignity, (2) names, (3) person, (4) offices, (5) two states, and finally, (6) his redemption.

The Exegetical Part

The text is resolved and explained.

II. The apostle presents the mediatorial dignity in Hebrews 9:15, in the words prefixed to this chapter, in which he speaks of:

    A. The Mediator: "And on account of this, he is the Mediator of the new covenant, or testament." Here is evident:

        1. The rationale on account of which he is the Mediator: διὰ τοῦτο, "on account of this," namely, what he had said in the previous verse, that is, that through the blood of beasts, there occurs no deliverance from sin truly and properly speaking; therefore Old Testament believers either had no deliverance from sin, which is absurd; or, they had it through the blood of this Mediator, that is, Christ: for there is no third option.

        2. The Mediator himself: μεσίτης ἐστίν, "he is the Mediator," that is,

Christ, about whom he had spoken throughout the whole chapter, indeed throughout the entire epistle. Moreover, he is the μεσίτης, from μέσος, middle. And Christ is in the middle, first with respect to his person, through the participation of both natures, as much of the divine as of the human, and thus he is in the middle between God and man, bound equally to both, and consequently constituted without any party spirit, which is entirely necessary in any mediator; and then in relation to his office, through which he intercedes in the middle between the offended God and the offending man, so that he may reconcile them to one another (1 Tim. 2:5; Heb. 7:22), insofar as, from the counsel of the Father, he undertook the guilt of the elect sinner upon himself (Ps. 40:6–8), insofar as once undertaken he paid it by making satisfaction in time (2 Cor. 5:18–19, 21), and in this way by his death sealed the covenant of grace (Heb. 9:16).

3. The covenant of which he is the Mediator: "of the new covenant," καινῆς διαθήκης. Διαθήκη means either a covenant, that is, a pact among parties, or a testament, which is established by one party. In this passage, whether you translate it by "new covenant" or by "new testament," it will result in nearly the same thing, because the covenant of grace absorbs the testament, inasmuch as it is a dispensation of the covenant of grace through the death of the testator. Although at the same time, by διαθήκη, here I prefer to understand a testament, not on account of this only, that the apostle mentions in the following verse the death of the testator which confirms a testament, which is not so characteristically required in a covenant, insofar as it is such, but also on account of this, that the apostle mentions transgressions that were under the previous testament. So then he calls it new inasmuch as it is distinguished from the Old Testament, so that it means that the blood of the Mediator was shed not only for the transgressions of the present church, but of the past church as well, namely that of the Old Testament. At the least, it does not mean that there are three testaments, as many want, but only two.

B. The mediation, either the ἔργον μεσιτικόν, work of mediation, or the use of the mediation, which is related as twofold, that is:

1. The removal of evil: "so that by a death intervening for the redemption of the transgressions that were under the previous testament." There is here:

a. The means of removal: ὅπως θανάτου γενομένου, "so that by a death accomplished." He calls death the means of deliverance, because χωρὶς αἱματεκχυσίας, "without shedding of blood," or without a death, "there is no remission" (Heb. 9:22), namely the death that in the eternal covenant of grace he had undertaken to offer. It means the death which all the elect had deserved through the violation of the covenant of nature. Therefore, deliverance does not happen by some sort of declaration alone, nor by surety or expromission alone, but by the promised death, or by satisfaction through death. But he recalls a death γενομένη, accomplished, certainly not with the intention to mean that prior to the accomplished death no one under the Old Testament had obtained remission, for he would contradict himself when he says that by a death were removed the transgressions of those under the previous testament. So why then? He wants to signify that without a death either future or present, no one ever has obtained or does obtain deliverance.

b. The deliverance accomplished through death: ἀπολύτρωσις, "redemption." Thus it means that he intends not just any deliverance —not one such as occurs by mere intercession, or through force— but one such as occurs by the payment of a price, λύτρῳ, by a ransom, by a redeemer (1 Cor. 6:20; 1 Peter 1:18–19), by a soldier's price, which when paid, captive soldiers were customarily freed and released (Eph. 1:7, 14; Col. 1:14), whether that deliverance frees here and now from guilt, or hereafter from punishment.

c. The terminus *a quo* of the deliverance: τῶν ἐπὶ τῇ πρώτῃ παραβάσεων, "of those transgressions that were under the previous testament." Here is shown that by the death of the Mediator satisfaction was made for sins not only of present and future persons, but also of those in the past, and accordingly, that the Mediator is the same yesterday, and today, and forever (Heb. 13:8). He speaks of the διαθήκη πρώτη, previous testament, in order to distinguish it from the present one, and to divide the whole time of the church into two testaments.

2. The conferring of good: ὅπως τὴν ἐπαγγελίαν λάβωσιν οἱ κεκλημένοι τῆς αἰωνίου κληρονομίας, "so that those who are called might gain the promise, an eternal inheritance."

a. The possessors of this good: οἱ κεκλημένοι, "those who are called," certainly not each and every person, but only the called. Those called, not only outwardly, by the Word, or by the common calling, but also inwardly, by the Spirit, or by the effectual calling proper to the elect, and this certainly in such a way that by the calling to receive the Mediator by faith, they have gained that good. As to the rest, many are called, but few are chosen (Matt. 20:16).

b. The good possessed or to be possessed, which is:

    i. An inheritance: κληρονομία, "inheritance," from κλῆρος, "lot," and νέμω, "I distribute," because the goods of an inheritance, both in the past and now, are customarily distributed by lot (Ps. 16:6), as is evident in the distribution of the land of Canaan. Moreover, by this inheritance is understood the heavenly kingdom (Matt. 25:34; Eph. 5:5), so that we should understand that eternal life obtains for the elect not from their works or merits, but from the testament of Christ the testator, which has been confirmed by his death.

    ii. An eternal inheritance: αἰώνιος, "eternal." The adjective is added so that this inheritance may be distinguished from any temporal one, even that of the land of Canaan, and in addition that it may designate such an inheritance as was destined for them from eternity, and will be present for all eternity.

    iii. A promised inheritance: τὴν ἐπαγγελίαν, "the promise." Here "promise" means the thing promised (as in Luke 24:49; Acts 1:4; 2:33; Rom. 4:13; and elsewhere). Promised, that is, before the foundations of the world were laid (Matt. 25:34), and to be conferred, with respect to the firstfruits at least, in this life (Rom. 8:23–24), and with respect to the full harvest, after this life in death (2 Cor. 5:1), and in the last judgment (2 Tim. 4:8).

The Dogmatic Part

A true, fitting, and sufficient mediator was necessary for the covenant of grace.

III. Thus a true, fitting, and sufficient mediator was necessary for the covenant of grace. For otherwise, from the judgment of the text, it could not have occurred that the sins of the previous testament would be taken away, and that those called would gain an eternal inheritance. I say that one was necessary, yet certainly not by: (1) a most absolute necessity, such as that by which God exists, for it could have occurred that no one would be created, fallen, redeemed, and beatified; nor by (2) a natural necessity, such as, for example, that by which a person seeks blessedness, whether true or artificial; for God did not sanction the covenant of grace by nature, but by the choice of his good pleasure; but by (3) a hypothetical necessity, that is, with the decree presupposed to create man, to permit his fall, and to confer salvation to him once fallen. For the covenant of grace cannot be established between God and the sinner without an intervening mediator to make peace (John 14:6; 1 Tim. 2:5–6).

The sort of mediator that was necessary for the covenant of grace
IV. In this way a mediator is necessary, not just of any sort, but one that is: (1) true, not typical, as the high priest once was (Heb. 5:1); (2) fitting, that is, squarely in the middle, as much with respect to his person, as the Son between the Father and the Holy Spirit, as with respect to his natures, as the θεάνθρωπος, God-man, between God and man; (3) sufficient, one who can perfectly and by his own strength reconcile the disagreeing parties, God and man (Heb. 10:1, 14). Moses was certainly a mediator under the Old Testament (Gal. 3:19 with Deut. 5:23ff.), but neither true, nor fitting, nor sufficient. He was not true, because he was typical, being only a form of the true Mediator (Heb. 3:5). He was not fitting, because he was not squarely in the middle, being a mere man, and thus closer to man than to God, and only a servant, not a son (Heb. 3:5–6). He was not sufficient, inasmuch as he himself needed a mediator (Acts 4:12). The same, *mutatis mutandis*, can be said of Joshua.

That a mediator sufficient and perfect in all ways was necessary
V. Therefore, a mediator that is true, fitting, and perfect in all ways is necessary (1 Tim. 2:5; cf. John 14:6; Acts 4:12; 10:43). For without a mediator, and indeed without this kind of mediator: (1) the eternal decree of God concerning the true, spiritual, and eternal blessedness of sinners could by no means have been committed to execution. For just as all things concerning that blessedness have been predetermined by an eternal decree (Eph. 1:11), so they are not predetermined other than in the Mediator (Eph. 1:3–5). Then, (2) without a mediator, and also one of this kind, so many prophecies, promises, and types that once were made throughout the entire Old Testament concerning him would fail, with the most present danger to the divine truthfulness—indeed, at its expense. Furthermore, (3) also in this way the covenant of grace would become just as, and even more so, incomplete, uncertain, and inconstant, as was the covenant of works. For the sinner has by his own merit been stripped of all strength by which he could supply the condition of the covenant (Rom. 8:3). In addition, (4) nor could the enmity which through sin thrives between God and the sinner ever have been happily removed without this kind of mediator (Heb. 7:25–27). Nor also

(5) could satisfaction have been made by the merit of sinners to the natural holiness of God, to his avenging justice, to his governing wisdom, to the demand of the law. Nor finally, (6) could fallen man, dead in his sins, have been effectually called, regenerated, converted, justified, sanctified, adopted, glorified, without this kind of mediator.

What a mediator is in general

VI. Therefore so that we may more rightly understand the nature and character of this mediatorial dignity, before all things we must think that a mediator, in its conception, is one who intercedes in the middle between disagreeing parties, so that he may reconcile them. To the Hebrews a mediator is termed אמצעי, to the ancients, a *sequester*,[1] to the jurists, an *interventor*,[2] *internuncius*,[3] *interpres*,[4] or *advocatus*,[5] to Ulpian, an *interreconciliator*.[6]

---

1. According to H. E. Dirksen in his *Manuale Latinitatis fontium juris civilis Romanorum. Thesauri Latinitatis Epitome in usum Tironum* (Berlin: Duncker & Humblot, 1837), 879, a *sequester* and *interpres* are synonymous with an *internuncius*. Dirksen cites a classical definition of a *sequester*: "one who has custody of a disputed object." The role of a *sequester* occurs within the context of a property or financial dispute, frequently within the context of a divorce process.

2. According to Ulpian (*Digest* XV.1.iii.5–6, 9) an authorized son who acted for the family as an *interventor*, that is, who acted as a surety or third party who held a deposit and assumed liability for the deposit between two parties, obligated the *paterfamilias* as well. See Paul Krueger and Theodor Mommsen, *Corpus Iuris Civilis*, 10th ed. (Berlin: Weidmann, 1905), 1:193. Cf. David Johnston, "Limiting Liability: Roman Law and the Civil Law Tradition" in *Symposium on Ancient Law, Economics & Society Part I: The Development of Law in Classical and Early Medieval Europe/ Symposium on Ancient Law, Economics & Society Part I: The Development of Law in the Ancient Near East*, vol. 70 (June 1995): 1515–1538.

3. Also *internuntius*. "internuncio: 1. A messenger between two parties. 2. One who serves as agent of both parties to a transaction." E.g. *Black's Law Dictionary*, ed. B. A. Garner, 9th ed. (Eagan, Minn.: West, 2009), 893.

4. Although Dirksen (cf. n1) considers the role of an *interpres* and *sequester* as synonymous, one difference is that the *interpres* has a duty to explain the application of the laws or even the terms of a contract to both parties, whereas the role of a *sequester* is simply a temporary custodian of a disputed object. Theoretically the same person may have both roles, but the terms do not have identical functions. Cf. Dirksen, *Manuale Latinitatis*, 494, 879. In this regard, another similar term that Mastricht does not mention from Greek law is the *proxenetas*, which is defined by the Romans as a *conciliator et interpres negotii contrahendi, munerisve impetrandi*, one who reconciles and explains the terms of business being contracted or the one who procures the collateral from both parties, cf. Dirksen, *Manuale Latinitatis*, 785. Commenting on *Digest* L.14.i–iii, *De Proxeneticis*, the seventeenth century jurist Dionysius Gothofredius notes that a *proxeneticon* is the collateral due to the *proxenata* or *intercessor* who acts as an agent for a foreigner. See note a, col. 1921 in the 1627 edition of the *Digest* in the volume entitled, *Corpus juris civilis quo jus universum Justinianeum comprehenditur* (Paris: Antoine Vitray, 1628). The Vitray edition of the series is entitled *Corpus juris civilis cum Notis D. Gothofr. IC.… suo nitori restitutum* (Paris: Antoine Vitray, 1627).

5. Cf. Digest II.16.ix.1–6, Krueger & Mommsen, *Corpus Iuris Civilis*, 93.

6. For the specific uses of these sometimes overlapping or even synonymous terms, see

The Mediator is in the middle between the offended and offending party.
VII. Accordingly, in this matter there is, first, the offended party, God (Ps. 51:4): theologically, God three in persons (Isa. 63:9–10), then economically, the Father, insofar as he is the supreme Lawgiver, Lord, and Judge (2 Cor. 5:19). Second, there is the offending party, certainly not each and every person (John 17:9), but all so beloved by the Father that they were given to the Mediator to be redeemed (John 17:11, 24; 3:16). Third, there is the Mediator (μεσίτης, 1 Tim. 2:5; Heb. 8:6–8; 9:14–15; 12:24), who is in the middle: (1) between the offended persons (Matt. 28:19; 1 John 5:7); (2) between the disputing parties, God and man, as עמנואל, Immanuel (Isa. 7:14 with Acts 10:38), bearing the natures of both equally, as the God-man, God revealed in the flesh (1 Tim. 3:16), the middle ladder, joining heaven and earth (Gen. 28:12); (3) by office, pleading the cause of each with the other (1 Tim. 2:5; Heb. 5:1), first of God with man (2 Cor. 5:20), and in turn of man with God, satisfying and interceding for him (1 John 2:1). Thus not unwisely do many observe that Christ from almost any perspective is viewed as in the middle: he is born, as some think, in the middle of the night; he suffers in the middle of the world, in Jerusalem; he is crucified in the middle of thieves; he died in the middle between heaven and earth; after the resurrection he stands in the middle of his disciples; he promises that where two or three are gathered in his name, there he would be in the middle of them; he walks in the middle of the candlesticks; and like the heart in the middle of his mystical body, he imparts spirit and strength to his members.

So that the Mediator may be fitting and sufficient, three things are required.
VIII. Furthermore, so that the Mediator may be fitting and sufficient, three things are especially required: (1) that he be legitimately called to it, for no one takes this honor to himself, but he who is called, as was Aaron (Heb. 5:4–6);

Dirksen, *Manuale Latinitatis*, e.g. 494, 879. There is a legal concept in classical Roman works of someone who functions as a peacemaker between hostile forces. Livy utilizes the phrase *reconciliator pacis et disceptator* in *Ab urbe condita* (XXXV.45) as well as *interpres arbiterque concordiae civium* (II.33). Valerius Maximus speaks of one who functions as *de pace disceptator* in *De dictis factisque memorialibus*, vol. 1, (Paris: Nicolaus Eligius Lemaire, 1822), II.x.4. Ulpian utilizes the term *disceptatio* more as a judgement or a decision of an arbiter, rather than as the work of a mediator (*Digest* II.15.viii). However, one possible source for the citation is that Mastricht's section is almost verbatim with respect to Frans Burman (1628–1679), *Synopsis theologiae et speciatim oeconomiae foederis gratiae* (Utrecht: Cornelius Jacob Noenardus, 1671), II.ii.14 §2, which reads "A Mediator, μεσίτης, or אֶמְצָעִי is called one who is the middleman between two disagreeing parties for the purpose of reconciling them, or one who stands between God and man like Moses did in Deuteronomy 5:5. By the ancient jurists, such is a person is termed a *sequester, intercessor, internuncius, interpres*, or *advocatus*, and by Ulpian, an *interreconciliator*." Burman provides no citation as to his source for this assertion.

that is, that he be (a) chosen from eternity by the Father, and separated to this work, as the end (Isa. 42:1); (b) foreordained to all things that aim at this end, as the means (1 Peter 1:20; Acts 4:27–28); (c) sent in time for its execution (John 3:17). From all of these things, he is said to have been sealed (John 6:27), anointed (Isa. 61:1), given to the world (John 3:16). (2) That he promptly admit and receive that office (Ps. 40:6–8). (3) That he be equipped with the necessary things required for this, from which he is said to have been sanctified (John 10:36); in particular, it was required that he would be: (a) true God (John 1:1–2), so that he might be able more fittingly to conduct the part of God with men (John 1:18), as the perfect Lord of his own life, to spend it by his death for sinners (John 10:18), to compensate for the death of so many myriads of people by his one death (1 John 1:7; Acts. 10:28), to procure for them infinite good, then through vivification, regeneration, conversion, sanctification, and glorification, to apply the procured good to them, concerning which application we will say more expressly in its own place.[7] (b) True man (1 Tim. 2:5), so that he might be able to take on the guilt of men (Ex. 32:33; Heb. 2:11, 14), to suffer death for them (Heb. 9:15). (c) A righteous man, so that he would not have the necessity first to satisfy for his own guilt (Heb. 7:26–27), and thus be rendered unfit to take away the sins of others. (d) God and man in one person, that is, so that we would have one Mediator (1 Tim. 2:5), for otherwise we would have none who would be God and man. Concerning each of these we will speak individually in their own places.[8]

The Mediator discharges his function: First, by pledging surety

IX. Moreover, the Mediator discharges his parts, first, by pledging surety (for which reason, the one who in Hebrews 8:6 is called the Mediator of the new covenant, in Hebrews 7:22 is addressed as the surety of the new covenant), when in the eternal counsel of peace, which is mentioned in Zechariah 6:13, through a certain singular pact between the Father and himself (Isa. 53:10), according to the will of the Father, he took upon himself the guilt and entire cause of the elect, and the Father in turn accepted this, of which pact the formula, as it were, is presented in Psalm 40:6–8: "Sacrifice and offering" (that is, from sinners themselves, and that indeed typical) "you have not desired, but my ears you have pierced" (that is, a sign of perpetual obligation); "burnt offering and sacrifice you have not required" (namely, that by it satisfaction might be made for sins). "Then I said, Behold, I come; in the volume of the book it is written of me, that I would

---

7. 1.6.1–9
8. 1.5.4 §§V, XVff.

do your will, O my God." Here stands forth the will of the Father, at which the Son arose with his surety.

Not by a conditional surety, but by an absolute surety
Moreover, he pledged not by a *fidejussio* or conditional surety properly speaking, by which the one pledging admits the guilt of the debtor only under the condition that the debtor himself has not paid or satisfied it, and thus reserves for himself the rights of order and seizure, so that the debtor himself would first be prosecuted and have goods seized, and therefore the principal guilt would remain with the debtor; but rather, he pledged by an *expromissio* or absolute surety, although this extraordinary absolute surety in a capital case must not be so rigidly held to the laws of the jurists' ordinary *expromissio*. We have already vindicated this absolute surety in the preceding chapter, §XXXIV.

Second, by announcing
X. Second, he discharges his office by announcing: "He sent me to announce to the meek" (Isa. 61:1; Ps. 40:9; John 1:18). Specifically: (1) by opening the aforementioned counsel of peace (Zech. 6:13; Isa. 53:10, 12), the covenant of grace held forth in the gospel (2 Tim. 1:10); (2) by revealing the conditions by which, from the counsel of peace, the covenant of grace may be established between God and the sinner (John 3:16; 1:12); (3) by inviting, with amassed arguments, sinners to accept those conditions (Matt. 11:28–30; Rev. 3:20; 22:17; Song 5:4); (4) by promising the success of those conditions when accepted (John 6:37). From this announcing especially, he is spoken of as an ambassador sent by God, throughout John (3:17, 34; 4:34; 5:23–24, 30, 36–37; 9:4; 10:36; etc.), the messenger of the covenant, מלאך הברית (Mal. 3:1), likewise ὁ λόγος, the Word (John 1:1; 1 John 5:7; דבר in Ps. 33:6), not only because he was spoken or promised to the Old Testament fathers as the future Messiah (Heb. 11:39), nor only from his mode of subsisting,[9] by which he is the wisdom of the Father (Prov. 8:22), from which he was also customarily spoken of as the λόγος ἐνούσιος and οὐσιώδης, the essential and substantial Word; but also because he is the

---

9. τρόπῳ ὑπάρξεως; cf. (Pseudo-)Justin Martyr, "Ἔκθεσις πίστεως περὶ τῆς ὀρθῆς ὁμολογίας, Expositio fidei de recta confessione, sive de sancta consubstantiali Trinitate" in *Opera* (Paris: Claudius Sonnius, 1636), 373: ὅτι τὸ μὲν ἀγέννητον καὶ γεννητὸν καὶ ἐκπορευτὸν οὐχ οὐσίας ὀνόματα, ἀλλὰ τρόποι ὑπάρξεως ὁ δέ τρόπος τῆς ὑπάρξεως, τοῖς ὀνόμασι χαρακτηρίζεται τούτοις, "wherefore 'unbegotten,' 'begotten' and 'proceeding' are not names of essence, but modes of existing (*modi existentiae*), and the mode of existing is characterized by these names." Cf. R. V. Sellers, "Pseudo-Justin's 'Expositio Rectae Fidei': A Work of Theodoret of Cyprus" in *The Journal of Theological Studies*, vol. 46, no. 183/184 (Oxford: Oxford University Press, July/October, 1945):145–60.

interpreter, messenger, spokesman, and ambassador of the Father (John 1:18), who declares the will of the Father to us, as much in his own person (Heb. 1:1) as through the prophets (1 Peter 3:18–19; 1:11), the apostles, and so forth; which two things appear to be conjoined in Matthew 11:27. Accordingly, also throughout the Aramaic paraphrase he is called מימר, the Speech (in Ps. 110:1; Isa. 45:17; Hos. 1:7), and in the Syriac New Testament, in place of λόγος, מלתא, the Word; from this he is called, among other things, the wisdom of the Father (Prov. 8:22; 1 Cor. 1:24), because by announcing to us the wisdom of God (1 Cor. 2:6–7), he has been made wisdom from God (1 Cor. 1:30). We will have more about this, Lord willing, in chapter 6.

Third, by placating

XI. Third, he discharges it by placating, reconciling, redeeming, satisfying, as he is the one who, as the only Mediator between God and men, gave himself as an ἀντίλυτρον, ransom (1 Tim. 2:5–6), and by himself accomplished the purging of our sins (from which sins came all the disagreement; Heb. 1:3). As the faithful high priest, he expiated the sins of the people (Heb. 2:17); by offering himself, he obtained eternal redemption (Heb. 7:27; 9:12, 14; etc.). Thus he is called εἰρηνοποιῶν, the one making peace (Col. 1:20), our peace (Eph. 2:13–14), by which God has made us acceptable to himself in the Beloved (Eph. 1:6); likewise the גואל, *Goel*, avenger (Job 19:25; Isa. 59:20), which in its emphasis denotes such a kind of champion, avenger, deliverer, and redeemer, who moved by right of consanguinity maintains the cause of his slain relative and avenges his blood, or claims for him again, by right of original ownership, that which in whatever way has been devolved and implicated in some contract, as witnessed by Salomon Glass, *Oration on the Necessity of the Hebrew Language* (cf. Lev. 25:25; Ruth 2:20).[10] For this reason, in Greek he is called ὁ ῥυόμενος, the deliverer

---

10. In November 1621, the Lutheran theologian, Salomon Glass (Glassius) delivered an oration entitled, "The Knowledge of the Hebrew Language is so necessary for a future theologian that one cannot lack it or lack it without difficulty." See Salomon Glassius (1593–1656), *Philologiae Sacrae Veteris et Novi Testamenti Scripturae*, 5th ed. (Frankfurt: sumtibus Johannes Theodore Fleischer, Jena), 361–76. Cf. Stephen G. Burnett, "Lutheran Christian Hebraism in the Time of Solomon Glassius (1593–1656)," *Hebraistik - Hermeneutik - Homiletik. Die 'Philologia Sacra' im frühneuzeitlichen Bibelstudium*, eds. C. Bultmann and L. Danneberg, Historia Hermeneutica. Series Studia, vol. 10 (Berlin: De Gruyter, 2011), 441–67; idem, "Chapter 1: Birth of A Christian Hebrew Reading Public" in *Christian Hebraism in the Reformation Era (1500–1660): Authors, Books, and the Transmission of Jewish Learning*, Library of the Written Word Series, vol. 19 (Brill: Leiden, 2012), 11–47; idem, *From Christian Hebraism to Jewish Studies: Johannes Buxtorf (1564–1629) and Hebrew Learning in the Seventeenth Century* (Brill: Leiden, 1996); Aya Elyada, "Protestant Scholars and Yiddish Studies in Early Modern Europe," *Past & Present*, no. 203 (May 2009): 69–98.

(Rom. 11:26), and the λυτρώτης, ransomer, because he gave his soul as a λύτρον ἀντὶ πολλῶν, a ransom for many (Matt. 20:28; Mark 10:45); ὁ μέλλων λυτροῦσθαι τὸν Ἰσραήλ, the one who would redeem Israel (Luke 24:21; cf. Titus 2:14; 1 Peter 1:18); in Latin, *redemptor*, redeemer, he who delivers by paying a price (1 Cor. 6:20). More will be seen in its own place, in the chapters on redemption, 7 and 18.

Fourth, by ratifying the covenant of grace

XII. Fourth, he discharges it by ratifying and sanctioning with his own death the established covenant of grace, so that from this arises a testament, by aid of which those called gain the promised inheritance, for where there is a testament, it is necessary that the death of the testator should intervene (Heb. 9:15–16; cf. Gal. 3:15). So then therefore it is not without reason that he will be termed a testator, because: (1) the testamentary Mediator by his death sealed, as it were, the testament or covenant of grace (the testamentary covenant); (2) he confers to his own all the benefits of the covenant of grace, just like so many legacies, once he is alive from death; (3) and that according to the Scriptures, inasmuch as they are the Word of Christ, as the testamentary instrument (Jer. 31:31); (4) written down through the prophets, apostles, and other divinely inspired amanuenses, as his notaries and scribes; in addition, (5) it was sealed with the sacraments, as seals of the New Testament (Matt. 26:27–28); and (6) not without witnesses (1 John 5:6–10), in heaven as well as on earth; and indeed, (7) alive again from the dead, he himself has also become the executor of this testament, through his Spirit efficaciously conferring and applying the benefits of the testamentary covenant (Luke 22:29).

Fifth, by interceding

XIII. Finally, he discharges it by interceding: (1) by praying for his own, while still existing on the earth (throughout the entirety of John 17); (2) by appearing for them before the Father in heaven (Heb. 9:24), that is, so that there he may diligently plead their entire cause (Rom. 8:34); (3) by offering their prayers, and commending them to his Father (Rev. 8:3–5); in addition, (4) by presenting his merits to the Father (Zech. 9:11). And from these things, he is called the παράκλητος, advocate (1 John 2:1), he who advocates to defend someone; likewise, מלאך פנים, the angel of the presence (Isa. 63:9), and מלאך מליץ, the angel-mediator (Job 33:23), because, as has been said, he appears for the sake of his own before his Father (cf. Matt. 18:10).

The mediatorial function embraces three offices.
XIV. From all these things and perhaps others, the mediatorial dignity is divided into three distinct offices: the prophetic (Deut. 18:15; Acts 3:22), priestly (Ps. 110:4; Heb. 5:6; 7:17), and kingly (Ps. 2:6; John 18:33, 36). And for this reason, so that as Mediator, he could easily assist: (1) their ignorance, insofar as he is a prophet; (2) their enmity and alienation from God, insofar as he is a priest; and (3) their impotence and infirmity, insofar as he is a king. We will expressly treat each of these one by one in their own place.[11]

Our Jesus alone is the Mediator.
XV. One thing remains, namely that our Jesus alone, and that indeed as the God-man, is that Mediator which we have so far delineated (Heb. 9:15; 1 Tim. 2:5–6; 1 John 2:1; John 14:6; Acts 4:12; etc.). For he alone: (1) by the eternal counsel of God, has been called (Heb. 5:4–6), foreordained, sanctified, sent, and anointed to this end, as we have said. (2) In him alone do all the prophecies and promises of the Old Testament about the Messiah Mediator converge. (3) He alone answers all the types and figures of the Messiah Mediator given under the Old Testament. (4) He alone enjoys the testimony of this dignity, not only that of John the Baptist, his forerunner by divine mission (Mal. 3:1; John 1:29), but also that of the Holy Trinity itself (Matt. 3:17), of the Father who seals him (John 6:27), and thus offers testimony (John 5:37), of the Son who offers testimony to himself by his miracles (John 5:36; Matt. 11:2–7; Acts 2:22), and likewise of the Holy Spirit, by his descent upon Jesus (Matt. 3:16–17), upon the apostles (Acts 2:2–4, 32–33, 36), who testifies in the consciences of all Christians (1 John 5:6). (5) He alone enjoys all the requisites of the true, fitting, and sufficient Mediator, as we have already said. (6) He alone has discharged all the mediatorial parts which we have spoken of. More things on this point will occur in the elenctic part.[12]

Jesus is the Mediator as God and man.
XVI. Not only is he the Mediator, but he is also so as the God-man, with his two natures concurring, not only for the qualification of the person, which even the Romanists themselves acknowledge, but also for the very discharging of the mediatorial office. This is so in such a way that the human nature for the most part supplied the mediatorial work, and the divine nature added its value and worth, for which reason it is said that God redeemed the church with his own

---

11. 1.5.6–8
12. §XIX, below

blood (Acts 20:28), and that the blood of Jesus Christ the Son of God cleanses us from all sin (1 John 1:7). And what is more, that the mediatorial work itself—insomuch at least as it attains to the application of the accomplished redemption through vivification, regeneration, conversion, sanctification, the conveying of saving faith, its operation—demands the aid of the divine nature, we will expressly demonstrate in its own place.[13]

The Elenctic Part

It is asked: 1. Is Christ such a mediator who, without any middle status of person, without the participation of both natures, without the eternal surety, without the placation of the offended party, is a mere messenger?

XVII. It is asked, first, whether Christ is such a mediator who, without any middle status of person, without the participation of both natures, without the eternal surety, without the placation of the offended party, is a mere messenger. The Socinians, out of hatred of the eternal deity and satisfaction of Christ, affirm this, with Socinus as proof, in *Jesus Christ the Savior* (bk. 1, ch. 1).[14]

The orthodox reasons

The Reformed on the contrary state that he is the Mediator because he is in the middle between the Father and the Holy Spirit, he bears the nature of both hostile parties, and he not only by announcing opens the will of the offended God to men, but also by his satisfaction has placated God toward man; and moreover, that Socinus's heresy regarding Christ as a mere messenger—who declared the way of eternal salvation to us, confirmed it, and plainly displayed it in his very own person, first by the example of his life, and then by rising again from the dead, and who himself will give eternal life to us who have faith in him; but that he neither satisfied, nor was it necessary that he should satisfy, the divine justice through which we deserved to be condemned as sinners for our sins[15]—is repugnant: (1) to the text, which says that he is the Mediator not only by ἀπολύτρωσις or redemption, but also by the taking away of sins that were under the previous testament; which to have been accomplished only by announcement, clearly cannot be conceived of, nor will be admitted by Socinus himself. It is repugnant (2) to those things by which in both pledging

---

13. 1.5.4 §IV

14. Faustus Socinus (1539–1604), *De Jesu Christo Servatore, hoc est, cur et qua ratione Jesus Christus noster Servator sit…disputatio* (Alex. Rodecius, 1594), 11–22; idem, *Opera omnia in duos tomos distincta* (Irenopolis [Amsterdam]), 2:124–27.

15. Socinus, *De Jesu Christo Servatore*, 2, 64.

and placating he performed the mediatorial parts, as we taught in the dogmatic part.[16] It is repugnant (3) to satisfaction, which in its own place, in the chapter on redemption, we will teach expressly.[17]

Our adversaries' objections
Nor is it any hindrance: (1) that (and here in this controversy they especially can allege this) from this hypothesis he acted as a mediator with himself. For it is not repugnant for a certain member of an injured society to intercede on behalf of the one injuring with the whole wounded society, and in that consequently with himself. Nor (2) that God, injured by sin, in giving the Mediator for the one injuring, now seems to have been placated toward him, and for this reason does not need the placation of a mediator. For: (a) it is not repugnant for one who loves the one injuring to be not reconciled to the one injuring, but still in need of being reconciled, as is seen in the case of David toward Absalom (2 Sam. 14:21). Then, (b) the love of benevolence, by which the one injured seeks to make reconciliation, does not argue for the love of complacency, or a reconciliation already made (2 Cor. 5:20). The remaining objections will occur in the chapter on redemption.[18]

2. Was the eternal surety of the Mediator a conditional or absolute surety?
XVIII. It is asked, second, whether the eternal surety of the Mediator was a conditional or absolute surety. We considered this controversy in the preceding chapter, §XXXIV; here we only point it out, so that you may have before you the matters that are controverted on this topic.

3. Is our Jesus the Mediator and Messiah?
XIX. It is asked, third, whether the Messiah promised long ago had to have been the Mediator, and whether our Jesus is that Messiah. The pagans, because they are devoid of revelation, either out of sheer ignorance or hatred of the Christian religion, deny both a Messiah, and a mediator, and Jesus, unless they considered their own demons as mediators. The Muslims do consider Jesus as an eminent prophet, but out of hatred of the Christian religion, and love for their Muhammad, they do not accept Jesus as the Mediator. The Jews, out of hatred of the Christian religion and our Jesus, deny both, that is, that the Messiah had to have been the Mediator, and that Jesus is the Messiah.

------

16. §§IX, XI
17. 1.5.18 §§XXVI, XXXIII–XXXIV
18. 1.5.18 §§XXVI, XXXIII–XXXIV

That the Messiah would be the Mediator

The Reformed affirm both. And they prove the first claim: (1) from the terms which are asserted for him in the Old Testament, when he is called the angel of the covenant, that is, the ambassador and messenger of the covenant (Mal. 3:1), likewise the angel of the presence, who appears on behalf of the covenanted before the face of God (Isa. 63:9), the גואל, *goel*, the avenger and kinsman Redeemer of the covenanted (Job 19:25; Isa. 43:14), עמנואל, Immanuel, God with us (Isa. 7:14), the one who joins God with man by mediation; (2) from the parts of the mediatorial office attributed to him, when he is called a prophet (Deut. 18:15), priest (Ps. 110:4), and king (Ps. 2:6), as we taught above;[19] (3) from the requirements of the Mediator, when he is called God and man in one person, עמנואל, Immanuel (Isa. 7:14), a child and a son (Isa. 9:6; etc.), the righteous one (Isa. 53:11); (4) from the mediatorial functions, the expromissory pact (Isa. 53:10–11), the announcing of the gospel (Isa. 61:1), the placating of God through undertaking our guilt (Isa. 53:12), the sealing of the covenant (Dan. 9:24, 27), the intercession for the covenanted (Jer. 30:21). For convincing pagans and Muslims will serve what we will consider below, in chapter 18, §XXIII.

That our Jesus is that promised Messiah

Second, they deny that our Jesus is the Messiah promised to them. That we might wrench the confession of this from them, solid arguments will be insufficient unless they also be sent against them in a fitting order, to which end it is necessary that we demonstrate the following three things distinctly: (1) that the Messiah promised to them has already appeared in the flesh, the truth of which we will obtain more certainly than certain by these ancient testimonies of Scripture, which teach that: (a) the scepter would not depart from Judah, nor a lawgiver from between his feet, before Shiloh come (Gen. 49:10); (b) the Messiah would be given after seventy weeks of years (Dan. 9:24–26); (c) while the second temple was still standing (Hag. 2:7; Mal. 3:1); and so forth. (2) The Messiah who has now appeared in the flesh is none but our Jesus. For if there is another, the Jews should show it, or if there is not, it is necessary that they confess ours, especially since there is no one whom the requirements of the Mediator designated in the Old Testament more exactly fit than ours: (a) a virgin parent (Isa. 7:14; Gen. 3:15), (b) birthplace in Bethlehem (Mic. 5:2–3), (c) the seed of Abraham, Isaac, and Jacob (Gen. 22:18; etc.), (d) from the family of David (Isa. 11:1; 2 Sam. 7:12; Ps. 132:10), (e) prophet, priest, and king, as was demonstrated above,[20]

---

19. §XIV
20. §XIV

(f) a king poor and needy, riding on a donkey (Zech. 9:9), (g) renowned for miracles (Isa. 29:18; 35:4–6), (h) to be rejected by his own (Ps. 118:22), (i) to be crucified and die for the sake of others (Ps. 22; Isa. 53; Dan. 9:24, 26–27), (k) to be resurrected from the dead (Ps. 16:10; 110:7), (l) to ascend into heaven and sit at the right hand of God (Ps. 68:18; 110:1; etc.). And (3) since in the application of these and other prophecies it is necessary to call for aid upon the Gospel history, if not as divinely inspired and canonical writing (which for the sake of order should to this point be set aside), at least as universally true history, we should have before us those things which we set forth on this matter in book 1, chapter 2, §XXX.

Jewish objections

Nor is it valid on the contrary to argue: (1) that the Elijah to come has not yet come (Mal. 4:5). Since that the Tishbite himself was promised is incumbent upon them to prove, and that he has come spiritually is evident (Luke 1:17 with Matt. 11:14; 17:12). (2) That the Mt. Zion to be exalted under the Messiah (Isa. 2:2–4) has not yet been exalted. For the church, which is understood by the mountain, both has been exalted, and is daily exalted, and will be exalted till the end of days, by the calling of the nations to participate in Christ. (3) That the temple to be built by the Messiah (Zech. 6:12, 15) has not yet been built. But that a material temple is to be built by the Messiah is incumbent upon the Jews to prove; however, the mystical temple, the church, by the calling of the nations, both has been built by the Messiah, and is being built daily. The rest of their objections are not of any consequence.

4. Besides Christ, are there other mediators, at least with respect to intercession?

XX. It is asked, fourth, whether besides Christ, there are other mediators, at least with respect to intercession. The Romanists, to disguise their idolatry: (1) distinguish between a mediator of redemption and of intercession, to this end, so that (2) besides Christ, they may have other mediators in heaven, the angels, the blessed Virgin, other departed saints, if not for redemption at least for intercession; they affirm this. And even so, (3) to these mediators they also assign merits, arisen from supererogatory actions and passions, which they can dispense for their clients. And accordingly, they teach (4) that they are for these reasons to be called upon, and in fact that God can be called upon through their merits, and those of their guardian angel, that God would confer upon them this or that petition.

The state of the controversy. Arguments
We Reformed, although we acknowledge: (1) that believers while on earth, on the basis of the divine command, by their prayers can and must intercede for one another (1 Tim. 2:1); and likewise although (2) we do not deny that it could occur that the blessed inhabitants of heaven pray for the militant church in an indefinite way, although certain testimonies of this are not yet obvious to me. Nevertheless, (3) that there are, from the style of Scripture, mediators of intercession, who are not mediators of redemption; or (4) that in heaven there are, besides Christ, mediators who intercede for believers on earth in particular; much more (5) who dispense for others their merits or good works; and for that reason (6) are to be called upon by us—all these things we think are contrary to Scripture, inasmuch as in it: (1) there is not a mediator of intercession who is not likewise a mediator of redemption; nor is there but one Mediator, as much of intercession as of redemption (1 John 2:1; 1 Tim. 2:5; John 14:6). Nor is there (2) anyone besides Christ who can boast of merits, much less of supererogatory ones that they could dispense for others. Nor accordingly (3) ought anyone besides Christ to be called upon for intercession, because invocation presupposes the knowledge both of the heart and of needs (which does not apply to the blessed inhabitants of heaven, Isa. 53:16), and religious worship is proper to God alone (Matt. 4:10).

Objections
Nor is there anything by which the papists might with any appearance of truth defend their mediators, for if they should allege: (1) that saints on earth legitimately intercede for saints, I respond, This God commanded (1 Tim. 2:1), the other he forbids as we have said; nor do they intercede as intercessors by office, but as brothers for brothers. (2) That it is not customary that we would burst into the presence of a king without interceding agents. I respond, We have an Agent, one worth them all, Christ (1 John 2:1).

5. Is Christ the Mediator only with respect to one of the natures, or according to both? A comparison of opinions
XXI. It is asked, fifth, whether Christ is the Mediator only with respect to one of the natures, or according to both. The papists, so that they may more easily conjoin many mediators to the one, think that though in his mediatorial person come together the two natures, the divine and the human, yet this is not so in the discharging of the mediatorial office, and thus that Christ the God-man, although he is in this matter the *principium quod,* as they say, the principle which

acts, yet the two natures are not *principia quo*, principles by which he acts.[21] Colluding with them, at least in thesis, is the Lutheran professor at Königsberg, Francesco Stancaro, whether carried away by love for Peter Lombard, or only by hatred for his colleague, Osiander.[22] So also the Socinians, in addition by denying the eternal deity of the Mediator. The Reformed on the contrary, because they hold to a Mediator who is the God-man, whose two natures are as many *principia* of his mediatorial operations, in such a way that each *principium* has its own particular efficacy in these operations, and through this efficacy, every mediatorial work flows from both natures, and from the proper efficacy particular to each, state that he is the Mediator according to both natures.

The orthodox reasons

Urging this is: (1) the constant tenor of the Scriptures, when they implicate the divine nature and its divine operation in the mediatorial functions (Acts 20:28; 2 Cor. 5:19; John 10:17–18). Urging it is (2) the end and goal of the personal union of the two natures in the one Mediator, which could not be anything else than that by the concurrent energy of each nature,[23] he could fully and entirely perform the mediatorial functions, that for example, he could assume the human nature, and thus be manifested in the flesh (1 Tim. 3:16), expend his soul by dying to redeem men (John 10:17–18), offer himself to God through the eternal Spirit (Heb. 9:14), rise again from the dead by his own strength (Rom. 1:4), and sit at the right hand of God (Ps. 110:1). (3) The nature and character of

---

21. This distinction is grounded in classic philosophical discussions regarding the nature of principles of being, knowledge, and action (ἀρχή among Greek philosophers, *principium* among Latin ones). Cf. Aristotle, *Metaphysics*, IV.1. For a brief discussion of the difference between a *principium quod* and *principium quo*, see William Fleming, *Vocabulary of Philosophy, Psychological, Ethical, Metaphysical; With Quotations and References* (n.p.: Griffin, 1890), 321. John F. Boyle succinctly defines the distinction between the two principles thus: "the *principium quod* and the *principium quo*, that is, the principle which acts (the agent) and the principle by which the agent acts," "St. Thomas and the Analogy of *Potentia Generandi*" in *The Thomist*, no. 64 (2000): 583. Cf. Giuseppe Zama Mellini, *Lexicon quo veterum theologorum locutiones explicantur theologiae tironibus accomodatum* (Cologne: J. M. Heberle, 1855), 63; "*Principium quod* est persona, vel suppositum, cui attribuitur operatio, seu denominatio operantis. *Principium quo*, est id, quod agit ut pars, vel virtus suppositi, hoc est, illud, a quo immediate oritur actio. Ita v. g. persona Petri est *principium quod* volitionum Petri, voluntas vero Petri est *principium quo*." Theologians utilizing the distinction include Gregory of Rimini, *Super Primum et Secundum Sententiarum*, Text Series No. 7 (New York-Louvain-Paderborn: Franciscan Institute, 1955), d. 7, q. 1, a. 2; John Owen (1616–1683), *Of Communion with God the Father, Son, and Holy Ghost* (Glasgow: W. & E. Miller, 1792), 74; Charles Hodge, *Systematic Theology* (Grand Rapids: Eerdmans, 1940), 2:458.

22. Francesco Stancaro (Franciscus Stancarus, 1501–1574), *De Trinitate et Mediatore Domino Nostro Jesu Christo* (H.G.V. Werdenstein [1562]).

23. *concurrente utriusque naturae* ἐνεργείᾳ

all the mediatorial functions urge that we should believe that the divine nature also cooperates with them. For he could not (a) have promised absolute surety from eternity for sinners; (b) by illuminating and persuading our hearts have declared the entire will of God regarding the covenant of grace, and the things that concern it; much less (c) by his one death have placated and reconciled to God so many myriads; (d) by his death have confirmed and ratified the covenant of grace; and finally, (e) by interceding, by presenting his own merits to the Father, have efficaciously enough pled the cause of his own—if he had not been God, and his deity had not cooperated with his humanity in the mediatorial functions. I need not add that (4) he could not have been such a prophet, namely one who taught both internally and externally; such a priest, who offered a sacrifice of infinite value; such a king, who by regeneration, conversion, and sanctification, efficaciously applied the salvation gained for his people, who for their sake routed such a mob of spiritual enemies—Satan, sin, the world, and so forth—unless his deity had most effectively cooperated with his humanity.

The adversaries' objections
Nor does it assist our adversaries to say: (1) that the Mediator of God and of men is called a man (1 Tim. 2:5); because in that passage he is also said to be such a Mediator who gave himself as the price of redemption for many, from which he is also certainly God. (2) That thus he would not have been in the middle between the offended and offending parties; for he would not have been so if he were only God, just as he would not have been so if he were only man, but now since he is both God and man, he is perfectly in the middle, through the participation of both natures. (3) That if he had been the Mediator as God, he would not have been different from the Son, either in person or in nature. He certainly would have been, and is, with respect to the economic state, by which the divine person exists under another form (Phil. 2:7). (4) That if he had been the Mediator only as God, then also the Father and the Holy Spirit would have been the Mediator. For this does not follow, because neither the Father nor the Holy Spirit are man, just as it does not follow either that if he is incarnate according to the divine nature, then also the Father and the Holy Spirit will be incarnate. For the mediatorial dignity is not fitting to the divine nature as a nature, but as he is endowed with such a mode of subsisting which is not fitting to the Father and the Spirit.[24] (5) That it seems to imply a confusion of operations, if the two natures exert influence upon the work. For this does not imply a confusion more than the fact that body and soul concur in the same completed

---

24. *Patri et [sic] Filio*

human work.[25] Compare the fourth chapter of this book, on the person of the Mediator.[26]

6. Is Christ the Mediator according to the divine nature only?
XXII. It is asked, sixth, whether Christ is the Mediator according to his divine nature only? Andreas Osiander, so that he might more comfortably hold that believers are justified and saved on account of the righteousness of the divine nature united to them by faith, stated that Christ was the Mediator only according to the divine nature. The Reformed certainly admit that he is the Mediator according to the divine nature, but not according to the divine nature only.

The orthodox reasons
For the contrary opinion: (1) is diametrically opposed to the Scriptures, as they not only expressly declare that the Mediator is a man, but also that he is such a Mediator who was so by the payment of a price (1 Tim. 2:5), who had to have been a partaker of flesh and blood, so that through his death he might abolish him who has the authority of death, and so forth (Heb. 2:14–17), who bore our sins in his body (1 Peter 2:24), who died for us (1 Cor. 1:13), who bore our infirmities (Isa. 53:4–6)—and who might show all the Scriptures that declare this? (2) It enervates all his procured righteousness, and renders it useless and unnecessary for us, since the righteousness of the divine person, all other things being equal, cannot but be sufficient. Indeed, (3) it quite thoroughly destroys the whole mediatorial office, for why then would he intercede as the Mediator, unless perhaps for this reason, that he might urge and persuade us to faith, by aid of which we should be either essentially or personally united with him, and thus be rendered partakers of his divine righteousness? I need not add that (4) the hypothesis of this error, that is, the essential or personal union of us with Christ, is utterly blasphemous, because not only does it make us God-men[27] as well as Christ, but it also makes all the sins of those so united with him, personal to him.

Objections
I do not see what with any kind of appearance of truth could be produced for this opinion, other than: (1) that absurd and blasphemous personal or essential union of us with Christ, for which, we will teach elsewhere,[28] must be substi-

---

25. *ad idem* ἀποτέλεσμα *humanum*
26. 1.5.4 §XV
27. θεανθρώπους
28. 1.6.5 §§VIII, XIV, esp. XX

tuted only a mystical and relational[29] union, from the thought of Scripture. (2) That in Jeremiah 23:6 he is called יהוה צדקנו, "Jehovah our Righteousness," and in 1 Corinthians 1:30, he who was made for us righteousness from God. For the prior passage does not hint at anything except that the Messiah, not only *as* he is Jehovah, but *who* is Jehovah, namely, our righteousness! And the latter passage does not say that he is our righteousness through the divine essence, but that he was made righteousness for us, that is, through his satisfaction and merit (cf. Rom. 5:15 with v. 18).

7. Is Christ the Mediator of each and every person?

XXIII. It is asked, seventh, whether Christ is the Mediator of each and every person. The Pelagians, together with the Socinians and the semi-Pelagians, the Jesuits, Remonstrants, Anabaptists, and Lutherans, so that they may more conveniently suspend the efficacy of grace upon free choice, state that Christ is equally the Mediator of each and every person. The Reformed universalists, so that they may hold to at least objective universal grace, state that Christ is certainly the Mediator of each and every person, but yet unequally: certainly of all, if they will to receive him by faith, but additionally of the elect, in order that they will to do so. The rest of the Reformed state that he is the Mediator of the elect only. For he is said to be: (1) in the text, the Mediator of the new covenant, so that those who are called may gain the inheritance promised them; likewise, (2) the Mediator who gave himself as the price of redemption "for many" (Matt. 20:28, 23); (3) who redeemed his people (Matt. 1:21), his sheep (John 10:11), his church (Acts 20:28), and so forth; and certainly in such a way (4) that it excludes the world (John 17:9).

Objections

Nor is it any hindrance: (1) that he is said to have been given to the world (John 3:16), because he is also said to have shut out the world (John 17:9), and accordingly, it does not understand *world* in any other way than insofar as it is distinguished from the Jewish church, just as is also done in Romans 11:12. (2) That he is said to have died for all (1 Tim. 2:6; Rom. 5:18), because it is not speaking of each and every person, but of the ranks of all, of kings and those placed in eminent positions, or of all in a certain kind (2 Peter 3:9). For which reason, what is said about all is restricted to many (Rom. 5:15 with v. 18). Other

---

29. σχετικήν

points of this kind occur in book 2, chapter 17, §§XXXII–XXXIII, and will occur in their own place in the chapter on redemption.[30]

8. Is Christ the Mediator of angels?
XXIV. We will join to the controversies some problems. It is asked therefore, eighth, whether Christ is the Mediator of the good angels, if not of their reconciliation, at least of their confirmation.

The negative reasons
It is denied: (1) because according to the text, he is the Mediator of the new covenant, of which the participants are men (1 Tim. 2:5), the called (Heb. 9:15), the world (2 Cor. 5:19), his people (Matt. 1:21), sheep (John 10:11), and the house of Israel (Jer. 31:31ff.), but nowhere in the Scriptures angels. (2) He is the Mediator of reconciliation (1 Tim. 2:5–6; Heb. 9:15; 12:24) and of intercession (1 John 2:1), such things as angels do not need. Thus the angel says in Luke 2:10–11, "Unto *you* is born this day a Savior." (3) He did not assume the nature of angels (Heb. 2:16).

The affirmative reasons refuted
Nor is it valid to argue on this point: (1) that he is said to have gathered all things which are in heaven and on earth (Eph. 1:10; Col. 1:20). For those only must be understood, from the constant tenor of the text, who are gathered to him after having fallen, from the force of the word ἀνακεφαλαιοῦσθαι, "to gather into one," those who are reconciled through his blood (Col. 1:20), and that by the gathering accomplished through the proclamation of the gospel and the efficacy of the Holy Spirit (Eph. 1:9–10), which likewise implies redemption, calling, justification, sanctification, from the context of Ephesians 1. Much less is it valid to argue here: (2) that he is the Mediator of the church, to which the angels belong (Heb. 12:22–23). For nowhere are angels called members of the church, although, through the adduced text, they do pertain to the universal assembly of the glorified. Nor (3) from this, that he is called the head of all authority and power (Col. 2:10), because that dignity belongs to him from creation, by which all things must be subject to him (Phil. 3:21), or from that authority which has been given him over the church, and on that account, over all things which are in heaven and earth (Matt. 28:18), from which everything that is in heaven and on earth must bend the knee to him (Phil. 2:9–10), which authority followed his mediatorial functions.

---

30. 1.5.18 §XL

9. Problem: Was he the Mediator for Old Testament believers?

XXV. It is asked, ninth, whether he was also the Mediator for Old Testament believers. The Socinians, out of hatred as much for his eternal deity as for his satisfaction, simply deny that he existed then; others acknowledge that he did exist under the Old Testament, and was also the Mediator virtually, but they deny that he was so actually, because this would require that he be man (1 Tim. 2:5).

The extent to which he was and was not the Mediator
under the Old Testament

It certainly seems that it must be affirmed both that he existed and that he performed mediatorial operations, provided that this be understood regarding those operations that depend more upon the divine person than upon the human nature, of which sort are: (1) the absolute surety made from eternity; (2) the declaration and appearance frequently made to the patriarchs (Isa. 61:1); (3) placation, at least virtually, that is, insofar as it depends upon the absolute surety, from which the Father is said to have cast our sins upon him (Isa. 53:4–5; 6:9; 2 Cor. 5:21); (4) intercession (Zech. 3:1–3). And provided that it not be extended to those operations which depend on the presence of the human nature, such as: (1) the actual placation, or expiation of sins accomplished through death (Heb. 9:15); (2) the sealing of the covenant through the interposition of death (Heb. 9:16; 1:3). From the prior functions: (1) even under the Old Testament, he is called the messenger of the covenant (Mal. 3:1), the angel of the presence (Isa. 63:9), the avenger, גואל, *goel* (Job 19:25), by whose grace (2) Old Testament believers are also said to have been saved (Acts 15:11). From which it is evident (in which is the chief difficulty of this case) to what extent in the Mediator the presence of the human nature is necessary.

10. Should Christ be worshiped insofar as he is the Mediator?

XXVI. It is asked, tenth, whether Christ should be worshiped insofar as he is the Mediator. Socinians, papists, Lutherans, and some Reformed,[31] with a different goal and different hypotheses, affirm it: the Socinians (those at least who, with Socinus, teach that Christ should be called on in prayer) do so because they do not acknowledge his divine nature; the papists, so that they may more conveniently assert for the blessed inhabitants of heaven the glory of intercession

---

31. Willem J. van Asselt, *Introduction to Reformed Scholasticism* (Grand Rapids: Reformation Heritage Books, 2011), 157, "Maresius, along with Ames and Walaeus, permitted prayer to Christ as mediator. Voetius, Maccovius, and Rivet, by contrast, argued that Christ could be worshiped only according to His divine nature."

as well as of invocation; the Lutherans, because they teach that divine properties, upon which the glory of invocation is constructed, are communicated to the human nature; those Reformed, because they do not adequately distinguish the concept of the Mediator, which implies deity, and the concept of pure deity. Therefore just as we acknowledge that Christ, *who* is the God-man Mediator, and *because* he is, must be worshiped, so *insofar as* he is the Mediator (such that, namely, mediation would be the sort of foundation of worship that when posited, worship is posited, and when removed, worship is removed), we accordingly deny it.

The negative reasons
We do so because: (1) if he were not the Mediator, he still would have to be worshiped as God. (2) The Father and Holy Spirit then ought not to be worshiped, because they are not the Mediator. (3) If the eternal deity of the Mediator is not established as the sole foundation, we will lose the efficacy of the argument for the eternal deity both of the Son and of the Holy Spirit which is sought from their worship (Matt. 4:10). Whatever can be produced to the contrary does not reach further than to prove that Christ *who* is the Mediator, or *because* he is the Mediator, must be worshiped. The hypotheses proper to each of our adversaries will be routed in their own places.[32]

The Practical Part
Practice: 1. It displays the glory of God's various attributes.
XXVII. With respect to practice, first, in the necessity, sufficiency, and perfection of the Mediator is evident the divine glory, that of severity toward sin, then of kindness toward the sinner (Rom. 11:22; 3:25). Of severity, I say, by which he did not will to pass over sin without satisfaction, the violation of the law without death, the threat of punishment without fulfillment. For justice had to be satisfied, or the sinner would die; the sinner could not do it, and so a Mediator promising an absolute surety had to take his place (Rom. 8:3). Moreover, of goodness toward the sinner (John 3:16; Rom. 5:8), by which the guilty might not perish: (1) he himself sought out and solicited the reconciliation (2 Cor. 5:19–20). (2) He himself gave and established the Mediator, expromissor, reconciler, Redeemer, and intercessor (John 3:16; Rom. 5:8). (3) He designated his own and only begotten Son for this work (Rom. 8:32; John 3:16). (4) He handed

---

32. On the Socinian denial of Christ's divine nature, see 1.5.4 §XIV; on the papist doctrine of the intercession of saints in heaven, see this chapter, above, §XX; on the Lutheran communication of divine properties, see 1.5.4 §§XXIII–XXIV.

over his only-begotten to death of every kind (Rom. 8:32), and he made him sin (2 Cor. 5:21). From this kindness, Salvian of Marseille says with great pathos in *The Government of God* (bk. 4), "God loves us more than a father loves a son. The reality of this indeed is evident, that God loves us beyond an affection for sons, for on account of us he did not spare the Son; and what is more, I add: and this the righteous Son, and this the only begotten Son, and this the Son who is God. And what more can be said? And this for us, for the wicked, for the most impious, for the iniquitous. Who can value this love of God toward us, except to say that the righteousness of God is so great that upon him something unrighteous cannot fall?"[33]

How these attributes should be contemplated
Therefore, (1) let us consider with the greatest attention, let us contemplate this stupendous union of severity and mercy in this matter: "Behold therefore the kindness and severity of God" (Rom. 11:22). (2) Let us abhor the latter (Rom. 11:20–22), and marvel at the former, with the Savior (John 3:16); and also (3) declare and glorify it (Rom. 5:8; 1 John 3:1). Finally, (4) let us imitate the latter severity against our sins, that we may grind them down, crucify them, and mortify them without having any mercy upon them (Col. 3:5; Gal. 5:24); let us imitate the former kindness toward our neighbor (Luke 6:36; Matt. 6:12, 14–15; 18:27, 35), namely by intercession for him (1 Tim. 2:1–2 with v. 5).

2. It brings forth very many secret things of the gospel.
XXVIII. Second, also in the same necessity, sufficiency, and perfection of the Mediator, very many secret things of the gospel are evident, from which the Mediator is denominated "Wonderful" (Isa. 9:6), and his teaching, the "without controversy great mystery of godliness," and also the "pillar and ground of the truth" (1 Tim. 3:15–16). For what great mysteries there are! (1) In the choice of the person, in which the one precisely in the middle in the Trinity was selected as Mediator, the one in the middle as well by the participation of both natures, that by mediation he might unite the disagreeing God and man; the true Immanuel, who was given as a marvelous sign, and represented to King Ahaz (Isa. 7:14; Matt. 1:23); the ladder joining heaven and earth, at which the patriarch was astounded with pious reverence (Gen. 28:12, 16–17).

---

33. Salvian (Salvianus, born c. 400), *De gubernatione Dei, et de justo praesentique ejus judicio libri VIII* (Paris: Officina Nivelliana, 1651), 118–19; idem, *De gubernatione Dei libri octo ad Solonium episcopum* in *Patrologia Latina (PL)*, ed. Jacques-Paul Migne (Paris, 1841–1855), 53:81; idem, *The Writings of Salvian, the Presbyter*, trans. Jeremiah F. O'Sullivan, *The Fathers of the Church (FOTC)* (Washington, D.C.: The Catholic University of America Press, 2008), 21–232.

Concerning this more will be said in the chapter on the person of the Mediator.[34]
(2) In the mediatorial office itself: he is the offended God and also the Mediator
between the offended God and offending man. He is the expromissor as well
as the testator of the New Testament (Heb. 7:22; 9:14–16). He is the covenant
(Isa. 49:8; 55:3), and at the same time the Mediator of the covenant (Heb. 8:6;
9:15). He is the prophetic and priestly King, the prophetic and kingly Priest,
and the priestly and kingly Prophet, more excellent than Melchizedek, who was
only a priest and king, and than David, who was only a prophet and king. He
is the priest, the sacrifice, and the altar, all at the same time. He died as a priest
and yet lives forever, a priest after the order of Melchizedek (Heb. 7:24). He was
ἀναμάρτηλος, sinless, and yet was made sin (2 Cor. 5:21). He cannot suffer and
yet suffered death. He is the Lord of glory and yet the most abject slave; innocent
and yet condemned; the life and yet died; the resurrection and yet buried. He
descended into the deepest abyss of misery and ascended to the highest throne
of glory. How mysterious are all these things! (3) In the mediatorial effects: we
as slaves are by his help redeemed; as enemies, are reconciled; as foreigners, are
adopted; as dead, are made alive; as buried, are resurrected; as condemned, are
blessed. (4) In the mode of procuring all these things: for the Mediator procured
them by his own slavery, condemnation, rejection, death, burial, and curse, and
because he was made sin, and so forth.

3. It stimulates to gratitude.

XXIX. So then furthermore, third, in the Mediator is evident the most effective
argument for gratitude, if we devoutly think on the fact that: (1) such a one gave
him, namely God (John 3:16), and with such a heart, with pure, unadulterated
love and mercy: "God so loved the world!" God, that all-sufficient one, אל שדי,
El Shaddai (Gen. 17:1; Ps. 16:2), for whom no more advantage could have been
hoped from the life of a sinner than from his death, from his salvation than from
his destruction. (2) He gave such a Mediator, not some illustrious and perfect
man, not some angel even of first rank, not a servant or a friend, in some manner
pleasing to him, but the Son, his very own Son, not adopted, but the only begotten (John 3:16; Rom. 8:32), the innocent, most obedient, most good, most
beloved (2 Cor. 5:21; Phil. 2:8; Matt. 3:17; cf. the example of Abraham offering
his son, Gen. 22:12). (3) He gave him for such people, for sinners, covenant
breakers, enemies (Rom. 5:6–8; 3:12–20). (4) He gave him to such ends, not
that he would be served, but that he would serve (Matt. 20:28), to all the worst
ends (Isa. 53:2–8), to death, the death of the cross (Phil. 2:7–8), to the curse

---

34. 1.5.4 §XXXV

(Gal. 3:13). (5) He gave him unto such uses, that he would promise an absolute surety for us; that he would convey the covenant of grace and its conditions to us; that he would placate the Father for us; that he would seal the covenant of grace, in which, as in a testament, we are recorded as the heirs; that he would continuously plead our cause before his Father; that he would be for us wisdom, righteousness, sanctification, and redemption (1 Cor. 1:30); and that from his fullness we would draw grace for grace (John 1:16), in such a way that we would be complete in him (Col. 2:9–10).

The duties of this gratitude
For these reasons so many and so great, it raises us to gratitude, in which: (1) we should readily receive such and so great a Mediator given for us (John 1:11–12). (2) To the one who has been given, we should give ourselves over to be redeemed (Acts 15:26), as those who have been given by the Father to him (John 17:9). (3) We should eagerly admit the word of reconciliation, made in the name of God and the Mediator for us (2 Cor. 5:19). (4) We should acknowledge the grace of reconciliation accomplished through the Mediator, and glorify the one accomplishing it (Rom. 5:8). Moreover, (5) we should conduct ourselves in all our life as those reconciled and redeemed by the help of the Mediator (Titus 2:11–12, 14–15).

4. It offers the sweetest argument for comfort.
XXX. From this, fourth, there is evident in this Mediator the sweetest argument for comfort. For as the sealing of the covenant of grace fell extremely bitter upon the Mediator, so it is extremely sweet and pleasant for the covenanted. It was extremely bitter for the Mediator, if you would devoutly think of his agony in the garden of Gethsemane, his bloody sweat, his head lacerated with thorns, his beatings, his pierced hands and feet, his wounded heart, his desertion by God, his supplications as if in vain, without access to the Father. But on the contrary it is extremely sweet and delightful for the covenanted, since it obtains for them all goods of every sort, temporal, spiritual, eternal; it obtains for them the Mediator, and all that belongs to the Mediator; it obtains God, and the things that are in God, and flow from God. How splendid and blessed an appropriation of all these things befalls the dependents of this Mediator! His agony is their victory; his condemnation, their justification; his anguish, their rest; his beatings, their medicines; his wounds, their bandages; his curse, their blessing; his death, their life; his shameful crowning, their glorious exaltation. O how sweet the fruits of such a bitter root!

To what persons this comfort is applicable

Here in specific must be considered the persons to whom this argument for comfort is applicable, namely: (1) those who have the sense of their own hostility with God, as well as of the evils emerging from it, and thus are seized by the desire for reconciliation (Matt. 11:28–30; Isa. 55:1–2; Rev. 22:17), namely that they may have a Mediator who makes peace (Col. 1:20), who takes away sins (John 1:29), which like dividing walls separate them from God (Isa. 59:2), as well as enmity (Eph. 2:16–17). Then (2) also to those who by the intervention of the Mediator have already been reconciled to God (Rom. 5:1).

Against what evils

To these is supplied from this Mediator an argument for comfort: (1) against their own daily infirmities (1 John 2:1), because they have in him an advocate who continuously pleads their cause before his Father (Rom. 8:33–34; Heb. 9:7); (2) against the fear of total and final apostasy (Luke 22:31; John 17:12, 15; 6:39); (3) against all kinds of temptations, because as tempted men we have a Mediator who certainly is God, but in addition, a man tempted in all things like his brethren (Heb. 4:15; 2:17–18); (4) against any wants and lacks, of both body and soul, because in our prayers, through the Mediator we have boldness and access to approach the throne of grace (Eph. 2:18; 4:12; Heb. 10:19), and moreover, an advocate to commend our prayers to the Father, that he may hear them, and indeed, a Mediator whose intercession is never not admitted (John 14:13; 16:23; 1 John 5:14–15); (5) against the pains of death (Job 19:25; 1 Cor. 15:25, 26; John 11:25); (6) against the terrors of the last judgment and eternal condemnation (John 5:24; 3:17).

5. It declares the misery of those who lack the Mediator.

XXXI. Furthermore, fifth, in the necessity, sufficiency, and perfection of the Mediator is evident the extreme misery of all who lack this one and only Mediator, such as: (1) all who are unbelievers by their own profession—pagans, Muslims, modern Jews—who thoroughly reject any mediator, concerning whom see Ephesians 2:12. (2) Those who do admit of a Mediator, but one that is inept, insufficient, and thus imagined, one who without any middle status of person, or the participation of both natures, without the eternal surety, without the placation of the offended party, performed the role of a mere messenger, those whom we noted and refuted in §XVII. (3) Those who do profess with their mouth the true and sufficient Mediator, but in reality deny him in many ways: when they admit the God-man to the mediatorial office either as God or as man only, or conjoin to the Mediator mediators, angels and men, those whom we noted in

§§XX–XXII. (4) Those who do grant to him the title of the necessary, sufficient, and perfect Mediator, but snatch from him the mediatorial functions by their satisfactions, merits, good works, and strength of free choice, which is a familiar fault of the Pelagians and Pelagianizers, of all the moralists and perfectionists.[35] (5) Those who do none of these things by profession, but at the same time are ignorant of the Mediator and are not diligent to learn (John 1:10, 26; 8:19; 4:22; 2 Thess. 1:8; Isa. 53:11; John 17:3). (6) Those who do not love him (1 Cor. 16:22; Matt. 10:37), neglect him, do not receive him, reject him (John 1:11–12; 5:40, 43; Matt. 22:3; Acts 13:46; John 5:44), tread underfoot the Son of God, and count the blood of the covenant an unclean thing (Heb. 10:29). (7) Those who do approach the Mediator with their mouth and honor him with their lips, but in heart remain far from him (Isa. 29:13; Matt. 15:8), who thunder with full mouth, "Lord, Lord" but do not do his commands (Matt. 7:21–22), who take up the name of Christ, but do not withdraw from their unrighteousness (2 Tim. 2:19), who assure themselves of Christ's promises, but do not walk as he walked (1 John 2:6; 3:3), and so make him, instead of the Mediator, the minister of sin (Gal. 2:17), and in their own way tread underfoot the Son of God (Heb. 10:29). (8) Those who would receive him in some manner, but not as must be done, as the whole Mediator, according to all the parts of the mediatorial office: as the Priest who would reconcile them to the Father, but not as the Prophet whom they should heed in all things (John 10:27), and not as the King to whom they should subject themselves (Luke 19:27). (9) Those who do not receive him by those laws by which he wills to be received (Luke 9:23 with Matt. 16:24).

What sort and how great their misery is
The misery of all these: (1) certainly in an abridged but graphic way, the apostle presents in Ephesians 2:11–12: "At that time you were without Christ, alienated from the commonwealth of Israel, strangers from the covenants of promise, having no hope, and without God in the world" (cf. Col. 1:21). In specific, (2) they are ἄθεοι, without God (Eph. 2:12), insofar as they are alienated from God by sin (Isa. 59:2), they cannot regain God except through the Mediator (John 14:6), and they have no access to him except in the Mediator (Rom. 5:2; Eph. 2:12), whom they lack. Indeed, (3) they do have God, but by their wickedness, they have him as their enemy (Rom. 5:10; 8:7), a consuming fire (Deut. 9:3; Heb.

---

35. *justitiariis et perfectistis*; cf. Melchior Leydecker, Ἡ Ἀλήθεια Εὐαγγελικὴ θριαμβευομένη *sive Exercitationes selectae historico-theologicae*, tome II (Amsterdam: Samuel Schoonwald, 1712), 262; Martin Luther, *Lectures on Romans* (Louisville: Westminster John Knox Press, 1961), 266; Marten Schoock, *Exercitationes variae, de diversis materiis* (Utrecht: Gisbert a Zyll, 1663), fol. c, recto.

10:27), a bear robbed of her cubs (Hos. 13:8; Amos 5:19). And (4) since they do not have the Mediator, in whom all the promises of God are yes and amen (2 Cor. 1:20), and from whose fullness should be drawn grace for grace (John 1:1, 16), they have entirely nothing. Nor only (5) do they have nothing, but they can also receive nothing, since without a Mediator, neither is the approach to the throne of divine grace open to them (Heb. 4:16; Eph. 2:18), as there is no one to approach on their behalf as their mediator (Rom. 8:34; 1 John 2:1). And even if they should most eagerly approach him with their prayers, without the Mediator to offer them, even their prayers would be an abomination to God (Rev. 8:1, 4; Isa. 1:13–15; Prov. 28:9). In fact, (6) not only do they have nothing, and can acquire nothing from God, but also without the Mediator, they can do nothing for themselves and their own salvation (John 15:5; Phil. 4:13). For this reason, (7) they are without hope of any salvation (Eph. 2:12), because there is not any salvation in any other than in the Mediator (Acts 4:12; John 14:6; 1 Tim. 2:5). I would add that (8) those separated from the covenant of grace and its benefits are under the rigidity and curse of the legal covenant (Gal. 3:13–14). So then, (9) they are under the enmity, wrath, hatred, and fury of God, and of those things which are subject to God (Eph. 2:5; Col. 1:21; Ps. 5:5–6), because they do not have the Mediator who makes peace. In addition, (10) they are by so many sins debtors to God, to be bound in hellish chains forever (Matt. 18:25, 34–35), and there is not for them a Mediator to promise an absolute surety or to make payment for them.

6. It persuades us to examine ourselves, whether or not the Mediator is ours.
The motivating reasons
XXXII. Therefore, sixth, there is also evident in the Mediator the necessity of examination, whether or not that one, necessary, sufficient Mediator who is perfect in all ways, is ours. For what, (1) I pray, does it help for him to be the Mediator, and such and so great a Mediator (since he is not the Mediator of all, as we taught in §XXIII), if he is not mine, nor I his (Song 2:16; Acts 8:21)? Or (2) if I enjoy no certain knowledge of this (Gen. 28:13, 16)? And on the contrary (3) how sweet it is, in any circumstance, to be able to say with boldness, "I know that my *Goel*, Redeemer, lives" (Job 19:25), "I am persuaded that neither life nor death…will separate me from the love of God which is in Christ Jesus" (Rom. 8:38–39). Moreover, (4) how will we approach God with boldness and obtain grace, if we do not know that he is the Mediator for us (Heb. 4:14–16)? And how will we know, except by examining ourselves whether Jesus Christ is in us, and is our Mediator (2 Cor. 13:5)?

Signs

But finally, by what indicators will we gain this knowledge with certainty? By these especially: (1) if we are his disciples (Luke 9:23; Matt. 16:24), we acknowledge his voice, heed it, depend upon it totally (John 10:16). If hearing him, we promptly follow him (Luke 9:23), imitate him (Matt. 11:29), walk just as he walked (1 John 2:6; 3:3). (2) If as disciples of the Mediator, for his sake we readily deny ourselves (Luke 9:23), we crucify the flesh with its lusts (Gal. 5:24). (3) If we sense his Spirit communicated to us (Rom. 8:9), to efficaciously convince us regarding our sins (John 16:9–11), to make us who were dead in sins alive (Rom. 8:10), to sanctify us, purify us (1 Cor. 6:11), to drive us, on account of the Mediator, to address God as Abba, Father (Gal. 4:6; Rom. 8:15). (4) If we have become new creatures (2 Cor. 5:17–18), if as those who were once God's enemies, we have now been reconciled by the Mediator (Rom. 8:7 with 5:10), if we who were once children of wrath are now vessels of mercy (Eph. 2:3 with Rom. 9:23), we who were once dead in sins are now made alive in Christ (Eph. 2:1, 5), we who were once under the power of Satan are now under the dominion of God (Acts 26:18), we who were once blind (Eph. 4:18) are now light in the Lord (Eph. 5:8; Acts 26:18), we who were once averse to and alienated from him (Eph. 2:12; Rom. 8:7) have now been made near by the blood of the Mediator (Eph. 2:13). (5) If we give ourselves back to him by sincere faith and love (Song 2:16; 2 Cor. 8:5).

7. It stirs us up to receive the Mediator by faith.

XXXIII. Especially also, seventh, it is evident in such a perfect, sufficient, necessary Mediator, that we must receive him with a living faith and ardent love: "He came to his own, and his own did not receive him. But as many as did receive him, he gave to them authority to become sons of God" (John 1:11–12; cf. Ps. 2:12; 24:7–10; Rev. 3:20; Gal. 4:14). Moreover, what it is to receive the Mediator, we have taught above (bk. 2, ch. 1, §XII), as well as in the *Syntagma on Saving Faith* (ch. 6, §§4–13).[36]

The motivating reasons

Furthermore, by what motivating reasons we should receive him, we likewise explained in book 2, chapter 1, §XLIV, but especially also in the *Syntagma on Saving Faith* (ch. 16, principally in §8), to which could be added without any trouble other arguments, for example: (1) from his perfection of every sort, and most absolute sufficiency, by which he is able to save perfectly as many as

---

36. Mastricht, *De fide salvifica syntagma*, 87–103.

approach God through him (Heb. 7:25–26, εἰς τὸ παντελές, "to the utter-most"; 10:14; Col. 2:10); (2) from his indescribable usefulness (1 Cor. 1:30; John 1:16; Matt. 11:25); (3) from his inflexible necessity (John 3:16, 36; 14:6; Acts 4:12; 1 Tim. 2:5; etc.).

The method of receiving
We have also spoken of the method of receiving him, above in book 2, chapter 1, §§XVII–XVIII, as well as in the *Syntagma on Saving Faith* (ch. 6, §§11–14).

8. It teaches that the Mediator who has been received must be diligently employed.
XXXIV. So then also, eighth, when we have already received the Mediator with faith and love, it is evident that we must carefully and constantly employ him who has been received, according to our need, indeed in every circumstance, that is, so that we would not receive that grace in vain (2 Cor. 6:1), if indeed only in vain (Gal. 3:4).

The motivating reasons
For (1) what does it help to have so great and such a Mediator, if you do not employ him? Is that not surely the same as if you did not have him? (2) Surely by not employing him, by neglecting the one whom you have received with your mouth, do you not in reality deny him (Titus 1:16)? (3) Surely by neglecting the one who is the savor of life unto life, will he not become to you the savor of death unto death (2 Cor. 2:16)? And the one who is given for the rising again of many, will he not result in your fall (Luke 2:34; Rom. 9:33)? Therefore, let us employ the Mediator given to us in every necessity, for he is (4) the faithful Mediator (Heb. 2:17), whose name is faithful and true (Rev. 19:11; 1:5; 3:14). He is (5) the merciful Mediator (Heb. 2:17; σπλαγχνίζομαι, "I have compassion," Matt. 15:32; 9:36; 14:14), such that the misery of men moves him to tears (Luke 19:41). He is (6) the most powerful Mediator (Heb. 7:25; אל גבור, "the mighty God," Isa. 9:6; Matt. 28:18; Ps. 89:19). He is (7) the perpetual, indeed the eternal Mediator, who is always able to help (Heb. 7:24–25; Matt. 28:20). He is (8) the omnipresent Mediator (Matt. 18:19–20; Ps. 139:7ff.).

The method of employing him
Adduced by all these reasons, let us employ our Mediator: (1) by approaching him as the Mediator, just as he invites us to himself, and gently draws us by his promises (Matt. 11:28–29; Isa. 55:1; Rev. 22:17). Then (2) by approaching God through him (Heb. 4:16). In specific, (3) if ever we, conscious of our natural treachery, are frightened away from the throne of grace: by approaching him as

our surety, our ἔγγυον (Heb. 7:22), our *Goel* (Job 19:25). We should present him before God as our security (Job 17:3). (4) If ever we, devoid of counsel, do not know what must be done: by going to him as the λόγος, the Word of the Father (John 1:1), as our counselor (Isa. 9:6), who was made unto us wisdom from God (1 Cor. 1:30). (5) If ever the guilt of sins vexes our heart: by fleeing to our Mediator, who gave himself as the price of redemption for all (1 Tim. 2:5–6), who was made sin for us, and so forth (2 Cor. 5:21), on whom God cast the sins of us all (Isa. 53:3–4). (6) If ever there is lacking either in us or in that which belongs to us, in body or soul, that which is necessary and useful, let us approach the throne of grace through the Mediator (Heb. 4:16; 1 Tim. 2:1, 5; John 14:13–14).

9. It exhorts us to imitate the Mediator who has been received.
XXXV. Finally, ninth, when we already employ and enjoy the received Mediator, there is also in him reason that we should imitate him, on account of which we should walk even as he walked (1 John 2:6; Col. 2:6). For to this end: (1) he came to us, and set himself as an example for us (John 13:12–14). (2) To those who come to him and who will enjoy his mediation, he commends imitating his example (Matt. 11:29). (3) In this imitation and walking he established the highest perfection of his followers (John 15:20; Matt. 5:48). (4) Without this we are unworthy to be called disciples and followers of the Mediator, for which reason the apostle commands us to "walk worthy of the Lord unto all pleasing, being fruitful in every good work" (Col. 1:10). Accordingly, (5) in this is a mark of our communion with him, if we walk even as he walked (1 John 2:6; John 15:10). Indeed, (6) without this we are excluded from all hope of communion with him, for whoever has this hope present in himself, purifies himself even as he is pure (1 John 3:3).

The method of imitating him
But how will we imitate him and walk even as he walked? I respond: (1) By acknowledging our Mediator, and his will and manner of living, as our example, by continuously holding him before our eyes, "that you may be filled with all knowledge of his will, in all wisdom and spiritual understanding, that you may walk as is worthy of the Lord" (Col. 1:9–10; John 10:14; 17:3; Phil. 3:7–10; Eph. 3:18–19). (2) By giving our attention that in the Mediator who has been acknowledged we may be more and more rooted and strengthened: "Just as you have received Jesus Christ the Lord, so walk in him, rooted and grounded" (Col. 2:6–7; Eph. 3:17–18). (3) We should continually carry around his footsteps, his deeds and words, indeed to whatever extent they can and should be represented

for our imitation, to the end that we may walk even as he walked (1 John 2:6), for example: (a) in gentleness and humility of heart (Matt. 11:28–29); (b) in righteousness and truthfulness (Isa. 53:9; John 8:26); (c) in zeal and obedience in completing the things committed to him (John 4:32, 34; 2:17); (d) in eagerness for serving and doing good to all (Acts 10:38; Matt. 4:23; 9:35; Mark 6:6); (e) in spirituality and heavenly manner of life, which he also took every occasion to impress upon his own (John 4:30, 33–34; 15:1–10); (f) in prayers (Matt. 14:23; Mark 6:46; Matt. 26:36; John 17:1ff.; Heb. 5:7); (g) in mercy and sympathy (Heb. 2:17; 5:2; Matt. 9:36; 14:14; Mark 1:41; Luke 7:13; 15:20); (h) in patience and tolerance of any injury inflicted upon him by his enemies (1 Peter 2:21–24; Isa. 53:7; Luke 23:34). (4) By studiously shunning any evil: let us cast off all the works of darkness, let us put on the Lord Jesus (Rom. 13:12–14; Gal. 5:24). (5) By seeking heavenly things that are above, where he is, sitting at the right hand of God (Col. 3:1; Phil. 3:20). (6) In all these things, by daily making progress more and more (2 Peter 3:18). And (7) by standing ready with eagerness for his glorious return to judge the living and the dead, and our beatification with him (1 Thess. 4:17; Phil. 3:20–21; 2 Tim. 4:7; 2 Peter 3:11–12; John 14:2–3; Song 8:14; Rev. 22:23). Meanwhile, (8) by striving, whether we are present with him or absent, that we may please him (2 Cor. 5:6–9), that we may live as well as die for him (Rom. 14:8–9). And thus (9) in all these things, through him who is the way, the truth, and the life, by striving toward the Father (John 14:6).

CHAPTER THREE

The Names of the Mediator

Men who have risked their lives for the name of the Lord Jesus Christ.
—Acts 15:26

The transition from the previous to the next things
I. Regarding the Mediator of the covenant of grace, we spoke of the first topic, namely his mediatorial dignity; now the second topic follows, which will address the names of the Mediator, so that by their influence we may know the named Mediator more distinctly. The more common of these the Jerusalem Council mentions in Acts 15:26.

The text is resolved and explained.
II. In these words is contained a certain commendation of Barnabas and Paul, from their piety toward the name of the Lord Jesus Christ. In which occur:
  A. The godly men commended: ἄνθρωποι, "men," namely those two apostles, Paul and Barnabas, emissaries and stewards of the mysteries of God (1 Cor. 4:1). They are called "men," *homines*, in the sense of the Hebrew אישים, *viri*, that is, not common but outstanding men (Ex. 15:3; Judg. 7:14; 1 Sam. 26:15), burning with zeal, as if from אש, fire, those who by pure and unadulterated zeal for the name of Christ did not have regard for their own life (cf. Ps. 69:9; John 2:17 with Acts 20:24).
  B. The godliness of those commended, or the duty of godliness: "who gave up their lives,"[1] regarding which is displayed:
    1. The giving up: παραδεδωκόσι. Παραδίδωμι is *trado*, "I give up," as if *transdo*, "I give over." And it occurs either with an inimical mind or hatred, from which it denotes *prodere*, to betray, like Judas betrayed Christ (Matt. 10:4), or it occurs with an amicable mind or love: thus

---

1. *qui tradiderunt animas.* Cf. chapter text, *qui exposuerunt animas.*

God gave up his only begotten Son for us (Rom. 8:32); thus Christ gave himself up for us (Eph. 5:2, 25); thus Paul and Barnabas gave themselves up—except that Christ gave himself up for us as a ransom (1 Tim. 2:5), an offering and a sacrifice (Eph. 5:2); they did so only to be used by Christ. But at the same time the giving up occurs on both accounts voluntarily and freely. And at the same time, *tradere*, to give up, connotes as if *transdare*, to give over, or *traducere*, to surrender oneself out of love for another for whom something is given up, to deprive oneself of that which is given up.

2. What was given up: τὰς ψυχὰς αὐτῶν, "their lives," that is, not their fortunes, not fame, not anything separable from them, but themselves, and in themselves not only their body and bodily things, but also their soul and its faculties. Ψυχὴ, "soul," denotes: (1) sometimes, any of our internal faculties, especially our will (Eph. 6:6; Phil. 1:27), as distinguished from our external faculties; (2) natural life itself (Matt. 2:20; 6:25; Luke 12:23; John 10:15), just as the Savior is also said to have come δοῦναι τὴν ψυχὴν αὐτοῦ λύτρον ἀντὶ πολλῶν, "to give his life a ransom for many."[2] Thus the sense is that these apostles so committed themselves and all they had to Christ that they were prepared to dedicate to him not only all their internal faculties, but even their very life.

C. The advantage of godliness, or also its motivating cause: ὑπὲρ τοῦ ὀνόματος τοῦ κυρίου ἡμῶν Ἰησοῦ χριστοῦ, "for the name of our Lord Jesus Christ." There is here:

1. The name: ὑπὲρ τοῦ ὀνόματος, "for the name." There is ὑπὲρ here, not ἀντὶ, which always expresses something vicarious (whenever it does not denote something adversarial), in which way it is generally used regarding Christ (Matt. 20:28), from which it is said that he was an ἀντίλυτρον, ransom, and that he underwent death in our place, although ὑπὲρ does occur regarding him (1 Tim. 2:6), yet not so properly that it is not said of others (e.g. Col. 1:24), concerning whom the employed particle ὑπὲρ does not denote anything except, "for some advantage and benefit": thus in this passage it does not denote anything except, "for some advantage to the name of Christ." Moreover, ὄνομα, "name," sometimes denotes the one named (Matt. 6:9, and frequently elsewhere); sometimes all that by which the one

---

2. Matt. 20:28; Mark 10:45

named is made known to others, for example, those words by which the one named is customarily distinguished, and likewise attributes, operations, and other things by which this occurs; also in particular, the gospel (Acts 8:12 with 8:25), inasmuch as through it the name of Christ was to be carried to the Gentiles (Acts 9:15–16). And so it is in this passage, such that ὑπὲρ τοῦ ὀνόματος does not denote anything except that the apostles spent their lives for the advantage of the gospel.

2. The one named: "the Lord Jesus Christ." Here the one named is distinguished with three titles, or as many names. Of these:

   a. The first presents him with respect to his lordship, with which he is distinguished throughout the New Testament (Acts 2:36; Col. 2:6; etc.), though he is never called δεσπότης, "master."[3] Within the Old Testament, the Septuagint translators translate the name *Jehovah* by τὸ κύριος, "the Lord." Moreover, there is a double lordship applicable to Christ: one divine, which as God he has over all creatures, the other mediatorial, by which he is throughout Scripture hailed as "our Lord" (on which see Matt. 28:18; Phil. 2:9–10; Eph. 1:20–22); this latter lordship is especially in view in this passage.

   b. The second presents him with respect to his benefit: "Jesus," because he is by office the Savior, about which we will have more in what follows.[4]

   c. The third presents him in relation to his office, when he is pointed out as "Christ," about which likewise we will treat expressly in what follows.[5]

The Dogmatic Part

In the Scriptures, various names are attributed to the Mediator.

III. Therefore it is evident that with a deliberate design the Mediator of the covenant of grace is described by various names in Scripture, among which the most common are *Jesus*, *Christ*, and *Lord*. For (1) it is not a rash occurrence in the text that not only is a "name" expressly attributed to him, but also several

---

3. Cf. 1.3.4 §II.B.4.a.i. where δεσπότης in Jude 4 is said to speak of the Father. Cf. 2 Peter 2:1; Rev. 6:10.

4. §§VIII–X

5. §§XII–XVI

names are heaped together, when he is denominated Lord, Jesus, Christ. Nor (2) does it occur without deliberate design that plural names are as if in one breath piled upon him: "And his name shall be called Wonderful, Counselor, the mighty God, the everlasting Father, the Prince of Peace" (Isa. 9:6). This occurs precisely so that by this variety of names, the various benefits of his mediatorial office may be heaped together upon him (1 Cor. 1:30). (3) Nor without cause are these three names—Lord, Jesus, Christ—commonly conjoined in the New Testament (Rom. 1:3, 7; 6:23; 13:14; 15:6, 30; 1 Cor. 5:5; etc.) And (4) this all happens not by any man, but by God himself, who does nothing rashly or without a deliberate design (Matt. 1:21; Luke 1:31; 2:21; Acts 2:36; etc.).

The reasons why such a great variety of names is attributed to him.
IV. But with what design then is this done? I respond, So that he may be distinguished from all others to whom the mediatorial dignity does not belong (Acts 4:12; 1 Tim. 2:5). For names are placed upon all things to the end that they may be distinguished from others, either as different species within the same genus, or as individuals within the same species. Different names are attributed in particular to the Mediator: (1) so that he may be more fittingly distinguished (for a *nomen*, name, is like a *notamen*, means of marking): (a) with respect to his divine person, from the Father and the Holy Spirit. To this end he is called the Son (Matt. 28:19), the λόγος, Word (John 1:1), the express image of the person of the Father (Heb. 1:3), the Son of Man (Matt. 16:13), because among the divine persons, he alone is man. (b) With respect to his human nature, from all other individuals, for although among men there have been those besides him who disjunctively bore either the name Jesus, such as Joshua (Heb. 4:8; Hag. 1:1) or Jesus Sirach; or the name Christ (Ps. 20:6); yet there has been none besides him who was conjointly named Jesus, Christ, and Lord. (c) With respect to his mediatorial office; although Moses is also called a mediator (Gal. 3:19), yet no one is called that one Mediator, the man Jesus Christ (1 Tim. 2:5). And although the Father also is sometimes said to save us, and consequently is a Savior, yet nowhere is the name of Mediator attributed either to him or to the Holy Spirit. (2) So that he may be more distinctly acknowledged and recognized by us (for a *nomen*, name, is like a *novimen*, means of knowing)—"that they might know you…and Jesus Christ" (John 17:3)—and that individually with respect to his natures, person, offices, estates, and benefits, for which reason with respect to each of these individually, analogous names are attributed. (3) So that what we have learned broadly about the person, in the names as in summaries we may commit more deeply to memory, for which reason names are called memorials (Ex. 3:15; Ps. 135:13; Hos. 12:5). (4) So that he may be more

carefully worshiped: "that at the name of Jesus every knee should bow" (Phil. 2:9–10). Thus in the text the apostles are said to have given up their lives for the name of the Lord Jesus Christ. But more about these things will occur in the practical part.[6]

Different meanings of the word name

V. Moreover, the word *name* expresses: quite frequently the named Mediator, without a distinct regard for anything belonging to him (so e.g. in Acts 4:12; Phil. 2:10); sometimes some property intrinsic to the one named, for example, his nature, person, office, and so forth; sometimes that which is clearly extrinsic to the one named, in which sense his name indicates the gospel (Acts 9:15).

The more general division of Christ's names

VI. Yet since (as Dionysius the Areopagite rightly observes in *On the Divine Names*)[7] the intent of these names is to represent the sum of all those things that are incumbent upon us to believe and profess regarding the one named, in the Scriptures are given to us various names by which the most absolute Mediator is distinctly represented according to the various perfections which are required for the mediatorial dignity. Thus we observe certain names that concern his two natures, either the divine or the human; certain ones to the whole person; certain ones to his offices (prophetic, priestly, or kingly); certain ones to the estates in which he discharges his office, that of humiliation or of exaltation; certain ones to the benefits arising from the offices. Furthermore, all these names designate either figuratively and metaphorically, by the words taken from other matters to which those words are proper, although the things signified by them apply in a more excellent degree to the Mediator; or properly, when both the thing signifying and thing signified equally apply to him.

A more special distribution of the names by classes

VII. Now since the things required of the Mediator, which the names serve to designate, are so many and so various that to review them separately would be almost endless, it will be much more helpful to reduce the chief names to certain classes, so that if opportunity should arise to teach them more specifically, the

---

6. §§XXVIII–XXII, below

7. Pseudo-Dionysius the Areopagite (fl. late-5th to early-6th c.), *De divinis nominibus* in *PG* 3:585–88; idem, *Pseudo-Dionysius: The Divine Names and Mystical Theology*, trans. John D. Jones (Milwaukee, Wis.: Marquette University Press, 1980), 107–16.

emphasis of each individual name can in some way be made known, either from the titles, or from those chapters where those titles are dealt with.

Class 1

So then, there are names which: (1) represent his divine nature, and that either properly, such as God, true God, the great God, Jehovah, Lord, the Son of God, his very own Son, the only begotten, and so forth; or figuratively, such as the λόγος, Word, the Word of the Father, the Image of God, "the brightness of his glory, and the express image of the Father's person," and others.

Class 2

There are (2) those which designate his human nature, either properly, such as the Man, the Son of Man, a man, a child, son of Abraham, son of David, Shiloh, the firstborn of Mary, and so forth; or figuratively, such as the seed of the woman, the seed of Abraham, of Isaac, of Jacob, of David, the fruit of the loins of David, the rod or shoot from the root of Jesse, *Zemach* or the Branch, the second Adam, the Lion of the tribe of Judah, and similar names.

Class 3

There are (3) those which refer to the whole person, arising from the union of both natures, such as Immanuel, Lord of all, the heir, and so forth.

Class 4

There are (4) those which express the function of the God-man in general, and that either properly, such as Mediator, Redeemer, the desire of the nations, salvation, the messenger of the covenant, the author and finisher of our salvation, and similar names; or figuratively, as the bridegroom, the head, the cornerstone, the foundation, the vine, the Rock, the bread from heaven, the Sun, the Light, the morning star, the tree of life, and so forth.

Class 5

There are (5) those which specifically express his prophetic office, such as the Prophet, the great Prophet, the Shepherd, the ἀρχιποίμην, chief Shepherd, master, Rabbi, teacher, the Apostle, a minister of the circumcision, the Amen, Counselor, the Overseer of souls, the faithful witness, wisdom, and so forth.

Class 6

There are (6) those which express his priestly office, such as the Priest, the High Priest, an advocate, a sacrifice, the Lamb of God, the passover, the angel of the presence, the ark, the scape-goat,[8] the mercy seat, the bronze serpent, and so forth.

Class 7

There are (7) those which express his kingly office, such as the King, the Prince of peace, a ruler, a leader, the Judge, the head of the church, King of kings and Lord of lords, and so forth.

Class 8

There are (8) those which designate his estate of humiliation, such as worm, child, servant, the bronze serpent, a sign which is opposed, sin, a curse, and so forth. There are those which exhibit his estate of exaltation, such as all those which we have already applied to the kingly office, with the addition of the Lion of the tribe of Judah, Melchizedek, Wonderful, the Judge, the *gibbor*, mighty one,[9] and so forth.

Class 9

There are (9) those which present his mediatorial benefits, in which, because they are almost infinite in number, the Scriptures exceedingly abound, on account of the prophetic, priestly, and kingly office, and also of redemption, calling, union, communion, justification, adoption, sanctification, confirmation, sealing, glorification: from which, in the explanation of these names, these topics should be explored. So, for example, from the benefits of the prophetic function, he is named: the Light, the way, the truth, the witness, the Amen, Counselor, wisdom, the Sun of righteousness, and so forth. From the benefits of the priestly function: salvation, a sacrifice, the propitiation, the intercessor, the angel of the presence, the blessed seed, the λυτρώτης, Redeemer, the ῥυόμενος, Deliverer, and so forth. From the benefits of the kingly function: the governor, the ἡγεμών, leader, the shepherd, the shelter (Isa. 32:2), the pillar of cloud and fire. From the benefits of redemption: the Redeemer, Mediator, physician, kinsman-redeemer (*goel*), the antitype of Moses and Joshua, redemption, the bronze serpent. From the benefits of calling: a gathering hen, the arm of God stretching itself forth

---

8. *Hircus Hasaël*, lit. "the male goat *Azazel*" (עֲזָאזֵל, Lev. 16:8) cf. Isidore Epstein and Leo Jung, eds., *Tractate Yoma*, vol. 6 in the *Hebrew-English Edition of the Babylonian Talmud* (London: The Soncino Press, 1974), 67b.

9. Cf. גבור, Ps. 24:8.

(Isa. 53:1; Prov. 1:20–22). From the benefits of union: the bridegroom, the vine, the head. From the benefits of communion: a bundle (Song 1:13), a horn of salvation (Luke 1:69). From justification: יהוה צדקנו, Jehovah our Righteousness, the plague of death, the Prince of peace, our peace, the price of redemption. From adoption: a brother, the firstborn, the everlasting Father. From sanctification: the Holy One of God, the Holy One of Israel, sanctification, the holy of holies (Dan. 9:24). From confirmation and strengthening: the stone, the foundation, the Rock, Mighty God, the Lion of the tribe of Judah. From sealing: manna, the bread of life, the passover, an ensign (Isa. 11:10). From glorification: the glory of Israel, the everlasting Father, the life, the ladder to heaven, the book of life, the wood or tree of life, and so forth. We are not subjoining individual passages of Scripture, not only because it would be endless, but also because by the assistance of concordances they can be tracked down with little trouble.

One thing to mention
One thing remains that must be mentioned. There are several names that simultaneously have in view his person and his office, the account of which depends upon the goal of the incarnation: for to this end was the Word incarnated, that he could execute the office of the Mediator (for which the properties of the divine and the human nature are required), and convey to his own the benefits of this execution. Although at the same time, certain of these names more directly and primarily concern his person, and indirectly and secondarily his office and benefits, and vice versa.

Regarding the name Jesus
VIII. In this crowd of names, three stand out conspicuously in the text as well as in the creed: *Jesus, Christ, Lord.* Among them the first name is that of benefit, the second of office, the third of rule. Accordingly, these will be examined a little more distinctly.

Improbable and perverse derivations
With respect to the etymology of the name Jesus, various writers supply various kabbalistic games rather than true derivations, perhaps arising from the superstitious veneration of the name. There are those who (1) if they do not derive it from, at least desire it to have an affinity with, the Hebrew יֵשׁ, which expresses existence and subsistence, because the Mediator has only one subsistence in two natures, or because all the promises of God have their subsistence, as it were, in him (2 Cor. 1:20; cf. Heb. 11:1). (2) Others from ἰάω and the Syriac אסא, which mean "I cure," so that Ἰησοῦς would mean ἰατρός, a healer—thus Basil in his

Ascetics, Cyril in his *Catechetical Lectures* (lecture 10).[10] (3) Osiander in his *Gospel Harmony* stated that it is the very name יהוה, *Jehovah*, which, because it was ineffable, was made utterable by the insertion of the letter ש from the word שילה, *Shiloh* (Gen. 49:10). Thus by this name is signified that the Mediator is true God, on account of the name יהוה, and true man, on account of the letter ש from שילה; and that these two natures were united in one person, just as from the names of the divine and human nature, one name is made. Furthermore, it is signified that the incomprehensible God, when the human nature was assumed, began to be knowable to us. Therefore, he says, it should be properly written with its letters as יהשוה, and by contraction ישו.[11] (4) We will not delay at all on the blasphemy of the Jews, who do not pronounce this name because it is prohibited in Exodus 23:13 for them to remember the name of strange gods, and if perhaps they might have uttered it, they beat themselves with their fists and say ישו, understanding by apocopation ימח שמו, "may his name be destroyed," as Fagius testifies on Exodus 23.[12] In addition, in place of ישו, which in numbers makes 316, they read וריק, "and vanity," which yields the equivalent numbers (see Anton Margaritha in his book *On the Faith of the Jews*).[13]

The authentic derivation of the name *Jesus*

IX. The angel in Matthew 1:21 discloses the genuine derivation of the word: "You shall call his name Jesus, for he will save his people from their sins." For this reason Rabbi Haccados in *Galei Rezaya*, speaking to the Consul Antoninus says, "Because the Messiah will save people, he will be called Jeshua; however, tribes of another nation which will follow his faith will call him Jesus, and therefore you will find this name designated as *Jesu* in Genesis 49:10, יבא שילה ולו, for if you take the first letters of each word, ישו, the same letters will make the name Jesu."[14]

______

10. Basil of Caesarea (330–379), *De grammatica exercitatione liber unus* (Basel: Oporinus, 1553), 12; Cyril of Jerusalem (c. 313–386), *Catecheses* X.13 in *PG* 33:677–78; idem, "Lecture X," *Catechetical Lectures* in *NPNF2* 7:61. For a usage of the same sources for the same point, see Cornelius á Lapide (1567–1637), *Commentaria in omnes Divi Pauli epistolas* (Antwerp: Henricus & Cornelius Verdussne, 1692), 575.

11. Andreas Osiander (1498–1552), *Harmoniae evangelicae libri IIII* (Paris: Robert Estienne, 1545), fols. aa.v r–bb.v r.

12. Fagius on Ex. 23:12, *Thargum, hoc est, paraphrasis Onkeli Chaldaica*, vol. 1, fol. P[1]r.

13. Anton Margaritha (1490–1537), *Ganz Judisch glaub mit sampt eyner grundtlichen und warhafftigen anzaygunge aller Satzungen, Ceremonien* (Leipzig: Melchior Lotter, 1531), fol. Y iiii r.

14. The pseudepigraphic account of Rabbi Haccados as cited from bk. 8, ch. 24, Pietro Galatino (1460–1540), *De arcanis catholicae veritatis* (Frankfurt: Joannes & Andreas Marnius, 1612), 495–96. cf. Robert J. Wilkinson, *Tetragrammaton: Western Christians and the Hebrew Names of God* (Leiden: Brill, 2015), 204–5; P. E. Hughes, "The Jewish Cabala and the Secret Names of God," *Philosophia Reformata*, 21, no. 1/4 (1956): 81–94.

Therefore Ἰησοῦς and Jesu, or as others more correctly write, Jesus, coincide with יהשע, Jehoshuah, or through a euphonic crasis, ישוע, Joshua (just as, not only the son of Jehozadak, who in Haggai and Zechariah is called יהשוע, elsewhere in Ezra 2:2 and Nehemiah 7:7 is called ישוע; but also the son of Nun, whom Moses calls Joshua, Paul calls Jesus in Hebrews 4:8). Both descend from ישע and its Hiphil form הושיע, which means to preserve or save, when in the Greek form, the sheva under the yod, the formative of a proper name, on account of the elided ה and cholem-vav, is changed into a tzere, to which corresponds the Greek η and the Latin e; and finally, the guttural ע, which cannot be pronounced by the Greeks, is changed into s, just as in place of ה, likewise having an uncertain sound, in the word *Messiah* they put s. Some Latins write *Jesu*, which, in order to deflect the blasphemous calumny of the Jews which we noted in the preceding paragraph, others do not tolerate, and prefer to say *Jesus*. Others sprinkle in the aspirative h, regarding which Jacques Lefèvre d'Étaples says, "In the name Jesus, the aspiration must be placed afterwards because in the tetragrammaton" (from which he wrongly presupposes it is derived) "the י precedes ה, not ה the י."[15] Others think that it should be put in on account of the ה in יהושע, which the Jesuits especially urge, so that they may defend the symbolic sign of their society, IHS, upon the middle letter of which they build a cross. Bünting supposes that it hardly matters whether it be written with or without the aspiration, because ישוע without the ה is also represented in various places.[16]

The reasons why the Mediator is called Jesus
X. Thus *Jesus* expresses nothing but σωτήρ, Savior, in Latin *Servator* or *Salvator*, of which they judge the former to have more Latinity, but the latter to be more emphatic. Moreover, he is said to be such because: (1) he does not act as a typical savior, like Moses formerly, or Joshua, Othniel, and others, but one truly and properly called such. Because (2) he freed his own from misery, not only corporeal misery, as those typical ones did, but also from spiritual misery, from sins, death, and the curse (Matt. 1:21; 1 Cor. 15:55–57). Nor (3) did he only free from misery, as Moses only led his people out of Egypt, but he also brought in a blessedness of every sort, just as Joshua led the people out of the desert into Canaan (Heb. 4:8). (4) He did both not only through merit, by redeeming, but

---

15. See Jacques Lefèvre d'Étaples (1455–1536) on Ps. 71:17, *Quincuplex Psalterium* ([Paris]: [Henri Estienne], 1509) fol. 109 r. cf. P. B. Copenhaver, "Lefevre d'Etaples, Symphorien Champier, and the Secret Names of God," *Journal of the Warburg and Courtauld Institutes*, 40 (1977): 189–211.

16. Heinrich Bünting (1545–1606), *Harmonia Evangelistarum. Das ist, Ein sehr schöne Und eindrechtige zusamen stimmung der heiligen vier Evangelisten* (Magdeburg: Kirchner, 1612), 123–24.

also through efficacy, by applying, from which he deserves to be called not merely יֵשׁוּעַ, Savior, but also יְשׁוּעָה, σωτηρία, σωτήριον, salvation itself (Gen. 49:18; Isa. 49:6; Acts 13:47; Luke 2:30). Nor (5) did he do these things only through merit and efficacy, but also perfectly, and in addition, he alone did them (Heb. 7:25; Acts 4:12). All of these points will perhaps be more distinctly expanded upon in the chapter on redemption.[17]

On the name Christ

XI. So far the first name of the Mediator, the proper name Jesus, sought from his benefit. Next follows the second, the appellative name taken from his office: *Christus*, מָשִׁיחַ, *Messiah*, the anointed one. Both have the same force (John 4:25), the latter being Hebrew, the former Greek. The former is very often conjoined with the name Jesus, perhaps for designating that he is not only the Messiah of the Jews, but the Savior of the Gentiles as well (Eph. 2:14–15; Rom. 3:29–30). Furthermore, just as מָשִׁיחַ is from מָשַׁח, so χριστὸς is from χρίω, both meaning entirely the same thing, namely "to anoint." There are not lacking among the ancients, those who, by an etymology that is allusive rather than true and proper, appear from χράομαι to have read *Chrestus*, which means useful and convenient (see Justin's *Second Apology for the Christians*, p. 24).[18]

What the ceremonial anointing was

XII. Moreover, the anointing of the Old Testament economy was a ceremonial inauguration by which, through the pouring out of holy oil, the things anointed were solemnly consecrated to God and to divine use. It was an inauguration, or solemn introduction to a holy use, for which reason it was applied to things anointed at the beginning, and only once. It had a holy oil, שֶׁמֶן הַמִּשְׁחָה, consisting of four aromatic ingredients: myrrh, cinnamon, calamus, and cassia. It was used first for holy things to be consecrated to God, such as the holy of holies and its vessels, the ark, the table of showbread, the candlestick, the altar of incense, and other such things, insofar as they displayed a type of the future Messiah (Ex. 30:26–29), upon which things oil was poured; then for persons: prophets (1 Kings 19:16), priests (Ex. 30:30; Lev. 4:3), and kings, as is evident in the history of Saul, David, Solomon, Jehu, and others. Upon these the oil was poured on the head such that from there it flowed to the rest of the members (Ps. 133:2–3).

---

17. 1.5.18

18. See instead Justin Martyr (c. 100–c. 165), *Apologia prima pro Christianis*, ch. 4, in *PG* 6:331–34; idem, *The First Apology* in *Ante-Nicene Fathers* (*ANF*), ed. Alexander Roberts and James Donaldson (New York: Christian Literature Co., 1885–1896; reprint Peabody, Mass.: Hendrickson, 1994), 1:164–65.

Generally it signified the consecration of the things anointed, by which they were dedicated to God and to divine uses, and would be fitted for them through a blessing and a conveyance of an aptitude sufficient for those uses. Specifically in persons it signified that they were lawfully called to their functions, and that by the gifts of the Holy Spirit they would also be sufficiently qualified (Ps. 45:7). In a choice way it also prefigured the calling of the Messiah to the mediatorial office. Thus in the rite of anointing a twofold sign occurs: a representing sign, the oil, and an applying sign, its pouring out. The thing signified by the oil is the Holy Spirit and his gifts; and by the pouring out, the communication of those gifts. The basis for the signifying is in the analogy which is observed between the oil and those gifts of the Holy Spirit—prudence, wisdom, ardor, joy, zeal, fortitude, and others—all so necessary for carrying out those three functions (cf. Isa. 11:1–2).

The difference with which the title *anointed* is attributed to the
Mediator and to others
XIII. Moreover, the name *anointed* is attributed to different persons in the Old Testament, not only to Hebrews but also to Gentiles, such as Cyrus (Isa. 45:1), but it is employed preeminently regarding the Mediator of the covenant of grace, and with the greatest distinction, with regard to: (1) the efficient cause, for while the former were anointed by mere men, prophets and priests, the latter was anointed by God immediately (Ps. 45:7); (2) the material, for whereas they were anointed with corporeal oil, he was anointed with spiritual oil, even the Holy Spirit himself; (3) the goal, for whereas they were anointed for earthly and passing functions, he was anointed for a heavenly and eternal function (Ps. 110:4); (4) the effect, for whereas their anointing subsisted and terminated in the ones anointed, his anointing also flowed to others, as from the head to the members (Ps. 133:2–3; John 1:16). For this reason, Athanasius in *Against the Arians* (oration 1) says, "Not like Aaron and David, or any of the rest, was he thus anointed with oil itself, but in a different way surpassing all his companions. That this oil is the Holy Spirit, he explains through the prophet: 'The Spirit of the Lord is upon me, because he has anointed me'" (Isa. 51:1).[19]

What the anointing signifies with respect to the Mediator
XIV. With respect to the Mediator, the anointing denotes two things: first, his calling to his office (Heb. 5:4–5), accomplished in a certain eternal pact between

---

19. Athanasius (c. 293–373), *Orationes versus Arianos* in *PG* 26:109–10; idem, *Four Discourses Against the Arians* in *NPNF2* 4:333–34.

him and the Father (Isa. 53:10), through which before all others he alone was chosen to be the Mediator (Isa. 42:1), was foreordained (1 Peter 1:20), for performing all that was required for the redemption of the elect, and was sent in time (John 3:17). And from all these things, the anointing is synonymously termed a sealing (John 6:27), a sanctification (John 10:36). Second, it denotes his qualification, by which he is outfitted with the gifts necessary for the mediatorial function (Ps. 45:7; Isa. 61:1). Accordingly, he was anointed with respect to both natures insofar as anointing designates calling, but with respect to the human nature only insofar as it denotes qualification.

The office to which the Mediator was inaugurated by the anointing
XV. The office to which he was inaugurated by this anointing is that of the Mediator (Heb. 8:6; 12:24; 1 Tim. 2:5), which three functions, as if three parts, sum up: (1) the prophetic (Deut. 18:15ff.; Acts 7:37; Isa. 61:1–2), by which he makes ignorant sinners, externally by the Word and internally by his Spirit, to learn the way of obtaining salvation, from which he is called the doctor, the apostle of our confession, the Light, the way, the truth, and the life; (2) the priestly (Ps. 110:4; Heb. 7:17), by which he reconciles sinners alienated from God (2 Cor. 5:19); and (3) the kingly (Ps. 2:6; Luke 1:32–33), by which he governs and protects the reconciled (John 10:27–28). The Lord willing, these offices will be treated in their own place explicitly and individually.[20]

He received the gifts of anointing not only for himself alone,
but also for his people.
XVI. Finally, the gifts of the Holy Spirit which he procures by this anointing, he received not for himself alone, but additionally for his people, so that by these gifts he might fill all things (Eph. 4:8; Joel 2:28–29). Thus Psalm 45:7, "Your God has anointed you with the oil of gladness מחבריך," that is, as Illyricus observes, not only "above your companions," but also "for your companions," which was also prefigured in Aaron (Ps. 133:2), with the balsam descending from his head upon his beard and garments, even to their lowest fringes.

Accordingly, they are called disciples and Christians.
From this, those who follow this anointed one are not only everywhere called his disciples, but even his companions (Ps. 45:7), on account of their participation in the anointing; and also Christians (Acts 11:26; 26:28; 1 Peter 4:16), inasmuch as his anointing belongs to them (2 Cor. 1:21; 1 John 2:20, 27), through which

---

20. 1.5.6–8

they become partakers of an anointing not the same in all things with their head (1 Tim. 2:5; Isa. 63:3), but yet not dissimilar in all things either, inasmuch as through it they also in their own way are: (1) prophets (Acts 2:17; Joel 2:28), those who (a) reverently inquire into the doctrine of our highest Prophet (John 5:39; Ps. 1:2); (b) faithfully make known to others the same doctrine, according to their office and the measure of their strength (Col. 3:16; Luke 22:32; 1 Thess. 5:11); or at least (c) profess the name of Christ vigorously and eagerly (Matt. 10:32; 1 Peter 3:19). They are (2) priests (Rev. 1:6; 5:10; 20:6; 1 Peter. 2:9; Isa. 61:6; 66:21), those who offer (a) themselves to God, as a spiritual sacrifice of gratitude (Rom. 12:1; 15:16); (b) their prayers and thanksgivings (Hos. 14:2; Heb. 13:15); (c) alms (Phil. 4:18; Heb. 13:16); and (d) their life for the name of Jesus (Acts 15:26; Phil. 2:17; 2 Tim. 4:6). They are (3) kings (Rev. 1:6; 1 Peter 2:9), those who (a) while they are here, strenuously fight for Christ and under Christ (2 Tim. 4:7), against Satan (1 Peter 5:8; 1 John 2:13; Rom. 16:20), sin (Gal. 5:17), and the world (2 Tim. 2:26; 1 Cor. 15:32); and (b) hereafter, gloriously triumph with him (Rom. 8:17; Rev. 3:21; 4:4; 2 Tim. 2:12).

The third name of the Mediator, our Lord
XVII. The third name of the Mediator remains, by which he is called *our Lord,* not only in our text, but throughout the entire tenor of Holy Scripture (Ps. 110:1; Mal. 3:1; 4:5; Matt. 3:3; 22:43–44, 46; Luke 2:11; John 20:28; Acts 2:36; 1 Cor. 8:6; Eph. 4:5; Phil. 2:11; Rev. 11:8). In it the Greek κύριος ἡμῶν corresponds to the Hebrew אדוני, in such a way that it denotes the lordship and authority that someone obtains by just title over someone or something, such as legitimate magistrates obtain over subjects, or masters over servants. Some possess this by nature, through generation, but others procure and possess it for themselves by various means, such as by right of military oath, of contract, of purchase, and so forth.

The double lordship of the Mediator
XVIII. A double lordship belongs to the Mediator: a lordship natural to him,[21] as he is God, by title of creation, preservation, governance, for which reason he is hailed as the Lord of all (Acts 10:36), such that by this very title is designated the dignity of the person, who, just as in the Old Testament he is called יהוה, the name absolutely proper to God, so in the New Testament he is called κύριος (Matt. 22:44); and a lordship acquired by the mediatorial function, by which: (1) he redeemed his own when they were set under the power of Satan

---

21. *congenitum*

(Col. 1:13; John 8:36). (2) When they were alienated from him by sin, he called them back to himself, to be his very own (1 Cor. 6:20; 7:23). And the price by which he accomplished this is customarily called a λύτρον, ransom, that by which captive soldiers are freed from their slavery to the enemy (Matt. 20:28; Rom. 3:24; 1 Cor. 6:20), which was supplied not with gold or silver but with his very own and precious blood (Acts 20:28; Eph. 1:7; 1 Peter 1:18–19; Rev. 5:9). With the same emphasis he is called a ruler (Mic. 5:2), unless the title Lord rather expresses power, right, and authority to rule, or to act according to his will, since he is called a ruler with respect to the exercise of ruling, and he is also given the title King in the same sense, for which reason those things that will occur in their own place regarding his kingly office should be transferred to here, just as vice versa what we have taught regarding his lordship should be referred to there. [22]

Why he is called *our* Lord

XIX. Finally, he is also designated as *our* Lord, that is, neither of all indiscriminately, nor of only some one person, but of many, either of some certain order of men, who are from this everywhere called his own (John 1:11), namely of that order in which Paul and Barnabas were, that is, of all the elect, as those: (1) who have been given to him by his Father (John 17:9); (2) whom he purchased for himself by the price of his blood (1 Cor. 6:19–20); (3) whom he claimed out from under the authority of spiritual enemies for himself as his own possession (Heb. 2:14–15); (4) who have been conjoined and united with him, as members of the same mystical body with their head (1 Cor. 12:12), like a bride to the bridegroom (Hos. 2:20); (5) for whom he gave up himself, in all that he is, through the covenant of grace (Eph. 5:2); just as (6) they in turn by the same covenant reciprocally gave themselves to him (2 Cor. 8:5). From all these things there belongs to him a certain proper lordship from which they are called his, and he theirs (Song 2:16), such that from all these things he is by every right denoted as "our Lord."

The Elenctic Part

It is asked: 1. Is it necessary to bow the knee at the saying
and hearing of the name Jesus?

XX. It is asked, first, whether it is necessary to bow the knee at the saying of the name *Jesus*. The papists and Lutherans—I do not know by what superstition—think it necessary, or at least that the uncovering of the head should be substituted

---

22. 1.5.8

for it. The Reformed, although they acknowledge that no veneration is too much which is devoted to the person of Jesus, nevertheless hold the opinion that it is superstitious to devote that veneration which belongs to the person to this word, because: (1) it reeks entirely of superstition to refer the veneration which belongs to the person to this one name, passing by other names of the same person: for example, not to the name God, or Christ, or Immanuel. And to this is added (2) that the uneducated common people, accustomed to this veneration of the name, also religiously apply the same to creatures: Joshua, when he is called Jesus (Heb. 4:8), to Jesus the high priest (Zech. 3:1), Jesus Sirach, and others. I need not add (3) that it is manifest idolatry to transfer that religious worship which belongs to the person to a name or word.

Objection

The only protection for this superstition they mistakenly seek in Philippians 2:9–10, for in that passage: (1) the apostle has entirely nothing about the saying and hearing of a word, at which he would want the knee to be bowed or the head uncovered. (2) He speaks of such a bowing of the knee which also occurs among spirits, as much heavenly as hellish ones, that is, of a spiritual bowing of the knee, which consists in subjection, whether spontaneous or unwilling. At least (3) he has nothing about the covering of the head.

2. Does there belong to the name Jesus *a peculiar effectiveness for driving away Satan, and so forth?*

XXI. It is asked, second, whether there belongs to the word or name *Jesus* a certain peculiar effectiveness, for example, for driving away Satan, and so forth. The papists, for disguising the superstitious and idolatrous veneration of the word Jesus which we spoke of, ascribe to it an effectiveness for driving away Satan, for removing diseases and enemies not only from men but also from beasts. From this, that word is continually in their mouth whenever something unusual occurs; indeed what is worse, they write the name Jesus on a piece of parchment and hang it around their neck or suspend it on their gates, frequently with the added words *Maria* and *Anna*, as prophylactics against the plague. The Reformed, although they leave every kind of efficacy to the person, yet leave none to the name, except that of signifying the one named. The papists are not mindful enough that: (1) to names, as they are words, belongs no other force than that of signifying, and moreover, not that of physically producing or effecting this or that thing. (2) The people are in this way made accustomed to profaning that name, and thus also to despising it. (3) It tends toward magic, which is so severely prohibited by God, to desire by the pronunciation of little words and analogous actions to drive out Satan and diseases. I do not see even a whit of protection produced for this superstition by its own authors, whether from Scripture or from nature. But if they should object passages such as Acts 16:18 and similar ones, where the apostles are said to have cast out Satan by the name of Jesus, the response is easy, that by the name of Jesus, his person is understood, not simply that word, as Peter teaches in Acts 4:10: "By him this man stands before you whole" (cf. Acts 19:13, 15).

3. Is it permissible to name oneself after the name Jesus?
XXII. It is asked, third, whether it is permissible to name oneself after the name *Jesus*. The followers of Ignacio de Loyola, through an intolerable arrogance, not content with the common title of *Christians*, are eager to be hailed, from the name Jesus, as *Jesuits*, or as being part of the *Society of Jesus*. The Reformed hold that the disciples of Christ must not be named after any other than the name Christ, or as Christians, because: (1) the name Jesuit is entirely absent from Scripture. (2) It breathes a spirit of contempt for the rest of Christians. (3) It snatches to itself what Christ asserted for himself alone (Isa. 63:3, 5). I need not add that (4) this name is (a) an innovation, (b) superstitious, (c) schismatic, and (d) incongruous, as it is not fitting to the thing named, (e) disapproved of by the saner papists themselves, for which reason in the convent of Poissy, in the name of the entire French church on December 15, 1541, it was publicly proclaimed that they should entirely abstain from that name.

The pretext of the Jesuits is removed.
The Loyolites allege this one thing for themselves: If believers are rightly named Christians after Christ, then they also, as well as the associates of their order, are no less rightly named Jesuits after the name Jesus. But they do not consider that the reckoning is dissimilar, because: (1) we are called Christians in Scripture, but Jesuits nowhere. (2) We are called Christians from Christ because we are partakers of his spiritual anointing; whereas we cannot be called Jesuits because in the meriting or conferring of salvation, Christ allows no associates. If they should insist further that they are not called Jesuits actively, but passively, we will respond that in this sense all who are truly Christians are indeed Jesuits, but they ought not be named such, because Scripture refuses to do so, and it sounds evil; and also much less ought anyone appropriate this name to himself.

4. Do they genuinely profess Jesus who, either totally or partially,
do not seek their salvation in him?

XXIII. It is asked, fourth, whether they do genuinely profess Jesus who, either totally or partially, do not seek their salvation in him alone. The unbelieving pagans especially do not seek their salvation in Jesus at all, but neither do they profess him. Likewise modern Jews; in addition, they detest Jesus. Muslims do profess him as an eminent prophet, but they do not seek their salvation in him. The Socinians do profess him, but they seek salvation in their own works. The papists, with the Pelagians, do profess him, and partially seek their salvation in him, but partially pursue it in their own satisfactions, merits, strength of free choice, in the intercessions of angels, of the blessed Virgin, of the saints, supererogatory works, papal indulgences, purgatory, the Mass, and other things of that sort. Now, it is asked whether these latter ones genuinely profess Jesus. They affirm that they do. The Reformed deny it, because Jesus is so named not only on account of the fact that he saves his own (Matt. 1:21), but also that he alone does it (Acts 4:12; John 14:6; Isa. 63:3, 5; Acts 5:31). Next should come the fact that those who do not acknowledge that Jesus is the perfect Savior, to that extent deny him, and cannot promise themselves salvation from him (Gal. 5:3–4; Rom. 10:3). Nor do I see what, at least with any appearance of truth, they could allege for themselves, except their empty hypotheses, which we have routed or will rout in the proper places.[23]

5. Was the Messiah promised to be a spiritual Savior?
And is our Jesus such a Savior?

XXIV. It is asked, fifth, whether the Messiah was promised to be a spiritual Savior, and whether our Jesus is such a Savior. The Jews do acknowledge that the Messiah will be a Savior, but only a temporal one, who will deliver Israel from their temporal enemies; so then they also more strongly deny that our Jesus is a spiritual Savior. The Reformed affirm both: the prior because (1) a Savior is promised (Hos. 1:7) who ought to be called, and is, צדקנו יהוה, *Jehovah our Righteousness* (Jer. 23:6). (2) It is predicted that he will be a light of the Gentiles, to open the eyes of the blind, to bring captives out from captivity, and those who are in darkness from the prison house (Isa. 42:6–7). (3) Such a Savior is predicted who will destroy transgression, seal up sins, expiate iniquity, and bring in everlasting righteousness (Dan. 9:24), who will confirm the covenant with many (Dan. 9:27), who redeems souls (Ps. 72:13–14; cf. Ps. 49), redeems from all iniquities (Ps. 130:7–8), redeems from death, from hell (Isa. 25:8–9; Hos. 13:14),

---

23. 1.5.1 §XXVIII; 1.5.2 §XIX

and that by an eternal redemption (Isa. 45:17). He will be a Savior poor and needy, riding on a donkey (Zech. 9:9–10). From all these things (4) he is called a priest (Ps. 110:4), *goel*, kinsman-redeemer (Job 19:25), ישועה, *Jeshua*, Salvation (Gen. 49:18), and Redeemer (Isa. 44:6). If they oppose those passages which seem to breathe of a temporal deliverance by the Messiah, they should consider that (a) things subordinate do not conflict, for he is a universal Savior (Ps. 103:2–3), both bodily and spiritual; (b) also, spiritual deliverance is quite frequently spoken of figuratively through bodily deliverance. With these things presupposed, the latter is also evident, namely that our Jesus is such a Savior, by all those arguments by which we demonstrated that our Jesus is the promised Messiah, above in chapter 2 of this book, §XIX. To these arguments we will not add anything except this instruction: if you wish to deal in summary form with a Jew, let him outline for you the criteria by which he would one day recognize the coming Messiah, and prove them by the Scriptures; then once proven you will be able to apply them without any trouble to our Jesus. If he should hesitate regarding the authority, or even the historical authority, of the New Testament, and accordingly not admit the credibility of any history, you should ask by what helps he will someday perceive that the supplied marks of the true Messiah are applicable to his Messiah, and likewise by what helps the Jews would want to teach him to others who are absent or live at a later time, if they spurn the credibility of all history, such as our New Testament is. This controversy is related to that which we already treated in chapter 2, §XIX, and that which we will treat in chapter 8, §XI.

6. Does the name Jehovah *belong to Christ?*
XXV. It is asked, sixth, whether the name *Jehovah* belongs to Christ. The Jews, so that they would not be compelled to admit that the promised Messiah is God from eternity, since they admit that this name is altogether proper to God, deny that this name is attributed to the Messiah. The Socinians and all anti-Trinitarians, so that they would not be compelled to confess that Christ and the Holy Spirit are God consubstantial with the Father,[24] sometimes deny that this name is proper to God, and sometimes, if it is proper to God, they deny that this name is attributed to Christ. The Reformed profess both, that it is attributed expressly both to the Messiah and to Christ, just as we have said in its own place (bk. 2, ch. 4, §§VIII, XIV; likewise ch. 26, §IX). To these we add that Scripture speaks against the anti-Trinitarians: (1) by nearly express testimonies, for example in Isaiah 41:14, where not only does the substance itself teach that the words

---

24. *Deum Patri* ὁμοούσιον

must be understood regarding the Messiah, but also the Aramaic paraphrase explicitly accommodates them to the Messiah.[25] Likewise in Isaiah 45:17, "Israel shall be saved ביהוה, in Jehovah, with an everlasting salvation"; in Hosea 1:7, "I will have mercy upon the house of Judah and I will save them in Jehovah their God"; in Jeremiah 23:6, "And this is the name by which they shall call him, יהוה צדקנו, Jehovah our Righteousness" (2) By the comparison of passages in the Old Testament, in which the subject is undoubtedly Jehovah, with passages in the New Testament where those passages are applied to our Mediator. Thus the one who delivered the people of Israel from Egypt was the true Jehovah—Deuteronomy 32:12, "Jehovah alone led him, and there was no foreign strong one with him"—but in Jude 5 this is attributed to the Mediator: "I want to remind you, though you once knew this, that the Lord" (in the Vulgate the name Jesus is added), "when he had delivered the people from Egypt," which Lord verse 4 affirms is Jesus Christ. Thus the one who promulgated the Law from Sinai was Jehovah (Ex. 20:2), but he was the Son of God (Acts 7:37–38). Again, the one who was tempted in the wilderness was Jehovah the Most High (Ex. 17:2, 7; Num. 11:1; 14:3; Ps. 78:17), but he was the Mediator (1 Cor. 10:9). (3) By those passages in which he is called κύριος, Lord (Luke 1:76; John 10:28; Jude 4), by which name the Septuagint customarily translated the name Jehovah, as is well known. We have dispelled the objections in their own place.[26]

7. Does the name θεός, God, *belong to Christ with the emphasis by which it denotes the highest God?*

XXVI. It is asked, seventh, whether the name θεός, God, belongs to Christ with the emphasis by which it denotes the highest God. The Socinians acknowledge that the name *God*, and even *true God*, belongs to him, yet so that they would not be compelled to acknowledge that he is God from eternity and consubstantial with his Father, they deny that this name belongs to him insofar as it denotes, as they themselves say, the highest God. Thus Socinus in his *Refutation* of Wujek (ch. 6, class. 4, arg. 1) says, "The name *God* is by its own nature an absolute name, and therefore applicable to many, but yet it is attributed par excellence in a singular way to that one highest Creator and Author of all things, such that in the New Testament when it absolutely obtains the place of the subject, whether with the article or without the article; or when it obtains the relation of the predicate, if it has an article simply, or without such an adjunct or construction as would diminish the force of the article, it is never found attributed to any

---

25. Montano, *Biblia Sacra*, 4:122–23.
26. 1.2.26 §XVIII

except him alone, not even Christ himself excepted."[27] Compare the same author in his *Animadversions,* chapter 4.[28]

The arguments of the orthodox

The Reformed on the contrary state that the name θεός, God, is attributed to him in its full efficacy, insofar as it denotes the highest God, because: (1) he is designated God with a specification[29] or additional element that is exegetical and amplifying: thus "the great God," "the true God," and "God blessed over all" (Titus 2:13; 1 John 5:20; Rom. 9:5). (2) He is named God not only attributively, but also subjectively (Acts 20:28; 1 Tim. 3:16). (3) He is named God with the article, ὁ θεός (Matt. 1:23; Luke 1:47; Acts 20:28; Titus 1:13; Heb. 1:8). (4) He is named God not only equally, but also equivalently with the Father,[30] in Colossians 2:2, "to the acknowledgement of the mystery of God, both of the Father and of Christ" (cf. 1 Thess. 1:3). (5) He is named God diacritically, indeed antithetically to "those that are called gods" and "those which by nature are no gods" (1 Cor. 8:5; Gal. 4:8; 1 Thess. 1:9; cf. Matt. 16:16; 1 John 5:20). (6) He is named God not only from his exaltation and glorification, as our adversaries want, but in the midst of his emptying[31] (Matt. 1:23; 1 Tim. 3:16). (7) He is called the God of Israel (by which name even the Socinians confess that no one besides the highest God is designated), in Luke 1:16 and Malachi 4:5, where the one whom John the Baptist preceded was undoubtedly the God of Israel, but the one whom John preceded is Christ (cf. Luke 1:17, 76). (8) David (Ps. 110:1) and Thomas (John 20:28) call him their Lord and their God, the emphasis of which the Savior urges (Matt. 22:43–44); and Paul also (Phil. 4:19).

---

27. Faustus Socinus, *Responsio ad libellum Jacobi Wujeki Jesuitae, Polonice editum, De divinitate Filii Dei, et Spiritus Sancti* (Raków: Sternacki, 1624), 353. Also found in *Bibliotheca Fratrum Polonorum quos Unitarios vocant* (Irenopolis [Amsterdam]: 1656), 2:599. Compared to Mastricht's citation, the first sentence of Socinus's original reads *nomen Deus sua natura esse nomen appellativum,* "the name *God* is by its own nature an appellative name." Jakub Wujek (1541–1597) was a Jesuit known for translating the Sixto-Clementine revision of the Vulgate into Polish, *Biblia to iest Księgi Starego y Nowego Przymierza według Łacińskiego przekładu Starego y Nowego Testamentu* (Krakow: Drukárni Łázárzowey, 1599).

28. The *Animadversiones* is Socinus's response to the theses *Assertiones theologicae de Trino et Uno adversus novos Samosatenicos* (1581). Socinus, *Assertiones theologicae…una cum animadversionibus* (Raków: Sternacki, 1618), 40–41; *Bibliotheca Fratrum Polonorum,* 2:423–92.

29. *cum* προσδιορισμῷ

30. *non solum aeque, sed etiam aequaliter cum Patre*

31. *in media exinanitione.* Cf. Phil. 2:7.

The Practical Part

THE GENERAL PRACTICE OF THE
NAMES OF THE SAVIOR

General advice on the practice of the names of Christ
XXVII. Before we hasten to practice, it should be mentioned in advance that it is not so much from names as from the ones named that the practice of the individual names must be sought; and so also that it should be cautiously observed whether a name signifies this or that: a nature in the Mediator, either divine or human; or his office, either prophetic, or priestly, or kingly; or a state, that of humiliation or exaltation; or this or that benefit. Then, the arguments for practice will come to be sought by comparing those chapters where the things signified are treated. For example, because the name Jesus expresses the benefit of redemption, so then the arguments for the practice regarding the name Jesus should be sought from the chapter on redemption. With this set down, for the twofold contemplation, general and special, of the names of the Mediator, also a twofold practice of this chapter will come before us.

The names of the Mediator generally invite us: 1. To know him.
XXVIII. The more general contemplation of the names of the Mediator invites us, first, to know the Mediator. For this is the first use of names, that they lead us to the knowledge of the thing named, from which a *nomen*, name, is called as it were a *novimen*, a means of knowing. So then, the name of Christ is particularly utilized in the Scriptures in place of the knowledge of Christ (John 17:6, 26; Rom. 1:5; Acts 9:15). To this same end points such a great aggregation of his names as is common in the Scriptures (Isa. 9:6; 1 Cor. 1:30; 1 Tim. 6:15).

Motives
For the knowledge of the Mediator is: (1) most excellent (Phil. 3:8); (2) most useful, for justification (Isa. 53:11), for eternal life (John 17:3), whereas ignorance of him is especially destructive (2 Thess. 1:8); (3) especially necessary for believing, loving, and worshiping the Mediator, without whom there is no salvation, nor is there another name given (Acts 4:12). In particular, thinking of the Mediator's names leads us to the knowledge of his: (1) person, as the God-man, to which refer names such as Immanuel and Ithiel; (2) divine nature, to which refer names such as Jehovah, θεός, God, λόγος, Word; (3) human nature, such as man, Son of Man, and the Branch; (4) office, to which point names such as Christ, *goel*, kinsman-redeemer, λυτρώτης, Redeemer, prophet, priest, king, and so forth; (5) state of humiliation, from which, for example, he is identified as a

servant, a worm; (6) state of exaltation, from which for example he is spoken of as King, Lord, King of kings, and Lord of lords; (7) benefits, from which he is denominated Jesus, Redeemer, Jehovah our Righteousness, Counselor, wisdom, righteousness, sanctification, redemption, Shepherd, Sun, shield, and so forth. Compare §§VI–VII of this chapter.

The manner of knowing

Moreover, it invites to a knowledge of the Mediator that is not just of any sort: (1) not purely speculative and idle, but powerful and working (Gal. 5:6); (2) not cold, but affectionate and loving, by which he is precious to us (1 Peter 2:7) above all things that are in heaven and upon earth (Ps. 73:25), by which even his reproach is for us above all the treasures of this world (Heb. 11:25); and so forth.

2. For distinguishing him from any others

XXIX. Second, for distinguishing him from any spurious and counterfeit mediators. For to this end names are imposed on things, first proper names and then appellative names (and from this the name of God is said to be one, Zech. 14:9): so that they may be distinguished from other things with respect to species as well as individuals (Isa. 42:8); from this a *nomen*, name, is called as it were a *notamen*, a means of marking. Namely, so that: (1) we would have only one Mediator (1 Tim. 2:5); (2) we would pass by others, and all other things (Ps. 16:4); (3) we would cling to the one, and place in that one our trust, hope, salvation, and all things (Ps. 16:6; Acts 4:12; John 14:6); (4) we would worship and heed only that one (Matt. 23:9–10; 4:10); (5) we would choose one bridegroom for ourselves, one head, one Lord (Song 5:10; Eph. 1:21–23; 1 Cor. 8:6; Eph. 4:5), passing by all others, after the manner of conjugal love (Ps. 73:25).

3. For glorifying him. The motivating reasons

XXX. Third, for celebrating and glorifying the Mediator. For since (as we have observed and demonstrated previously in bk. 2, ch. 4, §XVIII): (1) "name" throughout the Holy Scriptures denotes fame, glory, and great estimation and celebrity; (2) "men of name" are those renowned for whatever special privilege, even though for only one; and (3) to "have a name" is to be commended and celebrated by all; also, (4) "children without a name" are considered disgraceful children of the earth—how would such not apply to the Mediator? For (1) on him God heaped up in the Scriptures so many names, each of which presents a certain particular dignity, perfection, and eminence. (2) To him the most glorious God has given the name which is above every name, that at his name every knee should bow, of those who are in heaven, in earth, and under the earth (Phil. 2:9–11). And that (3) not only by pure and unadulterated grace, but in addition by his own merit: διό, "Wherefore" (Phil. 2:9–11). Indeed also, (4) he has given him again the glory that he already had with him before the foundations of the earth were laid (John 17:5). Especially since (5) from this duty, we are throughout the Scriptures commanded to do our works in the name of Christ, that is, for his glory and praise (Col. 3:17).

How he ought to be glorified

Therefore, in regard to this eminence of our Mediator, which by the amassing of so many and such great names can never be sufficiently represented, surely we should: (1) acknowledge it with our heart (Ps. 18:1–2; 103:1), because the intrinsic dignity and eminence of anything supplies the foundation of all its honor and glory. We should (2) celebrate it with our mouth (Ps. 116:17–19; 40:9–10; 22:22, 25; Phil. 2:10–11). We should (3) demonstrate it with our work, with reverence, worship, and every other duty that belongs to us (1 Peter 2:9). We should boast in him alone (Phil. 3:3).

4. It explains his all-sufficiency

XXXI. Fourth, such a great aggregation of names for the Mediator in the Scriptures as if by pieces unfolds and recalls to our minds his most absolute all-sufficiency, by which he is able to save to the uttermost (Heb. 7:25), inasmuch as he is for us the way, the truth, and the life (John 14:6); wisdom, righteousness, sanctification, and redemption (1 Cor. 1:30); Counselor, the mighty God, the everlasting Father, the Prince of Peace (Isa. 9:6); upon whom rests the spirit of wisdom and understanding, the spirit of counsel, the spirit of knowledge and of the fear of the Lord (Isa. 11:2); out of whose abundance we can draw grace for grace (John 1:16); in whom we can be complete (Col. 1:28; 2:9–10); such that there is salvation in no other, nor is there another name under heaven given to us (Acts 4:12).

To what end

All these things are impressed upon us with such a great mass of names, and represent the all-sufficiency of the Mediator, to the end that: (1) we would receive him by faith without hesitation or trouble, that we would believe on his name (John 1:12). (2) We would magnify him before all things (Phil. 3:8–9; 1 Peter 2:7). (3) We would love him with our whole heart, before any of the most beloved things (Matt. 10:37; 1 Cor. 16:22). (4) We would cling to him inseparably (Ps. 63:8). (5) We would seek him with all eagerness, we would desire him (Ps. 63:1;

62:6–7). (6) We would rest in him (Ps. 62:1, 6; 73:25). (7) In any necessity we would flee to him (Ps. 62:8). (8) We would kiss him (Ps. 2:12); and so forth.

5. They nourish and stir up the memory of the Mediator.
XXXII. Fifth, let us ceaselessly carry his memory with us. For names function to this end: that they may be memorials (Ex. 3:15; Ps. 135:13; Hos. 12:6), which the apostle so carefully impresses upon his Timothy (2 Tim. 2:8); that we may never forget him (Deut. 8:11).

Motives
For (1) this remembrance of the Mediator feeds our faith, as well as our hope, love, trust, comfort, and so forth (Col. 2:2, 7, 10). (2) By it Christ as it were dwells in our hearts (Eph. 3:17; Col. 3:16). And so (3) this remembrance makes Christ continuously present to us (Matt. 28:20; 1 Cor. 13:12). Thus (4) in any circumstance or need, we can enjoy the perfections of the one named, to the indescribable sweetness and solace of our soul (1 Peter 1:8). And so forth.

What sort of remembrance this ought to be
If only this remembrance of Christ, which is renewed by his names, should be: (1) not frigid, but affectionate (Ps. 42:4); (2) not inert and idle, but full of action, "Remember and do" (Rev. 2:2, 5); (3) not fluctuating and fleeting, but constant and always present, always flourishing, by which we keep him in remembrance (2 Tim. 2:8), and never forget him (Deut. 8:11; 32:15; etc.).

THE PRACTICE OF THE NAME *JESUS*

The practice of the name Jesus: *1. Makes known six abuses of the name* Jesus.
XXXIII. That was the general practice of the names of the Mediator; the special practice follows, that of his chief names: Jesus, Christ, Lord.

First
Therefore, the consideration of the name Jesus, first, condemns the abuse which is committed: (1) by the Jews, who despise and blaspheme this name, when due to hatred of his person, instead of "Jesus" they read and say "Jeshu," which means liar and impostor. In fact when the saying of his name is heard, if made by Christians, they are said to spit three times, adding these words, "May his name be

destroyed." Unless they should repent, Jesus will spew them out of his mouth (Rev. 3:16).[32]

Second

(2) By magicians, because they blasphemously abuse the name Jesus for their incantations and sorceries, when, for example, intending to adjure a flow of blood, they say with cyclopic impiety,[33] "Stay, blood, in your veins, just as Jesus in his pains";[34] likewise, by aid of it they labor to cure sick sheep. In their own way the papists approach these magicians, when by the saying of it they labor to drive away Satan and any adversities, for which reason, when exposed to any unforeseen circumstance, the name Jesus is continually in their mouth. That is, after the example of the exorcists who are mentioned in Acts 19:13–14, who attempted to cast out demons through the name of Jesus, and by the just judgment of God obtained the punishment for that profanation from the very same demons.

Third

(3) By the same papists, together with the Lutherans, who transfer the worship and glory which belongs to the one named to the name, when they suppose that the name Jesus is holier than the other names of the Mediator, indeed even than the very name Jehovah, and command at its pronunciation the bowing of the knee or the uncovering of the head. These we have already noted and refuted above in §XX of this chapter.

Fourth

(4) By the Loyolites, for whom it is insufficient to be named after Christ with others, unless before others and with contempt of others they name themselves Jesuits after Jesus, which we have already noted in the elenctic part.[35]

Fifth

(5) Once more by the papists, when, although they continuously profess the name of Jesus with their mouth, even to superstition, they yet in fact (insofar

---

32. Cf. §II, above.

33. Cf. Euripides, *Cyclops* in *LCL* 12:96–99, where the cyclops Polyphemus catalogs his impiety. John D. Mikalson, *Honor Thy Gods: Popular Religion in Greek Tragedy* (University of North Carolina Press, 1991), 157–58.

34. Various versions can be found in, e.g., *Memoirs of Samuel Pepys* (London: Henry Colburn, 1828), 2:236–37; R. Po-chia Hsia, *The Myth of Ritual Murder: Jews and Magic in Reformation Germany* (New Haven, Conn.: Yale University Press, 1988), 145; A. W. Moore, *The Folk-lore of the Isle of Man* (London: D. Nutt, 1891), 98.

35. §XXII

as they seek salvation in themselves or elsewhere than in Jesus) neglect him, and also well enough deny him. These we have also noted in the elenctic part.[36]

Sixth

(6) By the same papists and the Lutherans, when they excessively revel in the elevation of this name, while they not only declare it more holy and excellent than all the rest, first of the Mediator and then of even God himself, as we just taught, but they also transfer to this name the things that are proper to the one named, when they exclaim that the name is invincible, adorable, marvelous, and attribute to it that it would deliver us from the treacheries and temptations of Satan, and from all calamities, although all those things are applicable only to the person, by whatever name he may be designated.

The evils of this abuse

Devout meditation upon the name of Jesus condemns, I say, all this abuse, because: (1) the corruption of the best through abuse is always the worst (1 Peter 2:7; 2 Cor. 2:16–17). (2) The abuse of the name tends toward a superstition by which the things that belong to the one named are attributed to the name, and thus the uneducated common people become accustomed to worship the name instead of the one named (Rom. 1:25). And this (3) results in the despising of the person named (Acts 19:13–14). And so forth.

2. The name Jesus *commends the one named.*

XXXIV. Second, the consideration of the name Jesus commends to us the named Mediator, as: (1) most ancient, for this name is most ancient, even known well enough then to the patriarch Jacob when he established his testament (Gen. 49:10), from which passage, and from the first three letters of the three words יבא שילה ולו, Rabbi Haccados in Galatino gathers the name Jesus,[37] about whom in verse 18 Jacob says, לישועתך קויתי יהוה, which the Aramaic paraphrase translates, "the redemption of Christ, the Son of David, who is to come," and the Septuagint, "I await σωτηρία, salvation," and the Targum, "My soul looks for redemption." (2) Most pleasant, for which reason Paul was so delighted by the use of this name that he repeated it more than five hundred times in his epistles. And Bernard says, "honey in my mouth, a song in my heart, a joyful melody,"[38] and likewise, "Jesus, a sight to the vision, honey to the taste, balsam to

---

36. §XXIII

37. Pietro Galatino, *De arcanis catholicae veritatis* (Frankfurt: Jacob Gottfried Seyler, 1672), 154. Cf. §IX, above.

38. Bernard of Clairvaux (1090–1153), *Opera omnia*, ed. J. Mabillon, 4th ed., 2 vols. in 4

the smell, and a delightful flower to the touch."[39] (3) Marvelous, since when the apostles were to accomplish miracles, they most often used this name (Mark 16:17; Acts 3:6; 9:34; 16:18; etc.). (4) Unconquered and invincible (cf. Ps. 20:7; Prov. 18:10; 1 Sam. 17:45). (5) Adorable (Joel 2:32 with Acts 7:59). (6) Blessed, and blessing our endeavors (Luke 5:5; Col. 3:17), and also saving (Acts 4:12).

To what end?

It commends, I say, the Mediator in these and other ways, to the end that we may: (1) make him great (Phil. 3:8); (2) celebrate him (Phil. 2:11); (3) submit ourselves to him more promptly, bow the knee of our heart to him (Phil. 2:10); (4) boast in him (Phil. 3:3; 1:26; Ps. 35:9; etc.).

3. The name Jesus offers comfort.

XXXV. Third, it supplies in all adversities the sweetest comfort. For it is a horn of salvation (Luke 1:69). Anselm says, "Jesus is all things to us: if you desire to be cured, he is the physician. If you are burdened with iniquity, he is righteousness. If you need help, he is strength. If you fear death, he is life. If you flee darkness, he is light. Taste therefore how sweet the Lord is."[40] And Bonaventure says, "Jesus, salvation's offering, salvation's sacrifice. Jesus, salvation's grace, salvation's benefit. Jesus, the safe confidence, and the safe refuge. Jesus, the bestower of forgiveness. Jesus, the solace of the sorrowful. Jesus, the hope of the penitent. Jesus, the sweet memory, the affection full of thirst. Jesus, the sweet confidence, the refreshment full of joy. Jesus, the doorway of salvation. Jesus, the safest gate. Jesus, the protector of all men. Jesus, the wholesome truth, and the light illumining the mind. Jesus, the blessedness of life, the sweetness rejoicing in the heart. O goodness itself, good Jesus, you who are our righteousness! O truth itself, true Jesus, you who are our knowledge! O love itself, beloved Jesus, you who are our redemption! O holiness itself, holy Jesus, true sanctification, pray remove us from our guilt, and grant to us the light of life."[41]

(Paris, Gaume Fratres, 1839), 2-1:1295.

39. Albert the Great (c. 1193–1280), *Compendium theologicae veritatis*, bk. 7 ch. 30, 2 vols. (Deventer: Richard Paffraet, c. 1480–1482), fol. [s viii] r. For the (pseudo-)Bernardine reception of this quote in Paul Gerhardt, see J. A. Steiger, *"Geh' aus, mein Herz, und suche Freud": Paul Gerhardts Sommerlied und die Gelehrskamheit der Barockzeit (Naturkunde, Emblematik, Theologie)* (Berlin: Walter de Gruyter, 2007), 64n122.

40. See exact quote instead in Ambrose of Milan (c. 340–397), *De virginitate liber unus*, bk. 3, ch. 99 in *PL* 16:291.

41. Bonaventure (1221–1274), *De septem verbis dominis in cruce* in *Opera omnia…cura et studio A.C. Peltier…tomus decimus quartus* (Paris: Ludovicus Vives, 1868), 175. On the "uncertain or spurious" authorship of this work, see Pietro Maranesi, "The Opera Omnia of Saint Bonaventure:

The evils against which it offers comfort
Namely, it offers comfort: (1) in sins (Matt. 1:21; Acts 10:43); (2) in the snares of the devil (Rom. 16:20; Luke 11:21); (3) in temptations (1 Cor. 10:13; Heb. 2:18; 4:15); (4) in all adversities (Prov. 18:10). For he saves: (1) from fault, by forgiving (Acts 10:43); (2) from battle, by defending (Ps. 20:1, 7); (3) from adverse health, by healing (Mark 16:17–19; Acts 3:6); and so forth.

The requirements of those whom he comforts
These things are true provided that (1) we be of his people (Matt. 1:21), his sheep (John 10:7, 11); (2) we come to him (John 10:9; Matt. 11:28; Rev. 22:17; Isa. 55:1); (3) we believe in him (John 1:12; Acts 10:43); (4) we offer ourselves compliant to him (Rev. 22:14; Heb. 5:9); (5) we rest in him (Ps. 73:25); and (6) we call upon him (Ps. 25:3).

4. The name Jesus *raises us up to various duties to be rendered to the one named.*
XXXVI. Fourth, it urges us to carefully direct this name to our own uses, toward heightening: (1) our gratitude toward God, because out of pure love he gave such a Jesus (John 3:16; Isa. 9:6; Luke 1:68), and deigns through him to save us (Hos. 1:7); (2) the knowledge and sense of our sins and misery (Matt. 11:28), from which he would deliver us (Matt. 1:21); (3) desire for salvation (Rev. 22:17; Ps. 42:1; Isa. 55:1; John 7:37); (4) faith in him (Acts 10:43); (5) repentance from sins, hatred of them, zeal for good works (Titus 2:14; 2 Tim. 2:19); (6) glorification of him (Phil. 2:11; Luke 1:32); (7) worship, reverence, and submission to him (Phil. 2:10; Ps. 2:11–12); and so forth.

Motivating reasons
For, if we neglect these things: (1) he will be useless to us (Gal. 5:4; John 5:40); in fact, (2) he will be harmful and destructive (Rom. 9:32–33; Ps. 2:12); whereas (3) used diligently, he will supply a fullness from which we may draw grace for grace (John 1:16), that in him we may in all things be complete (Col. 1:19; 2:9–10); and so forth. Compare the preceding points, and those that will occur in their own place, Lord willing, in the chapter on redemption.[42]

History and Present Situation" in Jay Hammond, Wayne Hellmann, and Jared Goff, eds., *A Companion to Bonaventure* (Leiden: Brill, 2014), 71, 78.
    42. 1.5.18 §LII

THE PRACTICE OF THE NAME *CHRIST*
AND *CHRISTIAN*

The practice of the name Christ *must be sought elsewhere*
XXXVII. Next comes the practice of the name Christ, which, because it does not speak of anything but separation, qualification, and inauguration to his mediatorial office, advises us that its practice should be sought from the chapters on the Mediator and the mediatorial functions.[43] Nor does there belong to this topic anything except those duties which result from the communication of the name, by which we are designated Christians, and are made partners as it were in his anointing (Ps. 45:7; Heb. 1:9).

The practice of the name Christian *is: 1. To boast in Christ.*
This communication supplies us with an argument, first, for boasting (1 Peter 4:16; Phil. 1:26; 3:3; Isa. 61:3, 6; 62:2), because (1) he named us after himself (Deut. 28:10; Jer. 7:10–11, 14, 30). (2) By this he caused us to become his own possession (Isa. 43:6–7; 44:5), his spouse, his children, his members, inasmuch as those are customarily named after their husbands, their parents, their head (cf. John 1:12; 1 John 3:1; Heb. 2:10, 13). (3) He made us partakers of his own anointing, from which we are called companions, חברים, fellows (Ps. 45:7), μέτοχοι, partners (Heb. 1:9). By this anointing (4) he communicated the dignity of a prophet (Acts 2:7; Joel 2:28), of a priest (Rev. 1:6; 5:10; 20:6; 1 Peter 2:5, 9; Isa. 66:21), and of a king (Rev. 1:6; 1 Peter 2:9). In addition, (5) he anointed us together with him with the same Spirit (2 Cor. 1:21). Thus from all these things, however much we are despised and downcast in the world, we can boast in the title, "the Lord's anointed ones" (Ps. 105:15), and boast in the Lord (Jer. 9:23–24).

2. To be consoled in any adversities. Circumstances in which it comforts
XXXVIII. Second, for consolation: (1) in any of the common miseries of this life arising from sin, such as tiresome labor, anxious worry, disease, poverty, contempt, wars, death, and other such things which the apostle recounts in Romans 8:35, and the list he experienced in 2 Corinthians 11:23–33. (2) In the miseries specific to Christians: hatred, insults, persecutions of enemies, which are inseparable consequences of the name Christian (Matt. 10:38; 16:24; 2 Tim. 3:12; Luke 24:26; Acts 14:22). For which reason Tertullian in his *Apology* (ch. 3) says, "This name is the most hated without cause. A man may be a good Gaius or

---

43. 1.5.4–8

Sejus, but he becomes evil only because he is a Christian; the name, not wrong-doing, is condemned in us, and a mere word precondemns an unknown sect, because it is named, not because it has been convicted. An innocent name, in innocent people, is despised."[44] Compare Tacitus (bk. 15), "Therefore to obliterate the rumor" (namely that Nero had ordered the burning of Rome so that he might watch a type of the burning of Troy), "he arraigned and afflicted with the most exquisite punishments those detested for their abominations whom the common people called Christians."[45] (3) In temptations of Satan (2 Cor. 12:7; 11:3), to which Christians are especially exposed (Eph. 6:12; 2 Cor. 10:3–4). (4) In spiritual desertions (Ps. 13:1; 43:2; 77:7–9; 88:14–17); and so forth.

Consoling arguments

In these or any other circumstances, it is extraordinarily comforting: (1) to suffer as a Christian (1 Peter 4:16); (2) as a disciple (which coincides with a Christian), to carry the cross of Christ, indeed to take it up (Luke 9:23), in the cross to be made like Christ (Rom. 8:17, 29); (3) through the Christian name to have become Christ's own, as his possession (Isa. 49:15–16; Jer. 14:9); (4) that accordingly in adversities he cares for us, as though for himself (Acts 9:4; cf. Deut. 32:10; Zech. 2:8; Ps. 17:8), and that he is the one who suffered for this reason, that he could sympathize with us (Heb. 4:15); moreover, (5) that he anointed us as his companions (μέτοχοι) with the same Spirit of gladness (Ps. 45:8; Heb. 1:9), that he might present to us the Comforter (John 14:16, 27; 15:26), who pours out the love of God into our hearts, so that we may boast in adversities (Rom. 5:3, 5), who helps our infirmities (Rom. 8:26); and so forth.

3. To rebuke. Whom?

XXXIX. Third, for rebuke, of those who: (1) take the name of Christian without the substance, who say, "Lord, Lord," but do not do, and so forth (Matt. 7:22), who are Jews in public but not in private, whom the apostle notes in Romans 2:28–29; who (2) profess Christ with their mouth, but also deny him with their deeds (Titus 1:16), who have a name that they are living, but show by their works that they are dead (Rev. 3:1), who say that they are Jews, but in reality are of the synagogue of Satan (Rev. 3:9); who (3) profess Christ with their mouth, but in their living pursue Satan, the world, the flesh (John 8:44; Ps. 17:14; 1 John 2:15;

---

44. Tertullian (c. 155–c. 220), *Apologeticus adversus gentes pro Christianis* in *PL* 1:279-80; idem, *Apology* in *ANF* 3:20.

45. Cf. Tacitus, *Annals,* XV.44 in *The Loeb Classical Library* (*LCL*) (Cambridge, Mass.: Harvard University Press, 1979) 322:282–83.

Phil. 3:19), and so show themselves to be, instead of Christians, in fact Satanic, worldly, carnal; who (4) boast in any other than in Christ (Phil. 3:3), and crave to be named after someone else than Christ, for example, the Lutherans after Luther, about whom Paul speaks in 1 Corinthians 1:12.

By what arguments

These in fact: (1) show themselves to be liars (Rev. 3:9), (2) deny Christ (Titus 1:16), (3) in turn will be denied by him (Matt. 10:33), (4) deceive themselves (Gal. 6:3; James 1:22), (5) will be condemned by him in the last judgment (Matt. 7:22; Ps. 50:16).

4. To exhort. To what duties

XL. Fourth, for exhortation, that by every effort, as we are in name, so we may show ourselves to be Christians in substance. That is: (1) because from the imposition and reception of the name, we have been made his own possession, let us live and die no longer for ourselves, but for him (Rom. 14:7–8; 1 Cor. 6:19–20), that is, (a) for his glory (Phil. 1:20), (b) by his precept (Heb. 5:9), (c) by his internal leading (Gal. 2:20). (2) Because through communion with his anointing, sealed by the name Christian (Ps. 133:2), we have been made (a) prophets (Acts 2:17), let us fearlessly name, that is, profess his name (2 Tim. 2:19; Matt. 10:32; 1 John 2:23); (b) priests, let us sacrifice to him our entire selves (Rom. 12:1), and the calves of our lips (Hos. 14:2; Heb. 13:15), and also alms (Heb. 13:16); (c) kings, let us fight the good fight for Christ (2 Tim. 4:7). (3) Because we are Christians, and therefore disciples of Christ, which two names were once synonymous (Acts 11:26), (a) let us heed Christ in all things, as our one Teacher (Matt. 23:8, 10; Deut. 18:18–19); (b) let us deny ourselves and all our own things (Luke 9:23; Phil. 3:7–9); (c) let us follow Christ (Matt. 16:26) and pursue his footsteps (Matt. 11:29; 1 Cor. 11:1; Phil. 2:5; Eph. 5:1–2). (4) Because we name the name of Christ, let us forsake all unrighteousness (2 Tim. 2:19). (5) Because we are Christians, let us give ourselves to every Christian virtue, so that we may be pure, even as he is pure (1 John 3:3; 2 Cor. 7:1).

By what motivating reasons

In this way: (1) we will be members of Christ, and the mystical body of Christ (1 Cor. 12:12); (2) we will die with Christ, and in death itself we will be Christ's (Rom. 14:7). Otherwise, (3) we will pollute the members of Christ (1 Cor. 6:15); indeed, (4) we will deny him (Titus 1:16); (5) then in turn we will be denied by him (Matt. 7:22–23). Compare §XXXIX, and Casmann's *The Christian in Name and Substance*.[46]

THE PRACTICE OF THE NAME *OUR LORD*

The name our Lord *supplies:* 1. An argument for glorification
XLI. The practice of the name *our Lord* brings up the rear. Material for it is also supplied from the chapters on Christ's kingly office and on the glorified state.[47] This title likewise supplies an argument, first, for glorification, from which he is called the Lord of glory (1 Cor. 2:8), to whom belong majesty and glory (Ps. 45:3–4), and likewise, King of kings, Lord of lords (Rev. 17:14; 19:16), whom to this end God has made Lord and Christ (Acts 2:36; Isa. 49:5; 55:5; Jer. 30:21; Mic. 5:4), namely that we would honor the Son as we honor the Father (John 5:23), inasmuch as his lordship is: (1) heavenly (1 Cor. 15:47; John 18:36); (2) omnipotent (Matt. 28:18; Ps. 8:6); (3) universal (John 5:22, 27), to the ends of the earth, and even of the heavens (Phil. 2:10); (4) eternal (Dan. 2:44; 7:14); (5) spiritual, even over souls and consciences (John 18:36; 1 Cor. 6:20); and so forth.

The duties of glorification
Moreover, we glorify the Lord: (1) by acknowledging with our heart the nature and excellence of his lordship (Ps. 103:1; Heb. 8:11; Isa. 45:3, 5); (2) by proclaiming it with our mouth (Phil. 2:11; Rev. 4:10–11); (3) by demonstrating it with our work (Matt. 7:21; cf. §XLV); and so forth.

2. *An argument for comfort.* The comforting arguments
XLII. Second, it supplies an argument for comfort in any calamity, as much bodily as spiritual, as much public as private, as much in life as in death. To this end points that mass of evils in Romans 8:35–39, over which the apostle triumphs at length, in thinking of that love which is "in Christ Jesus, our Lord." And what at last could blunt the sting of any evil more effectively than to consider that: (1) in body and soul (1 Cor. 6:20), in life as well as in death (Rom. 14:7–8), we belong to the Lord Jesus? (2) Our Lord, whose special possession we are, is (a) most wise, who intimately perceives all of our misery (John 2:4; Isa. 46:1; Mark 8:3); (b) most powerful, who can save to the uttermost (Heb. 7:25), of whom we read that by a little word alone he repelled the most serious

---

46. Otto Casmann (1562–1607), *Christianus nomine et re, sorte et morte, suspiriis plenus* (Frankfurt: Collegium Musarum Palthenium, 1606).

47. 1.5.8; 1.6.9

evils, and even death itself, through whom his own can also do all things (Phil. 4:12–13); (c) most clement and most merciful (Heb. 4:15), from which comes that word common in the Gospels, σπλαγνίζομαι, "I have compassion" (Matt. 15:32; 20:34; Mark 1:41; etc.; Isa. 44:8; 49:14–15)? Accordingly, (3) we have a Lord, who (a) is able to save, as the mighty God (Isa. 9:6); and who (b) is willing to save, as a merciful and most ready Redeemer (Matt. 8:2–3; Mark 1:40; Luke 5:12; Matt. 15:28); indeed, (c) who already bought us with his own blood (1 Peter 1:18–19), and redeemed us from the power of the devil (Heb. 2:14–15)? In addition that we have such a Lord who is able and willing to powerfully preserve those already delivered (John 10:28), to the point that without his will not even the least hair can fall from the head of his people (Matt. 10:30; Luke 21:18); and moreover, to govern them in such a way that every evil turns not to their detriment, but to their benefit (Rom. 8:28), so that they can even boast in adversities (Rom. 5:5–6).

3. An argument for rebuke. The sins that must be rebuked
XLIII. Third, for rebuke, of those who: (1) do not acknowledge Jesus as Lord, such as pagans, Jews, and others who are openly unbelievers (1 Cor. 2:8); or (2) acknowledge him only with their voices, but not with their deeds (Matt. 7:21; Titus 1:16); moreover, (3) reject and despise him (Luke 19:14); indeed, (4) openly resist him (Ps. 2:1–3); and even (5) persecute him in his own (Acts 4:4–5); or at the least (6) although they profess him with their mouth and even to some degree embrace him with their heart as Jesus, as Christ, as priest, nonetheless they do not embrace him as Lord (Matt. 7:21; Acts 2:36; Col. 2:6), who want indeed to reign with him, but not to suffer with him (Matt. 20:21–22, 25–26, 28; 2 Tim. 2:12).

The reasons for rebuke
All of these (1) are enemies of Christ, either publicly or secretly (Phil. 3:18; Luke 19:27); (2) willing or unwilling, shall experience him as Lord, ruling in the midst of his enemies (Ps. 110:1–2; Acts 2:34–35; Phil. 2:10); and (3) bruising them with his rod of iron, and once broken like a potter's vessel, scattering them (Ps. 2:9); and finally, (4) utterly slaying them (Luke 19:27; Ps. 2:12).

4. An argument for exploration. Motives
XLIV. Fourth, for exploration: because (1) not all who say, "Lord, Lord" (Matt. 7:21) are of the Lord (Rom. 14:7), and many by their own profession shamefully deceive themselves (James 1:22); in fact, (2) they deceive themselves to their own eternal ruin (Matt. 7:22; 25:44, 46); and whereas on the contrary, (3) it is the

sweetest as well as the most useful thing to be persuaded in spirit and in truth that Jesus is their Lord (John 20:28; Gal. 2:20)—there is altogether reason for us to explore ourselves in earnest, whether Christ is personally our Lord.

Marks

But by what evidences at length will we certainly achieve this? I respond, Among them the first is knowledge of him (John 10:14; Jer. 31:34; Isa. 53:11; 2 Thess. 1:8), not of course just any sort, an inactive and idle knowledge, but an experimental and practical knowledge (Phil. 3:8, 10). Second, denial of self (Luke 9:23), of the flesh and carnal lusts (Gal. 5:24), of all worldly things (Ps. 16:5; 73:25–26). Third, the receiving of Christ accomplished through faith (John 1:11–12; Col. 2:5–6; Gal. 2:20), inasmuch as by it, from the promise, Christ becomes ours (Rev. 22:17). Fourth, the giving back of our own selves (2 Cor. 8:5). Fifth, covenanting, as it were conjugally (Song 2:16). Sixth, superlative love (Matt. 10:37, 39). Seventh, love with neglect and contempt for all others (Phil. 3:7–8; Song 5:9). Eighth, obedience (John 10:27; 2 Thess. 1:8). Ninth, zeal for imitation and for holiness (1 John 2:6; 3:3).

5. *An argument for exhortation.* Duties

XLV. Fifth, for exhortation: if he is the Lord and is our Lord, (1) we should acknowledge ourselves as his servants (Rom. 1:1; Phil. 1:1; Eph. 6:6); consequently, (2) we should obey him (Eph. 6:5; Col. 3:22; Heb. 5:9; 2 Thess. 1:8); furthermore, (3) we should honor and revere him (Mal. 1:6; Ps. 22:23; John 5:23); in addition, (4) we should submit ourselves to him (Eph. 5:24; 1 Peter 5:5; Heb. 2:8; Phil. 2:10); also, (5) we should love him; furthermore, (6) we should seek his glory at all times (Phil. 1:20; James 2:1); as well as these, (7) we should act for his cause in earnest (Phil. 2:21; 2 Cor. 5:15). And we should genuinely observe the further duties that are of this sort, those of servants toward their masters.

Manner

But we should pay attention that we do this: (1) in heart and spirit (Rom. 6:17; Eph. 6:6; Col. 3:22); (2) not only in speech, but also in deeds (Matt. 7:21–22; 15:8); (3) not for a time, but constantly (Phil. 2:12; Ps. 16:8); (4) not in this or that case only, as Herod heard John (Mark 6:20), but in all things (Col. 3:22). (5) Not only in the sight of men, with eye-service, as people-pleasers (Col. 3:22), just as the Pharisees (Matt. 6:2, 5), but in simplicity of heart, fearing God (Eph. 6:5–6). (6) Not under coercion, but freely and willingly (Eph. 6:7; Jer. 30:21; Ps. 110:3); and so forth.

Motives

For to this end: (1) Christ died, rose again, and was made alive, that he might be Lord both of the dead and living (Rom. 14:9). (2) He obtained us for himself with such a great price (1 Cor. 6:20; 1 Peter 1:18–19; Titus 2:14). (3) He redeemed us from the power of Satan (Heb. 2:14–15 with Luke 1:74–75). (4) We have devoted ourselves to Christ (2 Cor. 8:5; Rom. 6:16–19). And (5) what also is easier and more pleasant than to serve the Lord Jesus (Matt. 11:30; 1 John 5:3)? Indeed, (6) what is more useful (Isa. 49:3–4; 1 Cor. 15:58)? And at last, (7) what is more necessary (1 Cor. 16:22)? And so forth.

CHAPTER FOUR

The Person of the Mediator

The Word became flesh.
—John 1:14

The connection with the previous chapters
I. From the names of the Mediator, we advance directly to the one named, or to the contemplation of the person. We will consider the union of the two natures in the one person, following the lead of this portion from John 1:14.

The Exegetical Part
The text is opened and explained.
II. In this portion the assumption of the human nature, which was accomplished by the second person of the deity, that is, the union of the two natures in the one person of the Mediator, is presented in three particulars, namely:

 A. The person assuming: ὁ λόγος, *verbum,* "the Word," *sermo,* "the Speech." Without a doubt, the Son of God is meant (1 John 1:1; Rev. 19:13; Luke 1:2 with 2 Peter 1:16; as also, as I believe, in Acts 20:32; Heb. 4:12, either from Ps. 33:6 or from the history of creation, where it is quite frequently repeated, "And God said, and it was made," inasmuch as through him God created all things). Nowhere is he called ῥῆμα, also rendered "word," because λόγος signifies something more perfect, for whereas the former properly expresses *vocabulum,* a word, the latter expresses *oratio,* speaking; the latter properly concerns the mind and will, whereas the former never refers to such. In Hebrew it is דבר (Ps. 33:6; 148:8; cf. Maimonides, *The Guide for the Perplexed,* part 1, ch. 23, 65–66).[1] In Aramaic, not only in those passages where it is דבר in

---

1. Moses Maimonides (1135–1204), *The Guide for the Perplexed,* trans. M. Friedländer, 3 vols. (London: Trübner & Co., 1881/1885), 1.23 "On יצא and שוב," 1:84–85; 1.65 "On the

Hebrew, but also in others, especially those about miracles, prophecy, or the singular help of God, as well as where in Hebrew "the face of God," "the hand of God," "the eye of God" occurs, they employ מימרא, as Grotius observes.[2] For example, in Isaiah 45:12 for "I made the earth," the Aramaic has, "In my word I made the earth"; and in Isaiah 48:13, "My hand made the earth," the Aramaic has, "By my word I founded the earth"; Peter follows these in 2 Peter 3:5, "By the word of God the heavens existed." The same Aramaic also throughout for יהוה puts מימר יהוה, the Word of the Lord (as in Gen. 3:8; 6:6; Ex. 19:17; Job 42:9; Ps. 2:4). For λόγος, the Syriac has מלתא. Also, the term λόγος, Word, was known to the philosophers, especially the Platonists: so Heraclitus according to Amelius; and Zeno, praised by Tertullian in his *Apology*: "It is undisputed also among your wise men that the λόγος, that is, speech and reason, is considered the maker of the universe. For Zeno concludes that this λόγος is the fabricator who shaped all things in their arrangement."[3] Seneca, who followed the Stoics, hints at the same (Epistle 65),[4] as do many others, especially Amelius, who when he read the words of John, said, "By Jove! This barbarian perceives with our Plato that the Word of God was established in the rank of beginning."[5]

---

phrase 'God spake,'" 1:243–47; 1.66 "On Exod. xxxii. 16," 1:247–49. A more recent and common reprint of the 1963 and 1974 edition is idem, *The Guide of the Perplexed*, trans. and ed. S. Pines, 2 vols. (Chicago: University of Chicago Press, 2010), 1.23 1:52–53, 1.65 1:158–60, 1.66 1:160–61. Mastricht refers to "*More Nebuch.*" rather than the original Arabic entitled دلالة الحائرين. The Hebrew translation, entitled מורה נבוכים, was completed in Maimonides' lifetime. For a recent collection of essays on the Arabic original, and Hebrew, Latin, and English translations of Maimonides, see J. Stern, J. T. Robinson, and Y. Shemesh, *Maimonides' "Guide of the Perplexed" in Translation: A History from the Thirteenth Century to the Twentieth* (Chicago: University of Chicago Press), 35–54, 209–24, 241–56.

2. Hugo Grotius (1583–1645), *Annotationes in libros Evangeliorum* (Amsterdam: Blaeu, 1641), 849; idem, *Opera omnia theologica*, 4 vols. (Basel: E. & J. R. Thurneysen, 1732), 2:474. The 1972 Frommann-Holzboog edition is a reprint of the Grotius, *Opera*, Amsterdam edition (1679). The Basel edition (1732) has multiple and more extensive indices than the 1679. In loc. cit. Grotius states "Vide Maimoniden *Duce Dubitantium*, lib. 1, cap. XXIII. & LXV & LXVI," which is materially the same reference Mastricht supplied. The first complete Latin edition of Maimonides is *Rabbi Mosei Aegyptii Dux seu Director dubitantium aut perplexorum* (Paris: Agostino Giustiniani, 1520); for an early modern critical Latin translation from Ibn Tibbon's Hebrew translation (1204), see Johannes Buxtorf, Jr. (1599–1664), *Doctor perplexorum* (Basel: Ludovicus König, 1629).

3. Cf. Tertullian, *Apologeticus pro Christianis* in *PL* 1:398; idem, *The Apology* in *ANF* 3:34.

4. Seneca the Younger, *Epistles, Volume I: Epistles 1–65* in *LCL* 75:444–45.

5. Cf. bk. 11, ch. 19, Eusebius of Caesarea (c. 260–339), *Eusebius of Caesarea: Praeparatio Evangelica (Preparation for the Gospel)*, trans. Edwin Gifford, 5 vols. (Oxford: Clarendon Press, 1903), 3-1:540b–541a; idem, *Praeparatio Evangelica* in *PG* 21:899–900.

If you should ask why John did not name him *the Son of God*, one could respond that this name *Word*, to the learned as much among the Jews as among the Greeks, was neither strange nor disagreeable, while the Jews despised the name *Son* with respect to divine things, as contrary to the divine unity; then also, it was better accommodated to his proposition, that all things were made through him (John 1:3), insofar as it was known to all from Psalm 33:6 that by the word of the Lord all things were made. If you should ask further why John calls the Son of God the Word, it could be said, first, that he is similar to a person's internal speech, that is, either to the implanted and natural reason of the mind, or to its effect, namely its thought, or the speaking of the mind; then rather, because God completed all things which concern the work of either creation or redemption, not by putting his hand to it (which is a mark of human frailty), but only with a nod and word, or through the Son (Rev. 4:11); perhaps also, so that it would signify that he is the Messiah who was so many times spoken of or promised in the Old Testament (2 Sam. 7:21 with 1 Chron. 17:19); it could be added, because he is the sole interpreter of the Father or of the fatherly counsel, like the vocal word is the interpreter of our mind and will (John 1:18; Matt. 11:27), provided this is not asserted as the only reason, like the Socinians want (e.g. Socinus in his *Refutation of Wujek*, ch. 5;[6] Ostorodt, *Institutes of the Christian Religion*, ch. 17;[7] and others), serving their own hypotheses: they argue, namely, that he is spoken of in this way only from the mediatorial office, because he acts as the ambassador, voice, and spokesman of the Father before men. The Reformed certainly admit this as a less principal reason, from John 1:18, but they add that he is described in this way principally from the eternal existence of the person, by which he is the eternal Word of the Father, subsisting through himself, and

---

6. Faustus Socinus, *Refutatio libelli, quem Jac. Vviekvs…de divinitate filii Dei, et Spiritus sancti* (1594), 203–370; idem, *Responsio ad libellum Jacobi Wujeki*, 189–344; idem, *Opera omnia* (1656), 2:567–98. Cf. Jakub Wujek, *O Bóstwie Syna Bożego i Ducha Świętego* (Cracow: Andrzeja Piotrkowczyka,1590). For secondary literature, see J. Misiurek, "Ks. Jakub Wujek Jako obrońca Synostwa Bożego Chrystusa," *Ruch Biblijny i Liturgiczny*, 36, no. 5 (1983): 392–400; G. H. Williams "The Christological issues between Francis Dávid and Faustus Socinus during the Disputation on the invocation of Christ, 1578–1579," in *Antitrinitarianism in the Second Half of the 16th Century*, ed. D. Pirnát (Budapest: Akadémiai Kiadó, 1982), 318.

7. Christoph Ostorodt (Ostorodus, d. 1611), *Unterrichtung Von den vornemsten Hauptpuncten der Christlichen Religion* (Raków: Sebastian Sternacki, 1604, 1625), 96–98; in Dutch, idem, *Onderwyzinge van de Voornaamste Hooftpunkten der Christelyke Religie*, trans. Hendrik van Heuven (1688), 78–80.

consubstantial with him,[8] as is evident even from this, that the Father is said to have created all things through him (John 1:1–2). In this sense he is even named his wisdom (Prov. 8:22), his image (Col. 1:14–15), and the express image of the hypostasis of the Father (Heb. 1:3).[9] So that by this one name, these four things are denoted: (1) a person of the Trinity; (2) specifically the second person; (3) a divine person, not created but creating; (4) who acts as the Mediator or the spokesman of the Father.

B. The thing assumed, or the human nature: σάρξ, "flesh." Here this certainly does not mean: (1) carnal corruption (as in John 3:6; Rom. 7:5), which can in no way befall the Mediator, the God-man; nor (2) only one of the two essential parts of human nature, namely the body (Rom. 9:5), nor that he did not assume a human soul, as Apollinaris impiously stated. Rather, it denotes: (1) what in Christ is distinguished from the Spirit or the divine nature, namely, the entirety of his human nature (1 Tim. 3:16; 1 Peter 3:18), for man and humanity are signified by "flesh" throughout the Scriptures (Gen. 6:12; Ps. 65:2; Isa. 40:5–6; 49:26; 66:16; Matt. 24:22); next, (2) the parts of human nature, the body and the soul (Eph. 2:15; Heb. 2:14); finally, (3) bodily ailments and infirmities,[10] yet without sin (Heb. 5:7; Ps. 56:4; 78:39; etc.). But, because he wanted human nature signified by "flesh," why did he not say, "The Speech became *man*"? I respond: (1) So that he might more effectively prove the truth of his human nature; (2) so that he might more carefully distinguish the human and the divine nature, for the Jews were accustomed to oppose "flesh and blood" to God (Matt. 16:17; Gal. 1:16); furthermore, (3) so that he might more fully magnify the depth of his humiliation, insofar as he assumed flesh, the baser part of human nature; (4) so that he might apply a medicine suitable to our disease, that he might heal the flesh despoiled of every good and shamefully depraved, as Justin notes, and from him, Nicholas of Lyra.[11]

C. The assumption, or act of assuming: ἐγένετο, "was made," or "became," "The Speech became flesh." Certainly not by a mutation of the divine nature or person into flesh or human nature, as many Anabaptists want,

---

8. *eique* ὁμοούσιος

9. *character* τῆς ὑποστάσεως *Patris*; Dutch: *het gedruckte beeldt van 's Vaders zelfstandigheit*

10. *affectiones et infirmitates corporeas*; Dutch: *de lighamlyke aandoeningen, gesteltheden, hoedanigheden, en zwakheden*, lit. "the bodily ailments, dispositions, constitutions, and infirmities."

11. E.g. Justin Martyr, *Second Apology*, ch. 13 in *ANF* 1:193, "…since also He became man for our sakes, that becoming a partaker of our sufferings, He might also bring us healing"; idem, *Apologia secunda*, ch. 13 in *PG* 467–68. A reference in Nicholas of Lyra could not be found.

because the divine person is by nature immutable (Mal. 3:6; James 1:17), nor also by a confusion of natures, as once the Eutychians wanted. Rather, the Word became flesh in such a way, not that he ceased to be what he was, but that he began to be what he was not, that the Word or Son of God was made truly man, just as Theodoret abundantly discusses in his three dialogues on immutability, inconfusability, and impassibility;[12] according to that maxim, "I am what I was, but was not what I am; now I am called both."[13] Since therefore the Word became flesh without mutation or confusion, how then? By assumption (Phil. 2:7; Heb. 2:14, 16), by which is not signified anything but the personal and individual union of the assuming divine person with the assumed human nature.

The Dogmatic Part

There are two natures in the one person of the Mediator.

It is proved from the Scriptures.

III. Therefore, there are two natures, divine and human, in Christ the Mediator, so united with each other that from this union results his one person. For ὁ λόγος, the Word (the divine person) is said to have become flesh, not by mutation, but by assumption, so that namely with that flesh he might constitute one person. Thus he is called: (1) עמנואל, Immanuel, God with us (Isa. 7:14; Matt. 1:23); (2) a child and a son (Isa. 9:6), the former with respect to the human nature, the latter with respect to the divine nature; also, (3) איתיאל, Ithiel, God with me (Prov. 30:1); (4) for him in the Scriptures are distinctly asserted: (a) the divine nature, as we have taught above (bk. 2, ch. 26);[14] (b) the human nature, when he is called a child (Isa. 9:6), a Branch (Isa. 11:1; 53:2), a human being (Isa. 53:3), a man (1 Tim. 2:5), and all things human are asserted for him; (c) the union of both, from which it is said that the Word became flesh, that he assumed the seed of Abraham (Heb. 2:14, 16; Phil. 2:7), that God was manifested in the flesh (1 Tim. 3:16), so much so that by that assumption he was made the one Mediator (1 Tim. 2:5), Immanuel, Ithiel, as we have already shown.

---

12. Theodoret (c. 393–c. 458), *Eranistes seu Polymorphus* in *PG* 83:31–318; idem, Dialogues 1–3 in *The Dialogues* in *NPNF2* 3:161–244.

13. *Sum quod eram, nec eram quod sum, nunc dicor utrumque.* The source of this line is unknown; it appears throughout the medieval Scholastics, frequently summarizing patristic theologians: see, e.g., John of Damascus (c. 675–749), bk. 3, ch. 17 of *Exposition of the Orthodox faith* in *NPNF2* 9:65–66; idem, *Expositio accurata fidei orthodoxa* in *PG* 94:1067–72.

14. 1.2.26 §§IX, XVIII

The union of the two natures is confirmed with reasons.

IV. Not only was the Mediator in fact such, but he also necessarily had to be, so that he could be the Mediator (ὄφειλε, "He had to be," Heb. 2:16–17), namely: (1) so that he might act as the Mediator between God and men (1 Tim. 2:5), it is evident that it was necessary that by the participation of both natures he be the middle between both (cf. Gen. 28:12); (2) so that he might make men sons of God, it was necessary that he himself be the Son of God, and also a man (Gal. 4:4–5; Rom. 8:29); and (3) so that according to the mediatorial function he might make satisfaction for men to God from the rigor of his justice, about which we will speak expressly in its own place.[15]

Why the Mediator had to be God

To do this, it was necessary (4) that on the one hand he be God consubstantial with the Father, so that he might: (a) have authority in himself to lay down his life as the price of redemption (John 10:18), which authority over human life belongs to no one except God alone (Gen. 9:6)—from this he claims for himself the authority of life and death (Rev. 1:18); (b) in laying down his own life, offer a price of infinite value (1 John 1:7; Acts 20:28); (c) remove the infinite guilt belonging to every sin from the infinity of the injured majesty; and that (d) for the nearly infinite sins of each of the elect; and also (e) for the nearly infinite number of the elect; moreover, (f) obtain an infinite good, the union, communion, and enjoyment of the highest and infinite good, for each of these, and be for them all in all (1 Cor. 15:28 with 1 Cor. 1:30; John 1:16; Col. 1:19), so much so that in him they might be complete (Col. 2:9–10); (g) powerfully confer the prerequisites for participation in this infinite good—vivification, conversion, sanctification, faith, and so forth—and consequently apply the acquired infinite good; and also (h) powerfully preserve those vivified against the nearly infinite attacks of infinite spiritual enemies (Eph. 6:12, 16; Matt. 16:18; 1 Peter 1:5). For these, I say, and all other reasons, on the one hand, it was entirely necessary that the Mediator be God.

Why he had to be man

And on the other hand, it was necessary (5) that he be true man, so that he might: (a) take away the guilt of men who sinned (Ex. 32:33; Ezek. 18:4, 20); and that (b) by suffering and dying, which was the righteousness of the law (Gen. 2:16–17 with Rom. 8:3; Isa. 53:10; Heb. 2:9, 14); (c) be subject in addition to the divine law, in order to fulfill all righteousness (Gal. 4:4; Matt. 3:15; 5:17); also

---

15. 1.5.18 §§X–XIII

(d) be a merciful high priest, able to sympathize (Heb. 2:17–18; 4:15); and that (e) as our גֹּאֵל, *goel*, kinsman-redeemer, our ἔγγυος, surety (Ruth 3:12–13; 1 Kings 16:11 with Job 19:25); and in addition (f) as our brother (Heb. 2:10–12). For these reasons the Mediator had to be not only God, but also man.

Why the two natures had to be united
Finally, (6) the union of these two natures was necessary, so that: (a) they would make one person; (b) we would have one Mediator (1 Tim. 2:5), who is undivided (1 Cor. 1:13); (c) all salvation would be in this one (Acts 4:12); (d) God in the fullness of time would gather into one all things in Christ; and (e) we would have one Lord (1 Cor. 8:6; Eph. 4:5).

The assuming divine person
V. Now, so that we may more skillfully attain to the nature of this mystery, we must consider a little more distinctly, on the one hand, the extremes united, and on the other, the union of the extremes.

Not the nature
In the extremes, first there occurs something divine, that is: (1) not the divine nature considered in its breadth, for in that way: (a) not only the Son, but also the Father and the Holy Spirit would have been incarnated, inasmuch as to them belongs the same divine nature. (b) With both natures united, it would be necessary for a certain third nature to be produced, which the Eutychians wanted. (c) The Mediator would not be a person, because he would not have received personhood,[16] either from the divine nature, which does not have it, or from the human nature. Yet this distinction must be made in such a way that the nature is not excluded, so that it can be said that God was manifested in the flesh (1 Tim. 3:16), and that God redeemed the church with his own blood (Acts 20:28).

But a person. And one person
Rather, (2) a divine person, so that from it the Mediator might have his personhood, for from two natures a person does not result. And indeed, (3) only one person, for just as one divine person cannot assume two human natures, because in that way one person would become several human beings, so also several persons cannot assume one human nature, for in this way: (a) more than one person would become one human being; then also, (b) since the assumed human nature

---

16. *personalitatem*

is adequately delimited by the person assuming, to the whole extent it is able to be delimited, it cannot be delimited again by another assuming person.

Moreover, precisely the second person of the Trinity
What is more, (4) that assuming person: (a) could not have been the first person, the Father, because by that rationale the same divine person would be the Father and the Son simultaneously; nor (b) the third person, the Holy Spirit, because in that way there would be two Sons enumerated in the Trinity, the second person with respect to the divine nature, and the third with respect to the assumed human nature; so accordingly, it was (c) precisely the second person, namely (i) so that the Son would make sons (Gal. 4:4–5), (ii) so that the one who is the middle between the divine persons by negation would be the middle between God and man by participation in both natures.

The assumed human nature. Not a person
VI. Second, in the extremes of the union occurs something human: (1) not indeed a human person, for in that way the Mediator would not be one (1 Tim. 2:5), but two, on account of his two natures, divine and human; and because neither of these would be God and man simultaneously, by this reasoning we would have no Mediator at all.

But a nature
But (2) only a nature, indeed one that has all that is necessary for the constitution of human nature, and therefore with respect to nature, like us in all things, with only sin excepted (Heb. 2:16–17; 4:15), but nevertheless thoroughly devoid of personhood, through which a nature becomes incommunicable and complete. I say thoroughly, that is, devoid not only of a personhood proper and peculiar to it, which would import a double personhood, but also of a participated personhood, through which some describe the nature as enhypostatic,[17] because by this reasoning, the human nature would subsist by means of the divine personhood, and thus the human nature would be a divine person.

Moreover, a true human nature
(3) Moreover, it is a human nature that is true, of the same condition and essence as ours, with only sin excepted (Heb. 4:15), not only seeming and apparent,[18] such as once the Cerdonians, Marcionites, Manicheans, and others of that sort

---

17. ἐνυπόστατος. Cf. §§XXI–XXIII, below.
18. *non* δοξαστικήν *et apparentem tantum*

wanted, but true, such as the Gospels impress upon us: (a) by telling of his conception, birth, life, vigils, griefs, joys, and death; (b) by teaching that he was made a partaker παραπλησίως, most closely, of flesh and blood (Heb. 2:14);[19] and (c) that he also demonstrated this same nature by the resurrection (Luke 24:39).

One like ours in all things

A human nature (4) consubstantial with our nature,[20] or in all things like it (Heb. 2:17; 4:15). Concerning this we will have more in the elenctic part, Lord willing.[21]

Regarding the hypostatic union, these are explained: 1. Its nature
VII. Finally, there follows the union of the extreme parts, and what distinctly belongs to it, first, the hypostatic union itself, from which the parts, or natures, constitute one person, and one Mediator (1 Tim. 2:5), who is undivided (1 Cor. 1:13). Regarding this union, these must be considered: (1) its nature, which is not anything but a certain ineffable relation of the divine person to the human nature, through which this human nature is specifically the human nature of the second person of the deity. This relation is customarily described on many rational accounts because there is not just one by which its perfection can be sufficiently represented. Through it, the human nature is made: (a) on account of the assumption, to be as it were an adjunct proper to the divine person; likewise, (b) as it were a member of the whole Immanuel or God-man, whose divine person is as it were the other part; (c) with respect to existence, as it were an effect singularly sustained by the divine person; finally, (d) as it were a subject in which the divine nature singularly dwells (Col. 2:9). Yet we temper all these terms in which the sources of this unity are contained with the limitation "as it were," since this mystical and most close union has nothing similar to it in the nature of things, and so it cannot be represented adequately with just one term, but rather must be outlined to some extent with many.

2. Mode

(2) Its mode, which can barely be expressed more adequately than by those adverbs which the ancients, in order to steer judiciously between the two rocks of the heretics, were accustomed to use, distinctly delimiting that: (a) in the God-man, the natures are conjoined ἀδιαιρέτως καὶ ἀχωρίστως, without

---

19. Cf. §XVIII, below
20. *nostrae* ὁμοούσιον
21. §XVIII, below

division or separation, that is, against the Nestorians who state that there are two persons in the Mediator, and who accordingly deny that God was crucified and that the blessed Virgin is the θεοτόκος, the God-bearer.[22] (b) Against the Eutychians who conflate the two natures into one and confuse their properties,[23] they asserted that the natures were united ἀτρέπτως καὶ ἀσυγχύτως, without mutation or confusion. Thus we understand that this union was not made: (a) συνουσιωδῶς, consubstantially, such as is the union of the divine persons among themselves, with respect to the same essence; nor (b) φυσικῶς, physically and naturally, as form is united to matter; nor (c) merely σχετικῶς, relationally, such as is the union of a friend with a friend; (d) nor δραστικῶς, efficiently, or περιστατικῶς, circumstantially, through mere efficacy and omnipresent assistance; nor (e) μυστικῶς, mystically, only through the presence of grace, such as is the union between God and the elect (John 17:21); but rather, (f) altogether ὑποστατικῶς, hypostatically, insofar as the assumed nature coalesced into the same person with the assuming Word, with the properties of both natures preserved (Maresius, *Systema theologicum*, loc. 9, §24).[24] Accordingly, it is a personal union, not on account of a terminus *a quo*, that it is a union of persons, as Nestorius wanted, but on account of the terminus *ad quem*, that it results in a person. Furthermore, it is certainly a union of natures, but not a natural union.

The uniting is explained, with respect to: 1. Its denominations
VIII. Second, the uniting, which the ancient Greek fathers called the ἐνσάρκωσις, "enfleshment," ἐνανθρώπησις,[25] "enhumanization," ἐπιφάνεια, manifestation, and θεοφάνεια, manifestation of God. To the Latins it is called the *incarnatio*, incarnation, first the active incarnation, whereby God incarnated, then the passive, that whereby Christ was incarnated. The former, according to the reckoning of a work *ad extra*, belongs to the whole Trinity, and from this he is said to have pierced his ears, or prepared for him a body (Ps. 40:6; Heb. 10:5). The latter belongs only to the Son, who thus is said to have come in the flesh (Heb. 10:7; 1 John 4:2–3), and to have assumed the seed of Abraham (Heb. 2:16). The ancient fathers usually explain these things with a crass, albeit fitting, similitude, that of three together sewing one garment to be worn by one

---

22. Dutch: *Godts-baarster*

23. *idiomata*

24. Samuel Maresius (1599–1673), *Systema theologicum* (Groningen: Aemilius Spinneker, 1673), 464–66.

25. E.g. Epiphanius, *Panarion*, bk. 2, tom. 2, haer. 69, §42, 2 in *PG* 42:269–70, συνηνωμένη ἡ ἐνανθρώπησις αὐτοῦ εἰς μίαν ἀπάθειαν, *in unam passionis expertem naturae conditionem consociata natura hominis*; idem, *The Panarion of Epiphanius of Salamis*, trans. F. Williams, 2 vols., 2nd rev. ed. (Leiden: Brill, 2009, 2013), 2:370, "the human nature is united in one impassibility."

member of their society, which similitude must by no means be extended beyond its intention and proportion.

2. Its four parts: Incarnation

Therefore there is in this unity: (1) an incarnation (the one we called active), by which the whole Trinity prepared both essential parts of the human nature, body and soul, then conjoined the prepared parts to each other, and at the same time personally united the conjoined parts with the divine person. All of these things, as we said, are signified when it is said that he pierced the Son's ears (Ps. 40:6), and prepared a body for him (Heb. 10:5), gave him to men (John 3:16), and lastly, sent him forth (Gal. 4:4).

Assumption

(2) An assumption, by which the Son of God appropriated to himself the humanity prepared by the Trinity. From this assumption, it is said that the Word became flesh (John 1:14), came in the flesh (1 John 4:2–3), assumed the form of a servant (Phil. 2:7), was made a partaker of flesh and blood (Heb. 2:14).

Conception

(3) The conception of the human nature and its sanctification, which is appropriated to the Holy Spirit (Luke 1:35), who made the female seed fruitful, and either overturned or purged its intemperateness, from which moral corruption of the soul could have arisen, so that it might be born a holy thing (Luke 1:35).

Birth

Finally, (4) the birth, from which the blessed Virgin is named the God-bearer. We will speak expressly concerning these last things in their own place.[26]

This uniting does not argue: 1. That the whole Trinity was incarnated.
IX. Yet by this union: (1) the whole Trinity was not incarnated. For although (a) the entire Trinity produced the flesh or human nature, yet the Trinity did not produce it for itself in its entirety, but for only one of its fellowship.[27] And although the entire Trinity prepared the flesh, yet the entire Trinity did not assume it. Likewise, although (b) the second person, who assumed the human nature, connotes the entire deity, yet it does not connote the entire deity entirely, that

---

26. 1.5.10

27. *sed uni tantum e societate sua*

is, in all its breadth, but rather that deity characterized, that is, expressly imaged,[28] and as it were restricted to the one person through his personal property.

2. Nor does this assumption import any change in the one assuming.
Nor (2) was the second person, by assuming a human nature, changed, because: (a) this assumption was only an action, and not a passion, since change occurs by passion (which certainly here is only in the nature assumed), and not by action (which is in the one assuming). (b) The product of this assumption, or the personal union, at least with respect to the one assuming, is nothing except a mere relation, which does not import a genuine change properly speaking, although in the nature assumed it does import the greatest change, inasmuch as that nature by this assumption and union has been elevated to the highest perfection, as we will soon speak of expressly.[29]

3. Nor from this was a new subsistence born.
Nor (3) from the union of the two natures did there arise some kind of new subsistence or personhood, to whose constitution each nature conveyed its own part. For in that way: (a) the eternal subsistence of the Word would either cease or would be added to this new one; (b) a composite and more imperfect subsistence would succeed one that was eternal and most simple.

4. Nor has the personal union once accomplished ever ceased.
To these points we add that (4) the union of the two natures, once accomplished through the assumption, will continue wholly indivisible to eternity (Acts 2:27; Ps. 16:10), a union that was not disturbed even in death, when a separation of the essential parts of the human nature occurred, because those parts, however rent asunder, notwithstanding remained united with the Word, insofar as the flesh remained the flesh of the Word, and the spirit, his spirit. Much less did the union cease in the ascension of Christ, by a setting aside of the body, as Socinus imagines with the Manicheans, because in Acts 1:11 it says that he will come just as he departed.

5. The entire deity is also beyond the humanity.
I should add one thing, that (5) although by this union the entire fullness of deity is in the human nature (Col. 1:19; 2:9), notwithstanding the entire deity is also beyond it, because it is infinite, and accordingly in an adequated way cannot be indwelt by the finite.

---

28. Latin: *characterizatam*; Dutch: *gekenmerkt (gecharacterizeert)*
29. §XI, below

The four consequences of this union: 1. The communion of the natures

X. Third, there follows the thing united, or rather the consequences of this union, namely: (1) the communion of the natures in the person, which is called a μετοχή, partaking, in Hebrews 2:14: παραπλησίως μετέσχε αὐτῶν, "he most closely shared in the same things"; through which the two natures constitute the one person of Immanuel. For although in the Mediator there is one thing and another thing, yet there is not one person and another person.[30] So then, this communion, properly speaking, does not exist between the natures themselves, such that the divine nature was communicated to the human nature, and vice versa, for in that way a Eutychian confusion would have occurred.

2. The grace of union in the human nature

XI. (2) The grace of personal union, communicated to the human nature, from which furthermore flows the communication of gifts,[31] or a most full conveying of habitual grace to the assumed nature (spoken of in Isa. 11:1–2; Ps. 45:7; John 1:14; Col. 1:19; 2:3, 9), one indeed without measure (John 3:34), but still not thoroughly infinite, because the infinite can neither be communicated, nor received by the finite, for which reason it is said that he advanced in wisdom, stature, and favor (Luke 2:52). Namely, it was: (a) the grace of holiness (Luke 1:35), such grace by which he never sinned, nor could he have sinned, because that would imply that the God-man sins. (b) The grace of wisdom (Col. 2:3), which still was not omniscience (Luke 2:52; Mark 11:13; 13:32). (c) The grace of power and authority, from which he is called איתיאל and אֻכָל, Ithiel and Ucal, "God with me" and "I will prevail" (Prov. 30:1).[32] Yet properly speaking this is not divine and infinite, because in the exercise of his power he employed prayers (John 11:41–42).

3. The communication of attributes, in which there is:

The communion of properties

XII. The *communio idiomatum,* communion of properties, by which the properties of both natures coincide in one and the same person, and thus also are

---

30. *licet enim in Mediatore sit aliud et aliud, non tamen est alius et alius*

31. *communicatio charismatum*

32. On *Ithiel,* cf. §III, above. On both names, cf. Franciscus Junius (1545–1602) on Prov. 30:9, n. 9, *Testamenti Veteris Biblia Sacra* (London, 1593), 3:64, "That is to say, 'Christ who is God,' who is present with us, and through whom we can do all things. For *Ithiel* is a word composed of three parts, as if you should say, 'The strong God is with me,' just like *Immanuel* (Isa. 7:14); and similarly, *Ucal* is a name made from the verb that means 'to be able': and thus by these two appellations the godly are instructed regarding their sanctification through the presence and infinite power of God in Christ, as is unfolded in the five subsequent verses." Cf. 1.5.14 §XVII.

enunciated of the person. Thus, concerning this, two points should be observed: (1) the communion of properties itself, which is not (a) a real transfusion of them, through which the properties of one nature pass over to the other, and the human nature receives divine properties, and vice versa. For in that way the human nature would become divine, and on the contrary the divine would become human, and thus Eutyches would triumph. Nor is it (b) a real donation, by which one nature has appropriated its properties to the other, the kind that we have already observed in the communication of gifts in the human nature. For in this way one nature could employ the properties of the other at will; yet the opposite of this is evident from the ignorance of the human nature (Mark 13:32), and from prayer (Matt. 26:39, 42). (2) The predication built upon this communion, by which the attributes of one nature are certainly not enunciated of the other in the abstract, but the attributes of both natures are spoken of the person in the concrete. Yet this occurs in two modes, either: (a) more directly, when the attributes (i) are enunciated of the person denominated from both natures equally, such as when the Mediator is spoken of as God or man, or (ii) unequally, of the person denominated from only one nature, such as, the Word is eternal and omnipotent, the Son of man is mortal. Or (b) more indirectly, when the attributes are indeed enunciated of the person, but of the person denominated from that nature to which those attributes in no way belong, such as: in Acts 20:28, God redeemed the church with his own blood; the Son of man while existing on earth simultaneously is in heaven (John 3:13). Thus it is evident through this communion of properties that such predications must not be allowed that: (a) argue for a created personhood, because this is proper to the Word; (b) attribute human imperfections to the divine nature; or conversely, (c) attribute divine perfections to the human nature. With these things heeded, we assert that the communion of properties is: (1) real, with respect to its foundation, that is, the hypostatic union, through which the properties of both natures do in fact belong to the person; (2) verbal, as concerns predication or the mode of speaking; indeed, as it were figurative, and very close to a synecdoche. For when there are several forms or natures united in the same subject or *suppositum*, even if they are not able to be predicated mutually of each other in the abstract (since they are disparate), yet they can be asserted of that subject in the concrete.

4. The communion of effects

XIII. The *communio* ἀποτελεσμάτων, communion of effects (1 Tim. 2:5), which is nothing other than a concurrence of both natures for the mediatorial operations, such that those works proceed from the person of the God-man through the distinct efficacy of both natures; in which these four things must be noted: (1) the producing cause, the person of the God-man, the ἐνεργῶν, the one working; (2) the two *principia* ἐνεργητικά, operative principles, of the producing cause, which are the two natures in the Mediator; (3) the double efficacy, according to the number of the two principles, or the double ἐνέργεια, operation, that of the divine nature and that of the human nature; (4) finally, the one work, the ἐνεργούμενον, the thing worked, or the ἀποτέλεσμα θεανδρικόν, divine-human effect,[33] which the one Mediator produces according to his two natures through an efficacy peculiar to each. Thus for example, the one Mediator, the λυτρώτης, Redeemer, with both natures concurring as *principia* λυτρωτικά, redemptive principles, through a double efficacy or λύτρωσις, work of redemption, the human nature by conferring the death, and the divine nature the value of the death, procured one λύτρον or λύτρωμα, redemption.

---

33. Cf. Canon 15 of the Lateran Council (649), which exposited the Council of Chalcedon and condemned Monothelitism by defending two wills in Christ as well as a twofold operation of the divine and human nature, in Henry Denzinger, *The Sources of Catholic Dogma*, trans. R. J. Deferrari (Fitzwilliam, N.H.: Loreto Publications, 1955), 103, "Can. 15. If anyone according to the wicked heretics unwisely accepts the divine-human operation, which the Greeks call θεανδρικήν, as one operation, but does not confess that it is twofold according to the holy Fathers, that is, divine and human, or that the new application of the word "divine-human" which has been used is descriptive of one but not demonstrative of the marvelous and glorious union of both, let him be condemned." In part the debated meanings arise from terminology in Pseudo-Dionysius the Areopagite, *The Works of Dionysius the Areopagite* (London: James Parker & Co., 1897), 1:143–44; idem, *PG* 3:1072. See "Pseudo-Dionysius the Areopagite and Maximus the Confessor," in *The Oxford Handbook of Maximus the Confessor*, ed. P. Allen and B. Neil (Oxford: Oxford University Press, 2015), 180–81. On Reformed and Lutheran debate on the person of Christ at the Montbéliard Colloquy (1586) between Theodore Beza (1519–1605) and Jakob Andreae (1528–1590), see Beza, *Ad Acta Colloquii Montisbelgardensis Tubingae Edita, Theodori Bezae Responsionis*, 2 vols (Geneva: Jean Le Preux, 1588), 1:78–181; Andreae, *Lutheranism vs. Calvinism: the Classic Debate at the Colloquy of Montbeliard, 1586*, ed. J. Mallinson, trans. C. J. Armstrong (St. Louis, Miss.: Concordia Publishing House, 2017), 235–436. See also Jill Raitt, *The Colloquy of Montbéliard: Religion and Politics in the Sixteenth Century* (Oxford: Oxford University Press, 1993), 110–33; Richard Cross, *Communicatio Idiomatum: Reformation Christological Debates* (Oxford: Oxford University Press, 2019), 226–55. On the Reformed reception of these questions, e.g. on the *apostelesmatum communio*, Christ's *opera mediatoria* as ἀποτελέσματα θεανδρικὰ and the necessary distinctions between ὁ ἐνεργῶν, the person of the God-man, the *principium* ἐνεργετικόν, and the twofold ἐνέργεια, see Samuel Maresius, *Systema theologicum*, 474; on the *communicatio idiomatum* and the debates with the Lutherans, see Francis Turretin (1623–1687), *Institutio theologiae elencticae*, 3 vols., 2nd ed. (Geneva: Samuel de Tournes, 1688–1690), 13.8 (2:349–61); idem, *Institutes of Elenctic Theology*, ed. J. Dennison, trans. G. M. Geiger, 3 vols. (Phillipsburg, N.J.: P & R Publishing, 1992–1997), 13.8 (2:321–32); Georg Sohn (c. 1552–1589), *Theses de Incarnatione Filii Dei* (Heidelberg: Jacobus Mylius, 1586); Bartholomäus Keckermann (1571–1608), *Systema SS. Theologiae* (Hanover: Guilielmus Antonius, 1607), 315–21; Girolamo Zanchi (1516–1590), *Opera omnia*, 8 vols. (Geneva: Jean Tournes, 1649), 8:170–296.

The Elenctic Part
The controversies of this chapter are divided.
XIV. The elenctic part of this chapter is a seedbed of controversies and questions, of which some concern the assuming person, some the assumed nature, some the union of both natures, and finally some the consequences of the union.

QUESTIONS CONCERNING THE ASSUMING PERSON

It is asked: 1. Did the Mediator with respect to his divine nature exist from eternity?
A comparison of opinions
Concerning the person who assumes, it is asked, first, whether the Mediator is God, true and ὁμοούσιος, consubstantial, with the Father, existing from eternity. These once denied that the Mediator had existed before his birth from the blessed Virgin: Cerinthus, Ebion, Paul of Samosata, Photinus, Muhammad, and the Jews. The Carpocratians, Basilidians, and Arians did admit that he had existed before his birth from the blessed Virgin, but denied that he had existed from eternity and was consubstantial with his Father, and thus they perpetually had in their mouth, "There was a time when he was not,"[34] and consequently said that he was ὁμοιούσιος, of similar substance, but not ὁμοούσιος, of the same substance; you could call them Heteroousians. In addition there were those who said that he was of the same substance, but still of unequal essence, such as the Aetians and Eunomians, whom you might not unfittingly call Anomoeans, because they opposed the Arians with respect to the idea of similarity of substance.[35] The Socinians of our day, together with the first group, deny that he had existed before his birth from the blessed Virgin.

The opinion of the Reformed
The Reformed on the contrary state that with respect to his divine nature he existed from eternity. We vanquished the opinion of our adversaries in book 2, chapter 26,[36] and do not have anything to add to what has been said.

2. Did the divine nature or the person assume the human nature? Arguments
XV. Second, whether the divine nature of the Mediator, or the person, assumed flesh. Here we agree with the Lutherans at least with respect to the substance, but the Lutherans disagree with respect to the phraseology, tenaciously asserting that it is more correct to say that the nature was incarnated rather than the

---

  34. ᾖ, ὅτε οὐκ ἦν
  35. Cf. Socrates Scholasticus (c. 380–c. 439), *Ecclesiastical History*, 2.35 in *NPNF2* 2:60; Theodoret, *Ecclesiastical History*, 2.24–25 in *NPNF2* 3:89–91; Gregory of Nyssa (c. 335–c. 395), *Against Eunomius* 1.17–22, 34 in *NPNF2* 5:54–65, 79–81.
  36. 1.2.26 §XVIII

person, and even ridiculing the orthodox, as if they supposed that the mode of subsistence was incarnated without the divine nature. As far as the state of the question, it could be observed from the dogmatic part that we do not deny that the nature was incarnated, but that the nature in its breadth, with its personal modification abstracted, was incarnated. The reasons for the orthodox opinion we have already mentioned in §V, to which we add nothing at present except to note the style of Scripture (John 1:14; Phil. 2:7; Heb. 2:14–16).

Objections
Nor is there any substance to what they allege for themselves: (1) passages of Scripture (Col. 2:9; 1 Tim. 3:16) which expressly make mention of the incarnated divine nature; (2) that the divine nature and essence is so common to the three persons that it is nevertheless whole and undivided in each of them, and thus when the second person was incarnated, so also the divine nature was incarnated; (3) that the hypostasis and the divine essence in any of the persons do not differ really, and so then, when a person is incarnated, the nature must also be incarnated. I respond, We do not deny that the nature was incarnated, but that the nature in its breadth, considered without personal modification, was incarnated. Therefore, since the Lutherans acknowledge that the divine person assumed the human nature, and the Reformed in turn acknowledge that the divine nature, insofar as it is connoted in the person, assumed the human nature, the question seems to degenerate into a mere battle over words, arising from only an itch to contradict, and hatred toward the Reformed—we will not be delayed any longer on it.

3. *When the Son was incarnated, were the Father and the Holy Spirit incarnated?*
XVI. Third, it is asked whether when the Son was incarnated, the Father and the Holy Spirit were incarnated. Once the Patripassians guarded the affirmative with these two reasons especially: (1) that the divine essence is common to the three persons, and therefore when the essence of the Son was incarnated, both the Father and the Holy Spirit were also incarnated; (2) that the incarnation is a work *ad extra*, common to the three persons.

The orthodox arguments
The orthodox defend the negative, because: (1) not the nature in its breadth, but the nature as it is the Son's, and so as it were restricted by the personhood, was incarnated, to which therefore something could be added according to the hypostasis,[37] which was not added to the Father and the Holy Spirit. (2) The

---

37. καθ᾽ ὑπόστασιν

works *ad extra* are indeed common with respect to operation, although they are not with respect to the terminus of the operation. With these things carefully observed, a response can be easily made to the reasons to the contrary.

4. Apart from the sin of man, would the Son of God have been incarnated?
The difference of opinions
XVII. Fourth, whether apart from the sin of man, the Son of God would nevertheless have been incarnated. Some of the Scholastics have defended the affirmative: Alexander of Hales, Aquinas, Occam, Bonaventure, and others;[38] whom in the last century Andreas Osiander followed in his own little book, in which he intended to confirm the dogma of the Scholastics with ten arguments; and finally also, the Socinians.[39] The primary falsehood of the Scholastics seems to be the idea that he was incarnated not only for us, but also so that he might merit glory for himself; of Osiander, that he thinks that man was created according to the image of Christ who was to be incarnated; of the Socinians, that they might detract from satisfaction as the chief end of the incarnation. With these things carefully noted, not much difficulty remains regarding the question.

The arguments of the orthodox
Therefore, with Scripture, the orthodox maintain the negative (although some of the Reformed seem to hold a different opinion: Zanchi, *On the Works of the*

---

38. Alexander of Hales (1185–1245), pars III, q. 1, memb. 13, "An si natura humana per peccatum lapsa non esset, adhuc fuisset ratio et convenientia ad Christi incarnationem?" in *Summa universae theologiae*, 4 vols. (Venice: Franciscus Franciscius, 1575), 3:11v. Thomas Aquinas (1225–1274) maintained that Scripture only gives sin as the reason for the incarnation, but he also notes that God's power is not so limited to the reason of man's sin that God could not have become incarnate, idem, *Summa theologiae* (*ST*), III, q. 1, art. 3; William of Occam (Ockham, c. 1280–c. 1349), bk. 3, q. 1, *Quaestiones* in *Opera philosophica et theologica*, ed. S. Brown, 17 vols in 2 parts (New York: St. Bonaventure Press, 1967–2001) pt. 1, vol. 6:1–42; Bonaventure, bk. 3, dist. 1, art. 2, q. 2, resp. 1–9 and concl., *Opera omnia*, 10 vols. (Quarrachi: St. Bonaventure, 1882), 3:22–23, 24–28. Both Alexander of Hales and Bonaventure allude to or quote pseudo-Augustine, *De spiritu et anima*, ch. 9, in *PL* 40:785, "Wherefore God became man so that he might beatify the whole man in himself, and the whole orientation (*conversio*) of man would be toward himself, and the whole delight of man would be in him, because he would be seen from the sense of the flesh through flesh, and from the sense of the mind he would be seen through the contemplation of divinity. Moreover, this was the entire good of man, whether he went inward or outward, he would find pasture in his maker; pasture outwardly in the flesh of his Savior and pasture inwardly in the divinity of his Creator."

39. Andreas Osiander (1498–1552), *An Filius Dei fuerit incarnandus, si peccatum non introiuisset in mundum* (Königsberg: Haeribus Joannis Luftt, 1550), fols. [A4r–v]; here Osiander briefly evaluates the positions of Augustine, Bernard of Clairvaux, Alexander of Hales, Thomas Aquinas, Bonaventure, John Duns Scotus, and Giovanni Pico della Mirandola. Cf. P. Wilson-Kastner, "Andreas Osiander's Theology of Grace in the Perspective of the Influence of Augustine of Hippo" in *The Sixteenth Century Journal*, vol. 10, no. 2 (Summer, 1979): 79.

Six Days, pt. 3, bk. 3, ch. 2; Bucanus, *Institutions*, locus 10; Willet, *On the State of Man*, bk. 1),[40] because: (1) the promises and sacrifices, which prefigured the Messiah who was to come, only presuppose the sin that was to be expiated by his advent or incarnation (Gen. 3:15; Ps. 22; 40; 69; 110; Isa. 53; Dan. 9; Zech. 9:9). Nor is there a passage that is dissimilar. (2) No other goal of the incarnation is taught in the New Testament than the expiation of sins (Matt. 1:21; Luke 1:67ff.; 2:30; John 1:29; Matt. 9:13; 20:28; Gal. 4:4–5; 1 Tim. 3:16; Heb. 2:14; 1 John 3:8; etc.). Also, (3) the mediatorial office, which alone he came into the world to discharge, presupposes sin and sinners: so for the prophetic office (Isa. 61:1), the priestly (Isa. 53:2, 10; Matt. 20:28), and the kingly (Zech. 9:9).

The objections of the Scholastics
Meanwhile, the Scholastics object: (1) that he merited glory for himself (Phil. 2:9). I respond: (a) Yet by passive obedience (v. 8), which presupposes sin; or if by active obedience also, on behalf of sinners (Gal. 4:4). (b) He merited a glory of the creature, as man, which he would not have lacked if he had not been incarnated, no more than the Father and the Holy Spirit. (2) That he was incarnated so that he might show his love for men (Prov. 8:31). I respond, Certainly, but for them as sinners (Eph. 5:2; John 3:16). (3) That in the Old Testament he often assumed flesh so that he might appear to men, without respect to sin

---

40. Girolamo Zanchi, *De operibus Dei intra spatium sex dierum creatis opus* (Neustadt: Matthew Harnis, 1591), 618–28; idem, *Opera omnia*, 8 vols. (Geneva: Jean de Tournes, 1649), 3:693–704; Gulielmus Bucanus (d. 1603), *Institutiones theologicae seu Locorum communium Christianae religionis* (Geneva: Samuel Chouët, 1648), 99–102; idem, *Institutions of Christian Religion Framed out of Gods Word*, trans. R. Hill (London: George & Leonell Snowdon, 1606), 104–6; idem, *Christelicke Institutie ofte Grondige verklaringe vande gemeene Plaetsen der Christelicer Religie*, trans. W. L. (Amsterdam: Joannes van Ravesteyn, 1651), fols. 45v–46v. Andrew Willet (c. 1561–1621), *Synopsis Papismi* (London: Felix Kyngston, 1613), 843. Mastricht's citation of Andrew Willet (*Willet. de stat. hominis lib. 1.*) is oblique (cf. F. B. Westcott, *The Epistles of St. John: The Greek Text*, 4th edition (London: Macmillan and Co., 1902), 317n2). Mastricht's citations of Zanchi, Bucanus, and Willet are identical to Johann Gerhard (1582–1637), *Loci theologici* (Frankfurt and Hamburg: Zacharias Hertel, 1657), 1:456; idem, *Theological Commonplaces: Volume 4, On the Person and Work of Christ* (St. Louis, Mo.: Concordia Publishing House, 2009), 139. Gerhard, and thus Mastricht, referenced a Latin translation of selections from the fourth and fifth book of Willet's English work, *Synopsis Papismi*, known in the Netherlands and in Germany as Andrew Willet, *De gratia generi humano in primo parente collata, de lapsu Adami, et peccato originali, de praedestinatione, et de gratia et libero arbitrio: Disputationes theologicae, Bellarmino oppositae, ex V. tomo Synopseos Papismi Anglice conscriptae* (Leiden: Andries Clouck (Cloucquius), 1609). The subtitle of the first controversy of bk. 4, controversy 17 in the whole work, is "the state of man in paradise. This controversie containeth three questions. First of the state of mans soule by creation. Secondly, of the quality and condition of his body. Thirdly, of the place, namely of paradise." Cf. idem, *Synopsis Papismi*, 841.

(Gen. 18:31; etc.), so accordingly he could also have assumed it so that he might be personally united to it. I respond: (a) It is not valid to argue from what can be to what is. (b) There was also some use of those appearances with respect to sin.

The objections of Osiander
Osiander opposes this because: (1) we were created according to the image of Christ. I respond: (a) He claims this without Scripture; indeed, (b) contrary to Scripture, which speaks of the image of God as that of the Creator (Eph. 4:24; Col. 3:10; Gen. 1:26). (2) Otherwise he would have lacked the prerogative of being head over angels and men. I respond, He would not have lacked it any more than the Father and the Holy Spirit.

The objection of the Socinians
Finally, the Socinians oppose this because Christ had to deliver glory to man also in his integrity. I respond: They should prove it, because the triune God could have done this. Compare §IV.

QUESTIONS CONCERNING THE ASSUMED NATURE

It is asked: 1. Was the assumed nature true and consubstantial with ours?
XVIII. Next follow the controversies concerning the assumed nature. It is asked, first, whether the human nature that the Word assumed was true and consubstantial with ours in all things? In accord with the Scriptures the Reformed affirm this.

The opinions of heretics: (1) The Docetists
These in fact deny it directly: immediately upon the demise of the apostles, the Docetists and Phantastici, heretics, who teach that the Son of God did not assume a true humanity, but only its φάντασμα, an appearance which you would think was true, which opinion was later revived by the Manicheans and Marcionites. Thus regarding the Cerdonians, Augustine in *On Heresies* (ch. 21) reports that they taught, "Christ himself was neither born of a woman nor had flesh, nor truly died or suffered anything, but only feigned to do so."[41]

Objections
They assert this because: (a) angels frequently appeared thus in the flesh. I respond: (i) But nowhere did they assume the seed of Abraham, such that they

---

41. Augustine, *De haeresibus ad Quodvultdeum liber unus* in *PL* 42:29; idem, *The De Haeresibus of Saint Augustine: A Translation with an Introduction and Commentary* (Washington, D.C.: Catholic University of America Press, 1956), 73.

were made like their brethren in all things (Heb. 2:17). (ii) There is the greatest distinction between an appearance and an assumption (Heb. 2:16), as well as an incarnation. (b) The Holy Spirit appeared as a dove, yet did not become a dove. I respond, The appearance of the Holy Spirit is a whole heaven different from the union of the natures in the Mediator, for (i) the former was only symbolic, the latter personal; (ii) the former for a time, the latter indissoluble (Heb. 7:17); (iii) the former did not concern the deliverance of doves, as the latter did the deliverance of men. (c) He is said to have been sent "in the likeness of flesh" (Rom. 8:3). I respond, It does not say simply "of flesh," but "of sinful flesh." (d) That he emptied himself, "taking on the form of a servant, made in the likeness of men, and being found in fashion as a man" (Phil. 2:7–8). I respond, This is to say that he hid the divine nature and majesty for a time by the form of a servant, by the nature and likeness of other human beings, and by a common demeanor, yet in such a way that notwithstanding he was, together with infants, truly made a partaker of flesh and blood (Heb. 2:13–14; John 1:14).

(2) The Heteroousians

The Heteroousians, who did acknowledge in him a true humanity, but denied that it was consubstantial with ours. Thus the Valentinians, about whom Irenaeus testifies in *Against Heresies* (bk. 1, ch. 7) that they stated, "Christ passed through Mary like water passes through a pipe."[42] Eutyches also colludes with this idea. In their footsteps today the Anabaptists, Schwenkfelders, enthusiasts, and finally the Socinians follow, stating: (a) that Christ was begotten as much from the blood of Mary as from a material conveyed by God for begetting a body: thus Smalcius, in *Examination of 157 Further Errors* (error 18).[43] (b) That he laid aside his flesh in the ascension: thus Ostorodt, *Institutes* (ch. 18).[44]

---

42. χριστὸν διὰ μαρίας διοδεύσαντα, κατάπερ ὕδωρ διὰ τῆς σωλήνος ὁδεύει, Irenaeus (c. 130–c. 202), *Adversus haereses libri quinque* in *PG* 7:513–14; idem, *Against Heresies* in *ANF* 1:325. Cited originally as *Advers. Haeres. l. 1. c. 1.*

43. Latin: *Smal. Examin. Error. Francii. Errore 18.* There are two works, 1615 and 1616 respectively, by Valentinus Smalcius (Walenty Schmalz, 1572–1622) that could be reduced to this short citation. The work Mastricht cited is Smalcius, *Examinatio centum quinquaginta septem reliquorum errorum* (Raków: Sternacki, 1616), 8; contrast with: idem, *Examinatio centum errorum, quos Martinus Smiglecius Jesuita ex duabus libri nostri, nuper adversus monstra ipsius editi, partibus collegit* (Raków: Sternacki, 1615), 10. The eighteenth error in the 1615 work does not address this question Mastricht raises. These works were part of an ongoing dispute which includes the works: Smiglecius, *Nova monstra novi Arianismi seu absurda haereses a novis Arianis in Poloniam importatae* (Nysa: Schaffenberg, 1612); Smalcius, *Responsio ad librum Martini Smiglecii Jesuitae... nova monstra novi Arianismi* (Raków: Sternacki, 1613); Smiglecius, *De erroribus novorum Arianorum libri duo adversus responsum Valentini Smalcii, quod dedit pro novis Arianorum suorum monstris* (Krakow: A. Piotrkowczyk, 1615).

44. Ostorodt, *Unterrichtung*, 98–106; idem, *Onderwyzinge*, 80–86.

(3) The Apsychi

The Apsychi, who either denied that Christ had any soul, as the Arians did; or only denied that he had a rational soul, as the Apollinarians did (that is, so that the divine nature would replace the rational soul); or denied that his rational soul had its own will, as the Monothelites did: in so many ways, the true humanity of the Mediator is more directly denied. These however deny his humanity indirectly: (a) the Lutheran synusiasts, and (b) the papist metusiasts, who, in order to make a crust of bread into Christ,[45] fashion for him such a body which (i) is either diffused everywhere and not circumscribed by any space, (ii) or is invisible, impalpable, without location or extension, hidden under an invisible point, in many places separate from each other, actually present without location or circumscription,[46] and all that without the multiplication of itself, and without the occupation of a middle space, a body indeed which is made from bread by the force of certain little words magically muttered over it, a body which is accordingly not like us in all things except for sin.

---

45. Cf. §XXXIII, below. In the ancient church, Synousiasts, sometimes called Polemians, were a sect of Apollinarians "who held the incarnation was effected by a commixture of the divine substance with the substance of human flesh," J. H. Blunt, *Dictionary of Sects, Heresies, Ecclesiastical Parties and Schools of Religious Thought* (London: Rivingtons, 1874), 589. The term comes from a sentence in Theodoret, *Hareticarum fabularum compendium*, 4.9 in *PG* 83:427–28, συνουσίωσιν λέγει γεγενῆσθαι καὶ κρᾶσιν τῆς θεότητος καὶ τοῦ σώματος, "and he said a confusion of substances had occurred and a mingling of divinity and the body"; idem, "Compendium of Heretical Mythification" in *Theodoret of Cyrus*, trans. I. Pásztori-Kupán (New York: Routledge, 2006), 221–22; cf. Cyril of Alexandria (c. 376–444), *Against the Synousiasts* (fragments), in *Library of the Fathers of the Church* (LFC), 48 vols. (Oxford: James Parker & Co., 1838–1885), 47:363–77; idem, *Ex libro contra Synusiastas* in *PG* 76:1427–38; idem, *Quod unus sit Christus*, *PG* 75:1253–56; idem, *That Christ is One*, trans. P. E. Pusey in *LFC* 47:237–319. For a Reformed refutation of Lutheran synusiasts and Roman Catholic metusiasts on the Supper, see Zacharias Ursinus (1534–1583), "De controversia verborum Coena," *Prolegomena in religionis Christianae catechesin* in *Opera theologica*, 3 vols. (Heidelberg: Johannes Lancellotus, 1612), 1:268–69; idem, "Compendiosa Explicatio Totius de Coena Domini Controversiae inter synusiastas et orthodoxos," *Explicationum catecheticarum D. Zachariae Ursini…necnon miscellanea catechetica* (Neustadt: Wilhelmus Harnisius, 1598), 114–29. Johannes Pincier, Sr. (1521–1591), *Antidotum adversus Enthusiastarum, Meusiastarum, et Synusiastarum cavillos et calumnias in causa Eucharistica* (Basel: Johannes Oporinus, 1565); Marcus Beumier (1555–1611), *De duabus gravissimis quaestionibus: conjunctione videlicet sacramentali et vera communion corporis sanguinisque Christi adversus novum synusiastarum figmentum et futilem consensus orthodoxi refutationem* (Zürich: Christoph Froschouer, 1584). On the Lutheran and Reformed debates, see H. Hotson, "Irenicism and Dogmatics in the Confessional Age: Pareus and Comenius in Heidelberg, 1614," *The Journal of Ecclesiastical History*, vol. 46, no. 3 (July, 1995): 432–56.

46. *vel invisibile, impalpabile, illocatum et inextensum, sub puncto invisibili latens, in multis locis a seinvicem discretis, actu praesens illocabiliter et incircumscriptive*

The basis of the orthodox opinion

To all these, we oppose this one general but invincible argument. If according to the Scriptures all the requirements of a humanity that is true and consubstantial with ours belong to something, then a humanity that is true and consubstantial with ours belongs to it; but according to the Scriptures all the requirements of a nature that is true and consubstantial with ours belong to the human nature of the Mediator; therefore, a humanity that is true and consubstantial with ours belongs to it. The major premise cannot be denied without contradiction, nor, I know well enough, will it be denied. The minor premise is evident in this way: if human names, essential parts, affections, and operations belong to something, then all the requirements of a nature that is true and consubstantial with ours belong to it, because all such requirements can be summed up under those headings; but human names, essential parts, properties, and operations belong to the human nature of Christ; therefore, all such requirements belong to it. The minor premise here is evident by parts, in this way: (1) with respect to names, when he is called a human being (1 Tim. 2:5), a man (Zech. 6:12), a child (Isa. 9:6), the son of Abraham and David (Matt. 1:1), the seed of the woman (Gen. 3:15), from the tribe of Judah (Rev. 5:5), the fruit of the loins of David (Acts 2:30), the Branch of David (Jer. 23:5), the Son of Man (Dan. 7:13). (2) With respect to the essential parts, the soul (Matt. 20:28; 26:38; Luke 23:46), the body (Matt. 26:26; Col. 1:22). Moreover, the integral parts of the body: flesh (Luke 24:39), blood (Matt. 26:28), bones (John 19:33), hands, feet, eyes, head, face, ears, mouth, chest, side, and so forth. (3) With respect to properties: (a) of the soul, an intellect to which knowledge and ignorance are attributed throughout the Scriptures (Isa. 7:15; Luke 2:40; Mark 13:32), a will (Matt. 26:39) to which virtues are attributed (Isa. 11:1ff.; Matt. 11:27), as well as affections, love, hatred, desire, aversion, joy, sorrow, anger, fear, and so forth, which are everywhere asserted for him; (b) of the body, locality, visibility, finitude (Luke 2:7; Mark 16:6), palpability (Luke 24:39); (c) of the body and soul, infirmities common to the human species: to thirst, hunger, be wearied, suffer, die, and so forth (Heb. 4:15). (4) With respect to operations: to will, refuse, speak, preach, eat, drink, and so forth. Compare what we first touched upon in the dogmatic part, §VI.

Objections

Nor is it a hindrance to all these things: (1) that he is said to have come down from heaven (John 3:13; 1 Cor. 15:47; John 6:50), for this must be understood regarding the divine nature, which while it was manifested in the flesh (1 Tim. 3:16) is said to have come down (cf. Gen. 18:21). (2) That the nature is devoid of subsistence, since that is properly not demanded of a nature but of a person.

2. Did the Son of God assume a human person? The diversity of opinions
XIX. It is asked, second, whether the assuming Word assumed not only a human nature, but also a person, or whether the nature that the Word assumed was devoid of subsistence or personhood. Regarding the latter question: (1) the Nestorians deny it, admitting two persons in the Mediator that are also separable. (2) The Lutherans limit it, by certainly denying a subsistence proper to it, but granting a divine subsistence communicated to the human nature by the personal union. The orthodox affirm it, by abrogating entirely all subsistence from the human nature. At the same time they grant to it an existence, and certainly one that is substantial, although not incommunicable, and therefore not subsisting.[47] We have adduced the arguments of the orthodox party in the dogmatic part, §VI. Nor does the lack of subsistence diminish: (1) the truth of the human nature, or (2) its perfection; because the things that are proper to a person are not required for the truth and perfection of a nature.

QUESTIONS CONCERNING THE
UNION OF THE NATURES

It is asked: 1. Is there a true personal union of both natures?
XX. Concerning the union of the natures itself, the following questions especially are customarily controverted. First, whether there is a true union of both natures in the one Mediator. All anti-Trinitarians, the Jews, Socinians, and so forth, stubbornly deny and mock this union. Christians affirm it. Because it has already been demonstrated that: (1) the Mediator is God from eternity and consubstantial with the Father; (2) the same is also man true and consubstantial with us; notwithstanding, (3) he is only one person; and (4) from the mediatorial office, this necessarily had to be so—now follows of its own accord the union of the two natures, especially since Scripture teaches this throughout by so many testimonies and so clearly (e.g. John 1:14; Rom. 9:5; Col. 2:9; 1 Tim. 3:16; Heb. 2:14, 16; 1 John 4:2; etc.), and the church urges its necessity so constantly and with such great zeal (see Gerhard, *Exegesis*, loc. 4, §35).[48] Thus Hilary of Poitiers testifies in *On the Trinity* (bk. 9), "It is just as dangerous to deny divinity in Christ as to deny in him the flesh of our body: one without the other presents no hope

---

47. Cf. 1.2.24 §VI on the terms *existence, subsistence, personhood* or *personality*, and *person*.

48. The *Exegesis* is more elaboration upon volume 1 of Gerhard's larger *Loci theologici*, Johann Gerhard, *Exegesis sive uberior Explicatio Articulorum De Scriptura Sacra, De Deo, et Persona Christi in tomo uno* (Frankfurt and Hamburg: Zacharias Hertel, 1657), 410–11; cf. idem, loc. 8, ch. 3, "De personali duarum naturarum unione" in *Loci theologici*, 1:170–74.

of salvation. He is ignorant, utterly ignorant of his own life who does not know Christ as true God; so also he who does not know him as true man."[49]

Objections of our adversaries

If therefore they should allege: (1) He is man, therefore he is not God, which is what the Jews objected to Christ in John 10:33, we will respond, This does not follow, because Scripture attributes both to Christ. (2) There would be two contrary natures in Christ. I respond, Not contrary, but only different. (3) The humanity of Christ would be a monster devoid of personhood. I respond, We will deny this, because personhood is not required for a nature. (4) God can neither suffer nor die. I respond, With respect to the deity he cannot, but in his humanity he altogether can. (5) An essential mutation would have happened to God. I respond, By no means, because only a personal relation happened to him. (6) There would be two sons in one person. I respond, Only a double sonship, to his Father and to his mother, such as is observed even in us. (7) If this union were true, Matthew and Luke would have explained it. I respond, They surely did explain it, and if not so expressly as John and the other divinely inspired writers,[50] that was done for a specific reason, that their principal purpose was to weave the history of his humanity.

2. Does the formal nature of the union consist in this, that the subsistence
of the second person was communicated to the human nature?
The opinion of the Lutherans

XXI. It is asked, second, whether the formal nature of the union consists in this, that the hypostasis of the Word was made the hypostasis of the flesh. The Lutherans affirm this (Johann Gerhard, *Exegesis*, loc. 4, §115).[51] We deny this, in agreement with the Scripture. The primary falsehood of the Lutheran opinion is that they may more easily protect the communication of properties between the natures, through perichoresis, and that through it the flesh of Christ may be omnipresent, and thus also present in the Holy Supper. The question rests in two things: whether this communication of the divine hypostasis is the form of the union, or whether it is at least a consequence of it.

---

49. Hilary of Poitiers (c. 310–c. 367), *De Trinitate* in *PL* 10:282; idem, *On the Trinity* in *NPNF2* 9:156.

50. *scriptores* θεόπνευστοι

51. Gerhard, *Exegesis*, 443.

The opinion of the Reformed and its reasons

The Reformed deny both, because: (1) no hypostasis, whether proper or communicated, can belong to the human nature, for it would become a person. (2) The divine hypostasis is the very divine essence, and accordingly, if the divine hypostasis were communicated to the humanity, it would become the very divine essence. (3) If the divine hypostasis by a certain perichoresis were communicated to the human nature, then the human nature would become a divine person, for that to which a divine personhood belongs is without doubt a divine person. (4) Scripture nowhere represents that union by such a communication, but rather through the idea of taking on (Phil. 2:7) and assuming (Heb. 2:16), by which is signified that ineffable relation of the human nature to the divine person, by which the former has not only been inseparably conjoined to the latter, but also is sustained by the latter so that it may exist, not by a sustaining of common providence, but by a personal sustaining, by which the former together with the latter constituted the one person of the God-man.

Objections

Nor (1) for his own view does Johann Gerhard, with all his mustered strength from §115 to §121[52] produce even one argument, except that he presupposes, not proves, that there cannot be a personal union unless the personhood or hypostasis of the Word is communicated to the flesh. For the union can be sufficiently personal through that relation of the human nature to the divine person, by which the former together with the latter constitute one person. For this reason Scripture, when occupied with this union, teaches such things that do not proclaim some communication or perichoresis made with the human nature, but only an assumption, and a manifestation of him in the flesh. And if (2) you wish to argue in this way: Either the human nature had its own hypostasis, which is Nestorian; or it had none, and so would not have existed; or it had the hypostasis of the Word—I will choose the second; yet it did not therefore not exist, but only not subsist, which two things have a world of difference between them. And if (3) something with any appearance of truth could be urged for this communication, it will be Colossians 2:9, "For in him dwells all the fullness of the deity bodily," through which passage it seems to them that the deity indwells the human nature, but if you attend closely, you will observe that: (1) here no mention is made of a personhood or hypostasis, but of the deity; (2) it is not said to indwell the human nature, but the entire person, "in him"; and moreover,

---

52. Gerhard, *Exegesis*, 443–58.

(3) "bodily," that is, with the flesh, so that the sense is that in the one person of the Mediator, the deity and the flesh, or human nature, as it were, dwell together.

QUESTIONS CONCERNING THE CONSEQUENCES OF THE UNION

The absurdities of the Lutherans regarding the consequences of the personal union
XXII. From the idea that the hypostasis of the Word was communicated to the human nature, among the Lutherans there comes forth a long train of perverse hypotheses with respect to the consequences of this union. For since, even from their own hypotheses, the hypostasis of the Word does not differ really from the divine essence, it follows that when the hypostasis has been communicated, the divine essence has also been communicated; and furthermore, because the divine essence does not really differ from its properties, it follows that when the hypostasis has been communicated, the properties of the divine essence, and by the same stroke, infinite gifts[53] have also been communicated to the human nature. Therefore, these things must be laid open somewhat more distinctly.

It is asked: 1. Was the divine nature communicated to the human nature?
The opinion of the Lutherans, and of the Reformed with their reasons
XXIII. Therefore it is asked, first, whether through the hypostatic union the divine nature was communicated to the human nature. The Lutherans, so that they may more easily hold that the properties of the divine nature, and among them omnipresence, were communicated to the human nature, through which omnipresence the flesh of Christ would be present in the Holy Supper, both to the sacramental elements and to all those communicating, state that the divine nature through the hypostatic union was communicated to the human nature, and that the divine nature coincides with its properties—its omnipresence, omnipotence, and vivifying power. The Reformed, just as they acknowledge that through this union the two natures came together in his one person in such a way that in the one person exist two natures, both divine and human, so also they deny that the natures were communicated to each other, because: (1) regarding such a communication, Scripture has not even one whit, inasmuch as it continually speaks in the concrete about the person: Philippians 2:6–7, "Who though he existed in the form of God, …emptied himself, having assumed the form of a servant"; Hebrews 2:14, "And he (καὶ αὐτός) in a like manner took part (μετέσχε) of the same things," and v. 16, "For he does not assume

---

53. *charismata*

(ἐπιλαμβάνεται) the nature of angels, but he assumes (ἐπιλαμβάνεται) the seed of Abraham," and so forth. Nor is there a contrary example in the Scriptures. (2) The opinion of the Lutherans implies an open confusion of the natures, and thus Eutychianism. For (3) if the divine nature had been communicated to the human nature, then the human nature would have become the divine nature, for that which has the divine nature, is the divine nature, and thus the human nature would have ceased, and a manifest confusion would have followed. (4) If through the personal union the divine nature had been communicated to the human nature, then through the same union the human nature would have been communicated to the divine nature, and thus the divine nature would have become the human nature. And consequently, (5) just as, with the divine nature, divine properties have been communicated, so also vice versa, the properties of the human nature would have been communicated to the divine nature, and by this the divine nature would have become visible, palpable, passible, mortal, and not eternal. We should add, (6) if the divine nature had been communicated to the human nature, then the entire Trinity would have been incarnated, because the divine nature is common to the three persons. And so also, (7) if the divine nature had been communicated to the human nature, then the human nature would have been omnipotence itself, because the divine nature is omnipotence itself.

Objections

Nor do I see what those opposed could allege for themselves, other than: (1) that through this union the subsistence of the divine person was communicated to the human nature, which by it became enhypostatic,[54] because the divine subsistence is identical to the divine nature. I respond, We have already just expressly denied that the divine subsistence was communicated to the human nature. (2) That Colossians 2:9 says that in Christ dwells all the fullness of the deity bodily. We have already responded that all the fullness of the deity dwells in Christ the God-man, but not in the human nature. (3) That it is said that God was manifested in the flesh (1 Tim. 3:16). I respond, It is not said that the deity was communicated to the flesh, but that in the flesh, on account of the personal union, in the one person, it was as if the invisible God was made clearly visible, that is, through emperichoresis, about which the Savior speaks in John 14:9–10. (4) That at the same time, through that union some kind of communion[55] of natures occurred. I respond, Certainly in the person, but by no means in the

---

54. ἐνυπόστατος
55. κοινωνία

human nature. In addition, (5) that believers are said to be partakers of the divine nature[56] (2 Peter 1:4)—how much more the human nature of Christ? I respond: (a) If the consequence were valid, all believers would be God just as much as Christ is. But (b) "nature" is understood to be not the same nature which belongs to God, but a nature similar in some way, that is, in regard to the divine holiness.

2. From the union of the natures in the person, does a communication of properties in the natures follow?

XXIV. It is asked, second, whether from the union of the two natures in the one person there legitimately follows a communication of properties in the natures, such that the divine properties—omniscience, omnipotence, omnipresence, power to vivify, and so forth—were communicated to the human nature. The Lutherans, due to the communication of nature considered in the preceding question, if it were not false, would correctly infer the affirmative.

The opinion of the Reformed with their reasons

The Reformed certainly admit a communion of properties in the person, but deny a communication between the natures, because: (1) the divine properties coincide with the divine essence itself, as our adversaries themselves agree, and thus if the divine properties had been communicated, the divine nature would have been communicated to the human nature, which we refuted in the preceding section. (2) If through this union the divine properties were communicated to the human nature, then through the same union the properties of the human nature—composition, finitude, locality, and so forth—would have been communicated to the divine nature. (3) If certain properties—omnipresence, omnipotence, and so forth—had been communicated, then all the properties would have been, and thus the human nature would have existed from eternity, would have been most simple, immutable, impassible, and so forth, because the divine properties are inseparable, inasmuch as they all express the same undivided essence of God by way of inadequate concepts. I should add that (4) Scripture makes entirely no mention of this sort of communication.

Objections

Nor is there almost anything that they may allege to the contrary, except: (1) the hypostasis of the Word communicated to the human nature, and with it the divine essence, which includes the divine properties; this we have already refuted in the preceding sections. (2) Certain similarities, for example, that the

---

56. θείας κοινωνοὶ φύσεως

life of the soul is communicated to the body. I respond: (a) The soul does not communicate its life to the body, but produces life in the body. (b) Even if it did communicate it, still it would not follow. (3) That omnipresence, omniscience, omnipotence, and so forth, are attributed in the Scriptures to the human nature. Yet when we treated those attributes individually in book 2 we denied and refuted this.[57] They add (4) that the flesh of Christ, that is, his human nature, is said to be vivifying (John 6:54–55), which without a doubt is among the properties of the divine nature. I respond: (a) Likewise it is said in verse 63 that the flesh profits nothing, that is, that his words must not be understood carnally or properly, because it is the Spirit who vivifies, but spiritually or improperly, as concerning the spiritual communion which men have with him through faith, through which he is their life (Col. 3:4; Gal. 2:20; John 14:6). Then (b) Christ speaks about his entire person in verse 51, "*I am the bread of life which came down from heaven.*" So in verse 33, and verse 35, "*I am the bread of life: whoever comes to me will not hunger, and whoever believes in me will never thirst.*" They continue, (5) The Father has given to him to have life in himself (John 5:26), which pertains without a doubt to the divine properties, and necessarily must be referred to the human nature, because nothing can be given to the divine nature. I respond, This must be entirely referred to the divine person, to whom God has given independent life, not through the grace of union, but through eternal generation, by which, with the essence, independent life was communicated to the second person of the Trinity. Yet they do not stop, but add (6) that in John 17:5 he requests to be communicated to him that glory which he had with him before the world was; but this without a doubt is the divine glory, which since it cannot be communicated to the divine nature, must come to be communicated to him according to the human nature. I respond: (a) He requests such a glorification of himself which he did not then already have through the hypostatic union, yet the Lutherans intend such a glory as he did already have. Nor (b) does he request any glory to be given or communicated to the human nature, but he requests to be glorified, "Glorify me," that is, for the glory of the divine nature, which so far had been hidden through the assumed form of a servant, to be manifested, insofar as it would be acknowledged by men. They allege (7) that the Father has given the Son the authority to execute judgment, ὅτι, "because" he is the Son of Man, that is, insofar as he is the Son of Man (John 5:27). I respond, The text does not mean anything other than that the Father has given the authority to judge to the Son as Mediator, because he alone among the divine persons is the Son of Man, who through his human nature is suited to pronounce the judicial

---

57. 1.2.9 §IX; 1.2.10 §XIII; 1.2.20 §XXIV

sentence orally. Finally, they add (8) that God gave to the human nature to sit at his right hand (Mark 16:19; Matt. 26:64), which glory is certainly the divine glory. I respond: (a) It is denied that to sit at the right hand of God is the divine glory, for in that way both the Father and the Holy Spirit would be robbed of that divine glory, and consequently would not be God, because it is not attributed to them that they sit at the right hand of God. But (b) the mediatorial glory is understood, which from the eternal covenant he merited for himself by his humiliation (Heb. 1:3; Phil. 2:7–10). If they should object something else, it is so feeble that it would of its own accord refute itself.

3. From the personal union, did the Mediator receive infinite gifts, or such gifts to which nothing could be added?
XXV. It is asked, third, whether from the personal union the Mediator received infinite gifts,[58] or at least such gifts to which no degrees could afterward be added. The Lutherans, in order to more effectively protect their idea that divine properties were communicated to the human nature, in the worst way confuse gifts with divine attributes, so that from the fact that gifts cannot be bestowed upon the divine nature, they may more effectively deduce that infinite gifts were communicated to the human nature: they state that infinite gifts were communicated to him according to the human nature. The Scholastics with their followers do judge that the gifts were finite, but yet of such a kind that from the very first moment of conception nothing at all could be added to them. But there are not lacking among them those who distinguish between gifts with respect to habit and with respect to acts, such that in regard to the prior, they were perfect from the very first moment of conception, but in regard to the latter, they increased.

The opinion of the Reformed
The Reformed carefully distinguish gifts from the divine attributes, as effects from their causes. They also certainly admit that there were communicated to Christ as the Mediator, according to his human nature, gifts of such a sort and magnitude as can be bestowed upon a finite human nature, but neither simply infinite gifts, nor those given all at once, but rather those which had to advance over time little by little to their pinnacle. And so Scripture stated he was full of grace from the womb, yet in such a way that those gifts advanced with age. This is evident: (1) by express testimonies of Scripture (Luke 2:40, 52; Mark 13:32); and (2) by the fuller outpouring of the Holy Spirit, accomplished especially in his baptism, the symbol of which was the resting of the Holy Spirit upon him

---

58. *dona*

(Matt. 3:16–17; John 1:32; Isa. 11:1–2); (3) by the fact that he was in all things like us, except for sin (Heb. 2:17; 4:15).

The foundations of the Lutheran opinion
Nor does it help our adversaries that in John 3:34 God is said to have not given him the Spirit by measure. For this does not entirely exclude all measure, but that which is regularly measured to creatures (cf. Est. 1:8). If they should add that all authority in heaven and on earth has been given to him (Matt. 28:18), there will come an easy response, that it does not mean simply "all things," but all those things which are required for the governance of the church, as is evident from the following verse.

4. From this union, does the flesh also exist everywhere the divine person exists?
The negative reasons of the Reformed
XXVI. It is asked, fourth, whether from this union the flesh also exists everywhere the Word exists. The Reformed deny this, because: (1) Scripture expressly denies it (John 11:15, 32; Luke 2:12, 42; Mark 16:6; John 16:28; 17:11; Heb. 8:4; etc.). (2) The articles of our faith in many ways protest it, for in this way: (a) with respect to his human nature, he would not be in all things like us; (b) he could not have been born or come forth from his mother's womb; (c) he could not have died through the separation of body and soul; (d) he could not have risen again; (e) he could not return for judgment. I need not add (3) that through that adequated coexistence of the flesh and the Word, the flesh would become God.

The affirmative foundations of the Lutherans
The Lutherans, in favor of the oral eating of Christ in the Holy Supper: (1) invent a personal union which, as they love to say, involves a most profound perichoresis of the two natures, an immanence, permeation, *circumincessio*, most present presence of the natures, and communication of the natures, through which the natures as it were deeply permeate and pass through each other, indeed in such a way that the Word is and remains within the flesh, and the flesh within the Word, and thus neither is the Word beyond the flesh, nor the flesh beyond the Word, but everywhere the Word is, there also it has the flesh most present to it. We have already refuted such a union, however, in the preceding sections. (2) Through the same union, they suppose that the omnipresence of the Word has been communicated to the flesh, which communication of properties we have also already expressly dispatched, in §XXIV. They add (3) several testimonies of Scripture (Eph. 4:10; 1:23; Matt. 18:20; 28:20). But these are speaking about the presence not of the human nature, but of the entire person, or also about the presence not so much of a nature as of grace (2 Cor. 13:14). Finally,

(4) they urge that without this adequate coexistence of the Word and the flesh, the union is taken away, and the natures divided. I respond, This is excessively crass, since nowhere does the flesh exist where the Word does not coexist with it, and thus remains personally united to it, although the Word does exist where the flesh does not coexist with it, in the same way as the union between the soul and the head is not taken away because the head does not exist everywhere the soul exists, since the soul exists, for example, in the feet, where the head does not exist.

5. Does not the union of diverse natures import composition in the Mediator?
XXVII. Finally, fifth, whether the union of diverse natures does not import some sort of composition in the Mediator. I respond, We already taught that composition does not occur in the person of the assuming Word. Moreover, most theologians also think that it does not occur in the person of the Mediator, because God cannot enter into composition with the creature, since a whole always and necessarily exists more perfectly than any of its parts, as the perfection of each part comes together in the whole. This surely is most true in any ordinary composition of creatures, where one part does not include the perfection of the other, either formally or eminently. But if instead one is asking about an extraordinary composition, where one part absorbs the perfection of the other, not in fact formally, yet still eminently, I do not see by what reason it should be denied, either that God can enter into such a composition with the creature, or that the Word can concur with the flesh for the composition of the one God-Man Mediator. For by this reckoning the God-man will not signify something more perfect than the Word abstractly, because all the perfection of the flesh is eminently and more perfectly in the Word. Just as if you should conceive of God jointly with the creatures, you would even so not conceive of something more perfect than if you should conceive of God separately, because God eminently absorbs the perfection of all the creatures. And certainly it cannot be conceived by what reckoning any true union of diverse things, such especially as is observed in this personal union of the two natures, could occur without any composition, either ordinary, or such extraordinary composition as we have already represented.

The Practical Part

CONCERNING THE DIVINE AND THE HUMAN NATURE

The practice resulting from the human nature, 1. Presents the love: Of the Father
XXVIII. The practice of this chapter concerns, first, the assuming divine person, which we have already explained in book 2, chapter 26, and which can

be transferred from there to here.[59] Second, it concerns the assumed human nature, by which is presented to us in living color, first, the indescribable love for mankind,[60] first of the Father, who in the incarnation not only gave to men the Son, his very own, only begotten Son (John 3:16; Isa. 9:6), but also made him like men, in fact united him with men, and not that he might command men, but that he might become like a child (Isa. 9:6), indeed a slave (Phil. 2:7), and even a worm (Ps. 22:6), and not this only, but also exposed him to the law, to weaknesses and sicknesses of every kind (Gal. 4:4; Heb. 4:15; Isa. 53:2–6).

Of the Son
Then, that of the Son, by which fellowship with men delighted him so much (Prov. 8:31) that he not only desired to be made like men (Phil. 2:7; Heb. 2:17), but also to be made man, most close (παραπλήσιος) to man, indeed man's גואל, kinsman, even his brother (Heb. 2:12), and also one with men (Heb. 2:11), the same flesh and blood as them, that is, just as the children are partakers of flesh and blood, καὶ αὐτὸς παραπλησίως μετέσχε, "he himself also most closely partook" (Heb. 2:16). And he did that not for himself, that he might serve himself and his own comforts, but for men, that he might serve, and give himself as the price of redemption for men (Matt. 20:28).

To what end
This indescribable love for mankind, I say, both of the Father and of the Son, is presented to us in the incarnation, to the end that: (1) it may inflame us to reciprocal love toward God and toward Christ, through which in turn we may be φιλόθειοι καὶ φιλόχριστοι, lovers of God and lovers of Christ, just as they are φιλάνθρωποι, lovers of mankind (Titus 3:4 with 2 Tim. 3:4; Eph. 5:1–2). That (2) in turn we may strive more and more to be made like them, just as he willed in the incarnation to be made like us (Heb. 2:17), even to taking on the form of a servant (Phil. 2:7 with v. 5; Eph. 5:1; 1 Cor. 11:1). Indeed, that (3) we may strive by faith and the Spirit to be united with him, just as he willed to be united to us by flesh and blood (Heb. 2:14 with v. 11).

2. The profound humiliation of the Mediator
XXIX. Second, by the same human nature is presented to us the Mediator's profound lowering and condescension, through which, though he was the Son of God, his very own Son (Rom. 8:32), the only begotten Son (John 3:16), in the

---

59. 1.2.6 §XXff.
60. φιλανθρωπία

form of God, equal with God (Phil. 2:6), indeed, God himself, blessed forever (Rom. 9:5), the radiance of his glory, and the express image of his hypostasis (Heb. 1:3), he willed: (1) to assume a human nature, not an angelic nature, nearly countless miles more excellent than ours (Heb. 2:16). And that (2) not perfect, as it was in the state of integrity, but abject, as it had been made by sin, a nature which conveyed the form of a servant (Phil. 2:7), in which there displayed itself no form, no comeliness on account of which he could have pleased someone (Isa. 53:2). Indeed, (3) in that nature, and such an abject form of the nature, he who is holy, harmless, undefiled, separate from sinners, and made higher than the heavens (Heb. 7:26) willed to be united with us sinners (Heb. 2:11), though otherwise sins separate God and sinners (Isa. 59:2; 1:15). And what is more, he willed to assume (4) not only the nature and the natural affections of the nature, but also its weaknesses, and in addition all its weaknesses, however lowly, provided they are not shameful and sinful (Heb. 4:15), so much so that he was made not only equally as low, but even lower than us, who are in fact sinners (Ps. 22:6–7). And that (5) not for himself (Matt. 20:28), but for us, so that he might become our brother, as if there were so much excellence, so much glory in being the brother of the most lowly of men, which the apostle signifies with such great emphasis in Hebrews 2:11: "For which cause he is not ashamed to call them brethren."

To what end
And to what end was this condescension, this humiliation, this emptying? Except so that: (1) we might acknowledge his love and kindness toward mankind which we designated in the preceding section. (2) In turn for his sake we might not turn away from any humbling or emptying of ourselves, any contempt, disgrace, or similar such thing, no matter how hard or great (2 Cor. 11:23–30). Namely, (3) that we might not be ashamed of the gospel (Rom. 1:16) and the free profession of the name of Christ (Mark 8:38; Luke 9:26; cf. 2 Tim. 1:8, 12, 16), though it be conjoined with all manner of insult.

3. Our surpassing exaltation
XXX. On the contrary, third, in this descent of the Mediator to us, our ascent appears; in his humiliation, our exaltation (2 Cor. 8:9), insofar as through it we are now neighbors of the Son of God, his kin (Heb. 2:15), of his flesh and blood (Eph. 5:30), his brethren (Heb. 2:11), his sons (Heb. 2:10), one with him (Heb. 2:11). Surely in all these things, is there not the greatest exaltation of us (cf. 1 Sam. 18:23, 26–27)? How much greater an exaltation will also follow in its own time, when he shall change our vile body, that it may be fashioned like unto

his glorious body (Phil. 3:21)! Thus in this is supplied an argument for the greatest boasting for all Christians, no matter how lowly they are otherwise (Phil. 3:3; James 1:9).

4. Christ's more than brotherly care toward his own
XXXI. In addition fourth, in this same assumption of our nature, and in that which is visible in it, his love for mankind and condescension, there also appears his more than brotherly care for his own, which (1) he bears toward them as their neighbor, kinsman, brother, spouse, flesh of their flesh, and blood of their blood (Eph. 5:29; cf. Gen. 2:23; Isa. 58:7; Gen. 29:4; 37:27), surely more tenderly than Joseph toward his brothers, who were also once so hostile to him (Gen. 42ff.; Matt. 25:40; 10:40; 18:5; Mark 9:37). (2) He shows more clearly than the sun that he assumed this nature expressly to this end, that he might become a merciful and faithful high priest (Heb. 2:17), able to sympathize with our infirmities, inasmuch as he was in all points tempted as we are (Heb. 4:15). And also (3) to this end, that he might abolish death and deliver as many as through fear of death were all their lifetime subject to bondage (Heb. 2:14–15).

For the sweetest comfort in various cases
How much comfort from this is supplied to believers! (1) In the case of an ignoble and abject birth, because nevertheless they are neighbors, kinsmen, brothers, spouses of the Son of God. And because that very Son of God assumed his human nature from an ignoble and scorned maiden (Luke 1:48), and assumed it to this end, that he might exalt our nature. (2) In the case of poverty, because the Son of God also became poor, and indeed to this end, that he might make us rich (2 Cor. 8:9). (3) In the case of weaknesses and diseases, because the Son of God also assumed our nature, which was exposed to our weaknesses and diseases (Isa. 53:3–4, 10), so that he might heal our infirmities and diseases (Matt. 4:23). (4) In the case of satanic temptations, because the Son of God in our nature was also in all points tempted as we are, and certainly to this end, that he might be able to commiserate with us (Heb. 4:15). (5) In the case of death or the fear of death, because the Son of God also was made a partaker of our flesh and blood to this end, that through his death he might destroy him who had the power of death (Heb. 2:14). (6) In the case of the last judgment, because we await him as the Judge who is our neighbor, our kinsman, flesh of our flesh, blood of our blood, and likewise our brother and bridegroom, indeed who is one with us.

5. It excites in us a just concern
XXXII. At the same time, fifth, it offers an opportunity for a just concern, since:
(1) the Mediator assumed not only your own human nature, but also that common to all, yet to them is not supplied one whit of advantage or comfort, so lest perhaps the same thing happen to us; in fact, (2) lest it result in our loss and destruction, since we violated the nature which Christ assumed (1 Cor. 6:15), there is therefore reason that we should carefully inquire whether or not to us a child is born, and to us a son is given (Isa. 9:6; Luke 2:11), whether the benefits so far remembered pertain specifically *to us.*

Signs
But how at last will this be made known to us? From this, if: (1) through the assumption of our flesh, not only have we been made his (John 1:11), but also he in turn made ours (Song 2:16). If (2) just as by the assumption of the human nature he himself has been made one flesh and blood with us, we in turn, by the assumption of him which is made through faith (John 1:12), are made one spirit with him (1 Cor. 6:17; Rom. 8:9, 11). If (3) just as he by the assumption of our flesh has in all things been made like us with respect to nature, with only sin excepted (Heb. 2:17), so also we strive to be made more and more like him with respect to morals (Phil. 2:5; Eph. 5:2; 1 Cor. 11:1; Matt. 11:29). If (4) just as he willed to become a partaker of our human nature (Heb. 2:14), so also we in turn strive to become partakers of his divine nature (2 Peter 1:4). If (5) just as he, inflamed by pure love, assumed our nature (Prov. 8:31), so also we strive for his nature and do whatever we do by pure love (2 Cor. 5:14).

6. It dissuades from various abuses. What they are
XXXIII. Sixth, at the same time there is reason here that we should take careful heed, namely: (1) that we not neglect, not despise the Son of God who comes to us by the assumption of our nature (John 1:11; Rev. 3:20). Then (2) that we not rest only in his assumption of our human nature, because he also assumed the nature of the reprobate, insofar as it is human nature, for in this way the flesh will not profit us (John 6:63). Furthermore, (3) that we not seek salvation in a union of Christ with our nature, and in an assumption of the flesh, or of his human nature, which happens in any sort of oral eating, with the transubstantiating papists and consubstantiating Lutherans. For in this way, in the opinion of the incarnate Christ himself, his flesh will not profit us (John 6:63).

By what reasons

And so that we would more carefully avoid these abuses, it will assist us to consider: (1) that the abuse of the best is always the worst (Luke 2:34; Rom. 9:32–33; 2 Cor. 2:15–16). And (2) to those who rightly use it, by his incarnation he came for salvation (Zech. 9:9; Luke 2:11), but to those who abuse it, he will one day come for altogether dreadful judgment (2 Thess. 1:7–8).

7. It inflames us to various virtues: Holiness, purity, love of
neighbor, humility, kindness

XXXIV. Finally seventh, the union of the Mediator with our human nature most effectively inflames us: (1) generally, to a zeal for holiness, which the apostle impresses upon us in Hebrews 2:11: "For he who sanctifies and those who are sanctified are all of one, for which cause he is not ashamed to call them his brethren." Specifically, (2) to a zeal for purity, namely, that we not make the members of Christ members of a harlot (1 Cor. 6:15), and that we not contaminate by any fleshly impurity (2 Cor. 7:1; 1 John 3:3) that body one day to be transfigured, that it may be made like his glorified body (Phil. 3:21). Furthermore, (3) by the example of Christ's love for mankind (Prov. 8:31), by which alone he willed to be incarnated, we also should pay attention to love toward the members of Christ (Eph. 5:2), and not hide ourselves from our own flesh (Isa. 58:7). In addition, (4) by the example of Christ's humility, by which he emptied himself (Phil. 2:7), even to taking on the form of a servant, we also should pay attention to humility and lowliness of mind, that the same mind which was in Christ may also be observed in us (Phil. 2:3–5; Matt. 11:29). Finally, (5) by the example of Christ's kindness, by which he assumed human nature and human infirmities, not for himself, but for us, each of us also should seek not the things that are his own, but the things that are of the other, that the same mind that was in Christ may also thrive in us (Phil. 2:4–5).

THE PRACTICE OF THE UNION
OF THE TWO NATURES

In the practice of the union of the two natures occurs, 1. An argument for admiration, from the various mysteries: Of the union

XXXV. That was the practice of the united natures; the practice of the union itself follows. In it there occurs an argument for us, first, for admiration. For it is called: (1) by the apostle, the mystery of godliness, that is, of the Christian religion, the mystery that is great, and without controversy great: God manifested in the flesh (1 Tim. 3:16). It is called (2) "the preaching of Jesus Christ according to the revelation of the mystery, which was kept secret since the world began" (Rom. 16:25; cf. Col. 1:26; Eph. 3:4, 10–11). From which (3) the child born and the son given obtains as his first name "Wonderful" (Isa. 9:6). At which union also, (4) prefigured in the bush that was burning yet not consumed, in which was the angel of Jehovah (the angel of the presence, Isa. 63:9; the angel of the covenant, Mal. 3:1), Moses marveled in Exodus 3:2–3, "I will now turn aside, and see this great sight." And if (5) you should attend to the union itself, is it not stupendous for God to become man, for him who was from eternity to be made in time, for him who is omnipotent to be subjected to human weaknesses, for him who fills heaven and earth to be enclosed in the womb of a virgin, for him who has neither father, nor mother, nor genealogy, yet to acknowledge both a father, and a mother, and a genealogy; and so forth? So that Augustine not without cause states (sermon 12, *On Time*), "O miracles! O wonders! God is born, a virgin made with child, without a man!"[61] And Bernard in his *Sermon on the Vigil of the Birth of the Lord*, "That omnipotent majesty, in the assumption of our flesh, did three works, made three mixtures, so singularly miraculous and miraculously singular, that such things neither have been nor will be done again upon the earth, namely, there were conjoined to each other God and man, mother and virgin, faith and the human heart."[62] And John of Damascus in *On the Orthodox Faith* (bk. 3, ch. 1) calls this mystery, "the newest of new things under the sun."[63] "I am what I was, but was not what I am; now I am called both."[64]

Of the virtues of God conspicuous in the union:
Righteousness, holiness, wisdom, power, mercy
And furthermore, if (6) you should observe the source of this union, you will marvel at the confluence and collection of the mysteries: (a) of the avenging justice of God, which so that he might not dismiss sin unpunished, took not some outstanding man, not an angel, and not some sort of friend, but a son, his very own, only begotten, most beloved Son, and as it were drove him from the throne into this misery, so that he might make him who knew no sin, to be sin in the place of sinners (2 Cor. 5:21). (b) Of his holiness and hatred toward sin, by which he now slew not two sons of Aaron (Lev. 10:2–3), nor ten myriads of

---

61. Attributed to Augustine, "Sermo CXXVIII. In Natali Domini, XII" in *PL* 39:1997; on the sermon's provenance as a composite of several passages from Augustine, see 39:1997, note b.

62. Bernard of Clairvaux, "Sermo III" in "In Vigilia Nativitatis Domini" in *Sermones de tempore* in *PL* 183:98.

63. τὸ πάντων καινῶν καινότατον, ὑπὸ τὸν ἥλιον. John of Damascus, *Expositio accurata fidei orthodoxae* in *PG* 94:981–83; idem, *On the Orthodox Faith* in *NPNF2* 9:46.

64. Cf. §II.C, above.

Bethshemites (1 Sam. 6:19), but thrust the only begotten Son from the throne, so that he might punish him for the sins of men. (c) Of his wisdom, by which in the union of himself with human flesh he found out the way of reconciling his own avenging justice with the eternal salvation of the sinner, through the union of himself with the sinner, from which the Savior is called the wisdom of God (1 Cor. 1:24). (d) Of his power, by which he could personally unite deity with humanity, a greater thing than which can neither be thought of, nor exist. So that from this you can proclaim what is recorded in Exodus 10:14, that something such as it did not exist before, nor shall thereafter. Especially (e) of his infinite mercy toward the miserable, by which through the incarnation he gave to the miserable his only begotten Son (John 3:16), such that from this the apostle in Romans 5:8 not without cause says, "God commends his own love toward us, in that, while we were sinners, Christ died for us" (cf. 1 John 4:9). And if you should weigh these things devoutly, what is the Mediator, except the very love of God incarnate, love born from a virgin, love coming down from heaven and walking about in human flesh?

2. An argument for modesty
XXXVI. Second, an argument for modesty, by which we may repress fleshly curiosity in the investigation of this mystery; which seems to have been found and been rebuked in Moses, who desired to draw near so that he might investigate the miraculous sight of the bush in which was the angel of Jehovah, a bush though burning, yet not being consumed: "And Jehovah saw that he turned aside to see; he cried out to him from the midst of the bush, 'Do not come nearer. Take off your shoes…'" (Ex. 3:3–5). The angel seems to do the same before the blessed Virgin, who was perhaps too curious in the investigation of the same mystery, "How can this be?" (Luke 1:34), for he responds, "The power of the Most High shall overshadow you," signifying that the Holy Spirit would accomplish that union as with a covering and under a shadow, and would conceal it, which accordingly would not be fitting to investigate, and to uncover, as it were. That modesty the very majesty of this mystery also urges, namely because there is found no example of this union in all of nature, that we, persuaded of the infallible truth of this union by the very testimony of God, should not be excessively troubled concerning its mode.

3. It provides an immovable foundation for faith and confidence in the Mediator.
XXXVII. Third, it provides for us an immovable foundation for faith and confidence in Jesus the Mediator, because: (1) from it we infallibly realize: that he is our Mediator, from the fact that the Mediator cannot be one who is not God

and man in one person, that our Jesus is God and man, and that besides him there is no one who is such. (2) Our Mediator is sufficient, he who can save to the uttermost as many as come to God through him (Heb. 7:25), on account of the fact that as God he is able to save, and as man he wills to sympathize with us. (3) He both willed to save us, for to this end he already willed to be made like us, to become one flesh with us, our brother, our bridegroom, and so forth; and is able to do so, because the one made like us is also God. Accordingly, (4) in him, as both God and man, we can have whatever we may desire to drive away any misery and to confer any benefit, in soul or body.

4. It provides a foundation for resting in the one Mediator.
XXXVIII. Fourth, it supplies an argument for resting in him alone, forsaking all others, because from the union of the divine and human natures, he has been made for us one Mediator (1 Tim. 2:5), one Lord (1 Cor. 8:6; Eph. 4:5), and accordingly in him alone can we place our confidence, inasmuch as he alone is our way, our truth, and our life, without whom none of us can come to the Father (John 14:6), in whom is all our salvation (Acts 4:12; Ps. 16:11; 73:25), such that we ought to pass by and reject all other creatures, our own strength, merits, and so forth (Phil. 3:7–9).

5. Fifth, it summons us to a zeal for unity and harmony. Motivating reasons
XXXIX. Fifth, it kindles in us a zeal for unity and union. For in God we observe such a great affection and zeal for union that: (1) not only have the persons of the Holy Trinity, in one and the same essence, willed to be one (1 John 5:7); but also, (2) those three persons, each by their own specific economic operation, willed to procure the union of the divine person with our human nature, when in this union of the incarnation, the Father gave the Son (Isa. 9:6; John 3:16), and sent him in the flesh (John 12:49; 14:24); the Son came in the flesh (1 John 4:2; 5:20); the Holy Spirit, by overshadowing the blessed Virgin, prepared the flesh, and united it with the soul, and both of these with the divine person; finally the whole, undivided Trinity fitted for him a body (Heb. 10:5; Ps. 40:6–7). In addition, (3) the Son of God came down from heaven (1 Cor. 15:47; John 6:41, 50), so that he might be united with the flesh (John 1:14), be manifested in it (1 Tim. 3:16). And he did so (4) to this end, that from the two united natures, we might have one Lord (1 Cor. 8:6; Eph. 4:5). In addition, (5) to this end, that we might be united to him (Heb. 2:11), that together with him might be made one body (1 Cor. 12:12), and one spirit (1 Cor. 6:17). And all these things (1) the Savior, united with us by the incarnation, urges, in order to procure union among us: "That they may all be one, as you, Father, are in me, and I in you, that

they also may be one in us, that the world may believe that you have sent me" (John 17:21). (2) The apostle urges: "Endeavoring to keep the unity of the spirit in the bond of peace, one body, one spirit...one hope of your calling, one Lord... one God and Father of all" (Eph. 4:3–7). (3) The matter itself urges: for what thing more incongruous could be imagined than for those who are united in the same humanity, in the same mystical body, through the same Spirit, to live among themselves so divided, so dissimilar and disagreeable?

6. *It stimulates to gratitude.* Motives

XL. Finally, sixth, the union of the two natures in the Mediator stimulates to gratitude, because by this union of the incarnation: (1) the Father so loved us that he gave his only begotten Son for us (John 3:16; Isa. 9:6), and with the Son, all things (Rom. 8:32). (2) The Son came to us, and in coming willed to be made the Son of Man, that he might make us sons of God (Gal. 4:4–5), indeed his firstborn sons (Heb. 12:23 with Ex. 4:22–23). Regarding this, Irenaeus says (bk. 5), "The Son of God, on account of his immeasurable love, was made to be what we are, that he might make us altogether what he is. He was made to be a partaker of our nature, that we might become sharers of the divine nature."[65] (3) That same Son of God willed to unite himself not only with our nature, but also with our natural infirmities and imperfections, that he might bear our infirmities (Heb. 4:15; Isa. 53:4), and substitute for them his own perfections (1 Cor. 1:30; Col. 2:9–10).

Manner

Accordingly, in this gratitude of ours: (1) let us embrace with a reciprocal love this God, who out of pure love gave his Son to us (Ps. 18:1), a love by which we yield our whole selves back to him (2 Cor. 8:5). (2) Let us receive with living faith the Son, who descended and came to us by this union (John 1:11–12), let us in turn now come to him (Isa. 55:1; Matt. 11:28), and let us kiss the Son (Ps. 2:12). And just as he in coming willed to be united with us in our flesh, so also let us be united to him in our spirit (1 Cor. 6:16–17; Eph. 4:4–5), so that the union may become reciprocal, as is customary in marriage (John 15:5; Song 2:16). In addition, (3) let us abhor all sins of any sort, inasmuch as they are apt to divide from him those united with him (Isa. 59:2), and on account of them the Father as it were separated the Son from him, and shut him out to take on such a miserable nature as our own (Rom. 8:32), and likewise by them we as much as lies in

---

65. Irenaeus, *Adversus haereses* in *PG* 7:1120; idem, *Against Heresies* in *ANF* 1:526.

us bring insult and dishonor to the human nature of the Son of God, to which he united himself, and we as it were defile it (1 Cor. 6:15–16; Heb. 6:6; 10:29). Furthermore, (4) because the Son of God delighted so much to be with us and to dwell with us (Prov. 8:31; cf. John 17:24) that he willed to be united with our nature (Heb. 2:11, 14), in turn let us delight to be with him, to dwell with him (Phil. 1:23; Matt. 18:20; cf. Luke 2:49), and cling to him, that we be made one spirit with him (1 Cor. 6:16–17). Compare the things which will occur, Lord willing, in the chapter on the incarnation of the Mediator.[66]

---

66. 1.5.10, esp. §XXXV

CHAPTER FIVE

The Threefold Office of the Mediator[1]

For which reason, holy brethren, partakers of the super-heavenly calling, consider the apostle and high priest of our confession, Jesus Christ.
—Hebrews 3:1

The transition to the following matters
I. We have considered the Mediator of the covenant of grace, first with respect to his names, and then with respect to his person. Now it is time for us to consider him with respect to his mediatorial office, which he performed by a threefold function: prophetic, priestly, and kingly. Of these the apostle mentions two in the text, not because he does not recognize the third (as the Socinians desire in order to serve their own hypotheses), inasmuch as he declares it elsewhere (Heb. 7:1–2), but because mentioning it did not seem so relevant to him for his present purpose.

The Exegetical Part
The text is resolved and explained.
II. In the text is contained a commendation of Christ as prophet and high priest, written to the Hebrews for this reason, that they might heed him. There is in it:
   A. The foundation of the commendation: ὅθεν, "For which reason," which is relative to what he had said throughout the previous chapters, in which he had demonstrated the divine and the human nature of the Mediator, inasmuch as in them are contained the unavoidably necessary requirements for the function of the mediatorial office, the contemplation of which he was now preparing himself for.

   B. The persons to whom he commends Christ, whom he names:

---

1. *De Trinitate Officii Mediatorii*, lit., "On the Threeness of the Mediatorial Office."

1. "Brethren," that is, Christians, who, just as when their teacher was still present with them they were called disciples, so also now that he was taken away from them through the ascension were usually called brethren, because they were now equals, and recognized the same heavenly Father among themselves as well as with their teacher Christ (John 20:17; Heb. 2:11), such that accordingly they treated each other with a brotherly spirit.

2. "Holy," ἁγίους. The term is judged by several to be a composite from the privative a and γῆ, earth, such that it would denote such a person who is "without earth," that is, not earthly. To others it descends from ἄζω, I worship, and thus means "venerable," and speaks of such a one who is venerable from his integrity and perfection. To others it is from ἄγω, I lead, such that it speaks of such a one who is active and devoted to struggles—that is, with the breathing changed, and an iota interspersed. In the antiphrastic sense, it sometimes denotes something contaminated and impure, from which comes the saying, *auri sacra fames*, "an accursed greed for gold."[2] Here it denotes someone who abhors impurity and is prone to purity and holiness. Moreover, Christians are named in this way partly from covenantal holiness, whereby, for example, the entire people of Israel was once called holy, and under the New Testament the infants of believers are said to be holy (1 Cor. 7:14), and adults, "called to be saints" (Rom. 1:7)—these you might not inappropriately deem "ecclesiastically holy," because they are admitted into the communion of the church and enjoy the privileges of the church; partly from real holiness, accomplished by the sanctification of the Spirit—all should be considered as such by the judgment of charity who are members of the church, as long as they do not reveal the marks of their own profanity, because they are partakers of ecclesiastical privileges.

3. "Partakers of the super-heavenly calling," κλήσεως ἐπουρανίου μέτοχοι. Κλήσεως, "of the calling," that is, not to just any office, whether civil or ecclesiastical, but to the communion of redemption and grace, the first step of which is calling. Ἐπουρανίου,[3] "heavenly" or "super-heavenly": not an earthly or human calling that occurs through an external proclamation of the Word only, but also an

---

2. Virgil, *Aeneid* 3.57; cf. Seneca, *De vita beata*, ch. 26.
3. Emended from Mastricht's ὑπουρανίου, per the Greek of Heb. 3:1.

internal calling that occurs through the illumination and renewal of the Holy Spirit. The apostle describes this calling as ἐπουράνιος on account of: (1) its origin, for it is accomplished by the Holy Spirit, or by the Father who is in heaven (Gal. 5:8; Phil. 3:14); then (2) on account of the means by which we are called, which is spiritual and heavenly, namely, the Word and the Spirit; (3) on account of its goal, which is heavenly glory, as if he should say, a calling which does not, like the law of Moses, leads us to an earthly possession of the land of Canaan, but to super-heavenly things, to the inheritance of the heavenly homeland. He calls them μέτοχοι, "partakers," of this calling so that he may signify that they have been made partakers together with him and with all other true Christians, and accordingly that they have a share in the same lot. Moreover, he heaps up all these titles upon the Hebrews, not only for this reason, that he may reveal to them his affection that is more than fraternal toward them, as well as obtain their reciprocal affection toward him, but also that he may distinguish Hebrews from each other. For there were Hebrews who were professed enemies of Christ and Christianity. There were also those who had crossed over to the profession of the Christian religion, but yet were still weak, those who thought that the Mosaic law should be joined with the Christian religion, and from this were more than lightly offended that Christians abrogated the ceremonial law given by God through Moses. The apostle is concerned with this second class throughout this entire epistle. Finally, there were Hebrews who were entirely and genuinely professing Christianity: it is these that the apostle usually seems to want to distinguish from the former ones with so many descriptions.

C. The argument of the commendation, or the duty commended, of which is noted:

1. The action: κατανοήσατε, "consider." Κατανοέω does not mean simply to understand or to examine something, but to direct the mind toward a matter with great exertion. It is usually joined with words which denote seeing (Acts 11:6; James 1:23). Κατανοήσατε, "diligently stir up your mind," "consider," that is, "how great and of what sort he is who abrogated the ceremonial law, namely, God, the very one who once introduced it at Sinai; and also a man, not a common man, but one who is united with God, greater than Moses himself: it was not Christians, mere men, who abrogated it on their own

initiative. Therefore, there is no reason for you to take such offense that the ceremonial law given by God through Moses has been abrogated." This at last is the chief goal of the entire epistle.

2. The object of the action, which he describes from:

a. A double office:

 i. Prophetic, when he calls him the ἀπόστολον, "apostle." Many think the term descends from στόλος, which expresses a nautical fleet, according to Demosthenes, Harpocration, and others. By others it is more correctly derived from ἀποστέλλω, and thus denotes a public emissary, as much civil (John 13:16) as ecclesiastical (thus throughout the New Testament). Moreover, first in an ordinary sense, it refers to emissaries of Christ (1 Cor. 15:7; Matt. 10:5, 16) for the declaration of the gospel, and thus to the church's extraordinary ministers of the first rank,[4] such as the prophets were under the Old Testament. In an extraordinary sense, it refers to Christ himself, because he was sent by the Father to declare to men, and also to dispatch, the business of redemption (Matt. 21:37; John 3:17; 6:57; 7:29; 9:7). Moreover, he is named this first because he acted among men as the Father's ambassador or Mediator (1 Tim. 2:5), and then because he functioned as his interpreter and spokesman (from which he is also designated the λόγος, Word), who revealed his hidden mind to men (John 1:18), so that with one term both his mediatorial office may be designated generally, and in specific, his prophetic function.

 ii. Priestly, when he names him the ἀρχιερέα, *pontifex*, "high priest." Among the Romans such a person was in charge of sacred matters and of those who presided over sacred rites. To the Hebrews it is כהן הגדול, the highest priest, to whom belonged all the duties of the common priests, but in addition it was his specific duty each year to enter the holy of holies, and to be in charge of both the sacred things and the priests. The antitype of this high priest was Christ, surpassing him in excellence

---

4. *primipilos*. The *primipilus* (official title in the Roman Republic: *primus princeps prioris centuriae*) was the first centurion or senior centurion in a legion that possessed approximately sixty centurions. See Juvenal, *Aquila* xiv.197; T. S. Carr, *A Manual of Roman Antiquities* (London, 1836), 225–27.

as much as a body does its shadow. The apostle adds by way of distinction,[5] namely so that he might distinguish this our high priest under the New Testament from that one under the Old Testament—he adds, I say, τῆς ὁμολογίας ἡμῶν, "of our confession." The word ὁμολογία is from legal or covenantal usage, expressing an agreement, a compact, a covenant, where the one who stipulates ἐπερωτᾷ, asks, and the one who pledges ὁμολογεῖ, agrees, and thus an agreement is made with words. In divine things, the misery of man as well as the righteousness of God demanded, and the mercy of the Son of God promised, the work of redemption. Or, it is from ecclesiastical usage, and thus again it expresses either a profession, that is, "of the faith and religion that with one mind you profess with us," or a confession, that is, "of the apostle and high priest whom we confess with one heart and mouth."

b. Names: "Jesus Christ." Of these we spoke of expressly in ch. 3 of this book.[6]

The Dogmatic Part

The Mediator executes his office as a prophet, priest, and king.

III. From this it is evident that the Mediator as the God-man executes the mediatorial office in different ways, namely as a prophet or ἀπόστολος, apostle, and a *pontifex* or ἀρχιερεύς, high priest, to which we will add from other Scripture passages (inasmuch as it is set beyond controversy among all, at least who accept the Scriptures, even the Jews and Socinians themselves), as a βασιλεύς, king (Ps. 2:6; Zech. 9:9). For this reason, he is distinctly designated in the Scriptures as (1) a prophet (Deut. 18:15; Acts 3:22; Isa. 61:1–2; cf. Luke 4:16–21); (2) a priest (Ps. 110:4; Heb. 7:15, 17, 24, 26; Zech. 6:12–13); (3) a king (Rev. 17:14; John 18:33, 36).

Six reasons

IV. Teaching the same are: (1) the Old Testament types prefiguring those three functions in the Mediator, specifically, the prophetic, which Moses especially prefigured (Deut. 18:15–20; Acts 7:37); the priestly, which the priests, the high priest, and Melchizedek prefigured (Heb. 2:17; 5:4–6; Heb. 7); and the kingly,

---

5. διακριτικῶς
6. 1.5.3 §§VIII, XI

which Melchizedek king of Salem, David, and Solomon prefigured (Heb. 7:2; Jer. 23; Isa. 9:6–7; Luke 1:32–33; Rev. 19:16). In addition, (2) this triple function of the Mediator is required by the triple necessity of a sinner who is to be redeemed by the Mediator. Through it the sinner labors under: (a) crass ignorance (Eph. 4:17–18; 1 Cor. 2:8–9, 14; Rev. 3:17); (b) extreme alienation from God and from all salvation, indeed bitter enmity toward God, his law, and all things that concern God (Eph. 2:11–12; Col. 1:21; Rom. 8:7); (c) total powerlessness to turn back toward God (Rom. 5:6; 8:3; Eph. 2:1–3). Now, the prophetic function heals the ignorance; the priestly, the alienation and enmity; the kingly, the powerlessness. The same is shown by (3) the order of conveying salvation through the Mediator, inasmuch as: (a) it had to be revealed to the ignorant, (b) procured and acquired for the alienated, and (c) applied to the powerless. For if it were revealed and not also acquired, it would be like a remedy which consists only in the speculation and imagination of the physician. If it were revealed and procured, but not applied, it would be like a drug that was ever so effective, but not applied to the wound. Now, salvation is revealed by the Mediator as a prophet, acquired by him as a priest, and applied by him as a king. Thus (4) the Mediator also first declared salvation in his life, then acquired it by his death, and finally applies it by sending the Holy Spirit after his ascension. Again, (5) first he taught as a prophet, then offered himself as a priest, and finally entered into glory as a king. Last, (6) his anointing, from which we have already pointed out that he is denominated *Christ*, the anointed one, evinces this triple function of the mediatorial office. For it is well known that only prophets (1 Kings 19:16), priests (Ex. 28:41; 30:30), and kings (1 Sam. 16:12–13) were anointed.

The Elenctic Part

It is asked: 1. Was the Messiah promised in the past to have
but one function, that is, the kingly one?

V. It is asked, first, whether the Messiah promised in the past was to have but one function, that is, the kingly one. The Jews, out of pure hatred for our Jesus as the Messiah, deny that the Messiah was to have any other besides the one kingly function. The Reformed acknowledge three, because: (1) since in the past, as the Jews acknowledge, the anointing was occupied with a triple function— prophetic, priestly, and kingly—and the Messiah is also called the anointed one par excellence, it does not seem suitable that it be extended to only one or another function, but to all the functions, that it may absorb the perfection of them all. Especially since (2) the effect[7] of the triple function seems to be represented of

---

7. ἀποτέλεσμα

the Messiah in Daniel 9:24–26, where it is said that the Messiah is to be anointed, and to seal up the vision and prophecy, to expiate iniquities, and to usher in righteousness, and be נגיד, the Prince. The same (3) seems to occur in Zechariah 6:12–13, where it is said that the man צמח, the Branch (whom the Jews themselves understand as the Messiah), shall build the temple as a prophet, shall be a priest, and finally shall sit and govern on his throne as a king. Add that (4) since there were in the past not lacking those who simultaneously sustained a double function—as Melchizedek did the priestly and kingly (Gen. 14), David the prophetic and kingly, Samuel the prophetic and priestly—these by reason of their function would be, among those anointed, more perfect than the Messiah, whom nonetheless the Jews themselves confess as the anointed one par excellence. Indeed, for the anointed one par excellence, how could it be more fitting than if he should be said to have been inaugurated to a triple function? For this reason the Jews celebrate the triple crown, שלשה כתרים in *Pirkei Avot* 4:9, "Rabbi Shimon speaks of the crown of the law, of the priesthood, and of the kingdom."[8] Especially (5) because he is expressly called a prophet in Deuteronomy 18:15, and such who is likened to Moses, כמני, "like me," and in verse 18, "I will raise them up a prophet from among their brethren, *like you*, and I will put my words in his mouth," whereas in 34:10 it is expressly said that a prophet did not arise equal to Moses. In fact, he is such whom they are commanded to hear, אליו תשמעון, "To him shall you listen" (Deut. 18:15). And he is also expressly called a priest in Psalm 110:4. This Psalm Rabbi Saadia Gaon confessed should be understood about the Messiah, in his *Commentary* on Daniel 7:13.[9] Likewise in Zechariah 6:12–13, והיה כהן, "And he shall be a priest," which passage the Jews everywhere explain as about the Messiah. Let there be added that (6) both prophetic and priestly things are no less attributed to him than kingly things. For what did the prophets do? They taught (Jer. 7:25–26; Neh. 9:26); and this belongs to the Messiah (from Isa. 61:1; 42:1–2). What did the priests do? They expiated (Lev. 4:20–21); and this is attributed to the Messiah (Dan. 9:24).

---

8. Pirkei Avot 4:9, משניות (*Mishnayoth*), 7 vols., 2nd rev. edition corrected and enlarged (Gateshead: Judaica Press, Ltd. 1990), 4:521, "Rabbi Shimon said, 'There are three crowns: the crown of [the study of] the Law, the crown of priesthood, and the crown of royalty, but the crown of a good name surpasses them all.'" Cf. C. Albeck, H. Yalon, et al., eds., ששה סדרי משנה (*Shishah sidre Mishnah*), 6 vols. (Jerusalem: Mosad Byalik; Tel Aviv: Devir, 1952–1959), 4:371, רַבִּי שִׁמְעוֹן אוֹמֵר. שְׁלֹשָׁה כְתָרִים הֵם, כֶּתֶר תּוֹרָה וְכֶתֶר כְּהֻנָּה וְכֶתֶר מַלְכוּת, וְכֶתֶר שֵׁם טוֹב עוֹלֶה עַל גַּבֵּיהֶן.

9. Saadia ben Yosef Gaon (892–942), *The Book of Daniel: The Commentary of R. Saadia Gaon Edition and Translation*, ed. and trans. J. Alobaidi (Bern: Peter Lang, 2005), 541–43. Alobaidi's edition contains extensive commentary and notes upon forty extant Hebrew and Arabic manuscripts, their location, condition, and integrity. Regarding Rabi Saadia on Daniel 7:13, cf. Hugo Grotius on Matt. 1:22, in *Opera*, 3 vols. (Amsterdam: Joannes Blaeu, 1639), 2:12.

The objections of the Jews: The first
Nor do they have anything they may object except: (1) that Deuteronomy 18:15 and 18 ought not to be understood of the Messiah, but either of Joshua, as Ibn Ezra supposes, or of any prophet after Moses, as Rabbi David Kimchi and Rashi suppose; or of Jeremiah in particular, as some others suppose.[10] To these we respond: (a) that Joshua certainly was the successor of Moses, but nowhere is he named a prophet singularly and distinctively. Nor (b) is it said that God spoke in such a way through him as he did through Moses (Deut. 18:18). Nor (c) was it either Joshua, or Jeremiah, or any other, who comes to be likened to Moses (cf. Deut. 34:10). Nor (d) of all the subsequent prophets can those things be understood, because not only is "a prophet" mentioned, in the singular, not "prophets," but also, "I will raise up," אָקִים (Deut. 18:18; יָקִים in v. 15), seems to breathe of something singular. We will perhaps supply more on this matter in chapter 6 to follow.[11]

The second
(2) That Psalm 110:4 should be understood not of the Messiah, but either of Abraham, as Rashi and Rabbi Lipmann desire, or of David, as Ibn Ezra and Kimchi think.[12] Against them the text itself speaks, and in more than one way,

---

10. See Deut. 18:11–15 in Abraham ben Meir Ibn Ezra (c. 1089–c. 1164), *Ibn Ezra's Commentary on the Pentateuch: Deuteronomy (Devarim)*, trans. H. N. Strickman (New York: Menorah Publishing Co., 2001), "The latter refers to Joshua 'unto him ye shall hearken' (ibid.), which is later followed by 'and the children of Israel hearkened unto him' (Deut. 34:9) is proof of this. The fact that we do not find any other prophet but Joshua entering Canaan is additional proof of this. It is also possible that our verse lays down a general rule for each and every prophet who will arise after Moses." See Deut. 18:15, vol. 5 of Rashi (1040–1105), *Pentateuch with Rashi's Commentary Translated into English*, trans. M. Rosenbaum and A. M. Silbermann et al., 5 vols. (London: Shapiro Valentine & Co., 1929–1934; Jerusalem: Routledge & Kegan Paul, 1973). E.g. Isaiah 53, Kimchi (Radak, 1160–1235), *Commentary of David Kimchi on Isaiah*, trans. L. Finkelstein, vol. 20 in Columbia University Oriental Studies (New York: AMS Press, Inc., 1985). For almost the exact same list of authors and points that Mastricht raises, see John Owen, "Exercitatio IX: Promises of the Messiah Vindicated," §10 in *Exercitations on the Epistle to the Hebrew, also concerning the Messiah* (London: Robert White, 1668), 99; cf. idem, *The Works of John Owen*, ed. William H. Goold (London: Johnstone and Hunter, 1853), 18:190–91.

11. 1.5.6 §II

12. See Ps. 110:4 in *Rashi's Commentary on Psalms*, trans. Mayer I. Gruber (Philadelphia: Jewish Publication Society, 2007); Ibn Ezra, *Rabbi Abraham Ibn Ezra's Commentary on Books 3–5 of Psalms: Chapters 73–150*, trans. Norman Strickman (New York: Touro University Press, 2016); *The Commentary of David Kimhi on the Fifth Book of the Psalms. CVII–CL*, trans. Jacob Bosniak (New York: Jewish Theological Seminary of America, 1954). Yomtov Lipmann Muelhausen (fl. 1420), wrote a polemical work against Christianity, whose title translates "Book of Victory," *Liber Nizachon* סֵפֶר נִצָּחוֹן, ed. T. Hackspan (Nuremberg: Wolfgang Endterus, 1644), 199–200; 508–11. On Hackspan's printed edition and procurement of the Hebrew manuscript by deceit and

because (a) they have not been placed at the right hand of God; nor (b) has their rod been sent out of Zion; nor (c) were they constituted priests; nor (d) that also with an oath; nor (e) are they eternal; nor (f) does it speak in particular of David, since according to the title, David is speaking of his Lord. Compare chapter 7.[13]

2. Instead of the threefold office of the Mediator in Christ, ought a double office to be admitted?

VI. It is asked, second, whether instead of a threefold office of the Mediator in Christ, a double office ought to be admitted. The Socinians, since they mix the priestly office with the kingly, to the end that he would not be a priest truly and properly so called, nor accordingly would have sacrificed himself on earth for our sins, and by sacrificing have atoned for them, recognize only two offices—the prophetic and the kingly—and mix the priestly with the kingly, such that only at length in heaven did he offer himself to the Father. The Reformed on the contrary enumerate three different offices of Christ, because: (1) without a doubt the priestly and kingly are distinct functions, which are also distinctly attributed to the Mediator (Ps. 2:6; 110:4), nor does any reason demand mixing in Christ functions that are distinct in themselves. (2) That he was a priest truly and properly so called, who supplied on earth all things priestly, will come to be expressly demonstrated in the controversies of chapter 7.[14] We will presuppose here from those sections that the priestly office was not in fact the same as the kingly.

Objections

Nor does it help them that in Hebrews 3:1 only two functions are mentioned, the prophetic and the priestly, for it is not accordingly concluded either that he did not have the third, since the kingly function is expressly attributed to him, not only elsewhere in the Scriptures, but also in the very Epistle to the Hebrews (1:2, 8), or that the priestly function coincides with the kingly, because the acts of the latter clearly differ from those of the former, just as, from a review of both, will be evident to the eye.

The Practical Part

The practice: 1. Convinces us of the truth and sufficiency of Christ's mediatorial office.
VII. The practical part of this observation convinces us, first, of the truth and sufficiency of Christ's mediatorial office. For since, on the one hand, he cannot be

---

theft from a rabbi, see "Lipmann, Jomtob" in J. Strong and J. McClintock, eds., *The Cyclopedia of Biblical, Theological, and Ecclesiastical Literature* (New York: Harper & Brothers, 1880).

13. 1.5.7 §II treats Ps. 110:4 in detail.

14. 1.5.7 §§XV–XVI

a sufficient Mediator who is not a prophet, that he may inwardly and outwardly teach his own; a priest, that he may reconcile them with God; a king, that he may govern, sanctify, glorify them; and on the other hand, there has never been anyone who has borne this triple function—there have indeed been those who sustained one, or even two, of the three, but we read of none second to our Mediator who sustained the three of them simultaneously—it cannot but be that he, and indeed he alone, is the most sufficient Mediator, who is able to save to the uttermost (Heb. 7:25), who was made for us wisdom from God, as a prophet; righteousness, as a priest; sanctification and redemption or glorification, as a king (1 Cor. 1:30). Who alone is for us the way, as a prophet; the truth, that is, of the priestly and ceremonial types (John 1:17), as a priest; and the life, as a king, in such a way that no one can come to the Father, but by him (John 14:6).

To what purpose
And to what purpose does it convince us of this truth and sufficiency of Christ's mediatorial office? Except that: (1) we would take hold of the true and most sufficient Mediator with a true and living faith (John 1:12; Phil. 3:7–9); (2) we would securely rest in him as the one and only Mediator (1 Tim. 2:5), with all others neglected and rejected (John 6:68; Ps. 16:4–5; 73:25); and so forth.

2. It comforts us in any adverse circumstance.
VIII. Second, this threefold mediatorial office, and the fullest sufficiency of our Mediator which emerges from it, supplies the most effective consolation in every adverse circumstance, as from this he is able to save to the uttermost (Heb. 7:25). Namely, in a spiritual circumstance, if we are vexed by: (1) ignorance, blindness, and sluggishness of mind (1 Cor. 2:14; Eph. 4:17–18), nor is a suitable teacher available (Ps. 74:9); because in the Mediator we have as our teacher the one prophet worth them all (Matt. 23:10), who can teach us externally (Matt. 4:17; 22:16), and illuminate us internally (John 1:4–5, 7–9), who has been made for us wisdom (1 Cor. 1:30), and liberally supplies wisdom to those who ask (James 1:5). If we are vexed by (2) enmity with God, we have a priest who reconciles us to God by the offering of himself (Rom. 5:10; Eph. 2:14–16). If (3) any things necessary are lacking, we have a priest who has entered for us into the holy of holies, so that he may appear for us before God (Heb. 9:11–12), and has procured for us access with confidence (Eph. 3:12), so that we may come with confidence to the throne of grace, that we may obtain mercy, and find grace to help in time of need (Heb. 4:16), so much so that whatever we ask in his name, we will more certainly than certain gain (John 16:23). If in a bodily circumstance (4) we are pressed by the abundance, power, and cruelty of any enemies

(Ps. 3:1–2), we have a king who can break them with a rod of iron, like a potter's vessels (Ps. 2:6–9). And thus in all other remaining necessities, as will be evident in the particular explanation of the individual functions.[15]

3. It exhorts us: (1) To seek the Mediator who is three in offices. (2) To retain him. (3) To love him. And (4) to use him.

IX. Accordingly, third, it persuades us to strive with all our strength that: (1) we may certainly become partakers through faith of the Mediator (Phil. 3:7–9), who from his threefold office is abundantly sufficient for all our necessities (Phil. 4:19). (2) Having been made partakers, we may inseparably cling to him, and never desert him (Gen. 32:26; Ps. 63:1, 8; Luke 24:29). (3) We may love him above anything else (Matt. 10:37), with a love (a) of concupiscence and desire (Ps. 42:1; Rev. 22:17, 20); (b) of complacency or acquiescence (Ps. 73:25; 16:5–6); (c) of benevolence and obedience (2 Cor. 5:9). And finally, that (4) we may turn the sufficiency of this threefold mediatorial function in every circumstance to our use, by resting upon him (Isa. 10:20; Song 8:5). And so forth. Compare the practice of chapter 2, on the Mediator.

---

15. 1.5.6 §XXVII; 1.5.7 §§XXIX–XXXI; 1.5.8 §XXVII

CHAPTER SIX

The Mediator as a Prophet

The Lord your God will raise up for you a prophet from your midst, from your brethren, like me; him you shall hear.
—Deuteronomy 18:15

Progressing to the prophetic office
I. As a preface, we have examined in a more general way the threefold office of the Mediator; now we come to consider individually its individual functions, and among these, first, the prophetic function, about which Moses prophesies in Deuteronomy 18:15.

The Exegetical Part
The text is resolved and explained.
II. In these words is contained a famous prophecy concerning the Messiah, the prophet to come. In it two things occur:

A. The promise of a certain exceptional prophet. In which is designated:

1. The promised prophet: נביא, from נבא in the Niphil, which signifies the receiving of the prophecy from God, and the command to speak to others. For which reason נביא denotes a prophet, a seer, a scribe, and even an interpreter (Ex. 7:1); in Greek, προφήτης. Properly it speaks of such an extraordinary minister of the church who speaks for God, having been moved infallibly by God (2 Peter 1:20–21), who likewise predicts future contingencies; although sometimes it speaks of anyone occupied in interpreting the prophets of the Old Testament (1 Cor. 14:1). In this passage it denotes a certain exceptional prophet. But who then is it? There are: (1) those who want Joshua to be understood, others Jeremiah; these we rejected in the preceding chapter, §V. There are those who prefer any prophet to be understood, such as, with the Jews, the renowned Grotius and several others—except that they think Christ should also be enumerated

with these prophets. This they gather (a) from the preceding words, "Do not consult diviners," as if it were saying, "Because there will not be lacking prophets whom you may consult when it will be necessary"; which reasoning would not be appropriate if the passage is understood about Christ alone. (b) A response is being made to the demand of the Israelites that God might speak to them through an interpreter, which God assented to. (c) Here he opposes the prophet to a false prophet. From this (2) others do understand the passage about the prophets as types, but about Christ as the truth, first and foremost. (3) Others prefer the passage to be understood as about Christ alone, because the properties of this prophet taken together fit Christ alone, namely, (a) it is predicted that this prophet would be raised up from the brothers of the Israelites (v. 15), which, as all acknowledge, even the Jews, applies to the Messiah (Isa. 11:1). (b) He would be no less great than Moses (v. 18), whereas even the Jews acknowledge, from Deuteronomy 34:10, that since Moses none similar to him has arisen. So Maimonides on the Mishnah, and likewise in the *Guide of the Perplexed* (pt. 2, ch. 35), and Manasseh ben Israel in his questions on Deuteronomy (q. 11).[1] Now, that only the Messiah is similar to Moses, indeed greater, the Jews themselves acknowledge: thus Rabbi Isaac ben Abraham in *Hizzuk Emunah*, throughout the whole book.[2] (c) This prophet is said to be the Mediator between God and Israel, through whom God would speak to them (vv. 16–17), which cannot be said of any common prophet. (d) This prophet would perform the teaching office (v. 18), which is declared about the Messiah (Isa. 50:4; 61:1–2; 42:2–3), as Rabbi Manasseh ben Israel acknowledges in *On the Resurrection* (bk. 3, ch. 3).[3] (e) As the Jews willingly concede, hearing this

---

1. See Maimonides (Rambam), Sefer Ha'Madda (The Book of Knowledge), Hilchot Teshuvah (The Laws of Repentance), ch. 9, sect. 2, in *Mishneh Torah: A New Translation with Commentaries and notes*, trans. E. Touger, 14 vols. in 23 (Jerusalem/New York: Moznaim, 1992–2007), vol. 1; see ב .פרק תשיעי ,חלכת תשובה ,ספר מדה in idem, משנה תורה, 4 vols. (Venice: Meir Parenzo for Alvise Bragadini, 1574), vol. 1; idem, *Guide for the Perplexed*, 223–25; Manasseh ben Israel (1604–1657), *Conciliator, sive de convenientia locorum S. Scripturae, quae pugnare inter se videntur* (Frankfurt, 1633), 235–40; q. 189 on Deut. 33:10–12, idem, *The Conciliator of R. Manasseh ben Israel; A Reconcilement of the Apparent Contradictions in Holy Scripture*, vol. 1, *The Pentateuch*, ed. E. H. Lindo (London: Duncan and Malcom, 1842), 300–307.

2. Isaac ben Abraham Troki (c. 1533–c. 1594), חזוק אמנה (Breslau, 1873); idem, חזוק אמונה *or Faith Strengthened*, trans. Moses Mocatta, (London: J. Wertheimer and Co., 1851).

3. Manasseh ben Israel, *De resurrectione mortuorum*, 2nd ed. (Groningen: Aemilius Spinnikir, 1676), 263–69.

prophet par excellence is the same as what is owed to the Messiah. (f) This prophet is understood to be such who would not speak on his own impulse, but by the divine instinct and command (v. 18). And this the Jews grant concerning the Messiah. (g) This prophet is promised to be such about whom God threatens that he will punish anyone who will not hear him (v. 19), which even the Jews acknowledge about the Messiah, so much so that they think Gog and Magog will be eradicated by the Messiah since they will refuse to obey him. (h) The Jews themselves, at the beginning of the New Testament, acknowledged that this passage was to be understood concerning the Messiah (John 6:14; 1:45), and with them Peter also interpreted it concerning the Messiah (Acts 3:22–26), as did Stephen before the Jews (Acts 7:37; cf. Matt. 17:5; John 5:46). From these three opinions, the second, in the middle, seems the most pleasing to me, because: (1) the first, which excludes Christ, or does not include him except as some ordinary prophet, is manifestly false by the reasons of the third opinion; but the third is manifestly false by reasons of the first opinion; nor (2) do the reasons of the third extend further than to prove Christ is involved as the primary prophet; moreover, (3) the second is most congruent both with the goal and with the whole analogy of the context.

2. The properties of this prophet, namely his:

    a. Genealogy: "from your midst," "from your brethren." The people had sought that God would not afterwards speak to them immediately, as had happened at Horeb: God assented, and promised to them a prophet who would be a man, and indeed one from their midst, in fact their brother, whom they could consult with boldness, and who would respond to them with brotherly affection, as one of like passions, who would be the God-man, to whom accordingly they could safely submit, as the God who would not know how to deceive or be deceived, and as a man who could open wide the truth to them with a living voice, yet not so terribly as God.

    b. Authority: כמני, "like me," similar to me, equal, indeed greater. Such in fact was the Messiah, and certainly he alone, with respect first to: (1) person, insofar as both were true men and Jews from the midst of their brethren. Then with respect to (2) office, insofar as both were, although in a different degree, mediators interceding between God and the Israelites (Gal. 3:19; 1 Tim. 2:5).

(3) Faithfulness in the performance of their office (Heb. 3:2, 5–6). (4) Miracles, in which both were abundant, and the latter certainly much more abundant than the former. (5) Excellence, by which both conversed quite familiarly with God (John 1:18; 3:13).

3. The calling of this prophet, belonging to which are noted:

    a. The one calling, namely: (1) "Jehovah," one in essence, about whom we have spoken elsewhere;[4] (2) "God, אלהים, three in persons; (3) "your God," that is, through the covenant of grace. For no man takes this honor to himself, but he who is called (Heb. 5:4).

    b. The calling, יקים לך, "He will raise up for you." "He will raise up," he will establish, that is, by a legitimate calling, foreordination, and sending. "For you," for Israel, that is, first the bodily one, and then the spiritual Israel.

B. The prescribing of the duty that must be observed with respect to this prophet: אליו תשמעון, "Him you shall hear." שמע, to hear, in Greek ἀκούω and ὑπακούω, either with the ears or with the mind, and thus it expresses, to obey, to believe what has been said, and to do what has been prescribed.

The Dogmatic Part

That the Messiah is a prophet: It is proved by the Scriptures.

III. Therefore it is certain and indubitable that the Messiah promised to Israel is a prophet, because: (1) he is so named expressly in the text, and in Acts 3:22 and 7:37, and in those passages which on this matter we added in the explanation of the text. (2) He is named a great prophet (Luke 7:16; 24:19). (3) He is synonymously called a teacher sent by God (John 3:2), Rabbi, master,[5] teacher (Matt. 23:8, 10), the apostle of our confession (Heb. 3:1), a shepherd (Ezek. 34:23; 37:24), the good shepherd (John 10:11), that great shepherd of the sheep (Heb. 13:20), the ἀρχιποίμην, chief Shepherd (1 Peter 5:4), our lawgiver (Isa. 33:22), Counselor (Isa. 9:6), a minister of the circumcision (Rom. 15:8). (4) The acts of the prophetic office are attributed to him throughout both Testaments: the announcement of the gospel (e.g. Isa. 61:1–2; Ps. 40:9–10), the prediction of future things (Rev. 1:1; Matt. 24), and so forth.

---

4. 1.2.4 §VIII

5. *magister*, a master of students, as opposed to *dominus*, a master of servants

It is confirmed by reasons.

And also, being a prophet was fitting to: (1) his person, insofar as he is the eternal and substantial wisdom of the Father (Prov. 8:12, 22, 24), the λόγος ὑποστατικός, hypostatic Word, to whom it is fitting to act as the interpreter of God with men (John 1:18)—and such interpreters were called prophets (Ex. 7:1). (2) Our natural ignorance, which nothing can more effectively aid than the God-man, the very light of the world, illuminating every person coming into this world (John 1:9). (3) The things to be taught, for which no one is more sufficient than the Son of God, the prophet (Heb. 2:3), who is in the bosom of the Father (John 1:18).

What a prophet is in general
IV. Now, where the word προφήτης, *prophet*, comes from, whether from προφάναι, to show forth or to foreshow; and what prophecy is in general, namely, a faculty conferred by the Spirit of God upon some certain people, without human instruction, of knowing divine, sublime, and hidden things with certainty, and explaining them to others for the edification of the church; furthermore, out of a desire for brevity, we set what degrees there are in prophecy and similar such things aside. If someone is anxious to know, he can go to Peter Martyr Vermigli on 1 Samuel 19:24, or Caspar Peucer, *On Divination*, or Pierre Du Moulin, *The Seer*; and others.[6]

What the prophetic function of the Mediator is
It will be sufficient for us here to have defined the prophetic function of the Mediator, that it is that part of the mediatorial office in which, as much under the Old Testament as under the New, he reveals to men the whole counsel of God regarding their restoration and salvation.

The inauguration to the function
The inauguration to this function, by which he was solemnly declared by his Father himself the supreme teacher of the church, appears in Matthew 3:16–17, and is repeated with the addition, "Hear him," in Matthew 17:5: that is, as is fitting to him who is the eternal and substantial wisdom (Prov. 8:1ff.; 1 Cor. 1:24),

---

6. Peter Martyr Vermigli (1499–1562), *The Common Places of the Most Famous and Renowned Diuine Doctor Peter Martyr* (London: Henry Denham and Henry Middleton, 1583), 17–24; idem, *Loci communes*, 11th ed. (Geneva: Petrus Albertus, 1624), 5–8; Caspar Peucer (1525–1602), *Commentarius de praecipuis divinationum generibus* (Zerbst: Bonaventura Faber, 1591); Pierre Du Moulin (1568–1658), *Vates, seu de praecognitione futurorum* (Leiden: Joannes Maire, 1640).

and who in time was made for us wisdom (1 Cor. 1:30), and thus is the Word and spokesman of the Father to mankind (John 1:1).

He performed the prophetic function by revealing teaching: 1. Immediately,
(1) under the Old Testament, and (2) under the New Testament
V. He performed his prophetic office partly by revealing and promulgating his teaching, and partly by illuminating the minds of his own so that they may receive the teaching. He reveals and promulgates his teaching in his Word, which is from this also called the Word of Christ (Col. 3:16), first immediately, and that under a twofold period: (1) of the Old Testament (1 Peter 1:10–11), where he opened the will of God, concerning the restoration of the sinner to be procured through the future Messiah, to the patriarchs, prophets, and holy men of God, in visions, dreams, Urim and Thummim, inspirations, oracles, and so forth (Gen. 46:2; Dan. 7:1; 1 Sam. 28:6; cf. Acts 7:38), until finally that teaching, by the inspiration of the Holy Spirit, was consigned to writing and sealed. (2) Of the New Testament, where, as the God-man, in whom lie hidden all the treasures of wisdom and knowledge (Col. 2:3), he revealed to mankind the manifold wisdom of God (Eph. 3:10), and so great a salvation, which at first was declared by the Lord (Heb. 2:2–3), the wisdom of God in a mystery, even the hidden wisdom (1 Cor. 2:7–10).

By preaching to all
And that (1) by personal preaching, when, after his baptism, approximately in his thirtieth year, through three and a half years (which years Baronio, Tornielli, Salian,[7] and others most effectively gather from the four Passovers which intervened, as we read in John: the first we read in John 2:13, the second in 5:1, the third in 6:4, and the fourth, the funerary feast at his death,[8] in John 12:1), he declared the gospel (Mark 1:9, 14), interpreted the law and vindicated it from the corruptions and perversions of the Pharisees (Matt. 5), erected a new dispensation of the covenant of grace, which is called the New Testament, doing so, namely, as the Mediator of the new covenant (Heb. 8:6; 9:15; 12:24).

---

7. Cesare Baronio (1538–1607), *Epitome annalium ecclesiasticorum* (Venice: Io. Antonius Franzinus, 1602), 6–22; Agostino Tornielli, *Annales Sacri*, 4th ed., 2 vols. (Antwerp: Plantin, 1620), 2:646, 648, 655, 665–66; Jacques Salian (1557–1640), *Annalium ecclesiasticorum Veteris Testamenti epitome* (Rouen: Ioann. et David Berthelin, 1655), 1085, 1094–95, 1097, 1101.

8. θανάσιμον, Dutch: *doodfeest.* Cf. Johannes Marckius "De Paschate," *Compendium Theologiae Christianae Didactico Elencticum* (Amsterdam: R. & G. Wetstenius, 1722), 566.

By instructing the apostles
(2) By the instruction of the apostles, inasmuch as (a) he informed their mind (Luke 24:45); (b) he gave them commandments to preach the gospel (Matt. 10; 28:19–20); (c) he directed them by the Spirit (John 16:13–14; 14:26); finally, (d) he committed the canon of the New Testament, by the Spirit, to be committed to letters and sealed (Rev. 22:18–19). And in this way our prophet revealed the doctrine of salvation immediately under both Testaments.

2. Mediately, under (1) the Old Testament as well as (2) the New
VI. Second, he does so mediately, and that again: (1) under the Old Testament, when he taught the church by a ministry that was either extraordinary, first by patriarchs and prophets, then by his own Spirit (1 Peter 1:10–12; 3:18–20), or ordinary, namely that of the priests and Levites (Mal. 2:7). (2) Under the New Testament, when: (a) he planted the church by the extraordinary ministry of the apostles, prophets, and evangelists (Eph. 4:11–13; Matt. 28:20; 2 Cor. 4:6–7); (b) he cultivates and preserves it by the ordinary ministry of pastors and teachers (Eph. 4:11–13), who are all ambassadors of Christ, through whom he pleads that we be reconciled to God (2 Cor. 5:19–20). And thus by revealing and promulgating did the Mediator perform his prophetic office.

He performed his prophetic function also by illuminating.
VII. He also does the same by illuminating the mind (Luke 24:45) and bending the will of his own, so that they may understand and receive the revealed teaching (John 17:8). This is the chief effect[9] of the prophetic office, this anointing from the Holy One, which teaches us all things (1 John 2:20, 27), from which we are said to have been taught by God (John 6:45). This anointing happened more obscurely under the Old Testament, and as it were hidden under a veil (2 Cor. 3:12–14), whereas under the New Testament, most clearly, with unveiled face, we as it were beholding as in a mirror the glory of the Lord (2 Cor. 3:18).

The objects of the prophetic function
VIII. These acts of the prophetic function were distinctly occupied with: (1) the will of God in general, which he revealed in its entirety to his own (John 15:15; 1:18). (2) Future things, by foretelling them (Matt. 24:4–5ff.) and revealing them to his own (Rev. 1:19). (3) The law, by explaining and vindicating it, as we have said (Matt. 5). (4) The prophecies of the prophets, by interpreting and applying them (Luke 24:25, 27): for example, he interpreted Psalm 110:1

---

9. ἀποτέλεσμα

(Matt. 22:43–45), he applied Daniel 9:27 (Matt. 24:15), he explained Isaiah 61:1 and 42:7 (Luke 4:17–18). (5) The gospel (Matt. 11:5), until then set forth more obscurely under the Old Testament, and as it were hidden under a veil, by bringing it out into the open light (2 Tim. 1:10), and also by first commencing the gospel of fulfillment (Matt. 4:17). To all these is added (6) that by various and stupendous miracles, he confirmed the truth of his function, teaching, and person (John 5:36).

The virtues evident in the prophetic function
IX. In all these things, throughout the whole course of his earthly life, he was occupied: (1) prudently, employing familiar parables, such as those that come from the seed, the weeds, the mustard seed, the leaven, the hidden treasure, the pearl, the casting of a net into the sea (Matt. 13 and elsewhere). (2) Freely, without partiality,[10] as even his enemies confessed (Matt. 22:16). Furthermore, (3) effectively, such that no one could resist his wisdom (Matt. 21:25, 27; 22:19, 22, 32–34; Matt. 7:29). In addition, (4) eloquently, even to the point of a miracle (Ps. 45:2; Luke 4:22; John 7:45–46). Finally, (5) with such great zeal, that he therefore frequently neglected food (Mark 3:20), and there was nothing that he did not do to provoke his hearers to repentance (Matt. 23:37; Luke 19:42).

The Elenctic Part
It is asked: 1. Is the Messiah a prophet?
X. It is asked, first, whether the Messiah promised in times past would be a prophet. The Jews, out of pure, unadulterated hatred of Christ and the Christian religion, deny it; Christians affirm it. We have spoken of the Christians' reasons in the preceding chapter, §V, vindicated them in the exegetical part of this chapter, and confirmed them through his prophetic acts (from Isa. 61:1–2; Ps. 40:9–10). Nor is there available for the Jews anything to argue to the contrary, besides their frivolous evasions on Deuteronomy 18:15.

2. Is he alone that great prophet? Or is Muhammad also?
XI. It is asked, second, whether our Jesus alone is that great prophet promised in times past to Israel, or whether Muhammad should be counted with him, indeed preferred to him. The Christians affirm the prior, and declare not only that Muhammad was not that great prophet, but that he was no prophet at all, indeed rather that he was a false prophet and a most vile impostor. The Muslims

---

10. *citra* προσωποληψίαν

on the contrary do profess that Moses was a great prophet, and Christ a greater one, but that their Muhammad was the greatest, indeed, distinctly that one whom Moses designated in Deuteronomy 18:15–18. However, because the Muslims: (1) admit the authority of the law and the gospel, in which Christ expressly testifies that he is the only teacher of his own (Matt. 23:8, 10), and because likewise (2) they confess that Moses was a great prophet, and Jesus a greater one, it is incumbent upon them to prove that their Muhammad was the greatest prophet, indeed that very one whom Moses designated in Deuteronomy 18, on which point they have not yet, as far as I know, even tried to do so by any arguments. To these things, out of abundance we add that Muhammad could not be a true prophet, and much less that greatest one whom Moses predicted, because he is a whole heaven different from Moses and from Jesus, whom they themselves confess to be true prophets. Indeed moreover, by the filth and frauds of his life, he proves that he is not a divinely inspired prophet, but one possessed by an unclean spirit. Compare what we already have considered on this topic in book 1, chapter 2, §§XXIV–XXVI.

3. Besides Christ, is the pope also an infallible interpreter of Scripture?
XII. It is asked, third, whether, because Christ is that only Master of ours (Matt. 23:8, 10), that highest prophet of ours, about whom Moses speaks—whether, I say, he is not for this very reason also the only infallible interpreter of the Scriptures and judge of controversies, or whether the Roman pope, with and under Christ, is also an infallible interpreter of the Scriptures and judge of controversies. The Reformed affirm the prior, by those things which we have set forth in the dogmatic part; the latter the majority of papists affirm, whom we have already refuted above in book 1, chapter 2, §§LII–LV.

4. Did he exercise the prophetic function also in the Old Testament?
XIII. It is asked, fourth, whether Christ exercised his prophetic office also under the Old Testament. The Socinians, because due to hatred of the eternal deity of Christ they state that he did not exist before he was born of the blessed Virgin, deny this. The orthodox affirm it, and prove it, because: (1) in 1 Peter 1:11 the Spirit of Christ is said to have been in the prophets. (2) In 1 Peter 3:19 he is said once in the days of Noah to have preached to those who are in prison. (3) In Acts 7:37–39 he is said to have spoken to Moses and the Israelite fathers on Sinai, and to have given them the words of life. (4) In 1 Corinthians 10:9 he is said to have been tempted by the Israelites (cf. Isa. 63:9; Gal. 3:19–20).

Objections

Nor is this hindered by the fact: (1) that he is said to have begun to preach under the New Testament (Matt. 4:17), since he began to do so as a man. (2) That in the last times God is said to have spoken to us through the Son (Heb. 1:2), since he is understood to have spoken in the Son, not simply, but as manifested in the flesh. Which also, with the necessary changes, ought to be said in response to the objection from Hebrews 2:3. (3) That under the Old Testament, it is promised that he will be a prophet (Deut. 18:15), therefore he was not. I respond, It is promised that he will be in the flesh, or with respect to the human nature, yet not simply.

5. Was he taken up into heaven before he began his function, to be taught there?

XIV. It is asked, fifth, whether, when he was about to exercise his prophetic function on earth, he was for the forty days of his fasting taken away into heaven, so that he might be fully taught there of the mysteries of the gospel. Affirming this from hatred for the omniscient deity of Christ are the same Socinians; denying it are the orthodox, because: (1) as the eternal Word (John 1:1) and the wisdom of the Father (Prov. 8:14), he did not need such a rapture and instruction, inasmuch as he was set in the bosom of the Father (John 1:18). (2) He was anointed with the Spirit without measure (John 3:34; Ps. 45:7; Heb. 1:9), with the Spirit, namely, of knowledge, understanding, and wisdom, the Spirit who is Jehovah (Isa. 11:2). (3) He is said to have been anointed on the earth, not in heaven, with respect to the conferring of the necessary gifts, and that before his ministry had begun (Luke 3:22; 4:1, 14–15). (4) Only one ascension of Christ into heaven, that supernal sanctuary, is mentioned in the Scriptures (Heb. 9:12).

Objections

Nor does it help them to argue: (1) that he was the Speech, the ambassador, the one to proclaim most fully to mankind the will of God, for it is not rightly concluded from this that he had to be informed of the will of God from elsewhere, since as the God-man he understood it most exactly; much less also is it concluded from this that he had to have been taken up into heaven for this reason. (2) That Scripture testifies that he came down from heaven (John 6:38, 62; 3:13, 31; 8:23; 16:28), since those passages must be understood about him with respect to his divine nature, which is said by the manifestation of him in the flesh to have come down, even as God did (Gen. 18:21). (3) That Moses and Paul are said to have been taught by God in heaven, since not only is the reckoning clearly dissimilar between mere men and the God-man, between those who received the Spirit in measure and him who possesses it without measure, but also, it is false that Moses was taken away into heaven.

*6. Did the Messiah have to change anything concerning the
ceremonial law and worship?*

XV. It is asked, sixth, whether the Messiah had to change anything concerning
the ceremonial law of Moses and the Levitical worship of God. It was in the time
of Paul among the chief stumbling blocks and most effective hindrances to the
Jews' coming to a Christian profession, that he abrogated the ceremonial law and
worship solemnly commanded by God through Moses. The Jerusalem Council
toiled over its removal (Acts 15), and Paul was occupied with it in various epistles,
especially those to the Galatians, Philippians, Colossians, Romans, and expressly
in the epistle to the Hebrews, by showing that: (1) our Jesus who abrogated it, the
Son of God, is God, and thus is that very one who had introduced the law once
at Sinai; and also (2) from the nature of the matter, that ceremonial worship must
be abrogated, because it did not have anything except shadows and types of things
as they were yet to be, which accordingly, when the things were no longer yet to
be, but present, had to cease. To these things is added that (3) that prophet whom
Moses promised (Deut. 18:15–19), our Jesus, who abrogated the ceremonial worship, is of the same and even greater authority than Moses who introduced it,
inasmuch as he is the one whom (a) God raised up just as he did Moses, (b) in
whose mouth he willed to place his words, who (c) would tell the Jews all things
that God had commanded him, and whom accordingly (d) they ought to heed
in all things, (e) with the added threat against him who would not listen, that
he would require it of him. One thing we will add, that (4) in Daniel 9:27 it is
expressly predicted that the Messiah, after he had confirmed the covenant with
many, would cause the sacrifice and the offering to cease.

Objection

To all these things, I do not see anything that the Jews could oppose, at least with
any semblance of truth, than that throughout the Pentateuch the ceremonial
statutes are described as eternal (Ex. 12:14; Lev. 6:18, 22; Num. 15:15; and so
forth), but they think too little on the fact that עולם does not always mean a
duration that is simply unbounded, but one that does not cease only within a
certain period (Ex. 21:6), and thus it designates nothing other than that those
ceremonial rites would be unceasing as long as the period of the Jewish state
continued. But we will say more about these things expressly in their own place.[11]

7. Did Christ thoroughly abrogate the entire law?
XVI. It is asked, seventh, whether he thoroughly abrogated the entire law, even

---

11. 1.5.8 §XVIII; 1.8.2 §XLIX

the moral law. Affirming this are the Antinomians, under the pretext of Christian liberty, first those who once were in Germany, whose leader was Johann Agricola of Eisleben, an Epicurean man, about whom Micraelius speaks in his *Syntagma of Church History* (p. 3 of §48),[12] then those who are now in Britain, under the pretext of extolling grace, and because in the matter of justification they observed that the law is opposed to grace.

Arguments

The orthodox, although they confess that the entire law has been abrogated in regard to the ability to justify, with respect to all, and also in regard to its power to curse, with respect to believers, yet deny that it has been abrogated in regard to its power to direct, because: (1) Christ himself expressly denies that he came to abolish the law (Matt. 5:17). In fact, (2) in the same chapter, v. 18, he expressly declares that till heaven and earth pass, one jot or one tittle shall not pass from the law. (3) Paul concludes the same thing in Romans 3:31. (4) The moral law, inasmuch as the greatest part of its right is natural in part to God and in part to man, cannot be abrogated as long as God and man remain, as we will teach expressly in its own place.[13]

Objections

Nor is it incompatible: (1) that in John 1:17 the law is referred to Moses, and grace to Christ, because there through *law* is not understood anything except either the ceremonial law, which was typical, or the dispensation of the covenant of grace which was somewhat more legal under the Old Testament, and which has now been abrogated by Christ. Nor (2) that law constantly appears to be opposed to grace, and thus believers are said to be not under the law, but under grace, because this ought to be restricted only to the matter of justification, and to the covenant of works.

8. Did Christ correct or augment the moral law?

XVII. It is asked, eighth, whether Christ corrected or augmented the moral law. The Socinians, so that they may make the gospel from the law, and more easily obtain that man is justified not from the works of the law but from the works of the gospel, state that Christ added some things to the individual commandments

---

12. Johann Micraelius (1597–1658), *Syntagma historiarum ecclesiae omnium*, 2nd ed. (Stettin: Georgius Rhetius, 1644), bk. 3, sect. 2, quest. 48, p. 348, on Johann Agricola (1494–1566).

13. 1.8.2 §XLVIII. On a common distinction among the Reformed between *lex* and *jus*, cf. Franciscus Junius, *The Mosaic Polity*, ed. A. M. McGinnis, trans. T. M. Rester (Grand Rapids, MI: CLP Academic, 2015), 8, 55.

of the Decalogue, and three things to all of them: the denial of self, the bearing of the cross, and the imitation of Christ (Luke 9:23; in this last point the Arminians collude with them). In addition, they state that he sanctioned the augmented commandments with new spiritual promises of the forgiveness of sins and eternal life, so that by obedience to this gospel, we may gain justification.

The reasons of the orthodox
The orthodox on the contrary do not acknowledge that he is a lawgiver according to its true and proper name, or that he added any new commandment to the moral law, because: (1) the ancient law of Moses is so perfect (Ps. 19:7) that by its observance our first parents could have merited eternal life (Lev. 18:5; Ezek. 20:13, 25; Luke 10:28). (2) Those new duties that our adversaries want him to have added are already evidently commanded under the Old Testament, as we will teach in particular in its own place.[14] (3) By those new duties by which the law is converted into the gospel, the satisfaction of Christ is excluded, justification is suspended upon works, and the covenant of works is confused with the covenant of grace, which are all fatal to the Christian religion.

Objections
Nor does it help them to argue: (1) from the fifth chapter of Matthew, since there he does not correct or augment the law of Moses (as is evident to the eye, even if only from v. 43, inasmuch as not only is it nowhere present in Moses, but also its contrary is expressly prescribed, Deut. 32:35; Prov. 25:21), but he only vindicates it from the twisted interpretations of the Pharisees, as is evident from the adduced verse 43. Nor (2) that the New Testament repeatedly makes mention of a new commandment (John 13:34; 1 John 2:7–8), because to John the adjective *new* not rarely designates something outstanding and splendid (Rev. 2:17; 5:9; 14:3; etc.). More things of this sort will occur, Lord willing, in their own place.[15]

9. Was Christ the first to preach the gospel?
XVIII. It is asked, ninth, whether as a prophet he was the first promoter of the the gospel. The Socinians, from the hypotheses of the prior controversy, through which the gospel for them is nothing except the law of Moses augmented, and sanctioned with spiritual promises of the forgiveness of sins and eternal life, affirm this.

---

14. 1.8.2 §XLVIII; cf. 1.8.3 §§XLVI, VIII
15. 1.8.2 §XLVIII; cf. 1.8.3 §§XLVI, VIII

The orthodox reasons

The orthodox on the contrary, having rejected these perverse hypotheses, deny it, because: (1) the gospel is expressly said to have obtained even under the Old Testament (Rom. 10:8, 16; John 12:38 with Isa. 53:1). (2) The heads of the gospel are found in entire sections of Scripture throughout the Old Testament (Isa. 53; Gen. 3:15). (3) By the same gospel by which we are now saved under the New Testament, Old Testament believers are also said to have been saved (Acts 15:10–11). (4) That Socinian gospel is in fact not written in the Scriptures; indeed, it is a false gospel,[16] condemned by the apostle (Gal. 1:6, 8).

Objections

Nor does it help them to argue: (1) that Mark commemorates "the beginning of the gospel of Jesus Christ" (1:1), because the beginning of the preaching of Christ is not understood to be that of the gospel itself (cf. Matt. 4:17). (2) That in 2 Timothy 1:10 it is said that he brought to light the gospel, because (a) to bring to light is nothing other than to bring forth into clear light the gospel that was revealed more obscurely under the Old Testament, and in ceremonial shadows, as if covered by a veil (2 Cor. 3:14); or (b) not the entire gospel is understood, but the gospel of fulfillment as distinguished from the gospel of promise (about which Rom. 16:25–26 and Titus 1:1–3 speak). (3) That it is called the gospel hidden from the times of the ages (Rom. 16:25–26; Eph. 3:9; Col. 1:26–27), because (a) the gospel of fulfillment is understood, as has been said; (b) or it is understood with respect to the mystery of the fulfilled calling of the Gentiles (Eph. 3:8 with v. 9). (4) That it is said that the way of the saints was not yet made manifest, while the first tabernacle was yet standing (Heb. 9:8), because by "the way of the saints" is not understood the entire gospel, but Christ as he has been manifested in the flesh, who is the way, the truth, and the life (John 14:6), without whom none of the saints comes to the Father.

The Practical Part

The practice of the prophetic function: 1. Acknowledges the indescribable grace of the one giving.

XIX. The practice of the prophetic function of Christ, first, acknowledges the indescribable grace of God and glorifies it, saying that a great prophet has risen up among us, and that God has visited his people (Luke 7:16). By this grace: (1) he gave the prophet (Jer. 3:15). (2) The prophet promised and expected for

---

16. ἄγραφον, *imo* ψευδευαγγέλιον

so many ages (Deut. 18:15; John 5:46; Acts 3:20–24; 7:37). (3) The prophet so great and excellent, equal to Moses (Deut. 18:15, 18, "like me," "like you")—and how great was Moses? (Deut. 34:10)—indeed, greater than him (Heb. 3:2–6). (4) The inspired prophet par excellence, in whose mouth God has put his words, that he may speak all that God commanded him (Deut. 18:18). (5) The prophet, who even in the confession, though hypocritical, of his adversaries was a master (not an uneducated person), and also a teacher, and one who has been sent by God, that he may teach the way of God, and that indeed in truth, without partiality (Matt. 22:16). (6) The prophet who is in the bosom of the Father (John 1:18), mighty in deed and word before God and all the people (Luke 24:19). (7) The prophet, who not only can teach, but do so thoroughly, not only persuade, but do so utterly, not only speak externally, but also illuminate internally (John 1:9). To say it in word, (8) the prophet who is one among thousands (Job 33:23; Song 5:10), one worth them all (Matt. 23:8), without whom the rest can do nothing (John 15:5), and through whom they can do all things (Matt. 28:20; Phil. 4:13; Rom. 15:18).

The manner of acknowledging
The practice acknowledges, I say, the grace of such a prophet, such that it: (1) glorifies God with a grateful heart (Luke 7:16), (2) readily receives the prophet who has been sent (Matt. 10:40; John 13:20), (3) hears the one received with all submission (Deut. 18:15, 19), and (4) kisses him (Ps. 2:12).

2. It acknowledges the prophet himself.
XX. Secondly, it acknowledges (1) the prophet himself, after the example of the Samaritan woman,[17] "Sir, I perceive that you are a prophet" (John 4:19), from: (a) his revelation of secret things, and manner of dealing with us (John 4:19), (b) his miracles (John 6:14; 9:17; 3:2), (c) his excellence in teaching (John 7:40). It acknowledges him (2) as that great prophet who was once promised, "This is truly that prophet who is to come into the world" (John 6:14). It acknowledges him (3) as its own prophet (John 20:16, "Rabboni, Master"). It acknowledges him (4) as a disciple does his master (Matt. 23:10), for which reason Christians were once called disciples (Acts 11:26; thus throughout the gospels, e.g. Luke 14:26). It acknowledges him (5) as the only infallible Master, upon whose mouth alone it may depend without worry (Matt. 23:8; Job 33:23). It acknowledges him (6) in all things that he speaks to it, whether they are favorable or adverse (Deut. 18:18–19 with 5:27; Jer. 42:5–6).

---

17. *Cananaeae*

3. It receives Christ as a prophet. In what manner

XXI. Third, the practice of the prophetic function of Christ receives him as a prophet (Matt. 10:41; John 5:43; Luke 9:48; Matt. 18:5), not only in mouth (Matt. 7:22), but in substance, by faithfully rendering to him the duties owed to such a great prophet and teacher, namely: (1) love (Gal. 4:14–15; Matt. 10:37); (2) reverence (Phil. 2:29; 1 Tim. 5:17; 1 Cor. 4:1; Matt. 13:57 with John 13:13), for which reason he is greeted throughout the gospels by his disciples, and even repeatedly by the Pharisees, as Master and Lord; (3) faith, by which we believe his words to be most exactly and universally true (Isa. 53:1; Rom. 10:16; John 4:19, 29, 39, 41; 5:24, 46–47); (4) obedience (Heb. 13:17; Josh. 1:17; Rom. 6:17; 2 Cor. 2:9; Deut. 17:8–13 with Heb. 5:9; 2 Cor. 10:5–6); (5) imitation (Heb. 13:7; 1 Cor. 4:16; Phil. 3:17; 2 Thess. 3:8–9 with 1 Thess. 1:6; 1 Cor. 11:1; Matt. 11:29); (6) sustenance (Gal. 6:6; 1 Cor. 9:7, 11), to be offered to our prophet not indeed in his own person (Ps. 50:12), but in his members (Matt. 10:41 with 25:40, 45); (7) desire for presence and conversation (Judg. 13:18 with Song 1:7; John 4:40; Luke 24:19 with v. 29; Rom. 10:15).

By what reasons

For if in these duties: (1) we are obligated to receive any ordinary prophets, doctors, and teachers (Phil. 2:29; 3 John 8), indeed if we are obligated to receive even a little child in his name (Mark 9:37; Luke 9:48), surely, and indeed more so, we would receive this prophet, so great and so excellent, whom we have already presented in part in §XIX. Especially because (2) he who receives him at the same time receives the Father who sent him (Matt. 10:40; Mark 9:37; Luke 9:48; John 13:20). And (3) he who receives him obtains the authority to be a son of God (John 1:12). While on the contrary, (4) those who do not desire to receive him, draw upon themselves his just fury, and manifold destruction (Ps. 2:12; Luke 9:53–54). I need not add (5) the highest right and equity, by which the one who comes to his own, sent by his Father to act among them as a prophet and spokesman, deserves to be received (John 1:11–12).

4. It hears Christ as a prophet. The motivating reasons

XXII. Fourth, the practice of the prophetic function, in particular, hears the one who was sent by the Father and who comes to us as a prophet. For this is demanded by: (1) the very preeminence of the prophetic dignity, by which he is not only a prophet, but also one so great and of such a kind as we have already presented (Matt. 12:42; Luke 11:31). (2) The commandment of the Father who promises him (Deut. 18:15, 18). (3) The severest threat added against those who would not listen to him, in verse 19, "And it shall happen that whoever will not

listen to the words which he shall speak in my name, I will require it of him."
(4) The solemn inauguration by the Father who displays and confirms the promised prophet (Matt. 3:17 with 17:5; Luke 9:35). Because (5) from this we are able to gather certainly that he is our shepherd and we are his sheep (John 10:3, 16), indeed those born of God (John 8:43 with v. 47). Because (6) by hearing him we are able to obtain for ourselves eternal life (John 5:24). This is to add nothing of (7) the excellency of his words (Matt. 13:17).

The manner of hearing
But how does it hear? (1) With admiration and amazement (Matt. 7:28–29; 22:33; John 7:46), with applause and celebration (John 7:40; Luke 24:19); (2) with assent and faith (John 5:24; 8:45–46); (3) with joy (Matt. 13:20; Heb. 6:5); or even (4) with fear (Mark 10:24, 26; Isa. 66:2); (5) with obedience (Luke 6:47; Matt. 7:24; James 1:22); (6) with constant remembrance of what has been heard (Luke 2:49 with v. 51).

5. It attends to the things this prophet has said. Why?
XXIII. Fifth, the practice of the prophetic function also receives the word of this prophet that has been heard, so that the Word of Christ may dwell in us richly in all wisdom (Col. 3:16), and that we may "give the more abundant heed to what we have heard, lest at any time we drift away. For if the word spoken by angels was made steadfast, and every transgression and disobedience received a just recompense of reward, how shall we escape, if we neglect so great a salvation, which at the first began to be declared by the Lord…?" (Heb. 2:1–3).

To what things? In what manner?
Therefore, whether: (1) he interprets and vindicates the divine law (Matt. 5; 22:24–29), or (2) teaches the gospel (Matt. 4:23; Isa. 61:1; Luke 4:43; 2 Tim. 1:10), or (3) prescribes duties (John 15:14, 17), or (4) predicts future things (Mark 13:22–23; John 16:20), or (5) promises benefits to his people (Matt. 28:20; John 16:23; 2 Cor. 1:20), or (6) threatens punishments (Matt. 23:13–15ff.; 18:7; Luke 6:24), and so forth, let us always pay attention, "to give the more abundant heed to what we have heard (Heb. 2:1), such that that we receive what has been heard with the affection suitable to each of them.

6. It also receives his emissaries. The duties of reception that must
be rendered to his emissaries
XXIV. Sixth, the practice of the prophetic function not only receives that prophet himself, and what he has said and taught, but also his emissaries,

prophets, apostles, pastors, teachers (Gal. 4:14). And that indeed with the same duties of love, reverence, faith, obedience, sustenance, and appetite for presence and conversation, by which it receives him as the supreme prophet and teacher, which we have already spoken about in §XXI, which for the sake of brevity will not be repeated here in more detail.

Motives

For (1) he teaches us, at least externally, by them (1 Peter 1:11; 3:19–20), as his συνεργοί, fellow workers (1 Cor. 3:9), from which ministers are called fellow workers in the Lord (Rom. 16:3, 9, 21), with whom he is said to work together, συνεργεῖν (Mark 16:20; Rom. 15:18), and who on the other hand work together with Christ (2 Cor. 1:24). (2) They are his emissaries, his ambassadors (2 Cor. 5:20; Matt. 10; 1 Cor. 1:17). (3) Whatever they do, they do in the name of Christ (Matt. 18:20; 28:19; 1 Cor. 5:4; Matt. 7:22; Acts 5:40). (4) They who receive them, receive him, and indeed the Father who sent them (Matt. 10:40). And on the other hand, whoever do not receive them, and spurn them, reject and spurn Christ himself, and his Father (Luke 10:16; Mark 6:11; Luke 9:5). (5) Whatever is done to them, he views as done to himself, and also wills to reward them fittingly (Matt. 10:41–42; cf. 25:35–36, 40, 43). (6) They perform the same work with Christ (Phil. 2:30; 1 Cor. 15:58). (7) They work together with Christ to their advantage (2 Cor. 1:24).

Manner

Nevertheless, at the same time we must take heed that while the same duties are offered to Christ and to his emissaries, we nonetheless do not offer them in the same way: (1) they are to be offered to him as to the Lord, as to the Master; to them as to servants, as to ministers (1 Cor. 3:5); (2) to him on account of himself, because he deserves it (John 13:13); to them on account of him (Mark 9:41); (3) to him in a degree even more intense than the absolutely greatest; to them comparatively in the least degree (Mark 1:7; Heb. 3:1–7).

7. It instructs church ministers to imitate Christ as prophet.

XXV. Seventh, the practice of the prophetic function of Christ instructs vicarious prophets, that is, church doctors and pastors, his ministers, to endeavor to imitate their Master in his functions (John 13:13, 15; 1 Cor. 11:1; Luke 6:40), by doing the same thing that the Master did, so that their work may be the work of Christ (Phil. 2:30; John 6:28), that is, just as the Master himself did the work of his Father who sent him (John 10:37; Luke 2:49).

By which duties

And what did the Master do? (1) He interpreted the law and vindicated it (Matt. 5:17; 22:36); they also should do the same (Rom. 3:31). (2) He promulgated the gospel (Isa. 61:1); they also should promulgate it, that they may do the work of an evangelist (2 Tim. 4:5; Rom. 1:1, 5; 1 Cor. 1:17). (3) He administered the sacraments, he baptized (Matt. 3:11; Luke 3:16), he administered the Supper (Matt. 26:26–29); they also should administer them, "as the ministers of Christ, and stewards of the mysteries of God" (1 Cor. 4:1), they should baptize (Matt. 3:11; Luke 3:16), they should administer the Lord's Supper (1 Cor. 11:23ff.). (4) He taught the ignorant (Matt. 4:23), reproved the stubborn (John 8:44), raised up the downcast in heart (Isa. 61:1); so they also should reprove, exhort, and comfort (2 Tim. 4:2). (5) He foretold the future judgments of God (Matt. 24:4–5ff.); they also should foretell them, but from his Word (2 Tim. 3:1–6). (6) He showed himself as an example to his hearers (John 13:13–14); they also should thus show themselves (Titus 2:7). (7) He confirmed his teaching by his works (John 5:36); they also should confirm theirs by their works (John 5:36; Matt. 5:13–18; 7:21–22). (8) In all these things, he did not seek himself and his own advantages and benefits, but those of his Father and his people (John 5:41; 8:50; Matt. 20:28); they also should not seek themselves, but those things which are Christ's (Phil. 2:4–5, 21).

In what manner

Nor should they only do those things that Christ did, but also in the same way: just as he performed his prophetic office (1) prudently, according to the capacity of his hearers, by employing familiar parables (Matt. 13), piercing their hearts carefully (Matt. 21:28 with v. 45); so they also should act prudently (Matt. 10:16; 2 Sam. 12:1–13). (2) Freely, without partiality (Matt. 20:16); they also should act freely (2 Sam. 12:7; Mark 6:18; Acts 4:19). (3) Effectively (Luke 24:19; Matt. 7:29); they also should act effectively, so that they may convince, may judge, so that the secrets of the heart may be made manifest, and their hearers may fall down on their face and worship God (1 Cor. 14:24–25; cf. Heb. 4:12). (4) With great zeal (John 2:17); they also should act with holy zeal (2 Cor. 11:2). (5) With exceeding great affection, by lamenting, weeping, and so forth (Luke 19:42; Matt. 23:37); they also should act with great affection (Phil. 3:18; 2 Cor. 5:20).

By what reasons

And so that they may do all this with greater diligence, they should consider: (1) that otherwise they will not be prophets, but false prophets (Matt. 7:15; 24:11, 24; Luke 6:26; 2 Peter 2:1; 1 John 4:1), false apostles (2 Cor. 11:13), ravening wolves (Matt. 7:15), dogs, evil workers (Phil. 3:2), not shepherds, but hirelings (John 10:12–13); and not (2) emissaries sent by him, but those running of their own accord (Rom. 10:15; Jer. 23:21); and therefore (3) those who will be rejected by him (Matt. 7:21–23).

8. It commands all to prophesy.

XXVI. Eighth, because from our participation in his anointing (1 John 2:20, 27), all we Christians are prophets (Joel 2:28; Acts 2:17), the practice of the prophetic function of Christ also commands us all to prophesy (1 Cor. 14:1, 24, 31, 39; Num. 11:26, 29), even the women (1 Cor. 11:5); that is, to cultivate that teaching which our highest prophet handed down.

By which duties

This is done: (1) by learning the teaching of Christ (1 Cor. 14:31; Eph. 4:20; 1 Tim. 2:11), as those taught by God (Jer. 31:34; Isa. 54:13; John 6:45). (2) By searching the Scriptures and interpreting them, for this is the meaning of prophesying, according to the apostle (1 Cor. 14), and the prophet Joel (2:28). And that in accordance with our office and the measure of our gifts, whether publicly to others (1 Cor. 14:4), or privately to ourselves, by discerning what is that good, pleasing to God, and perfect will of God (Rom. 12:2). (3) By testing the spirits (1 John 4:1; 1 Thess. 5:21; Acts 17:11; John 5:39). (4) By teaching our neighbor, each according to his office and gifts, so that the Word of Christ may dwell in us richly (Col. 3:16). (5) By bravely and intrepidly confessing the name of Christ.

By what helps

And so that we can do these things, we ought to strive: (1) that before all things we be truly rendered companions (μέτοχοι, Heb. 1:9; חברים, Ps. 45:7) in Christ's anointing, which teaches us all things (1 John 2:27), and that we receive it from Christ (1 John 2:27; 5:20). Then (2) that we come to our highest prophet, that we may be taught by him (Mark 2:13), in the temple (Mark 14:49), on the Sabbaths (Luke 4:31), in schools (Lk. 6:6), that also to this end we wear him out with prayers, "Lord, teach us" (Luke 11:1; Ps. 25:4–5; 86:11), that he would teach not only externally, through his own, but also internally, through himself, by illuminating (Eph. 5:14). Furthermore, (3) that the Spirit of Christ, who was in the prophets (1 Peter 1:10–11), be also in us (Rom. 8:9) and communicated to us, just as the spirit of Moses was communicated to the seventy elders, so that they prophesied (Num. 11:25), and that it be communicated to us not for a short time, as to them, "They prophesied, and did not continue"[18] (Num. 11:25), but constantly, as to Eldad and Medad (v. 26); and not as to Saul, through a sort of lightning flash, which ceased after a short time (1 Sam. 10:6, 10–13), but as to Christ the highest prophet, that the Spirit may rest upon us (Isa. 11:2). To this end, (4) that we wear him out with fervent prayers, that he give to us his Spirit (Luke 11:13), that he obtain him by his intercession with the Father (John 14:16), that he send him (John 15:26), so that he may guide us into all truth (John 16:13), so that he may abide with us forever (John 14:16–17), after the example of Elisha, who asked for a double measure of the spirit of Elijah, and obtained it (2 Kings 2:9, 15).

9. It supplies comfort. In what circumstances
XXVII. Ninth, finally, the last practice takes the most efficacious comfort from the prophetic function of Christ, in various circumstances, if: (1) we should be afflicted, if poor, if spiritually deserted, if in any way captive, spiritually or bodily, if under fear of divine wrath, if sorrowful, if anxious in spirit, because the Spirit of the Lord Jehovah is upon him, and he has anointed him to preach good news to the afflicted, because he has sent him to bind up the brokenhearted, to proclaim liberty to the captives, and the opening of prison to those who are bound, to proclaim the year of Jehovah's goodwill, and the day of vengeance for our God, to comfort all who mourn, to provide for those who mourn in Zion glory and the oil of joy, and instead of mourning a garment of praise, to those who are anguished in spirit (Isa. 61:1–3). If (2) we should be destitute of prophets, of teachers, so that we ought to mourn for ourselves, "There is no more any prophet; there is no more anyone who knows" (Ps. 74:9), if we should be deprived, either by force of persecutions or by divine providence, of our faithful teachers (Acts 20:37). If (3) our prophets and teachers should be hirelings (John 10:12), be ravening wolves (Matt. 7:15; Isa. 10:1), if ignorant, lying, seducers, dumb dogs, such that night prevails over us from the vision, that it bring darkness upon us, that we not prophesy, and the sun go down over our prophets, and the day grow dark over them, that the prophets blush, and the diviners be covered in shame, and they cover their lips, however many they will be, because there is no answer from God (Mic. 3:5–7), such that we are constrained to wail with Jeremiah, "As concerns the prophets, my heart within me is broken; all my bones are out of joint…because both prophet and priest defile…" (Jer. 23:9–18). If (4) we also should be blind, so that we do not understand spiritual things, but rather, they are foolishness to us (1 Cor. 2:14; Eph. 4:17–18); and so forth.

---

18. *prophetarunt, et non addiderunt*

Consoling arguments
How much comfort does it then provide to think that: (1) notwithstanding, we have a prophet, a messenger, one among thousands, to show to us the equity of God (Job 33:23). (2) We have a prophet, one worth them all (Matt. 23:8, 10), as he is the very wisdom of God (Prov. 8), and has been made for us wisdom (1 Cor. 1:30), who is in the bosom of the Father, and therefore alone is able and willing to reveal the things which are necessary to know (John 1:18). (3) We have a prophet who not only can teach externally, but also illuminate internally (John 1:9), by opening the heart (Acts 16:14). (4) We have a prophet who for us obtained and sends the Spirit, who leads us into all truth, that he may abide with us, indeed be in us (John 14:16–17). (5) We have a prophet who will abide with us, even to the consummation of the ages (Matt. 28:20).

CHAPTER SEVEN

The Mediator as a High Priest

The Lord has sworn and will not repent, You are a priest forever, after the manner of Melchizedek.

—Psalm 110:4

The connection of this chapter with the previous

I. We have examined the first function of Christ's mediatorial office, that is, the prophetic, by which he expounded the counsel of God regarding the reconciliation of the sinner. Now we proceed to the second, the priestly, by which he accomplished the expounded reconciliation, and we will present it according to the leading of the prefixed text.

The Exegetical Part

The text is resolved and explained.

II. In this text there is contained a solemn inauguration, or conferral of the priestly dignity, made by Jehovah to the Messiah, wherein occur:

A. The one conferring, or the person inaugurating: "Jehovah," economically the Father (Ps. 2:7). For by him in the eternal covenant of grace he was constituted and called, and by him in time he was sent, to be a priest (Heb. 5:4–5). And he indeed alone did this, for he alone was offended by sin (Ps. 51:4), he alone had to be reconciled by the priesthood, and so then he alone was able to constitute the priestly reconciler, nor was he bound to assent to anyone not constituted by himself.

B. The twin conferral, or act of constituting the priest:

1. One act, positive: "He has sworn," נשבע from שבע, seven, the most perfect number, because an oath is the most perfect confirmation of a matter. The oath of God presupposes a matter that is not trivial or common, but rare, unusual, and incredible, one of great moment, for it was unusual to constitute a priest who was not from the tribe of

Levi, but from the tribe of Judah (Heb. 6:16; 7:11–13). Without a doubt God swore this oath so that by it he might repress our hesitation. So then this oath regards three things: (1) it signifies the immutable character of his counsel (Heb. 6:17; cf. Isa. 45:23; 54:9–10); then (2) it commends the excellence of this priesthood compared with any other, inasmuch as it is sealed as it were with a divine oath (Heb. 7:20–21; cf. John 6:27); and finally, (3) it aims at confirming the sinner in his confidence (Heb. 6:17, 11).

2. The other act, negative: "and he will not repent." He will not retract, will not change this counsel, he will not suspend it upon the obedience, or disobedience, of men, namely, as he did in other matters, by changing his counsel (Jer. 18:7–8; 1 Sam. 15:11; Isa. 38:1, 5), and in particular, in the Aaronic priesthood, for which, once it was antiquated, he substituted this eternal, evangelical priesthood. Furthermore, repentance belongs to God in a way worthy of him,[1] not with respect to the affection, but with respect to the effective operation, as we have taught elsewhere.[2]

C. The thing conferred, or rather, the formula of conferring it, in which is designated:

1. The person to whom it is conferred: אתה, "you," that is, the one whom he had described in the previous verses, namely, David's Lord, the Messiah. So all Christians understand the passage: (1) on the authority of the New Testament (Matt. 22:42; Acts 2:34; 1 Cor. 15:25; Heb. 1:13). The Pharisees seemed to have thought the same, as did all the Jews in common of that time. (2) From the entire context, for the entire Psalm speaks about such a one: (a) who would sit at the right hand of God, (b) who would be a priest forever, (c) about such a one who would be the Lord of King David, and thus superior to him, (d) who would be a king and priest simultaneously, (e) who would not be a Levitical priest, but one after the order of Melchizedek. (3) From the consensus of the ancient Jews.[3] Thus Rabbi Yoden in the name of

---

1. *poenitentiam Deo competere* θεοπρεπῶς

2. 1.2.15 §XIX

3. For a highly similar and prior usage of subsequent rabbinic sources, see e.g. John Owen, *Exercitations on the Epistle to the Hebrews*, 129–32; idem, *An Exposition of the Epistle to the Hebrews*, ed. W. H. Goold, 7 vols. (Edinburgh: Johnstone & Hunter, 1854), 3:218–24; idem, *Works*, 20:218–24.

Rabbi Chiya on Psalm 18;[4] Rabbi Yitzhak on Genesis;[5] thus in Midrash Tehillim on this very Psalm: "And he said to the Messiah"; thus Rabbi Ovadiah: "The psalmist composed this Psalm about the Messiah."[6] Rabbi Saadia Gaon, on Daniel, interprets this Psalm as about the Messiah.[7] Thus also the ancient masters of the Jews, Barachias and Rabbi Levi, cited by Rabbi Moses Nachmanides.[8] The Hebrews who lived after the rise of Christianity began to deny this only due to hatred of Christianity. Yet Rabbi Kimchi[9] and others contradict them, as does Trypho in Justin: they interpret the second Psalm, which is of the same kind, as regarding the Messiah.[10] The more recent Jews, so that they may distort the Psalm, contort themselves into various shapes. There are those who: (1) think that Eliezer, the servant of Abraham, spoke this Psalm about his lord Abraham, after he had returned from the conquest of the five kings, and they

---

4. *Midrash Tehillim*, Ps. 18:35, "Rabbi Yoden, in the name of Rabbi Chiya, said, 'In the world to come, the blessed God shall place Messiah the king at his right hand, as it is said, 'The Lord said to my Lord.'"

5. On Ps. 110:4, Salomon Yitzhak (Rashi, תהלים / *Psalms*, ed. and trans. A. J. Rosenberg, 3 vols. (New York: Judaica Press, 1991); idem, *Rashi's Commentary on the Psalms with Notes*, ed. and trans. M. I. Gruber (Leiden: Brill, 2004), 652.

6. On Psalm 110, Ovadiah ben Sforno (c. 1475–1550), באור על ספר תהלים ([Venice], [1585]), fol. 1 18 recto–verso.

7. On Daniel 7:13–14, Saadia Gaon, *The Book of Daniel*, 260–64, 547–50; idem, דניאל עם הועד להוצאת ספרי רס״ג תרגום ופירוש רבנו סעדיה בן יוסף פיומי (Jerusalem: / *Ha-Va'ad le-Hotsa'at Sifre Rasag*, 1980/1981); for his Arabic translation of Daniel, see Sa'adia ben Yosef, *The Book of Daniel with Saadia's Arabic Translation. A Babylonian-Yemenite Manuscript*, ed. S. Morag (Leiden: Brill, 1973). For an early modern scholarly edition of the Hebrew biblical text and many rabbinic commentaries, including Saadia Gaon, see דניאל ז, [*Biblia Hebraica Rabbinica*], Bomberg 2nd ed., rev., 4 vols. ([Venice]: [Israel Cornelius Adelkind], [1547–1549]), 4:[361–62].

8. On Gen. 14:18 and Ps. 18:36, see Joshua ben Levi (fl. 200–250) in Moses ben Nachman Girondi (Ramban or Nachmanides, 1194–1270), *Commentary on the Torah*, ed. and trans. C. B. Chavel, 5 vols. (New York: Shilo Publishing House, 1971–1976), 1:188–190. A renowned disputation at Barcelona (1263) between Ramban and a Jewish convert to Christianity and the Dominican Order, Pablo Christiani (fl. 1261–1265), before the court of James I of Aragon (1208–1276) is an important reference point in Jewish-Christian debate on Christology from biblical and rabbinic sources. For Nachman's account, see Ramban, *The Disputation at Barcelona*, trans. C. B. Chavel (New York: Shilo Publishing House, 1983); in Hebrew with a Latin translation, see "Disputatio R. Nachmanidis cum Fratre Paulo" in J. C. Wagenseil, *Tela ignea Satanae* (Altdorf: J. H. Schonnerstaedt, 1674).

9. See Ps. 110 in Kimchi, *Commentary on the Fifth Book of the Psalms*; idem, ספר תהילים עם פירוש רבי דוד קמחי (Isny: Paul Fagius, 1542).

10. Cf. Matthew Poole (1624–1679), *Synopsis criticorum aliorumque Sacrae Scripturae interpretum et commentatorum* (Utrecht, 1684), 2:1244; citation of Trypho in Justin Martyr, *Dialogus cum Tryphone Judaeo* in PG 6:687–88; idem, *Dialogue of Justin, Philosopher and Martyr, with Trypho, a Jew* in ANF 1:244.

twist all the ingredients of this Psalm to fit this view. However, neither is the author of the Psalm Eliezer, but David, from the title, nor was Abraham a priest after the order of Melchizedek. Others (2) prefer to think that David spoke this Psalm about his lord Saul. But neither did Saul ever sit at the right hand of God, nor was Saul a priest, nor one after the order of Melchizedek, nor did he bear or have an eternal priesthood, nor did the people sacrifice to him, nor after he had drunk from the brook did he lift up the head. Others (3) refer this to Hezekiah. However, neither was he David's lord, nor did he sit at the right hand of God, nor was he himself a priest, nor such who was after the order of Melchizedek, nor did he exist when David composed this Psalm, nor was sacrifice ever made to him. Others (4) prefer to understand Solomon. But neither was he the lord of David his father, nor did he sit at the right hand of God, nor was he a priest, nor such who was after the order of Melchizedek, nor did he have an eternal priesthood, nor did his subjects ever sacrifice to him. There are not lacking those who (5) want to think that David is not speaking here, but his soldiers spoke this Psalm of him, because they said, "You shall not go down with us to battle, that the lamp may not be extinguished in Israel" (2 Sam. 21:17), and they distort the contents of the text to fit him. However, besides the fact that the Jews cannot prove by even one jot that the soldiers are speaking here, also none of the ingredients of the Psalm with any appearance of truth can be declared about David, according to the things we have already said. Therefore nothing remains except that here this אתה, "you," is none other than our Messiah.

2. The office which is conferred: "You are a priest," or "You shall be a priest." כהן denotes an honored minister, as much among political as among ecclesiastical ministers, and sometimes a prince (2 Sam. 8:18; 20:26 with 1 Chron. 18:17; and from Job 12:19; Gen. 41:45; Ex. 2:16), but this is by an analogical meaning, in which the proper and principal signification is a priest or ecclesiastical minister, and the improper and less principal one a political minister, that is, because the priesthood is as it were the most noble and divine function, also because the care of sacred matters, and thus the priesthood, was incumbent upon princes and heads of families, and in addition upon the first born under the patriarchs, and finally because the care of divine worship and sacred matters is incumbent upon princes, so then

by analogy the prince is also called a כהן (cf. Menochio, *On the Republic of the Hebrews*, bk. 7, ch. 7).[11] Accordingly, Rabbi Kimchi, so that the Messiah would not be a priest, explains it as "king," "prince," or "leader." The Socinians follow him, so that they may hold that the priestly and kingly offices of Christ are one and the same, to the end that Christ would not have acted as a priest on earth, and not have satisfied for us by making an offering, but only in heaven at the right hand of God, as a king, by offering himself to the Father; they state that from this passage Christ is called a prince or king rather than a priest. On the contrary to Christians, in its proper, principal, and ordinary meaning, it denotes a priest or ecclesiastical minister, because: (1) the term in Genesis 14:18, from which it is cited here, without doubt in Melchizedek denotes a priest, insofar as he is called a king and a priest. (2) In very many other passages, the Messiah is named a priest (Zech. 6:13; cf. Jer. 30:21; 33:15, 18; likewise Isa. 53:10, where sacrifice is attributed to him). (3) Thus Ibn Ezra and the ancient rabbis thought, as Rabbi Kimchi testifies.[12] (4) They will never prove that the term is employed of a king, still less of a king who sits at the right hand of God. David as a king had כהנים, princes, under him (2 Sam. 8:18; 1 Chron. 18:17): how therefore would David, about whom Kimchi wants this passage to be understood, be called a כוהן, prince, who is less than a king? (5) The Messiah performed all priestly things, for (a) priests taught (Lev. 10:11; Mal. 2:7); the Messiah also taught (John 1:18). (b) They offered sacrifices to placate God, as is well known; the Messiah also sacrificed (Heb. 10:5; Eph. 5:2). (c) They prayed and interceded for the people, as well as blessed them (Ps. 118:26; Num. 6:23); the Messiah also prayed, interceded, and blessed (Rom. 8:26; Heb. 7:25). (6) In Hebrews 5:6 and 7:17, 21, it is translated as ἱερεύς, "priest." I need not add, (7) it is not permitted to depart from the proper meaning of words to an improper one without a pressing necessity arising either from the analogy of faith or from the analogy of the context, but such necessity does not obtain here. And thus כוהן does not denote here anything but a priest. Nor should it be passed by that here the Messiah is simply called כוהן, a priest, and not a high priest, כוהן הגדול, the greatest

---

11. Giovanni Stefano Menochio (Menochius, 1575–1655), *De republica Hebraeorum libri octo* (Paris: Antoine Bertier, 1648), 677.

12. See Ps. 110:4 in *Ibn Ezra's Commentary on Books 3–5 of Psalms*.

priest, not because he was not such, for he was, and that indeed par excellence, but so it may be signified that he was the antitype not only of the high priest, by reason of his entrance into the holy of holies, but also of the common priests, by reason of his offering on the earth, contrary to what the Socinians state, to serve their own hypotheses.

3. The duration of the office, לעולם, "forever," that is, in contrast to the Levitical priesthood, which ceased after its own period. Yet he will not perform his priesthood except for the period of this finite world, after which he will deliver up the kingdom to the Father, that God may be all in all (1 Cor. 15:24, 28).

4. The exemplar of the priestly office: על דברתי מלכי־צדק, "according to," or "upon the word of Melchizedek." Paul in Hebrews 7:11 trans-lates the words as κατὰ τάξιν Μελχισεδέκ, "after the order of Melchizedek." Here must be considered: (1) who Melchizedek was. As regards the word, מלכי־צדק expresses either "my king" (supply, "who is") "the king of righteousness" or simply "righteousness," and thus the י will be a pronominal suffix, and the sense will emerge as, "my king Melchizedek, who in a figure is righteousness," that which the Messiah was in truth (Jer. 23:6; 33:16; 1 Cor. 1:30). Yet to others, on the authority of Paul, the י is paragogic, as also seems to occur in the preceding word דברתי, as we will soon observe, and then it will say, "king of righteousness," according to Paul. מלך, by the force of the word, means "consul," and in Hebrew ordinarily denotes a king or monarch. In all Oriental languages, צדק means equity, propriety, and righteousness or agreement with the law. The Suda thinks Melchize-dek was descended from Sidus, the son of the king of Libya, and that his mother was Astaroth or Asteria, and so perhaps he is called צדק from this.[13] Moreover, that this was his proper name, and not an appellative name by which Abraham commended him, is apparent from the fact that: (a) it is not said that Abraham called him this. (b) By the Maqqef accent the two words מלך and צדק are as it were united into one proper name, and hence they are always pronounced in one word, Μελχισεδέκ, "Melchizedek" (Heb. 5:6, 10; 6:20; 7:11, 17, 21). In addition, (c) Salem is the proper name of a city, yet צדק is not, for which reason he is ὁ βασιλεὺς Σαλήμ, "the king of Salem"

---

13. Cf. Μελχισεδέκ in *Suidas* (Geneva: Chouët, 1619), 2:127–28, and writing against the Melchizedekians, Epiphanius, *Panarion*, §55 in *PG* 41:973–74; idem, *The Panarion of Epiphanius of Salamis, Books II and III. De Fide*, trans. F. Williams, 2nd rev. ed. (Leiden: Brill, 2013), 78–87.

(Heb. 7:1), from which it is evident that βασιλεὺς is an appellative name, though Σαλὴμ is a proper one. With respect to his biography, Rabbi Jonathan the Jerusalemite,[14] Nachmanides,[15] and indeed the oldest and best of the Hebrew rabbis, think that Melchizedek was Shem, that is, lest such a great person, more excellent than Abraham himself, be a foreigner to their own race, for Noah had established Shem as lord of the land of Canaan, and he accordingly came there, built the city of Salem, and ruled there—with them Jerome,[16] Primasius,[17] and others seem to agree.[18] Didymus and Origen prefer that he was an angel.[19] The Melchizedekians say that he was the Holy Spirit;[20] others that he was at least the great power of God; and finally others that he was not a man, but the Son of God, who appeared to Abraham in the form of a man, which opinion Cunaeus expressly

---

14. See Gen. 14:18 in (Pseudo-)Jonathan, *Targum Pseudo-Jonathan of the Pentateuch: Text and Concordance*, ed. E. G. Clarke, W. E. Aufrecht, J. C. Hurd, and F. Spitzer (Hoboken, N.J.: Ktav Publishing House, 1984); idem, *Targum Pseudo-Jonathan, Genesis*, ed. and trans. M. Maher, 1 volume in 2 parts (Collegeville, Minn.: Liturgical Press, 1992), 1B:58.

15. On Gen. 14:18, Nachmanides, *Ramban (Nachmanides): Commentary on the Torah: Genesis*, ed. C. B. Chavel (New York: Judaica Press, 2005).

16. Against the view that Melchizedek was the Holy Spirit, but instead more likely Shem, in agreement with the rabbis, the most direct reference is Jerome, *Ep. LXXIII ad Evangelum* in *PL* 22:679. Jerome also complained about a book of questions in *Ep. LXXIII, PL* 22:676, "You sent me a volume of unknown authorship, and I do not know whether you left out the name from the title or whether the one who wrote it did not want to admit he was the author so he might escape the risk of disputing [with me]." Jerome probably was interacting with a question from this work, wherein Melchizedek was viewed as the Holy Spirit (Pseudo-Augustine, q. 109, "De Melchisedech," *Quaestiones Veteris et Novi Testamenti* in *PL* 35:2324–30. Current scholarship holds the pseudonymous Ambrosiaster as the author of the *Quaestiones Veteris et Novi Testamenti*. On the question of Jerome and Melchizedek, see A. Souter, *A Study of Ambrosiaster* (Cambridge: Cambridge University Press, 1905), 11–12, esp. 11n4. Cf. Gen. 14:18–19, Jerome, *Liber Hebraicarum quaestionum in Genesim* in *PL* 23:961; idem, *Saint Jerome's Hebrew Questions on Genesis*, ed. and trans. C. T. R. Hayward (Oxford: Clarendon Press, 1995), 47.

17. On Hebrews 7, see Primasius of Hadrumetum (d. ca. 560), *In Epistolam ad Hebraeos Commentaria* in *PL* 68:725–31. Primasius's authorship of this commentary, however is in question as is Migne's attribution to him, see J. Haussleiter, *Leben und Werke des Bischofs Primasius von Hadrumetum: Eine Untersuchung* (diss. Erlangen: Universitäts-Buchdruckerei, 1887), 29; on the acceptance of Primasius's authorship, e.g. B. F. Westcott, *The Epistle to the Hebrews: The Greek Text with Notes and Essays*, 3rd ed. (New York: Macmillan & Co., 1903), vii; on its rejection, e.g. E. Riggenbach, *Der Brief an die Hebräer* (Leipzig: A. Deichert, 1913), L.

18. For further documentation of ancient rabbinic views of Melchizedek, see John Bowker, *The Targums and Rabbinic Literature: An Introduction to Jewish Interpretations of Scripture*, reprint (Cambridge: Cambridge University Press, 1969, 1979, 2009), 196–99.

19. Origen's and Didymus's view as reported in Jerome, *Ep. LXXIII*, n16 above.

20. Against the Melchizedekians, and for an outline of their view, see Epiphanius, *Panarion*, §55.

contends for in *On the Republic of the Hebrews* (bk. 3, ch. 3).[21] Against all those opinions militate the following: (a) Scripture in Genesis 14 does not speak about him other than as about some mere man, whom it describes by his proper name, by his office, kingly as well as priestly, and by the place where he reigned, Salem. (b) That he was not Shem is evident from this, that it cannot be said of Shem that he was "without father, and without mother, and without genealogy, having neither beginning of days, nor end of life" (Heb. 7:3). (c) That he was not some angel is evident because it is nowhere attributed to an angel that he is a priest. (d) That he was not the Holy Spirit is evident because neither is he called anywhere a priest or king, nor did he appear in human form, or prepare a feast for a man. Nor (e) was he the Son of God, because he is said to be ἀφωμοιωμένος, "made like" the Son of God. If you should say that he is said to be "made like" him because he formed for himself the appearance and habit of a body, which afterward he bore in reality on the earth, I would oppose to it that the apostle does not place the similitude in the appearance, but in that he did not have beginning of days, and so forth. If in addition you should say that Christ is said to have been like man in Philippians 2:7, although he was true man, I will respond, It is said in this way because though he was the God-man, yet he was like a common man. Who therefore was Melchizedek? He was a common man, king and priest in Salem, greater than Abraham, inasmuch as he blessed him, and Abraham offered him a tenth, he was "without father and without mother, without genealogy, having neither beginning of days, nor end of life," not because he did not in fact have them, but because these things, by the determined counsel of the Holy Spirit, were not mentioned in the Scriptures, for this reason, that in these things he might bear a type of the Son of God. Moreover, with regard to his priesthood, the apostle himself attributes these things to him so that it might be signified that there was a whole heaven of difference from the Levitical priesthood, namely because that depended upon a Levitical and Aaronic pedigree. Now that we grasp who Melchizedek was, it must be asked (2) what kind of order was that of Melchizedek, על דברתי, "after the order," or the manner, or rite, or arrangement, or condition, or business, or form of the order. Several want the י in דברתי to be a pronominal suffix, so that the sense would be, "after my word," that is, to Melchizedek or

---

21. Petrus Cunaeus (1586–1638), *De republica Hebraeorum* (Leiden: Elzevir, 1632), 274–95.

about Melchizedek. So argues Grotius, that he may gain favor for the Jews, who state that the Psalm speaks of David.[22] But others more correctly believe that it is paragogic and redundant, as frequently occurs elsewhere, as Buxtorf testifies in his *Thesaurus Grammaticus* (bk. 2, ch. 3), and as Rabbi Kimchi and Ibn Ezra acknowledge.[23] Thus the apostle (Heb. 5:6, 10; 6:20; 7:11; etc.) translates it κατὰ τάξιν, "after the order," or κατὰ τὴν ὁμοιότητα, "after the similitude."[24] And perhaps the paragogic י was added for the sake of meter. Therefore it denotes that Melchizedek was certainly not a Levitical or Aaronic priest, but one a whole heaven different; just as Christ was not. To say it in word, "after the order of Melchizedek" means κατὰ δύναμιν ζωῆς ἀκαταλύτου, "after the power of an endless life" (Heb. 7:16). That is to say, not by some corporeal anointing, or legal ceremony, or intervening ordination of man, but by a heavenly institution, an immediate anointing of the Spirit of life, in an extraordinary way. There remains (3) to be observed in a few words the analogy between Melchizedek and Christ, which the text indicates with the little word עַל, "after," "according to." By this particle, on the one hand is excluded the identity of the Melchizedekian and Levitical priesthoods, and is intended the distinction between the two. On the other hand is intended the agreement between the priesthood of Melchizedek and that of the Messiah, as well as the excellence, perfection, and perpetuity of Christ's priesthood compared with the Aaronic priesthood (Heb. 7:11–12; 8:6). We will present this agreement more precisely, Lord willing, in our dogmatic part.[25]

The Dogmatic Part

The Messiah is a priest truly and properly so called. His various names

III. It is therefore from the text without question that the Messiah is a priest truly and properly so called. From which he is also named a minister of the sanctuary, and of the true tabernacle (Heb. 8:2), our advocate with the Father (1 John 2:1–2; Heb. 7:25), the Passover sacrificed for us (1 Cor. 5:7), the lamb

---

22. Grotius, *Annotata ad Vetus Testamentum* (Paris: Sebastian Cramoisy, 1644), 1:484.

23. Johann Buxtorf, Sr. (1564–1629), *Thesaurus grammaticus linguae sanctae hebraeae* (Basel: J. J. Decker, 1663), 342, "Videntur quaedam esse cum Jod paragogico, ut, דִּבְרָתִי מַלְכִּי צֶדֶק *secundum ordinem Melchisedeci.*" Cf. nn. 9 and 12, above.

24. Heb. 7:15

25. §IV, below

slain (John 1:29 with Ex. 29:38–39; Rev. 13:8), a propitiation[26] (Rom. 3:25), the propitiation for our sins (1 John 2:1–2), λύτρον καὶ ἀντίλυτρον, a ransom and price (Matt. 20:28), אשם, an offering (Isa. 53:10), sin (2 Cor. 5:21), a priest forever, after the order of Melchizedek (Ps. 110:4), and so forth. In these final words is also contained a solemn inauguration to the priestly office.

The types prefiguring Christ's priesthood

IV. He had as types and figures of the priestly function: (1) all the common Levitical priests (Heb. 7:23–24), inasmuch as they offered goats, calves, bulls, heifers (Heb. 9:12–13, 21), and so forth, and also the Passover lamb (1 Cor. 5:7; John 19:36). (2) Melchizedek (Gen. 14:18; Ps. 110:4 with the whole of Heb. 7). He, moreover, was neither an angel, nor the Holy Spirit, nor some man immediately created by God, nor even the Son of God himself, as some imagine, because Moses speaks about him in Genesis 14:18–20 as a neighboring king, and one covenanted with Abraham, who came forth to meet him in order to congratulate him about his victory; rather, he was only a type of the Mediator, "made like the Son of God" (Heb. 7:3), as we discussed with more abundance in the exegetical part. This type he bore, not as the Romanists babble on about with respect to the sacrifice of the bread and wine of the Mass, since he brought out, הוציא, these things as provisions not for God, but for Abraham and his army (Gen. 14:18); rather, it is because: (a) he was called the king of righteousness, such as the Son of God was (Jer. 23:6; 1 Cor. 1:30); (b) the king of Salem, or of peace, such as the Son of God was (Isa. 9:6; Eph. 2:14); (c) at once a king of men and a priest of God (Zech. 6:12–13 with Ps. 2:6). (d) He blessed Abraham and received a tithe from him, and consequently signified an excellence in the priesthood beyond any of the Levitical priests, such excellence as obtained in Christ (Heb. 7:4–6, 8–10). (e) By the determined counsel of the Holy Spirit, the text is silent about his genealogy and age, and consequently he is called ἀγενεαλόγητος, "without genealogy," and ἀπάτωρ καὶ ἀμήτωρ, "without father" and "without mother," by which he might prefigure the ineffable generation of Christ, and especially his divine and eternal duration. (f) He did not have either any predecessors or any successors in the priesthood, just as Christ also did not have any partner in his priesthood before him, nor would have any after him (Heb. 13:8 with 10:2–4, 10–12; 7:23–24). (3) The high priest, or the greatest priest (Heb. 3:1; 5:1, 5), descending from Aaron by the alternation of succession, upon whom was incumbent a special worship and annual observance in the holy of holies, for which reason he was also a more illustrious type of Christ the priest (Lev. 16:2ff.; 21:12;

---

26. *propitiatorium*

Heb. 7:23; 9:6–7; etc.), by reason of: (a) the special attire, to which belonged the ephod and the breastplate (Ex. 28:2ff.), the headdress with the golden plate (Ex. 28:36–38), all which prefigured the most eminent dignity of Christ the high priest (Heb. 5:5–6); (b) the anointing (Lev. 8:10–11), which prefigured the anointing of our high priest (Ps. 45:7; 133:2–3; Heb. 1:9); (c) the annual entrance into the holy of holies, with another's blood, to make propitiation (Lev. 16:2–4), which prefigured the entrance of our high priest into heaven (Heb. 10:19–20); (e) the cleanness and gravity (Lev. 21:10–15), which foreshadowed the purity and holiness of our high priest (Heb. 7:26; 4:15).

The necessity of this priest is made known by four reasons.
V. The necessity of this sort of priest results partly: (1) from the injury inflicted by us through sin in so many ways against the infinite majesty of God, which demands the vengeance of a death of every sort (Rom. 1:32). Partly (2) from the most friendly conflict of avenging justice, which demands punishment for the offense to his majesty (Gen. 18:25 with Hab. 1:13), with mercy, which demands the preservation of the sinner (Ps. 103:8–15; Ezek. 16:3–7; Jer. 31:20), in the middle of which, as it were, the divine wisdom interposed itself as the reconciler, solving the conflict by finding the means by which both justice and mercy could be satisfied through the Son, as the priest who offers himself for the guilt of the sinner, from which Christ is named the wisdom and power of God (1 Cor. 1:24), as the one who found eternal redemption (Heb. 9:12). Partly (3) from the most amicable conspiracy of the divine mercy, which willed that man not be totally destroyed (Mic. 7:18; Ex. 34:6–7; Isa. 55:7; Jer. 9:24), justice, which willed that sin not be dismissed unpunished (Ps. 5:5; Zech. 8:17; Amos 5:21–22; Isa. 1:13–14), and truthfulness, which willed that violence not be done against his threatening by the impunity of the sinner (Matt. 5:18 with Gen. 2:17). At last, partly (4) from the eternal impotence of man to satisfy the avenging justice of God (Rom. 8:3; Ps. 49:7–8). From the conjunction of these things, there cannot but emerge a most absolute necessity for some priest who was sufficient to offer himself to the Father as the price of redemption for his own (Matt. 20:28).

What the priesthood is, and what its acts are
VI. That priesthood is nothing other than the mediatorial office of Christ, insofar as it is ordered to the expiation of sins and recovering for sinners the favor of God (Col. 1:20–22; 2 Cor. 5:15; Rom. 5:10). Its general act is to sacrifice, or to do that which is to be done for God with men and, in turn, for men with God. Its specifics are observed to be four altogether: (1) to teach the people (Mal. 2:7); since this was common to the prophets and belonged to them more excellently

than to the priests and Levites, we have already assigned it to Christ's prophetic function;[27] (2) to offer (Heb. 8:3); (3) to intercede (Joel 2:17; Heb. 5:1); and (4) to bless (Num. 6:23–24). Which four things are discerned to be, as prefigured in the types, so presented in the antitype.

The first act of the priestly office is offering.
VII. Therefore, the first act of Christ's priestly office is to offer (Heb. 5:3; 7:27; 9:14, 23), which is nothing other than (we speak of a propitiatory sacrifice[28]) to present to God, for the sinner and sin, something of such a kind in which he may rest, and on account of which he may be reconciled to the sinner. As in any offering, so in this one especially, four things occur to be considered: (1) the priest who offers, (2) the sacrifice offered, (3) the altar of offering, and (4) the goal of the sacrificing. (1) The priest in this present business is the God-man Mediator, with respect to both natures (Ps. 110:4 with Heb. 7:3). (2) The sacrifice, himself (Heb. 7:27), most properly speaking with respect to his human nature, for which reason it is attributed to his body (1 Peter 2:24; Col. 1:22), and his blood (Col. 1:20), and also his soul (Isa. 53:10; Matt. 20:28). (3) The altar, himself, with respect to his divine nature (Heb. 9:14; 13:10), because just as the value and efficacy of the sacrifice depended upon the altar (Matt. 23:19), so the worth and efficacy of Christ's death depends upon his deity (1 John 1:7; Acts 20:28). (4) The goal of this offering is: (a) satisfaction, by which through the transfer of guilt to the sacrificial victim, the sinner was delivered (Lev. 4:24; ch. 16 with Heb. 9:12–13; 2:9, 14–15, 17; Rom. 3:24–26). It will be incumbent upon us to treat this satisfaction expressly in the chapter on redemption.[29] Then from this follows (b) reconciliation with God, who has been offended by sin, by which, when guilt has been taken away through satisfaction, the sinner is restored to peace and friendship with God (Num. 16:46 with Rom. 5:1–2, 9, 11; Eph. 2:13–14). This offering our high priest consummated once and for all by dying on the wood of the cross (Heb. 9:26; 10:14).

The second act of the priestly office is intercession.
VIII. The second action of the priestly function is intercession (Heb. 5:1). Accordingly, he is called a παράκλητος, paraclete (1 John 2:1–2), which in reference to the Holy Spirit denotes a comforter (John 14:16–17, 26; 16:7), but in reference to Christ, an advocate (*advocatur*, who is called in, to plead someone's

---

27. 1.5.6 §V
28. *de sacrificio* ἱλαστικῷ
29. 1.5.18 §§X–XIII

case, specifically by appearing for and answering for him in judgment, and by pleading his case against his adversary), because against any of our adversaries (1 Peter 5:8 with Matt. 5:25; Rev. 12:10) he appears for us before God (Heb. 9:24; 7:25), answers for us, and pleads our case, ἐντυγχάνει, "makes intercession," at the right hand of God (Rom. 8:34), to the end that he may obtain what we desire. This intercession therefore is nothing other than the gracious and constant will of Christ before his Father (John 17:24; Heb. 9:24; Rom. 8:34), that, on account of his satisfaction and merits (1 John 2:1–2), the Father may receive into grace both the persons and the spiritual sacrifices of the persons (Heb. 7:24; Rev. 8:3; 1 Peter 2:5; Rom. 8:34) of each and every one of the elect (John 17:9–10; Luke 22:31–32), which the Father is also always willing and ready to do (Matt. 17:5; John 11:42).

The two periods of intercession: The beginning, and the consummation
IX. Two periods of this intercession are observed: the first, that of the beginning, which he completed while existing on the earth, in the deepest humiliation of soul and lowliness of attitude (John 17:9, 20; Luke 22:31–32; Heb. 5:7; John 17:1ff.; Matt. 26:37–39; Mark 14:35; Matt. 3:17), and the second, that of the consummation, which, being present in heaven, he carries out there, with the highest majesty: (1) by appearing before the Father for us (Heb. 9:24 with 8:6; 7:22), just as Judah did for Benjamin (Gen. 43:8–9), and Paul did for Onesimus with Philemon (Philemon 9–10), and the high priest once did in the holy of holies, adorned with the names of the twelve tribes on his breast (Ex. 28:9–12, 17–22), to which the bride alludes (Song 8:6). (2) By presenting his satisfaction and merits, so that on account of them the spiritual sacrifices of himself and of his people may be accepted in his Father's sight (1 John 2:1–2; Rom. 8:34; Heb. 7:25). This was once prefigured in the high priest, slaying propitiatory sacrifices and bringing in their blood, and as it were presenting it in the holy of holies before the ark of the covenant (Lev. 16:11–12, 15–16). Without this, as he would be constantly remaining on the earth, he would not be a priest, that is, not a perfect one (Heb. 8:1–4).

The properties and prerogatives of this intercession
X. So then furthermore, the incomparable properties and prerogatives of this intercession are made known to us, that: (1) it is built upon his satisfaction and meritorious propitiation (1 John 2:1–2; Rom. 8:34; Heb. 9:12ff.), which rests upon the worth of his person as the God-man. (2) It was not merely charitative, like our intercessions, but authoritative as well (John 17:2; Matt. 28:18;

John 5:21–22, 26–27), because he merited it.[30] (3) It universally prevails with the Father, who always hears the Son (John 11:42; Col. 1:13; Heb. 12:24; John 14:16; 16:23–24, 26), no accusations of divine justice, the law, or Satan obtaining anything to the contrary (Rom. 8:34). (4) It is exceedingly glorious, inasmuch as it is in heaven, done by the one seated at the right hand of God (Rom. 8:34). (5) It is general, for each and every one of the elect who are, who were, who will be (John 17:9, 20; Heb. 9:24). (6) It is perfect and saving (Heb. 7:25). Therefore, there is no intercession that can compare with this one: while we do not know what we should pray for as we ought (Rom. 8:26–27), he intercedes and obtains for us, with our names continually present on his breast and on his shoulders, as our great high priest.

The distinction between the intercession of the Son and of the Holy Spirit
XI. However, because both the Holy Spirit as well as the Son are our παράκλητος, paraclete, as is evident by a comparison of 1 John 2:1 with John 14:16–17, 26 and 16:7, and both are said to intercede for us (Rom. 8:34; Heb. 7:25 with Rom. 8:26–27), it will be helpful to observe the distinction between the intercessions of the two, namely that: (1) Christ intercedes before the Father without us (1 John 2:1; Rom. 8:34), whereas the Holy Spirit intercedes before God with us (Rom. 8:15). (2) Christ intercedes for us as our high priest and advocate, outside of us, by the presentation of his death, by the satisfaction of his death, by the power of his satisfaction and merit, by taking up our case, opposing any accusation against us (Heb. 7:24–25), whereas the Holy Spirit intercedes as one who assists, by his effectual work within us (Rom. 8:26–27; Rev. 22:17), efficiently, as they say, not formally. (3) Christ intercedes for us by the voice of his own blood, which speaks better things than the blood of Abel (Heb. 12:24), whereas the Spirit intercedes for us by stirring within us inexpressible groanings (Rom. 8:26–27).

The third act of the priestly office is blessing.
XII. The third act of the priestly office is blessing. For (1) not only did the priests once bless the people from the divine commandment (Num. 6:23); nor only (2) did Melchizedek, priest of the most high God (Heb. 7:1), as a type of our

---

30. Compare the distinction between a *charitativa benedictio*, or euctical blessing, which is more of a prayer of an inferior for a superior, and an authoritative blessing of a superior to an inferior, such as fathers and priests, in John Owen on Heb. 7:1–3, observation XXI, *A Continuation of the Exposition of the Epistle of Paul the Apostle to the Hebrews, viz. on the sixth, seventh, eighth, ninth, and tenth chapters* (London: Printed for Nathaniel Ponder, 1680), 104–7; cf. Heb. 7:1–3, observation XX, idem, *Exposition of the Epistle to the Hebrews*, 5:316–20; idem, *Works*, 22:316–20.

priest, bless Abraham (Gen. 14:19; Heb. 7:6–7); but also, (3) it is said that all the nations will be blessed in the seed of Abraham (Gen. 22:18), of Isaac (Gen. 26:4), and of Jacob (Gen. 28:14), which seed is our priest (Acts 3:25). And so then in addition, (4) it is said that the blessing of Abraham comes on the Gentiles in Christ Jesus (Gal. 3:14), namely, the same blessing in kind as that by which God blessed Abraham on account of this seed of his. So then, (5) appearing to his disciples after his resurrection, he bestowed a blessing upon them, by praying peace upon them (John 20:19, 21). (6) The apostle imitates this, throughout his letters not only praying grace and peace upon the churches, but also distinctly, "from our Lord Jesus Christ" (Rom. 1:7; 1 Cor. 1:3; etc.). Finally, (7) it is said that God blesses us with every spiritual blessing in Christ Jesus (Eph. 1:3).

What it is to bless
XIII. Moreover, to bless, בָּרַךְ, εὐλογεῖν, means (1) to praise, to commend, to give thanks, and thus we bless God (Ps. 100:4; 103:1–2, 20); (2) to wish all things favorable, to pray for them, just as parents bless their children (Gen. 9:26–27), pastors bless their people (Num. 6:23), all sorts of people bless each other (for example, Jacob blessed Pharaoh, Gen. 47:7); (3) to consecrate, to sanctify, to separate for holy use: thus God blessed the Sabbath (Ex. 20:11), thus Christ blessed the eucharistic bread and wine (Matt. 26:26); (4) to confer any sorts of benefits: thus Jesus blesses the Jews (Acts 3:26), thus it is said that the Gentiles will be blessed in Christ (Gal. 3:14). It is in this last sense that the word *blessing* comes to us here.

The benefits of the blessing: Spiritual benefits
XIV. And thus by blessing our priest confers benefits to his own: (1) all spiritual benefits (Eph. 1:3; 2 Peter 1:3), and specifically: (a) redemption (Gal. 3:13–14), (b) the communication of the long-promised Spirit (Gal. 3:13–14), (c) conversion from sin to God and righteousness (Acts 3:25–26), (d) adoption, by which we were admitted into the family of God (Gal. 4:4–5 with 1 John 3:1–2), (e) justification by faith (Gal. 3:8–9; Ps. 32:1–2), (f) covenantal communion with God (Gen. 17:7–8; Heb. 8:10ff. with Ps. 144:15), (g) eternal glorification (Luke 13:28–29 with 16:23), and so forth.

Temporal benefits
(2) All temporal benefits, as appurtenant and corollary to the spiritual benefits (Matt. 6:31–33; Rom. 8:32; 1 Tim. 4:8), as is evident in the blessing conferred upon Abraham (which is said to be turned upon all his seed in Christ Jesus, Gal. 3:14), by which he obtained (a) riches (Gen. 13:2; 24:35), (b) honors (Gen. 24:35;

23:6), (c) success in his affairs (Gen. 14:14–16), (d) numerous offspring and posterity (Gen. 17:5; Heb. 11:11–12). With all these benefits, our priest blesses his own, not only charitatively by his prayers obtaining those things from elsewhere, as we bless (Ps. 129:8), but authoritatively and operatively, from himself. Thus God blesses us with these benefits on account of Christ as the meritorious cause (Dan. 9:17), through Christ as the conferring cause (Phil. 4:13; 1:11), in Christ as in our head (Eph. 1:3; 2 Cor. 1:20).

The Elenctic Part
In the elenctic part of this chapter, these questions especially occur:
1. Was Christ named a priest truly and properly?
XV. In the elenctic part regarding Christ's priestly function, after the question whether the Messiah who was from the divine promise one day to come had to be a priest, which we have already determined in the elenctic part of chapter 5,[31] the first question that occurs is whether Christ was truly and properly named a priest. The Socinians, so that they would not be compelled to admit that he rendered a propitiatory sacrifice according to its true and proper name, and thus properly speaking made satisfaction for our sins through substitution, do at least admit that in the Scriptures he is sometimes called a priest, but notwithstanding they still assert he is named such improperly, according to some kind of analogy and likeness that he had with the high priest, who annually in the holy of holies offered himself to God.

The orthodox arguments
The Reformed on the contrary, together with the Scriptures, assert that he was named a priest truly and properly, and that by these reasons especially, because: (1) he is frequently called a priest, which they acknowledge, and without any compelling necessity this must not be twisted into an improper sense. (2) He is described as true priest, and one properly so called, and all the requirements of a priest properly so called belong to him. The description of a priest properly so called, which is found in Hebrews 5:1–11, is applied to him in the same passage, and in Hebrews 8:3. Taken individually, (a) a priest had to have a legitimate calling, for no one takes this honor to himself, but he who is called by God, as was Aaron (Heb. 5:4); and Christ had such a calling (Heb. 5:5, 10). (b) He has to be taken from among men (Heb. 5:1); and Christ was from among men (1 Tim. 2:5). (c) And that so that he might act for men with God (Heb. 5:1); and

---

31. 1.5.5 §§V–VI

Christ acted for men, then on earth, not only by reconciling us with God (Eph. 2:12–17; Col. 1:20–21), but also by interceding for us (John 17:9; Luke 22:32), and now in heaven (Rom. 8:34; 1 John 2:1–2). (d) He has to offer gifts and sacrifices (Heb. 5:1); and Christ offered himself (Heb. 7:27; Eph. 5:2). (e) He had to have an altar on which to offer sacrifice (Ex. 29:23ff.); and Christ had one (Heb. 13:10). (f) He had to have his own order (2 Kings 23:4; Luke 1:5, 9); and Christ had his own (Ps. 110:4). Nor can anything be adduced in the priest that was not in Christ. In fact, he was such a true priest that all the Levitical priests at his coming had to cease, like prefiguring shadows when the body appears (Heb. 10:1–2, 8). (3) He is called a far more excellent priest than all the Levitical ones (Heb. 7–10); so then, he is a true and proper priest. I would add that (4) the truth of all the things that were prefigured in the ceremonial law is in Christ (John 1:17; Col. 2:17; Heb. 10:1); therefore also the truth of the priesthood.

Objections

There is not anything to what they may object: (1) that only in the Epistle to the Hebrews is mention made of this priesthood. I respond: (a) For that reason, was he therefore improperly called a priest? (b) Mention of it is also made elsewhere, both in express words (Ps. 110:4), and in force, whenever it is attributed to him to be a Mediator (1 Tim. 2:5), an intercessor (1 John 2:1–2), a Redeemer through an offering, and to do priestly acts. (2) That the things that the priests according to the law did, he did not properly do: he did not sacrifice animals to God. I respond, From this is inferred only that he was not a priest according to the law, not that he was no priest. For in this way neither would Melchizedek have been a true priest, and one properly so called. (3) That the apostle attributes to Christ's priesthood an intercession, which is still not a sacrifice properly so called, through which sins are expiated, but only improperly, insofar as the intercession served for the expiation. I respond: (a) It is false to say that Christ's priesthood consists only in his intercession for us; rather, it also consists in the offering of himself for us (Eph. 5:2). Then also, (b) that very intercession which he performs for us in heaven, according to the example of the high priest interceding in the holy of holies for the people, presupposes a sacrifice offered on earth (Heb. 9:7 with vv. 11–15).

2. Was he a priest on earth?

XVI. Second, it is asked whether he was a priest also on earth. The Socinians, so that they would not be compelled to acknowledge that by the death of Christ accomplished on earth he offered himself for us, and by offering made satisfaction, think that he was not a priest on earth, but only in heaven, where he offered himself to the Father by interceding for us.

The orthodox arguments
The Reformed prove that he was a priest even while existing on earth, dying there, and offering himself by dying, because: (1) in Hebrews 9:11–12 it is said that by his own blood he entered into the holy place and obtained eternal redemption (cf. vv. 15–18, 22–23). (2) In Hebrews 9:25–28 it is said that having now once been made manifest to put away sin by his sacrifice of himself, he offered himself, which occurred without a doubt on earth. (3) In Hebrews 10:10 it is said that we are sanctified through the offering of the body of Christ, accomplished once, and without a doubt on earth. (4) In Hebrews 10:12 it is said that when one sacrifice had been offered for sins, he sat down at the right hand of God (cf. v. 14). Finally, (5) in Ephesians 5:2 it is said that he gave himself up for us as "an offering and a sacrifice to God for a sweet-smelling aroma," which beyond all doubt occurred on earth.

Objections
Nor does it prove the contrary: (1) that in Hebrews 7:26 it is said that our high priest would be higher than the heavens, such that, if he were on earth, he would not even be a priest (Heb. 8:4). I respond, From this it is only concluded that he had to complete the acts of his priesthood not on earth, but when his offering was made on the cross, he had to ascend with his own blood into the heavenly sanctuary, and intercede there for us; otherwise he would not be a more exalted and more perfect priest than the common Levitical priests. (2) That in Hebrews 7:16 it is said that he was made a high priest after the power of an endless life; therefore, they say, he was not a priest as long as he was mortal. I respond: (a) The apostle does not intend that he was not a priest when he had life that would be ended, but that for the purpose of perpetual intercession he had at some point to obtain an endless life. Moreover, (b) he also had an endless life on earth, by reason of his divine nature, and after the resurrection, even while still existing on earth, with respect to his human nature. (3) That in Hebrews 5:9–10 it is said that when he had been rendered perfect, he became the cause of eternal salvation to those who obey him, having been called by God a priest, and so forth. I respond, He was never simply imperfect, because he was always sufficient for himself and for his office, although through stages by succeeding actions he was made gradually more perfect, until at last in the heavens, seated at the right hand of the Father, and there gloriously interceding for us, and most effectively applying to us the procured redemption, he became a most perfect priest.

3. Was only the high priest a type of Christ's priesthood?

XVII. So then, third, it is asked whether only the high priest bore a type of Christ, or whether the common priests of the Old Testament also did. The Socinians, because they state that Christ became a priest by his entrance into the heavenly holy place, which was prefigured by the entrance of the high priest into the holy of holies, deny that the common priests sustained a figure of Christ.

The arguments of the orthodox

The orthodox teach that the common priests were also types of Christ, because: (1) he is not only called an ἀρχιερεύς, high priest, but also a ἱερεύς, כהן, priest, and he is compared with the common priests (Heb. 8:4). (2) The high priest and the common priests were of the same kind, differing nearly alone in degree of dignity, for which reason not only did all things (the entrance of the high priest into the holy of holies nearly alone excepted) also belong to the priests, but also, the high priest is designated throughout the Old Testament by כהן, the same name as that of the common priests. (3) Not only the sacrificing of the highest priest, which was done surrounding his entrance into the holy of holies, with the blood of goats and calves (about which the apostle speaks in Heb. 9:12), but also all sacrificing altogether, even that which was done by any of the priests, through the blood of bulls, of goats, and the ashes of a heifer (about which he speaks in v. 13), prefigured the sacrifice of the Mediator (cf. v. 19). (4) The Passover lamb, which was not sacrificed by the high priest alone, but by any of the common priests, also bore a type of Christ (1 Cor. 5:7; John 18:36). (5) The apostle in Hebrews 10:11 (cf. v. 10), compares every priest, in reference to sacrifice, offering, burnt offerings, and sacrifice for sins (vv. 5, 6, 8), with Christ, as the type with the antitype. (6) With regard to the entire ceremonial law it is pronounced that it had a shadow of good things to come, such that the body is Christ (Col. 2:17; Heb. 10:1), and accordingly this includes the common priests as well. I need not add that (7) from the contrary hypothesis, not even Melchizedek could have provided a type of Christ, because he was not a partaker of the entrance into the holy of holies.

An objection of our adversaries

Nor do I see what our adversaries could allege to the contrary, at least with any semblance of truth, except that a more express, frequent, and full comparison occurs between the high priest and Christ than between the common priests and Christ. However, from this can be concluded at the most nothing more than that the high priest bore a more illustrious type of Christ, and that by reason of his entrance into the holy of holies, yet not that he alone sustained a type of Christ.

4. Did he make an offering for himself?

XVIII. Fourth, it is asked whether Christ also made an offering for himself. Socinus, so that he might more effectively weaken the point that Christ made satisfaction for the sins of others by a priestly offering, stated that Christ made an offering no less for himself than for others: not indeed for his own sins, which he acknowledges he did not have, but for the infirmities of his flesh, that is, for his mortality and passibility.

The arguments of the orthodox

The orthodox deny this, from the fact that: (1) the offering is constantly described in the Scriptures as made on account of sins (Lev. 5:11; Heb. 5:3, 2:17), from which Christ was immune (Heb. 7:26). (2) Infirmity of the flesh, passibility, and mortality, to the extent that they are without sin (as they were in Christ, Heb. 4:15), do not require a sacrifice. This is not to mention that (3) even from the hypothesis of our adversaries, in which the offering of Christ was made in heaven, when he had set aside all infirmity of the flesh, passibility, and mortality, this offering for himself is absurd.

An objection

The sole point that could be adduced to the contrary with any semblance of the truth is found in Hebrews 5:2–3, "Who can have compassion on those who are ignorant and wayward, since he himself is also compassed with infirmity, and by reason of this infirmity he ought, as for the people, so also for himself, to offer for sins." However, Socinus does not observe that the apostle speaks about a sinful infirmity, which was common to the people and to the high priest, for which the high priest had to make sacrifice for himself as well as for the people; but in this respect it does not apply to Christ, nor can it apply, because he was not liable to infirmities of this sort.

5. Did Christ alone offer himself, and that only once, and does he
besides himself have no other priests properly so called?

XIX. Fifth, it is asked whether Christ alone offered himself, and that only once, and thus he alone is a priest after the order of Melchizedek, or whether he is also offered by others, and that more frequently, who therefore are priests with him, and indeed after the order of Melchizedek. The papists, for the sake of their Mass, state that Christ is daily offered by sacrificing priests for the sins of the living and the dead, and that they are therefore not only priests, but also priests after the order of Melchizedek.

The arguments of the orthodox
The Reformed state that Christ alone offered himself, and that only once, and therefore he alone is a priest properly so called, alone according to the order of Melchizedek, because: (1) Scripture nowhere teaches that Christ must be offered by any other than himself, nor more frequently than once, nor that he would have any priests truly and properly so called as successors, much less priests of the same order with him, namely after the order of Melchizedek. Indeed, (2) Scripture teaches the contraries of all these things, when it frequently relates that Christ by the one offering of himself has perfected all those who are being sanctified (Heb. 10:14). I need not add that (3) it implies the greatest absurdities, indeed the denial of that one and only sacrifice which Christ accomplished on the cross, if we say that Christ is offered by men, and that this one and only offering of himself is of no advantage to us if it is not repeated daily, and that by men who are priests of the same order with him, that is, after the order of Melchizedek.

An objection
Nor do they have anything that they may object except Malachi 1:11, "In every place incense is offered to my name, and a pure offering." However, they refuse to notice that by "incense" and "a pure offering" is understood nothing except the true and spiritual worship of the New Testament, and the spiritual sacrifices prefigured by these Levitical sacrificings in the Old Testament (cf. Zech. 14:16, 20). More points of this kind, Lord willing, will occur when we will expressly refute the Mass.[32]

6. As a priest, did he truly and properly make satisfaction?
XX. Sixth, it is asked whether Christ, as a priest, in offering himself by death on the cross, made satisfaction for sinners from the rigor of divine justice, by paying their debts with an equivalent price, and in that way reconciled them to God. Christians affirm this, Socinians deny it. This is certainly the most momentous controversy of this topic, but because this one controversy diffuses itself into several, namely, regarding the necessity, truth, universality, and so forth, of the satisfaction, which pertain to the chapter on redemption, we will set this matter aside for there.[33]

---

32. §§XXIII–XXV, below; and esp. 1.7.5 §XXIV
33. 1.5.18 §§XVIII–XXI

7. Does intercession for us belong to Christ alone?

XXI. Seventh, it is asked whether Christ alone intercedes for us. The papists transfer the dignity[34] of intercession also to angels and to departed saints, whom they also teach should be called upon for that reason. Protestants leave that dignity to Christ alone, because: (1) he alone is called not only the μεσίτης, Mediator (1 Tim. 2:5), but also the παράκλητος, advocate or intercessor (1 John 2:1). (2) The priestly dignity, in reference to all its acts, among which is also intercession, Christ has ἀπαράβατον, unalterable (Heb. 5:5–6; 7:4, 6–7, 11, 16–17, 21–22, 24; etc.). (3) Intercession is nothing other than an effectual presentation of an offering (Heb. 9:12, 24; Rom. 8:34). Therefore since the latter belongs only to Christ, so also does the former. (4) There is no need for members of his household to serve as agents, since the Son himself so kindly invites us to himself (Matt. 11:28), and so generously promises the hearing of our prayers made in his name (John 16:23–24), especially since no man comes unto the Father, but by him (John 14:6). (5) No one besides him fully sees either our hearts, because this belongs only to God (1 Kings 8:39), or our necessities (Isa. 63:16).

An objection of our adversaries

Nor is there any substance to what they allege to the contrary, that we are commanded to pray for each other (1 Tim. 2:1; James 5:16), for we are commanded to do so while we are together on earth and know our mutual needs, but not once we are brought into heaven, for those who are on earth, inasmuch as we do not know them (Job 16:21; Isa. 63:16).

8. Did Christ intercede for us while he existed on earth?

XXII. Eighth, it is asked whether Christ interceded for us even while he was still living on earth. The Socinians, because they restrict Christ's priestly function only to intercession, and want his priesthood to have begun only in heaven, deny that he interceded for us on earth. The orthodox affirm the contrary, because: (1) Scripture plainly teaches that he interceded also on earth (Luke 22:32; John 17). (2) The hypotheses upon which they build their opinion are patently false, namely: (a) that Christ's priesthood only consists in his intercession, whereas it was after the purging of our sins had already been accomplished that he sat down at the right hand of God (Heb. 1:3), there to intercede for us (Rom. 8:34). (b) That he began his priesthood only in heaven, the falsity of which we have expressly demonstrated in §XVI.

---

34. ἀξίωμα

9. Did Melchizedek sacrifice bread and wine?
XXIII. Ninth, it is asked whether Melchizedek, when he met Abraham after his victory, offered bread and wine as a sacrifice to God, so that by this he might prefigure Christ, as the priest according to the order of Melchizedek, sacrificing himself under the species of bread and wine (Gen. 14:18). The papists seek, if not the only, at least the chief stronghold for their sacrifice of the Mass, in this sacrificing of Melchizedek.

The arguments of the orthodox
Protestants deny that there occurred here sacrificing properly so called, because (1) Scripture makes no mention of sacrificing. (2) The text and the historical circumstances expressly speak against this, for הֶעֱלָה, which is employed in the Scriptures for sacrificing, does not occur here, but rather, הוֹצִיא, "he caused to come" or "he made to be brought," that is, bread and wine, and that not alone (since such a man, and in such a circumstance, does not customarily receive such a man with only bread and wine), but by synecdoche, all sorts of food. Nor did he himself do this so much as, by his command, his servants, who nevertheless did not by that fact make a sacrifice. (3) It is incompatible with the very hypotheses of the papists, which want Jesus the Savior to have sacrificed himself, his own flesh and blood, in the first Mass, and not bread and wine.

An objection of the adversaries
Nor do I see what the adversaries could allege for their case except the syntax, "He brought forth bread and wine, *for* he was a priest of the most high God." For which reason Johann Eck says, "He brought them forth so that he might offer them to God."[35] But they give no reasons, nor also is the rational conjunction *for* present in the text, and the act of his priesthood is expressly designated not in an offering, but in a priestly blessing (cf. Num. 6:23).

10. Did Christ offer himself to God in the Holy Supper?
XXIV. So then, tenth, it is asked whether Christ himself offered himself in the Mass under the species of bread and wine. The papists, for the sake of the sacrifice of the Mass, affirm this. Protestants deny it, because: (1) in the Scriptures, namely in the institution of the Holy Supper, according to all the Gospel-writers, and indeed in the Pauline repetition, there is not even one bit about this offering. (2) It is constantly said that he sacrificed himself on the cross, and that by his death. (3) Because the offering of a propitiatory sacrifice happens by the

---

35. Johann Eck (1486–1543), *Ad invictissimum Poloniae regem Sigismundum, De Sacrificio Missae contra Lutheranos, libri tres* (Cologne: Peter Quentel, 1526), fol. 7v.

destruction of the thing offered, Christ in offering himself in the Mass would have destroyed himself. (4) Such a bloodless propitiatory sacrifice as is asserted for our Savior by our adversaries implies a manifest contradiction (Heb. 9:22). (5) Instead of the institution of a sacrament, he would have offered a sacrifice, which stand a whole species apart from each other. It will be sufficient in this place to have pointed out these things that will be, Lord willing, discussed more fully in their own place.[36]

The Practical Part

Christ's priesthood: 1. Shows how horrendous and detestable sin is.
XXV. The practice of Christ's priesthood, first, shows us how horrendous and detestable a thing sin is, inasmuch as: (1) it makes us so adverse to God (Isa. 1:10–16; 59:2), such that it made a priest and reconciler, who would act on our behalf with God (Heb. 5:1), absolutely necessary for us. And not (2) some common Levitical priest, not Aaron, not Joshua, but one so great and of such a kind, after the order of Melchizedek, after the power of an endless life (Heb. 7:11, 16), the very Son of God, the God-man (Heb. 7:3). (3) It brought upon us so much guilt that a sacrifice was necessary for us, not of bulls and goats (Ps. 40:6–7; 51:16; Mic. 6:6–7; Heb. 9:13), but of the very Son of God, who would offer himself to God (Heb. 9:12). (4) It has made all our holy things, prayers, and best works, so hateful and abominable to God (Isa. 1:10–16; 64:6) that an intercessor was necessary for them, who would bring them before the sight of God (Rev. 8:3–4). (5) It has so deprived us of every blessing entirely, whether bodily or spiritual, that a priest was necessary who would bless us (Num. 6:23 with Eph. 1:3; Gal. 3:13–14). (6) It so armed the law, justice, and the power of God against us, that we could not have been reconciled unless by the cursed sacrificing of the very Son of God (Gal. 3:13–14).

To what purpose
So then, if sin is such a thing to be detested, and that in the sight of the most just Judge, certainly it is the case that: (1) we also should detest and abhor it (Gen. 39:9), (2) on account of it we should humble ourselves profoundly before God (Dan. 9:3–4ff.), (3) whose reconciliation we should earnestly seek in the sacrifice of our one and only high priest (Dan. 9; 2 Cor. 5:18–20), (4) we should pursue it with an irreconcilable hatred (Ps. 97:10; 119:128), and (5) from it we should cleanse ourselves more and more in the blood of our priest (Isa. 1:16; Jer. 4:4; 1 John 1:7; Heb. 10:22; Ps. 51:2, 7).

------

36. 1.7.5, esp. §XXIV

2. It presents the conflict between divine justice and mercy,
which is settled by our priest.

XXVI. Second, it presents, so that we may marvel, the harmonious discord and friendly combat between the various attributes of God, into which our priest, through the divine wisdom, interposed himself in the middle and as a mediator, so to speak. For God's avenging justice demanded an eternal condemnation from the sinner (Deut. 27:26; Gal. 3:10; Rom. 1:18, 32), and to its help came his immovable truthfulness, pronouncing upon the sinner death and every kind of evil as a punishment (Gen. 2:17, 3:17); on the other hand, grace and mercy contended for the preservation of the sinner, and his eternal blessing (Ps. 103:8; Isa. 55:7; Zech. 9:11), and to its help comes glory, sought from the good works of the redeemed, converted, sanctified sinner (John 15:8; Matt. 5:16), as well as from the celebration of his goodness and clemency, by which he does not delight in the death of the sinner, but that he be converted and live (Ezek. 33:11); and between these parties, the divine wisdom interposed itself in the middle as it were, to satisfy both contending parties, so that both the sin might be punished according to justice, and the sinner might be preserved according to mercy; it presented a priest who would satisfy justice and would save the sinner; and thus from this he is called the power and wisdom of God (1 Cor. 1:24), inasmuch as that wisdom, in this our priest, as it were reconciled grace with justice (Rom. 3:25), so that now grace and truth meet together, and righteousness and peace kiss each other (Ps. 85:10).

To what purpose
Thus in this conflict, and in the most friendly settlement made by our priest, at least four divine perfections offer themselves to us—justice, truthfulness, mercy, and wisdom—that here we should: (1) contemplate them (Rom. 11:22), (2) marvel at them (Rom. 11:32–33), (3) celebrate and glorify them (Rom. 11:36), and (4) imitate them, continually tempering the rigor of justice with mercy and gentleness[37] (James 2:13).

3. It moves us to gratitude. The motives
XXVII. Third, it most effectively moves us to gratitude, first toward the God who gives, then toward the Savior given to us to be a priest. That is, if we should distinctly consider: (1) the one who gives, Jehovah, "Jehovah has sworn" (Ps. 110:4), that all-sufficient God (Gen. 17:1), who induced not by any lack, but

---

37. ἐπιεικεία, lit. "equity," in Aristotle, *Topica*, 141a16 in *LCL* 391:572–73; cf. "gentleness" or "kindness" in Acts 24:4, 2 Cor. 10:1.

by pure, unadulterated abundance of grace, destined this priest in the eternal counsel, and gave him in time. (2) The one given, not just any sort of priest, not a Levitical or Aaronic priest (Heb. 7:11), not a man of just any kind or greatness, but one of this kind, and one this great, τοιοῦτος, "such" (v. 26), after the order of Melchizedek (vv. 17, 21), the very Son of God (v. 3), who is eternal (vv. 17, 21), the God-man, most sufficient, who is able to save to the uttermost (vv. 24–25), who is able to reconcile, to intercede, to bless, and to accomplish all things that must be done for us with God (Heb. 5:1). (3) The manner of giving, with such great solemnity, with an oath (Ps. 110:4; Heb. 6:16–17; 7:20–21), with a solemn declaration of an immutable counsel, "and will not repent" (Ps. 110:4; cf. Heb. 6:17; Isa. 45:23; 54:9–10; Ps. 89:34–35), which way of acting is neither in vain, nor breathes of common things, as it (a) most effectively persuades us of the immutability of his counsel (Heb. 6:17); (b) commends to us the excellency of this priest and priesthood, which the apostle extols throughout the Epistle to the Hebrews; (c) strengthens the heart of the sinner regarding the immutability of God's good pleasure toward him, "For men swear by the greater, and an oath for confirmation is to them an end of all controversy. Wherein God, willing more abundantly to show the immutability of his counsel, ἐμεσίτευσεν ὅρκῳ, guaranteed it by an oath, that by two immovable things, in which it is impossible for God to lie, we might have a strong consolation" (Heb. 6:16–18; cf. Mic. 7:20; Hab. 3:9). From this Tertullian in *On Repentance* (ch. 4) says, "What God commends so highly, and what he also, in a human way, testifies under an oath, we ought certainly to both approach and guard with the greatest gravity, so that abiding in the affirmation of the divine grace, and also in its fruit and benefit, we may be able accordingly to persevere."[38] (4) The persons to whom he gave it: little men (Ps. 8:4), dust and ashes (Gen. 18:27), public enemies condemned by the law itself, and dead in sins (Eph. 2:1, 5; Ezek. 16:3–6). From all these things, God commends his love toward us, while we were yet sinners (Rom. 5:7–8). (5) The uses for which he gave him, namely so that: (a) he might reconcile us to himself (Lev. 19:22 with 2 Cor. 5:19), (b) he might provide an agent through whom we might have boldness and access with confidence to the throne of grace (Eph. 2:18; 3:12), (c) he might heap up blessings of every kind upon us (Num. 6:23 with Eph. 1:3; Gal. 3:14).

The duties of gratitude

All these things, are they not of such a kind and so great that they should most effectively move us to gratitude? That is, a gratitude by which: (1) we pursue in

---

38. Tertullian, *De poenitentia liber* in *PL* 1:1234.

turn with sincere and ardent love the one who gives this priest to us, Jehovah, and gives him with such great solemnity and preparation, that is, by interposing an oath, and the declaration of an immutable counsel, and gives him out of pure, unadulterated love (Rom. 5:8, 11); (2) we promptly and eagerly receive the one given, this priest, and without care commit to him our cases to be pleaded before God (Heb. 5:1); (3) we in turn sacrifice ourselves and all we have to God (Rom. 12:1).

4. It teaches us to contemplate him. The motivating reasons
XXVIII. Fourth, it teaches us to contemplate this our priest with devotion, κατανοήσατε, "Consider" the high priest (Heb. 3:1), that is, pay attention to him; θεωρεῖτε, "See" how great this man was (Heb. 7:4). For to this use (1) pointed the annual sacrifice of the Passover lamb under the Old Testament (1 Cor. 5:7); (2) the Holy Supper under the New Testament (1 Cor. 11:26); (3) the so often repeated and so accurately impressed description of this priest and of this priesthood throughout the whole Epistle to the Hebrews.

The particulars of this contemplation
Namely, let us contemplate: (1) his necessity, which is altogether unavoidable, provided we want to become partakers of any good (Heb. 7:26, "He was fitting for us"), such that we feel this necessity, for by the lack of this feeling, so few, even among such as who profess him at least with their mouth, sincerely strive for participation in him, or gather any fruit from it (John 4:10). (2) His nature and excellence: "such" (Heb. 7:26; 8:1), "holy, harmless, undefiled, separate from sinners, and made higher than the heavens" (Heb. 7:26), "merciful and faithful" (Heb. 2:17), the very Son of God (Heb. 7:3), the God-man, and so forth. (3) His use: for reconciling a sinner, a public enemy, to God, for pleading all his case before God, for procuring every blessing for him, and so forth, of which matters we have already spoken in the preceding sections.

The method of contemplating
Moreover, we indeed should consider, κατανοοῦμεν, these things in such a way that: (1) we receive him faithfully by our profession, as the high priest of our confession (Heb. 3:1; 4:14–16; 10:23); (2) we securely repose upon him through faith (Isa. 10:20), as the one who is a merciful and faithful high priest (Heb. 2:17), in all points tempted as we are (Heb. 4:15); (3) we inseparably cling to him (Heb. 3:14; cf. 12:2–3; Ps. 63:8); (4) in any circumstance, we convert to our uses all the acts of his priesthood: in the case of sin, his offering and reconciliation;

in the case of necessity, his intercession; and in the case of any lack, his blessing. Regarding these things we will speak expressly in the following sections.

5. It urges the use of the offering. The circumstances in which
XXIX. Fifth, it calls for us to turn to our uses the offering of our priest, by which he strives for our reconciliation with God: (1) in the case of sin, if (a) it should burden and beset us (Ps. 38:4–5; 51:3–4); if (b) conscience should accuse, condemn, and gnaw (2 Sam. 24:10; Ps. 32:3–4); if (c) Satan, the accuser of the brethren, should accuse us day and night before God (Rev. 12:10); if (d) the law should run to his assistance with its curses (John 5:45); if (e) our own heart should join in (1 John 3:20; Rom. 2:15); if (f) the wrath and indignation of God should torture us (Ps. 90:11; Rev. 6:17); if (g) the fear of death and eternal condemnation should terrify us, should choke us (Heb. 2:14–15), should perpetually gnaw like a worm, and burn like an unquenchable fire (Isa. 66:24). (2) In the case of spiritual desertions, when we walk in darkness, so that we see no light (Isa. 50:10), so that we sigh, "Jehovah has forsaken me, Jehovah has forgotten me" (Isa. 49:14), "How long, O Lord? Will you forget me forever?" (Ps. 13:1–2; cf. Pss. 77; 88; etc.). (3) In the case of divine judgments, as much public—famine, plague, war (Num. 16:45; Jer. 24:10; 29:17)—as private (Ps. 32:3–4; 38:2–6).

The reasons on account of which
In these and other circumstances, what would more efficaciously comfort us, than: (1) to have a priest who offers himself for reconciling us (Num. 16:46); (2) to have such a priest, one who is the very Son of God, the God-man, after the order of Melchizedek, the king of righteousness and peace (Heb. 7), who offers not bulls, not calves, but himself (Heb. 10:1–15), who was in all points tempted as we are, and thus is merciful (Heb. 4:15); (3) such a priest who is able to save perfectly as many as strive toward God through him (Heb. 7:25)?

The manner by which
Therefore in every circumstance, what could be more prudent than to direct to our own uses such a great sacrifice of such a great priest? We do this (1) with a profound sense of our sin and misery (Ps. 51:3, 7; 2 Sam. 24:10), (2) by a humble confession of the same (Ps. 51:4; 32:5; Luke 15:18–19), (3) by a confident appropriation of the sacrifice provided (Gal. 2:20), and (4) in this way, by placing as it were our sins upon him (Lev. 4:4, 15, 24, 29, 33), because God has placed them upon him already (Isa. 53:4–5; 2 Cor. 5:21); and so forth.

6. It urges the use of the intercession. The benefits of the intercession
XXX. Sixth, let us similarly turn his intercession to our uses, as often as we have a case to be pleaded before God. Here it is incumbent upon us to unfold: (1) the benefits of this intercession, namely: (a) our communion with the Father and the Son (John 17:21), (b) the gift of the Holy Spirit (John 14:16–17), (c) protection against all spiritual enemies (Rom. 8:34; John 17:15), (d) our glorification, by which the one seated at the right hand of the Father will one day set us with him in the heavenlies, "made us sit together in heavenly places" (Eph. 2:6), because: (i) he is seated there in our flesh (Heb. 2:14; Eph. 5:30 with John 17:24; 14:23); (ii) he is seated for our sake (Heb. 6:20). And thus, he is so near to us: by nature, inasmuch as he is the same as we are; by office, as our expromissor; and by the Spirit, inasmuch as he procures his communion for us. (e) Strength against our sins, because from his priesthood in the heavens, which coincides with his intercession, the apostle infers the writing of the law upon our hearts (Heb. 8:4–6, 9–10). (f) The sanctification of our entire worship, prefigured in the Levitical priests, when they had to bear the iniquity of the holy things of the children of Israel, in all the gifts of their holy things (Ex. 28:38; cf. Rev. 8:3). For there is in us a triple impurity: (i) of our state, from the guilt of sins, which our priest remedies by the offering of himself for us, as יהוה צדקנו, Jehovah our Righteousness (Jer. 23:6; 1 Cor. 1:30). (ii) Of our nature and faculties, through our original stain, which he remedies through the Spirit, procured for us by his own intercession, who regenerates, renews, converts, sanctifies us (John 3:5; Titus 3:5). (iii) Of our worship and obedience (Isa. 64:6) which is remedied by the sweet-smelling aroma (Eph. 5:2), which being drawn from him is applied to all our worship (Phil. 4:18; Gen. 8:20), inasmuch as we have been made priests (Rev. 1:6), a holy priesthood, to offer up spiritual sacrifices, acceptable to God through Jesus Christ (1 Peter 2:5). (g) The internal intercession of the Holy Spirit (Rom. 8:26), whom our priest procured for us by his intercession. (h) Patience and indefatigable constancy in our duty (Heb. 12:1–3). (i) Confidence of coming boldly to the throne of grace (Heb. 4:14, 16; 10:12, 32).

The foundations of the benefits
All these benefits and others are certain and indisputable for us by virtue of the intercession of Christ, because: (a) the Father always hears him, and listens (John 11:42), because he himself destined him to the priestly office (Heb. 5:4–5). (b) He loves him (John 16:26–27). (c) He intercedes with authority, "Father, I will that," (John 17:24), and with power to confer what has been prayed, "I will send him" (John 16:7; cf. Ps. 68:18; Eph. 4:8). (d) He promised these benefits (Acts 2:33).

The uses of the intercession, or the means of participating in the benefits
(2) The means of participation, namely: (a) that we receive with living faith the priest who is our advocate (John 1:12), in whom all the promises of God are yes and amen (2 Cor. 1:20). Then (b) that without reserve we commit by prayers to him our case to be pleaded fully before God (Heb. 5:1; Phil. 4:6). In addition, (c) that we present our prayers with living faith to this our priest, that we pour them out in his name (John 16:23; Dan. 9:17), and place them upon him, as the true golden censer, to be brought before the sight of God, that they may be a sweet-smelling aroma (Rev. 8:3–4). Furthermore, (d) that we place upon this our priest the impurity and imperfection of all the duties of our worship, to be by both his merit and his intercession cleansed, corrected, and carried into the holy of holies, after the example of Aaron, about which we read in Exodus 28:38, "And Aaron shall bear the iniquity of the holy things, which the children of Israel shall sanctify in all the gifts of their holy things…to bring them favor before Jehovah." And thus they will be a sweet-smelling aroma, a sacrifice acceptable and well pleasing to God (Phil. 4:18; 1 Peter 2:5).

7. It urges the use of the blessing. The cases in which
XXXI. Seventh, also let us turn to our uses the blessing of our priest. The benefits of this blessing to be taken from its use, we already outlined in the dogmatic part, §XIV, from which are supplied the cases in which the use of this blessing is to be made, to which we add the case of persecution and cursing, threatening us from our enemies, insofar as through this blessing God promises to Abraham that he will curse all who curse him (Gen. 12:3; 22:17), an evident example of which he supplies in the glorious victory which he granted him against his enemies (Gen. 14), and in the preservation of his wife (Gen. 12:14ff.; 20:2–4, 18); which must not be restricted to bodily enemies, but extended also to spiritual enemies (Matt. 16:18; John 10:28; 2 Thess. 1:6–7); and so forth.

The method and means of obtaining the benefits of this blessing
The method and means of obtaining these benefits of the blessing are in these things, that: (1) we strive with all our strength that we may be of the spiritual seed of Abraham, for these benefits overtake the Gentiles in the blessing of Abraham (Gal. 3:14), inasmuch as it is promised not only to Abraham but also to his seed, and to it alone (Gen. 17:7; 22:17). That (2) we be in the covenant of grace, for this blessing is promised to Abraham and his seed through the covenant of grace (Gen. 17). That (3) we be in Christ, and united with him, for God confers the benefits of this blessing in Christ Jesus (Eph. 1:3), inasmuch as in him all the

promises of God are reckoned yes and amen (2 Cor. 1:20). Accordingly, (4) that by a true and living faith, we lay hold of the blessed seed (Gal. 3:14; John 1:12).

8. It teaches us to examine ourselves, whether or not he is our priest.
The motivating reasons
XXXII. Eighth, let us earnestly inquire whether or not that priest is ours, who sacrificed himself for us, who intercedes for us, and who blesses us. For since: (1) he is not the priest of all indiscriminately (because the apostle restricts it clearly enough, Heb. 4:15, "We have a high priest," as does the priest himself, John 17:9, "I do not pray for the world"), but of a certain sort of people; since (2) so great is the felicity and blessedness of those to whom this priest devotes himself, and so great and of such a kind are the benefits of his offering, his intercession, his blessing; since on the other hand, (3) so great is the misery of those who lack so great a priest, and are excluded from participation in benefits so necessary to them; and (4) so great is the tranquility of heart, the joy, the solace in a certain and infallible persuasion of this participation; since (5) the entirety of this depends upon a certain accurate scrutiny—who would doubt that it is altogether necessary to undertake an earnest examination of himself?

Its evidences
But by what evidences then will we gain this with certainty? I respond, The apostle offers some to us in Hebrews 3:1, "Wherefore, holy brethren, you who are partakers of the heavenly calling, consider the apostle and high priest of our profession." So then, those who have Christ as their priest are: (1) "brethren," not only among themselves (Matt. 23:8), but also, even especially, with Christ (Heb. 2:11), such that they have with him both one God and one Father, for thus, in order to intercede as their priest, he also ascended for them (John 20:17). (2) They are "holy," for he who sanctifies and those who are sanctified are all of one, for which cause he is not ashamed to call them his brothers (Heb. 2:11), namely that by this, as a brother is similar to his brothers, so also the brothers may be similar to their brother in all things, and accordingly also in holiness, that he may be for them a faithful high priest, in the things which must be performed for them before God, to make reconciliation for the sins of the people (Heb. 2:11, 17). (3) They are "partakers of the heavenly calling," for no one takes this honor to himself (namely, either to be a priest, or to have communion with Christ the priest), but he who is called (Heb. 5:4), not only by a common calling (Matt. 20:16), but by a heavenly calling (Rom. 8:30), that which is conjoined with election, by which we are made to be conformed to the image of the Son, to the end that he might be the firstborn among many brethren (Rom. 8:29). (4) They are

of the Christian confession, for he is "the high priest of our confession," that is, of the Christian confession, not Jewish, not pagan, and so forth. And that not only in name, but also in substance (2 Tim. 2:19). To these things I add, (5) They are not of this world, for he is not engaged in the intercession of the priesthood for those who are of this world (John 17:9). (6) They are of the number of those who have been given to Christ by the Father (John 17:9), that is, those who through faith have been made his own (John 17:20–21), who having been made his own, by denying themselves, by bearing the cross, they imitate him (Luke 9:23), they crucify the flesh with its lusts (Gal. 5:24). Compare, with the necessary changes made, what we said above in chapter 2, on the Mediator, §XXXII.

9. It binds us to the duties to be offered to our priest. The motives
XXXIII. Ninth, it binds us to present the duties owed to so great and such a priest as ours. For if (1) the Israelites owed their own dues to the common priests, for which reason we read of מִשְׁפַּט הַכֹּהֲנִים, the priests' due (1 Sam. 2:13);[39] if (2) to them as fathers (Judg. 17:10; 18:19; cf. 2 Kings 2:12; 6:21; 13:14; 1 Cor. 4:15) they owed paternal or filial duties, of honor, love, obedience, fidelity; if (3) to them distinctly as priests they owed the tithe, as it were a token of the homage to be presented not so much to the priests as to God, which tithe was thus called holy to the Lord (Lev. 27:32); if (4) Abraham himself, so great and such a patriarch, presented honor to Melchizedek (Gen. 14:20), as to one greater, and tithes as to a priest, which the apostle in one and the same chapter observes four or five times (Heb. 7:2, 4, 6, 8–9)—will we not surely present dues, priestly duties, and tithes to our priest, so great and so excellent, an inestimable distance greater than Melchizedek himself?

What these duties are
But what then are the dues, lawful duties and tithes that we owe to our high priest? They are: (1) honor fitting to such a high priest (Heb. 7:26), which Abraham himself offered to him in Melchizedek (Heb. 7:1, 4, 7), as did the Levitical priests in the loins of Abraham (Heb. 7:9). (2) Love toward our priest, as to a father (Judg. 17:10 with Matt. 10:37), as to a priest so faithful and merciful (Heb. 2:17; 4:15), who offered himself for us, intercedes for us, blesses us with every benefit, spiritual as well as temporal, as we have said (cf. 1 Cor. 16:22). (3) Compliance or obedience (cf. Hag. 2:12; Lev. 10:10–11; Deut. 33:10; Mal. 2:7 with Heb. 5:11; 2 Cor. 10:5). (4) Homage, in the place of tithes (Ps. 2:12), that is, as to a royal priest (cf. 1 Peter 2:9), which sort of priesthood Melchizedek

---

39. Cf. Deut. 18:3.

sustained (Heb. 7:1). (5) Sustenance, to be presented as if in tithes, not indeed to his own person, but to his members, his ambassadors, his poor (Heb. 7:5–6; 1 Cor. 9:13–14). In all these things and others (6) let us consider (κατανοοῦμεν) our high priest (Heb. 3:1).

10. It exhorts us to present ourselves also as priests. Why
XXXIV. Finally, tenth, after the example of our priest, let us also be priests, and act as priests, for: (1) we also are priests, made so by him (Rev. 1:6), indeed (2) a royal priesthood (1 Peter. 2:9), (3) anointed if not to a priesthood the same in all things, at least to a similar priesthood (2 Cor. 1:21), and from this his companions (μέτοχοι, Heb. 1:9; חברים, Ps. 45:7).

How. With respect to the personal requirements of priests
On this account we must struggle with all our effort to meet the personal requirements of priests, and even those of our highest priest himself, by which: (1) we must be genuinely called (Heb. 3:1, "partakers of the heavenly calling"). For no one takes this honor to himself, but he who is called, as was Aaron (Heb. 5:4), just as also was our highest priest (Heb. 5:5). (2) We must be ἄμωμοι, blameless (1 Cor. 1:8; Eph. 1:4; Phil. 2:15; Col. 1:22; 1 Thess. 5:23), just as the Levitical priests who were to be called had to be without bodily blemish, or any other defect from which disgrace could come upon their function (Lev. 21:18–21; cf. 22:22), just as our highest priest is also blameless (1 Peter 1:19; Heb. 9:14). (3) We must be anointed (2 Cor. 1:21; 1 John 2:20, 27), just like the legal priests (Ex. 29; Lev. 8; 4:5), and also our great highest priest himself (Heb. 1:9 from Ps. 45:7; Isa. 61:1). (4) We must be clothed with pure, white, priestly garments (Rev. 3:4–5, 18; 4:4; cf. Jude 23; Isa. 61:10), just as the Levitical priests also had to be clothed with בגדי לבן, white garments,[40] holy garments (Ex. 28:2, 4; 35:19, 21), washed garments (Lev. 11:25; Num. 19:7), which when a priest lacked, he was called מחוסר בגדים, one deprived of garments,[41] and was considered profane; just as our highest priest was also clothed (Isa. 11:5; Rev. 3:4). (5) We must be holy (1 Peter 2:9; Heb. 3:1; Rom. 11:16; 1 Peter 1:15), just as the Levitical priests also had to be holy (Ex. 19:22; Ezra 8:24, 28; Ps. 132:9), and our highest priest was (Heb. 7:26). Finally, (6) in all these things we must show ourselves purified and sanctified to our highest priest (cf. Matt. 8:4; Mark 1:44; Luke 17:14).

---

40. Cf. Eccl. 9:8.
41. Cf. Nachmanides on Ex. 28:35.

With respect to the priestly acts

And thus equipped with the personal requirements of the priesthood, let us also perform our priesthood, just as our priest has performed it: (1) by offering (a) ourselves (Rom. 12:1), just as our high priest offered himself (Heb. 5:3; 7:27; 9:25), certainly not as a propitiatory sacrifice, as he did, but as a thanksgiving sacrifice,[42] (b) a contrite and humbled spirit (Ps. 51:16–17), (c) the offerings of our lips, like calves (Hos. 14:2), (d) good deeds and sharing, in which God delights (Heb. 13:16); (2) by interceding (1 Tim. 2:1; 2 Cor. 1:11); (3) by blessing (Matt. 5:44; Luke 6:28; Acts 20:1; Rom. 12:14; 1 Cor. 4:12; 1 Peter 3:9).

---

42. *non quidem in sacrificium* ἱλαστικόν, *prout ille; sed in sacrificium* εὐχαριστικόν

CHAPTER EIGHT

The Mediator as a King

But I have set my king on Zion, the mount of my holiness.
—Psalm 2:6

The preceding points are connected to those that follow.
I. And so at last we come to the third function of the mediatorial office, that is, the kingly, through which the Mediator intends the application of the benefits acquired in the preceding two functions. The king himself who was established represents its nature from the decree and counsel of the Father who established him, in Psalm 2:6.

The Exegetical Part

II. In these words is contained the establishment or inauguration of the Mediator to his kingly function, in which is evident:

    A. The one establishing or inaugurating: וַאֲנִי, "And I." The prefix וֹ, "and," although it most frequently serves more for ornamentation than for meaning, yet here it adversatively signifies "but" or "yet" (as in Isa. 29:13; Mal. 1:4), so that this sense emerges: "Although the kings of the earth raise themselves up, yet I have anointed my king." The words are a sign of kindled wrath (as in Acts 23:3).[1] Moreover, the אֲנִי is emphatic, "I myself," even that one about whom we read in verses 2–3, "I Jehovah, who remove and establish kings" (Dan. 2:21). In this place, he is Jehovah not so much considered theologically, as God, but rather economically,[2] as the Father (because he speaks about the Son in v. 7), who in the eternal covenant of grace established the Son to be Mediator and king.

---

1. Greek: καὶ σὺ κάθη κρίνων, lit. "And do *you* sit to judge…?"
2. θεολογικῶς…οἰκονομικῶς

B. The establishment: נסכתי. To some it means in a passive sense, "I have been poured out," such that the Son is speaking of himself, but this is not necessary since the word in the Qal has an active meaning, as is evident from the following word מלכי, where making the ׳ paragogic seems extremely forced. Nor is it necessary to depart from the common sense, especially when, if you take it actively, the context becomes more elegant and easy, in this way: "Then he shall speak thus to his enemies, Yet I have anointed…." And moreover, what sense is there in saying, "I have been established my king"? For this reason the Vulgate was forced to translate the words, "I have been established the king *of him*."[3] The Aramaic translated it actively, רביתי, "I have made him great"; Symmachus, ἔκρισα, "I have anointed"; Acts 4:27, ὅν ἔκρισας, "whom you have anointed."[4] To others it is, more emphatically, "I have poured out," that is, not by smearing, as upon others, but by smearing and pouring out upon him, above his companions (Ps. 45:7; cf. John 1:16). To others it is, "I have appointed him,"[5] that is to say, "Know this, that the Messiah, though he displeases you, did not take this dignity to himself, or receive it by human counsels" (Heb. 5:4–5; cf. John 6:15; 18:36), "But I have solemnly appointed him," or "anointed him." Nor must it be missed that it is said, "I have anointed," in the past tense, so that it is intimated that this anointing happened in the past, in the eternal counsel of the persons, by which the Son was designated to be the mediatorial king (Isa. 42:1), or also, through an enallage of the past tense for the future, "I will establish, will anoint, will send him in his time, and that as certainly as if I had already anointed him."

B. The one established, of whom here is mentioned:

1. His kingly power[6]

---

3. *Ego constitutus sum Rex ejus.* Vulgate: *Ego autem constitutus sum rex ab eo;* from the Septuagint: Ἐγὼ δὲ κατεστάθην βασιλεὺς ὑπ' αὐτοῦ; from *The Holie Bible Faithfully translated into English out of the authentical Latin,* 2 vols., 2nd edition (Douay: John Cousturier, 1635), 2:16, "But I am appoynted King by him"; cf. Psalm 2:6 translated in an active sense, *Ego inungens regem meum, praefeci Tzijoni monti sanctitatis meae,* "I, anointing my king, have set [him] over Zion, my holy mountain," Immanuel Tremellius and Franciscus Junius, *Testamenti Veteris Biblia Sacra,* 4 parts in 1 vol., 2nd ed. (London, 1592–1593), 3:16r.

4. The Old Testament Greek translation of Symmachus (fl. late 2nd century) is included in Origen's fragmentary *Hexapla,* see Origen, *Origenis Hexaplorum quae supersunt, sive, Veterum interpretum Graecorum in totum Vetus Testamentum fragmenta,* ed. F. Field (Oxford: Clarendon Press, 1875), 2:89.

5. *creavi*

6. *Potestas,* cf. 1.2.20 §II.B, footnotes 2 and 5, on Mastricht's definitions and usage of *potestas*

a. "King," מֶלֶךְ, that is, the monarch, the head of the kingdom. But who is that king? Commentators are divided here, for there are: (1) those who interpret the entire Psalm with a single referent,[7] concerning only David. Thus the Jews—but only the more recent ones, and that due to hatred of Christ and the Christian religion. For example, Rashi says, "Our doctors explained that this was meant of King Messiah, but as it sounds, and so that a response may be made to the *Minim*"[8] (that is, "to the heretics," by which he means Christians, as is well known).[9] Although these words of his are not found in the editions of Buxtorf and Venice, no doubt erased by Christians, as Pococke discusses in his "Miscellaneous Appendix of Notes" on Rabbi Maimonides, *A Gate to Moses*.[10] Rabbi Kimchi is also inclined in this direction.[11] With them the Socinians of our day concur, out of hatred for the eternal deity of Christ. Others, (2) among whom are Calvin, Pareus, and Rivet, interpret at least most things in this Psalm of David in figure, and of Christ in truth, because many things in this Psalm also fit David.[12] Others (3) refer the entire Psalm only to Christ, because it speaks of one who: (a) is named the Son of God, absolutely, (v. 7, as in Matt. 3:17; 17:5), which is applicable to Christ alone

---

and *potentia*. In this chapter, *auctoritas*, *potestas*, and *potentia* require nuance, being differentiable but overlapping.

7. μονοτρόπως

8. *Minaei*. This is a Latinized form of the Hebrew term for the *Minim* (in Rashi הַמִּינִים), or heretics. Cf. Robert A. Harris, "Rashi and the 'Messianic' Psalms" in *Birkat Shalom: Studies in the Bible, Ancient Near Eastern Literature, and Postbiblical Judaism presented to Shalom M. Paul on the occasion of his Seventieth Birthday* (Winona Lake, Ind.: Eisenbrauns, 2008), 847–48.

9. Rashi continues, "…it is expedient to interpret this as regarding David himself." Quoted in Edward Pococke's (1604–1691) edition, "Appendix notarum miscellanea," in Moses Maimonides, בָּאב מוסי, *Porta Mosis sive, dissertationes aliquot a R. Mose Maimonide…una cum appendice notarum miscellanea* (Oxford: H. Hall, 1655), 307 (i.e. [315]).

10. Pococke, "Appendix," *Porta Mosis*, 318. The words in question are "so that a response may be made to the *Minim*."

11. For a critical Hebrew text, see *The First Book of the Psalms according to the text of the Cambridge MS. Bible Add. 465, with the longer commentary of R. David Qimchi critically edited from nineteen manuscripts and the early editions*, ed. S. M. Schiller-Szinessy (Cambridge: Deighton, Bell, & Co., 1883). For an English translation see *The Longer Commentary of R. David Kimchi on the First Book of the Psalms*, trans. R. G. Finch (New York: Macmillan, 1919), 14–15.

12. John Calvin, *Commentary on the Book of the Psalms* (Edinburgh: Calvin Translation Society, 1845), 2:13–17; David Pareus, *Calvinus orthodoxus*, 195–210; Andrè Rivet, *Commentarius in Psalmorum propheticorum, de mysteriis evangelicis, dodecadem selectam* (Rotterdam: Arnold Leers, 1645), 4–49.

(Heb. 1:4–5). (b) He is said to be the Son begotten by God, and indeed "today," that is, from eternity. Such a one who (c) will have the nations for his inheritance (vv. 8–9). (d) Religious worship is claimed for him (vv. 11–12). (e) In the New Testament it is applied to Christ alone (Acts 4:35; 13:33; Heb. 1:4–5; 5:5). (f) It is not evident by any indication that David, the author of the Psalm, is speaking about himself. (g) The destruction of rebellious nations and kings is suspended upon his wrath, when it is kindled but a little (v. 12). Finally, (h) their salvation is suspended upon trust in him (v. 12). It is most well-known that all of these things only fit Jesus. Nor does it help the case for David that some of the things in this Psalm could be applied to him, since it is a whole heaven different that some things can be applied to him, and for him to be the same one intended and understood by the writer.

b. "My," מלכי, "my king," that is, the very one who is my Messiah, who is mentioned in verse 2. The particle ׳ here means, in a passive sense, "the one anointed by me," who will reign at my command—thus in 1 Samuel 16:1, "a king for me," that is, who will fulfill my commands—but not in an active sense, like in Psalm 74:12, that is, "the one who has power over me." Accordingly, he is called the Lord's king, first (1) by reason of his eternal generation, "Today I have begotten you" (v. 7); then (2) by reason of his sending, just as he is called "my Shepherd" in Zechariah 13:7; furthermore, (3) by reason of the singularity of his kingdom, because he would have one entirely different from those of this world (John 18:36); also (4) by reason of its author, who was God immediately, not the civil state; I will add, (5) by reason of his excellence, "my king," that is to say, who is worthy of me, that he may rule in my name, and with me. For although kings are established by God, and thus are of God, and are called God's anointed (Isa. 45:1), yet God does not name anyone "my king"; however, he designates this one "my king" because he is with him one God, his very own and only begotten Son (Ps. 2:7), and he governs his kingdom (Matt. 6:10, 13; 1 Cor. 15:24–25).

2. His kingdom: "upon Zion, the mount of my holiness." This kingdom is represented:

a. By a proper name: "upon Zion." Zion was once a nearly impenetrable fortress of the Jebusites, and after David defeated them, he devoted it to be his royal city (2 Sam. 5:9; 1 Kings 8:1), and called it the city of David. In its vicinity was the hill Moriah (2 Chron. 3:1; Isa. 31:4), on which the temple stood, so that the kingly and priestly power might cohere, just as in Melchizedek and the Messiah (Ps. 110:4; cf. 1 Peter 2:9). Mystically Zion is the church, especially in the New Testament (Isa. 60:14; Heb. 12:22; Rev. 14:1), first by reason of its invincibility (Matt. 16:18), then also because the gospel would go forth out of Zion (Ps. 110:2; 87:3; 132:13; Isa. 2:3; Mic. 4:2; Zech. 9:9; Luke 24:47; Acts 1:4), just as David the king of Zion not rarely refers mystically to Christ (Jer. 30:9; Ezek. 34:23; 37:24; Hos. 3:5).

b. By an appellative name, or a certain description: "the mount of my holiness," that is, from the nearby Moriah, on which the temple was, which elsewhere is called "the temple of holiness" (Ps. 79:1), from which it was "the city of holiness" (Dan. 9:24; Matt. 4:5), and "the holy people" (Isa. 63:18). But it is spoken of in this way not from an inherent holiness, but a relative one. Moreover, mystically the mount of holiness is the church, which especially in the New Testament would be extended all the way to the ends of the earth (cf. Isa. 60:14; Heb. 12:22; Rev. 14:1). But it is named in this way because the most holy God as it were dwells in it (Isa. 31:9), because the most holy worship of God thrives in it (Rom. 12:1), because it is itself holy (1 Peter 2:9; 2 Cor. 1:1; Eph. 1:1), because it has been made holy by the blood and Spirit of Christ (1 Cor. 6:11), because zeal for holiness is incumbent upon it (Heb. 12:14), because one day it will be made perfectly holy (Eph. 5:26–27).

The Dogmatic Part

Regarding the kingly function is taught: 1. Its reality.

III. In the parts of the mediatorial office, finally there is its third function, the kingly one. First its reality is evident: (1) by so many prophecies made once under the Old Testament concerning him (Gen. 49:10; Ps. 2 with Acts 4:25–28; Ps. 132:11–12 with Luke 1:31–33; Acts 2:30; cf. Isa. 11:1–3; Hos. 3:5; Ezek. 34:23–24; 37:24–25; Dan. 9:25). (2) By so many types and figures: Melchizedek (Heb. 7), David (Jer. 30:9; Hos. 3:5; Ezek. 34:23–24), Solomon (Matt. 12:42; Luke 11:31). (3) By the kingly titles that are everywhere attributed to him, that he is head of the church (Eph. 5:23; 1:22), a ruler of Israel (Matt. 2:6; Mic. 5:2), ἀρχηγὸς τῆς σωτηρίας ἡμῶν, the captain of our salvation (Heb. 2:10), the

Prince of peace (Isa. 9:6–7), the Prince of life (Acts 3:15), the Lord of glory (1 Cor. 2:8), Lord of lords (Rev. 19:16), the judge and lawgiver (Isa. 33:22), the king of Zion (Ps. 2:6), King of kings (Rev. 19:16), and so forth. (4) By the very avowal and confession of Christ before Pilate (John 18:33–38), for which reason he was also condemned to death, with this inscription nailed to the cross, "Jesus of Nazareth, the King of the Jews" (John 19:12–23), and in addition, with one of the thieves who was crucified with him acknowledging and professing: "Remember me when you come into your kingdom" (Luke 23:42–43).

2. Its nature and species

IV. Second, its nature, insofar as it is that function of the mediatorial office by which he administers and governs with authority and power all things which regard the salvation of his own (Dan. 2:44; Luke 1:32–33). Moreover, it is: (1) essential or divine, common to him as God, with the Father and the Holy Spirit, which we dealt with in book 2, chapter 20, on the power and might of God. (2) Personal, economic, or mediatorial (Ps. 2:6; John 18:36; Eph. 1:20–22), delegated to him by the Father, as the God-man and the Mediator (Acts 2:36; Matt. 28:18; John 5:21–22, 26–27; Phil. 2:8–9). And this again is twofold: (a) universal, extending to all creatures, for the sake of his church (Eph. 1:19–23; Rev. 17:14; 1 Peter 3:22), which includes: (i) on the one hand, the supreme and most absolute right and authority[13] to rule and govern (Ps. 110:1–3; Matt. 28:18); (ii) on the other, the exercise of that right in the subjugation of his enemies, which will last until he has subjected them all under his feet (Ps. 110:1; Heb. 1:6; Phil. 2:9–11; 1 Cor. 15:27). (b) Particular, extending to only the mediatorial kingdom, that is, to the church, that he may gather, govern, defend, and raise it eternally (Luke 19:12, 15; Ps. 2:8; 28:9), which occurs: (i) in this age (Matt. 28:19–20; Acts 1:8; 13:47; 26:17–18), (ii) in the end of this age (Matt. 25; 1 Thess. 4:14ff.; 1 Cor. 15:24ff.; Rev. 20:2ff.; Eph. 5:27), and (iii) after this age, or in the age to come (Matt. 25:46; 1 John 3:2; 2 Tim. 4:8). From what has been said, it is now easy to conclude who the subjects of this kingdom are: generally, the whole world and all its contents; specifically, the church or the people of God.

3. Its kingly dignities: (1) Anointing

V. Third, its kingly dignities, namely: his anointing, customarily conferred especially upon kings (1 Sam. 16:12–13 with Ps. 45:6–7; Acts 10:38), by which he received the Spirit and power (Acts 10:38) not by measure (John 3:34), but by

---

13. *jus et* ἐξουσίαν

a fullness of every kind (Col. 1:19; John 1:14, 16), about which we have spoken more abundantly in its own place.[14]

(2) Inauguration

His inauguration, by which from the eternal decree he was designated king (Ps. 2:6–8), then promised and prefigured, as we have said in §III, then furthermore, as it were proclaimed at his birth (Luke 1:31–33; 2:10–11), indeed also acknowledged in his death (John 18:33–38; 19:12–23; Luke 23:41, 43), but then by a solemn investiture was declared king in the ascension to his throne and session at the right hand (1 Peter 3:22; Eph. 1:20–22).

(3) Coronation

His coronation, which first happened when he was about to die, with a crown of thorns (Matt. 27:29), then when rising from the dead, ascending into heaven, and sitting at the right hand of God, with a crown of glory (Heb. 2:9; Phil. 2:9–11).

(4) Throne

His throne or royal seat (1 Chron. 29:23; 2 Chron. 9:17–19 with Rev. 3:21; Eph. 1:20; Heb. 1:3; Col. 3:1), which he will occupy until the restoration of all things (Acts 3:21; Ps. 110:1; 2 Thess. 1:9–10), and then will possess to all eternity (Heb. 1:8; Ps. 45:6–7).

(5) Scepter

His scepter, the royal rod, the sign of royal majesty and sovereignty (Est. 5:2 with Heb. 1:8; Ps. 45:6). Moreover, there belongs to him a double scepter: one as it were of gold, by which he governs his subjects, first outwardly by the Word, especially that of the gospel (Ps. 45:6; 110:2), then inwardly by the Spirit, who from this is called the finger and arm of the Lord (Luke 11:20; Matt. 12:28; Isa. 53:1); the other of iron, by which he breaks and crushes his enemies (Ps. 2:9; Rev. 2:27).

(6) Laws

His laws, which are just, holy, and good (Rom. 7:12), whereby he is called the lawgiver (Prov. 8:15 with James 4:12), which he not only introduces externally by the Word, but also writes internally on the heart (Heb. 8:10).

---

14. 1.5.4 §XI

(7) Prerogatives

His royal prerogatives, for example, tributes (Rom. 13:6–7 with Ps. 96:8), armaments against enemies (Isa. 39:2 with Eph. 6:11–19; Rom. 13:12; 2 Cor. 10:4), ambassadors (2 Chron. 32:31 with 2 Cor. 5:20–21), coercive judicial power (John 19:10 with 5:22), to which pertains the power, exercised at least by kings, to forgive evildoers, which belongs to Christ truly and preeminently (Mark 2:5, 9–11).

4. Its administration: Of his essential kingdom

VI. Fourth, the administration of the kingly function, on account of the twofold kingdom, is also observed to be twofold: the first, that which regards the essential or divine kingdom, extending to all creatures, with respect to the church, is exercised: (1) by upholding them (Heb. 1:3; Col. 1:17; Eph. 1:22) until all the elect are gathered in; (2) by permitting trials and persecutions of his subjects, for the wisest uses (Rev. 2:10; 12:2, 4, 17; 13:6–7; 19:19; 20:7–9); (3) by restraining the fury and assaults of his enemies (Rev. 2:10; 20:1–3); (4) by protecting (Rev. 12:2–16; 14:1–6); (5) by ordering even all the worst things to the good of his own (Rom. 8:28; 2 Cor. 4:17; Phil. 1:12–14); (6) by avenging, and destroying his enemies (Ps. 2:9; 110:1–2; 1 Cor. 15:25); and finally, (7) by delivering his people totally and finally (Rev. 21:1–4).

Of his personal kingdom, with respect to the period of the current age

VII. The latter administration, which regards his personal or mediatorial kingdom, specifically with respect to his church, according to its three periods (noted in §IV), is occupied, first, with this present age: (1) by pouring out his Spirit abundantly and efficaciously, to procure the application of the merits of his redemption, and of his benefits (John 7:38–39; Acts 2:2–4, 33; John 16:7–16); (2) by sending out his ministers, first extraordinary, then ordinary (Eph. 4:8–13; Matt. 28:19–20); (3) by establishing the ecclesiastical rites of the New Testament, to be religiously observed by his ministers who have been sent, such as: the preaching of the gospel (Mark 16:15), the administration of the sacraments (Matt. 28:18–19; 1 Cor. 11:23), public prayers (1 Tim. 2:1–3; Acts 6:4), public psalm-singing[15] (Col. 3:16; Eph. 5:19), ecclesiastical censures (Matt. 18:15–22; 1 Cor. 5ff), the hallowing of the Lord's Day (Acts 20:7; 1 Cor. 16:1–2), the gathering of the church (Matt. 22:2–11; Acts 26:17–18), the upbuilding and strengthening of the gathered church (Acts 14:22), until we all come unto a perfect man, unto the measure of the stature of the fullness of Christ (Eph. 4:10–13).

---

15. Latin: *psalmodia*; Dutch: *Psalmgezang*

With respect to the period of the consummated age
VIII. Second, concerning the consummated age: (1) by descending for judgment (1 Thess. 4:16; 1 Cor. 15:52); (2) by raising the dead, and changing the living (1 Thess. 4:16; 1 Cor. 15:52); (3) by lifting the elect into the air to meet him (1 Thess. 4:16–18); (4) by gathering all nations to his judgment seat and separating the sheep from the goats (Matt. 25:31ff.); (5) by pronouncing the sentence of acquittal or condemnation (Matt. 25:31ff.); (6) by renewing and purifying the whole creation, so that there comes forth a new heaven and a new earth, in which righteousness dwells (2 Peter 3:10–13; Rev. 21:1, 2, 5).

With respect to the period of the eternal age
IX. Third, concerning the eternal age: (1) by distributing eternal rewards according to works (Rom. 2:6–17; Jude 6); (2) by taking the elect to be with him forever, beholding him in his glory (John 17:24; 1 John 3:1–2; 1 Thess. 4:17); (3) by casting the reprobate from his sight into the lake burning with fire and brimstone (Matt. 25:30, 41; Rev. 20:10, 14–15); (4) by reigning immediately over the church triumphant, his people also reigning with him (Luke 1:32–33; Rev. 22:5; 2 Tim. 2:12), after, when all his adversaries have been subdued, he has delivered up his mediatorial kingdom to the Father (1 Cor. 15:24), indeed not simply with respect to the very essence of the kingdom, since it is said to be eternal (Luke 1:32–33; Heb. 1:8), but with respect to the instrumental mode of administering it: through ministers, the Word, sacraments, discipline, and so forth.

The properties of the kingdom
X. Finally, from what has been said, you will easily deduce the chief properties of this kingdom, namely that: (1) it is universal, with respect to (a) all ages (Heb. 13:8; Matt. 22:43–45), (b) all kinds of persons (Dan. 7:14; Rev. 17:14), (c) all creatures, insofar as they can look to promoting or illustrating the salvation of his people (Matt. 28:18; Phil. 2:10 with Eph. 1:1, 12). (2) It is spiritual, extending even to the very soul and conscience of men (John 18:36 with Rom. 14:17; 1 Cor. 6:19–20). (3) It dispenses eternal life and death (Rev. 1:18). (4) It is eternal (Dan. 2:44). (5) It brings profound peace, tranquility, and perfect blessedness to all those who are truly its subjects (Rom. 14:17; Isa. 9:6; Eph. 2:16). From these properties it is called throughout the Scriptures the kingdom of God, the kingdom of peace and glory, the kingdom of light and glory, the kingdom of heaven, and the world to come (Heb. 2:5).

The Elenctic Part

It is asked: 1. Did the Messiah have to be a temporal king? The Jews affirm this.

XI. Regarding the kingly function it is disputed, first, whether the Messiah, promised in the past had to govern a spiritual or a temporal kingdom. The Jews, so that they may more easily obtain that our Jesus is not the Messiah, inasmuch as he did not have such a kingdom, choose the latter, and with them, in the first infancy of their Christianity, the apostles themselves agreed (Matt. 20:21; Luke 24:21).

Christians deny it. The arguments of the Christians

Christians, with Christ (John 18:33, 36), choose instead the prior, because: (1) our Jesus is the true Messiah, which we have already taught with invincible arguments in chapter 2, §XIX, yet he did not govern a temporal kingdom. (2) It is foretold that the Messiah would come once the temporal kingdom or kingly power was already taken from the Jews (Gen. 49:10). (3) It is foretold that he would come as a king poor and lowly, riding on a donkey (Zech. 9:9). (4) It is said that he would be despised and rejected by his very own people (Isa. 53:2–3, 8; Ps. 69:7), indeed even slain by them (Dan. 9:26; Zech. 12:10), which the Jews try in vain to remedy with a ridiculous fiction about a double King Messiah, one Messiah ben Joseph, from the tribe of Ephraim, who would be slain by Armilus,[16] and another Messiah ben David, from the tribe of Judah, a glorious and triumphing warrior: that is, instead of the two natures of the one Messiah, and instead of his two states, they rave about two Messiahs. (5) It is foretold that he would reign without temporal arms, horses, or chariots (Zech. 9:9–10; Hos. 1:7; Isa. 9:3–5). (6) Instead of physical weapons, he would use the rod of his mouth, and the breath of his lips (Isa. 11:4). (7) Without external violence, with nothing except kindness and gentleness, it is said that he would subdue the nations to himself (Isa. 65:1–2; 42:1–4). (8) He would perform spiritual things entirely impossible for temporal kings: for example, (a) he would subdue the devil (Gen. 3:15), (b) bless all the nations (Gen. 22:18), which promise is repeated at least seven times,[17] (c) procure salvation for believers (Gen. 49:18; Isa. 49:6), (d) finish transgressions, seal up sins, expiate iniquities, bring in everlasting righteousness (Dan. 9:24; Zech. 13:1), (e) justify by his knowledge (Isa.

---

16. In some strands of medieval Jewish eschatology, Armilus is an anti-Messianic figure who will lead the world in a final apocalyptic war against the Jews. It is uncertain whether the name derives from Romulus, in which Rome is the source of ancient Jewish persecution, or Ahriman, which would be a Persian source of Jewish persecution. Cf. Isidore Singer, *The Jewish Encyclopedia*, 12 vols. (New York: Funk and Wagnalls, 1901–1906), 2:118–20.

17. Gen. 12:3; 18:18; 22:18; 26:4; 28:14; Ps. 72:17; Jer. 4:2; cf. Acts 3:25; Gal. 3:8

53:11), (f) free his own from death (Isa. 25:8), indeed (g) from hell (Hos. 13:14). (9) Throughout the entirety of Psalm 72, which (with the agreement of the Targum and the ancient Jews, as Rashi and Ibn Ezra attest)[18] describes the kingdom of the Messiah, nothing but spiritual benefits are evident: that, for example, he would lead his people to justice and deliver the poor (v. 2), that in his time it would be that the righteous flourish, and abundance of peace, until there was no moon (v. 7), that all kings would adore him and all nations serve him (v. 11), that he would deliver the needy when he cried, and the afflicted who has no helper (v. 12), and so on throughout the whole Psalm. If you should gather all these things together, this will emerge as an invincible argument: that king who would be poor, lacking temporal weapons, rejected by his own, and slain, would perform all his works by the rod of his mouth and the breath of his lips, would subdue the nations with gentleness and kindness, would procure spiritual benefits for his own, and so forth—without a doubt is not a temporal, but a spiritual king. But the promised Messiah is such; hence, he is not a temporal, but a spiritual king.

The objections of the Jews

Of those things which could be brought forth to the contrary by the Jews, the chief are: (1) that it is said that he would wage temporal wars against Gog and Magog (Ezek. 38–39; Ps. 2:9) and the fictitious Armilus or Antichrist. But besides the fact that it is nowhere said that the Messiah would fight against Gog and Magog, there is also nothing preventing him, if he is said to fight, from fighting spiritually, as a spiritual king. (2) It is foretold that he would build a third temple (Ezek. 40ff.). But (a) there is no mention of any third temple in the Scriptures. Moreover, (b) that the second temple, to which it is predicted the Messiah would come (Mal. 3:1; Hag. 2:7, 9), would be the last, is gathered from Daniel 9:26. Indeed, (c) it is not said in Ezekiel that the Messiah would build any temple. And, (d) the temple that is delineated by Ezekiel is nothing but the mystical temple, that is, the church, especially of the New Testament, namely that mountain of God that would be exalted above all the mountains (Isa. 2:2), which temple has so far been built, is still being built, and will be built hereafter, even to the end of the age, by our Messiah.

---

18. See Ps. 72 in *Rashi's Commentary on Psalms*; *Abraham Ibn Ezra's Commentary on the Second Book of Psalms: Chapter 42–72*, trans. H. Norman Strickman (Boston: Academic Studies Press, 2009).

2. Is the Mediator only a subordinate and dependent king?

XII. Second, it is asked whether the Mediator Jesus is only a subordinate and dependent king. The Socinians, because they reject the eternal deity of the Mediator, do not acknowledge in him any other than a conferred, subordinate, dependent kingship. The orthodox, although they acknowledge in him a mediatorial kingship that is conferred and dependent (Matt. 28:18; Phil. 2:9; Ps. 2:6), yet in addition acknowledge a natural, divine, independent kingship, which, presupposing the eternal deity of our King Jesus (which we expressly demonstrated elsewhere bk. 2, ch. 26, §§VIII–XII), not even the Socinians would deny (cf. 1 Tim. 1:17 with 6:14–16; Rev. 19:16), on account of all those passages from both Testaments in which an independent kingdom, and power, and glory are attributed to God forever (Matt. 6:10, 13).

3. Was the Mediator, while living on earth, a temporal king, either
de jure or *de facto?* The state of the controversy

XIII. Third, it is asked whether the Mediator, while living on earth, was a temporal king, either *de jure* or *de facto.* The canonists, parasites of the Roman pontiff, so that they can more easily assert for him not only spiritual but also temporal power, state that the Mediator had temporal power, if not *de facto*, at least *de jure*, over the whole earth, for if he did not have it, then it could not be derived from him to Peter, and from Peter to the pope.

Arguments of the orthodox
Protestants, although they assert all power entirely for him as God, and likewise although they humbly acknowledge that he as Mediator after the resurrection received from the Father all power in heaven and on earth (from Matt. 28:18; etc.), yet before that time, that he possessed temporal power either *de jure* or *de facto*, or handed it down to Peter, they deny, because: (1) he was registered in the census of Augustus (Luke 2:4–5), which registration paid homage as it were to Augustus. (2) He expressly protests that he did not come to be ministered to, as a temporal king, but to minister, and to give his soul a ransom for many (Matt. 20:28). (3) He testifies that he has nowhere to lay his head (Matt. 8:20; Luke 9:58). (4) He expressly declares that his kingdom is not of this world (John 18:36).

Objections of our adversaries
Against these things the Romanists object in vain: (1) that the throne of his father David was promised to him (Luke 1:32; 2 Sam. 7:12; Ps. 132:11; Isa. 9:6), since this must be understood mystically regarding such a kingdom that

is not only eternal but also infinite (Luke 1:33; 2 Sam. 7:13–16). (2) That he was descended from the seed of David according to the flesh (Rom. 1:3; 2 Tim. 2:8). For (a) not all who are descended from royal seed are immediately kings, either *de jure* or *de facto*. Especially since (b) before the birth of the Messiah this right had long perished in the family of David, with the rule of Judea having been transferred through many changes after the captivity, first to the Hasmoneans, then Herod, then finally to the Romans, to whom also, as lawful lords, taxes were to be paid, as he himself taught (Matt. 22:21). This is not to add (c) that Jeconiah, from whom the Messiah descended legally through Joseph, the betrothed husband of his mother (Matt. 1:12), already had the kingdom of Judea removed from him (Jer. 22:30).

4. Does any temporal royal power belong to the pope? The difference of opinions XIV. Accordingly, fourth, it is asked whether temporal royal power over kings, princes, kingdoms, principalities, persons, and the secular affairs of all Christians belongs in any way to the pope. The papalists separate here into factions, for there are those who simply remove all temporal power from the pope, such as the Gallican papists. There are those who claim all power for him, and that directly and simply, such as Alessandro Cariero in *On the Power of the Pope*,[19] Azor in *Moral Instructions* (pt. 2, bk. 4, ch. 19),[20] and most of the Italian and Spanish papists. There are those who bestow on him all power, but only indirectly in reference to spiritual matters: thus Bellarmine, book 5, *On the Temporal Power of the Pope*, even to the point that he can remove kings and princes from the throne, and absolve their subjects from an oath of fealty.[21]

Protestants deny this.

Protestants certainly acknowledge that some spiritual power has been derived from Christ to the legitimate heralds of the gospel (Matt. 16:19; 18:18; John 20:22–23), yet no power that is temporal, much less kingly, but instead only spiritual, and that ministerial, because: (1) the Mediator himself, at least prior to his resurrection, did not possess it, as shown in the preceding section. Therefore, he also did not communicate it to Peter, much less to the pope, who was

---

19. Alessandro Cariero (1543–1626), Italian jurist and professor at the University of Padua, *De potestate Romani Pontificis adversus impios politicos, libri duo* (Padua: Francisco Bolzeta, 1599).

20. Juan Azor (1536–1603), Spanish Jesuit theologian and presbyter, *Institutiones Morales* (Cologne: Antonius Hierat, 1616), 2:585–600.

21. Robert Bellarmine (1542–1621), controv. gen. 3, bk. 5, "De temporali dominio et potestate ejusdem Pontificis," *Disputationes de controversiis Christianae fidei*, 4 vols. (Ingolstadt: Adam Sartorius, 1601), 1:1063–98; idem, *Omnia Opera* (Naples: J. Giuliano, 1856–1862), 1:524–40.

nonexistent. (2) He removed it from his apostles (Matt. 21:25–26). (3) The apostles themselves reject it clearly enough (Acts 6:2), after the example of Christ himself (Luke 12:14). (4) They reprove the same in others (2 Tim. 2:4). (5) Our opponents do not even try to produce any records, indeed not even one whit, from Scripture for this temporal power of the pope.

The papists affirm it, with these weak reasons.

The weak reasons of our adversaries are of entirely no significance, such as: (1) "Temporal power is subject to spiritual power, because temporal things are subject to spiritual ones, and not vice versa, from which it follows that if a secular prince should undertake something in his administration that is contrary to a spiritual good, he can be brought back into order by the spiritual power"—thus Bellarmine reasons in the place cited. I respond: (a) Therefore does the pope have temporal power? (b) By these hypotheses, would not the lowest sacrificing priest have this temporal power? (c) Spiritual power (at least the royal kind) to bring aberrant secular power back into order belongs only to God and Christ. (d) Finally, the power that brings aberrant temporal power back into order is not anything but a spiritual power, and one acting in a spiritual way. (2) "Otherwise, the ecclesiastical commonwealth[22] would not be sufficient for itself and its own end." I respond, The head of the ecclesiastical commonwealth is Christ, in whom it is entirely sufficient for itself without any power of the pope. (3) "The judging of a king who is a heretic and overturns the church, who is to be deposed, belongs to the pope, and therefore so does temporal power." I respond: (a) a king who is a heretic and overturns the church is to be deposed only by one superior to him, namely God and Christ. (b) Judging a heretical king does not pertain to the pope, who is a heretic and the Antichrist. (c) Even if judging did pertain to the pope, yet temporal power would not follow from this, just as it belongs to those who mint coins to judge a counterfeit coin, yet there does not belong to them power over the counterfeiters. (4) "All Christian kings, by an agreement either express or tacit, have subjected their scepters to Christ, even under penalty of losing their power to rule." I respond: (a) Therefore have they subjected them to the pope? (b) Therefore, when they stray in any way from the duty belonging to Christ, should they be deposed by the pope? (c) By this reasoning, would there not belong to the pope the power to strip away goods, indeed to deprive of life, all Christians not living in a Christian manner? (5) "It is necessary for a pastor to have the authority to ward off a wolf." I respond: (a) Thus any common pastor will have temporal power over a heretical prince. (b) He has the power

---

22. *Respublica ecclesiastica*

to ward off a wolf, but only a spiritual power, and that of driving him away in a spiritual way, of convincing from the Word of God, and not a temporal power that of deposing. (6) "Uzziah, on account of his leprosy, was by the priest judged, ejected, and thus deprived of his power to rule." I respond: (a) If it is valid to use examples from the Old Testament in these cases, then from the example of Solomon judging and deposing Abiathar the highest priest (1 Kings 2:27), you would more evidently conclude that to kings belongs power over pontiffs. (b) Uzziah was not deprived of his royal power but only impeded in its use, and that not so much by the priest as by God, who inflicted leprosy upon him. Indeed, (c) perhaps not even in its use, for he could also have ruled through others, just as, according to the papists, the pope can through bishops. (7) "Jehoiada the high priest ordered Queen Athaliah to be killed, and Joash to be made king (2 Chron. 23)." I respond: (a) She was not a legitimate queen. (b) Nor were these things done by Jehoiada alone, but by the whole covenanted congregation. (c) What Jehoiada did, he did not precisely as the high priest, but as, from affinity, the guardian of the legitimate king. (d) And, if the consequence of this example is solid, it will also be permitted for the pope to kill kings, which the papists (whatever they may actually think) would not dare attribute, even to him.

5. Is the Mediator alone the king of the church? The opinion of the Romanists
XV. Fifth, it is asked whether the Mediator alone is the king and monarch of the church. The papists, so that they may establish the pope as the universal king and monarch of both the church and the world, want it to be that King Jesus handed over his own kingly power to Peter, as his vicar on earth, and because Peter was the Roman bishop, and the popes are his successors to the Roman episcopal throne, that at the same time he entrusted his royal power to all the Roman pontiffs.

The opinion of Protestants with its grounds
On the contrary, Protestants: (1) receive only Christ as their king and head (Matt. 23:8, 10–11; 1 Tim. 2:5; Ps. 2:6). Nor (2) with respect to the kingly dignity do they allow either any deputy or any successor of him, because (a) he himself expressly prohibits this (Luke 22:25–26). (b) Even the one who is alleged to be his vicar, Peter, rejects any such dignity (1 Peter 5:1–3). (c) Christ himself, who is immediately present in his own affairs, does not need any (Matt. 18:20; 28:20). Nor, accordingly, (3) did he ever confer a vicariate upon Peter, because not only are there no records of this conferral, but he also wanted all the apostles to be equal (Luke 22:25–26). Nor (4) do they judge that it can be demonstrated by solid reasons that Peter was the Roman bishop; indeed, he was not even ever in

Rome. And (5) even if he were most certainly so, they think that it cannot be proven that from the ordinance of Christ this dignity of the vicariate transfers to Peter's successors any more than the dignity of the apostolate. Furthermore, (6) they deny that the Roman pontiffs are the true successors of Peter, because they differ a whole heaven from his doctrine. They add that (7) such a succession, if there was one, was quite frequently interrupted, through interregna, antipopes, and so forth. And thus it is incumbent upon the papalists to demonstrate all these things before they can obtain that the pontiff is the king and monarch of the whole, universal church.

The grounds of the Romanist opinion
The entire grounds of our adversaries' case is in the monarchy which is said to have been: (1) promised to Peter in Matthew 16:18–19. I respond, (a) It is not evident that with these words any authority is promised to Peter, because by the word *petra*, "rock," could be understood either Christ himself (1 Cor. 3:11), or Peter's confession about Christ. (b) If it is granted for no reason that an authority was promised, yet it is not kingly and monarchical, for a priestly authority could suffice, as the old Scholastics acknowledged, together with the Master of the Sentences.[23] Nor (c) does the Sorbonne and the theological faculty of Paris admit that kingly authority is promised to Peter. (2) Transferred to him in John 21:17, "Feed my sheep." I respond: (a) Here there is not even one hint about a kingly and monarchical power, but rather, (b) an office common to all apostles and ministers of the divine word (1 Peter 5:1–3; Matt. 28:19; Jer. 3:15) is being impressed upon Peter with singular emphasis. To these things (3) they add certain scraped-together prerogatives of Peter, for the most part fictitious, all foolish, which would imply what is to be implied, namely a monarchical authority, though Paul expressly testifies that he is equal to Peter (2 Cor. 11:5; 12:11).

The grounds of the Protestants' opinion
The grounds of the orthodox opinion have already been designated, and to them we do not add anything except the parity of the apostles, which not only does the Savior command, but also the apostle impresses, in the passages just cited (and Gal. 2:6–9, 11, 14). Therefore we wait upon the Romanists to establish the grounds of their opinion.

---

23. Peter Lombard (c. 1100–1160), e.g. bk. 4, dist. 19, ch. 1, *Libri IV Sententiarum* in *PL* 192:889–92; idem, *The Sentences*, trans. G. Silano, 4 vols. (Toronto: Pontifical Institute of Medieval Studies, 2007).

6. Was the Mediator made king only from his ascension?

XVI. Sixth, it is asked whether the Mediator was made king only from his ascension. The Socinians, because they confuse the priestly office with the kingly, and state that the priestly office began with his ascension, to the end that he would not have offered himself on earth, and by offering have made satisfaction, are also compelled to deny that he was king before his ascension. For this reason Smalcius in *Refutation of Franz's Theses* (disp. 3, thesis 84) concludes, "Therefore at the ascension begins not only the manifestation and use of the power of Christ, but also his power itself, which beforehand he never in fact had, and which beforehand he could in no way use."[24] Protestants distinguish three things in a king: the right or authority to rule, which he had from eternity by reason of his deity, the exercise, and the manifestation. Then they refer the exercise, or at least the total exercise, of his kingly authority, and also its manifestation, or at least its full and complete manifestation, to the state of exaltation (Matt. 26:63–64; cf. John 17:5; Acts 2:36; Phil. 2:9–10), but the right of it they assert for him from his very birth.

The arguments of the negative part
For: (1) the Magi search for him as the one who was born King of the Jews (Matt. 2:2). (2) He himself confesses before Pilate that he was born a king (John 18:37). (3) The child born is said to have authority upon his shoulders (Isa. 9:6–7). (4) He conducted himself like a king even before his ascension, although according to his state of humiliation (Matt. 21:4–5). (5) The Jews are commanded to receive the king as one coming in the flesh (Ps. 24:7–10; Zech. 9:9). (6) He had all authority in heaven and on earth before his ascension (Matt. 11:27; 28:19). (7) Immediately from his birth, he was the Son of God (Gal. 4:4), about which we read in Psalm 2:6–7, "I have set my king…'You are my Son.'"

The objections of the affirmative part
There is not anything that they can object, other than: (1) that Christ was not a priest on earth (Heb. 8:4); therefore, he was also not a king. I respond, The argument rests upon a double false hypothesis: (a) that the kingly function of Christ is the same as the priestly, which we have expressly rejected above in chapter 5, §VI. (b) That the Mediator was not a priest on earth, which we refuted in chapter 7, §XVI. (2) That all that authority in heaven and on earth, which coincides with his kingly authority, about which we read in Matthew 28:19, was conferred

---

24. Valentinus Smalcius, *Refutatio thesium D. Wolfgangi Frantzii…de praecipuis Christianae religionis capitibus* (Raków: Sternacki, 1614), 77.

on him only after the ascension, when the apostles were sent throughout the whole world, which occurred only after the ascension. I respond, On the contrary, he expressly declares that the authority *was* given to him, in the past tense, while he was still living on earth with the apostles, and he also already exercised that authority when he derived from himself to the apostles the authority of declaring the gospel throughout the whole earth, which was to be exercised only after the solemn outpouring of the Holy Spirit at Pentecost (Acts 1:4). (3) That he did not exercise kingly acts while he existed on earth. I respond: (a) Someone can have a right and authority and not exercise it. (b) And he also exercised it, as has been already demonstrated, although according to his humiliated state, he did so not as fully as in his glorified state.

7. Will the kingdom of the Mediator last forever? The difference of opinions
XVII. Seventh, it is asked whether the kingdom of Christ will last forever. The Socinians, I do not know by what fit of dizziness, sometimes assert an eternal kingdom for him (Smalcius, *On the Divinity of Christ*, ch. 15),[25] and sometimes teach that he will set aside the kingdom in the last judgment, undoubtedly to the end that they may more powerfully obtain that he was not God from eternity, as one who would at some point lack the authority to rule.

The affirmative arguments
The orthodox distinguish between kingly power or the authority to rule, and the last stage of the mediatorial economy, or that mode of ruling which is now in force. Then they deny that he will ever set aside the power to rule, although they acknowledge that he will set aside the mode of ruling, because: (1) an eternal kingdom is promised to him (2 Sam. 7:12–13). (2) It is described as an eternal kingdom (Dan. 7:27). (3) It is foretold as eternal, by the angel (Luke 1:33; Rev. 11:15).

An objection
Our adversaries seek the only defense for their negative opinion in 1 Corinthians 15:24, "When he shall have delivered up the kingdom to God, even the Father." But they do not consider that those words, as we have said, do not deal with kingly power and the authority of kingship, but with the final stage of the mediatorial economy, and with the glorified church to be presented before the Father,

---

25. Valentinus Smalcius, *De divinitate Jesu Christi* (Raków: Sternacki, 1608), 93–96.

which is spoken of objectively as his kingdom, because he has been anointed as king over it. Compare Cloppenburg, *Anti-Smalcius* (disp. 55, §30ff.).[26]

8. Did the Mediator abrogate the ceremonial and judicial law only as a king?
The difference of opinions: What do the Jews think? The Socinians?
The orthodox?
XVIII. Eighth, it is asked whether the Mediator abrogated the ceremonial and judicial law only as a king. The Jews simply deny that the Messiah as king would possess the authority to abrogate either the ceremonial or the judicial law; Daniel refutes them in exact terms (Dan. 9:26–27), and we will expressly refute them elsewhere.[27] The Socinians, because they remove Christ's priesthood on earth and confuse it with his kingly function, which he only obtained and exercised after his ascension to heaven, refer this abrogation only to his kingly function, and state that it was completed only after the aforementioned ascension (see Smalcius, *On the Divinity of Jesus Christ*, ch. 20).[28] The orthodox distinguish this abrogation according to its right and according to its accomplishment; then they refer this abrogation, first according to right, to his priesthood, insofar as by it he fulfilled the types and figures of the Old Testament, and thus removed them, according to the prediction in Daniel 9:27. Christ both testified to this in word while hanging on the cross (John 19:30), and proved it in very fact, with the rending of the temple veil (Matt. 27:51). At the same time he well enough removed the Jewish state, upon which the judicial laws depended. But then according to its accomplishment, they refer this abrogation to his kingly function, in which, partly through the preaching of the gospel, he took care to promulgate immunity from the burden of the typical ceremonies, which were now fulfilled by his death, and partly also through the destruction of the Jewish temple, city, and polity, he declared that their end had come. Thus now that the abrogation of the ceremonial laws accomplished through the priesthood on the cross, according to right, has been proven, the Socinian opinion fails, in which that abrogation is imagined to have occurred through the kingly authority alone. And their reasons accomplish nothing against the orthodox, inasmuch as they do not deny that these ceremonial and judicial laws have *de facto* been abrogated through the kingly authority.

---

26. Johannes Cloppenburg (1592–1652), "Elenchus cap. XXII Disp. LXV," §§XXX–XLII, *Anti-Smalcius: De divinitate Jesu Christi* (Franeker: Idzardus Balck, 1652) in idem, *Theologica opera omnia*, 2 vols. (Amsterdam: Gerard Borst, 1684), 2:886–88.
27. 1.8.2 §XLIX
28. Smalcius, *De divinitate Jesu Christi*, 120–24.

9. Will the administration of the mediatorial kingdom, after the ascension
until the end of the world, be uniform? The difference of opinions
XIX. Ninth, it is asked whether the administration of the mediatorial kingdom will be uniform from the ascension of Christ until the consummation of the ages. The crasser chiliasts, whose founder was Papias, stated that after a universal resurrection, Christ with his saints would reign on earth for a thousand years, to be spent not so much in spiritual blessedness as in carnal delights. With the Epicurean delights removed, many from the more ancient fathers, for example, Justin Martyr, Irenaeus, Tertullian, Lactantius, Victorinus, and infinite others, indeed even Augustine, at least at first, and Jerome, inclined toward the same opinion. Several more recent theologians depart not very far from them, except that they terminate the beginning and end of these thousand years before the last judgment. Indeed Johann Piscator urges that some indefinite period of time after the destruction of the Antichrist there will be certain bodily resurrection of the martyrs, preceding the general resurrection of the dead by a thousand years, and these martyrs will reign with Christ not on earth but in heaven.[29] Johann Henrich Alsted, a disciple of Piscator, in his *Diatribe on the Millennium*[30] differs from his teacher in two things: (1) he thinks that this millennial reign of the martyrs will be not in heaven but on earth. (2) He determines that its beginning will be in the year 1694. Those in England and elsewhere who profess the fifth monarchy state that the saints of the first resurrection will remain on earth and will converse familiarly with surviving Christians, with Christ visibly and personally ruling both of them from the city of Jerusalem, where he will erect the seat and throne of this fifth monarchy.[31] The renowned Cocceius thinks that for an indefinite period before the last day the state of the church will be by far most blessed, and will be conjoined with the universal conversion of the Jews, and so there will be a new heaven and a new earth, in which righteousness dwells (according to Rev. 21:1ff.).[32]

---

29. Johann Piscator, *Commentarii in omnes libros Novi Testamenti*, 3rd ed. (Herborn: [Christoph Corvinus], 1638), 821–23.

30. Johann Heinrich Alsted (1588–1638), *Diatribe de mille annis Apocalypticis, non illis Chiliastarum et Phantastarum, sed B B. Danielis et Johannis* (Frankfurt: Eifrid, 1630), 30, 37–38; idem, *The Beloved City, or The Saints Reign on Earth a Thousand Yeares*, trans. William Burton (London, 1643), 13, 56, 70–72.

31. The Fifth Monarchy Men were an English sect active 1649–1661, bearing influence in Oliver Cromwell's Parliament. The name refers to the prophecy of Daniel that Messiah's kingdom should arise after the four kingdoms of Babylon, Persia, Greece, and Rome. The sect was eager to use political means to institute Christ's imminent, personal, visible reign on earth.

32. Johannes Cocceius (1603–1669), *Cogitationes de Apocalypsi S. Johannis Theologi*, in *Opera*

The common opinion of the orthodox. The arguments of the orthodox

The common opinion of the orthodox, although in the circumstantials of the church it freely admits of certain variances, nevertheless in the substantials of the kingly administration, especially with respect to a personal millennial kingdom of Christ himself on earth, and a blessedness of the church so great that it excludes all persecutions of enemies, or even vices of the church itself, admits of no variety at all, because: (1) Scripture presents the last times to us as the most difficult, as much with respect to spiritual things (Luke 18:8) as to temporal things (2 Tim. 3:1–5). (2) Scripture, as it acknowledges a triumphant church only in heaven, so it acknowledges none but a militant church on earth (Job 7:1; 2 Tim. 4:7–8). (3) Scripture teaches that the Antichrist, the most atrocious persecutor of the church, will not be consumed except in the appearing of Christ, with the spirit of his mouth (2 Thess. 2:8). (4) The chiliast opinion interposes a space of at least a thousand years between the destruction of the Antichrist and the consummation of the ages, although Paul nevertheless joins those two things together immediately (2 Thess. 2:8). (5) The chiliast hypotheses presuppose one of two things: either the souls of the martyrs before the last judgment will be drawn back and reunited with their bodies on earth, so that they may reign there with Christ, or their bodies will be taken up into heaven. (6) They introduce another resurrection of bodies besides that universal one which according to the Scriptures will occur in the last judgment. (7) Scripture foretells that there will be a uniform administration of the mediatorial kingdom through the declaration of the gospel even to the end of the age (Matt. 24:14).

The objections of the chiliasts

To all these things, those of the contrary opinion have scarcely anything to oppose except the rather obscure passage of Revelation 20:1–8, which contains a prophecy, which are hardly ever understood before they take place. At the least, in this passage: (1) it is not said of Christ that he will begin any new kingdom, but only of the martyrs that they will reign with Christ for a thousand years. (2) There the place is not expressed where that kingdom will be, that it will be on earth, as most of the chiliasts want; however, the martyrs can reign with Christ, although Christ is not with them on earth. (3) Those thousand years can be understood to have already passed, whether they be computed from the incarnation or the passion of the Savior, or from the destruction of Jerusalem, or from the reign of Constantine the Great. If from the incarnation, the thousand

omnia theologica, exegetica, didactica, polemica, philological, 9 vols., 3rd ed. (Amsterdam: Peter Blaeu & Joan II Blaeu, 1701); 6:109–10.

years stop at Sylvester II, the renowned magician; if from the passion, then at Benedict IX, who was suffocated in the woods by the devil; if from the destruction of Jerusalem, then at Gregory VII, the most wretched thing upon two feet; if from the beginning of Constantine the Great, then at the rise of Boniface VIII and the Ottoman dynasty, and the dire persecutions of the Waldensians, around the thirteenth century. See Cornelius à Lapide on Revelation 20.[33] Furthermore, (4) the resurrection of the martyrs could be understood as a spiritual resurrection that happens from sins through faith and repentance (on which see John 5:25), which in the text is called the first resurrection, in distinction to the second, bodily resurrection, which will occur at the last judgment. Furthermore, (5) by the reign of the martyrs with Christ could be understood the reign of grace to be conducted here, distinguished from the reign of glory to be received in heaven hereafter. Finally, (6) the binding of Satan could be understood not as such by which he simply could not undertake anything against the church, but such by which he could not seduce entire nations (v. 3). Thus the sense of the whole passage emerges that Satan was bound either from the incarnation of Christ, or rather from the rule of Constantine the Great, to the extent that he would no longer seduce entire nations to idolatry or such cruel persecutions of Christians, until the time of Boniface VIII, in the year 1300. Then for a brief time, that is, until the time of the Reformation, he was loosed so that he might seduce entire nations, partly through the Antichrist, who was then especially growing strong in the West, and partly through the Muslim empire which was then arising. And throughout the thousand years in which Satan was bound, the martyrs who were slain before Constantine were spiritually resurrected, not as individuals, but as a class; and thus they also reigned spiritually, that is, they were held in value and in honor, as priests of God and Christ.

The Practical Part

In the kingly function is evident: 1. The glory of the king
XX. In the kingly function of the Mediator is evident, first, the glory of the king (from which he is expressly greeted as the king of glory, Ps. 24:7–10, and the Lord of glory, 1 Cor. 2:8), so magnificently promised and prefigured to him in the glory of David and Solomon, in Psalm 89:24–25, 27, where there is distinctly promised to him (1) a glory that will be exalted, "In my name shall his horn be exalted" (v. 24), with *horn* (as Calvin explains) designating glory, dignity, authority, and so forth (Luke 1:69); (2) sovereignty and power, extending to seas and

---

33. Cornelius à Lapide, *Commentaria in Apocalypsin S. Johannis Apostoli* (Leiden, 1627), 291–97.

rivers, "I will set his hand on the sea, and his right hand on the rivers" (v. 25); (3) eminence over the kings of the earth, "I will make him my firstborn, more eminent than the kings of the earth" (v. 27).

By various similar things
This glory is also distinguished by various similitudes, namely: (1) of a horn, inasmuch as in it consists the splendor and power of wild beasts; (2) of a lamp (Ps. 132:17; Luke 2:32), which spreads splendor or glory (cf. 1 Kings 11:36; 15:4; Job 18:6); (3) of a flourishing crown (Ps. 132:18, "Upon him shall his crown flourish"; Song 3:11; cf. Prov. 16:31; Ps. 89:40); (4) of a throne (Luke 1:32–33; Ps. 45:6), on which monarchs manifest their glory (cf. Jer. 14:21; 17:12; Job 36:7). This glory of the Mediator was prefigured in the magnificence of David and Solomon (2 Chron. 1:1, 12, 15; 6:23–24; 9:26 with Matt. 12:42).

It is conspicuous in three things especially.
But this glory will more powerfully strike us, if we should more distinctly think about: (1) the one reigning, who not only (a) is most wise, indeed the very wisdom of God (Prov. 8; 1 Cor. 1:24), given to us for wisdom (1 Cor. 1:30), the Counselor (Isa. 9:6), so then most apt for ruling; (b) most righteous (Isa. 53:11), given to us for righteousness (1 Cor. 1:30), indeed righteousness itself (Zech. 9:9; Jer. 23:6); (c) most humane, most merciful, most beneficent (Matt. 11:29; 12:19–20; Zech. 9:9); (d) most powerful (אל גבור, the mighty God, Isa. 9:6), the very power of God (1 Cor. 1:24), to whom belongs all authority in heaven and on earth (Matt. 28:18), all of which make this king glorious; but also is very God and man, in one person. If (2) we should think about his kingdom, which is: (a) most full, extending to seas and rivers (Ps. 89:25), to the uttermost ends of the earth (Ps. 2:8), indeed to the very heavens (Matt. 28:18; Phil. 2:10; Eph. 1:21–22); (b) most lasting, and altogether eternal (Luke 1:33; Dan. 2:44; Ps. 145:3); (c) most flourishing (Ps. 132:18); (d) most peaceful (Rom. 14:17; Ps. 55:14); (e) most obedient, most good (Ps. 110:3; Matt. 6:10; etc.). If (3) we should think about his reigning, or manner of ruling, which is most agreeable to this king, that is, wise, most righteous, most clement, most powerful (Ps. 45:6–7; 9:8; 96:13; 98:9).

To what end it is evident
But this glory of our king is evident to this end, that: (1) we may see and acknowledge it (John 17:24; Ps. 97:6; 102:15–16), (2) we may refer it back to him (Ps. 29:2; 1 Tim. 1:17; 6:16), (3) we may glory in him (Phil. 1:26; 3:3; Jer. 9:23). Compare book 2, chapter 22, §XVI, and likewise book 5, chapter 3, §XXX.

2. The blessedness of the kingdom and its subjects
XXI. Hence is evident, second, the blessedness and happiness of the kingdom, and of the subjects of this kingdom (Ps. 33:12). Thus it is called: (1) the kingdom of God, throughout Scripture (Rom. 14:17; Luke 14:15), likewise (2) the kingdom of Christ (Eph. 5:5), (3) the kingdom of heaven (2 Tim. 4:18), (4) the kingdom of light (Col. 1:12), (5) the kingdom of peace and joy (Rom. 14:17), (6) the kingdom of glory (Matt. 19:28; 25:31; 16:27).

In what that blessedness consists
That blessedness is evident, namely: (1) in the nature of the king, inasmuch as he is most wise, most just, merciful, most powerful (which we designated in the preceding section); (2) in the nature of the kingdom, for it is most wide, most constant, most holy, most abundant in all good things (Rom. 14:17), which we likewise discussed in the preceding section; (3) in the method of its administration, through: (a) the scepter of the gospel (Ps. 110:2; 45:6), (b) the most righteous laws (Deut. 4:8), (c) the sweetest manner of ruling, by the internal bowing of the heart (Gen. 9:27, יפת, "he shall draw";[34] cf. Prov. 21:1; Jer. 31:33), for which reason it is said that the kingdom of God is within us (Luke 17:21) and his yoke is easy (Matt. 11:30). (4) In the results of the kingdom: (a) the security of its subjects (Matt. 16:18; Heb. 12:28), (b) while we live here on earth, peace and joy in the Holy Spirit (Rom. 14:17), and (c) hereafter in heaven, a crown of glory (2 Tim. 4:8; Heb. 12:28; Matt. 25:34).

To what end it should be considered
There is therefore in this blessedness, reason on account of which: (1) its true subjects should give thanks and rejoice (Zech. 9:9). (2) We should strive with every effort to become and be the children of this kingdom (Matt. 13:38), which happens: (a) by regeneration (John 3:5), (b) by repentance and faith (Mark 1:18), (c) by seeking the kingdom of God and his righteousness (Matt. 6:33), and so forth. (3) By the consideration, communion, and hope of this kingdom, we should encourage ourselves against any persecutions (Luke 12:32; Acts 14:22), of any enemies, as much physical as spiritual.

---

34. Cf. *Alliciet Deus Jephethum*, "God shall draw Japheth," in Immanuel Tremellius and Franciscus Junius (1510–1580), *Biblia Sacra* (Amsterdam, 1633), 6. Poole, *Synopsis criticorum*, 1:115, attributes this interpretation also to Henry Ainsworth (1569–1622), *Annotations upon the first book of Moses called Genesis* (Amsterdam: G. Thorp, 1621), fol. [H4 verso], and Piscator, *Commentarius in Genesin*, 237.

3. The misery of those who are not subject to Christ the King. Who they are
XXII. And from this also is evident, third, the misery of all those who are not subject to this king, such as are: (1) those who reject him by their very profession (Luke 19:11, 27; Job 21:14), that is, all unbelievers, pagans, Muslims, Jews. Those who (2) oppose themselves to our king, like the Antichrist (2 Thess. 2:4), the kings of the earth (Ps. 2:2–3; Acts 4:26–27), and those who put their power at the disposal of the beast (Rev. 17:12–13). Those who (3) instead of doing what they ought, in taking the crowns from their own head and casting them at the feet of our king (Rev. 4:10), well enough take his from him and as it were place it on their own head, following the example of the Antichrist (2 Thess. 2:4), when they snatch for themselves his spiritual and ecclesiastical rule, as well as the rights of Christ's kingdom. Those who (4) indeed cry out with a loud voice, "Lord, Lord" (Matt. 7:21–22), that is, those who as far as their profession are children of the kingdom (Matt. 8:12), but do not do this king's will, and thus in reality deny him (Titus 1:16). In a word, (5) all those who are not truly born again (John 3:5).

How great their misery is
The misery of all of these is evident in this, that: (1) they are utterly deprived of all the blessedness and happiness of Christ's kingdom, and of all the benefits which belong to his believing subjects (per the preceding section; Eph. 2:12). (2) They are the enemies of him who is the King of kings and Lord of lords (Phil. 3:18), who will rule in the midst of his enemies, and that until he has made them all a footstool for his feet (Ps. 110:1). (3) They have a most loathsome king, the prince and god of this world (John 12:31; 2 Cor. 4:4). (4) They are under the power of darkness (Col. 1:13). (5) They are slaves of Satan (Heb. 2:14–15), under his snares (2 Tim. 2:26; Acts 26:18). And thus (6) slaves of perdition (2 Peter 2:19). (7) Those whom our king will crush with his iron scepter in his fury (Ps. 2:5, 9, 12).

What the remedies are
Therefore it is the case that: (1) we should earnestly search ourselves, whether or not we may be of the number of these who are enemies of Christ, slaves of Satan, liable to such great misery (Zeph. 2:1; 2 Cor. 13:5). (2) If we discern that we are so far still under the kingdom of darkness, then we should strive with all our strength to be rescued from it, and transferred into the kingdom of the Son of God (Col. 1:13), which is done: (a) by God, as the one who delivered us (Col. 1:13); (b) by the Mediator, who took away the power of Satan (Heb. 2:14); (c) by means of faith (John 1:12); (d) with the preaching of the gospel assisting

like a midwife (Acts 26:18). (3) If we have been rescued, we should offer ourselves in heart, mouth, and deed grateful to God (Col. 1:12–13). (4) We should carefully take heed of the fiery darts and hidden snares of Satan (1 Tim. 3:7; Prov. 13:14; 14:27), indeed we strive against him with all our strength (Eph. 6:11–12).

4. It rouses us to seek the kingdom of Christ.

What seeking the kingdom of Christ intends

XXIII. From the three preceding points, fourth, a most effective motive is supplied for zeal to seek the kingdom of Christ (Matt. 6:33). This zeal includes: (1) a love toward it (Ps. 26:8; 122:6–7); then (2) a labor (a) to receive it, or that the kingdom of God may come (Matt. 6:10, 33), that is, that the church may be planted everywhere (1 Cor. 3:6–8; Ps. 80:8, 15; Rom. 15:18–19), (b) to retain it, against the attacks of enemies (Matt. 16:18; Rev. 2:25–26), (c) to build up and reform it (Ps. 51:18; 80:13–14), (d) to propagate and extend the kingdom of grace, or the militant church, even to the ends of the earth (Ps. 2:8; 22:27; 72:8; 47:8–9).

In what actions it consists

All these things are intended and obtained: (1) by praying (Ps. 122:6–7; 51:18). (2) By using the means that God customarily employs to procure them, such as: (a) the preaching of the Word (Matt. 4:23; Luke 8:1, 10; Acts 19:8; 20:26; 28:23, 31); (b) the raising up of churches (1 Cor. 3:6–8; Mark 12:1; Ps. 80:15; Isa. 5); (c) the sending out of faithful laborers (Matt. 20:1, 2, 4; Luke 20:9); (d) the cooperation of God, or his blessing of the labors (1 Cor. 3:6–7; Rom. 15:18; Gal. 2:8); (e) the planting of schools and seminaries (Gal. 6:6; Ps. 34:11); (f) the establishment of a faithful magistrate, to be a nursing father for the church (Isa. 49:7, 23); (g) household discipline (Eph. 6:4; Deut. 6:7, 20; 2 Tim. 1:5 with 3:15). (3) By combating and conquering the enemies of this kingdom (Eph. 6:10ff.; 1 Tim. 6:12; 2 Tim. 4:7; Rev. 12:11).

What sorts of things move us to seek it

Moreover, so that we may seek the kingdom of Christ in this way, these things ought rouse us: (1) the glorification of the king, which we spoke about in §XX (cf. Prov. 14:28); (2) the blessedness of the kingdom, which we spoke about in §XXI; (3) the misery of those who are not subjects of this kingdom (Eph. 2:12); the blessing which the psalmist invokes upon seekers (Ps. 122:6) and the King himself promises (Matt. 6:33). Compare writers on the second petition of the Lord's Prayer.

5. *It binds us to the duties owed to this king.* What they are

XXIV. In addition, fifth, the kingly dignity of the Mediator binds us to offer to him lawful duties, specifically: (1) the kiss of homage (Ps. 2:6, 12), customarily conferred upon new kings, and a sign of religious worship (Job 31:26–27; 1 Kings 19:18; Hos. 13:2). This is a kiss (a) of love, and as it were on the mouth (about which, see Song 1:2; 8:1), by which we love him above all things (Matt. 10:37; 1 Cor. 16:22); (b) of dependence, and as it were on the hands (about which, see Sirach 29:5), through which in all things we depend upon him alone, inasmuch as without him we can do nothing (John 15:5), through which we look for life, salvation, and every blessing from his hands, as it were (Acts 4:12; John 14:6; 2 Cor. 1:20); (c) of submission, and as it were on his feet (about which, see Luke 7:46), through which we depend upon his mouth alone (Deut. 18:15), we reverently do his pleasure (2 Cor. 5:9; Matt. 6:10), we cast ourselves and all we have at his feet, as it were (Rev. 4:10; Ps. 115:1; Phil. 2:21). (2) Honor and esteem, whereby this one is to us above father and mother (Matt. 10:37), above ten thousand (2 Sam. 18:3), indeed above heaven and earth (Ps. 73:25). (3) Fear and reverence (Ps. 2:11; 33:18; Rev. 15:4; Mal. 1:6). (4) Trust, in his wisdom, power, and goodness (Ps. 2:12; 20:6–7). (5) Obedience and observance (Ps. 2:11; Rom. 1:9; Col. 3:24; Rev. 7:15; 22:3). (6) Our gifts and services (Ps. 72:10; 76:11; 96:8; Matt. 2:11). (7) Celebration and glory (Rev. 5:12; 1:17; 6:16).

To what end they should be bestowed

All these duties should be bestowed upon our king because: (1) they rightfully belong to him (Rev. 4:11), namely, as he is King of kings and Lord of lords (Rev. 19:16; 1 Tim. 1:17; 6:16), the Lord of glory (1 Cor. 2:7). (2) He himself bestows glory and benefits upon his subjects, insofar as it is by his grace that they are worthy, and so forth (Rev. 3:4; 16:6). (3) Bestowing them is, to the bestowers themselves, most useful for all things (Matt. 19:27–29; cf. Job 21:10; Mal. 3:14; Matt. 6:33). (4) Bestowing them is especially necessary, if we wish to safely and successfully turn away his just vengeance (Ps. 2:12).

6. *It urges kings and princes to the imitation of Christ the King:*

(1) With respect to justice in ruling

XXV. Especially sixth, in the kingly function of our Mediator, all kings, princes, and magistrates of this world have that which they should imitate, so that together with kings David and Solomon, who were types of our King, and also with our King himself, they would govern justly and religiously: 2 Samuel 23:3, "The God of Israel said to me, the Rock of Israel spoke to me, 'A ruler among men will be just, a ruler in the fear of God.'" Whether you render the Hebrew text, which is ambiguous from the omission of the substantive verb, imperatively, so that it prescribes to David the duties of justice and piety, "You will be" or "You shall be a just ruler," or prophetically, so that it promises a just ruler, "There will be a just ruler," and also whether you take it regarding David as a type, who was in fact a just ruler and God-fearing man, or regarding the Messiah as the antitype, that he was the ruler preeminently just and religious (Ps. 45:2–6; 72:1–4, 7, 12–14; Isa. 11:1–10; Jer. 23:5–6; Zech. 9:9–10), the true מלכי־זדק, Melchizedek, King of Righteousness (Heb. 7:1–3)—in whatever way, I say, you take it, you will at least have this, that rulers over men must follow the example of king David and King Messiah.

The justice of the person of kings
And therefore, they must study in their governance, first, a twofold justice, namely (1) of their person, by which they should be just, not only outwardly, through actual justice, but also inwardly, through habitual justice (about which see Ps. 101:1; Prov. 20:28 with 29:4), through which they should be prone to exercising justice and clemency toward all, without respect of persons (Prov. 24:23; 28:21; Ps. 82:2; Deut. 1:16–17), above fear or hope of reward, by which they would pervert justice (Deut. 1:16–17; Isa. 1:23; Prov. 29:4). Within this habitual justice various virtues are enfolded, for example: (a) zeal for knowing right and justice (Ps. 2:10; Prov. 28:16; Eccl. 10:16; Isa. 3:4–5). (b) Clemency and mercy (Prov. 20:28), by which he comes to the help of the oppressed (Isa. 1:17, 23). (c) Fortitude, by which he is not terrified by others, but is a terror to evildoers (Prov. 20:2; Rom. 13:3). (d) Modesty and humility, so that he would not lift himself above his subjects in order to oppress them (Deut. 17:9, 20), like Rehoboam did (1 Kings 12:14ff.). (e) Chastity, so that he would not be turned away from justice by his lusts (Deut. 17:17; Prov. 31:3). (f) Temperance and sobriety (Prov. 31:4–5; Eccl. 10:13–14). (g) Contentment,[35] and a zeal for shunning avarice (Deut. 1:16–17; 17:17; Prov. 28:16). And by all these things a ruler among men must study, first, the justice of his person.

The justice of the kingly calling and the justice of kingly rule,
in protecting and in governing
Then in addition, he must study (2) the justice of his office and rule, which includes these two things, namely: (a) the justice of his calling, in which he should govern by a just title, as a legitimate ruler, not by mere usurpation, as a tyrant, like Athaliah (2 Kings 11:1–3); just as the Messiah was anointed, that is, legitimately

---

35. αὐτάρκεια

called (Ps. 2:6; Heb. 5:4–5). (b) The justice of its execution, in which (i) he should protect and defend the just (Isa. 32:1–2), that is, against (1) enemies, as much internal as external (Ps. 101:5, 7–8), (2) violence, oppression, and injuries of any kind, and done by anyone (Ps. 101:3; 82:3–4; Isa. 1:17), (3) any lack, as much of spiritual as of bodily necessities (Job 29:14–15; 2 Kings 6:25–27). (ii) He should govern (Rom. 13:3–4; 1 Tim. 2:2), (1) by establishing and promulgating just and useful laws (Amos 5:15; Ezra 1:1; 6:1–3), (2) by rewarding the good (Rom. 13:3–4), (3) by punishing the evil (Rom. 13:3–4; Judg. 18:7; Ps. 101:8). Thus kings or rulers among men must, according to the example of David and Messiah, study justice.

(2) With respect to godliness in ruling
They must study, second, the fear of God, through which they should govern not only justly, but also piously and religiously. They should have concern for religion, not neglect it (Acts 18:14–16), but devote themselves entirely to it, which chiefly concerns these three things: (1) to have a heart faithfully possessed with the fear and reverence of God, throughout their entire governance (Gen. 42:18; 2 Chron. 17:3–6; 34). Next (2) to direct the entire contour of their governance according to what has been prescribed in the divine Word, to which end the king of Israel was bound to write for himself a book of the law (Deut. 17:18–20; 2 Chron. 17:6). Furthermore, (3) to set before them as the chief goal of their entire governance the glorification of our King, the propagation and amplification of his kingdom, to provide in every way for its prosperity of both kinds, spiritual and temporal (Rom. 13:3–4; Isa. 60:10, 16; 1 Tim. 2:2). All this is generally obtained by these helps: (1) by cherishing and stirring up the exercise of religion and divine worship (2 Chron. 15:9–16; 20:7–9; 29–31; 34–35; Deut. 17:18–20). (2) By removing any impediments to religion, with respect to doctrine, worship, discipline: the sorts of impediments that generally arise from idolatry, heresy, profanity, persecutions, and so forth (Deut. 13:1–6; Zech. 13:3; 1 Kings 15:14 with 2 Chron. 15:17; 1 Kings 22:44; 2 Kings 12:3; 23:8, 13, 19–20, 24–25). (3) By reforming the church, if ever it has been corrupted in doctrine, worship, or morals (examples of which are evident in Ex. 32; Josh. 24; 2 Chron. 15; 17; 2 Kings 18; 23). (4) By calling together synods for reforming and directing matters of the church (1 Chron. 13:1–2; 23:1–2; 29:4; 1 Kings 8:1; 2 Kings 23:1–2). (5) By establishing the laws and statutes of Christ by their own civil authority, and by appointing and inflicting penalties upon violators (2 Chron. 29:5, 24; 30:1; 34:33; Neh. 13:7ff.; Dan. 3:28–29; 6:26–27). (6) By providing for the church whatever is necessary for it with respect to external matters: the support of ministers, schools, and so forth (1 Chron. 22; 2 Chron. 3ff.; 34ff.; 1 Tim.

5:17–18; 1 Cor. 9:6–15 with 2 Kings 31:4–9). (7) By punishing violators, not only of the second table, but of the first table of the law as well (Deut. 13:1–6; Zech. 13:3; Ex. 22:1–15; Lev. 20:11–12, 14, 17, 19–25). And so forth. To say it in a word, by all these things they should serve Christ the King (Ps. 2:11), they should cast their crowns, that is, their entire authority and power at the feet of Jesus the King (Rev. 4:10), they should devote their resources to him (Matt. 21:3, 7–8), by the example of David, Solomon, and others, and thus they should make their monarchies to be theocracies, in which God, and his anointed, is the supreme king (1 Sam. 8:7; 12:12; Rev. 11:15; Ps. 82).

Motivating arguments
And so in order that the kings of this world may more readily will all these things, they should earnestly consider that: (1) Jesus is that King of kings and Lord of lords (Rev. 19:16), whose are the kingdoms of this world (Rev. 11:15), even to the end of the earth (Ps. 2:8), to whom belongs all authority in heaven and on earth (Matt. 28:18; Eph. 1:21–22; Phil. 2:10). (2) From him accordingly they have received whatever they possess of dignity and authority (Dan. 2:37), which ought accordingly to be faithfully referred back to him (Rom. 11:36). (3) Through him they rule (Prov. 8:15), that is, everything required for ruling— power, wisdom, blessing, prosperity, and so forth—they obtain from him alone. (4) If they neglect their duties toward this king, they will more certainly than certain be deprived of their kingdoms (1 Sam. 13:13; Dan. 6:26, 28), and be cast down to the beasts (Dan. 4:33), and at last be shattered and crushed with an iron scepter (Ps. 2:9, 12; Rev. 19:15, 19). On the contrary, (5) if they faithfully render the duties owed, they will be established in their kingdom (2 Sam. 7:12–13; 1 Kings 2:24, 46; 9:5; etc.), and also be blessed by God with all kinds of good things, so that the crown flourish upon their head (Ps. 132:18).

7. It rouses all sorts of persons to imitate Christ the King. In which matters
XXVI. Also seventh, in the kingly function of the Mediator, to all sorts of Christians is supplied what they should imitate: (1) in regard to the person of our King, that insofar as he was wise, just, brave, merciful, fair,[36] so also all sorts of Christians, as partakers of his royal dignity, should pay attention to the same virtues (Phil. 4:8). Then (2) in regard to his rule, as our King commands all things, so also they should command themselves, and their affections and lusts (Gal. 5:24; Rom. 5:21; 6:12–13), nor should they allow themselves to be brought under the power of anything (1 Cor. 6:12). Also (3) in regard to his contest

---

36. ἐπιεικής

and fight, as our King fought with spiritual enemies, with Satan (Matt. 4:1–11; John 12:31; 14:30; Rom. 16:20; 1 John 2:13), with the world (John 16:33), so also they should fight a good fight (2 Tim. 4:7) with spiritual enemies, Satan (1 Peter 5:8–9), the world (1 John 5:4–5; Rom. 12:2), the flesh (Gal. 5:17), and to do so indeed that by fighting, with the help of King Jesus (Rev. 5:3; 17:14), they also overcome those spiritual enemies (Rom. 12:21; 1 John 2:13–14; 5:4; Rev. 2:7, 11, 26; 3:5, 21; 21:7). Finally, (4) in regard to his manner of life, as our King did not lead a worldly kingdom (John 18:36), nor lead with worldly pride (Zech. 9:9; Luke 17:20; cf. Acts 25:23), and thus even when a kingdom was also offered to him, he shunned it, so they also should be spiritual (Gal. 6:1), they should spurn pride and other worldly things (1 John 2:15–16), as things that are beneath their royal dignity (1 Peter 2:9).

By which motivating arguments
And so in order that in all these things they may more readily will to imitate their King, it will help to consider: (1) that they were made partakers (μέτοχοι) of his royal dignity (Heb. 1:7–8; Rev. 5:10), to the end that also in these things they might become more and more similar to him (Rom. 8:29). (2) Their highest perfection consists in this, that also in this royal perfection they may be made similar to their most perfect King (Luke 6:40; Matt. 5:48). (3) If in all these things they have been made similar to Christ the King by grace, they will also be made similar to him with respect to eternal glory (Luke 22:28–29; Rom. 8:17; 2 Tim. 2:12; 4:8; Luke 22:29).

8. It provides comfort. In which cases. By which consolatory arguments
XXVII. Finally, eighth, in the kingly function of Christ is supplied a most effective consolation (Zech. 9:9). In the circumstance of: (1) poverty and oppression (Ps. 72:13), (2) satanic temptations (Rev. 12:7, 9), (3) persecutions, when we are vexed by the abundance, strength, and cunning of our enemies (Ps. 3:1–2), what else in these and a thousand other circumstances can more powerfully support and raise our spirit, than that: (1) we have a king, so (a) righteous (Ps. 45:6; 9:8; 96:13; 98:9; Jer. 23:6 with Ps. 43:2–3), (b) so powerful (Isa. 9:7; Matt. 28:18; Eph. 1:20–22), (c) so kind (Zech. 9:9) and merciful (Heb. 2:15; Ps. 72:13). (2) We have a king who reigns in the midst of his and our enemies, and will make them as a footstool for his feet (Ps. 110:1–2). (3) He will act according to his faithfulness, so that we may gloriously triumph over his and our enemies (1 Cor. 15:54–55), and being set free from every evil (Rom. 8:37), we may fully enjoy the deepest peace and the sweetest rest.

CHAPTER NINE

The Humiliation of the Mediator

Who, being in the form of God, did not consider it robbery to be equal with God, but emptied himself, having taken the form of a servant, was made like men, and was found in appearance as a man; he humbled himself, having become obedient to death, even the death of the cross.
—Philippians 2:6–8

The transition from the preceding things to those that follow

I. We have contemplated the Mediator of the covenant of grace with respect to the mediatorial dignity, to names, to person, and to offices. Now we must consider the same Mediator with respect to the twin states in which he performed those offices, namely, the state of humiliation and of exaltation. Regarding then the state of humiliation, we will examine it first more generally, and then more specifically. The more general contemplation belongs to this place, and the words of the apostle in Philippians 2:6–8 will lay the foundation for it.

The Exegetical Part

The text is resolved and explained.

II. With these words the apostle presents to the Philippians as an example of humility the humiliation of the Son of God, in which two things occur:

A. The one humiliated, or the person humbling himself: "Who, existing in the form of God." In which words, the following things are recorded of the one humiliated:

1. The person, in the relative pronoun: ὅς, "Who," namely that same one who had been commended in the preceding verses as an example of self-denial and self-humiliation: τοῦτο φρονείσθω ἐν ὑμῖν, ὅ καὶ ἐν χριστῷ Ἰησοῦ, "Let this thinking be in you, which also in Christ Jesus," supplying, "which *thinking was* also" or "which *was* also." And what then was that? He had already said, "nothing through strife or

vainglory, but in humility considering each other greater than yourselves," ὑπερέχοντες ἑαυτῶν, to which he immediately adds, "Let this mind be in you, which was in Christ Jesus." Therefore the one humiliated is Jesus Christ, the God-man, not with respect to only one or the other nature, but with respect to the whole person, and to both natures of his person, the divine and the human, albeit in different ways: with respect to the former, through the concealment of the divine majesty; with respect to the latter, through the acceptance of the humility.

2. The pre-existing form, adduced for the elaboration of the humiliation, because "existing in the form of God," ἐν μορφῇ θεοῦ, "he humbled himself." Here it is preeminently disputed what this μορφὴ θεοῦ, "form of God," means. The Arians and Photinians, who deny the consubstantial[1] deity of Christ, and with them Erasmus, Grotius, and the Socinians, understand by it a certain external and only accidental ὁμοιότης, likeness, תמונה or תבנית, which was in his outstanding power of working miracles, of casting out demons, of raising the dead, and so forth. More correctly, those who receive the eternity of his deity think that it designates his very essence, his nature with its essential properties, namely, the same as οὐσία and φύσις, except that οὐσία means the bare essence, φύσις means the same essence as clothed with its properties—majesty, power, wisdom—whereas μορφὴ adds, in creatures, the accidents that are consequent to the nature of the thing, in which as it were by outlines its οὐσία and φύσις, its nature, is confirmed and depicted, just as it also expresses the human nature considered with its properties. And so then this seems to be the reason that he said μορφὴ θεοῦ, "form of God," μορφὴ δούλου, "form of a servant," and σχῆμα ἀνθρώπου, "appearance of man," rather than θεός, God, and ἄνθρωπος, man. The reasons they hold their opinion are: (1) it is the antithesis of the "form of a servant," which undoubtedly denotes the human nature; so then also "the form of God" denotes, to the apostle, the divine nature. (2) He explains this phrase by εἶναι ἴσα θεῷ, "to be equal with God." (3) The word ὑπάρχειν, to exist or to subsist, demands a substance, for a thing does not subsist in its accidents. (4) All the fathers, whom Zanchi and Erasmus summon, agree on this point.[2] To these reasons

---

1. ὁμοούσιον
2. On Phil. 2:7–8, see Girolamo Zanchi, *In d. Pauli Apostoli Epistolam ad Philippenses*

is added what has been demonstrated in its own place,[3] the truth of the eternal deity in Christ; with that presupposed, there is nothing that compels us to restrict μορφὴ to accidents. Nor is it valid to argue on the contrary: (1) that it is not probable that the apostle used μορφὴ in a meaning known only to philosophers. For its cognate in Galatians 4:19, ὡς μορφωθῇ χριστὸς ἐν ὑμῖν, "that Christ be *formed* in you,"[4] as well as its synonyms, φύσις, nature, οὐσία, essence, χαρακτὴρ τῆς ὑποστάσεως, express image of the hypostasis, εἰκὼν θεοῦ, image of God, were known to them, and if they were not known to the common people, they could have been explained by their teachers. (2) That μορφή, form, ὁμοίωμα, likeness, and σχῆμα, appearance, mean the same thing to the apostle, yet the latter two speak not of nature but of accidents, because Christ set aside the μορφὴ δούλου, form of a servant, in his ascension. I respond, Christ did not set aside the form of a servant, but only its humility; then also, μορφὴ denotes, with the essence, also the attributes.

3. Existence: ὑπάρχων, "existing," or "subsisting." Namely, even before he assumed the form of a servant, that is, the human nature (John 8:58). Thus from this we understand two things, namely that a person who subsists from eternity, that is, who is God from eternity, humbled himself, and that such a person was from eternity in possession of his own right, by which he was able to humble himself, or likewise was able not to: so accordingly, he humbled himself by pure, unadulterated choice, from which his ταπεινοφροσύνη, humility, is also increased.

B. The humiliation, which includes:

1. An abnegation, or a certain negative act in which he did not recognize as his own, or at least he did not consider as his own, what in fact was his own: οὐχ ἁρπαγμὸν ἡγήσατο τὸ εἶναι ἴσα θεῷ, "He did not consider it spoil to be equal with God." In these words are:

a. The act of abnegating: οὐχ ἁρπαγμὸν ἡγήσατο, "he did not consider as spoil." Translators unanimously are accustomed to translate

---

commentarius, 103–11, in idem, *Opera omnia theologica*, 8 tomes in 3 vols. (Geneva: Samuel Crispin, 1619), vol. 2, tom. 5; Desiderius Erasmus (c. 1466–1536), *Annotationes* in *Opera omnia*, 9 vols. (Basil: Frobenius, 1540), 6:622–24.

3. 1.2.26 §§VIII–XII

4. Mastricht's Greek here differs from that of Gal. 4:19; as elsewhere, he is not quoting but paraphrasing. Cf. 1.5.10 §XLI, where he makes an exact quotation of the same verse in Greek.

ἁρπαγμὸν as "plunder" or "spoil," and in such a way one has it by force and injury. Nevertheless, I think a distinction must be made between personal plunder, which is never acquired without injustice, such as occurred in the case of Achan (Josh. 7:21), and public plunder gained in a just war, such as is observed in the case of the Israelites plundering the goods of the Canaanites, which occurred due to God's grant. The former the plunderers are accustomed to hide, as is evident in the aforementioned case of Achan, but the latter the victors were accustomed to display in triumphal procession, as is clear in the case of the Romans in their triumphs. That the latter is understood here seems evident from the scope of the clause, for in it is intended the abnegation of the glory to be gained from spoils, through a just victory. Ἡγεῖσθαι is to "consider as" plunder, as if spoils justly gained, and to boast in them, so the sense emerges that Christ, in his majesty which he had in the form of God, did not desire to boast as those who triumph in their spoils, but rather to abnegate the honor of equality with God, which truly belonged to him, by not displaying it or taking pride in it.

b. The object abnegated: τὸ εἶναι ἶσα θεῷ, "to be equal with God." There are those who think that an ellipsis of ἑαυτὸν, "himself," or τὰ ἑαυτοῦ, "the things of himself," should be supplied so that the sense would be that he himself and his own things, which he had from the form of God, are equal with God, that is, so that in the plural word ἶσα they would not be bound to admit an enallage of the plural number for the singular, which others are bound to assert, such that ἶσα is in the place of ἴσον, or adverbially, in the place of ἴσως, "equally." The prior is more satisfying to me, as it is more agreeable to the ordinary construction. However, the ἰσότης here does not mean ὁμοιότης, likeness (as the Socinians would desire, with the Arians and Photinians, so that instead of ὁμοούσιος, of the same substance, they would have ὁμοιούσιος, of similar substance); rather, it means equality, namely that of essence and essential majesty (cf. 2 Cor. 8:9, 14; Col. 4:1). The word θεῷ could be taken here either essentially, so that it would mean that he is equal to the whole Trinity with respect to the divine essence and all the divine perfections; or it could be taken personally, that he is equal to his Father, which seems more suitable to the analogy of the context, in which sense it occurs in verse 9.

2. An emptying, or a positive act of humbling himself, in verse 7: ἀλλ᾽ ἑαυτὸν ἐκένωσε, "but he emptied himself," namely, with respect to all his glory and equality with the Father, not of course with respect to the κτῆσις or possession of it, but with respect to its χρῆσις, its use; not with respect to his right to it, but with respect to the ordinary manifestation of it: ordinary, I say, because he also did manifest it extraordinarily, as opportunity arose, in his miracles. The ἀλλὰ here without any doubt means the adversative "but," in the most fitting sense: "Though he was God in essence and majesty, and equal to him, he was not proud of these things, as of spoils in a triumph, but emptied himself." Ἐκένωσε, he emptied, הריק, he evacuated, as if he reduced himself from everything to nothing, he deprived himself of equality with God; not simply and absolutely, as if he ceased to be God and equal to God, but with regard to status, comparatively, by hiding his divine glory as if he did not have it; not by setting it aside, properly speaking, or utterly abnegating it, for God cannot deny himself (2 Tim. 2:13): thus it does not say οὐδένωσε, he annihilated himself. Ἑαυτόν, "himself," means that he was emptied not by another, by his Father, not unwillingly on account of his own sins, but he emptied himself of his own accord. This emptying is made known by degrees to be threefold:

a. In origin, which emptying is in the assumption of the human nature: μορφὴν δούλου λαβών, ἐν ὁμοιώματι ἀνθρώπων γενόμενος, "taking on the form of a servant, being made in the likeness of men." There is here:

i. The thing assumed: μορφὴ δούλου, "the form of a servant." Μορφὴ here: (1) to many, means the *likeness* of a servant, just as to them in the previous phrase it denoted "the likeness of God," so that he was not made a true servant, but similar to a servant. Thus Erasmus, and others who plot against the hypostatic union of the two natures. However: (a) this is contrary to the goal of the apostle, for how is he said to empty and evacuate himself, who only assumed the likeness and not the true form of a servant? Who likewise (b) would believe that μορφὴ is said here only of that which he seems to be, but in fact is not? Others (2) prefer it to be understood as a servile, humble, and abject condition, just as μορφὴ θεοῦ is understood as a divine state, a view which we already refuted in what preceded. Nor also, as we have said, is it valid to claim for this opinion that when he ascended into heaven he undoubtedly set aside the form of a servant, because he did not set aside the form of a servant itself, but only the humility of that form. Most accurately, therefore (3) do they think who judge that by "the form of a servant" here is understood his human nature itself, but clothed in its servile qualities, just as by "the form of God" they understand the divine nature itself, together with its properties, the divine majesty and glory. Moreover, Christ is the servant or slave of God (Isa. 53:11), not only from the fact that in the eternal covenant of grace he took upon himself the entire guilt and cause of elect sinners, from which servitude he nevertheless already discharged himself, now that payment has been fully made, but also from the human nature, according to which all men are slaves of God.

ii. The assumption: λαβών, "assuming." This means that Christ took this form to himself, or he assumed it for himself into the unity of his person, through the personal union, which is what ἐπιλαμβάνεται, "he took on," means (Heb. 2:16), and accordingly, that the nature assumed was not a part of the person assuming.

iii. The mode of assuming, ἐν ὁμοιώματι ἀνθρώπων γενόμενος, "made in the likeness of men." From which the Marcionites and others once wrongly inferred that Christ was not made a true man, but only bore the appearance and phantasm of a man, and accordingly that he also did not truly die, rise again, and so forth. But they did not adequately observe that one man is similar to another man in nature and appearance, as an egg is said to be similar to another egg, and likeness does not always exclude identity (Rom. 8:3; Heb. 4:15), in which sense it is said that Christ is similar to his brothers (Heb. 2:17), and that Adam begat his son Seth after his own image or likeness (Gen. 5:3), who from the hypothesis of the Phantasiasts would not have been a true man. Therefore, Christ was in the likeness of men, either of those who were common and abject, who are often simply called "men" (Judg. 16:7, 11; Ps. 82:7), or of other men of all sorts, not one of whom was not a mere man, and a sinner. Nor should it be missed that he is said to be γενόμενος, "made," by which the hypostatic union of the divine person with the human nature is signified, without which uniting, it could not be said that he was made man, but only that he was joined to man.

b. In life: καὶ σχήματι εὑρεθεὶς ὡς ἄνθρωπος, "and being found in appearance as a man." That is, in appearance, in carriage, and in the entire external manner of living and conducting himself, he was discovered to be a man. Σχῆμα, from σχέω, just as *habitus* from *habeo*, denotes habit, carriage, appearance, and every external thing which befalls the senses, by which something is recognized: by this Christ everywhere demonstrated the reality of his human nature (Luke 24:39; John 20:27). It is not the same as μορφή, "form," or ὁμοίωμα, "likeness," not an empty shape and appearance of a body, as if Christ were not a true man, but such an appearance that demonstrates the truth of the matter, just as τύραννον σχῆμα ἔχειν, to have a tyrannical appearance, in Sophocles means to show or demonstrate oneself to be a tyrant. Accordingly, he is said to be εὑρεθεὶς: "found" or "proven," by the most certain arguments, ὡς ἄνθρωπος, "as a man," namely a true, common man, such that ὡς here is a mark of one affirming, or of truth, not of mere likeness (and thus is used here as in John 1:14), as if it were saying, "bearing before him through his whole life and conduct the habit of a man, namely, all that which he truly was, that is, a man."

c. In death: "He humbled himself, having become obedient to the point of death, even the death of the cross." Here is:

   i. The humiliation: ἐταπείνωσεν ἑαυτόν, "He humbled himself." Who? Christ, the Son of God. Whom did he humble? Himself. He was not humbled by another whether he wanted it or not, but he humbled himself of his own accord, and that indeed as the God-man: with respect to the divine nature, by hiding, and as it were by withdrawing, the majesty of his equality with his Father; with respect to the human nature, by undertaking an estate and lot that was lowly, abject, and as if that of an evildoer, and also in this estate, by bearing himself most humbly (v. 5).

   ii. The argument or matter of the humiliation: "having become obedient to the point of death." "Obedient," ὑπήκοος, from ὑπακούω, "I submissively hear," namely, as regards the will of a superior, I first perceive it, then I promptly follow it. Christ was obedient, first to God his Father, then also to men, to his parents, to the Jewish and Roman magistrate. "To the point of death": μεχρί, "to the point of," here should be taken not exclusively but inclusively, so that it means that he was obedient not only to the point of death, but also in death, indeed that his obedience was so great that it extended even to death, a death in fact of every kind: natural, spiritual, and eternal.

iii. The degree of the humiliation to death: θανάτου δὲ σταυροῦ, "even the death of the cross." Not an ordinary and natural death, nor even a violent death of some kind—of burning, of stoning, and so forth—but precisely of the cross. Σταυρός, *stauros*, "cross," named after the letter T, *tau*, the shape of which the cross bears, means a fixed stake, namely that upon which extraordinary evildoers were hung. For Christians it denotes that wood on which Christ died (Matt. 27:32, 40), and by metonymy not rarely means Christ's entire passion, of which the cross had the chief part (Heb. 12:2; Eph. 2:16). Here is it that most disgraceful kind of death Christ died, which the Latins call the wicked cross,[5] the wretched tree,[6] the notorious stake,[7] the damned stake, which, in the thought of Appian (*The Civil Wars*, bk. 1), was prescribed for slaves,[8] and to the Hebrews in addition was accursed (Deut. 21:23), which Christ had to undergo, so that he might free his people from the curse (Gal. 3:13).[9]

---

5. *malam crucem*, e.g. Plautus, *Curculio*, act 5, scene 2, line 693.

6. *infelicem arborem*, e.g. Livy, 1.26, *History of Rome* in *LCL* 114:92–93, B. O. Foster's translation, "a barren tree." Compare, however, the 1914 Roberts translation of *infelici arbori reste suspendito*, "hang by a rope on the fatal tree," and thus the 1857 Spillan translation "hang him by a rope from the gallows." Cf. "the deadly wood of the cross" in Minucius Felix, *Octavius* in *ANF* 4:177; *crucis ligna feralia* in idem, *Octavius* in *PL* 3:231–366.

7. *infamem stipitem*, e.g. *Noxius infami districtus stipite membra*, from *Elegia de spe*, attributed to Seneca the Younger: cf. John Granger Cook, *Crucifixion in the Mediterranean World*, 2nd ed. (Tübingen: Mohr Siebeck, 2019), 149–50.

8. *sententia Appiani Civil. lib. 2*; instead, for an account of crucifixion of Spartacus and his slave army in Appian, *The Civil Wars*, 1.4.120, see *LCL* 5:238–39, and also for Antony's crucifixion of slaves and execution of free citizens by casting them headlong off of the Tarpeian rock, see 3.1.3, Appian, *The Civil Wars* in *LCL* 543:6–7.

9. For an important early modern work on the history of crucifixion with many of the same points, see Justus Lipsius (1567–1606), *De Cruce libri tres ad sacram profanamque historiam utiles, una cum notis* (Antwerp: Plantin, 1597).

The Dogmatic Part

The Mediator humbled himself, even to the cursed cross.

III. Therefore from what has been said, it is evident that the Son of God, Jesus Christ, brought himself down by various degrees even to the extreme curse of the cross. For it is said that existing in the form of God, that is, in the essence and majesty of God, he did not consider it spoil that he was equal with God; he emptied himself, assumed the form of a slave, made himself like common people, and humbled himself in his birth, life, and death.

It is proved: 1. By the Scriptures

The apostle sets forth things similar in substance elsewhere (Heb. 2:7, 9–10, 17–18; 2 Cor. 8:9), as does the Savior himself (Matt. 17:22; Mark 9:31; 10:33–34; Luke 9:44; 24:26), things which are also read to have been previously foretold (Isa. 53; Ps. 22; 8:5–6).

2. By reasons

The basis of this extreme humiliation is in Christ's absolute mediatorial suretyship,[10] for: (1) since our first parents, by transgression of the divine commandment and violation of the legal covenant, and all of us in them, had elevated ourselves above God and his law, and therefore had deserved extreme humility, even to death and the eternal curse (Rom. 5:12ff.; Gal. 3:10; Deut. 27:26), it was therefore necessary that an absolute surety undergo extreme humiliation for those to be redeemed (Isa. 53:2–7; 2 Cor. 5:21; Gal. 3:13; 4:4–5). Also (2) since these ones to be redeemed were through him to be raised to the utmost degree of height and glory (Eph. 2:4–6), he thus had to be humiliated to the extreme (2 Cor. 8:9; Gal. 3:13–14). (3) Since in this humiliation of his Son, there was to be manifested, on the one hand, God's most rigid avenging justice toward the absolute surety (2 Cor. 5:21; Rom. 3:25), and on the other hand, his inexhaustible mercy toward the sinner to be redeemed (Eph. 2:4, 7–8), it was entirely fitting that the absolute surety be cast down to extreme humility and misery, through which he would become a servant (Phil. 2:7; Isa. 53:10–11), and what is worse, a worm (Ps. 22:7), and indeed what is the worst, a curse (Gal. 3:13) and sin (2 Cor. 5:21).

---

10. *expromissio.* Cf. 1.5.1 §XXXIV. See also W. J. van Asselt, *"Expromissio* or *Fideiussio?* A Seventeenth-Century Theological Debate between Voetians and Cocceians about the Nature of Christ's Suretyship in Salvation History"* in *Mid-America Journal of Theology,* 14 (2003): 45.

What the state of humiliation is

IV. Moreover, the state of humiliation is that state in which the Mediator as the God-man, first with respect to the divine nature, deprived himself of the use and manifestation of the glory that otherwise belonged to him, then with respect to his human nature, was subject with extreme humility to the divine law, to endure and to accomplish all things that were required for the restoration of the sinner (Phil. 2:7–8; Gal. 4:4–5). Here we assert this humiliation for the whole God-man, because it belongs to him as the Mediator, which office he performs as the God-man, as we have expressly demonstrated elsewhere, in chapter 2 of this book.[11]

With respect to the divine nature

And this we assert indeed with respect to both natures: first with respect to the divine nature, by way of concealment, by which he hid himself in the human nature as in a tabernacle (ἐσκήνωσε, "he tabernacled," John 1:14), and deprived himself of the manifestation of his glory which he had with the Father from eternity (John 17:5), such that there was observed in him no form, no comeliness by which he could be either honorable or acceptable (Isa. 53:2), except when extraordinarily, in the performance of miracles and in other ways, he at times manifested himself (1 Tim. 3:16; 1 John 1:1–2; Luke 2:9, 11–12; Matt. 17:2–5; John 14:8–11).

With respect to the human nature

We assert this also with respect to the human nature, by way of the intrinsic depreciation and misery which he received (on which see Isa. 53:2ff.), by which he was more abject than the vilest slave (Phil. 2:7), "a worm, and no man, a reproach of men, and despised of the people" (Ps. 22:7), the goal of which humiliation was that he might be made subject to the law (Gal. 4:4), in order to offer its δικαίωμα, righteous requirement, for those to be redeemed (Rom. 8:3–4), first by acting, then by suffering, as we will expressly show, Lord willing, in its own place.[12]

This humiliation is apparent: 1. In his conception.

V. This humiliation is apparent, first, in his conception, insofar as: (1) in assuming the human nature into the unity of the same person with him, the eternal Son of God, the Creator of all things, was as it were made in time, and of a

---

11. 1.5.2 §§XVI, XXI–XXII
12. 1.5.18 §XIV

woman, whose Creator he himself was (Gal. 4:4 with 1 Tim. 3:16), and in that way he was as it were hidden in the flesh (John 1:14). (2) He assumed this human nature from the substance of a virgin, and indeed one descended from the royal blood of David, but yet one of an especially poor, humble, and abject condition (Luke 1:48; Matt. 13:55; Mark 6:3).

2. In his birth

VI. Second, in his birth, inasmuch as: (1) he who was from eternity to eternity the living God, blessed forever, nonetheless in the fullness of time willed to be born of a woman (Ps. 90:2 with Matt. 1:25), and he who gives to all life, and breath, and all things (Acts 17:25), received life and breath from a poor young woman. (2) His birth itself was troubled with the most despicable circumstances, since he was born, not at the house of his mother, but among foreigners (Luke 2:4–6), not in a palace but an inn, not in one of its comfortable bedchambers, but in a stable among the cattle, because there was no room for him in the inn (Luke 2:6–7); because the splendor of his divine glory and majesty was wrapped in swaddling clothes and laid in a manger (Luke 2:6–7).

3. In his life

VII. Third, in his life, in which: (1) he who was the highest lawgiver (Isa. 33:22) was made subject to the law (Gal. 4:4; Matt. 5:17; Gal. 3:19). (2) He who reserves Satan bound in chains of darkness for the judgment of the great day (Jude 6) was exposed to the most violent and subtle temptations of Satan (Matt. 4:1–12; Luke 4:1–14). (3) He who is the Lord of glory (1 Cor. 2:8), God blessed forever (Rom. 9:5), experienced from all kinds of men, even the most vile, so many hatreds, disgraces, persecutions—indeed, what did he not experience? (John 15:18; Matt. 13:55; Ps. 22:6; Heb. 12:2–3; Mark 3:21; Matt. 12:10, 24; 26:14–16). (4) He who had done no evil, as the judge himself (though otherwise quite unjust to him) pronounced, and that indeed before the tribunal, in the face of his adversaries (Matt. 27:23), nonetheless endured every evil (Heb. 4:15), that is, not only those infirmities to which we all in general are liable from the condition of human nature—hunger, thirst, sorrows, troubles, and so forth—but also all other evils more specific to that most abject position to which he exposed himself for us (Isa. 53:2ff.), to the point that his entire life was nothing but a sewer of miseries and sufferings.

4. In his death

VIII. Fourth, in his death, where: (1) he was treacherously betrayed by his very own disciple (Matt. 26:14–16; 27:4). (2) He was shamefully deserted by all his disciples (Matt. 26:56). (3) He was denied by his most beloved disciple, and that in such an egregious way (Matt. 26:69ff.). (4) He was harassed most undeservedly by false testimonies, mockeries, beatings, blows, and so forth (Matt. 26:59, 67). (5) Without any cause, he was most unjustly condemned to the ultimate punishment, as much by the Jewish court as by the Gentile court of Pilate (Matt. 27:11–27). (6) He was barbarously treated by the soldiers (Matt. 27:27–35). (7) He was crucified in the most shameful way, in the middle of two thieves, outside of the city, at Golgotha, a notorious place (John 19:17–18; Matt. 27:38). (8) While hanging on the cross, he was tormented with the most awful tortures while drawing breath, and was also sarcastically mocked by every kind of onlooker (Matt. 27:39–44). (9) He allowed precisely this cursed kind of death, so that he would be made a curse for cursed sinners (Gal. 3:10, 13). And so by this death, the light of the world was extinguished, the health of the world was wounded, the life was killed, and the Savior of the world, who knew no sin, was made to be sin for sinners (2 Cor. 5:21).

5. *In his burial*

IX. Fifth, in his burial, in which: (1) he who possesses the key of hell and death (Rev. 1:18; 1 Cor. 15:55–57), who ought not see corruption, notwithstanding was cast into the pit of corruption (Isa. 38:17); (2) he who was the King of kings and Lord of lords was buried without any stately funeral rites; nor (3) in a tomb suitable for his ancestors, but in a stranger's tomb, as one who had nowhere to lay his head (Luke 9:58); nor (4) by his own relatives, but by strangers, though secretly disciples, Joseph of Arimathea and Nicodemus (John 19:39–40).

6. *In his descent into hell*

X. Sixth, in his descent into hell, inasmuch as through it not only (1) was he for three days a captive as it were of death, no differently than if he had himself committed sin (Act. 2:24–27, 31; Ps. 16:10; Rom. 6:9), and as it were under the triumph of Satan, sin, the world, and the power of darkness (Heb. 2:14; Rom. 6:23, 9; Matt. 27:62ff.). But also (2) in his soul he sustained the hellish punishments owed to our sins, as much by way of loss (Matt. 27:46 from Ps. 22:1) as by way of sense (Matt. 26:38; John 12:27). We adduce all these things for one purpose, at least here, that we may perceive the extreme humiliation of the Mediator, intending in the subsequent chapters to explain each of them in their breadth.

The Elenctic Part

It is asked: 1. Was the Mediator humiliated only with respect to the human nature?
The difference of opinions

XI. The controversies of this chapter concern the particular components of this humiliation: his conception, birth, and so forth, which will be spoken of specifically, Lord willing, in their own topics. Regarding this topic, there are only three questions to be determined. First is whether the Mediator was humiliated only with respect to the human nature. The Socinians, because they do not accept the divine nature, the papists, because they declare that he is the Mediator only according to the human nature, and the Lutherans, because they want the emptying to be nothing other than the evacuation of the divine majesty that was communicated to the human nature, all uphold the affirmative. The Reformed on the contrary state that the Mediator was humiliated with respect to both natures: with respect to the divine nature, by reason of the hiding of the glory, that is, with respect only to the use of it, just as the sun is said to be darkened when because of clouds or something else opaque interposed, it does not disperse its rays to us; but with respect to the human nature, due to its intrinsic lowering.

The negative is proved

And so they answer the question in the negative, because: (1) the κένωσις, emptying, either of the μορφὴ θεοῦ, form of God, or the ἰσότης θεοῦ, equality with God, when the μορφὴ δούλου, form of a servant, was assumed, cannot but mean the hiding of glory, which cannot but concern the divine nature. (2) The Savior himself clearly enough signifies the hidden glory and majesty of the divine nature, when he seeks from the Father that he might be glorified with it (John 17:5). (3) The apostle testifies in 2 Corinthians 8:9 that when he was rich (undoubtedly according to the divine nature) he became poor, certainly not by privation of the riches of the divine nature (Col. 2:9), so accordingly, by hiding, which without any doubt concerns the divine nature. (4) As all confess, the divine nature of the Mediator was throughout the period of humiliation hidden under a veil, and as it were under the tabernacle of the flesh, except when it was at times made evident extraordinarily, and only to his own (John 1:14–15). (5) If the divine nature and majesty had not been hidden by the flesh that was assumed, then certainly he would have been evident and manifest to all as the Lord of glory; yet, however, he was not evident to all (Isa. 53:2–3; 1 Cor. 2:8; Phil. 2:7–8).

The objections to the negative are refuted

To argue the contrary, the papists generally allege two things, namely: (1) that from our hypothesis the divine nature would have been changed, and (2) it also would be imperfect. The falsity of both inferences is more than adequately perceived from what has been said, for from the hidden glory of the divine nature, some intrinsic mutation or imperfection of it is not inferred. The opinion of the Socinians topples by the reality of the divine nature, asserted elsewhere.[13] Likewise the opinion of the Lutherans topples by what has been denied in chapter 4, that the properties of the divine nature were communicated in the hypostatic union to the human nature.[14]

2. Does "the form of God" mean the nature or the majesty of God, or both?

The difference of opinions

XII. So then also second, it is asked whether by μορφὴ in Philippians 2:6 a substantial form or an accidental form should be understood, or whether "the form of God" denotes the essence of God, or the majesty of God, or both, and if the final option is true, whether it is primarily the glory and majesty of God, and secondarily his very essence. It is agreed among all—as much the ancient as the more recent, as much the Reformed as the Lutherans (for we will not tarry here with the anti-Trinitarians)—that "form" is double, substantial and accidental, and thus by "the form of God" can be understood the nature itself, or that by which he is God, such that to be in the form of God is to be God by nature; and also that the majesty and glory of God are the same thing as his nature. The only difference is whether in the text by "the form of God" ought to be understood the nature or the majesty of God. Some from the ancients and from the Reformed, such as Johann Piscator, state that not the nature but the glory is understood by the apostle.[15] With these the Lutherans agree, although hesitantly: "On this passage," says Johann Gerhard (*Exegesis*, loc. 4, §295), "We deny" (that is, regarding μορφὴ θεοῦ) "that primarily and properly[16] by this phrase is signified the very divine essence, considered in itself and absolutely according to its quiddity,[17] but

---

13. 1.2.26 §§IX, XVIII

14. 1.5.4 §§XXIII–XXV

15. Johann Piscator, *Analysis logica sex Epistolarum Pauli, videlicet ad Galatas, Ephesios, Philippenses, Colossenses, utriusque ad Thessalonicenses* (Herborn: Christopher Corvinus, 1602), 171–73.

16. πρώτως καὶ κυρίως

17. τὸ εἶναι: Gerhard utilizes a shortened form of the phrase τὸ τί ἦν εἶναι, most likely referencing Aristotle, *Metaphysics*, 1029b; literally "the what it was to be," which is frequently translated as *essentia* by scholastic theologians. A similar but shorter phrase is τὸ τί ἐστι (see Aristotle, *Metaphysics*, 1030a), literally "the what it is", which was distinguished from *essentia* or *quidditas* as *haecceitas*, as interpreted by Duns Scotus, *Ordinatio* II, d3 p1 q2 n48. The fine distinction between

we say that by it is understood the divine state or divine condition, namely, the divine glory and majesty."[18] Therefore he admits that secondarily and less principally, the nature and essence of God is also understood. On the contrary, the Reformed in common, together with most of the fathers, understand by μορφὴ θεοῦ, first and principally, the nature of God; second and less principally, the majesty of God.

The orthodox arguments
For: (1) undoubtedly by μορφὴ θεοῦ, the form of God, is first and primarily and understood that by which he was ἴσος θεῷ, equal with God; but he was equal with God by the divine nature. (2) By the form of God is primarily understood that which, in the antithesis of the following corresponding clause, is understood by μορφὴ δούλου, the form of a servant; but by that is primarily understood the nature of a servile human being. (3) Then also it will bind us more effectively to the goal of the apostle if he should argue in this way: "Christ, though he was God, and accordingly in equal glory with the Father, yet so lowered himself that he assumed the nature of a servant, that is, of man, and became a servant to God the Father, even to the most shameful death of the cross." I will not add (4) the nearly unanimous consent of antiquity, and that (5) there is nothing to the contrary that would oppose it.

Objections
But if they should allege: (1) that our meaning of the phrase is excessively philosophical; I will reply that it was common among the Greek Philippians, from the received philosophy of Aristotle. (2) That in Mark 16:12 it has another meaning; I will certainly admit that, but will say that it does not necessarily have the same meaning in this passage. (3) That the three terms in the text—μορφή, ὁμοίωμα, and σχῆμα—are synonyms; it will be incumbent upon them to prove this, because we have distinguished them fittingly enough in the exegetical part. (4) That by "the form of a servant" in the antithesis is understood not the very nature of man, but only a servile condition, because he set aside the form of a servant in his exaltation; I will deny that in his exaltation he set aside the form of a servant, because he constantly remains the servant of God; rather, he only set aside the humility of the form. (5) That a form and being in a form are distinct,

---

quiddity and haecceity can be broken down into the qualities that are universal in nature to a genus and those that are particular either to the species or to the individual.

18. Gerhard, *Exegesis*, 527; cf. loc. 4, ch. 6, "De statu exinanitionis"; idem, *Loci theologici*, 1:183–84.

since the same thing cannot be said to be in itself, and therefore because the Son of God is the form of God itself according to the divine nature, he cannot be said according to the same nature to be in the form of God; I will acknowledge that the form is not in the form, the deity not in the deity, the nature not in the nature, but I will deny that the Son of God, as he is the second person, *is* the very form, deity, or nature of God; rather, he *has* the same form, deity, and divine nature with his Father, and in that sense is said to be in the form of God. (6) That if to be in the form of God is nothing other than to be God by nature, then the Father and the Holy Spirit can also be said to be in the form of God; I will say that nothing in this is absurd, just as there is not if they should be said, from our adversaries' opinion, to be in the majesty and glory of God. (7) That by the form of God is understood such glory which the Philippians could see, that they might imitate his emptying, such a glory about which John 1:14 speaks; I will reply that that nature is understood by which the person was equal to God, and that glory of which they were persuaded from the instruction of Paul, not from the seeing of the eye, because it was hidden in the incarnation by his extreme humiliation, which they ought to imitate. Compare the exegetical and the dogmatic part.

3. Does the humiliation consist in this, that Christ set aside the divine majesty and glory communicated to the human nature?

XIII. Third, it is asked whether the humiliation of the Mediator consists in this, that he set aside the majesty and glory communicated to the human nature in the personal union, certainly not with respect to its possession and substance, but with respect to its use and authority.[19] The Lutherans, in favor of masticating the omnipresent flesh of Christ in the Lord's Supper, and of their opinion that there were communicated to the human nature divine properties, among which is the divine majesty and glory, answer in the affirmative. On the contrary, the Reformed answer in the negative, because: (1) that Christ was humiliated not only according to the human nature, but also according to the divine nature, we have already taught in §XI. (2) The basis of the Lutheran opinion, namely that the divine proper qualities were communicated to the human nature, we have expressly demolished in chapter 4, §XXIV. Add to this that (3) the Lutherans, who are making an affirmation, and upon whom accordingly, from the law, proof is incumbent, have neither proved, nor attempted to prove, that his humiliation consists in this.

---

19. *non quidem quoad* κτῆσιν *et* οὐσίαν, *sed quoad* χρῆσιν *et* ἐξουσίαν

The Practical Part

The practice of the humiliation of Christ: 1. Commends to us the grace of the Mediator.

XIV. Just as the elenctics of the humiliation of Christ concern its particular components—his conception, birth, and so forth—which are to be specifically taught in their own places, so also does the practice. Nevertheless, a more general contemplation of this humiliation commends to us, first, the indescribable grace of the Mediator, according to the apostle: "You know the grace of our Lord Jesus Christ, that for your sakes he became poor, that you through his poverty might become rich" (2 Cor. 8:9).

The arguments for commendation

We will also perceive that grace more evidently if we should carefully consider: (1) the person, either as humbled or as humbling, which was not just any man, whether lowly or illustrious, nor also an angel, even of the highest rank, but the very Son of God, existing in the form of God, equal to his Father as much with respect to his nature as to his glory, the brightness of his glory, and the exact imprint of his person (Heb. 1:3), the image of the invisible God (Col. 1:13), he who was rich (2 Cor. 8:9), in whom all treasures are hidden (Col. 2:3). If (2) we should consider his humiliation itself, in which he did not consider it plunder to be equal to God, he did not take pride, like triumphing victors, in his spoils, but ἐκένωσε, he emptied himself thoroughly of all his native majesty and glory, and in this way humbled himself, even to the most shameful death of the cross. If (3) we should consider the degrees of his humiliation in each of its components: with respect to his conception, birth, and so forth; with respect to the beginning, middle, and end of his life, and so forth. If (4) we should add the impelling causes of the humiliation, first inwardly, pure unadulterated grace (2 Cor. 8:9), then outwardly, the extreme misery of man, contracted by haughtiness toward God (cf. Isa. 14:11–20; Matt. 11:23). If (5) we should compare the goal of the humiliation, that he might exalt the wretched and downcast (2 Cor. 8:9).

The use of the commendation

If we should devoutly gather all these things together, it will certainly supply to us reason that: (1) with our mind we should deeply marvel at the riches of grace (Eph. 1:7), indeed the overflowing riches of his grace in kindness upon us (Eph. 2:7). (2) With all our voice we should declare them, by exclaiming, "Who is like the Lord our God, who dwells on high, who humbles himself to look down on heaven and earth, who raises up the poor from the dust, who lifts the needy from the dunghill, that he may make him sit with the princes of the people?" (Ps. 113:5–8). (3) With all gratitude we should most readily repay them (Ps. 116:12).

2. It supplies comfort. In what cases
XV. Second, the humiliation of the Mediator supplies the sweetest comfort to those: (1) who are in the form of a servant, that is, extremely humiliated, or cast down and despised in the world (1 Cor. 4:13; Rom. 8:36; cf. Isa. 53:2–3); to those (2) who with Christ have been humiliated to the most shameful death of the cross, that is, those whom the enemies of Christ pursue to a most shameful death (1 Cor. 4:9; Ps. 45:23); to those (3) who are like little worms in the world (Isa. 41:14; cf. Ps. 22:6); to those (4) who are poor in the world, and as it were servants and slaves, people of the lowest condition (2 Cor. 8:2, 9; Rom. 15:16; Ps. 22:25).

By what consoling arguments
In these and other cases of humiliation, how greatly it helps them to devoutly consider that: (1) our Mediator also, although existing in the form of God and equal to God, was emptied of all glory and honor. And that (2) for their sake (2 Cor. 8:9), that he might exalt them. And thus (3) in this their humiliation they are conformed to the image of the Son of God (Rom. 8:29), in which consists their highest perfection (Luke 6:40); they carry the cross of Christ, and thus prove themselves to be genuine disciples of Christ (Luke 9:23). Also, (4) it is unbecoming for a disciple to be in a better condition than his master (Matt. 10:24). Finally, (5) if with their master they are humbled, they will also with him be exalted (Rom. 8:17 with Phil 2:10), because for this purpose he himself was humbled and became poor, that he might lift them up, or make them rich (2 Cor. 8:9). By these arguments they can rejoice in their poor King (Zech. 9:9), and even glory in their humility (James 1:9–10; Rom. 5:3).

By what laws
Provided: (1) that according to the example of Christ, who not only was humbled by someone else, by his Father (Isa. 53:3–4, 6), but also emptied and humbled himself, we not only allow ourselves to be humbled by others, God or men, but also of our own accord humble ourselves (1 Peter 5:6), of our own accord take up our cross (Luke 9:23), that in this also we may follow Christ, and be made like him. Provided (2) that with Christ, in our humiliation we obey God, by not murmuring against him, that we obey to the point of death, even to the death of the cross, that is, to all the most shameful and the worst things (1 Cor. 4:9, 13).

Provided (3) that with Christ, we do not consider this our humiliation, or anything good and excellent that may be present in us, as plunder, that is, that we are not lifted up by it, or proud of it (1 Cor. 4:6–7; 15:10; Ps. 115:1).

3. It rebukes. What sinners

XVI. Third, it rebukes the pride and perversity of those who: (1) though they are in fact in nothing but the form of a servant, strive to be in the form of a lord, indeed in the form of God (Gen. 3:5; Isa. 14:12–14), insofar as, instead of how Christ, existing in the form of God, emptied himself, humbled himself, these, puffed up and inflated in mind (2 Cor. 12:20; 2 Tim. 3:4), lift themselves up (a) above God (Ex. 5:2; Isa. 14:12–14; Acts 12:22–23; 2 Thess. 2:4), and spurn God (Job 21:14–15; Jer. 44:16–17); (b) above themselves, insofar as, being high-minded (Rom. 11:20–21), they make themselves greater than in fact they are, by arrogating to themselves what they do not have (Rev. 3:17; Gal. 6:3), or by elevating above measure what they do have (2 Kings 10:16); (c) above others (1 Cor. 4:6; Luke 18:11). Those who (2) consider that which they possess, or arrogate to themselves, of what is divine or good, for example, authority and power, strength, wealth, and so forth, to be as it were spoil, that is, by external pride, as victors do their spoils, they make them a display. And that: (a) with puffed-up mouth and speech (Ex. 5:2; 2 Chron. 32:11–20; Ps. 73:6, 8–9, 11; Jude 8; Ps. 12:3; 17:10); (b) with a haughty carriage ("The Pharisee stood," Luke 18:11; "I sit as queen," Rev. 18:7; Ps. 101:5; Prov. 21:4); (c) with haughty appearance and dress (Isa. 3:19–20); and (d) with a proud manner of life (Jer. 48:29; Ps. 30:7).

By which rebuking arguments

Now think for me: (1) how unjust, shameful, and perverse it is that the Son of God, existing in the form of God, equal with his Father, should empty himself, assume the form of a servant, humble himself, even to the most shameful death of the cross, and that a son of man, being in the form of a servant, should as it were assume the form of God, and make himself equal to God, fill himself with empty pride, and childishly and foolishly display his goods and gifts. (2) How just it is that such a one should be emptied of all the form which he has, be humbled all the way to the most abject form of a servant, be rendered similar to the most abject persons, be subject to death, even the most shameful death of the cross. (3) How abominable this pride is in the sight of God (1 Peter 5:5; Prov. 6:16–17; 16:5; Luke 16:15; 18:11, 14), so that he sees it with roaring (Job 40:6–7), he hears it with indignation (Job 42:2–3), he breaks it with anger (Lev. 26:19; Isa. 2:12), he destroys it with his furor (Ezek. 30:6). (4) How horrendous the judgments are by which he has punished pride, in Babel (Isa. 14:4–27), Nebuchadnezzar (Dan. 4:29–34), Herod (Acts 12:21–23), and so forth.

4. It encourages us to humility. The duties of humility

XVII. Fourth, it encourages us to strive to have the same mind which was in Christ. This is the goal of the entire argument proposed here. It is the mind, namely: (1) of modesty, by which with Christ ("He did not consider it plunder") neither should we arrogate to ourselves that excellence which does not belong to us (Rev. 2:9; 1 Cor. 4:6), nor boast about that which does truly belong to us (1 Cor. 4:7), nor from our prerogatives pursue vain glory and elevate beyond measure that which is ours (Gal. 5:26), nor seek after honors and dignities (Ps. 131:1). (2) Of emptying, by which with Christ ("He emptied himself") we should empty ourselves, ἐξουδενῶμεν, consider ourselves as nothing, especially compared to God (1 Cor. 1:28; Gen. 18:27), just as Herod (Luke 23:11) and the nobles of the Jews did to our Savior, emptying him, even as he emptied himself, from which he is called the stone ἐξουθενηθεὶς ὑπ' οἰκοδομοῦντων, "the builders have rejected" (Acts 4:11 from Ps. 118:22). (3) Of humility, by which with the Savior ("He humbled himself") we should be lowly in heart (Matt. 11:29), deny ourselves (Luke 9:23) and our own will, and as it were cast ourselves at the feet of God (Matt. 26:39). (4) Of obedience, by which with Christ ("obedient to") we should submissively hear God, and most humbly compose ourselves to do his will (John 5:30; 1 Sam. 3:10; cf. Jer. 42:5–6), to death, indeed even the most shameful death (Acts 20:23–24). (5) Of the appearance and form of a δοῦλος, a bondservant, by which even in externals, with the Savior, in all our conduct we should bear ourselves not as lords but as servants, with respect to: (a) voice and speech, without any grandiloquence (Jude 8), garrulousness, or clamoring (Isa. 29:4; Matt. 12:19), we should speak abjectly about ourselves (Ps. 22:6; 1 Sam. 24:14), we should confess our vileness and unworthiness before God (Dan. 9:5–6). (b) Gestures, in which also the Savior was found "in appearance as a man," for example, kneeling (Matt. 26:39; Phil. 2:10), bowing (Gen. 18:2), lowering the eyes (Ps. 121:1), and so forth. (c) Our external comportment, that it be humble (Matt. 3:4), as in the Old Testament sackcloth signified (1 Kings 21:27; 2 Kings 19:1; Ps. 30:11). (d) The whole manner of life, that it be familiar, mild, and fair (Matt. 11:29; Acts 20:19; Job 31:34). And this is that "mind which was in Christ Jesus," for which, from the commandment of the apostle (Phil. 2:5), we ought to strive with every effort, that it may also be in us.

The arguments persuading to humility

For in this way: (1) we will be made more and more like Christ (Matt. 11:29) in which all our perfection consists (Matt. 10:25). Indeed, (2) we will be united with Christ, for where the mind of Christ is and lives, there Christ himself is and lives as well (Gal. 2:20). Also (3) we will obtain tranquility of soul, Matthew 11:29, "Learn of me, for I am lowly in heart, and you will find tranquility for your souls," because Christian humility composes agitated affections, from which all disturbances of soul result, and also in every state, condition, and lot, it composes a person to the will of God (Ps. 39:9). In addition, (4) from the promise of God, we will obtain grace (1 Peter 5:5; Luke 1:53), that of justification and forgiveness of sins (Luke 18:14), and that of the divine presence and union (Isa. 57:15). Finally, (5) having been humbled with Christ, we will also be exalted with him (Phil. 2:9; James 4:10; Luke 18:14; Prov. 22:4).

The means for obtaining humility

Moreover, the following helps will most effectively procure that mind of humility which was in Christ: (1) to have Christ before our eyes lighting the way, whom the apostle sets forth to his Philippians in the text to this end, which the Savior himself also commends (Matt. 11:28; John 13:12–16). (2) To devoutly compare our vileness with the immeasurable perfection, majesty, and glory of God (Gen. 18:31; Prov. 30:1–2; Job 42:3–4; Isa. 6:1–2; Rom. 9:20–21). (3) To earnestly consider ourselves: "What is man?" (Ps. 8:4), "Who are you?" (Rom. 14:4), "What do you have?" (1 Cor. 4:7). Individually: (a) who and what sort we were by creation, and from what degree of perfection and glory we have fallen (Rom. 3:23; cf. Ezra 3:12); (b) who and what sort we are after sin, children of wrath, dead in sins (Eph. 2:3, 5), most evil (Titus 3:3), most wretched (Rom. 7:24); (c) what sort we will soon be by death and eternal condemnation (Matt. 25:41), unless by pure, unadulterated mercy God averts them. (d) To attentively consider the multitude of our sins, their shamefulness, their punishments (Luke 18:13).

5. It urges us to exalt the humbled Christ. The duties of this exaltation

XVIII. Fifth, the deeper the Mediator humbled himself for us, it urges us to lift him up higher (Phil. 1:20). This occurs: (1) by raising him up above all things in our heart, just as God, for this cause, ὑπερύψωσε, "highly exalted" him (Phil. 2:9); by setting him first before all the most outstanding things (Matt. 10:37; Phil. 3:7–8; Ps. 73:25). (2) By attributing to him a name which is above every name (Phil. 2:9; Eph. 1:21), because there is no other name of the same kind and efficacy under heaven (Acts 4:12); by naming his name with nothing but the highest reverence (2 Tim. 2:19), by confidently laying down our lives for the name of our Lord Jesus Christ (Acts 15:26). (3) By reverently bending the knee, both of our body and our heart, to him (Phil. 2:10), that is, by totally submitting all that we are to him (Eph. 5:24; 1 Peter 3:22), as to our Lord, to whom God gave all authority in heaven and on earth (Matt. 28:18), whom he established as head over all things (Eph. 1:21–22), under whose feet he put all things (Ps. 8:6–8; 1 Cor. 15:27). (4) By confessing with our tongue that Jesus Christ is Lord (Phil. 2:11; Matt. 10:32–33; John 1:20). (5) By asserting for him as fully as possible the form of God, and the equality with God, of which he emptied himself (Matt. 16:16). (6) By restoring to him as liberally as possible the form of God, in which he existed from eternity (John 17:1, 5), in place of the form of a servant which he assumed, by receiving him as Lord (Acts 2:36; Col. 2:6), indeed as Lord of lords (Rev. 17:14; 19:16), as the Lord of glory (1 Cor. 2:8). (7) Since he submitted himself to the Father, and became obedient to him even to the death of the cross, in turn by submitting ourselves to him, and obeying him to the point of death, and even the most shameful death of all (Heb. 5:8–9; Acts 20:24).

Motivating arguments

And this because: (1) God himself, on account of his humiliation, decreed and conferred this exaltation to him (Phil. 2:9, "Wherefore God also has highly exalted him"). (2) The μορφὴ θεοῦ, the form of God, and equality with God belong to him by nature, and from eternity he had them by right (John 17:5). (3) For us, so that he might exalt us (2 Cor. 8:9), he emptied himself of all glory, and lowered himself into this depth of humility and misery: by all right we owe him out of gratitude an exaltation of this kind (Rev. 5:9–10). (4) He in turn will one day exalt us (Luke 22:29), so that we may reign with him (Rom. 8:17), and sit with him on thrones (Rev. 3:21; 4:4; Matt. 19:28).

CHAPTER TEN

The Incarnation of the Mediator

The Holy Spirit will come upon you, and the power of the Most High will overshadow you; therefore also that holy thing which will be born of you will be called the Son of God.

—Luke 1:35

The connection of the preceding things and those that follow

I. Thus far we have pondered the humiliation of the Mediator more generally; now the same humiliation comes for our consideration somewhat more specifically, through these four degrees: (1) his incarnation, (2) life, (3) death, and (4) descent into the tomb and into hell. So first, the incarnation involves these two things, the Mediator's conception and birth (for we already examined the assumption of the human nature made by the divine person and the union of the human nature with the divine person in chapter 4), which are pointed out in the pericope from Luke 1:35.

The Exegetical Part

The text is opened and explained.

II. In the words of this pericope, the angelic foretelling of the incarnation, or of the miraculous conception and birth of Christ, is contained. Thus regarding the Mediator is foretold:

    A. His conception, regarding which are noted:

        1. Its procurer, and his names:

            a. His proper name: "The Holy Spirit" (for which Servetus audaciously substituted ὁ λόγος, the Word),[1] about whom we have

---

1. Michael Servetus (c. 1511–1553), *De Trinitatis erroribus libri septem* ([Hagenau]: [Johann Setzer], 1531), 6, "potentissima Verbi Dei virtus." Against Servetus on Luke 1:35, see Theodore Beza, *Jesu Christi Domini Nostri Novum Testamentum* (Geneva: Eustache Vignon, 1598), 233–34.

expressly spoken in book 2, chapter 26. For which reason the procurement of the conception is specifically attributed to the third person, though it is common to the three persons, will perhaps be explained in the elenctic part.[2] In the meantime, here it must be observed, first against the Socinians, that the Holy Spirit is a person, because personal operations are asserted for him, namely coming upon and overshadowing; then against the Macedonians, the Pneumatomachi, and John Biddle, that he is a divine person from this, that the fecundity of the Virgin, which is designated by these operations, is a divine operation.

b. His appellative name: "the power of the Most High." Through this Christ himself must not be understood here, as if he by interposing his body overshadowed the Virgin, as several of the fathers understood, as Maldonado attests on this passage,[3] but rather, the Holy Spirit, because at that time the Savior did not yet have a body. So then the καί, "and," here is not copulative of different persons, but exegetical or explanatory of the one person. For this reason power and the Holy Spirit are frequently joined together in the Scriptures (as in Acts 1:8; 24:49; Luke 4:14; Acts 10:30; Rom. 1:4; 15:13; 1 Cor. 2:4; Eph. 3:16; 1 Thess. 1:15). However, by power is not understood some accidental potency, as the Socinians want, because accidents do not occur in God, nor is the attribute of omnipotence understood, as we have said elsewhere, book 2, chapter 27, §XVII. Nor is the ὑψίστου, "of the Most High," here diacritical, such that it distinguishes the highest God from a lower God, such as Christ is to the Socinians, but explanatory, such that it means the same thing as "God," he who is the highest in every class of beings, as is evident from the miraculous fecundity of the Virgin, which does not belong to any creature, as a subordinate god (Isa. 7:11, 14).

2. The procurement of the conception, of which a twofold act is denoted:

a. "He will come upon you," ἐπελεύσεται ἐπί σε, he will descend upon you, not in location, because he is omnipresent, but in efficacy: not of common providence, but of extraordinary providence,

---

3. Juan de Maldonado (1535–1583), *Commentarii in quatuor evangelistas*, 5 tomes in 2 vols. (Mainz: Balthasar Lippius, 1611), 2:48–50.

such an efficacy in which God once descended in Genesis 18:21 (cf. Judg. 14:6), such which supplies the part of a father's begetting. Yet I prefer to translate it, "He will come upon you," that is, spiritually he will do in you what a man in such a matter does carnally, namely: (1) he will separate some small portion of your flesh and blood to be the offspring; (2) he will prepare that portion for this use; (3) he will ward off from it all intemperateness from which sin could afterward arise, namely so that a holy thing might be born of her; (4) he will unite the human nature with the divine person. However, he will not mingle some heterogeneous and divine substance with your seed, from which what was born of you will be named the Son of God, as the Socinians want due to their hatred of the eternal and ineffable generation of Christ.

b. "He will overshadow you," ἐπισκιάσει σοί. There are among the fathers those who interpret this, "He will cover you," "he will cool your flesh," so that you may not conceive with any sense of libidinous desire. Thus Augustine, Gregory, and Bede: see Maldonado on this passage.[4] Indeed, the translators of the Septuagint customarily render the verb סכך, cover, by ἐπισκιάζειν (Ps. 91:4; 140:7; etc.). Nevertheless, Theophylact and others think more correctly that this is a metaphor taken from birds hatching their chicks, such that in this way the angel is showing that this offspring would arise by the same power by which the world took its beginning.[5] For in the history of Moses (Gen. 1:2), the Spirit of God מרחפת על פני המים, "moved upon the face of the waters," which verb the most learned Hebrew doctors explain as concerning the same sort of brooding; and here is openly evident the use of the same verb (cf. Deut. 32:11, where the Septuagint translators employ σκεπάσαι with an equal meaning). It is best, at least in my judgment, to say that the idea of a "shadow" is a mark of the secret and

<hr>

4. Augustine, Gregory, and Bede as cited in Maldonado, *Commentarii in quatuor evangelistas*, 2:48–50; cf. Augustine, *Homilia XLIIII* in *Opera*, 10 vols. (Antwerp: Christopher Plantin, 1576–1577), 10:199; idem, "Sermo CCXC: in natali Joannis Baptistae, IV" in *PL* 38:1315–16; Gregory I, *Moralia*, 27.12 in *PL* 76:411–12; 33.3 in *PL* 76:671–75; Bede on Luke 1:35 in *Expositio Lucae* in *PL* 92:318–322.

5. Theophylact of Ohrid (1055–after 1107), *Ennaratio in Evangelium Lucae* in *PG* 123:706; idem, *The Explanation by Blessed Theophylact of the Holy Gospel According to St. Luke* (Manchester, Miss.: Chrysostom Press, 1997), 17; Grotius, *Annotationes in libros Evangeliorum*, 610.

incomprehensible working[6] of the Holy Spirit, by which he performed this business of making her fertile in a way so secret that its manner was not made known even to the blessed Virgin, and he also willed that we be warned not to inquire too curiously into its manner. To this same end seems to point the overshadowing of the cloud in the tabernacle of the covenant (Ex. 40:35), and that the cherubim overshadowed the ark (2 Chron. 5:8; cf. 1 Kings 8:12; Num. 9:22).

B. His birth: "therefore that holy thing born of you will be called the Son of God." In these words is:

1. The one born, or about to be born: "that holy thing," διὸ καὶ τὸ γεννώμενον ἐκ σοῦ ἅγιον, "also what will be born from you holy." Ἐκ σοῦ, "of you," is in the Greek codices, but not in the ancient Latin versions nor in Theodotion, yet the Syriac and the Arabic have it, as do the ancient writers, Irenaeus, Tertullian, Novatian, Epiphanius, Athanasius, as Beza, Grotius, and others observe, and thus judge that it should be retained.[7] Τὸ ἅγιον, "that holy thing," that is, "which will be born of you," τὸ γεννώμενον ἐκ σοῦ, not any other thing, and accordingly the article seems to be employed diacritically. Ἅγιον, "holy thing," stands for ἅγιος, holy person, by the commonly used enallage of gender, to signify some ὑφιστάμενον, subsistence, which already existed with respect to the divine nature, and would be born with respect to the human nature. Moreover, it is called ἅγιον, "holy," not from this, that it would be born from a holy seed which the Holy Spirit cleansed from all original impurity, for it is speaking not about a holy seed, but about a holy person, nor also is a seed, as it is not a rational being, subject to moral impurity; but rather, because it is the Holy One of Israel (Isa. 10:20), whom the Father sanctified in the eternal covenant of grace, that is, separated from all other persons who would exist, and sent in time into the world to be the Mediator, and because he would be the one preeminently holy, who would be conceived in a most holy way, and would be exempt from all corruption, as much original as actual (2 Cor. 5:21).

2. The birth: γεννώμενον, "being born," an enallage of the present for the future, as in Matthew 2:4. It is not speaking properly of

---

6. ἐνεργείας

7. Beza, *Novum Testamentum* (1598), 234; Grotius, *Annotationes in libros Evangeliorum*, 610–11.

conception, for thus it would have said ἐν σοί, "in you," but of birth, ἐκ σοῦ, "of you." Thus Paul says, γενομενον ἐκ γυναικός, "born of a woman" (Gal. 4:4). Furthermore, here γίνεσθαι means the same thing as γεννᾶσθαι, "to be born" (Luke 1:13; Acts 7:20). The evangelists relate the birth of Christ by its circumstances, especially in Luke 2, so that from them it would be clear that he is the promised Messiah.

3. The name of the one born: "He will be called the Son of God." Διὸ τὸ γεννώμενον, "Therefore that which is born": not because the fundamental reason on account of which he ought to be named the Son of God is his extraordinary and miraculous conception and birth, as the Socinians want, in order to exclude his eternal generation, from which he is the Son of God properly speaking (Ps. 2:7; Mic. 5:2); but rather, because by means of this extraordinary conception by the Holy Spirit, the union of the divine person with the human nature occurred, from which the one born is, in the concrete, the Son of God, and from his birth, God was manifested in the flesh (1 Tim. 3:16). Κληθήσεται, "he will be called," therefore intends the same thing here as "he will be manifested": the Son of God already existing from eternity will be acknowledged as the only begotten Son of God (John 1:18). Therefore in the whole clause is signified that: (1) the Savior would take his own flesh *from* the substance of the blessed Virgin. (2) That flesh, by the operation of the Holy Spirit, would be united, both with a rational soul so that he would come forth a true man, and with the divine person so that at the same time he would be true God, and thus the God-man. (3) On account of this union with the second person of the deity, that man born from the blessed Virgin would be called the Son of God.

The Dogmatic Part

The incarnation of the Son of God occurred in an altogether extraordinary and wonderful manner.

III. Therefore, the incarnation of the Son of God occurred in an altogether extraordinary and wonderful way. For it is said to have occurred: (1) by a certain extraordinary efficacy of the Holy Spirit, which the phrase, "The Holy Spirit will come upon you" indicates; (2) by an overshadowing, that is, such an efficacy of the Holy Spirit which was procured under a shadow, in secret, in an altogether imperceptible manner; (3) contrary to the common order, with the human flesh produced only from the seed of the woman. For (4) a virgin gave birth and (5) she gave birth to the Son of God.

It is proved by the Scriptures.
For these reasons the incarnation is called a mystery, and also a great mystery, indeed without controversy (1 Tim. 3:16; cf. Rom. 16:25–26; Eph. 1:9; 3:9; Col. 1:26), and a new thing (Jer. 31:22) from which, the name "Wonderful" is attributed to the one to be incarnated (Isa. 9:6; cf. Judg. 13:18).

And by reasons
And an extraordinary and wonderful incarnation was surely fitting, because: (1) the person, both as he was to be incarnated, that is, the second person of the Trinity, and as he is incarnated, the God-man, is extraordinary and wonderful (1 Tim. 3:16; John 1:14). (2) The work for which he was incarnated, that is, the redemption of the human race, was extraordinary and wonderful (1 Tim. 1:15). (3) The condition of the Mediator to be incarnated, by which he had to be exempt from all original stain (2 Cor. 5:21), had to be extraordinary and wonderful.

The passive principle of conception: A virgin
IV. Moreover, this wonderful incarnation consists of two parts: conception and birth. In the conception, which comes before us for discussion in the first place, three principles concur: the passive, the active, and the material. The passive principle was: (1) a virgin, from whom the Mediator willed to be born, (a) so that there might be a fulfillment of the prophecies (Gen. 3:15; Isa. 7:14; Jer. 31:22; Song 4:12). (b) So that it might be evident that he was immune from the original stain, inasmuch as it is propagated by ordinary and natural generation (cf. Ps. 51:5; John 3:6 with Heb. 7:26). It is not that the virginity of his mother is the sole or formal cause of this immunity, but that the extraordinary conception and birth provides a certain argument of this immunity. (c) So that he might be "without father," as the antitype of Melchizedek (Heb. 7:3). (d) So that he might show that he was that γεννώμενον ἅγιον, that holy thing which would be born (Luke 1:35), about whom it says in Daniel 9:24, "to anoint the Holiness of holinesses," למשח קדש קדשים.

A virgin from the tribe of Judah
(2) A virgin from the tribe of Judah, of the seed of David (Rom. 1:3; Acts 2:33; Luke 1:27, where "of the house of David" can be referred to Mary as well as to Joseph; Heb. 7:14; Matt. 1:2–15; Luke 3:23–38), namely that he would be that

Lion of the tribe of Judah (Rev. 5:5; Gen. 49:9), that Son of David (Matt. 9:27; 12:23; 21:9; 22:41–42, 45; Jer. 33:15), indeed, David himself, as the antitype (Jer. 30:9; Ezek. 24:23–24; 37:25; Hos. 3:5).

A virgin who was betrothed
(3) A virgin who was betrothed (Matt. 1:18) to Joseph, a man from the tribe of Judah (Matt. 1:20), who from this betrothal (insofar as it is consent that makes a marriage) is at times called the father of Christ (Luke 2:48), that is, not only because Joseph was commonly considered to be his father (Luke 3:23), and because he had a fatherly affection toward him (Matt 2:14), but also because he was the true husband of his mother, with whom he did in fact enter into marriage (for which reason she is called "woman" in John 2:4),[8] a marriage that was confirmed, although not consummated. But whether or not she remained a virgin after the Savior's birth was completed cannot be determined with certainty from Scripture, because on one hand it seems less probable that the vessel once impregnated by the Holy Spirit was afterwards known carnally by a man (cf. Ezek. 44:1–2), and on the other hand the Scriptures do not lack statements that seem at first glance to suggest that it was consummated (Matt. 1:18, 25; 13:55–56; Mark 6:3). Although I do not deny that responses on the negative part can be made easily to those passages, it suffices that she more certainly than certain was a virgin before the birth and in the birth, and that it was at least not from a vow of virginity that it was not consummated, because not only does Scripture make entirely no mention of this, but also it would be absurd to promise virginity to God and marriage to Joseph, because a married woman is not in possession of her own right (1 Cor. 7:4). Moreover, the Savior willed to be born precisely from a betrothed virgin so that: (a) from the testimony of her cohabiting husband we might be more persuaded of the virginity of his mother, without which he could not have been the true Messiah; (b) he would not be rejected as one born illegitimately (cf. Matt. 1:18ff.); (c) by the work of Joseph, both mother and son might be more properly supported and defended.

A virgin who was godly, but not without sin
(4) A virgin who was certainly godly, and that surpassing all other women (κεχαριτωμένη καὶ εὐλογημένη, "highly favored" and "blessed," Luke 1:28), yet nevertheless not born either without original sin, because Scripture excludes only one from this, the Savior (Rom. 5:12; 1 Cor. 15:22), or without any actual sin (John 2:4).

---

8. The Latin *mulier*, like the Greek γυνὴ in John 2:4, can mean "woman" or "wife."

A virgin named Mary

(5) A virgin whose name is Mary. Whether you should derive it from מרר, to be bitter, so that it says that she is bitter (cf. Luke 2:35 with Ruth 1:20); or from ירה, to teach, so that it denotes that she is a teacher (Luke 1:46); or from אור, to be light, so that it signifies that she is illuminated (Luke 1:31, 45); or from רום, to be high, so that it means she is exalted (Luke 1:28 with v. 48); or by composition, as if מָרְיָם, so that it denotes that she is a *stilla maris*, a drop of the sea, from which the monks through ignorance of Hebrew made and applied to her the name *stella maris*, star of the sea—it hardly matters. You will find a sort of prosopography of the blessed Virgin in Nicephorus (bk. 2, ch. 23).[9]

The active principle of conception: The Trinity. The Holy Spirit

V. The active principle of Christ's conception was certainly the entire Trinity, insofar as it is a work *ad extra* (Acts 13:32–33): the Father, by preparing a body for him (Heb. 10:5; Gal. 4:4); the Son, by taking the form of a servant (Phil. 2:7), whom also several of the ancients want to be understood by "the power of the Most High" in Luke 1:35 (cf. 1 Cor. 1:18); the Holy Spirit, by overshadowing (Luke 1:35). Yet through appropriation, the active principle is the Holy Spirit, on account of his peculiar operation: (1) in making Mary fertile (cf. Gen. 1:2); (2) in sanctifying or procuring such that a holy thing would born of her (Luke 1:35).

The sixfold operation of the Holy Spirit

Moreover, the operation of the Holy Spirit signified in coming upon and overshadowing had in general the following components, that: (1) he separated some particle of the Virgin's substance, from which the body of Christ was formed (Heb. 10:5). (2) He bestowed a molding force[10] upon the separated particle, by means of which the Virgin's seed alone could do in the conception what from the order of nature both seeds, the male and female, can do. (3) He as it were cleansed the seed of the Virgin, not indeed from moral impurity or sin, inasmuch as a seed not yet ensouled[11] is not liable to that, but from physical intemperateness, from which, in its own time, sin could have resulted, or at the least he preserved the birth from all impurity, to the end that what would be born of her would be holy (Luke 1:35). (4) He gradually formed that seed of the Virgin into human members, in the way that they are formed in ordinary generation (Heb. 10:5).

---

9. Nicephorus Callistus Xanthopulus (1256–1335), *Ecclesiasticae historiae libri XVIII* in *PG* 145:815–18.

10. *vim plasticam*

11. *animatum*

(5) When the body was already formed, he joined to it a rational soul (Zech. 12:1). (6) In uniting the soul to the body, at one and the same time he inseparably joined the divine person to both united parts. However, from all these things, the Holy Spirit is not rightly called the Father of Christ, even according to the human nature, because: (1) the Holy Spirit did not supply the material cause from which Christ's flesh would have been formed, such as a father provides in the generation of a son, but only the efficient cause; (2) according to his human nature, Christ is not of the same species with the Holy Spirit; nor (3) is Christ anywhere in Scripture called the Son of the Holy Spirit.

The material principle of conception. What did not supply it. What did supply it. VI. The material principle of this conception was not: (1) the very essence of the Word,[12] which was converted into the human nature, since the essence of the Word: (a) was not only spiritual and entirely heterogeneous to the flesh; but also (b) the very immutable essence of God, consubstantial with the Father and the Holy Spirit (Mal. 3:6; James 1:17); and moreover, (c) the very deity, which if it changed, there would not now be a God. Nor (2) was it the essence of the Holy Spirit, for the same reasons. Nor (3) anything immediately produced in heaven by God and sent down into the womb of the blessed Virgin, because Scripture makes entirely no mention of that, nor could we know it from anywhere else. Rather, it is (4) the seed of the blessed Virgin, from which the one born is called "the seed of the woman" (Gen. 3:15), derived from Adam, through Abraham, Isaac, Jacob, David, and so forth, to Mary by ordinary transfer,[13] such that he was the seed of Abraham, of Isaac, of Jacob, of David, and so forth (Rom. 9:5). However, this seed, although it was propagated through sinners to Mary, yet was not liable to sin or moral wickedness, because this wickedness does not occur in something without a soul or reason,[14] although it could have a natural intemperance, which afterwards could offer an opportunity for sin, which we have said was for this reason removed by the Holy Spirit from the seed of Mary.

What the consequences of this are
And from this seed: (1) he was the true Son of Mary (Matt. 1:25; 13:55; Mark 6:3), and the Son of Man, as he is called throughout the Gospels (Matt. 8:20; 9:6; etc.). And (2) because the human nature born from the seed of Mary was united by the power of the Holy Spirit to the divine person, the blessed Virgin

---

12. *ipsa essentia* τοῦ λόγου
13. *traduce ordinario*
14. *inanimatum et irrationale*

is rightly called the θεοτόκος, the God-bearer[15] (Luke 1:43), just as the Savior, by reason of the divine person, from his eternal generation, is rightly called the θεότοκος, the one born of God.[16] Yet (3) the Savior was not on this account a double Son, because *son* is a description not of a nature but of a person. Although I do not yet see why a double sonship—one by reason of the divine nature and the other by reason of the human nature—could not be admitted in him, since sonship is nothing but a relation, and every person obtains a double sonship, one by reason of his father and another by reason of his mother: from which also our Savior is called the Son of God and the Son of Man.

The time of the conception
VII. From the first moment of this conception, when the personal union of the two natures was accomplished, Christ obtained the fullness of all habitual grace, that is, with respect to κτῆσις, possession, or οὐσία, substance; although, with respect to χρῆσις, use, and ἐξουσία, power, or with respect to second acts, and through extension to more objects, he made increases day by day (Luke 2:52). However, at what moment in time, whether the conception occurred at the point of the angelic announcement or after it, is asked out of curiosity and not determinable with certainty. This is certain, that it did not happen before the angel had completed his diplomatic mission (Luke 2:21 with 1:31). Thus far regarding the conception, the first part of the incarnation.

The birth: Temporal, predicted, prefigured, and presented
VIII. Next comes the birth, which is: (1) not that eternal birth which Psalm 2:7 and Micah 5:1 speak of, which belongs to him with respect to the divine nature, by which he is called the Son (Isa. 9:6) and has the first person of the Trinity as his Father (Matt. 3:17); nor (2) that spiritual birth which occurs by the Spirit and the Word in the hearts of believers, which is indicated in Galatians 4:19; but (3) that temporal birth by which he was conceived by the Holy Spirit of his virgin mother, and was brought forth into the light. This happened according to so many: (a) Old Testament prophecies (Gen. 49:10; Num. 24:17; Isa. 7:14; 11:1; 9:6; Jer. 31:22; Mic. 5:2; Hag. 2:8); (b) figures and types, in the burning bush (Ex. 3:3), Aaron's rod (Num. 17:8), Gideon's fleece (Judg. 6:37ff. with Ps. 72:6; Isa. 45:8); (c) recorded history (Luke 2; Matt. 1–2).

---

15. Dutch: *Godtbaarster*
16. Dutch: *Godtgeboorne*

The causes of the birth: God

IX. Regarding this birth, there come for our consideration, first, the procuring causes, namely: (1) on the one hand, God, who by this birth sent his own Son to us (Gal. 4:4) and gave him for us (John 3:16; Isa. 9:5), and so he is called the gift of God (John 4:10). God was in this giving led (a) by an inexhaustible love toward us (John 3:16; Rom. 8:32); (b) by a zeal to manifest his glory (Luke 2:14); (c) by a sense of our misery (Ps. 14:2ff.; Rom. 3:10–26). Yet God by this procurement of the birth must not be called the Father of Christ, for in this way Christ would not have been born "without father" (Heb. 7:3), and because, namely, he neither supplied from himself the matter or the seed from which he would have been born, nor is he of the same nature and species with the one born.

The Virgin Mary

(2) On the other hand, the blessed Virgin, the mother, whose prosopography we have touched upon in sufficient detail in §IV. Nor do we add anything here, except that God deigned to destine for this childbirth a poor virgin, the bride of a carpenter, the hewn-down trunk of Jesse (Isa. 11:1), and at the same time one of royal stock, so that he might designate the poorness of the son and the glory of the mother, as the one highly favored and blessed among women (Luke 1:28), who nevertheless in giving birth did not lose her virginity, inasmuch as it cannot be lost or injured except by intercourse with a man.

The one born: The Son by reason of the divine nature and a child
by reason of the human nature

X. Second, the one procured by God from the virgin Mary through the birth was a child and the Son (Isa. 9:6): (1) the Son by reason of the divine nature (Ps. 2:7), God's own Son (Rom. 8:32), the only begotten (John 3:16); (2) a child with respect to the human nature (Matt. 2:20; Luke 2:12, 16–17, 21, 27, 40, 43; Acts 3:13). Moreover, he willed to be born a child, so that: (a) he might show that he was the promised Messiah (Isa. 9:6); (b) he might lower himself more profoundly (Phil. 2:7; Heb. 2:14; Gal. 4:4); (c) he might as a brother to us be made like us also in this (Heb. 2:14; 4:15); (d) he might make known his love toward infants (Mark 10:14; Ps. 8:3); (e) he might commiserate and bring us help in our infirmities, even those of lowest infancy (Heb. 4:15).

The firstborn. God and man simultaneously

He was also the firstborn of his mother (Matt. 1:25). Not because there were more born of Mary after him, but because no one was born of her before him (cf. Num. 18:15–16; Ex. 13:2; Luke 2:23), and namely because he was the firstborn of the creatures (Col. 1:15) and the firstborn from the dead (Col. 1:18), the firstborn who was to be brought into the world (Heb. 1:6). Yet at the same time he was the Son of God (Matt. 16:16), the only begotten (John 3:16), indeed God himself manifested in the flesh (1 Tim. 3:16). Thus from this by all right his mother is called the *Deipara*, θεοτόκος, God-bearer; and he is called, with respect to his person, the θεάνθρωπος, God-man, and with respect to his office, the Redeemer of the elect, the Christ, the Lord (Luke 2:11).

The birth itself was: True, wonderful, miserable
XI. Third, the procurement, or the birth itself, which was: (1) certainly a true birth (Luke 1:35) and of the same kind as ours (Luke 2:6ff.; Ps. 22:9), through the opening of the womb (Num. 8:16; Luke 2:23), with pains and other things ordinary to childbirth, not only because the blessed Virgin on account of sin was liable to the same condition as Eve and other women (Gen. 3:16; John 16:21), but so that the Savior himself, as in all natural things, so also in this, might be made like us (Heb. 2:14 with 4:15). But yet (2) wonderful and extraordinary, for which reason it is called a new thing (Jer. 31:22), such that it can be compared with wonderful things, for example, with the production of Eve from one sex (Gen. 2:22–23), with the burning bush which was not consumed by fire (Ex. 3:2–3; cf. Deut. 9:3; 4:12; 5:4), with Aaron's rod blossoming and bearing fruit in the same night (Num. 17:8), with Gideon's fleece (Judg. 6:37). And surely indeed it is marvelous for (a) a virgin to give birth (Isa. 7:14; Jer. 31:22); (b) without a man, by the Holy Spirit (Luke 1:35); (c) to give birth to the God-man (Isa. 7:14); (d) to give birth to the one who pre-existed her from eternity (John 8:56–58). At the same time, (3) it was also miserable (Ex. 2:3), especially if you should attend to: (a) his wretched and poor mother (Luke 1:48, 53), (b) the place of his birth, in a lowly town, Bethlehem, in an inn, in a stable, in a manger, in swaddling cloths, and so forth.

The time of the birth. In general. The fourth monarchy. The year is uncertain. And even more so the day.
XII. The surrounding conditions and circumstances of the procurement, or of the birth. First, those antecedent to it or concomitant with it, among which is: (1) the time, which was certainly put off, according to God's manner (Ex. 2:23–25), in order to stir up desire (Prov. 13:19; Isa. 44:1), but yet not put away, or protracted longer than was fitting or than had been promised (Dan. 9:24–26; Num. 23:19). Specifically, it occurred: (a) under the fourth monarchy (Dan. 2:40, 44–45), under Augustus (Luke 2:1), when the scepter and lawgiver was transferred from Judah to the Romans (Gen. 49:10). Although (b) the year of

the birth cannot be so exactly settled, because our present method of calculation, by which our times are marked as those of Christ, was only taken up at a later period, at the initiative of Dionysius Exiguus,[17] for which reason the reckoning of times is recognized to be not a little confused, especially in the earlier centuries. However, the most common calculation of the chronologists places the birth of Christ, *anno mundi*, in the year from the world's beginning 3928, 3949, 3970, or 4020. Without any doubt, it must be referred to the reign of Augustus, which lasted for forty-four years after the victory at Actium; the most outstanding chronologists assert that the birth of Christ was in the thirty-first year of that reign. Moreover, it is computed that he was baptized in the fifteenth or the beginning of the sixteenth year of the reign of Tiberius, the successor of Augustus. And much less also (c) can the day of his birth be certainly designated, because Scripture, in those passages which contain a mark of the times of Christ (that is, Matt. 2:1; Luke 2:1–2; 3:1), relates only a general note of them, and determines nothing of the day. Ancient eastern Christians celebrated January 6 as the day of Christ's birth, which they called Theophany; Scaliger refers it to the feast of Tabernacles, customarily celebrated in the month of September; nor are there lacking those who designate for it April 22 or even May 22. The common opinion of those in the West celebrates December 25 as the day of his birth. This opinion, taken from the Roman census records, spread throughout the Christian world, and the most ancient of the fathers frequently cited these records (Tertullian, *Against Marcion*, bk. 4).[18] At the least, from Scripture scarcely anything certain can be determined regarding the day of his birth. At the same time, it is evident from Luke 2:8 that the birth occurred at night, but in what watch of the night is unknown.

The place of the birth

XIII. (2) The place of his birth was: (a) Bethlehem (Luke 2:4), an obscure κώμη,

---

17. Dionysius Exiguus (c. 470–c. 544), whose method in tabular form was adopted by Bede in *De temporum ratione*, which may be found in Latin in C. W. Jones, ed. *De temporum ratione* in *Bedae opera didascalia* 2, Corpus Christianorum Series Latina, 123B (Turnhout: Brepols, 1997), or in English translation in Bede, *Bede: The Reckoning of Time*, trans. Faith Wallis (Liverpool: Liverpool University Press, 2004). For a brief overview of the problems posed by calculating Easter and a bibliography on the Julian calendar, see *calendar* and *computus* in T. F. Glick, S. Livesey, and F. Wallis, *Medieval Science, Technology, and Medicine: An Encyclopedia* (New York: Routledge, 2014), 109–11, 139–41. Regarding the gradual adoption of this system, see also *The Catholic Encyclopedia* (New York: Robert Appleton Co., 1909), 6:738.

18. Tertullian, *Adversus Marcionem libri quinque* in *PL* 2:405; *Tertullian: Adversus Marcionem*, trans. Ernest Evans (Oxford: Oxford University Press, 1972), 4.19.10, pp. 362–63, "Also it is well known that a census had just been taken in Judaea by Sentius Saturninus, and they might have inquired of his ancestry in those records."

town,[19] on account of prophecy (Mic. 5:2) and perhaps foreshadowing (2 Sam. 6:12ff., 23:15 with John 4:14). (b) An inn of Bethlehem (Luke 2:7); but which inn, what sort it was, and where, whether in or outside the city, is asked with excessive curiosity by the idle. And indeed, (c) in the stable of the inn, because there was no room for them in the inn (Luke 2:7). This was to the end that: (a) from it we may more clearly perceive the depth of his humiliation (Phil. 2:7); (b) perhaps also, we may have in it a mystery, because בֵּית־לֶחֶם, "Bethlehem," means "house of bread" (cf. Ex. 16:15; John 6:33; 2 Sam. 23:15).

The consequent circumstances which concern his humiliation are, that:
His mother wrapped her son in swaddling cloths.
XIV. Then, second, the consequent circumstances of the birth were of two kinds: the one concerned designating the humility of the birth, and the other its glory, namely so that both natures of the Mediator, the humble human nature and the glorious divine nature, as well as both mediatorial states, that of emptying and that of exaltation, would be prefigured immediately in the very birth of the Mediator. To those circumstances, which refer to his humiliation, pertain the fact that: (1) the mother herself wrapped the little newborn son in swaddling cloths (Luke 2:12, 16), without doubt because she lacked both a midwife and a nurse, as Chrysostom observes (*Homily* 34 on John): "His mother wrapped him in swaddling cloths and laid him down herself, because Joseph did not dare touch him whom he knew was not begotten of him: he marveled and rejoiced at the child, but he did not dare touch the child."[20] That latter part is uncertain, but the former breathes of poverty and humility.

She laid him in a manger.
(2) Once wrapped, she laid him (for lack of a cradle, on account of their poverty) in a manger, the place for livestock fodder, undoubtedly to represent his extreme poverty, misery, and humility (cf. Matt. 8:20; 2 Cor. 8:9).

He was sought to be murdered.
(3) Soon after his birth, he was sought by Herod to be murdered, and also with such great fervor that on account of it the tyrant destroyed all the infants of the whole district of Bethlehem from two years old and under (Matt. 2:16). Undoubtedly this happened to the end that he might show as soon as his very birth that he was born to die (Matt. 20:28).

---

19. John 7:42

20. John Chrysostom, "De Nativitate Domini, Homilia XXXIIII" in *Opera*, 4 vols. (Basil: Froben, 1530), 2:118.

By flight into Egypt he looked out for his life.

(4) Therefore, by the flight into Egypt he had to look out for his life until the death of Herod (Matt. 2:13–15), so that he might fulfill the prophecies (Matt. 2:15 with Hos. 11:1), and at the same time signify that he was born for every kind of misery, so that he might lead us from the spiritual Egypt into the heavenly Canaan.

The consequences of this birth which concern the glory of the one born are, that:
He was sought by the wise men, pointed out by a star, proclaimed by angels, sought by shepherds, and revealed.

XV. The consequent circumstances of this birth which concern his glory were, that: (1) he was so fervently sought and adored by the eastern magi, after an extended journey, and enriched with gifts: gold, frankincense, and myrrh (Matt. 2:1–2, 11). But who these magi or wise men were, from which region of the east, how many in number, what they were named, whether they were kings, to what end precisely, and in what quantity they brought gold, frankincense, and myrrh, and other such questions, since Scripture is silent, are determined with excessive curiosity by idle monks. (2) By a particular star, whether recently created or recently assigned to this new use, God willed to reveal the one born king of the Jews even to the farthest Gentiles; it was therefore called his star (Matt. 2:2, 10; cf. Num. 24:17; 2 Peter 1:19; Rev. 22:16; 1:16). (3) By an angel, and one surrounded with the glory of the Lord, the birth was first revealed to shepherds keeping watch over their flocks by night (Luke 2:9–12), and by the heavenly host it was celebrated with a hymn (vv. 13–14). (4) By the shepherds he was eagerly sought, found, and revealed to Judea (vv. 15–17).

The ends of his birth: The glory of God, peace on earth, good will
toward men, our adoption, redemption and eternal life
XVI. Of this birth that has been narrated, there remain its ends, namely: (1) the glorification of God, from which the angel herald who would declare his birth appeared surrounded with the glory of the Lord (Luke 2:9), and the angelic host attributed glory to God above all in their hymn, "Glory to God in the highest" (v. 14). For in this birth, the glory of his wisdom, power, righteousness, goodness, and mercy shone in so many rays, as we will show more distinctly in its own place.[21] (2) Peace on earth, or the reconciliation of God with sinners (2 Cor. 5:19), to be procured by the satisfaction and merit of this one who was born (Eph. 2:11–14; Isa. 54:10; 66:12). Hence (3) εὐδοκία, good will, toward

---

21. §XXXIV, below

men (Luke 2:14), חפצי, "my will" (Isa. 62:4; 65:18), because in this one born, apprehended by faith, (a) we please God (Eph. 1:6; Heb. 11:6), and (b) obtain all manner of spiritual gifts, as fruits and witnesses of this good will (Eph. 1:3). Furthermore, (4) our adoption, because it was to this end that by this birth God sent his own Son into the world, that we might obtain υἱοθεσία, the adoption of sons (Gal. 4:4–5; John 1:12). Finally, (5) redemption and eternal life, for it was to this end that in the birth, God gave to the world his only begotten Son, that whosoever believes in him should not perish, but have eternal life (John 3:16). For all these reasons, and others that will be indicated in their own place,[22] the angel herald commands us to fear not, but rejoice, because he announces great joy for all the people, namely, that to them is born a Savior, Christ the Lord (Luke 2:10–11).

The effect of the conception and birth is: The incarnation and
the union of the two natures
XVII. Finally, that which pertains to the product of this conception and birth, is: (1) the incarnation of the Son of God, customarily designated by various names, partly scriptural and partly ecclesiastical: the ἐνσάρκωσις, enfleshment (from John 1:14), the θεοφάνεια, manifestation of God (1 Tim. 3:16; Isa. 40:5), the ἐνανθρώπησις, being made man (Phil. 2:7), the ἐξαποστολή, sending forth (Gal. 4:4), the ἐπιφάνεια, appearing (Luke 1:79; 2 Tim. 1:10), the visitation of the Son of Man (Ps. 8:4; Luke 1:78); or (2) the union of the two natures in the God-man Mediator, which was expressly the business for us in chapter 4.

The Elenctic Part
It is asked: 1. Is the incarnation common to the entire Trinity?
XVIII. Passing by then all those questions which concern the person of Christ and the union of the natures in it, it is asked, first, whether the cause of the incarnation is the entire Trinity, and its individual persons. The reason for doubting it is, on one hand, that the incarnation is an operation *ad extra*, and thus common to the entire Trinity, and on the other hand, that it seems to be attributed only to the Holy Spirit, who comes upon and overshadows the blessed Virgin (Luke 1:35), or even only to the Son, the person assuming, who was made flesh (John 1:14).

The active incarnation is common.
Therefore an answer must be made with a distinction: the active incarnation, which does the producing, is common to the entire Trinity, according to that

____
22. §XXXIX, below

maxim of Augustine, "For the visible nature, belonging only to the Son of God, the invisible Trinity has worked" (*On the Trinity*, bk. 2, ch. 10).[23] For not only is it an operation *ad extra* that is occupied with something different from God, but it is also asserted for the individual persons individually: for the Father who sent (John 10:36), who raised up the Branch of David (Jer. 23:5) and prepared the body (Heb. 10:5); for the Son, who assumed flesh, and by assuming was made flesh (John 1:14); for the Holy Spirit, who came upon and overshadowed the Virgin (Luke 1:35), yet through appropriation, on account of that particular mode of operating which the Holy Spirit supplied in coming upon and overshadowing, which we explained in §V. The active incarnation is common to the Trinity.

The passive incarnation is particular to the Son.
The passive incarnation belongs only to the second person (John 1:14; 6:38, 41–42; 16:28; 1 Tim. 3:16; Col. 2:9; Heb. 2:14; 10:5; 1 John 3:8; 4:2), insofar as the flesh produced by the active incarnation is terminated particularly upon the second person who assumes it, to whom it is united, and whose it becomes. We with several fathers declared this in its own place by the crass similitude of three people together sewing one garment to be worn by only one of them.[24]

*2. With respect to this birth, is God, or the Holy Spirit, rightly called
the Father of Christ?*
XIX. Second, whether God, or the Holy Spirit because he came upon and overshadowed Mary, is rightly called the Father of Christ, and Christ himself on that account is rightly called the Son of God. The Socinians, so that they more easily strip away from the Savior the eternal deity and his eternal generation, do admit that Christ the man was not begotten from God's very substance, indeed, that he received his essence from the substance of his mother no less than others receive it from their mothers, yet they devise the idea that the Holy Spirit sent another substance, which was immediately created, into the Virgin's womb, or that he created it there, from which substance Christ, once that which he received from the substance of the Virgin was joined to it, was begotten a true man, in such a way that from this, Christ as a man had not only a mother, but also a Father, God or the Holy Spirit, from which he is called the Son of God. They affirm the question.

---

23. Cf. Augustine, *De Trinitate libri quindecim* in *PL* 42:857; idem, *On the Trinity* in *NPNF1* 3:46, "…yet it is the *person* (*persona*) of the Son alone; for the invisible Trinity wrought the visible person of the Son alone."
24. 1.5.4 §VIII

The arguments of the orthodox
The orthodox deny it, because: (1) as even our adversaries confess, he was not born from the substance of God or the Holy Spirit. (2) He is not of the same nature or species as God. (3) Nowhere in the Scriptures is he called the Son of the Holy Spirit, nor the Holy Spirit called the Father of Christ. (4) From the Socinian hypothesis, there would be two Fathers in the Trinity. (5) Thus in no sense could he be said to be "without father" (Heb. 7:3). I need not add that (6) he is said to be materially from Mary, from her flesh and blood (Matt. 1:20; Luke 1:35; Gal. 4:4), because of which he is said to be the fruit of her womb (Luke 1:42).

The objections of our adversaries
Meanwhile, our adversaries allege: (1) that Mary is said to have been impregnated ἐκ πνεύματος ἁγίου, "of the Holy Spirit" (Matt. 1:18, 20). I respond, The preposition ἐκ in this passage does not denote a material cause, but an efficient cause (as occurs in Rom. 11:36; 1 John 5:1), because the substance of God and the Holy Spirit, which is immaterial, infinite, and immutable, cannot supply the material from which a body would be generated. (2) That the Holy Spirit is said to have come upon and overshadowed the Virgin (Luke 1:35). I respond, This occurred in no other way than that which we spoke of in §V. (3) That in no other way could he be called the Son of God. I respond, This is exactly their primary error, the contrary of which we have demonstrated above in book 2, chapter 26, §§XVI–XVIII.

3. Apart from the extraordinary operation of God, could a virgin conceive and give birth? The negative reasons
XX. Third, whether in order for a virgin to conceive and give birth, the extraordinary operation of the Holy Spirit was absolutely necessary. Some Jesuits affirm that it could happen that a virgin in mind and body would nevertheless be impregnated and conceive, from male seed brought to her apart from conjugal union. All Christians, and even the Jesuit Delrio in *Investigations into Magic* (bk. 2, q. 15), deny "that a woman can be known by a man without a loss of virginity, or be impregnated, if she be not known,"[25] because: (1) otherwise that extraordinary operation of the Holy Spirit which is mentioned in Luke 1:35 would have been superfluous. (2) God gives it to Ahaz as a miraculous sign

---

25. Martin Antoine Delrio (Del Rio, 1551–1608), *Disquisitionum magicarum libri sex* (Lyon: J. Pillehotte, 1612), 76; idem, *Investigations into Magic*, ed. and trans. P. G. Maxwell-Stuart (Manchester University Press, 2000), 89–91.

(Isa. 7:11, 14). (3) It exceeds the order of her particular nature that a virgin would give birth, and accordingly, an operation surpassing nature is required for it. (4) From the noted hypothesis, blood and semen outside of their vessels would not necessarily putrefy and lose their molding force, though this is the common opinion of natural philosophers and physicians. (5) From the same hypothesis, someone could have a father whom his mother never saw. I would add that (6) this profane immodesty of the Jesuits exposes the Savior's birth to the manifest calumnies of our adversaries. Moreover, they have nothing that they could adduce for their opinion, except some scrounged up examples that have never been proved.

4. Did the Messiah have to be born of a virgin? The affirmative is proved.
XXI. Fourth, whether the Messiah had to be born of a virgin. The Jews, out of hatred for Christ, obstinately deny it. Christians affirm it, because: (1) it is said in Isaiah 7:14 (cf. v. 11), "Therefore the Lord himself will give you a sign: behold, the virgin shall conceive and bear a son, and she shall call his name Immanuel." Here the following things must be observed: (a) a miraculous thing is promised, an אות, sign; (b) not only to the king, but also to the entire people, or to the house of David, to "you," in the plural, and thus something is promised that concerned everyone; (c) a sign that is altogether divine, to be displayed by God alone, "Therefore the Lord himself will give you a sign"; (d) a sign to be marveled at, "Behold"; (e) placed in this, that העלמה, the virgin, would bear; (f) that she would bear a son, Immanuel. Because all these things cannot be made to fit anyone other than the Messiah, it follows that here it is foretold that the Messiah would be born of a virgin. (2) In Jeremiah 31:22 it is foretold that the Lord would create something new in the earth, that a woman would encompass a man (that is, in her womb). Here it can be concluded that by נקבה is understood a virgin, not only because is it said that the Lord, יהוה, and that certainly by creation (ברא), would procure something both new, as it were, and unheard of in the earth, just as by גבר is understood a man who is strong and unique; but this name is attributed to the Messiah (Zech. 13:7; cf. Isa. 9:6), which is also confirmed from the scope of this and the preceding chapter, in which he intends to lift up the afflicted church through the coming of the Messiah, of King David, whom God would raise up for his people (Jer. 30:9; cf. Zech. 9:9). (3) Genesis 3:15 foretells such a seed of the woman that can crush the head of the serpent Satan, which without a doubt is applicable to no one except the Messiah. (4) In Genesis 49:10 the promised Messiah is called שִׁילה, Shiloh, from שִׁלְיָה, afterbirth, so that Shiloh is as it were "the son of the afterbirth," in which afterbirth the fetus is wrapped in his mother's womb (cf. Deut. 28:57). Thus the sense of the promise

is: until the son of that woman should come, whom she alone conceived without a man and bore, namely, that son who is called the seed of the woman (Gen. 3:15). You could add (5) Leviticus 12:2, where mention is made of a woman who has received seed (תזריע) and borne a male child, that she would be unclean, that is, by way of distinction, to signify that there would be at some point a woman who would not have received seed and yet would bear a male child, and that she would not be unclean. Among the ancient rabbis, (6) there are not lacking those who for this purpose employ the fact that in Isaiah 9:7, in the word למרבה, "of the increase," there is found a closed mem, contrary to the custom of the Hebrew language, in order to indicate that the mother of the Messiah would be a closed virgin (see Galatino, *On the Hidden Mysteries of Catholic Truth*, bk. 8, ch. 2).[26] From all these points you may gather an argument of this sort: that man who (1) would be born from an עלמה, a virgin, for a divine sign, whom (2) his mother would encompass in her womb in a new and unheard-of way, who (3) would be that great seed of the woman, who (4) would be procreated by a mother who did not receive seed—he had to be born without a doubt from a closed virgin; but the Messiah would be such a man; therefore, he had to be born from a closed virgin.

The negative is refuted. Exceptions to Isaiah 7:14: First
The declinatory exceptions of the Jews press against two of our fundamental passages. First, against Isaiah 7:11–14 they allege (1) that עלמה certainly frequently, but not always, means "virgin," and they only adduce a single instance, in Proverbs 30:19, "the way of a man with an עלמה," that is, "with a prostitute." I respond: (a) "The way of a man" does not denote anything except the amazing efforts or devices which a lover employs toward a virgin, so that he may possess her, which detracts entirely nothing from true virginity. (b) Even if we grant that in Proverbs 30:19 עלמה means a prostitute, yet it does not mean the same thing in Isaiah 7:14, for protesting against this are not only so many things surrounding the text, which we have already expressed, but even the Jews themselves, when they claim that it is understood as the wife either of the prophet or of Ahaz.

Second
(2) That there is not promised to Ahaz as a sign a birth that would occur only after so many centuries to come. For how could this raise up and sustain Ahaz's faltering spirit, since Ahaz would not see it? I respond: (a) The promise of this sign was not so much for raising up Ahaz, who had well enough despised it, but the entire house of David (vv. 13–14), which would last even to the coming of the

---

26. Galatino, *De arcanis catholicae veritatis*, 436–39.

Messiah. (b) He raises them up not only by a sign for prediction, which precedes the event (such as is evident in Judg. 6:37), but also by a sign for remembrance,[27] which follows the event and renews the memory of it (such as is evident in Ex. 3:12; 1 Sam. 2:34; 10:2–3; 1 Kings 22:25; Jer. 44:27, 29–30). So then the sense of the passage is: the house of David cannot be uprooted, because after so many centuries a certain virgin from the house of David will bear a son, whom she will call Immanuel, or the God-man, which is to the house of David as an infallible sign of its future liberation.

Third

(3) That the prophet understands עלמה as his own wife, as is evident from 8:2–4. I respond: (a) Several commentators want that passage to be understood not historically but prophetically, from its context, as in Hosea 1–3 and elsewhere. At the least, (b) the wife of the prophet was not the עלמה promised in Isaiah 7:14, because in his wife's conception and birth there was not that sign that could have comforted the whole house of David against threatening kings; nor was her son Immanuel, or the Lord of that entire region (Isa. 8:8).

Fourth

(4) That (according to Rabbi Kimchi)[28] by עלמה must be understood the wife of Ahaz, to whom God promises a son, namely Hezekiah, who would be the king of Judah. I respond: (a) This birth would not have supplied a sign by which the house of David could be strengthened in its present need. (b) This interpretation is incompatible, since Hezekiah was already at that time nine years old, as is evident by comparing 2 Kings 16:2 and 18:2. For it is said in the prior passage that Ahaz reigned for only sixteen years, and in the latter that Hezekiah began to reign in the twenty-fifth year of his own age. Therefore, if you subtract from these latter years the former years of his father's reign, it will remain that Hezekiah was nine years old when his father took up the kingship.

Fifth

(5) There is not lacking one who argues from the demonstrative prefix, העלמה, and thus that such a woman is signified who was known at that time in Judah, and present with him. I respond: (a) Although the name Mary was unknown to the Jews, and no prophet said in specific terms that the mother of the Messiah would be a virgin, yet she could have been known from the fact that the

---

27. *signo non tantum* προγνωστικῷ, …*sed* ἀναμνηστικῷ *etiam*

28. David Kimchi, *The Commentary of David Kimchi on Isaiah*, ed. Louis Finkelstein (New York: Columbia University Press, 1926), 49.

Messiah is called the seed of the woman (Gen. 3:15), and Shiloh, the son of the afterbirth (Gen. 49:9); and she could also have been made known from the live oral exposition of the prophet, if he had said, "That woman, that mother whose son the Messiah will be, will conceive and give birth to Immanuel." (b) But it is most false that the demonstrative or emphatic ה always denotes a thing present (see Mal. 3:1; 4:5).

Sixth

Some add (6) that Mary did not name her son Immanuel, but Jesus. I respond, He bore both names, the latter as a proper name, the former as an appellative name (Matt. 1:23, 25; cf. Isa. 9:6).

Seventh

(7) There is also one who constitutes the force of the sign in this, that the עלמה would conceive, which does not happen for all married women; nor only would she conceive, but also give birth, which does not happen for all who conceive, since many miscarry; nor only would she give birth, but specifically to a son, and to such a son who would eat butter and honey instead of milk, and finally such a son who would be named Immanuel. I respond, Of course, what a great and excellent sign this would be! A sign that ought to sustain and comfort the whole house of David in such dire straits, a sign which God had substituted the offered sign, for that which King Ahaz ought to have asked for, in heaven or on earth, in verse 11: "Ask for yourself a sign from Jehovah your God: make your request deep, or lift yourself on high."

Eighth

Also especially (8) they argue that the sign to be given had to have been fulfilled, and that son had to have been born, before the departure of the two enemy kings (v. 16). I respond, It is denied, because in verse 8 seventy-five years are fixed for when Ephraim, that is, the ten tribes of Israel, would be carried into Assyria, and thus the land which Ahaz abhorred (v. 16), namely the land of Israel, would be deserted. From this it would follow that the child, who according to the promise given would be born soon, would within seventy-five years of eating butter and honey not come to the point that he could discern between good and evil. Therefore the goal of the words in verse 16 is: As of yet the birth of Messiah is far distant; before he had been born, and before he had, by eating butter and honey, food familiar to the Jews, arrived at the years of discretion, the land of Syria, over which Rezin was head, and the land of Israel, over which Pekah, Ramaliah's son, was head (the men whom Ahaz feared so much), would be deserted, from which the house of David could easily gather for its comfort that by those two kings who were then assaulting it, it would not be uprooted, but would endure, so that from it the promised son Immanuel could be born. These generally are the points that the Jews object against this clear passage, which points we desired to represent more freely than usual because they occur more rarely among the writers of common places, and at the same time they touch upon the foundation of the Christian cause.

Exceptions to Jeremiah 31:22: First
Against Jeremiah 31:22, they object: (1) that the text is not speaking about the birth of a woman or virgin properly speaking, but by "a woman" is meant the Jewish people; by "a man" is meant the God of this people, whom by true repentance that people by a new example would seek, and continually embrace: that is, since ordinarily a man seeks a woman, here extraordinarily a woman would seek a man, and this then is that new thing that God so magnificently promises that he would accomplish. I respond: (a) It was not a new thing in Israel to seek God with true repentance, as is evident from the books of Joshua, Judges, Samuel, Kings, Chronicles, and so forth. Nor (b) is it true that the people sought their God with repentance before God sought the people with his grace, per verses 18–19, "Convert me, and I shall be converted, for you are my God.… When I will have been converted, I will repent." Nor (c) is it a new thing if a woman should seek a man, as is evident in Rebekah (Gen. 24), in Hagar (Gen. 16:9), in the spiritual bride (Song 3:1–3). Nor (d) can the words "a woman will encompass a man" mean the Jews' repentance itself, because they are adduced as the cause of that repentance: "How long will you turn back, O rebellious daughter? For Jehovah will create a new thing in the earth, a woman will encompass a man." Would the sense then surely not be, "Turn back, because you will turn back"? Finally, (e) it is not said, "A woman will turn back and will pursue a man," but "will encompass a man," by which repentance was never customarily designated in Scripture; and even if it were thus designated, yet this is not such a great new thing, for the repenting soul to embrace its Redeemer by faith, that God had to promise so magnificently that he would do this new thing in the earth. They object (2) that by the word נקבה is always understood a married woman, not a virgin. I respond, It is the name of the feminine sex, not of a state, just as זכר is the name of the masculine sex, not of a state; so then it is false that by נקבה is always understood a married woman (cf. Lev. 3:1; 12:7; Gen. 1:27; 6:19; with Spanheim, *Dubia Evangelica*, dub. 34).[29]

---

29. As background for the main points of this section, see Frederic Spanheim, Sr. (1600–1649), "Dubium XXXIV: An recte vel citetur, vel applicetur ab Evangelista Oraculum

5. Was Mary a virgin from a vow? The opinion of the papists
XXII. Fifth, whether Mary was a virgin from a vow of continence and celibacy. The papists, so that they may more easily protect monastic vows, and especially the vow of celibacy, affirm it, with a few fathers, but not without a great difference in their hypotheses, since some think that before the Virgin was born, or at least before she passed from infancy, she was consecrated by her parents to God, in which consecration was contained a vow of virginity. Others prefer that the vow was made before her betrothal, and still others, after it (see Maldonado on Luke 1:34).[30]

The opinion of the orthodox
The orthodox, just as they do not deny that it could have happened that she had the free purpose, with the consent of her betrothed, to abstain from the use of matrimony, yet they state that it can in no way be proved that she bound herself by a vow to perpetual virginity. The adversaries seek their only support for this vow in the words, "How will this happen, since I do not know a man?" (Luke 1:34). Here, they say, the word "I know" does not mean knowledge, but familiarity, and that not only about the past or present, but also about the future, as if she were saying, "I have neither known, nor can know," and moreover, they say that she is objecting not from natural but from moral inability; but such inability is contracted from nothing else than a vow. I respond with the words of Cardinal Cajetan on this passage: "She asks how she would become a mother, since she had no intercourse with a man. She did not say, 'I will not know a man,' but, 'I do not know a man,' because she had understood that the angel's words would be fulfilled at that time when the angel said, 'Behold, you will conceive': 'How will I now conceive, since I do not presently have knowledge of a man?'"[31] Or rather, in the words of Alfonso Salmeron: "In another way, perhaps no less probable, it could be said that the Virgin Mary, who was quite skilled and knowledgeable in the holy writings, understood that the mother of the Messiah would be a virgin, and therefore asked the angel how, with her virginity intact, she could become a mother; and once this was known, she immediately acquiesced and assented to the angel with a ready heart. And this sense directly sets forth the authority

Propheticum, Esa. 7:14, 'Ecce virgo uterum feret, et pariet Filium, et vocabis nomen ejus Immanuel,' Matt. 1.25" in *Dubia Evangelica in tres partes distributa*, 3 vols. (Geneva: Pierre Chouët, 1655), 1:270–325.

30. Maldonado, *Commentarii in quatuor evangelistas*, 2:47.

31. Tommaso de Vio Cajetan (1468–1534), *Evangelia cum commentariis* ([Paris]: Josse Badius, Jean Petit, Jean Roigny, 1532), cvii verso.

of Scripture, asserting that the mother of the Messiah would be a virgin" (Salmeron, vol. 3, tract. 7).[32] From these hypotheses, no vow is necessary.

6. Was Mary descended from the tribe of Aaron? The difference of opinions
XXIII. Sixth, whether the blessed Virgin descended from the tribe of Judah. The Jews, so that they may more effectively deny that our Jesus is the Messiah, falsely allege that Christians cannot show that his mother was from the tribe of Judah. Once Faustus the Manichean thought that Mary was descended from a father who was a priest (Augustine, *Against Faustus the Manichean*, bk. 23, ch. 9).[33] Baronio, from Augustine and other fathers, wants Anne, the mother of Mary, to have been the daughter of a priest, married to Joachim from the tribe of Judah, because the kingly and priestly tribes could be mixed (Baronio, *Apparatus*, §§30–32), namely so that "by a certain marvelous harmony, he might at once conjoin the mystery of both anointings, that is, the kingly and the priestly, in one and the same person of Christ, who took up the kingship and priesthood, and established a royal priesthood."[34] The imbecility of this reasoning, and the absurdities arising from it, Casaubon notes in *Exercises on Baronio* (ex. 1, no. 30).[35]

The reasons of the orthodox
All the orthodox uphold that she was descended only from the tribe of Judah, on account of: (1) prophecies (Gen. 49:10; Mic. 5:2), and (2) promises (1 Chron. 17:14; 2 Sam. 7:12–13, 16 with Luke 1:32–33; Isa. 11:1; etc.). (3) He is throughout Scripture called the son of David (Matt. 9:27; 15:22; Luke 20:41; Rom. 1:3). (4) His descent is nowhere asserted as from any other tribe than from the tribe of Judah, and he seems to have been so averse, as it were, to the tribe of Levi, that he called not even one of his apostles from it, which Casaubon observes in the cited passage. (5) The apostle declares this expressly in Hebrews 7:13–14, "He of whom these things are spoken pertains to another tribe, from which *no man* attended at the altar. For it is *evident* that our Lord arose from the tribe of Judah." (6) His priesthood is expressly referred not to the Aaronic order,

---

32. Alfonso Salmeron (1515–1585), *Commentarii in Evangelicam Historiam, et in Acta Apostolorum*, 16 vols. (Cologne: A. Hierat & J. Gymnicus, 1612), 3:62.

33. Augustine, *Contra Faustum Manichaeum libri XXXIII* in *PL* 42:471–72; idem, *Reply to Faustus the Manichaean* in *NPNF1* 4:315–16.

34. Cesare Baronio, "Apparatus ad Annales ecclesiasticos" in *Annales ecclesiastici* (Rome: Congregation of the Oratory of Holy Mary in Vallicella, 1593), 1:11–12.

35. Isaac Casaubon (1559–1614), *De rebus sacris et ecclesiasticis exercitationes XVI ad Cardinalis Baronii prolegomena in Annales, et primam eorum partem* (Frankfurt: Joannes Bringius, 1615), 70–72.

but to that of Melchizedek (Ps. 110:4; Heb. 7:11), from which also, with regard to the priesthood, he is said to be "without genealogy" (Heb. 7:3). (7) By both evangelists, Matthew in chapter 1 and Luke in chapter 3, the descent of Christ is referred to David and Judah. It is not a hindrance to this (a) that the genealogy of Joseph, not of Mary, seems to be explained by the evangelists, because: (i) the evangelists in their genealogy seem to embrace Joseph's descent at the same time as the blessed Virgin's, because, as all interpreters acknowledge, it was uncommon among the Hebrews to narrate genealogies through the women. (ii) Heli, who in Luke 3:23 is called the father of Joseph, could have been his father-in-law (as they are frequently called fathers), being in fact the father of Mary. (iii) Or that phrase, "who was of Heli," could be referred to Jesus himself, so that there would be a certain parenthetical opposition in the words, with this tenor, "Jesus himself, beginning to be about thirty years, being (as he was thought to be the son of Joseph) of Heli," namely, the son of Heli, that is, his grandson, because the evangelist did not have a father to put first, and he did not, from custom, have to refer to the mother in the genealogy. I need not add that (iv) Mary could have been a virgin heiress,[36] to whom, from the law (Num. 36:6, 8), it was not permitted to marry outside her tribe. Yet this does not satisfy Casaubon and other learned doctors, because not only was this regulation not observed, but it was restricted to that time in which the land was first distributed among the Israelites, and also because it could scarcely be proved that a poor virgin girl was an heiress. Nor is it hindered by (b) the diversity of the names which is observed in the genealogies of the two evangelists, because from it could not be solidly concluded that there were diverse tribes, "because most of the Jews had two names, and the υἵωσις, the receiving of someone as a son, and the giving of the name son, were contingent upon various causes, occurring, namely, either by nature, or from the law of Moses regarding raising up the seed of a dead brother, likewise by adoption or arrogation, and also on account of affinity, for a son-in-law was said to be a son to his father-in-law; add also succession to a kingship or a private inheritance, for such also are counted to be the sons of those whom they succeeded." These are the words of the most learned Casaubon.[37] It seemed good to represent these things at a little greater length, if perhaps they could shed some light on these most obscure genealogical quarrels.

The contrary objections

For the contrary opinion, namely that in which the blessed Virgin descended

---

36. ἐπίκληρος
37. Casaubon, *De rebus sacris*, 71.

either from the tribe of Levi, or from both Judah and Levi, it could be adduced: (1) that in Luke 1:36 Mary is said to be the συγγενής, relative, of Elizabeth, who is said to be of the daughters of Aaron (v. 5). But this is not a conclusive argument, for if the father of Elizabeth had joined to himself a wife from the tribe of Judah and the kin of the blessed Virgin, then certainly it would be correct to say that Elizabeth was related to Mary, but from this it would not be correct to say that Mary was descended from the tribe of Levi. (2) That among Joseph's ancestors, Luke mentions one named Levi. I respond, But those who read Ezra and Nehemiah attentively are not ignorant that the names of the patriarchs were common to all of the tribes. (3) That Christ was the highest priest, and therefore in his genealogy, Luke preferred to mention Nathan instead of Solomon, because the royal dignity was to be propagated to the descendants of David through Solomon, but the priesthood through Nathan. I respond, But, as we embrace with both arms that he was the highest priest, so from this we with Scripture deny that he derived his descent from the tribe of Levi, because he was a priest after the order of Melchizedek, not after that of Aaron (Heb. 7:11–13). Nor also can it be understood how David could have transferred to his son Nathan the Aaronic priesthood which he did not himself have.

7. Was the blessed Virgin free from all sin, and specifically, original sin?
The opinion of the papists
XXIV. Seventh, whether the blessed Virgin was ἀναμάρτητος, or free from all sin, as much original as actual. The papists here divide into factions: the Franciscans, Jesuits, and others think that she was entirely ἀναμάρτητος, lacking all sin. The Dominicans, although they agree with the others that she lacked actual sin, nevertheless vigorously defend that she was liable to original sin. This controversy caused the severest uproars in the papal realm, in the Council of Trent, in Spain, and elsewhere, as related by Paolo Sarpi in his *History of the Council of Trent*, and especially by Luke Wadding, the Irish Franciscan, in his particular volume *On the Legation of Philip III and Philip IV to Paul V and Gregory XV to Determine the Controversy over the Conception of the Virgin.*[38] Our Rivet presents

---

38. Paolo Sarpi (1552–1623), *Historiae Concilii Tridentini Libri Octo*, 5th ed. (Gorinchem: Paul Vink, 1658), 158–61. Regarding his thinly veiled pseudonym, Pietro Soave Polano, to avoid Venetian civil authorities, see D. Wootton, *Paulo Sarpi: Between Renaissance and Enlightenment* (Cambridge: Cambridge University Press, 1983), 105–106; Luke Wadding (1588–1657), ΠΡΕΣΒΕΙΑ *sive legatio Philippi III et Philippi IV Catholicorum regum Hispaniarum ad SS. DD. NN. Paulum PP. V. et Gregorium XV de definienda controversia immaculatae conceptionis B. Virginis Mariae* (Antwerp: Petrus Bellerus, 1641). Title translated according to Mastricht's own paraphrase.

the contents of this latter volume in summary form in his *Apology for the Virgin Mary* (bk. 1, ch. 5–8).[39]

The opinion of the Protestants

Protestants unanimously judge that she was not only liable to original sin, but also to actual infirmities. We have set forth the arguments on both sides in book 4, chapter 2, §XXVII. If anyone desires more on this matter, let him go to Chamier, *Panstratia catholica* (vol. 3, the whole of bk. 5),[40] Johann Gerhard, *Loci theologici* (vol. 2, loc. 12, §§112–121),[41] and Rivet's *Apology for the Virgin Mary* (bk. 1, ch. 4ff.).[42]

8. How could the Savior be born pure from a mother contaminated with sin?

The various opinions of various people

XXV. Eighth, how the Savior could be born sinless from a mother liable to the original stain, and also to actual infirmities. The Socinians cut the knot by thoroughly denying original sin and all propagation of sin, except that which occurs by imitation. The old Anabaptists, so that they may render the Savior immune from the original stain, state that he did not take his flesh in his conception and birth from the seed or substance of his mother, but brought it down from heaven. Among the fathers there are not lacking those who think that original sin is propagated only through the heat of lust in the begetting parents, which heat the Holy Spirit extinguished in the blessed Virgin, by overshadowing her, because shade usually makes one cooler. Others who hold to the propagation of the soul through seminal transfer think that it is only through the man's seed that the soul is propagated, and with it the original stain, or at least from the coinciding of the seed from both parents, and therefore, because the Savior was born from only a woman's seed, that original stain could not have been propagated to him. Still others think the propagation of that stain depends upon ordinary generation, and accordingly it does not pertain to Christ, who was born extraordinarily. Yet others want this to have been the case because the Holy Spirit purged the maternal seed from all corruption.

---

39. André Rivet, *Apologia pro sanctissima virgine Maria Matre Domini* (Leiden: Francis Heger and Francis Hackius, 1639), 30–58.

40. Daniel Chamier (1565–1621), *Panstratiae catholicae sive controversiarum de religione adversus pontificios corpus* (Geneva: Rovière, 1626), 109–56.

41. Gerhard, *Loci theologici*, 2:149–54.

42. Rivet, *Apologia pro Sanctissima Virgine Maria*, I.4, pp. 20–25.

The best opinion is chosen.
It would take forever to examine each of these and other opinions one by one; it should be sufficient to present the true cause of this immunity in a few points. Therefore, he was immune from the original stain, because: (1) he was not in Adam, at least not federally, when God contracted the covenant of works with him. He was certainly in him naturally, as in the head and root of human nature (from which Luke, recounting his genealogy in Luke 3, ascends all the way to Adam), but not federally, insofar as God did not reckon him in Adam (as God reckoned in Adam all his other posterity) when he prohibited him from eating of the fruit of the tree of the knowledge of good and evil, and thus contracted the covenant of nature. So then (2) he did not sin in Adam either, nor can that sin of our first parents be imputed to him. Accordingly, (3) he could not on account of this sin have been deprived of the original righteousness of the divine image, from the absence of which there exists in the mind that blindness by which a person does not perceive spiritual good in a spiritual way, and in the will that perverse propensity by which he is averse to all spiritual good, and inclined toward every evil. And in this consists the original stain. Therefore when it has been proved that he did not exist federally in Adam, the reason will be evident on account of which he was born immune to the original stain.

It is proved that the Savior was not federally in Adam.
Moreover, that he did not exist in Adam in this way is evident for these reasons, because: (1) God did not contract the covenant of works in Adam with the God-man, but with mere men. (2) He contracted it not with human nature as such, but with a human person, such as the Savior never was. (3) He contracted it with the first Adam, but not with the second, who for this cause is distinguished from the first. (4) He contracted with those who could sin (for to impute sin to one to whom sinning is repugnant is contrary to justice), but not with one who can in no way sin, such as Christ is, for this implies that the God-man is a sinner. I would add that (5) he contracted with those who, when the covenant was contracted, were to exist from the order of nature, but not with the Mediator who, when sin did not yet exist, was not to exist from the nature of things. I need not add that (6) he contracted with those who by the power of nature, in its ordinary manner, would be propagated from Adam, by which power and in which manner our Savior was not propagated from him. (Compare what we have said in book 3, chapter 12, §IX, and book 4, chapter 2, §XV).

9. Ought the blessed Virgin, the God-bearer, be adored? The opinion of the papists XXVI. Ninth, whether the blessed Virgin, because she is the God-bearer, ought to be attended with religious worship. The papists, emulators of the Collyridians, not content to have asserted for her the religious worship of *dulia*, reverence, by which they customarily attend the heavenly saints, allot to her the reverence of *hyperdulia*, special reverence, and although in their words they abrogate from her the glory of *latria*, divine worship that is proper to God, yet in deed they quite liberally arrogate it to her, when: (1) they load her with titles that require *latria*, by saluting her as *Domina Nostra, Regina Caeli*, Our Lady, the Queen of Heaven, to whom belongs a spiritual reign over all angels as well as men, and over their whole universe, in those things that concern grace and the goods of grace.[43] She not only has the right, that is, the authority, of jurisdiction over men, angels, and demons, but also the right of dominion, on account of which they truly and properly ought to be called bondservants made over to her, or slaves set under her dominion. For when that ought to be confessed regarding the son, it cannot reasonably be denied to the mother. Even all other irrational creatures are under the dominion of this great queen, and nothing is so proper to anyone that the Virgin does not have as it were an anticipated dominion over it, for no other judgment must be held regarding the mother other than that which is held regarding her son, the Lord Jesus Christ. These are the words of the Spanish Jesuit, Ferdinand Chirino de Salazar, in his commentary on Proverbs 31 (no. 202, 140).[44] (2) They define her religious worship by ten duties, which breathe of nothing but *latria*, divine worship: (a) external and internal honor, (b) the frequent repetition of the angelic greeting through the rosary, (c) invocation, (d) appointed holy days and feasts, (e) shrines, oratories, and altars erected to God in honor and memory of the Mother, (f) sacrifices for her glory, and offered in her honor to God, (g) vows made for her, and that terminate on her, (h) all sorts of images, whether sculpted or painted, whether located at crossroads and public squares or elsewhere, (i) pilgrimages to places holy to her and famous for miracles, which ought to be undergone with complete faith, great hope, fervent love, the purest intention, with a view toward the soul's enjoyment rather than the body's, and (j) confraternities established under her august name. All these duties of Marian worship are recounted in the *Manual of the*

---

43. Ferdinand Chirino de Salazar (1576–1640), *Expositio in Proverbia Salomonis* (Paris: Jerome Drouart and Denis Bechet, 1637), on Proverbs 31:29, no. 202, p. 603.

44. Summary of Salazar, *Expositio in Proverbia*, on Prov. 31:22, no. 140, p. 585; on 31:29, nos. 201–2, p. 603.

Confraternity of Blessed Mary collected by the Confraternity of Leige.[45] You could add to this (3) litanies, and especially the *Psalter of the Blessed Virgin*, in which all that is said of God in the Psalms is transferred to Mary, which is attributed to Bonaventure.[46]

The opinion of the Protestants
Protestants do freely attribute to her as much honor and civil worship as any creature allows: (1) by acknowledging and celebrating her eminent virtues, for which she was most renowned, also (2) by imitating them to the best of our ability through the grace of God, and especially (3) by acknowledging the grace whereby she surpasses all creatures, namely whereby she was chosen as the mother of the Messiah, of the God-man, and of God himself, whereby according to the angel she is highly favored, and blessed among women (Luke 1:28). But they dare not confer upon her the duties of religious worship, because: (1) God has reserved those for himself alone (Matt. 4:10; etc.); (2) they are beyond the nature and condition of every creature; and thus (3) they depart into manifest idolatry; (4) even the blessed Virgin herself, according to her singular modesty and humility (Luke 1:48), does not allow honor proper to God any more than the angels do (Rev. 19:10; 22:8). In favor of their Mariolatry, our adversaries cannot produce anything from the Scriptures—whether command, or example, or analogy of any sort—upon which to build the righteousness of this worship. And those things which they undertake to prove for this matter through scant logical consequences, as if from the nature of the matter, are so insignificant that they are not worthy to be recounted. I need not add that the extravagance of this worship is exceedingly distasteful to many papists in Spanish Belgium, on account of which many most severe quarrels have been stirred up against them by the Jesuits and others. Perhaps more points of this argument will occur in their own place, where we will speak expressly about religious worship.[47]

*10. From the operations of the Holy Spirit in the conception and birth, is the
Holy Spirit rightly called the Father of Christ, and Christ the Son of God?*
The opinion of the Socinians
XXVII. Tenth, whether from the operations of the Holy Spirit surrounding the conception and birth of Christ, the Holy Spirit is rightly called the Father of

---

45. François Véron (1575–1649), *Manuale sodalitatis B. Mariae V. …collectum olim a Sodal. Leodiens.* (Pont-à-Mousson Franciscus du Bois, 1608).

46. E.g. *Psalterium B. Mariae virginis, a S. Bonaventura editum* (Munich: Melchior Segen, 1642).

47. 2.2.1 §II. Cf. 2.2.13, on instituted worship.

Christ, and Christ the Son of God. The Socinians, who deny the eternal deity of Christ, so that they may more easily mock the Catholics' arguments in favor of this eternal deity, which are sought from those Scriptures that call him not only the Son of God, but also his own Son, and in addition the only begotten Son, state that in Christ's conception the Holy Spirit performed the role of a father properly so called, not only by making Mary fertile, but also by creating a certain substance, and sending it into the womb of the Virgin, from which, when it was conjoined with the seed of the Virgin, the Savior was conceived and born, who also from this operation of the Holy Spirit is called the Son of God.

The opinion of some of the orthodox. Their reasons are refuted.
Nor are there lacking those even among the orthodox, who though they receive the eternal deity of Christ, yet also affirm that from this operation of the Holy Spirit he can be called the Son of God according to the human nature. Their reasons are: (1) that there is promised an overshadowing of the Holy Spirit, through which there is modestly signified nothing other than the action of a father in procreating a son. I respond, It must not be presupposed but proven that, besides those operations of the Holy Spirit which we designated in the dogmatic part,[48] there was effected by the Holy Spirit any such operation as is signified by our adversaries. (2) That he is said to have been conceived *of* the Holy Spirit (Matt. 1:16, 20; Luke 1:35). I respond: The *of* is understood regarding Mary materially, and regarding the Holy Spirit only efficiently, with regard to power: "the power of the Most High," and so it occurs in Romans 11:36 and John 3:6. Moreover, (3) if on account of this generation of the Holy Spirit he was not the Son of God, then he would have become so afterwards, which both the text and the matter itself speak against. I respond, It would be true if he had not been begotten by the Father (Ps. 2:7; Prov. 8:22–31; Mic. 5:2), and not been the Son of God from that. (4) That in Luke 1:35 it is expressly said, "therefore also (διὸ καὶ) that holy thing which will be born of you will be called the Son of God." I respond, On account of that personal uniting of the divine person with the human nature, which was procured by the Holy Spirit, that entire complex consisting of the divine and the human nature will be called the Son of God, but not on account of that operation of the Holy Spirit alone. (5) That we are called sons of God because we are reborn of the Holy Spirit, so then much more must Christ be called the Son of God because he was conceived of the Holy Spirit. I respond, It is a most dissimilar reckoning, because Scripture everywhere declares regarding us that we are children of God through the grace of regeneration;

---

48. §V, above

regarding Christ it never says this. Therefore the orthodox more rightly deny that from this operation of the Holy Spirit surrounding the conception and birth of Christ, the Holy Spirit is his Father, and that from this operation of the Holy Spirit, either totally, as the Socinians want it, or partially with respect to the human nature, as others want it, is the Son of God.

The opinion of the orthodox is confirmed with reasons.
The reasons for this opinion we have previously noted in the dogmatic part, §V, to which we add that: (1) from the hypotheses of this opinion, in no way would he be "without father," contrary to Paul in Hebrews 7:3. (2) Scripture attributes to him only one Father, namely the first person of the Trinity (John 1:18; 5:17), from whom, by the mode of subsisting, the Holy Spirit is different. (3) Through his conception and birth, the Savior is said in the Scriptures to have been sent (John 3:16–17; Gal. 4:4; Rom. 8:3; etc.). But now, the Son is certainly said to send the Holy Spirit (John 15:26; 16:7), yet nowhere is he said to be sent by the Holy Spirit. (4) A father properly so called begets a son similar to himself through a communication of his essence, but the Holy Spirit by his operations did not produce one similar to himself, because he produced such a one who has flesh and bones, which do not belong to a spirit (Luke 24:39), nor also by these operations of his did he communicate his own essence to the one begotten, as even our adversaries confess. Also, (5) if the Savior, according to the human nature, on account of the conception of the Holy Spirit would be the Son of God, then in the one person, not only would the Son of God be distinguished from the Son of Man with respect to the natures, but also the Son of God would need to be distinguished from the Son of God, as the natures are distinguished in the person. I would add that (6) by this reasoning three sonships would be enumerated in one person, namely two divine—one with respect to the Father, the other to the Holy Spirit with regard to the human nature—and one human, with respect to his mother. I will go on to say that (7) in this way there would be two Fathers in the Trinity: the first, the first person with respect to the divine nature of Christ; the second, the third person with respect to his human nature. I need not mention that (8) from this opinion he would be *made* the Son of God, for he is said to have been made of a woman (Gal. 4:4), whereas according to the Scriptures (Psalm 2:7) and the Nicene Synod, he was *begotten*.

11. Did the formation of the body of Christ in the womb of his mother occur in a moment? The opinion of the Scholastics
XXVIII. Eleventh, whether the formation of the body of Christ in his mother's womb, procured by the Holy Spirit, was momentaneous or successive. The

Scholastics here distinguish between the separation and preparation of the matter, which the seed would provide; the formation of the body from that matter, with respect to the members; and the completion of the body and the development of the members. They admit that the separation and preparation did not occur in an instant, because it requires motion, which is not accomplished in a moment; and also they concede that the development occurred successively, because the mother bore the child for nine months; but they want the formation of his members to have been completed not only after forty-two days, in the usual manner, but in a moment, without delay or succession. The common people of papists follow them, so that from an extraordinary and miraculous method of conceiving, they may lend greater majesty to the Virgin; whereas the Scripture for the most part pursues those things which look to the greater humiliation of Christ.

The opinion of the Reformed
The Protestants, with several of the Scholastics, think that it is more agreeable to the Scriptures for the formation to have occurred successively, because: (1) in the history of the conception, gestation, and birth of John the Baptist the ordinary time is noted (Luke 1:38, 56–57), nor is anything different observed concerning the conception and birth of Christ (Luke 2:6). Therefore, since from these things they admit that the preparation and development of his body occurred successively, there is no reason for them to invent something extraordinary in the formation. (2) In the assumption of the human nature, which occurred through the conception and birth, it is said that he was made like us in all things except for sin (Phil. 2:6–7; Heb. 2:14–15, 17; 4:15). (3) The body of Christ when he was born grew outside the womb of the blessed Virgin according to the manner of others (Luke 2:40, 52). (4) Miracles ought not to be invented rashly beyond and outside of the Scriptures.

The reasons of the papists are examined.
On the contrary, most of the papists urge for their position: (1) that the Word assumed a human nature, not an unformed mass. I respond, We judge that the union with the divine person did not occur before there occurred a delineation of the organic parts and the union of them with a rational soul. (2) That the Holy Spirit could have formed him in a moment. I respond, It is not valid to argue from what can be to what is: the Holy Spirit could also have accomplished the separation and preparation of matter, and the development after birth, in a moment. (3) That the first Adam was formed suddenly, and so then the second also was. I respond: (a) Neither was the body of the first Adam formed in a

moment. (b) In that brief span of time in which the body of the first Adam was formed, it achieved its full stature, whereas the body of the second Adam achieved the fullness of this stature successively, as even our adversaries confess. (4) That if the body of Christ was not formed at one and the same time, the Word either was united to a body not yet formed or human (which, as everyone acknowledges, is absurd), or, if the Word was not united to it, this body existed unformed without the Word. I respond, It existed not yet formed, just as it existed when it was being prepared, and even before it was being prepared in the conception, that is, in its causes. But it did not subsist, just as it also did not subsist after the union with the Word; nor before the formation of the parts, or before it was a human body, did it exist personally sustained by the Word, as it began to exist when it was united with the Word, which happened at that time when the body was at last formed, and made a human body.

12. Was he born with the womb of Mary closed, and also without birth pangs?
The opinion and basis of the papists and the Lutherans
XXIX. Twelfth, whether he was born with the womb closed, and so then without birth pangs in the one giving birth. The papists, not only so that they may hunt for miracles in favor of their Mariolatry, but also so that they may more easily show how the body of Christ is in heaven and simultaneously in the sacrament, such that he is not in the middle, repeatedly teach that Christ was born not by passing through the middle, but by immediately leaping from one extreme to the other. The Lutherans also, so that they may more effectively demonstrate that the body of Christ in the resurrection passed through the stone of the tomb, and afterwards through closed doors, affirm that Christ was born with Mary's womb closed. The basis for this opinion is in this alone: that the opening of the womb and the hymen[49] would take away her virginity, when virginity is not actually taken away by anything other than marital congress.

The opinion of the Reformed with their reasons
On the contrary, the Reformed, according to the simple account of Scripture, teach that he was born in an ordinary way, because: (1) just as the children are made partakers of flesh and blood, Christ partook most closely of the same (Heb. 2:14). (2) He was quite openly numbered among those who opened the womb of their mothers (Luke 2:22–23). (3) Otherwise, he would not have been truly born, because being born is nothing but passing out of the womb. (4) The penetration of dimensions presupposes a contradiction, because (a) to be a body

____

49. *claustri virginalis*

is to have a part outside a part,[50] which parts are distinguished by a specific space; and thus a body in a body, by the penetration of dimensions, is not a body. (b) By this penetration of dimensions, or existence of two bodies in the same space, two bodies would be one body.

13. Was the body of Christ formed from the very substance of the blessed Virgin?
XXX. Thirteenth, whether the body of Christ was formed from the very substance or seed of the blessed Virgin. We have spoken about the various opinions of the ancient heretics above, in chapter 4, §XVIII. The modern Anabaptists think that the body of Christ received entirely nothing of the substance of the blessed Virgin, that is, so that they would not be compelled to admit that the Savior was liable with us to the original stain. The Socinians, so that they may not be compelled to grant that Christ is the Son of God from his eternal generation, and thus God from eternity, do admit that Christ as man was not begotten from the very substance of God, indeed that he received his substance from that of his mother, no less than others receive it from their mothers, but yet they also invent the idea that the power of God, the *virtus Dei*, that is, the Holy Spirit, sent into the womb of the Virgin a certain immediately created substance, from which, once it was joined with the Virgin's substance, a true man was begotten, who from this cause is called the Son of God.

The opinion of the orthodox with their reasons
The orthodox on the contrary state that he received his body only from the substance of the Virgin, because: (1) he is expressly said to be the seed of the woman (Gen. 3:15 with Heb. 2:14), the seed of Abraham (Gen. 22:18; Gal. 3:16), of the seed of David (Rom. 1:3; Acts 13:23). (2) He is said to be the fruit of Mary's womb (Luke 1:42), the fruit of the loins of David (Acts 2:30), according to the promise (2 Sam. 7:12; 1 Kings 17:11). (3) The terms conception, impregnation, and birth are employed by Scripture in this generation (Matt. 1:16, 18, 20, 23; and elsewhere). (4) He is throughout called the Son of Man preeminently (Matt. 8:20; 9:6; etc.), in fact the son of Mary (Mark 6:3), just as Mary in turn is called the mother of Jesus (Matt. 1:18; Luke 1:43; John 19:25). (5) His genealogy is drawn from Adam to the blessed Virgin and the husband betrothed to her.

The objections of our adversaries
It is no hindrance: (1) that he is said to have been conceived of the Holy Spirit (Matt. 1:18, 20). I respond: (a) the preposition *of* does not always designate the

---

50. *habere partem extra partem.* That is, to have spatial extension. Cf. 1.2.6. §VII; 1.3.6 §VIII; 1.5.15 §XVII.

material cause, but sometimes the efficient cause (Rom. 11:36). (b) The Socinians themselves do not admit that he was conceived of the substance of God or the Holy Spirit. (2) That he is said to be the bread of God which comes down from heaven (John 6:33, 51). I respond, He is spoken of in this way from the divine person, who came down by the incarnation, when he was manifested in the flesh (1 Tim. 3:16), just as God is said to come down when he makes manifest his extraordinary presence by a certain extraordinary sign (Gen. 18:2, 20–21). (3) That he is called the Lord from heaven (1 Cor. 15:47). I respond, Likewise with respect to the divine person, who, in the way that we have said, came down from heaven. (4) That if he had taken his body from Mary, it would be liable to the original stain (John 3:6). I respond, In what way he was nevertheless immune to this stain, we have already expressly explained in §XXV.

14. Was Christ from the first instant of his conception a pilgrim and simultaneously a comprehensor? The opinion of our adversaries. The opinion of the Reformed and its reasons

XXXI. Fourteenth, whether Christ from the first moment of conception was a pilgrim and simultaneously a comprehensor, lacking all ignorance and imperfection, with respect to the human nature. The papists answer in the affirmative,[51] with whom here the Lutherans collude in favor of their perverse communication of attributes. The Reformed admit that at the first moment of conception he received the fullness of grace with respect to the first act, as they say (John 1:14; Luke 2:40), yet in such a way that it could be augmented with respect to second acts, and through extension to new objects, because: (1) he is said to have increased in wisdom and stature (Luke 2:52); (2) he labored under a kind of unknowing, rather than ignorance (Mark 13:32; 11:13);[52] (3) he is observed in the Scriptures to be liable to various infirmities, although without any sin; (4) he is declared in the Scriptures to be liable to sadness, fear, and other affections which breathe of imperfection; (5) to be a pilgrim and simultaneously a comprehensor is to walk by faith and by sight simultaneously, which two things Scripture opposes to each other (2 Cor. 5:7; 1 Cor. 13:12; 2 Cor. 3:18). Nor do they have anything to object except those passages (John 1:14; Luke 2:40; etc.) which we have already sufficiently answered. We dispatched the controversies

---

51. Cf. Aquinas, *Summa theologiae* (*ST*), I, q. 113, art. 1, ad 1; IIa IIae, q. 17, art. 2, ad 1; III, q. 8, art. 4, ad 2.

52. *qualicunque nescientia, potius quam ignorantia*

about the personal union of the two natures in Christ in their own place, in chapter 4 on the person of the Mediator.[53]

The Practical Part

The conception and birth of Christ: 1. Strengthens our faith regarding the Messiah who has been exhibited. From testimonies

XXXII. We have already dealt with the practice of Christ's incarnation in chapter 4, and there is not anything remaining here except that we make somewhat of a gleaning. Therefore, first, the conception and birth of Jesus exceedingly strengthens our faith, because the Messiah once promised has undoubtedly come, and because our Jesus, and he alone, is that Messiah. For the following offer testimony to him: (1) the foretelling angel Gabriel, sent by God to Nazareth to his mother herself, that he might make known to her the Messiah's conception and birth (Luke 1:26, 31, 35). (2) The angel who announces that he had already been born (Luke 2:11). (3) The whole host of angels, with hymns celebrating God from the birth of the Messiah (vv. 13–14). In addition, (4) the experience of the shepherds, who at the instruction of the angel, diligently sought and found him (vv. 15–16). (5) The experience of the wise men, who with such great zeal and preparation, instructed through the extraordinary star, sought and found him (Matt. 2:1–13). (6) The experience of Simeon, who instructed by the oracle of the Holy Spirit in a prophecy, after he had taken him in his arms, full of joy praised God on this account (Luke 2:25–36). (7) The experience of Anna the prophetess (Luke 2:36). Let us add (8) the experience of John the Baptist, also pointing his finger to him (John 1:15, 19, 29). Thus in these we have every kind of witness: angels and men, male and female, learned and unlearned.

From the circumstances

To all these things is added (9) the testimony of the matter itself, when in the history of the conception and birth, we observe all those circumstances which were foretold of the Messiah. For if: (a) you should attend to the time, he was born to a Jewish people subjugated to the Romans, when Augustus, as an indicator of this fact, registered the nation under a census (Luke 2:1), so accordingly the scepter and lawgiver had been taken away, which had been foretold (Gen. 49:10), when the seventy weeks of years had just been fulfilled (Dan. 9:24), while the second temple was still standing (Hag. 2:9; Mal. 3:1). If (b) you should look to the place, he was born in Bethlehem, according to prophecy (Mic. 5:2). If

---

53. 1.5.4 §XXff.

(c) to the family, he was born from the tribe of Judah, as the Son and Branch of David (Luke 3:23ff.; Matt. 1:1–16), according to what was foretold (Gen. 49:10, Isa. 11:1; etc.). If (d) to the parent, he was born of a virgin (Luke 1:27, 34), so that he might be that seed of the woman which was foretold (Gen. 3:15; Isa. 7:14). If (e) to the forerunner, he was born after John the Baptist (Luke 1:13, 17), which was foretold (Mal. 3:1; 4:5; Isa. 40:3–5). Nor can there be shown from the Scriptures any circumstance foretold of the conception and birth of the Messiah which is not clearly seen in the conception and birth of our Jesus. So now no reason will allow even the least bit of hesitation concerning the double truth fundamental to the Christian faith, namely that: (1) the Messiah has already been born, and (2) our Jesus is that Messiah. Therefore, with faith well confirmed in these things, we will also be more prompt, first: (1) to hope for the benefits which are so abundantly promised to us in the Messiah, then (2) to give in return to the Messiah those duties which we owe to the Messiah, about which it will be our task to philosophize a little more abundantly in the things to follow.

2. It urges us to strive to fully explore the mystery of the incarnation. Motives XXXIII. Second, it urges us, now persuaded by so many testimonies of angels, of men, and of the matter itself regarding the truth of our incarnate Messiah, to stir up ourselves and others, as much as can be done, to examine and investigate the mystery of the incarnation, so great and excellent as it is. By the example: (1) of the shepherds (Luke 2:15), who when the heralding angels had first departed, stirred each other up, "Let us certainly go even to Jerusalem and see that word which the Lord has made known to us." (2) Of Moses (Ex. 3:2–3), who when the angel of Jehovah appeared to him in the midst of the bush that burned and was not consumed, stirred himself up, "I will now turn aside to see this great sight." (3) Of so many prophets and kings in the Old Testament (Luke 10:24), who longed to see what the apostles saw, namely the Messiah incarnate; and in particular the example of Abraham (John 8:56), and of the entire ancient church (Isa. 64:1). Indeed, (4) of the very angels themselves, "things into which the angels long to look" (1 Peter 1:12; cf. Ex. 25:20). Also inviting us to this is (5) the majesty of the thing itself, inasmuch as it presents to us a mystery, a great mystery, without controversy great, the mystery of godliness, or of the Christian faith (1 Tim. 3:16), a mystery enveloped in silence from the times of the ages (Rom. 16:25), from which the first name of the one incarnate is Wonderful (Isa. 9:6). And so also (6) its sweetness, apt for stirring up the sweetest joy, "Fear not, for behold, I declare to you great joy" (Luke 2:10).

To what end

Therefore let us endeavor to see it, and not only be content to hear it, so that: (1) we may know it more and more, so then that we may search into it carefully, like the prophets: "Of which salvation the prophets have inquired and searched diligently" (ἐξεζήτησαν καὶ ἐξηρεύνησαν, 1 Peter 1:10; cf. Luke 2:19). (2) We may marvel at it, with the blessed Virgin (Luke 1:34), with the shepherds and their hearers (Luke 2:15, 18; cf. above, ch. 4, §XXXV). (3) We may declare it to others, with the angel, "I declare to you" (Luke 2:10), and the shepherds, "And when they had seen it, they made it known abroad" (v. 17). (4) We may hold to it in an obliging way, that we may not with excessive curiosity pry into its component mysteries, for example, of the virgin birth, of the union of the two natures, so that we should say, "How can this be?" (Luke 1:34), as we are prohibited from this by God himself (Ex. 3:5; cf. ch. 4, §XXXVI).

3. It calls us to the glorification of God.

XXXIV. Third, It calls us to the glorification of God, by the example of the angelic host singing, "Glory to God in the highest" (Luke 2:13–14), and of the shepherds (Luke 2:20), of Simeon (Luke 2:28), and of the blessed Virgin herself (Luke 1:46). For this is the chief goal, as of the whole of redemption, so also of this incarnation (Eph. 1:6), and in this incarnation are evident the most glorious perfections of God. For example: (1) the glory of the divine faithfulness and constancy, in keeping his promises, from the fact that the Messiah who was promised so many times, in such a holy way, and also for so long a time, he presented so carefully, at the appointed time (Gal. 4:4) and place (Mic. 5:2–3), and in agreement with the other circumstances as foretold. (2) The glory of providence, by which he so wisely conjoined both Augustus and his registration of the world, and the parents of the Savior, that they might go to Bethlehem, so that at precisely that time and place the Messiah might be exhibited to the world. And also he so powerfully preserved him against the treacheries and attacks of Herod, so that they could not cause him one whit of harm. (3) The glory of wisdom, (4) the glory of avenging justice, (5) the glory of goodness, grace, and mercy, (6) the glory of omnipotence: about these we taught individually above in chapter 4, §XXXV.

4. It molds us in thankfulness toward God. Motivating reasons

XXXV. Fourth, it molds us in thankfulness toward God, who led by pure, unadulterated grace and love for mankind, by the incarnation of his Son, gave us a gift greater than which one can neither be thought of, nor exist (Isa. 9:6; John 3:16; 4:10). We will acknowledge this even more if we should more distinctly consider: (1) the giver, the all-sufficient God, אֵל שַׁדַּי, El Shaddai (Gen. 17:1), the one who could promise himself absolutely no benefit from such a gift (cf. Ps. 16:2; 50:8–13); (2) those to whom he gave, men who are nothing but dust and ashes (Gen. 18:27; Isa. 40:15, 17), horrendous sinners, liable to every kind of death and eternal condemnation (Rom. 5:6, 8); (3) the gift, which is (a) the product of grace and favor, not of the common sort, such as all earthly things are, but special and saving, "For God so loved the world" (John 3:16), which is incompatible with hatred, unlike all other gifts of God, no matter how excellent. It is (b) eternal, not only arising from eternal love, but also enduring for eternity, that is, of the kind of gifts that the apostle calls "without repentance" (Rom. 11:29), of which not even death can deprive us (Rom. 8:38). (c) Extending to the soul itself, and capable of satisfying it (Ps. 73:25; 16:5–6; cf. Isa. 55:2; Gen. 33:11 with v. 9). (d) Including all other gifts, from which he is called a bundle (Song 1:13–14), and the apostle says that God has blessed us with every heavenly blessing in Christ Jesus (Eph. 1:3), so that from his grace we can draw grace for grace (John 1:16; cf. 1 Cor. 1:30; 3:22). (e) Sanctifying all other gifts, and repairing the defects of all others, without which all others are "gifts that are no gifts, and do no good"[54] (cf. Gen. 15:2 with 12:3), for Christ is all in all (Col. 3:11), and in him the beloved, we and all that we have are beloved (Eph. 1:6). It is (f) an altogether wonderful gift (Isa. 9:6), profitable for all things, because you can get even more use from Christ than the apostle could from godliness (1 Tim. 4:8). For he is: (i) in any difficulty, the Counselor, (ii) in any hopeless circumstance, the Mighty God, (iii) in any inconstancy and changeability, the Father of Eternity, (iv) in any hostility, with God, with men, with our own conscience, in any restlessness, our Prince of Peace (Isa. 9:6). In all these things and many others, are there not abundant reasons that ought to stir us up to thankfulness?

The manner of this thankfulness

By this thankfulness: (1) from the heart we should love God (Ps. 18:1), who so loved us that he gave to us his only begotten Son (John 3:16). (2) As if constrained by this love (2 Cor. 5:14), we should readily render back to him all of our most beloved things, even to our very selves, and our own life (Matt. 10:37; 2 Cor. 8:5; Matt 16:24–25), just as he conferred his most beloved one to us (Matt. 17:5), and in him, his own self, out of pure grace. (3) We should also eagerly expend ourselves and all we have, for all his employments (Phil. 1:20–21;

---

54. δῶρα ἄδωρα, καὶ μὴ ὀνήσιμα. Sophocles, *Ajax*, 665.

Acts 20:24). (4) Even when lacking all other gifts, wealth, honors, pleasures, health, we should calmly rest in this one gift (Ps. 73:25; 16:5–6; Phil. 3:7–9).

5. It instructs us to inquire whether he is born for us, and given for us.
Motivating arguments
XXXVI. Fifth, we should inquire whether the child is born *for us*, and the Son is given *for us* (Isa. 9:6), so that to us also may be made the angelic proclamation, "*To you* is born this day the Savior" (Luke 2:11). For (1) what does it help for him to be born and given for all kinds of people, if he is not given and born for us? And (2) even if he is given and born for us, what joy or comfort will it bring us if we should not by certain indications be persuaded of it? And (3) how will we be certainly persuaded of it without a careful inquiry? And indeed, (4) will it not increase our anxiety immeasurably if there should be born for the world so great and such a kind of Savior, in whom we have no participation, no association? Who is set up for our fall (Luke 2:34)? For a stone of stumbling and a rock of offense (Rom. 9:33)? Concerning whom accordingly we must exclaim in horror with Satan, "What have I to do with you, Son of the Most High God? I adjure you not to torment me" (Mark 5:7), or, "Have you come to destroy us?" (Luke 4:34)?

Signs
But by what marks then will we certainly attain to this? I respond: (1) If we believe in him, "For God so loved the world that he gave his only begotten Son, that whosoever believes in him should not perish, but have eternal life" (John 3:16). If (2) by believing we receive him as he comes, for "He came to his own, and his own did not receive him, but as many as did receive him" (John 1:11–12). If (3) we receive him by such faith which is at work through love (Gal. 5:6). If (4) we sense not only that he has been given for us, but that in turn we have been given to him by the Father (John 17:9). Compare the things we said in chapter 4, §XXXII.

6. It encourages us to seek the one who was born. Motivating reasons
XXXVII. Sixth, if we should not yet detect that he was born for us, given for us, then let us seek him so that he may be ours, by the example of the shepherds of Bethlehem (Luke 2:15), and of the wise men (Matt 2:1ff.), that we may be (1) stirred up by the angels (Luke 2:12), with (2) the star summoning and guiding us (Matt. 2:2, 10; Num. 24:17), (3) his very enemies themselves informing us (Matt. 2:4–6), (4) God commanding us (Isa. 55:6; 2 Chron. 15:2), (5) the example of his parents leading us (Luke 2:44–45, 48), (6) the very excellence

of the thing to be sought urging us on (1 Peter 2:4, 6–7), as also its usefulness, inasmuch as he is all in all for us (Col. 3:11), in him alone we are complete (Col. 2:10), as well as its necessity, inasmuch as apart from him there is no salvation at all (Acts 4:12), without him no one comes to the Father (John 14:6), without him we can do nothing (John 15:5), and so forth.

In what manner
Let us seek him: (1) not with hatred, like Herod (Matt. 2:13), nor only with our lips, or all mere external duties (Isa. 29:13; Matt. 15:7–8), like Judas (Matt. 26:47–49), or for the sake of bread or profit (John 6:26), but with love and with our heart (Song 3:2), on his account (Ps. 73:25). Let us seek him (2) with a most ardent desire (Isa. 64:1), as if with hunger and thirst (Ps. 42:1; Isa. 55:1; Matt. 5:6). Let us seek him (3) with indefatigable toil and zeal, like the wise men (Matt. 2:1ff.), with an arduous and lengthy journey, with a diligent search; and like the shepherds (Luke 2:15–16), quickly, as soon as the heralding angels had departed, at night, having left their flocks, and stirring up each other to this end. Let us seek him (4) in Bethlehem (Luke 2:11, 15), in the temple (Luke 2:27), where he is according to his promise (Matt. 18:20; Ex. 20:24). Let us seek him (5) in the stable, in the manger, in the swaddling cloths (Luke 2:7), not in some splendid palace: that is, let us seek the lowly one in a lowly fashion, without pomp or pride (Matt. 8:19–20 with 20:20–24).

7. It stirs us up to eagerly receive the one who comes.
XXXVIII. Seventh, let us also readily and eagerly receive the one who comes to us in his incarnation, according to the example of Simeon (Luke 2:28), lest from us also be supplied to him that cause for his complaining, which was supplied from the Jews, "He came to his own, and his own did not receive him" (John 1:11), or we also fall into the ingratitude of Bethlehem, which had no room for him, but sent him to a stable with the livestock (Luke 2:7; cf. 9:52–54). Therefore, let us receive him in our cities, in our churches, in Bethlehem, in our homes and not our stables, in our families (Col. 3:16), in our arms, that is, in our hearts (Luke 2:28), that he may dwell in our hearts (Eph. 3:17).

The motivating reasons
For to this end: (1) we are so splendidly summoned, "Lift up your heads, O gates, lift up yourselves, O ancient doors, that the King of glory may come in" (Ps. 24:7–10). To this end (2) his forerunner, John the Baptist, was sent to prepare the way, that the Lord might come to his temple (Luke 1:76; Matt. 3:3; Isa. 40:3; Mal. 3:1). Inviting us to this in addition is (3) the very one to be received:

not some common man, not even an angel, but the Lord of glory (Ps. 24:7; 1 Cor. 2:8), the King of kings and Lord of lords (Rev. 19:16). And because (4) in receiving him he becomes ours, the one born to us, given to us (Isa. 9:6), so that we can say with the blessed Virgin, "God my Savior" (Luke 1:47), and apply to ourselves that angelic pronouncement, "*To you* this day is born a Savior" (Luke 2:11). In addition, because (5) in receiving him, he is united with us, and dwells in our hearts (Eph. 3:17), and becomes our brother (Heb. 2:11–13), and we, together with the one received and united to us, become the sons of God (Gal. 4:4–5; John 1:12; 20:17). Also because (6) in receiving him, we receive all that is his (Rom. 8:32; 1 Cor. 3:21–22). Furthermore, (7) if we receive his ambassadors for his sake (Matt. 10:41; Gal. 4:14–15; Matt. 18:5–6), would we not receive him all the more for his own sake? Let me add that (8) in receiving him, we will receive salvation (Luke 19:6; cf. 10:39, 42). This is not to mention that (9) if we have received him here by his grace, it will be that he in turn receives us into his glory (Matt. 25:34; Acts 7:59).

The manner of receiving

However, we must receive him: (1) with our arms (Luke 2:28), the arms of true and living faith (John 1:12), that by it we take him into our house, just as John took Christ's mother (John 19:27; Song 3:4), so that he may dwell with us (Eph. 3:17). We must receive (2) and lay him in the manger of our heart (Luke 2:7), that is, (a) with the tenderest love, or with great joy (Luke 19:6), (b) with the greatest esteem (Song 5:10; Phil. 3:7–8; cf. Phil. 2:29), (c) with an insuperable vigor, with our whole heart (Acts 8:37; Jer. 29:13). We must receive him (3) as the Savior (Luke 2:11; 1:69), and indeed as the one and only Savior (1 Tim. 2:5), in whom we place all our confidence (Acts 4:12), who is our all in all (Col. 3:11), who is our sun for warming us to life, and our shield for protecting us (Ps. 84:12), who is our nourishment (John 6:48, 55–56), and our covering (Rom. 13:14; Isa. 61:10). We must receive him (4) as our King (Luke 1:31–32), to whom we subject ourselves with the utmost devotion (Ps. 2:11–12; Luke 19:11, 27). We must receive him (5) not only as a king on the throne, in his glory (Matt. 20:20–21), but also as a child in the stable, in the manger, in his misery, that is, not only that we may reign with him, but also that we may suffer with him (2 Tim. 2:12; Rom. 8:17), not only that we may be possessed of his goods, but also that we may be stripped of our goods (Matt. 19:27; Phil. 3:7–8; 1 Cor. 4:13). Thus at last will we receive him by those laws by which he offers himself to us, and wills to be received by us (Matt. 16:24; Luke 14:26). We must receive him (6) in the correct way, whereby we receive not only his goods, but also his person, and first indeed his person, then his goods; first him, then from him, the adoption of sons (John

1:12); that is to say, let us receive him in that way in which the Father delivers him (Rom. 8:32): he delivers first his Son, then with him, all things.

8. It invites us to joy. The motivating reasons
XXXIX. Eighth, let us rejoice and delight in the one received. For to this end the angel proclaims great joy (Luke 2:10), that: (1) by his birth we may possess him for whom the ancients sighed under such great powerlessness, "O that you would rend heaven and come down, and the mountains would flow down at your face!" (Isa. 64:1), whose day, that is, whose day of birth, Abraham so eagerly desired to see, and when in spirit he had seen it from afar, he so greatly rejoiced (John 8:56; cf. Gen. 17:17). And after him, Jacob the patriarch, in his very anguish, was so greatly revived and delighted by the thought and desire of it that he abruptly cried out, "I wait for your salvation, O Lord" (Gen. 49:18). Moreover, though in false hope, Eve, when she had given birth to that wretch Cain, exclaimed, קניתי איש את יהוה, "I have gotten a man, the Lord!" (Gen. 4:1).[55] So that most deservedly the Savior pronounces his disciples so blessed on this account (Luke 10:24; cf. Heb. 11:13). Hence the blessed Virgin, due to the promise of the Messiah that would be born from her, so greatly exulted in God her Savior (Luke 1:47). (2) By this birth of the Savior, such a friendly approach of God has been made toward us (Luke 1:41, 43; cf. Isa. 59:2; Eph. 4:18 with John 14:6; 1:9; Isa. 9:2; 60:2). (3) By the same birth, such a close kinship has been made of us with God and the Son of God (Eph. 5:30; Heb. 2:11; 2 Peter 1:4; John 1:12). Indeed even (4) a certain spiritual betrothal (Isa. 62:5; Ezek. 16:8; Hos. 2:19; Eph. 5:29).

The means of seeking joy
Moreover, since joy of any sort arises for us especially from three things—from the excellence of the good possessed, from the certainty of the possession, and from the use of the good possessed—it will help, that we may be filled more sweetly with that joy: (1) to think frequently and devoutly upon the excellence and preeminence of the Savior born and given for us, after the example of Mary and Joseph (Luke 2:19, 33). (2) To take diligent care that we may be infallibly certain of our possession of him, or that we may be persuaded that he was born for us, given for us (Isa. 9:6; Luke 2:11), which will happen by careful exploration of ourselves, which we urged in §XXXVI. (3) In any presented occasion, to use and enjoy the Savior born and given for us: for example, in doubtful matters, as the Counselor; in hard and difficult matters, as our hero or the Mighty God; in matters troubled by enmity with men, with conscience, with God, as the Prince

---

55. Cf. on Gen. 4:1, Matthew Poole, *Synopsis criticorum*, 1:51.

of Peace; in the vanity of things, their inconstancy, or the fear of death, as the Father of Eternity; and so forth.

9. To the duty that must be offered to the one born

XL. Ninth, while we rejoice in the benefits of the Savior born and given for us, we should in turn faithfully direct our duties back to him, after the example of the blessed Virgin (Luke 2:7), of Joseph (Matt. 2:13–14), of the wise men (Matt. 2:11). For how will the Savior who was born bestow his benefits upon us, if we have withdrawn from him his duties? By what argument will we be persuaded that he was born for us, given for us, if we faithlessly take away from him the things that he is due?

The fourfold duty

But what then are these duties? I respond: (1) the duty of reverence and adoration, which the wise men offered to him (Matt. 2:11, "They fell down and worshiped him"), that is, as to God (Ps. 95:6; Matt. 4:10). (2) The duty of subjection and homage, as to a king (Ps. 2:12), by which we should kiss the Son, with a kiss: (a) on the mouth, or of love (Song 1:2; 8:1; 2 Sam. 19:39; Gen. 48:10); (b) on the hands, or of universal dependence (Sirach 29:5), because he sustains all things with his hands (Heb. 1:3; Ps. 8:3; 102:25); (c) on the feet, even of submission (Luke 7:38, 46), for under them God has subjected all things to him (Ps. 8:6; 1 Cor. 15:27; Heb. 2:8; Eph. 4:10). (3) The duty of giving gifts, by which with the wise men (Matt. 2:11) we should open our treasures, and from them bring out and offer to him: (a) gold, that is, we should expend all the most precious things among our goods for his uses, and for the preservation of his own (Prov. 3:9; John 12:3, 5; Acts 2:45); (b) frankincense, that is, sacrifices, prayers, praises (Ps. 141:2; Rev. 5:8; Ps. 50:14–15; Mal. 1:11); and (c) myrrh, that is, serious repentance, certainly bitter (Matt. 26:75), but quite fragrant (Luke 15:10). (4) Finally, the duty of celebration, of doxology, after the example of the angelic host crying out, "Glory to God in the highest" (Luke 2:14), of the blessed Virgin (Luke 1:46–55), of the shepherds (Luke 2:20), of Simeon (Luke 2:28–33; cf. Rev. 5:9–10; Eph. 5:19).

10. To the spiritual conception and birth of Christ in our hearts

XLI. Tenth, let us strive with every effort to conceive the spiritual Christ within us, in a spiritual way through conversion to bear and form him in our hearts, and finally to give birth to him and bring him forth in public in our manner of life. The apostle lays the foundation of this practice in Galatians 4:19, "My little children, for whom I labor in birth again until Christ be formed in you" (see also Rev. 12:1–2, 5), and perhaps also the Savior himself in Matthew 12:48–50, "Behold, my mother.... For whoever has done the will of my Father in heaven, that one is my...mother." For those things which occurred in the natural conception and birth of the natural Christ concerning the blessed Virgin, also occur in their own way in the spiritual conception and birth of the spiritual Christ (which occurs by regeneration and conversion). But here by the spiritual Christ we do not understand anything other than conformity to Christ, arising from his union with our soul, and by means of this, the life and strength of Christ communicated to it, from which we live for Christ, and Christ lives in us, as the apostle teaches (Gal. 2:20), which conformity is procured in our regeneration, conversion, and sanctification.

Its triple principle: (1) The passive principle, namely, a heart that is virgin, betrothed to God, perpetual in virginity

Therefore, so that we may perceive the analogy of this double birth of Christ, natural and spiritual, that which occurred outside of us in the blessed Virgin, and that which occurs inside of us in our hearts, it will help to compare, first, the triple principle of natural birth, namely: (1) the passive principle, the blessed Virgin and her womb, whose fruit Christ is declared to be (Luke 1:42), (2) the material principle, the seed of the blessed Virgin, from which his flesh was conceived and formed, (3) the active principle, the Holy Spirit who came upon her, and the power of the Most High which overshadowed her (Luke 1:35). Let us also note the triple principle, analogous to this one, in his spiritual generation, namely: (1) the passive principle, instead of the blessed Virgin, is the heart of each of the elect, from which he is said to be *in us* (ἐν ὑμῖν, "in you," Gal. 4:19) and to dwell in our hearts (Eph. 3:17). Moreover, just as: (a) in the natural birth, the mother was a virgin (Isa. 7:14), untouched and undefiled by a man (Luke 1:34), so in his spiritual birth, there is required a virgin heart, untouched by the world and worldly lusts (2 Cor. 11:2; Rev. 14:4; Jude 8). For just as the high priest of old, in order to beget a high priest, had to marry not a prostitute, nor a widow, but a virgin (Lev. 21:13), so also the high priest Jesus does not will to be conceived and born except in a virgin heart. Also just as (b) in his natural birth, his virgin mother was betrothed (Luke 1:27), so for the spiritual birth, a heart is required that is betrothed to God (Hos. 2:19; Ezek. 16:8; cf. Ruth 3:9). Furthermore, just as (c) in the natural birth, his mother remained a virgin (to which end the fathers employ Ezekiel 44:2), so for his spiritual birth, a heart is required that is constant in spiritual virginity (Song 4:12).

(2) The material principle, the Word of God. (3) The active principle, the Holy Spirit

(2) The material principle, instead of the seed of the blessed Virgin, in his spiritual birth is the Word of God (1 Peter 1:23; 1 John 3:9; James 1:18), from which the spiritual Christ, or conformity to Christ, is born. (3) The active principle, as in the natural birth (Luke 1:35), so also in his spiritual birth, is the Holy Spirit (John 3:5–6), without whose spiritual coming upon us and overshadowing us, neither the mother nor the seed can do anything toward this spiritual birth (Rom. 15:19; John 6:63; 1 Cor. 3:7), and so through the Spirit both the mother and the seed must be made fertile.

The triple period of spiritual birth: (1) Spiritual conception, or regeneration

Besides this triple principle in this spiritual birth, likewise as in Christ's natural birth, there occurs a triple period, that of conception, of formation, and of delivery. For just as (1) in his natural birth there was a conception that included the presence of a seed, and a vivification of the same (Matt. 1:20; Luke 1:31), so also the spiritual birth requires a conception, in which the spiritual seed: (a) is received, by the hearing of the Word (Matt. 13:23; Rom. 10:17), just as also in his natural conception the word of promise was received by the blessed Virgin from the announcing angel (Luke 1:30–39); (b) is vivified (John 6:63), because otherwise it is dead (2 Cor. 3:6). This spiritual conception is accomplished by regeneration more strictly so called, in which the Word is spiritually received, the heart is spiritually vivified, and, when the first act of spiritual life has been infused, the seeds of all saving virtues are conferred upon the soul (John 3:3, 5, 7).

(2) Formation, or conversion

Just as (2) in the natural birth of Christ there was a gestation or a formation of the members through the months needed for it, so also in the spiritual birth, as the apostle indicates in Galatians 4:19, "until Christ be formed in you." This is accomplished by conversion more strictly so called, in which those saving virtues (by the conformity to which, the spiritual Christ is understood), seminally conferred in regeneration, are formed through distinct habits, and that through various stages and paths, as we teach in its own place.[56]

(3) Delivery, or sanctification, in which are: (a) Sorrow

Just as (3) in his natural birth, after the conception and formation occurs the delivery (Luke 2:6), so also in the spiritual birth, the spiritual Christ, or the

---

56. 1.6.4 §IIIff.

conformity through which he lives in us, is brought forth, when the virtues conferred seminally in regeneration and habitually in conversion are by sanctification as it were brought forth in public in our manner of life (Matt. 5:16; 7:17–19; Gal. 5:22). And just as this natural delivery did not happen (a) without the sorrows natural to delivery, nor without manifold miseries in the circumstances, that she gave birth after a troublesome journey to Bethlehem, in the time (as is believed) of the winter solstice, in a stable with the stench of livestock, in extreme poverty, so also the spiritual delivery does not happen apart from sorrows (Gal. 4:19, "of whom I travail in birth again"). For in it is required: (i) contrition, a deep sense of sin and spiritual misery (Rom. 7:24), and the spirit of slavery to fear (Rom. 8:15); (ii) humiliation (Luke 15:21–22; Jer. 31:19; 2 Sam. 24:10); (iii) a godly hopelessness concerning ourselves and all other deliverers besides God and the Mediator (Acts 2:37; 16:30–31; Rom. 7:24); and that (iv) to these previous points in most cases there should be added, the contempt of neighbors and the persecutions of enemies (Matt. 2:13; Luke 2:35). So that from all these sorrows of delivery, they not rarely complain with Rebekah in Genesis 25:22, "If it be so, why am I with child?"

(b) Joy

Just as (b) the natural delivery did not happen without joy (John 16:21; Luke 1:47ff.), so his spiritual delivery will not happen without indescribable joy (1 Peter 1:3, 6; Acts 13:52; 16:34; Phil. 4:4; cf. Luke 15:9; 19:5–6). Therefore, in this way the spiritual Christ is spiritually conceived, formed, and born from us: in regeneration, conversion, and sanctification, when the virtues of Christ are conferred upon us seminally, formed habitually, and brought forth actually.

The motivating reasons

Now, we must give birth in such a way that we give birth to Christ. For in this way: (1) each of us will become a mother of the Lord, regarding whom the angel said, "Blessed are you among women" (Luke 1:28), that is, most blessed; and Elizabeth, "Why is this for me, that the mother of my Lord should come to me?" (Luke 1:43; cf. Luke 11:27). For if there is so much blessedness, so much glory in natural motherhood, certainly there is even more in a spiritual one, as the Savior himself acknowledges and declares (Matt. 12:48). From this Augustine (ch. 3 of his book *On Holy Virginity*) says, "Mary was more blessed by receiving the faith of Christ than by conceiving the flesh of Christ," and after this, "The maternal affinity of Mary would have been no use to her at all, if she had not borne Christ more blessedly in her heart than in her flesh."[57] (2) If we have spiritually conceived, formed, and begotten Christ, he will be as it were our son, and accordingly also: (a) he will take care of us in every circumstance, just as he did in the case of his natural mother, when he was about to die and entrusted her to John (John 19:26–27); (b) he will always hear our prayers, so that we will never be put to shame, as Solomon heard the petitions of his mother Bathsheba (1 Kings 2:20); and also, (c) one day at the last judgment he will as it were set up a throne for us at his right hand, just as Solomon did for his mother (1 Kings 2:19; cf. Rev. 3:21). On the contrary let us ponder (3) the misery and disgrace of spiritual barrenness, which spiritual eunuchs feel and complain of in Isaiah 56:3, "Let not the eunuch say, 'Behold, I am a dry tree.'" And if Rachel felt her natural barrenness with such great distress that she preferred death to it (Gen. 30:1), and Hannah on account of it thought that she was as it were dead, and living in hell (1 Sam. 1:10; 2:6), what will we not think of spiritual barrenness, in which we are bereft of this blessed fruit, not of the womb, but of the heart (Luke 1:42)? Finally, (4) what use will any fertility be to us, as much in offspring as in goods, if we should be bereft of this progeny which is blessed as well as blessing? Will we not complain with greater right than Abraham in Genesis 15:2, "Ah Lord Jehovah! What will you give me, since I go without children?" since in this one blessed seed, both we ourselves and all we have are blessed (Eph. 1:3), and without him, every blessing is nothing but a curse (Mal. 2:2).

11. That we may bear spiritual children for Christ

XLII. Finally eleventh, because Christ willed for us to be born as a child and to be given as a son (Isa. 9:6), then in turn we ought to take heed that we spiritually beget and bear children for Christ. The apostle hints at this practice in Galatians 4:19, "My children, for whom I labor in birth again," and from this calls himself a father, and attributes to himself begetting (1 Cor. 4:15; Philemon 10), and also the sorrows of birth (Gal. 4:19), and names those converted by him as his children (Gal. 4:19; 1 Cor. 4:17; 1 Tim. 1:2, 18; Titus 1:4; 1 Peter 5:13). And those who are spiritually begotten in this way are begotten for Christ, and are called his children (Heb. 2:13, Ps. 110:3; Isa. 53:6).

---

57. Augustine, *De sancta virginitate liber unus* in *PL* 40:398; idem, *Of Holy Virginity* in *NPNF2* 3:418; idem, *De bono conjugali and De sancta virginitate*, trans. and ed. P. G. Walsh (Oxford: Clarendon Press, 2001), 68–69.

What this birth is, and what its ingredients are
Moreover, this spiritual birth happens by the proclamation of the gospel and the conversion of souls (1 Cor. 4:15; Philemon 10). For there is also in this birth, just as we mentioned with regard to the preceding section: (1) a triple principle: (a) the passive principle, the mother and as it were the conceiving womb, the church (Gal. 4:26); (b) the material principle, the incorruptible seed of the divine Word (1 Peter 1:23), the heavenly dew (Ps. 110:3); and (c) the active principle, the Holy Spirit who as it were impregnates and vivifies the Word (John 6:63; 2 Cor. 3:6), and as it were confers the molding force (John 3:3). (d) The co-laborers of the Holy Spirit are ministers (1 Cor. 3:9; 2 Cor. 1:24), sowing as it were the seed (Mark 4:14), and also serving like midwives as it were for those being born. There are here (2) three periods: (a) of conception, in which the Word is first admitted by the hearers (Mark 4:20; 1 Thess. 2:13); (b) of gestation, in which it is preserved once admitted, and is formed (Gal. 4:19, "be formed in you"; Luke 2:19); (c) of delivery and bringing forth, in which they bear fruit (Mark 4:20).

Requirements
Now so that ministers may bear children for Christ in this way, in them are required: (1) labors and efforts of giving birth (2 Cor. 11:27; 2 Thess. 3:8); (2) sorrows of birth (Gal. 4:19, "for whom I labor in birth"), and fear of loss (Gal. 4:11; 2 Cor. 11:3); (3) joys (1 Thess. 2:19–20; 3:8; 2 Tim. 1:4); and also (4) in ministers who give birth, there is required an ardent desire to give birth for Christ, by an unwearied proclamation of the Word (2 Tim. 4:2; 1 Thess. 3:10; Acts 20:18–21).

The motivating reasons
And also, that they may more readily labor in this, it will help to seriously ponder that: (1) it is most equitable, because Christ willed to be born for us so that we might become children of God (Gal. 4:4), that we should also earnestly strive to beget children for him (cf. Heb. 2:10 with 2 Cor. 11:2). (2) Those children whom by the proclamation of the Word and by conversion they have begotten for Christ, will be their children (Gal. 4:19). And thus (3) will also be one day their honor and glory in Christ's presence (Phil. 4:1; 2 Cor. 1:14; Phil. 2:16).

CHAPTER ELEVEN

The Life of the Mediator

That the life of Jesus might be made manifest in our body.
—2 Corinthians 4:10

The second degree of Christ's humiliation is in his life.
I. We have already examined the first degree of Christ's humiliation, in his incarnation; now the second degree follows, in his life and conduct up to his death. The apostle will supply an opportunity for a synoptic consideration of it, in 2 Corinthians 4:10.

The Exegetical Part
The text is opened and explained.
II. There the apostle shows the scope and use of all Christian miseries and afflictions, namely that in them the miserable and afflicted life of Christ may be represented. In this representation there occurs:

A. The exemplar to be represented: ἵνα καὶ ἡ ζωὴ τοῦ Ἰησοῦ, "That the life also of Jesus...." There is here: (1) life, which generally is nothing except the actuality of an ensouled being.[1] It is threefold: (a) vegetative life, which operates without any knowledge of its object, the life by which, for example, plants, trees, and other things live, draw nourishment, grow, and put forth fruits; or (b) sensitive life, which certainly is conjoined with some knowledge, but only sensitive, or that which they have from their senses; by this life brute beasts live and are actualized; or (c) rational life, which is conjoined with rational knowledge, the life through which men live and operate. And this at last is the life properly belonging to this topic. Moreover, this life is considered either with respect to its first act, as they say, which life is nothing except the faculty or power

----

1. *actuositas animati*

of operating from themselves[2] in the order of second causes, the life through which they are only able to operate; or in the second act, the life through which they do operate in actuality. From this life comes among men their conversation, which frequently is called their life. That actuality of living things arises from a certain union of parts to be conjoined: for example, in natural life, from the union of the body with the soul, for when this is taken away, the one who lived is said to be dead; in spiritual life, from the union of the divine image, or original righteousness, from which a man can work spiritual things. This is the nature of life in general. Moreover, here there is (2) in particular, the life of Jesus, and that is indeed observed to be threefold: (a) divine life, or that of the divine person, regarding which we have philosophized above in book 2, chapter 12; but that does not properly belong to this topic; (b) human life, and that not only natural, which he lived from the union of the body with his soul, but also spiritual, which he lived from the union of the most perfect righteousness with his soul; (c) the mediatorial life, which properly speaking he lived for us, from the union of the two natures, the divine and the human. But what life of Christ does the apostle understand in this passage? He understands: (a) his internal life, whether the potency or the efficacy of living, whereby he also lives in us (Gal. 2:20), whereby from our mystical union with him, he confers to us the strength to work spiritually, for which reason he is called our life (Col. 3:4), and likewise the way, the truth, and the life (John 14:6), inasmuch as without him we can do nothing (John 15:5), and through him we can do all things (Phil. 4:13). Then (b) his external life, or his entire conduct, insofar as it is able to be represented in us, from which he commands that we should follow him (Luke 9:23), that we should learn of him (Matt. 11:29), from which we are imitators of him (1 Cor. 11:1; Phil. 2:5). And this life belongs especially properly to this topic. Moreover, in the passage is noted (3) "that life" of Jesus, ἡ ζωή. For since Jesus lived (a) a miserable life, all the way to his resurrection; (b) a glorious life, after his resurrection; although both can be understood here because both were united in him (Luke 24:26; Phil. 2:7–9), and ought to be united in us (Rom. 8:17–18; 2 Cor. 4:17), nonetheless here the prior is intended more, that is, his life full of misery and affliction, as is evident from the preceding context in verses 8–10, where he speaks of the afflictions of the apostles, that the life of Jesus may be made manifest in them.

---

2. *a se*

B. The image represented or that must be represented, wherein is noted:

1. The subject receiving the representation: "in our body." In the body, but certainly also in the soul, and that indeed principally: in it we bear the image of God (1 Thess. 5:23), with respect to the intellect (Col. 3:10), with respect to the will in righteousness and holiness (Eph. 4:24), and thus with respect to the whole man, which is by synecdoche at times indicated by "body" (Rom. 8:10; Heb. 10:5). Moreover, only the body is named, because in the preceding half of the verse mention is made of the νέκρωσις, "dying," which was accomplished through various afflictions, first in Christ as the exemplar (1 Peter 2:24–25), then in us as the image (Gal. 6:17), and because the afflictions of believers, which are treated in the preceding verses, principally touch the body. He adds, "in *our* body": certainly the body of all Christians, who are bound to bear the image of the life of Christ (Luke 9:23; Matt. 11:29), but in particular that of the apostles, whom Paul had spoken of in the preceding verses, inasmuch as in them the life of Christ was made manifest preeminently.

2. The act of representation: φανερωθῇ, "might be made manifest." Φανερόω is from φανερός, manifest, and this from φαίνω, I bring to light, which they derive from φῶς, light. It means to make it so that something may be conspicuous, or meet the eyes, just as how in an image, that which is imaged is conspicuous, though absent. Moreover, the life of Christ manifested among Christians is chiefly of three sorts: (1) his internal life, or his living and vivifying power, insofar as he makes us alive spiritually, so that we can do spiritual things, for without him we can do nothing in this kind of actions (John 15:5), and through him we can do all things necessary (Phil. 4:13), from which he is said to live in us (Gal. 2:20), indeed to be our life (Col. 3:4), as we have said. Then (2) his external life, or conduct, through the imitation of those virtues which he presents to us that they might be displayed, for example, fortitude, patience, gentleness, humility (Matt. 11:29; Phil. 2:4–6). Finally, (3) his glorious life, from his resurrection, inasmuch as through our mystical union with him it has an inseparable connection with his dying (Rom. 6:4–5), for which reason Paul says, "I have been crucified with Christ, and I live" (Gal. 2:20).

The Dogmatic Part

The Mediator lived not so much for himself as for us.

It is proved by the Scriptures.

III. Therefore, just as the Mediator was born not so much for himself as for us (Isa. 9:6), so also he lived on earth not so much for himself as for us. For he lives so that: (1) he may communicate his life to his own, that he may be their life (Col. 3:4), through which they also may live spiritually (Gal. 2:20); (2) by his life he may supply them an example for imitation throughout all their life (Matt. 11:29; John 13:14–16; 1 Cor. 11:1); moreover, (3) that he did not live for himself but for us, he testifies everywhere (Matt. 20:28; etc.).

And by reasons

For if (1) he had willed to live for himself, he would not have willed to descend into our life, for he was rich before he descended, and became poor for us when he descended (2 Cor. 8:9). (2) Also, if he had willed to descend for himself and not for us, he would have descended not to serve but to be served, the contrary of which is in Matthew 20:28. (3) He would have descended into glory, not into misery; whereas on the contrary, existing in the form of God, he did not consider it plunder to be equal with God, but emptied himself, took the form of a servant, and willed to be made like common, miserable men (Phil 2:6–8). He did so for this reason, that (4) he might acquire for us life, that of: (a) justification, that he might restore us, delivered from the guilt of death, into the state of life (John 3:16–17); (b) of sanctification, that by it he might vivify the spiritually dead (Eph. 2:5–6), from which he is called our life (Col. 3:4), without whom we can do nothing (John 15:5), and by whom we can spiritually do all things (Phil. 4:13); (c) of glorification, or eternal life (John 3:16, 36; Eph. 2:6; John 5:24), as we have said.

The twofold life of Christ: Eternal life. And temporal life: spiritual,
eternal, and natural

IV. This life, which he devoted not to himself, but to us, is twofold: the one life he possesses in himself from eternity as the second person of the Trinity, the life communicated to him by his Father by an ineffable generation (John 5:26); the other life he receives in time, as a man, by conception from the Holy Spirit and by birth from the blessed Virgin (Luke 1–2). This life, together with our common life, is nothing other than the faculty of operating from oneself in the order of second causes, arising from the union of parts to be conjoined, as we have just taught. And so: (1) from the union of the divine image and original righteousness with his soul, he possessed spiritual life, and the faculty of accomplishing all good, even spiritual good (which faculty we lost by sin, so that we are dead in sin, Eph. 2:1, and unfit for spiritual good, 2 Cor. 3:5), seeing as this faculty is derived from him to us (Col. 3:4), and from it we are able to do whatever we can (John 15:5; Phil. 4:13). So also (2) from his perfect union with God, he has eternal life, by which he can see God face to face (1 Cor. 13:12), and delight and rejoice in him (John 17:13; 3:29; 15:11). So (3) from the union of his soul with his body, he had natural life, which he was deprived of by temporal death. And this life especially is the subject of our current consideration. Compare what we have already said about these things in the exegetical part.

The threefold period of this life: 1. Its commencement, in which was
(1) His circumcision
V. This natural life, after his birth, occurred under three periods: the commencement, the continuation, and the conclusion.[3] The first of these is in his infancy, in which: (1) through his circumcision, performed on the eighth day of his life (Luke 2:21), he undertook and sealed a covenant with God, with respect to its initiation, namely a threefold covenant: (a) the national covenant, which was common to him with the entire Jewish nation; he acknowledged and demonstrated that he was from their midst and from his Jewish brothers, from whom God had promised he would raise the Messiah up as a prophet (Deut. 18:15, 18), and that he was that blessed seed of Abraham, of Isaac, of Jacob, promised so many times of old, and so splendidly. (b) A personal covenant, which is common to him with all the elect, by which God sealed to him that he was his God (Gen. 17:8, 10 with Ps. 22:1). (c) The mediatorial covenant, which was established between him and the Father in the eternal counsel of peace (Zech. 6:13; Isa. 53:10), by which he offered himself for us as surety and expromissor (Matt. 26:28; Luke 22:20). The sealing of this third covenant especially was accomplished in his circumcision: (i) by the amputation of the fleshly foreskin, by which he signified and sealed that the spiritual foreskin under which we by nature labor through sin (Deut. 10:16; Rom. 2:25–27) would be removed by his life (Deut. 30:6; Ezek. 16:30 with Col. 2:10–11). (ii) By the grievous shedding of blood, so that shortly after the beginning of his life he might foreshadow and seal that mediatorial covenant that would be ratified by his blood, which on this account is called the blood of the covenant (Ex. 24:8 with Matt. 26:28; Mark 14:24). And from this renewal of the mediatorial covenant, and its initial ratification accomplished through the

---

3. *ingressu, progressu et egressu*

shedding of blood, in his circumcision he obtained by divine authority that most sweet name *Jesus*, concerning which we expressly taught in chapter 3.[4]

(2) His dedication: The preceding purification of his mother
VI. Following his circumcision in infancy was (2) his dedication, on his fortieth day of life (Luke 2:22ff.), namely so that he who had already dedicated himself to God through the renewal of the covenant in circumcision might also, according to the divine command, be offered and dedicated to God by his parent. (a) The purification of the mother preceded this dedication, as it also did the circumcision, according to the law (Lev. 12:2–4, 6–8), because God did not want a gift to be offered to him with impure hands, and because she had to be cleansed first from her original impurity, which the ceremonial impurity of a woman who gave birth prefigured, before either she or the child made an appearance in the temple in the sight of God, or touched anything sacred. For this cause she had to bring forward either a lamb of the first year, with a young pigeon or turtledove, if she could afford so much, or if not, then either two turtledoves or two pigeons, to the door of the tabernacle, to the priest, who would sacrifice them, and in sacrificing legally expiate that ceremonial impurity, as a sign of the true purification that would be procured through the sacrifice of the Messiah at the proper time, regarding which we will speak expressly in its own place.[5]

The dedication of the son
(b) The dedication itself followed (Luke 2:22–23) in which, as the firstborn son, the one who opened the womb, he was particularly set apart to God, according to the law (Ex. 13:2; Num. 3:13; 8:16–17), and thus was brought to Jerusalem, the city of God, and into the temple of Jerusalem, into the house and sight of God, and not without some small gifts, according to the prosperity of the parents. That is, that it might be prefigured that he was God's firstborn (Heb. 1:6; Ps. 2:7), the firstborn of every creature (Col. 1:15), the firstborn among many brethren (Rom. 8:29), the firstborn from the dead (Col. 1:18; Rev. 1:5), more excellent than all the rest, and as it were, the one worth them all, and thus to be especially set apart and sanctified to God, so that in the one all the elect might be sanctified and set apart to God (cf. Rom. 11:16).

The blessing of Simeon and the confession of Anna
Following or accompanying this dedication was (c) the blessing of righteous

---

4. 1.5.3 §VIIIff.
5. 1.5.18

Simeon,[6] in which: (i) he was the first to receive Jehovah Messiah as he came to his temple (Mal. 3:1), with joy taking him in the arms of his body as well as of his heart (Luke 2:25–27), then (ii) he rejoiced both in the one who came, and in himself, with a hymn (vv. 29–33), furthermore, (iii) blessed his parents (v. 34), and finally, (iv) predicted the hard destiny that threatened them because of this their child (vv. 34–35). And finally, (d) the confession of Anna the prophetess, who realized he was the Messiah and made him manifest to others (Luke 2:36–38).

(3) The reverent visitation of the wise men

VII. If it did not follow the dedication, as several want, after the parents had set out for Bethlehem a second time, then (3) the reverent visitation of the wise men (Matt. 2:1–13), at the earliest, immediately preceded it. In it some number of magi, or wise men and philosophers of Persia, taught by divine revelation, with the assistance of an extraordinary star, of the birth of an extraordinary and spiritual king of the Jews, set out on a long and difficult journey to Jerusalem, the place of the temple, of the priesthood, and of all the most sacred holy things of the Jews. Once there, they diligently inquire of the one born king, and then instructed by men, and with the heavenly star lighting the way, they seek him out, and reverently adore the one sought out as God, and as man attend him with their gifts. Then, led by a divine oracle to avoid Herod, the hypocritical persecutor, they return to their own people. They were the first of the Gentiles converted to Christ, and thus the firstfruits of the nations, a prelude of the impending universal calling of the nations. On this we already previewed a few things in the preceding chapter, §XV.

(4) The persecution of Herod and the escape of Jesus

VIII. But this service of piety and reverent honor was soon followed by (4) the most terrible persecution of Herod the Great (Matt. 2:13ff.), continued until his death, wherein the tyrant, deceived in his own cleverness, sought the child to kill him, just as the wise men did to revere him, so that the child might show that honors and persecutions walk hand in hand. Therefore, in order that, according to the state to which he had lowered himself for us, he might in a human way look out for his life, he was removed by his parents, who had been warned in a divine dream, to Egypt, the house of slavery. Then from there, when the persecutor had died, he was returned to his homeland, so that from the beginning he might immediately make known that he was the one who, having assumed the form of a servant (Phil. 2:7), was driven from his throne into the house of slavery,

---

6. On the possible identities of "Simeon Justus," see Poole, *Synopsis criticorum*, 4:899–900.

and also that he would lead his people back from spiritual Egypt into the liberty and rest of the children of God (Gal. 5:1; Heb. 4:8).

(5) The return to Nazareth

IX. Finally, having returned from Egypt, (5) he settled in Nazareth as the place of his upbringing (Matt. 2:23; Luke 2:39; Matt. 26:71; Mark 14:67; Acts 3:6), where he had been conceived by the Holy Spirit. From this he was, indeed as an insult from the common people (cf. John 1:46), given the surname "of Nazareth" (John 19:19), but yet this was not apart from the counsel of God, namely that by it, even if only by sound and tone, the ears and hearts of believers might be taught that he is that נֵצֶר, *Nezer*, Branch, by which the Messiah is frequently signified in the Scriptures (e.g. Isa. 11:1), to which צֶמַח, Branch, is akin (Zech. 6:12; Jer. 23:5). From this afterwards, out of contempt, his disciples were called Nazarenes, and the sect of the Nazarenes (Acts 24:5). And these points are the entirety of what the Holy Spirit wanted us to know regarding the Mediator's infancy, so not undeservedly have both the ancients and the moderns, and even the papists who are otherwise too much addicted to nonsense of this sort, condemned the apocryphal book concerning the infancy of Jesus as spurious and inauthentic.

2. *The continuation of the life of Christ includes:*

His adolescence, in which are his: Growth

X. Following the commencement comes the continuation of the life of Christ, which has two periods: his adolescence, extended longer than usual, insofar as it contains his entire private life; and his adulthood, in which he led his public life. His adolescence is presented briefly in Luke 2:40–52: (1) with respect to the growth of Jesus (a) in stature; (b) in wisdom with respect to his intellect, in the habitual, actual, and experimental wisdom of the human nature, insofar as day by day it was extended to more objects; (c) in grace, or in the gifts and virtues of grace, with respect to his will; (d) in favor with God and men (Luke 1:80; 2:40, 52).

Conversation religious and civil

(2) With respect to conversation, as much: (a) religious conversation, wherein not only did he frequent the public rites of that economy, already at twelve years old ascending with his parents on foot to Jerusalem to celebrate the feast of Passover (Luke 2:41–42), but also he was active in holy things, inquiring into truth, instructing others, disputing[7] with the doctors in the temple, in which he offered a certain sample and advance witness of that public vocation by which he was

---

7. συζητήσεις…*ambiendo*

ordained and sent as the Doctor and Teacher of Israel, and also proved that his judgment, knowledge, and wisdom were drawn not only from human instruction over the course time, but from the divine union, in an extraordinary manner. By all these things he also revealed his piety, in which above his natural parents he loved his heavenly Father and considered it as his highest pleasure to be about his Father's business (Luke 2:49). As also (b) civil conversation, in which (i) he rendered himself subject and compliant to his parents, and thus made most manifest that he did not come to destroy the law, but to fulfill it (Matt. 5:17), because there is no part of moral obedience which could seem more foreign to the Lord of heaven and earth than subjection toward human beings. (ii) He was employed in the manual labor of a carpenter (Mark 6:3), so that he might manifest the humility and poverty he undertook for us (2 Cor. 8:9), and so that he might draw from us upon himself the curse arising from the violation of the divine law (Gen. 3:19), although even the most renowned of the Jewish doctors considered it an honor to themselves to join a trade with the contemplative life, by whose example even Paul was a tentmaker (Acts 18:3).

Being hidden in the wilderness
From this period of adolescence until his thirtieth year of age, in which the Savior began his public life, he was hidden in the desert (Luke 1:80). Yet he did not live in such great ease for himself alone, but he sanctified himself and his entire life for us, and devoted himself to us by his subjection to the law (Gal. 4:4), poverty (Luke 9:58; 2 Cor. 8:9), prayers, and continuous preparation for death and for his public office.

His adulthood, in which he performed the mediatorial office:
(1) Its initiation, or threefold preparation, accomplished by John the Baptist
XI. Finally, his adulthood followed, during which he led his public life (Luke 1:80), in his thirtieth year of age (Luke 3:23), that is, after the institution of the Levites (Num. 4:47). Regarding the mediatorial office which he undertook in this period of life, two things come for our consideration: its initiation and its completion. So first, its initiation includes three things: (1) the preparation accomplished by the ministry of John the Baptist, who was born not without a miracle to parents past the age of childbearing, Zacharias the priest and Elizabeth (Luke 1:5–26), and frequently promised in the past to the Israelites as the forerunner of the Messiah (Mal. 4:5; Isa. 40:3, which oracles the New Testament refers to the Baptist, Matt. 11:14; Luke 1:17; Matt. 3:3). Therefore by office it was incumbent upon him in the spirit and power of Elijah to go before the face of the Messiah, so that he might prepare the way for him (Matt. 3:3). Moreover, he

prepared the way: (a) by crying out for repentance (Matt. 3:1–2), that by it the Jews might not only correct their depraved morals, but also set aside their perverse errors regarding righteousness and justification, so they would more eagerly receive the Messiah as their Redeemer. (b) By baptizing, that is, his proselytes, as future disciples of the imminent Messiah (Matt. 3:11; Acts 19:4), according to the custom of the Jews, by purifying them with water, and consequently receiving them into the covenant of grace under the new dispensation now arising. (c) By offering such an illustrious testimony to the Messiah who was coming after him, indeed who was already present, by pointing to him as if with his finger, and by lifting him up infinitely above himself (John 1:27; Matt. 3:11), and that from the extraordinary revelation of God (John 1:33). By all these things, he concluded the old dispensation of the covenant of grace, and opened up the new as well, and deserved to be called greater than all who preceded him, and less than those who followed (Matt. 11:11).

(2) His inauguration, through baptism

XII. The initiation into the mediatorial office includes (2) the inauguration made by baptism (John 3:13ff.), inasmuch as it was nothing except a public and solemn introduction, by which the three functions of the mediatorial office: (a) are asserted by the testimony of the Father, who publicly declares that Jesus is his Son, and thus the king constituted by him upon his holy mountain (Ps. 2:6), likewise that he is the priest in whose propitiatory sacrifice he would rest (Isa. 42:1), and finally that he is the prophet, whom he wills to be heard most carefully in all things (Matt. 3:17; 17:5 with Deut. 18:15, 18). (b) They are confirmed by added signs, by the opening of heaven, by the descent of the Holy Spirit in the visible form of a dove, and resting upon him, and by the voice heard from heaven, in which the testimony of the Father was signified. To which there is also added another goal and use of this baptism, namely to seal the covenant of grace to the entire mystical Christ (that is, to him and all his own), of which covenant he himself was its very basis, consequently also to confirm and sanctify our baptism, and to show in whom its strength and efficacy ought to be sought and found.

(3) His examination, through the temptation of Satan

XIII. The initiation includes (3) the examination that occurred by the temptation of Satan (Matt. 4), in which after four of the heaviest attacks that were powerfully vanquished, triumphing over Satan, he made it indubitable to us that he was: (a) more powerful than the first Adam who succumbed to temptations; indeed, (b) even stronger than the devil himself; and thus (c) the true seed of the woman, which came to crush the head of the serpent (Gen. 3:15 with Rom.

16:20); (d) in all points tempted like we are, so that he can sympathize with us when we are tempted (Heb. 4:15), to the end that with that much greater confidence, in all temptations we might be able to flee to his help (Heb. 4:16).

The completion of his public life. It was accomplished:
(1) By preaching and teaching
XIV. The initiation into public life was followed by the completion of the same, or the discharging of his office, especially of the prophetic office, which occurred, first, by preaching and teaching, not new commandments, nor evangelical counsels, nor a mixture of commandments and counsels, but by interpreting and vindicating the law of Moses, by proclaiming the gospel, especially that of fulfillment, and by foretelling future things. To all these things the following were always conjoined: (1) with respect to him, first (a) grace and authority (John 7:46; Matt. 7:28–29), then (b) toil and trouble, insofar as he was occupied day and night with traveling from town to town (Mark 6:6; Matt. 9:35; Luke 13:22), then (c) faithfulness, in which he completed this work not only by himself, but also by his agents (Matt. 10:1ff.; Mark 6:7ff.; Luke 6:13ff.). (2) With respect to others, either the opening or conversion of the heart (John 2:23), or its hardening (Mark 4:11–12). We have spoken of all these things expressly in the chapter on the Mediator as a prophet.[8]

Why did he so frequently use parables?
XV. Specifically, it must be observed here that during his preaching he was so frequent in using parables borrowed from all manner of earthly things (Matt. 13; etc.), for which plan he had various reasons: (1) with respect to himself, (a) he willed to exhibit a mind that even in bodily matters was spiritual, in earthly matters heavenly, so that he could perceive something spiritual and heavenly in all fleshly and earthly things, and he also might commend and impart the same affection to us (cf. John 3:12); so that (b) he might satisfy the prophecies of the Scriptures (Ps. 49:4; Matt. 13:35ff.). (2) With respect to all others, so that (a) in this he might more freely and effectively restrain and correct (cf. Judg. 9:7ff. with Matt. 21:45–46), (b) so that he might more fittingly teach, because (i) similitudes illustrate (Jer. 13; 19; Ezek. 4:4ff.; 8), (ii) they influence, delight, and motivate (2 Sam. 12:1ff), (iii) they help the memory (Isa. 57:8). (3) With respect to the different character of his hearers: (a) to the pious and teachable, for clarity (Mark 4:33), and (b) to the reprobate, for concealment and ruin (Matt. 13:11ff; Mark 4:11ff cf. Ps. 109:17).

---

8. 1.5.6 §V

(2) By performing miracles. The requirements of miracles
XVI. The Savior spent his public life, second, by performing miracles, which is beyond doubt to all, at least who receive the gospel. Moreover, what a miracle is conceptually, we have already explained in book 3, chapter 10, §XXVI, to which we do not add anything at present, except that it requires: (1) that it be an astounding work, and one that surpasses the realm of nature, so that it may provide a suitable testimony to the divine power (Mark 1:27; 5:42; Luke 5:26; 9:43). (2) That it not happen in a corner, but openly in public view (Mark 1:23ff.; Matt. 14:14, 19). Also (3) not in many circuitous ways and with a lengthy effort, but suddenly, at a mere command (Matt. 8:26; 17:18; Mark 9:25). And (d) not by degrees or gradually, but in a moment, all at once (Matt. 8:3; 20:34).

What sort of miracles the Savior performed
XVII. Moreover, the Savior performed miracles in every kind of creature: (1) in unclean spirits, by casting them out (Matt. 8:16; 9:33; 12:22; 15:22, 28; 17:18; Mark 1:26, 39; Luke 4:35; etc.); (2) in men, by healing: (a) the sick (Matt. 4:23ff., 9:35; 12:15; 15:30; 19:2; Mark 1:34; Luke 4:40; 6:18), (b) the leprous (Matt. 8:3; Mark 1:42; Luke 5:13; 17:14), (c) paralytics (Matt. 8:6, 13; 9:7; Mark 2:3, 11; Luke 5:24; John 5:8), (d) those with dropsy (Luke 14:2, 4), (e) those with fever (Matt. 8:15; Mark 1:30–31; Luke 4:39; John 4:45 with v. 52), (f) the blind (Matt. 9:30; 12:22–23; 20:34; 21:14; Mark 8:25; John 9:7), (g) the deaf (Mark 7:35), (h) the hunchbacked (Luke 13:11–12), (i) the withered (Matt. 12:10, 13; Mark 3:1, 5; Luke 6:8, 10), (j) those suffering from bleeding (Matt. 9:20, 22; Mark 5:29; Luke 8:44), (k) the deaf (Mark 7:32), and those with a mutilated ear (Luke 22:51), (l) the dead, by raising them (Matt. 11:5; 9:25; Mark 5:41; Luke 8:54; 7:14; John 11:44; Matt. 27:52ff.); (3) in irrational things: (a) in the heavens (Matt. 27:45; Mark 15:33; Luke 23:44), (b) in the earth (Matt. 21:19; Mark 2:14; 6:41–42; 8:1, 8–9; Luke 9:17; John 6:12; Matt. 15:37; John 21:9; etc.), (c) in the waters (John 2:9; Luke 5:6; John 21:11; Matt. 17:27); (d) in the region of the air, by restraining the winds (Matt. 8:26).

The six goals of miracles
XVIII. Moreover, the Savior performed so many and such great miracles for this reason, so that: (1) he might demonstrate that he was neither pure man, nor pure God, but the God-man: for the ministry of his bodily members, the touch of his hands, the commands of his mouth, and other things clearly argued that he was a man; and the effects,[9] unheard of from the ages (John 9:32), done

---

9. ἀποτελέσματα

in such great abundance, in every part of nature, and also by his own strength (Matt. 8:2; 9:28), and for the glory of God alone, argued well enough that he had existed as more than a creature (John 5:17–24). (2) He might demonstrate that he was the Messiah who had been promised for such a long time, and also with such great preparation (John 5:36; 7:31), insofar as: (a) he performed all those works, which, according to the prediction of the Old Testament Scripture, were incumbent upon the Messiah to perform (cf. Isa. 35:5; 29:18 with Matt. 11:5). And (b) in such circumstances which, according to the observation of scholars, excellently confirm this: for example, that (i) before him for many centuries, entirely no miracles had been done; (ii) none of his ancestors was renowned for miracles; (iii) even in his own age, no one before him had done so many and such great miracles, or the very same miracles, not even his forerunner John (John 10:41); (iv) besides him (Matt. 21:14), no one ever is observed to have performed miracles in the temple; (v) no one's birth and death is ever read to have been ennobled with miracles, other than his alone; (vi) at his nod, whenever he wanted, all nature—angels, heaven, earth, and so forth—stood prepared to obey him when he willed to perform miracles. (3) He might confirm with deeds the truth of the doctrine of the gospel (John 10:38; 14:11), because God (whose works alone miracles are, Luke 11:20; Matt. 12:28), inasmuch as he is the first truth, who cannot lie[10] (Titus 1:2; Num. 23:19; 2 Tim. 2:13; Heb. 6:18), and who does not know how to deceive or be deceived, in no way can bear testimony to falsehood. (4) He might make known his universal authority over all creatures (Matt. 28:18; Eph. 1:20–22; Ps. 24:1), by miracles performed in all kinds of creatures. Especially also so that (5) he might display his indescribable goodness and mercy toward men, whom he had come to save, because he devoted all his miracles either to healing or to saving miserable men, except that he dedicated only two in special cases to severity, and those not even in men, but in the Gadarene swine (Matt. 8:31–32), and in the barren fig tree (Matt. 21:19). Also accordingly it is not read anywhere that he performed miracles for himself: not even when hungry or thirsty did he will to eat or drink other than with the hands of nature (Matt. 4:2, 4; John 4:6–7; 19:28–29). (6) He might assert for himself the strength of spiritual miracles that are analogous to the corporeal, the strength by which, for example, he could awaken the spiritually dead (Eph. 2:5–6), restore sight to the blind in mind by his illumination (Eph. 1:18), cleanse the spiritually leprous (Ps. 51:10), and heal those suffering with a spiritual paralysis, dropsy, fever, deafness, decay, or disease of any sort. With respect to spiritual miracles of this sort, greater power is not required than with

---

10. *utpote prima veritas* ἀψευδής

respect to any corporeal miracles, since infinite force is required for both, the sort that occurs in creation (Ps. 51:10).

Five reasons why he forbade the publicizing of his miracles
XIX. If you should ask why therefore he frequently forbade the publicizing of miracles he had performed (Matt. 8:4; 9:30; Mark 8:26; Matt. 17:9), then I will respond: (1) Because he wanted to be made known and become strong not suddenly but gradually, like the sun after dawn proceeds to morning and noon (Ps. 19:4–6). (2) Perhaps also so that by the abundance of miracles he would not as it were overwhelm the Jews, and so that he might give time to examine them one by one, and thus the Messiah might be made known to them more certainly and suitably (John 7:21). (3) Because he judged that the rest that had been revealed were sufficient for the present time (Matt. 16:1–2). (4) Because he appears to have selected the time after his resurrection to make manifest all kinds, indeed all of his miracles throughout the globe, so that from the greatest miracle of all, and the most splendid testimony of divine favor, the rest of his miracles and his entire teaching might receive weight and authority. For which reason he also went so far as to forbid too free of a dissemination, not only of his miracles, but also of the fact that he was the Messiah (Matt. 16:20; Luke 9:21). To the same end seems to point the fact that to the Jews who demanded a sign, he willed to promise none other than his resurrection after three days of death (Matt. 12:38–40). However, (5) he never willed to allow his miracles to be publicized by Satan (Mark 1:34–35; 3:11–12), because this could not do anything except defame his teaching.

He performed miracles through himself and through his people.
With what difference
XX. Finally, because the Savior performed miracles not only through himself but also through his people, with the power communicated to them of morally performing miracles (Mark 16:17), not only the same ones, but also in their own way (Matt. 10:1) even greater ones (John 14:12), it will be worthwhile to observe the difference between the miracles of Christ and those of the apostles, namely that: (1) Christ did miracles by his own power and for his own honor (John 5:17; 2:11); the apostles by the power of Christ and for his glory (Acts 3:6, 12–13). (2) Christ could communicate the faculty of performing them (Luke 10:19; Matt. 10:1, 8), the apostles by no means could. (3) Christ as it were habitually,[11] as often and wherever he wanted, had that faculty immediately at hand, whereas

---

11. *per habitum*; Dutch: *door ene hebbelykeheit*

the apostles in the moment,[12] according to some divine promise, had to request it from God with prayers. And thus (4) Christ physically performed a miracle by attaining to it immediately by his own power, whereas the apostles obtained miracles from elsewhere, by another's power,[13] only by their prayers, so that it was not so much they but Christ who was the author of their miracles.

(3) In suffering all sorts of adversities

XXI. Thus the Savior spent his public life in preaching and performing miracles. He also spent it, third, by suffering all sorts of adversities, from the womb to the tomb, so that his life was nothing but continuous suffering.

By whom he suffered

For he suffered (1) from his friends: (a) his God and Father, who not only decreed all his adversities for him from eternity (Zech. 13:7; Acts 2:23; 4:28), but also inflicted them (Isa. 53:4–6; Matt. 26:31), and forsook him (Ps. 22:1; Matt. 27:46). (b) The apostles, who tempted him (Matt. 16:22–23), betrayed him (Ps. 55:13–15; Matt. 26:21, 25, 47–48), forsook him (Matt. 26:31, 56), denied him (Matt. 26:69ff.). He suffered (2) from enemies of every kind: (a) the devil (Matt. 4:1–10); (b) men: (i) politicians: kings (Ps. 2:2), Herod (Luke 23:7–8, 11), Pontius Pilate (Matt. 27:2), and so forth, and their subordinates, the soldiers (Luke 23:36; John 19:2, 23), and so forth; (ii) ecclesiastics: the scribes, Pharisees, priests, chief priests, elders, and the entire Sanhedrin (Matt. 26:3, 62–63).

What sort of things he suffered

He also suffered: (1) in his soul (Isa. 53:11) which was frequently tempted (Matt. 4:1ff.; Heb. 2:18), troubled (John 12:27), sorrowful (Matt. 26:38), vexed by every kind of indignity (Matt. 11:19; 12:24; John 8:48), harassed with hellish torments (Matt. 26:37–38; 27:46; Mark 14:33–34; Luke 22:44; Heb. 5:7). Then (2) in his body, by enduring exile (Matt. 2:14–15), hunger (Matt. 4:2; 21:18), thirst (John 4:6–7), various perils of life (Matt. 2:16; Mark 3:6–7; John 7:1; 8:59; 11:53–54), arrest and chains (Matt. 26:50; John 18:24), spitting from the vilest men (Matt. 26:67; 27:30; Mark 14:65), blows (Matt. 26:67; 27:30; Mark 14:65; 15:19), scourgings (Matt. 27:26; John 19:1), the crown of thorns (Matt. 27:29; Mark 15:17; John 19:2), the cross (Luke 23:26; John 19:17), and its pain through all his members (Ps. 22:16; Matt. 27:35; Mark 15:24–25). Furthermore,

---

12. *per actum coruscationis*, fig. "in a flash"; Dutch: *door ene daadt van flikkeringe*
13. *virtute aliena*; Dutch: *door enes anderen kracht*

(3) in his reputation, through various calumnies (Matt. 11:19; 12:24; John 7:48), accusations (Matt. 26:59–67; 27:12), mocking words and actions (Matt. 27:27–32, 38–41), and so forth. Finally, (4) in his fortunes, he suffered extreme poverty (Matt. 8:20; Luke 9:58; 2 Cor. 8:9), deprived of his clothes (Matt. 27:35) and even of necessary nourishment (Matt. 27:34). He suffered such things, moreover, through his entire life, but especially through the last four years of his life, and their last four days, and four hours, regarding which we will expressly say more things in the following chapter.[14] From these points we see clearly that the Savior not only endured all things that were incumbent upon us to bear because of sin, but also more things than all of us were due, things plainly infinite in value and price (Lam. 1:12).

(4) By lighting the way with his life and all his actions.
By what rules the actions of Christ are to be imitated
XXII. Finally, the Savior spent his public life, fourth, by lighting the way with his life and actions as an example for all (Matt. 11:29; 1 Cor. 11:1; cf. 1 Thess. 1:6; Eph. 5:2–3, 25; 1 John 2:6; 1 Peter 2:21–23; John 13:14–15). Yet this must be taken with a grain of salt, for there were among his actions: (1) those of divine power, such as were evident in his miracles, (2) those of divine authority and prerogative, such as in the loosing of the donkey without greeting its owners (prescribed in Matt. 21:2–3), (3) those that are mediatorial, prophetic, priestly, kingly, which are discussed in their own places, (4) those that are accidental, occasional, incidental, and circumstantial, such as for example, that he celebrated the Lord's Supper at night, after the completion of an ordinary meal, with only males, and church ministers, and unleavened bread. There are at last (5) those that are moral (as in Matt. 11:29; Eph. 5:2–3, 25ff.), built upon reasons and moral foundations (John 13:14–15). Now to imitate Christ in actions of the first kind, is thoroughly impossible; in those of the second kind, unrighteous; in those of the third kind, sinful and disparaging to Christ the Mediator; in those of the fourth kind, superstitious. Thus only in those actions of the fifth kind did Christ light the way for us as an example for imitation, yet this is so in such a way that all the rest of his actions also provide us various uses.

The virtues by which our Savior lights the way for us: Piety toward God
Therefore he presented to us the moral virtues and their actions, that they may be imitated by us. He lit the way then (1) in piety toward God, and that (a) in the duties of the natural worship of God: (i) the knowledge of God (John 7:29;

---

14. 1.5.12 §§II, VI

1:18), (ii) glorification and reverence (John 8:49; 17:4), (iii) obedience (Phil. 2:7; John 5:30; 6:38), (iv) patience (Isa. 53:7; 1 Peter 2:23), (v) humility (Phil. 2:7; Matt. 11:29), (vi) trust in God (Matt. 26:53; 27:46), (vii) hatred of idolatry, even of the most subtle kind (Matt. 4:8–10), and so forth; (b) in the duties of instituted worship: (i) circumcision (Luke 2:21), in which was sealed the most exact observance of the entire ceremonial law (Gal. 5:3), (ii) the presentation in the temple (Luke 2:22), (iii) the celebration of the Passover (Matt. 26:17ff.), (iv) the sanctifying of the Levitical feasts (Luke 2:41–42), (v) the reception of baptism (Matt. 3:13ff.) and its institution (Matt. 28:19), (vi) the gathering of churches (Matt. 16:18), (vii) the sending of church ministers (Matt. 10:1ff.), (viii) the establishment of church discipline (Matt. 18:15–19), (ix) the commending of public prayers (Matt. 18:19), (x) the cleansing of the temple (Matt. 21:12), (xi) the proclamation of the Word (Matt. 4:17), (xii) frequent attendance upon holy things (Luke 2:49), and (xiii) aversion to all will-worship (Matt. 15:9); (c) in reverence, devotion, and singular zeal in divine worship (Matt. 21:12–13), and avoidance of all profaning of the divine name (John 8:49); (d) in the sanctifying of the Sabbath (Mark 1:21; Luke 4:31; 13:10), and its vindication from the superstitious institutions of the scribes and Pharisees that were adverse to mercy and kindness (Matt. 12:1–12; Mark 2:23).

Righteousness toward neighbor

(2) In righteousness toward his neighbor, which he presented: (a) in honor of his neighbor, reverence of his parents (Luke 2:51) and the magistrate (Matt. 22:21; 17:27), study of humility (Matt. 11:29), and avoidance of all pride (Phil. 2:6–7); (b) in kindness toward his neighbor, shown by love (Eph. 5:2; John 15:13), compassion (Matt. 15:32; 20:34), kindness (Matt. 4:23ff.; 9:35), by helping all sorts of miserable persons with so many miracles, as we have shown in its own place,[15] by hatred of all cruelty (Matt. 12:11–12); (c) in chastity, and detestation of even the slightest impurity (Matt. 5:27–29); (d) in commutative justice, by rendering to each his own (Matt. 22:21; 17:27); (e) in truthfulness (John 18:37; 8:40) and the execration of every lie (John 8:44); (f) in self-sufficiency,[16] in which content with his lot, even though most weak and abject, he never was high-minded, and was a stranger to any depraved covetousness (John 6:15).

---

15. §XVII, above
16. αὐταρκεία

Temperance toward himself

In temperance toward himself, wherein intent in heart upon heavenly things (John 6:27), and upon the will of the Father (John 4:34), he denied his own will (John 5:30; 6:38; Matt. 26:39, 42), freely took up the cross (Phil. 2:6–8), scorned worldly pride (John 18:36; 6:15). And in all these things he was so exact that he fulfilled all righteousness (Matt. 3:15; 5:17, 19), he did not even know any sin (2 Cor. 5:21), and he could challenge his most rigid observers, "Which of you charges me with sin?" (John 8:46). "For such a high priest was fitting for us, who is holy, harmless, undefiled, separate from sinners" (Heb. 7:26).

3. The conclusion of the life of Christ

XXIII. And so finally we reach the third period of the life of Christ, that is, the conclusion of this life, which occurred in his preparation for death, which John quite accurately presents in his Gospel (ch. 13–17). Pointing to this are: (1) so many and such clear predictions of his imminent death (Matt. 16:21; 17:22–23; 20:18; Mark 8:31; 9:31; 10:33; Luke 9:22, 44; 18:31), to the end that the disciples would not suspect that he was overwhelmed by death ignorant and unwilling. (2) His transfiguration on the mount (Matt. 17:1–9), so that the hearts of his disciples might be strengthened against the scandal of his imminent death, and at the same time have a foretelling sign[17] of the glorification which would follow his death (Luke 24:26). (3) The use of those sacraments which had singular respect to his death, namely of the Passover (Luke 22:15), and its abrogation (Matt. 26:17–21), so that he might signify that he was that Passover lamb to be sacrificed for men (1 Cor. 5:7); and the institution of the sacramental Supper, inasmuch as it was both a prediction of his death while it was imminent, and a remembrance of it once it was passed (Matt. 26:28; 1 Cor. 11:24–26). (4) The pattern[18] for developing humility and brotherly love,[19] in the washing of the disciples (John 13:4–12). (5) A farewell sermon, as it were, wherein he endeavored to buttress the minds of the disciples first against his impending death and then against the persecutions that would follow (John 14–16). Finally, (6) his prayers on the verge of death,[20] in which, as he was about to depart, he commended his disciples into the hands of his Father (John 17).

---

17. προγνωστικόν
18. ὑποτύπωσις
19. φιλαδελφίας
20. *preces emortuales*

The Elenctic Part

It is asked: 1. Are circumcision, offering, Passover, and other ceremonies fitting for the Mediator? The affirmative reasons

XXIV. It is asked, first, regarding Christ's infancy, whether circumcision, dedication, attendance at Passover, and other ceremonies are appropriate for the person of the Mediator. The reason for doubting is because all those ceremonies presuppose sin, from which the Mediator was free. Nevertheless, it must be said that they are appropriate, because: (1) he was a Hebrew infant under God's national covenant, and such were, from the divine precept, obligated to those ceremonies (Gen. 17:10 with Gal. 5:3). (2) His dealings were to be with the Jews, inasmuch as he was sent to save the lost sheep of the house of Israel (Matt. 15:24), which without circumcision and the other ceremonies, could not have happened as it did (cf. Acts 16:3). (3) It was incumbent upon him to fulfill all righteousness for us (Matt. 3:15; 5:17; Rom. 8:3–4). (4) All the ceremonies were shadows to be removed by his observance of them, as by the body itself (Col. 2:17; Heb. 10:1). Individually, (5) circumcision was fitting for him because it was a seal of the covenant of grace (Gen. 17:10–11; Acts 7:8; Rom. 4:11), of which he was the Mediator and foundation (Heb. 8:6; 9:15; 12:24). Also (6) offering was fitting for him because he was the firstborn of God (Rom. 8:29; Heb. 1:6), who had to bring us, who were alienated by sin from God (Isa. 59:2), back to God (Isa. 49:6), for which he had to offer himself to the Father (Eph. 5:2). Finally also, (7) the Passover was fitting for him because he had to show himself to be its antitype (1 Cor. 5:7). Nor is it a hindrance that all these ceremonies presuppose sin, for although he was personally free from sin, yet covenantally he was made sin for us, that we might be made righteousness in him (2 Cor. 5:21).

2. Was baptism fitting for him?

XXV. Second, it is asked whether baptism was also fitting for him. The reason for questioning it could be twofold: first because circumcision and baptism coincide in substance (Col. 2:11), insofar as both are a sacrament of initiation and introduction into the covenant of grace; second, because baptism seals the remission of sins (Acts 2:38; 22:16) and the regeneration of the Holy Spirit (Titus 3:5), which the Mediator did not need.

The reasons of the affirmative opinion

Yet these things notwithstanding, baptism was fitting for him, for to the extent that (1) baptism is the ordinary sacrament of introduction into the covenant of grace (Acts 2:38–39 with Gen. 17:10), for whom was it more fitting than for him who is the Mediator and foundation of the covenant of grace (Heb. 12:24)? Also, to the extent that (2) baptism was an extraordinary sacrament of introduction or inauguration into the mediatorial office (Matt. 3:16–17), for whom was it more fitting besides him alone, who is the one and only Mediator (1 Tim. 2:5)? To the extent, however, that (3) it was a sign of the remission of sins and of regeneration by the Spirit, he did not receive it in his own name, but in the name of a surety,[21] because he is the sole meritorious cause of all remission and of the Holy Spirit who regenerates. I need not add that (4) he willed to be baptized so that he might foreshadow that baptism would be instituted by himself, and so that he might commend and consecrate it to us.

The foundations of the negative

So then it is no hindrance: (1) that it sealed remission and regeneration, for it did not seal it for him personally, but for us. (2) That baptism was the same as circumcision. For it was the same with respect to the substance, yet it was not with respect to the circumstance, to the extent that the covenant of grace was indeed sealed by both as to the step of initiation, but yet with respect to the different economy of the Old and the New Testament.

3. In the time of his fast, was he carried up to heaven?

XXVI. Third, it is asked whether during his forty-day fast, which followed his baptism, he was taken up to heaven so that there he might be more fully taught about the gospel mysteries to be preached to men. I respond, With what intent and by what reasons the Socinians affirm and the orthodox deny this, we discussed above, in chapter 6, §XIV.

4. Is it incumbent upon us to imitate Christ's forty-day fast?

XXVII. Fourth, whether Christ's forty-day fast provides for us an example for imitation. The papists, due to a love for the superstition peculiar to their own sect, affirm the question: "By his own fast," Granada says in his Lord's Day sermon on the *Invocavit*, "he sanctified the forty-day fast and conferred on it a heavenly virtue and dignity."[22] The orthodox certainly confess that all the actions of Christ were recorded for us for our instruction, but not all for our imitation. This fast also occurred for our imitation with respect to its genus, such that

---

21. *non proprio; sed sponsorio nomine*

22. The *Invocavit*, based on the Latin of Ps. 91:5, "He shall call upon me and I will answer him," is a standard collect and lesson on the first Lord's Day in Lent. See Luis de Granada (1508–1564), *Opera*, 3 vols. (Cologne: Officina Quenteliana apud Joannes Krebs, 1626), 2:219.

when the occasion invites us we should fast with Christ; yet not with respect to its species, such that we should fast for forty days every year, only abstaining from meat.

The arguments of the orthodox

This is because: (1) the Savior, who not infrequently commends fasts to his followers (Matt. 6:16–17; 9:15; 17:21; Mark 2:20), yet never does so by setting forth this fast of his as an example. (2) This fast is included among his miracles, which were recorded not for imitation, but for instruction, as we taught in the dogmatic part.[23] (3) Not even our adversaries are either able or willing to imitate Christ's fast, insofar as: (a) Christ did not fast every year, but only did so once, nor (b) did he accustom or invite his followers to such a fast for forty days, nor (c) did he fast by eating only fish, but by abstaining from all food and drink. So then (4) the fast of the papists is nothing but pure, unadulterated will-worship,[24] condemned by Christ himself (Matt. 15:9), and exploded by the apostle (Col. 2:20–23). I need not add that (5) this fast of the papists is not even a fast, inasmuch as a fast requires total abstinence from all sustenance, as is evident by induction from all the fasts that are mentioned in the Scriptures.

The papists' foundation

Nor do the papists have anything to allege for themselves to the contrary other than the general precept of imitation (1 Peter 2:21; Phil. 2:5; 1 Cor. 11:1). Yet by what rules this should be restricted we already taught above in the dogmatic part, §XXII. Compare Chamier, *Panstratia catholica* (bk. 19, ch. 7).[25]

5. Did the temptation of Christ happen historically?

XXVIII. Fifth, it is asked whether the temptation of the devil, which the Mediator endured after his fast, happened historically, through a visible appearance of the evil spirit,[26] his speech, his presentation of a stone, his leading him to the highest mountain and the summit of the temple, and so forth, or rather, ecstatically, through internal suggestions. Of the Protestants, all the Lutherans and most of the Reformed, together with the papists, affirm that the narrative occurred historically and just as it was written.[27] A few of the Reformed, among whom are Oecolampadius, Bucer, and others, on the contrary acknowledge

---

23. §§XVIII, XXII, above
24. ἐθελοθρησκεία (Col. 2:23)
25. Chamier, *Panstratia catholica*, 3:727–36.
26. *cacodaemonis*
27. κατὰ τὸ ῥητόν

that Satan truly tempted Christ, but that he did not do this in the presence of his body, but rather in the presence of his mind or his imagination.[28] Bekker, because he holds the opinion that evil spirits do not operate outside of themselves, either through their own strength or through a connection[29] which God willed to exist between their thoughts and such effects outside of themselves, denies that Satan truly tempted Christ: rather, "God willed that here his own well-beloved Son, who had set out to find solitude, would at one point represent to himself the devil as the one who had brought so many adversities upon men, whose work he now stood against, and who also would be opposed to him with all his strength if he could. He who was in all points tempted as we are (yet without sin, Heb. 4:15), long exercised by fasting and prayers, saw (as it seemed to him) the tempter coming to him, to endeavor in this way or that to lead him into apostasy." These are his words in *The World Bewitched* (bk. 2, ch. 21).[30] Yet being not sufficiently satisfied, as it seems, with this figment of his, he concludes near the end in these words, "Does someone want me to say how I know this?" (that is, this account). "That would not be fitting here, unless I should declare my opinion in this chapter more fully, lest perhaps I am misunderstood."[31] And so he adds no interpretation of this narrative at all. Finally, there are not lacking among the Reformed those who take a middle path, among whom is the renowned Lightfoot, who states on Matthew 4, "It was a delusion of the devil and a deception of the sight…. The devil led Christ to a mountain not so that he might truly show these things to him, but so that he might give a false appearance of them to him, although Christ was not deceived in the least, nor did not receive them as true things like the devil wanted, but as fictitious representations. Therefore the devil casts before the eyes of Christ the airy horizon, in which the devil produces these phantasms, for he is the prince of the air…on which he works, at times by true effects, as when he stirs up storms, and at times by imaginary appearances, as he does here…(and in Egypt through magicians)…. In these phantasms he first condenses the air, then imposes on it shape and color…all which is easy for him to do, as he is a spirit…ready to deceive."[32] These are the words of Dr. Lightfoot.

---

28. *phantasiam.* Johannes Oecolampadius (1482–1531), *Enarratio in Evangelium Matthaei* (Basel: Andreas Cratander, 1536), 47r–v; Martin Bucer (1491–1551), *Enarrationes perpetuae, in sacra quatuor Evangelia* (Strasbourg: Georg Ulrich Andlan, 1530), 32v.

29. σύνταξιν, referring to the opinion of the Cartesians. Cf. 1.3.7 §XXVII.

30. Balthasar Bekker (1634–1698), *De Betoverde Weereld* (Amsterdam: Daniel van den Dalen, 1691–1693), II.xx §11, p. 123. For more on Bekker, cf. *TPT*, vol. 3, Preface, p. xviii, n. 51, and p. 194, n. 37 (1.3.7 §XXVII).

31. Bekker, *De Betoverde Weereld*, 124.

32. In Latin, Mastricht abridged Lightfoot's English comments, cf. the English and Latin in John Lightfoot (1602–1675), "Harmonia Quatuor Euangelistarum" in *Opera omnia*, trans. and ed.

The arguments
The first of these opinions is especially pleasing to me, because it has no true difficulty, as is evident by the following arguments: because, in Bekker's opinion, (1) Christ would have tempted himself, instead of what the history relates, that Satan tempted him. (2) Christ would have assaulted himself with those blasphemies which the text attributes to Satan. He would have said to himself, "If you are the Son of God, command that these stones be made bread," "Cast yourself down," "All these things I will give to you, if you will fall down and worship me." (3) By his own imaginations, Christ would have led himself to the pinnacle of the temple, to the highest mountain, would have showed himself all the kingdoms of the world, would have said to himself, "All these things I will give you, if you will fall down and worship me," would have refuted himself by adducing the Scriptures, "Man does not live by bread alone," "You shall worship the Lord your God," "Depart from me, Satan." (4) This would have been an extraordinary dispute, wherein Christ, meeting with himself, assaulted himself and conquered himself. (5) From this masked conflict, as Bekker wants it, Christ received so much sorrow, anguish, and fear. Yet notwithstanding all this, (6) Christ was more certainly than certain persuaded that the devil had from the first seduction of man been condemned to perpetual imprisonments in such a way that it was now no longer permitted for him to have any dealings with men. That is to say, Christ represented to himself a Satan coming to him and tempting him, who could not come to him and tempt him. Let there be added to this that (7) Dr. Bekker could not present any sense of this narration that would even satisfy himself.

Objections
Meanwhile, with great effort he hunts for difficulties whereby he may obtain that Satan properly speaking did not tempt the Savior, and that the text must not be understood historically. He alleges: (1) that in this way Satan would have been foolish to want to lead the God-man into sin. I respond: (a) He was foolish, and was made a fool by him who takes the wise in their own craftiness (Job 5:13), especially since the entire business of this temptation concerned nothing other than that Satan would be made a fool. (b) What if also with the Pelagians and Jesuits, he thought that the Son of God, as one having the power of free choice,

---

D. Bor, J. Hill, R. Kidder, et al., 2nd ed., 2 vols. (Utrecht: Guilielmus Broedelet, 1699), 1:372–74; idem, *The Harmony of the foure Evangelists…from the baptism of our Saviour, to the first Passeover after*, 2nd ed. (London: R. Cotes, 1647), 33–35; idem, "Harmony of the Four Evangelists…part the Second" in *The Whole Works*, 13 vols. (London: Dove, 1822–1824), 4:370–73.

could have sinned? (2) That it would have been too little for the glory of the Son of God if he had been exposed to the temptations of the vilest spirit. I respond: (a) Was it more for the glory of Christ that he was exposed to the temptations and mockeries of the vilest Pharisees, scribes, and soldiers? (b) It may not have been for the glory of Christ, provided it was for his humiliation, through which, being in the form of God, and equal to God, he assumed the form of a servant (Phil. 2:7–8). Also, (c) it was for his glory that by this conflict he demonstrated to his own that he could conquer and crush the most powerful spirit. (3) That the vilest spirit would have provoked the Son of God to a miracle, whereby he would make bread out of stones. I respond: (a) Is there not enough impudence in him to do this? (b) It does not seem to have been Satan's intention to provoke him to a miracle, but to upbraid him for his extreme necessity, wherein after so many days of fasting, and the hunger contracted from it, he the Son of God did not even have bread to throw to his growling stomach, and thus he would lead him to faintheartedness by which he would hardly believe that he was the Son of God. It is as if he said, "Are you the Son of God? Is God your Father? You who have fasted for so many days, are tormented with hunger, and do not even have bread by which you may nourish your spirit: devour stones, or if you are the Son of God, make bread from stones." Is this so absurd an interpretation? (4) That it is inexplicable how from the desert he could be transported to the highest mountain such that by day people would not see him, and by night he would see the kingdoms of the world. Or how from a mountain, no matter how high, the devil could have shown him all the kingdoms of the world, even those that are on the other side of the world? How would he have lifted him to the pinnacle of the temple so that he might throw himself down from it? I respond: (a) Say that neither you, nor we, nor anyone can solve those difficulties: therefore is it pious and Christian to call into doubt the trustworthiness of the entire history handed down in the unanimous judgment of nearly all the Evangelists (Matt. 4:1–12; Mark 1:12–13; Luke 4:1–14)? (b) Neither could you untie as many difficulties attending Satan's first temptation, or how he seduced our first parents, whether by counsel or by example, but even so you have not yet dared to deny that that temptation truly happened. (c) Indeed does there not come into use here what you have in §12, "I would prefer to say that I do not understand Scripture in matters of this sort"?[33] (d) What if also we should say that those transports were made in his imagination, in a vision, such as that in which it appears Ezekiel was transported to the river Chebar? But we have not yet descended to those extremes. (e) What if Satan led him on foot by ordinary ways

----

33. Bekker, *De Betoverde Weereld*, 123.

to the pinnacle of the temple or to the highest mountain, to which end seems to point the word παραλαμβάνει, "he takes" (Matt. 4:5, 8; cf. ἐπιλαμβάνει, Acts 9:27; 17:19; 23:19; Heb. 8:9), that which could easily be done over the passing of time; and did not snatch him through the air? But how could he show him all the kingdoms of the world, even the ones on the other side of the world? I respond, He shows him in words, by speaking to him, by presenting to him historically all the kingdoms of the world (in which sense the word δείκνυμι, "show," occurs in 1 Cor. 12:31; Acts 10:28), especially when the glory of the world could scarcely be shown otherwise. With these things posited, what difficulty still remains in the history? Finally, (5) that created spirits, as they are mere thoughts, do not operate beyond themselves, nor by their own strength (which is also true in the case of good angels), nor through the connection made by God, who willed that upon such thoughts of evil spirits would follow such operations. I respond, This is his primary falsehood, which we have expressly rejected above in book 3, ch. 8, §XXI. Compare our *Epanorthosis* to Bekker, §XXIII.[34]

6. *In preaching did he correct or augment the law?*
XXIX. Sixth, whether the Savior in preaching corrected or augmented the law of Moses, sanctioned it with spiritual promises, and therefore produced the gospel from the law? For what purpose and by what reasons the Socinians affirm this and the orthodox deny it, we have indicated above in chapter 6, §XVII.

7. *Is all that Christ preached true? The objections of the Jews: First*
XXX. It is asked, seventh, whether all that Christ taught in his preaching is infallibly true. The Jews, out of hatred both for Christ and for the Christian religion, deny it. Christians on the contrary affirm it, and the method of demonstrating this affirmation we have explained in book 1, chapter 2, §XXX, so that here nothing remains to be done other than to refute the chief slanders of the Jews in a few words. Therefore, they allege: (1) that what he taught in Matthew 5:43, "You shall hate your enemy," is contrary to Moses. Thus Rabbi Isaac ben Abraham Troki in *Faith Strengthened*.[35] I respond, Christ did not teach this, but only recounted the opinion of those of old, that is, of the Pharisees and scribes, and he censures and corrects that under the name of the righteousness of the Pharisees (Matt. 5:20).

---

34. Petrus van Mastricht, *Ad Beckerum epanorthosis gratulatoria occasione articulorum, quos venerandae classi Amstelodamensi exhibuit* (Utrecht: Anthonius Schouten, 1692), 11–15.

35. Troki, *Faith Strengthened*, 212; idem, "Munimen Fidei" in *Tela Satanae*, 362.

Second

(2) That what he says in Matthew 10:34, "Do not think that I have come to send peace on earth, but a sword," is contrary to the Messiah, since it is said about the Messiah, that he would teach the nations peace (Zech. 9:10; Isa. 2:4).[36] I respond, Christ, so that he might more effectually uproot the error received by the Jews about the Messiah, that he would be a temporal king, who, once all the nations were subjugated, would bring to his people a profound earthly peace (an error also too deeply rooted among his own disciples), declared that he had not come to bring such peace to the world, but rather that on account of his teaching, there would arise in the world the fiercest fights and wars (Matt. 10:21–22). Meanwhile he does not deny that he came to restore to the world the spiritual peace which the prophets foretell about the Messiah: in fact he expressly asserted this peace for himself (John 14:27; 20:19; etc.; cf. Rom. 5:1; Eph. 2:14). Moreover he everywhere inculcated peace in his people (Matt. 10:13; Luke 24:36; John 20:19, 21; 14:27; Rom. 12:18).

Third

(3) That Christ speaks against himself, when in Matthew 11:13 he says that all the prophets and the law prophesied until John, but in Matthew 5:17 he denies that he came to destroy the law and the prophets, but to fulfill them.[37] I respond, In the prior text he intends nothing other than that all the prophets until John spoke of the Messiah as future (Isa. 2:2; Jer. 33:15; Joel 3:1; Num. 24:17; Heb. 11:13), whereas John showed him as present (John 1:29, 36); but in the latter text he means that he did not come to take away from the legal and prophetic writings the authority of obligating, nor to abrogate the moral law, but to fulfill it for us most precisely. What is the contradiction in these things?

Fourth

Nor is there any more of a conflict in (4) what they charge, that Christ affirms that John is Elijah (Matt. 11:14), and John denies it regarding himself (John 1:21),[38] if only you should distinguish the spiritual Elijah who had been promised as the forerunner of the Messiah (Mal. 4:5; Luke 1:17; Matt. 17:10–12), from the bodily Elijah or the Tishbite. Christ affirms that John is the spiritual Elijah, and John does not deny this; John denies that he is the Tishbite, and Christ does not affirm that.

---

36. Troki, *Faith Strengthened*, 239; idem, "Munimen Fidei" in *Tela Satanae*, 403.
37. Troki, *Faith Strengthened*, 240–1; idem, "Munimen Fidei" in *Tela Satanae*, 405.
38. Troki, *Faith Strengthened*, 240–1; idem, "Munimen Fidei" in *Tela Satanae*, 405.

Fifth

They allege (5) that it is false what is recorded in Matthew 15:17–18, "It is not what enters a person that contaminates him," because what entered our first parents contaminated them (Gen. 3), unclean animals contaminate when they enter the mouth (Lev. 11:43), that which is strangled and blood contaminate (Acts. 15:29).[39] I respond, If you should distinguish (a) bodily impurity or ceremonial impurity, about which Leviticus 11:43 speaks, from spiritual or moral impurity, about which Christ speaks, you will acknowledge that there is no conflict. Again with respect to moral impurity, (b) if you should distinguish the food itself that enters, about which Christ speaks—for example, the fruit of the tree of the knowledge of good and evil, the wine of Noah—from the abuse of the food, you will grasp that it is most true that it is not the food that enters, but the abuse of the food, which proceeds from the heart, that contaminates, and that did contaminate our first parents and Noah.

Sixth

They charge (6) that in practice Christ was opposed to his own teaching, when in Matthew 5:39 he commands that to him who strikes you on the one cheek you should turn the other, which he himself did not do when standing before the high priest (John 18:22). I respond, In Matthew 5:39, Christ forbids private vengeance, with Moses (Lev. 19:18) and Solomon (Prov. 24:29), in favor of which, as if it were lawful, the Pharisees twisted Exodus 21:24 and Deuteronomy 19:19, 21, which speak about public vengeance. And so that his people may be more removed from this private vengeance, he prescribes that if one or the other must be chosen, either private vengeance or being struck on the other cheek, they should prefer the latter rather than the prior. He is not opposed to this when before the high priest, because he did not use vengeance, but only a calm rebuke; moreover, he well enough offered up not only his other cheek, but his whole body, as is evident from Matthew 26:68, with Isaiah 50:6.

Seventh

They falsely allege (7) that in his teaching Christ abrogated all criminal judgments in John 8, because he said in verse 7, "He that is without sin among you, let him first cast a stone at her" (the adulteress), and in verse 11, "Neither do I condemn you."[40] I respond, Christ's intention is not to abrogate criminal judgments, inasmuch as he elsewhere expressly confirms them (Matt. 26:52; cf. Rom.

---

39. Troki, *Faith Strengthened*, 241–42; idem, "Munimen Fidei" in *Tela Satanae*, 406–7.
40. Troki, *Faith Strengthened*, 261–62; idem, "Munimen Fidei" in *Tela Satanae*, 435.

13:1–4), but to prudently dodge the tricks of the plotting Pharisees, (which are noted in v. 6), to which end he skillfully reminds them of their own guilt, that by the conscience of it they might flee accusations against a neighbor; then furthermore, there being no public judgment, he denied that it was incumbent upon him by office to condemn the accused woman.

Eighth

Then (8) they charge that Christ in John 13:34 calls a commandment that is most ancient, new (Lev. 19:18).[41] I respond, But they do not notice that "new" is used to name something that is splendid (Isa. 62:2; 65:15; Mark 16:7; Ps. 33:3).

Ninth

Also (9) they charge that Christ prohibited divorce in Matthew 19:8–9, which Moses commanded (Deut. 24:1–2). I respond, Moses did not command it, but permitted it on account of the Jews' hardness of heart (on which see Ex. 32:9; 33:3; Isa. 48:4), whereby the Jews deserted their wives "for every cause" (Matt. 19:3). And God did permit it, not ethically, such that it would not be sin (inasmuch as it is noted to be expressly prohibited in Mal. 2:14, 16), but only politically, so that it would not be civilly punished; however, Christ does nothing except prohibit it ethically, from the original institution of marriage.

Tenth

They allege (10) that Christ in Matthew 19:22 willed that we sell everything and give it to the poor, which God nowhere commanded in the law. I respond, He did not command it universally, but particularly, for a cause particular to that young man, that he might wean his soul from wealth, to which it was excessively devoted.[42]

Eleventh

They allege (11) that Christ permitted the use of unclean foods, which Moses prohibited, and that he abrogated other ceremonies that God commanded. I respond, Christ did not abrogate anything but what God had commanded for a certain period (Dan. 9:27), and he did not abrogate them before that period ended.

---

41. Troki, *Faith Strengthened*, 267; idem, "Munimen Fidei" in *Tela Satanae*, 444.
42. Troki, *Faith Strengthened*, 242–43; idem, "Munimen Fidei" in *Tela Satanae*, 407–9.

Twelfth

Finally, they charge (12) that he violated the Sabbath in many ways, by healing the sick, by permitting the disciples to pick heads of grain, and so forth. I respond, This is an old slander of the Pharisees (John 5:16; 9:16), which he expressly refuted (John 5:16; 12:10ff.) by showing that works of charity were by no means prohibited on the Sabbath, but rather commanded, and so forth. These are the chief points that Rabbi Isaac ben Abraham Troki falsely alleges in his *Faith Strengthened*.

8. Did Christ perform miracles truly so called?

The foundations of Christians, who affirm it

XXXI. Eighth, it is asked whether those miracles which Jesus of Nazareth performed are miracles truly so called, that is, divine miracles, and such that are valid to prove the Messiah. Christians affirm it, because: (1) the New Testament, which as our adversaries agree, attributes such miracles to him, is of universal truth and divine authority, just as much as the Old Testament, which we have demonstrated elsewhere (bk. 1, ch. 2, §§XXX–XXXI). (2) Jesus of Nazareth is the true Messiah, just as we demonstrated above (bk. 2, §XIX), to whom the Old Testament, as even the Jews admit, attributed true miracles, and the greatest miracles — even the very ones that the New Testament attributes to our Jesus. (3) Flavius Josephus, a Jewish writer who was his contemporary, expressly attributes to him many miracles (bk. 18, ch. 3).[43] The Jews, out of hatred for Jesus of Nazareth, falsely allege different things against the miracles of Christ, things which also do not agree well enough with each other. We will briefly examine them.

The objections of the Jews, who deny it. First

For now they falsely allege: (1) that the miracles of Christ were nothing except figments of the apostles, such as those that the Turks everywhere attribute to their Muhammad, Lucian to Apollonius, and the papists to their saints. I respond: (a) Let them prove it; otherwise you could allege the same thing against the miracles of Moses, Elijah, Elisha, and others. Indeed, (b) by the same arguments by which the Jews will prove to us the truth of the miracles of Moses, Elijah, and others, given that they were true, we also will prove to them the truth of the miracles of Christ. (c) The truth of the miracles of Christ has a testimony not only from the apostles and evangelists, men of proven faith who sealed their testimony even with their own blood, but also from the Gentiles, for example,

---

43. Josephus, *Antiquities*, 18.3.

from Julian the Apostate, who does extenuate the miracles but still acknowledges them (bk. 6 of *Against the Christians*),[44] indeed even from the Jews: from Flavius Josephus,[45] from the Talmud, which in *Avoda Zara* acknowledges that the son of the sister of Rabbi Joshua wanted to be saved from poison in the name of Jesus (ch. 2, בשם רבי ישו, in the name of his teacher Jesus).[46] Even more, all the Jews who state that he performed his works by the שם־המפרש, *Shem ha-Mephorash*, the exhibited name,[47] presuppose that he performed miracles. Moreover, (d) the reckoning of the miracles of Muhammad, Apollonius, and the papists is a whole heaven different, insofar as their miracles—or more correctly their marvels— were not performed in a crowded public gathering, even of a multitude of adversaries, but here or there, in a private corner, nor do they rest on the presence of so many and such great weight of witnesses, but only of one or two.

Second

Now they falsely allege (2) that he performed miracles by magical arts, like Pharaoh's magicians, like Simon the Magician. I respond: (a) That must be proved. (b) Otherwise the same thing could be said, for the same reasons, of the miracles of Moses, Elijah, and Elisha. (c) The hostile Pharisees would have accused Christ on this account before the Sanhedrin, to whom it belonged to judge matters of this sort, as it says in *Sanhedrin* (ch. 1, דני ממנות, "Monetary Cases").[48] (d) As regards the magicians of Egypt, they were finally convicted and refuted by the finger of God (Ex. 8:19); Christ never was.

Third

Now they allege (3) that Moses performed much greater and more evident miracles. I respond: (a) If that were true, it still would not prove that Christ's miracles

---

44. This book is only extant in excerpts. For representative statements, see Julian the Apostate (331–363), *Against the Galileans*, trans. R. Joseph Hoffman (New York: Prometheus Books, 2004), 116–17.

45. Josephus, *Antiquities*, 18.3.

46. Babylonian Talmud, Avodah Zarah 27b:6; *New Edition of the Babylonian Talmud*, trans. Michael L. Rodkinson (New York: New Talmud Pub. Co., 1918), 18:49. Cf. Jerusalem Talmud, Avodah Zarah 2:2; Johannes Hoornbeeck, תשובה יהודה, *sive Pro convinciendis et convertendis Judaeis, libri octo* (Leiden: Petrus Leffen, 1655), 233.

47. *nomen expositum*. Cf. 1.2.4 §XIII.

48. סנהדרין, *Sanhedrin*, is an eleven-chapter treatise in the *Seder Nezikin* section of the Babylonian Talmud. In its first chapter it is said that a member of the Sanhedrin must be able to preside over matters of witchcraft. "Tract Sanhedrin," *New Edition of the Babylonian Talmud*, 8:40, "R. Johanan said: The persons who are chosen to be members of the Sanhedrin must be tall, men of wisdom, of good appearance, and of a considerable age; and, also, they should understand something in cases of witchcraft."

were not miracles truly so called. (b) It is also false that Moses performed more illustrious miracles, for if you pay attention to the number of them, Rabbi Manasseh ben Israel (*Conciliator* on Deut., q. 11) says that Moses performed, or there were performed on his behalf, seventy-six miracles,[49] whereas Jesus is said to have performed so many that the world would not contain the abundance of the books enumerating them (John 20:30; 21:25).

Fourth

Nor are there lacking (4) those who say that he performed the miracles by the *Shem ha-Mephorash*,[50] that is, the exhibited name, *Jehovah*, by which they do not understand anything but the Tetragrammaton. This name, they say, Solomon ordered to be engraved in his temple on a certain stone, and forbid it from being committed to memory; and so that this would not happen, he placed two bronze dogs before the doors of the sanctuary on two columns, so that he who tried to memorize it would, upon exiting, by their terrible barking became so terrified that he forgot the name; however, Jesus wrote this name upon a piece of parchment and inserted it into his lacerated thigh, from there refreshed his memory of the name, and by its power performed his miracles. I respond, Luther expressly refuted this old wives' tale in a specific treatise which he entitled *Vom Schemhamphoras* (in the Jena *Opera*, vol. 8),[51] and surely it is not of such great moment to merit being examined by more words.

Fifth

Also, there are not lacking (5) those who allege that many things happened accidentally which we make into miracles, and that this occurred by the providence of God so that the Jews might be tempted. I respond: (a) It is unheard of for the dead to be accidentally restored to life, the blind to sight, the deaf to hearing, the sick to health, and that in such a great abundance. (b) Could you not also take the same exception to the miracles of Moses, Elijah, and Elisha, and that with greater semblance of truth? These generally are the chief points that Rabbi Isaac ben Abraham Troki in *Faith Strengthened*, and Rabbi Lusitanus in

---

49. Manasseh ben Israel, *Conciliator*, 235–40 (on Deut. 34:10); idem, *The Conciliator*, 304–6.

50. שמ־המפרש

51. Martin Luther, *Vom Schemhamphoras: und vom Geschlecht Christi* (Frankfurt, 1543). The Jena edition of Luther's *Omnia Opera* by Rhodius (1564–1570) has four volumes; the Wittenberg edition (1552–1558) has seven volumes; neither edition has this work.

his *Middleburg Colloquy*,[52] produce against the legitimacy of Christ's miracles. Compare Hoornbeeck, *For Convincing and Converting the Jews* (bk. 3, ch. 1).[53]

9. Was the life of Christ free from all sin? The foundations of those who affirm it
XXXII. Ninth, it is asked whether Christ's life and conversation was free from all sin. Christians affirm it, resting on: (1) not only the testimonies of the New Testament, the universal truth and divine authority of which we have demonstrated (bk. 1, ch. 2, §§XXX–XXXI), but also (2) the condition of the office through which he is the Messiah, just as we also have demonstrated (bk. 5, ch. 2, §XIX), as it is foretold that our sins would be placed upon one who was innocent, or righteous (Isa. 53:4–6), who would make his soul אשם, guilt,[54] for the sins of others, and accordingly had to be free from all sin. From these points we argue in this way: If the Messiah had to be free from all sin, and our Jesus is the Messiah, then he was free from sin.

The objections of the Jews
On the contrary, the Jews both ancient and more recent, out of pure hatred, not only attribute sins to him, but also a wicked life, in which he was a Samaritan, a blasphemer, a seducer, a demoniac, seditious, crucified on account of theft, who did not honor his mother, but despised her by rebuking her (Luke 2:49; John 2:4; Mark 3:33). But they do not endeavor to prove all these claims except by the accusations (not testimonies) of the Pharisees, scribes, elders, priests, chief priests, which are cited throughout the New Testament, by which at least obliquely they seem to presuppose the truth of the New Testament. I respond: (1) the witnesses adduced were his sworn enemies. (2) It was by the reproaches of these enemies that those crimes were imputed to him. Moreover, we readily acknowledge from the Gospel narrative that he was accused of some of them before a judge; but that he was ever convicted of any crime before a competent judge, is incumbent upon them to prove. Indeed, for abundance, (3) he was declared innocent by the very sentence of the judge, which we prove by the trustworthiness of the same Gospels whereby they impugn him with sins (namely in Matt. 27:23–24); added to this is the divinely inspired testimony of Pilate's wife (Matt. 27:19), that of his betrayer (Matt. 27:4), that of the centurion guard (Luke 23:47), and so forth. Specifically, (4) he did not dishonor his mother, but

---

52. Jacob Judah Aryeh Leon Templo (Lusitanus, 1603–c. 1675) wrote a dialogue between a Jew and a Christian entitled *Colloquium Middelburgense*, most commonly found in the anthology of Johann Müller (1626–1672), *Judaismus oder Judentumb* (Hamburg: Zachariah Hertel, 1644).

53. Johannes Hoornbeeck, *Pro convincendis et convertendis Judaeis*, 231–34.

54. *reatum* (Isa. 53:10)

only rightly rebuked her; and he did not rebuke her as her son, but as her God, for which reason he does not say, "Mother, what do I have to do with you?" but "Woman," (John 2:4).

10. Did Christ also suffer in his soul? Two hypotheses of the papists are refuted.
XXXIII. Tenth, it is asked whether Christ also suffered in his soul, or at least in the higher part of his soul. The papists deny it, for two causes: (1) because they state that the soul of Christ, from the first moment of his conception, was perfectly blessed; which is contradicted by his growth (Luke 2:40, 52) and ignorance (Mark 13:32). Then (2) so that they may more conveniently defend the local descent of Christ's soul into hell, or to the limbo of the fathers, which descent very many of the Reformed locate in the sufferings of his soul; whereas both (a) history teaches that his body was either hung on the cross, or that once put in the tomb, it stayed there, but that his soul was received into the hands of his Father (Luke 23:46), and (b) even the matter itself argues against a descent of this sort, because it is useless to the souls of Old Testament believers, who had already been delivered before the time of Christ into heavenly glory, as is evident in Enoch (Heb. 11:5), Elijah (2 Kings 2:1), and others.

The foundations of the orthodox
The Reformed on the contrary state that he also suffered in his soul, because: (1) Scripture expressly teaches this (Matt. 26:38; John 12:27; Isa. 53:10). And (2) the matter itself urges this, for unless he had sustained the torments of soul which were incumbent upon us from sin, he would not have taken them away. We will have more to say about these things in their own place.[55]

11. Were the things Christ suffered before his last three hours satisfactory?
The difference of opinions
XXXIV. It is asked, eleventh, whether what Christ suffered before the last three hours of his life, or of the darkening of the sun, pertained to the satisfaction for our guilt as much as did those things which he suffered during those three hours. The Socinians do not want any of the sufferings of Christ to have been satisfactory, but only to have resulted in our good, namely that he might confirm his doctrine by them, offer an example of suffering for us, show us the way in which through extremities we may ascend to dignities,[56] that having by his sufferings been made a merciful high priest, he might promptly bring aid to us who have

---

55. 1.5.12 §X
56. *per angusta, enitamur ad augusta*

been tempted, that he might make satisfaction for the truth of the predictions and the signification of the types; however, in no way did he suffer that he might make satisfaction for our sins.

The hypotheses of a certain learned man
There is a certain man among the Reformed, a learned man, and also famous for his writings, who acknowledges against the Socinians that certain sufferings of Christ were satisfactory, namely only those that he bore during the last three hours of his life, but that the rest were only devoted to our good in a general way, and indeed that not even the temporal death of Christ was satisfactory.[57] So then he distinguishes between Christ's convicting sufferings, through which a person is convicted of his own sin, yet in such a way that by the endurance of them satisfaction was not made to the avenging divine justice, nor was our guilt taken away; and his compensating sufferings, by which satisfaction was made to the divine justice (which is discussed in Rom. 2:5–9), which is called "the wrath to come" (Matt. 3:7; 1 Thess. 1:10). Likewise he distinguishes between his martial sufferings, to which Christ was exposed while fighting with Satan, fleeing from Herod, enduring persecutions and reproaches of enemies, according to the pronouncement of God (Gen. 3:15); and his judicial sufferings, which were inflicted upon him by God as the strict Judge, for the compensation of his justice. He extends the prior ones to Christ's entire life and the latter only to the last three hours of his life. His hypotheses are principally these, that: (1) the death declared to the man if he would sin, was only that death that he experienced on the very day on which he sinned; but that was not bodily death, but the wrath of God, which he underwent on the very day in which he sinned, when he hid himself from the face of God in the thickness of the trees of the garden, not unlike those to be damned will one day desire to do (Rev. 6:15). Then (2) by this death of our first parents, satisfaction was made to God with respect to the truth of the threat, but not to the divine justice, which demanded full compensation: to this justice, from the mediatorial covenant between the Father and the Son, the longsuffering[58] of God intervened up to the day of wrath and the last judgment.

---

57. This distinction is maintained in Jacob Alting (1618–1679), Locus IX, "On the punishment of sin," in *Methodus theologiae didacticae* in *Opera*, 5 vols. (Amsterdam: Gerardus Borstius, 1685–1687), 5:91; cf. idem, "Epistola LXXVI," Alting to J. R. Wettstein, Sr., in *Opera*, 5:393–95. Hermann Witsius (1636–1708) had also referred to Alting as a *Vir Doctus* among the Reformed who made the same distinctions that Mastricht mentions here; Witsius, *De oeconomia foederum Dei cum hominibus libri quatuor*, 3rd ed. (Utrecht: Franciscus Hama & Gulielmus vande Water, 1694), bk. 2, ch. 6, pp. 177–201.

58. μακροθυμία

(3) This death of man, who was to that point still whole from the union of body and soul, Christ sustained in the fullness of time, when hanging on the cross he was abandoned by God, and at the same time experienced the most bitter wrath of God, who, while he demanded satisfaction from him, was delighted by his contrition. (4) This contrition men could not have noticed on account of the thickest darkness that surrounded them. (5) This death he sustained while still alive, until full satisfaction had been made to the divine justice. This happened at last upon the cross when he cried out, "Why have you forsaken me?" This was the approaching death that he feared in the garden, which fear is for this reason called προπάθεια, suffering anticipatory to that death, from which he was delivered when he said, "It is finished." (6) This alone is the death which he undertook for us as our surety in the eternal covenant of grace, and which he paid on the cross, and not any bodily death, which accordingly concerns not meriting the satisfaction, but representing it.

The common opinion of the Reformed, with their reasons
On the contrary, the common opinion of the Reformed holds that God declared every kind of death upon our first parents who would sin—death bodily, spiritual, and eternal—and every misery pertaining to it, either as a component or as a preparation. This death Christ in the mediatorial covenant diverted from the elect onto himself, by promising an absolute surety,[59] and paid it on the cross, and so then, all his miseries throughout his entire life up to his last breath, taken together, pay the ransom price[60] belonging to our sins. This is because: (1) all his weaknesses and sorrows, which he indubitably bore and carried throughout all his life, were ours (Isa. 53:4), he was wounded for our transgressions (v. 5), inasmuch as the Lord made them to fall upon him (v. 6). All those things without a doubt happened before his last three hours. So then (2) he is said to have been made perfect διὰ παθημάτων, through sufferings (Heb. 2:10), so that he might redeem (v. 15), certainly through all the sufferings of his entire life, from which sufferings he learned obedience (Heb. 5:8), and being made perfect, became the cause of salvation to all who obey him (v. 9). To this end (3) he is surely said to have suffered for us (1 Peter 2:21) all those things by which he left us an example of patience; and when those things are said to have been suffered ὑπὲρ ὑμῶν, for you, they are certainly pronounced to be satisfactory. Especially (4) his bodily death is spoken of as satisfactory in Isaiah 53:10, after he laid down his soul as an אשׁם, propitiation for sin. Christ teaches that his bodily death is understood

---

59. *expromittendo*
60. λύτρον

here (Matt. 20:28; John 10:15, 17). (5) Paul holds the same thing (Col. 2:22; Rom. 5:10; Heb. 9:15), and Peter does as well (1 Peter 3:18). And what is that death? It is certainly bodily, a death which confirmed a testament (Heb. 9:16–17). Pointing to the same conclusion are (6) his scourging and stripes, by which we are healed (Isa. 53:5; 1 Peter 2:24). (7) And especially also the λύπη, pain, τάραξις, turmoil, ἀδημονία, trouble, εὐλάβεια, timidity, θάμβος, astonishment, περιλυπία ἕως θανάτου, exceeding sorrow to death, about which the evangelists speak, which threw him to the ground upon his face, wrenched from him drops of blood, as well as prayers and supplications with tears and strong crying, all which certainly preceded his last three hours. Moreover, to refer all these things to προπάθεια, anticipatory suffering, is much too barren, and in addition devoid of all reason.

Objections of the learned man
With respect to the contrary hypotheses: (1) it is said gratuitously that the only thing that pertains to the punishment of the first sin is that which was inflicted on the very day of the sin: the text speaks against this (Gen. 3:16ff.). Neither in this way would there pertain to the punishment of sin those things which are discussed at greater length in Leviticus 26:14–40 and Deuteronomy 28:15ff. Yet we do not deny that our first parents contracted on the very day of the transgression the guilt of every kind of death, and the punishment itself of spiritual death, which the apostle speaks of in Ephesians 2:1, 3. With respect (2) to the distinctions between convicting and compensating sufferings, and likewise between military and judiciary sufferings, we think that they are distinctions without a difference, that is, they are not distinctions, because that wrath of God which he experienced during his last three hours, also convicted us of the weight of sin, nor can any convicting or military penalty be taught that would not at the same time be a compensating and judiciary penalty. With respect to his objections, he alleges (3) that the sin of the whole land was expunged in one day (Zech. 3:9), and that Paul testifies that by Christ's one offering, accomplished once on the cross, his expiatory sacrifice was completed (Heb. 9:28; 10:12, 14). We acknowledge that it was completed on the cross, but we do not acknowledge that it did not begin during the preceding sufferings: for from all his sufferings coalesces that single sacrifice accomplished and completed on the cross. Again, (4) that before the sufferings of the cross he was not a priest. Whereas from his very birth he was the Messiah, the anointed, the Christ (although the function of that priestly office in its chief part was completed on the cross; cf. John 19:37; Luke 2:49), and he also interceded for the church (John 17; Zech. 1:12–13). In addition, (5) that prior to the sufferings of the last three hours, he was under

the favor of God (Luke 2:52; Matt. 3:17; 17:2; Luke 10:21). I respond, He was, at intervals, so that he could also discharge other priestly duties, but from this it does not follow that being the beloved Son of God, and even so being under God's wrath, is contradictory, as is evident in Absalom with respect to his father David (2 Sam. 13:38–39 with 14:21, 24). For, as the Son, as the beloved, as the one obedient to the Father even to the point of death, Christ even while existing under wrath during the three hours on the cross nevertheless pleased the Father, although as the surety, on account of the sins of others which he undertook, he was under wrath. His remaining objections are of entirely no weight. Therefore our discussion here should be sufficient, especially since not only did the author himself regret this cause, as is evident from his letters published after his death, but also, he presently has no followers as far as I know. Our most renowned and closest colleague Dr. Witsius has dealt most clearly and solidly with this cause in his *Economy of the Covenants* (bk. 2, ch. 6, 3rd ed.), and we have consulted him for our discussion here.[61]

12. Is footwashing a sacrament? The opinion of our adversaries
XXXV. Finally twelfth, it is asked whether footwashing (which in the preparation of Christ for death occurred between the abrogation of Passover and the institution of the Lord's Supper) was made an ordinary sacrament of the Christian church. The Roman popes, in affectation of Christ,[62] on the fifth day of the week before the feast of Easter have customarily washed the feet of certain poor men. Also in the church of Milan and in several others this was the received custom, as Cornelius à Lapide testifies on John 13:7,[63] that the feet of those to be baptized were washed by the bishop, and then by the priests and clerics in the font that stood for this purpose before the doors of the temple. Next, he says, the bishop kissed the feet he washed and the bottom part of the foot was placed on the bishop's head. Among the Anabaptists there is a sect whom they call the ποδονίπτοι or "footwashers": they consider it as a sign, that is, as a sacrament of the church.

The opinion of the orthodox and its foundations
The Reformed acknowledge that Christ prescribed his example of humility and humanity for all his followers (just as he prescribes his example of longsuffering

---

61. Witsius, *De oeconomia foederum Dei cum hominibus libri quatuor*, 177–201.

62. κακοζηλία *Christi*

63. Cornelius à Lapide, *Commentaria in Quatuor Evangelia*, 2 vols. (Antwerp: Meursius, 1681), 2:448.

and humility in Matt. 11:29), but by a clearly extraordinary rite, and one that was to the eastern regions, and also to the patriarchs under the Old Testament, not sacred but civil. This can be evidenced: (1) from this, that after this first example of this rite, there is not any commandment or imitation of it found in the entire New Testament. (2) From this, that it could not be used decently and properly enough by both sexes in a church assembly, according to the custom of the sacraments. From which the Anabaptists themselves conclude in their own *Confession of the Most Principal Heads of the Christian Faith against Herman Faukelius* (p. 261), "Footwashing is not necessarily appointed for every person, and therefore must not be used in the public place of assembly."[64] (3) From this, that the rite of Christ, as it is presented at length in seven or nine circumstances in John 13:4–15, namely that Christ: (a) rose from supper, (b) laid aside his cloak, (c) took a towel, (d) girded himself, (e) poured water into a basin, (f) washed their feet, (g) wiped the washed feet with the towel with which he was girded; to which two others are additionally included, (h) that the Master himself (i) washed the feet of the disciples—this rite, I say, can scarcely be observed in all these particulars in the public assemblies, according to the custom of the sacraments.

The foundations of our adversaries
Our adversaries do not have anything to support their opinion except the one passage, John 13, and in it the example of Christ lighting the way, with the command of imitation; but without any difficulty both the example and the command can be fulfilled by the imitation and observance, not of an external rite as a sign, but of humility and humanity, as the thing signified. Compare 1 Timothy 5:10 with the marginal annotation of the Dutch translators.[65]

---

64. Claes Claesz (Nicolaus Claesz), *Bekentenisse van de voornaemste Stucken des Christelijcken Gheloofs, ende der Leere, dienende tot antwoort op het Boecken Harmani Faukeli Babel der Wederdooper* (Amsterdam: Jacob Aertsz Colom, 1624), 261; cf. Herman Faukelius (1560–1625), *Babel, dat is Verwerringhe der wederdooperen onder malkanderen over meest alle de stucken der Christelicke leere* (Middelburg: Hans vander Hellen, 1621), 211–12.

65. *The Dutch Annotations upon the Whole Bible: or, All the Holy Canonical Scriptures of the Old and New Testament*, trans. Theodore Haak (London: Henry Hills, 1657) on 1 Tim. 5:10, "… if she have washed the saints feet, [As this was very usual in those warm countries, where people went bare-footed and onely upon soles, and therefore being wearied, or fouled with dust, many were wont to use such services for refreshment. See Joh. 13. Ver. 5, 14. and by this one example of courtesie all manner of care and service is understood.]" cf. *Het Nieuwe Testament* (Leiden: Paulus Aertsz van Ravensteyn, 1637), fol. 124n18.

The Practical Part

*The practice of the life of Christ: 1. Offers an example for parents in the
raising of their children.* Bodily care

XXXVI. With respect to practice, first, the infancy of the Mediator, or his
entrance into this life, offers an example for Christian parents in the raising of
their children. For as in the raising of Christ, his parents supplied him with a
twofold care, bodily and spiritual, so also the same twofold care is incumbent
upon parents with regard to their own offspring. For with respect to his bodily
care, we observe that his parents provided for Christ: (1) nourishment, insofar as his mother without doubt supplied him sustenance from her own breasts
(cf. Luke 11:27), according to the example of Sarah (Gen. 21:7; Ps. 22:9); likewise
parents should provide suitable nourishment and sustenance for their children
(Luke 11:11–13). Then (2) clothing, insofar as they swaddled the newborn child
(Luke 2:7); likewise parents should provide the necessary clothing for their children, according to the example of Jacob (Genesis 37:3; cf. 27:15). Furthermore,
(3) advantages of living, insofar as once he was swaddled they laid him in a manger to sleep (Luke 2:7); so also parents should provide to an adequate extent
those things that pertain not only to the necessities of life, but also to its lawful
advantages; for example, in an honorable marriage (Jer. 29:6; 1 Cor. 7:26, 38),
and so forth. Finally, (4) bodily security, insofar as to avoid Herod's treachery
they fled with the young child into Egypt (Matt. 2:14), and also afterwards, for
their son to avoid poverty, they trained him in the work of a craftsman (Mark
6:3; Matt. 13:55); likewise parents should provide for their children bodily security of every sort, by which they may profit not only while they are alive but also
after their death: to this end they should take care that they may be seasonably
trained in some honorable vocation (Prov. 22:6; 20:11).

Spiritual care

With respect to his spiritual care, which was so much the more careful, we
observe that the parents of Christ took care that: (1) their young son would
be under the covenant of grace with them, and would receive its symbol, the
sacrament of initiation, that is, circumcision, according to the divine prescription (Luke 2:21); likewise parents should take pains that their children would
be covenanted with God and would in timely fashion receive the sacrament of
initiation, holy baptism (Gen. 17:10; Acts 2:38–39; 16:33; Ps. 22:10). (2) Then
their young son, whom God now had received into the covenant and to whom
he had given himself, they as it were would give back to him by his solemn dedication (Luke 2:22); likewise, and even more, parents should take care that their

children, who have been alienated from God by their own guilt, would be as it were restored and dedicated anew to God, by prayers (Gen. 17:18) as well as labors (Eph. 6:4; cf. 1 Sam. 1:11). To this end (3) they bring their young son from Bethlehem to Jerusalem to the temple (Luke 2:22), that is, to the house of God, where God dwelled, to the end that he might in timely fashion become a member of the household of God (Eph. 2:19), and be about his Father's business (Luke 2:49); all parents should do the same: they should bring their children in a timely fashion to the temple (Luke 2:42; 1 Sam. 1:22, 24; Joel 2:16), so that they would with them be gradually accustomed to God and conversation with God (Job 22:21). And also (4) for their own as well as for their son's impurity (the guilt of which the Son took from us upon himself), they sacrifice a pair of turtledoves and pigeons (Luke 2:24); all parents should do the same: they should offer for their own as well as their children's native impurity, together with the sighs of turtledoves and pigeons, that is, with true and profound repentance, the one sacrifice that was prefigured by the turtledoves and pigeons (Job 1:4–5). In addition, (5) they commit their own young son into the arms of Simeon, that he might in God's stead receive him and bless him (Luke 2:28, 34); all parents should do the same: they should commit their children into the arms of the priests, that they may receive and bless them, after the counsel and example of the Savior (Matt. 19:13–14; Mark 10:13–14; Luke 18:15–16) and of Hannah (1 Sam. 1:25); they should commit their children to the priests to be instructed and catechized (Prov. 22:6; Deut. 6:7–8; Eph. 6:4; Ps. 34:11–12). Finally, (6) in holiness and religious worship they light the way for their son, they go up every year to Jerusalem to celebrate the feast of Passover (Luke 2:41–42); all parents should do the same (Ps. 101:2; Josh. 24:15).

Motives

If all Christian parents would faithfully discharge all these duties toward their children according to the example of Christ's parents, then also with Christ's parents: (1) they will see with delight their children growing, and becoming strong in spirit, as those filled with wisdom, upon whom the grace of God rests (Luke 2:40). (2) They will have children that are compliant and obedient to them (Luke 2:51), on account of whom (3) they will be able to be blessed, and be celebrated as blessed (Luke 11:27), children in whom (4) or in whose reputation they will be able to rejoice and delight, as at a miracle (Luke 2:33; Prov. 10:1; 23:25), children who in turn (5) will faithfully take up the care of them until their death (cf. John 19:26–27).

2. Christ's adolescence should be an example for adolescents.
(1) Three gifts of Christ as an adolescent: Strength of spirit
XXXVII. Second, Christ's adolescence and youth (which the Holy Spirit certainly represents briefly but boldly in Luke 2:40ff.) presents an example for imitation to adolescents and youths. For in Christ's adolescence and youth there are evident: (1) three gifts especially necessary for adolescents and youths, and thus to be sought with every effort: (a) growth and strengthening of spirit, walking in equal step with the growth and strengthening of body: "And the child grew and was strengthened in spirit," ἐκραταιοῦτο πνεύματι (Luke 2:40). Whether you should translate those words, "He grew strong in spirit," namely in his own spirit, that is with respect to his mind and spiritual things, or, "He grew strong by the Spirit," namely God's Spirit, it makes little difference, because they can be easily conjoined, so that the sense would be: the boy, as he grew in his body, with the Holy Spirit strengthening his mind, so also he advanced and grew strong in spiritual matters (cf. Luke 1:80; 2:52). Therefore such a kind of strengthening of spirit is especially necessary in adolescents and youths, and so then must be most eagerly sought, because this period of life is most dangerously exposed to Satan's temptations, which require the greatest amount of spiritual strength to overcome (1 John 2:13–14; Eph. 6:10–12).

Fullness of wisdom
(b) Fullness of spiritual wisdom: "filled" or "replete with wisdom" (Luke 2:40), under which as the chief type are included all the rest of the intellectual habits: understanding, knowledge, prudence, and skill; indeed even civil wisdom, but nevertheless chiefly spiritual wisdom, which not only concerns spiritual things, but is itself spiritual, and is occupied in a spiritual way with spiritual things (the wisdom of which the apostle speaks in 1 Cor. 1:21; 2:6, 7, 13, 15). Such wisdom is all the more necessary and desirable for adolescent youths because adolescents and youths are prone to foolishness (Prov. 20:15; 7:7), which must be driven out of them to the end that they may be able more securely not only to obtain ability in the arts and sciences, but also to know and avoid the tricks of Satan and the seducing world (cf. Gen. 41:12ff.). Accordingly the most wise Solomon shows to youths the means of pursuing this (Prov. 1:4), namely: (i) the Word of God (Ps. 119:9; 19:7–8); he adds (ii) the fear of God (Prov. 1:7; 9:10; Ps. 111:10; 25:12); to which must be added (iii) prayers (James 1:5).

The communion of divine grace
(c) The communion of divine grace: "And the grace of God was upon him" (Luke 2:40), whether you understand by the grace of God here either, the favor itself

of God, or the grace freely given, or, the products of this favor, the spiritual gifts, or the grace freely given (concerning which 1 Cor. 12:4 speaks). For Christ was strong in both: in favor (Matt. 3:17; Isa. 42:1; Matt. 12:18; Luke 9:35; 2 Peter 1:17), as well as in spiritual gifts (Isa. 11:1–2). Both graces are especially necessary and worthy of seeking by adolescents, so that, as by the grace of age they may commend themselves to men, so also by the grace of virtue they may commend themselves to God; and accordingly, just as in Christ, so also in them, the two may be united: "grace with God and with men" (Luke 2:52).

(2) The religion of Jesus as an adolescent, through various acts:
Of natural worship
From this triple gift, there resulted in Jesus as a youth and adolescent: (2) religion, or the worship of God, through various acts: (a) those of the worship that is natural to God, namely, love toward his heavenly Father and his Father's business (Luke 2:49), which includes, according to his own thought (Matt. 22:37, 40), all the remaining duties, knowledge, reverence, obedience, confidence, submission, and so forth. Adolescents (Ps. 71:6) and youths (Eccl. 12:1; Lam. 3:27) ought to give themselves to this same religion, according to what is prescribed in the first commandment.

Of instituted worship
(b) The acts of instituted worship, through which he was present at the public sacrifices in the ecclesiastical assembly at Jerusalem, from the divine command, at the stated times, without any will-worship (Luke 2:41–42). Adolescent youths should do the same, after the example of Samuel (1 Sam. 2:18), from what is prescribed in the second commandment.

Zeal and devotion in worship
Moreover, (c) Christ did not do this perfunctorily, but with great zeal and devotion, at the tender age of twelve years old making such a great journey from Nazareth toward Jerusalem, and that on foot (Luke 2:41–42). Our young people should imitate his zeal and devotion in the divine worship, like Josiah (2 Kings 22ff.). And that from what is prescribed in the third commandment.

Sanctifying of holy times
(d) Jesus religiously sanctified the appointed times dedicated for divine worship, setting out every year for Jerusalem with his parents for the feast of Passover (Luke 2:41–42), staying there for the appointed time, and indeed from love for worship adding three days (vv. 43, 46), and devoting that time not only to

ceremonial and ordinary duties, but also to moral and extraordinary duties, to disputations (Luke 2:46). Our young people should offer similar things, according to what is prescribed in the fourth commandment.

Denial of the world

Besides these things (e) in our Jesus there is evident a singular denial of the world and of worldly things, wherein, out of love for his heavenly Father and for the things that belong to this Father, and likewise out of love for divine worship, he deserts his earthly parents and his worldly relations, which otherwise are the most dear and beloved things to us in this world, so that he could be free for divine worship (Luke 2:43, 46). Our young people also should imitate him, according to the thought of Jesus (Matt. 10:37; cf. 19:27, 29).

Zeal for knowing God and divine things

Moreover, (f) zeal for knowing God and divine things, by which, leaving his parents and relations, for three days he was occupied in inquiries and disputations with the doctors (Luke 2:46). Our youths also should imitate him, especially those who are preparing themselves for the sacred ministry, by the example of Timothy (2 Tim. 3:15).

(3) Righteousness toward men, and its four acts

Finally, there resulted (3) righteousness or humanity, especially directed toward his parents, through which: (a) he imitated the piety of his parents, going up with his parents to the feast (Luke 2:41–42). So also by all means our adolescent youths should unhesitatingly follow in the footsteps of their parents and ancestors, at least of the godly ones, just as is said of Josiah (2 Kings 22:2). (b) He patiently sustained the rebuke of his mother, although it was unfair, and refuted it mildly (Luke 2:49), and corrected her by reason. So also our young people should patiently bear the infirmities of their parents, teachers, and others, and never rail at them (1 Peter 2:18; 1 Sam. 20:34; cf. 2 Sam. 16:23–17:1 with 19:24, 26–28). (c) He renders proper obedience to them (Luke 2:51). So also our young people should render it as well (Prov. 1:8; Eph. 6:1, 5; Col. 3:20). (d) He submitted himself to his parents' instruction, in learning the skill of a builder, and also afterwards in exercising it (Matt. 13:55; Mark 5:3). So also our young people should be submissive, according to their parents' determination, to be trained in the manual trades, or in the liberal arts (Prov. 22:6; 20:11).

Motives

In all these things, if our young people would faithfully walk in the footsteps of Jesus as an adolescent and youth, then: (a) they will acquire for themselves a reputation by which they will be esteemed by all, just as the adolescent Jesus was (Luke 2:47). (b) They will surpass even their instructors, their parents, their doctors in knowledge (Ps. 119:99), just as the adolescent Jesus did (Luke 2:46–47, 50). (c) They will grow strong in grace and favor with God, so that with Solomon they may be called Jedidiah, "Beloved of Jehovah" (2 Sam. 12:25), just as the adolescent Jesus from that time grew strong in grace with God (Luke 2:52). Likewise (d) they will grow strong in grace and favor with men, just as Daniel did (Dan. 9:23; 10:11, חמודות איש, "a man of desires"; Rom. 14:17–18), in the same way the adolescent Jesus did (Luke 2:52).

3. His adulthood offers an example for ministers.

Regarding preparation for ecclesiastical function.

XXXVIII. Third, his adulthood, in which he discharged his public life and prophetic function, offers an example to those who undertake a public life, and especially an ecclesiastical life, in many points: (1) so that with unwashed hands they would not leap into a public function, especially into that of the ecclesiastical ministry, but for a sufficient time they would prepare themselves for it, so that they can provide a proof or specimen of one who should be brought into it (1 Tim. 3:10), and that they may have no cause for shame (2 Tim. 2:15). Just as Jesus, although in his twelfth year of age he had provided incomparable specimens of his aptitude (Luke 2:46–47), yet still willed to live privately from then until his thirtieth year, and to prepare himself for his public function (Luke 3:23).

Regarding legitimate calling

(2) So that without a legitimate calling they would not of their own accord rush into the sacred ministry (Jer. 14:14–15; 23:21, 32), much less that they would thrust themselves on churches by force, or by the strategems of simony, but rather wait for the lawful sending of God. Just as Christ did not undertake his public function in the church before he had by baptism been solemnly inaugurated to it (Matt. 3:16–17).

Regarding temptations

(3) So that those who should be brought into the sacred ministry would not promise themselves all manner of halcyon circumstances, but rather, every kind of the most dreadful temptations, struggles, persecutions, thorns in the flesh,

and buffetings of the devil (2 Cor. 12:7; 11:23ff.; 2 Tim. 4:7–8), and they would seasonably fortify themselves against such things by fastings and prayers (Acts 13:2–3). By the example of Jesus Christ, who having just been inaugurated to the prophetic function through baptism, and led away into the desert by the Spirit, before he was harassed by Satan in three of the strongest assaults, had wisely fortified himself against them by forty days of fasting (Matt. 4:1–12).

Regarding preaching
(4) So that now adequately prepared, lawfully called, and armed against all assaults, they would eagerly gird themselves for the preaching of the Word (2 Tim. 4:2). Just as Christ, adequately prepared through eighteen years of private life, and through studies, then solemnly inaugurated in baptism, and armed against temptations, straightway girded himself for his function (Mark 1:14–15). And ministers should do this faithfully and laboriously, ἐν κόπῳ καὶ μόχθῳ, in labor and toil, in many sleepless nights, in hunger and thirst and many fasts, in cold and nakedness (2 Cor. 11:27). Moreover, not only should they do this publicly, but also privately, from house to house, day and night (Acts 20:20, 31), just as Christ taught by traveling from village to village, as we showed in the dogmatic part.[66]

Regarding operations
(5) So that they would not only teach by speaking, but also by doing what they teach (Acts 20:35; Titus 2:7; cf. Matt. 7:22), and that they would at every point pursue the welfare of their people, not only spiritually, but also, as much as is in them, temporally (Heb. 13:17; 1 Thess. 2:7), just as Christ not only cared for the souls of his people by preaching, but also for their bodies by healing them and casting out demons, as we have shown in the dogmatic part.[67]

Regarding sufferings
(6) So that they would not only teach, and do it faithfully, but also bravely suffer all adversities (2 Cor. 11:27ff.; Acts 20:22–24), just as Christ endured all adversities against his reputation, his prosperity, his body, and especially his soul, just as we have shown in the dogmatic part.[68]

---

66. §XIV, above
67. §§XVII–XVII, above
68. §XXI, above

Regarding lighting the way for others, and the example of their life

Finally, (7) so that by their life's example they would light the way for their people (Titus 2:7; 1 Cor. 11:1), and not, like the Pharisees, place burdens upon others, which they do not touch even with one finger (Matt. 23:3–5; Rom. 2:21–23), just as Christ, who in all things that he prescribed for others to do, lit the way for them by his own example, as we have shown in the dogmatic part.[69]

4. Christ's later life offers an example of preparation for death, in seven particulars

XXXIX. Fourth, Christ's later life[70] or preparation for death offers an example for imitation for all, but especially for those more advanced in years, and thus closer to death. For just as in this preparation of his own, Christ: (1) frequently and earnestly meditated upon his approaching death, when he so many times foretold to his disciples that it was impending, just as we have shown in the dogmatic part,[71] and consequently gradually accustomed himself to death, so that he might not be overwhelmed by it, as by a snare; so we also, by a frequent and earnest contemplation of our death, should accustom ourselves to it (Ps. 39:4–5; 90:12; James 4:13–14 with Eccl. 7:2; 1 Cor. 15:31), so that we may not be overwhelmed by it suddenly (1 Thess. 5:6; 1 Peter 4:7; Rom. 13:13).

(2) Just as Christ did not bear with any annoyance others' discussions and warnings regarding his impending death, but willingly received them, namely from Moses and Elijah when they spoke of his departure (Luke 9:31), so we also should not shrink from conversations and warnings about our own approaching death (Isa. 38:1). Especially from Moses, that he would recall to our mind the wages of our sins (Gen. 2:17), so that we may be profoundly humbled before God regarding them, and in a timely fashion before death be converted from them to God, so that we would not die in sins (Luke 21:34, 36). Then also from Elijah, Christ's forerunner, that he would prepare our heart to receive Christ with living faith before we depart (Isa. 40:3; Mark 1:3 with Luke 2:28–29).

(3) Just as Christ in his preparation willed to be transfigured (Matt. 17:2), and therefore to experience a foretaste and firstfruits of the glorification to follow after death, and by it to be fortified against the horror and bitterness of his impending death, so we also should strive with all our strength to be transfigured before death (Rom. 12:2), striving not only for true repentance (Rom. 12:2), but

---

69. §XXII, above
70. *senectus*, lit. "old age"
71. §XXIII, above

also for the firstfruits and foretaste of the heavenly and eternal glory which will follow after death (Acts 7:55–56; 2 Cor. 5:1–2), so that the sting of death would be blunted (1 Cor. 15:54–57) and the desire for death would replace it (Rom. 8:23; Phil. 1:21, 23).

(4) Just as in his preparation Christ wanted with great desire to solemnly renew the covenant with his God before his death, and once renewed, to certify it with the sacramental seals of Passover and the Supper (Luke 22:15), so we also before we depart from here should also long to renew our covenant with God, and (if it can be done fittingly) to experience its sacramental seals (Matt. 22:32; Ps. 39:12–13).

(5) Just as in his preparation Christ was the promoter to his disciples, both in word and example, of love, humility, and humanity, by washing their feet (John 13:15), so we also, when we are about to die, should promote our own piety toward God, and righteousness and humanity toward our neighbor (1 Kings 2:2; Isa. 38:1).

(6) Just as Christ in his preparation attempted with many reasons in a certain most ample sermon to soften the sorrows and fears of his disciples which would arise from his departure, and to fortify them against the persecutions and treacheries of this world in a farewell sermon (John 14–16), so we also should strive to lighten the sorrows of our people (Luke 23:27–28), and to fortify them against all impending evils (Gen. 49; Acts 20:28–31).

Finally, (7) just as in his preparation Christ commended himself, when he was about to die, and his disciples to his Father with the most ardent supplications (John 17), so we also, when we are about to die, ought with most fervent prayers to pray against our sins (Ps. 143:1–2; 130:1, 3), to place our souls into God's hands (Acts 7:59; Ps. 31:5), and to commit our own who will survive us to the care and custody of God (Acts 20:32).

5. Christ's sufferings offer for us in our sufferings an example of:
Patience, confidence, prudence
XL. Fifth, we should especially take Christ's sufferings, which he endured in his circumcision, in his Egyptian exile, throughout his entire life, from God and from men, from friends and from enemies ecclesiastical, political, and martial, in soul, in body, in reputation, in goods, as an example of: (1) patience and longsuffering (1 Peter 2:23; Isa. 53:7; Rev. 1:9), to be imitated in any adversities

(Heb. 10:36; James 5:10–11); (2) faithfulness and comfort (1 Peter 2:23; Matt. 27:46), which comfort we can draw the more effectively in any of our adversities from the very sufferings of Christ because whatever he suffered, he suffered for us, so that he might thoroughly remove all harm from our sufferings (Isa. 53:4–5; 1 Cor. 15:55–57); (3) prudence, through which we should carefully discern those sufferings which we must necessarily bear—either from the known will of God (Matt. 26:53–54), or from our office (Heb. 2:17–18), so that we may approach them fearlessly (Matt. 26:45–46), and even freely undertake them (Luke 9:23)—from those which can be avoided, so that we may prudently avoid them by an escape, or other remedies which God and nature supply, by the example of Christ (Matt. 2:13–14; Mark 3:6–7), and the commandment of Christ himself (Matt. 10:23).

6. The temptations of Christ show us: To what temptations we are liable
XLI. Sixth, in the temptations of Christ (Matt. 4:1–12; 16:22–23) is supplied to us an example to show: (1) to what kind and what strong temptations all Christians—and especially ministers of the divine Word—are liable (Job 7:1; Eph. 6:12), namely: (a) to unbelief, "If you are the Son of God" (Matt. 4:3), as if he should say, "You certainly think that it was already said to you, 'This is my beloved Son'" (Matt. 3:17): "you should not believe this, for how could the Son of God be oppressed by hunger?" So any true Christians—and especially ministers of the Word—are tempted by need, persecutions, and the worst evils which meet them, to believe that they are not sons of God (Judg. 6:13), or have been deserted by God (Isa. 49:14; Ps. 13:1). (b) To distrust, "Make these stones become bread" (Matt. 4:3), as if he should say, "You lack the necessary means of living, bread and other things: eat stones." So also any true Christians situated in dangers and adversities are tempted to distrust (1 Sam. 27:1; Matt. 6:25; 8:25–26). On the contrary, (c) to presumption, "If you are the Son of God, cast yourself down, for it is written" (Matt. 4:6). So any Christians are tempted to presumption whenever either in spiritual or in bodily matters they freely expose themselves to dangers (Matt. 26:58; 2 Sam. 11:2). (d) To pride and greed, "He showed to him all the kingdoms of this world and their glory, and said, 'All these I will give to you, if…'" (Matt. 4:8–9); so any Christians are tempted (2 Tim. 4:10; 1 John 2:15; James 1:13–14). (e) To idolatry, "If you will fall down and worship me" (Matt. 4:9); so also any Christians are tempted (1 John 5:21), either to that crass idolatry into which Solomon fell (1 Kings 11:4), or to the subtle kind in which they worship their belly as God (Phil. 3:19).

By what method we must strive against the temptations of Satan
(2) By what method we must strive against all these temptations, namely that:
(a) whenever we are led into these temptations by divine providence, we should
not cry out and murmur against God (Matt. 6:13; Rev. 3:10), just as Christ,
led by the Spirit into the desert so that he might be tempted by Satan, did not
resist, but yielded and went. (b) We should strive against them with fastings and
prayers (1 Peter 5:8; Matt. 17:21; Eph. 6:18), just as Christ, when he had fasted
for forty days and nights and had prepared himself by this method to undergo
Satan's temptations, proceeded into the desert so that he might be tempted.
(c) We should boldly cling to the divine words and promises (Heb. 12:4–5;
13:5), just as Christ, when tempted as to whether he was the Son of God, constantly and immovably clung to the divine declaration that was made to him at
his baptism (Matt. 3:17). (d) We should use the sword of the divine word (Eph.
6:17), and oppose every one of Satan's temptations with fitting portions of Scripture. For example, if we are tempted toward greed, we should oppose it with
Hebrews 13:5 and 1 Timothy 6:9–10; if toward an angry temper, Ecclesiastes
7:9; if toward haughtiness and pride, Proverbs 16:18 and James 4:6; if toward
drunkenness and gluttony, Proverbs 20:1; if toward lust, 1 Thessalonians 4:3–5
and Hebrews 13:4; if toward verbosity, then Psalm 39:1 and James 3:2; and so
forth, just as Christ opposed each of Satan's attacks with his "It is written" (Matt.
4:4, 7, 10). (e) Especially against more frightful temptations and thoughts, we
should not tarry and not dispute, but at the first moment they arise, we should
instantly repel them with detestation, and immediately extinguish Satan's fiery
darts (Eph. 6:16), just as Christ, when tempted toward idolatry, said, "Depart
from me, Satan" (Matt. 4:10).

By what supports we ought to strengthen and raise our soul against
the horrors of satanic temptations
(3) By what supports we ought to strengthen and raise our soul against the horrors of satanic temptations, about which Paul speaks (2 Cor. 12:7; Isa. 43:17),
namely, we should consider that: (a) we are led by divine providence into temptation (Matt. 6:13), and the Holy Spirit is present with us by his power and
strengthening (Isa. 43:2; Ps. 23:4), just as Christ was led by the Spirit of God into
the desert so that he might be tempted by Satan (Matt. 4:1), and the Spirit was
also constantly present with him. (b) Christ also was tempted, and was tempted
in all points like us, and was tempted to the end that he could sympathize with
us (Heb. 4:15). And we his disciples ought not be in a better condition than our
Master (Matt. 10:24–25). Also, in this way we are being conformed to the image
of the Son of God (Rom. 8:29), in which the highest perfection of a Christian

consists (Matt. 10:25). (c) We are exposed to the temptations of Satan, not so that we may be subjugated by him, but so that we may be adapted to performing the duties of our Christianity (Acts 9:16; James 1:2–3), just as Christ was exposed to the temptations of Satan to the end that he might be qualified for his mediatorial office (Heb. 4:15; 2:10, 18). (d) These temptations will not last forever, but we more certainly than certain will be delivered from temptations (2 Peter 2:9; 1 Cor. 10:13), just as Christ, after he boldly repulsed Satan's three attacks, was delivered from Satan (Matt. 4:11). (e) When we have blessedly triumphed over temptations, we will possess the glory of having conquered and triumphed over Satan (1 John 2:13; 1 Cor. 15:55–57), just as Christ possessed this glory (John 14:30). Finally, (f) when the temptations have been overcome, there will one day be a most joyful conclusion (Rev. 7:13–14; 2:7, 11, 17, 26–27; 3:5, 12, 21), just as the angels came to Christ, after he had routed Satan's temptations and assaults, and ministered to him (Matt. 4:11).

7. Christ's entire life rouses all Christians to imitation. In which particulars XLII. Seventh, Christ's entire life teaches all Christians that they should with all their gathered strength strive for this, that the life of Jesus may be made manifest in them (2 Cor. 4:10), that is: (1) that they would set forth to themselves Christ's life and conduct as an example for imitation in all things, with the Savior urging this very thing (Matt. 11:29; John 13:14–15), as well as the apostles (Eph. 5:2; 1 Cor. 11:1; 1 Thess. 1:6; 1 Peter 1:21ff.). Moreover, we must present by imitation the outlines of Christ's life and conduct, with respect to: (a) first his virtues, religion toward God, righteousness toward neighbor, fortitude and temperance toward ourselves. With respect to (b) their exercise,[72] with regard to his infancy, adolescence and youth, adulthood, and later life, as we have said. Likewise, (c) with respect to the discharging of his office, accomplished by teaching, doing good, suffering, and lighting the way. With respect (d) to all manner of sufferings and adversities. With respect (e) to the temptations of spiritual enemies. And so finally (f) in life as well as in death. The outlines, I say, of his conduct, we already presented in the previous sections,[73] so that in them we may set for ourselves an example to be imitated. Then (2) they should also draw the very power of imitating from Christ's life, so that the life of Christ not only offers to them the example but also the principle, with the apostle commending this (Phil. 2:5; Gal. 2:20), from which Christ is called our life (Col. 3:4; John 14:6; 1:4; 11:25); for without Christ's life communicated to us, not only can we do nothing to produce

---

72. ἄσκησιν
73. §XII, above

the imitation of him (John 15:4–5), but also, even if we were especially able, it would not be pleasing to God unless it was done in the Beloved (Eph. 1:6), for whatever is born of the flesh is nothing except flesh (John 3:6). Therefore in this double way, we must strive with our every effort that the life of Jesus may be made manifest in us.

By what motivating reasons
We must do so because: (1) to this end the Savior came in the flesh and led his whole life among us, that he might not only justify us, but also sanctify us (1 Cor. 1:30; Titus 2:11–12, 14), and provide in his life and conversation an example of his holiness to be imitated (Rom. 8:29). (2) This is an invincible argument of our union and communion with Christ, if his life is made manifest in us, for whoever says that he abides in him, ought (ὀφείλει) to walk as he walked (1 John 2:6), and everyone who has this hope in him sanctifies himself, even as he (the Christ who will appear) is holy (1 John 3:3), so that in this way Christ may live in him (Gal. 2:20; 4:19), insofar as the same life is in the members united with the head, which is in the head itself (1 Cor. 12:27; Heb. 2:11). (3) From this we are called Christians (Acts 11:26) and disciples of Christ, because the manner of living prescribed by Christ and the example offered in life is fitting for us to imitate (Luke 9:23; Matt. 10:38; 16:24; Mark 8:34; Luke 14:27); and thus if we did not imitate it, by that very fact we would deny the entirety of our Christianity (2 Tim. 2:19), and in turn would be denied by him (Matt. 10:33), and slain (Luke 19:27). (4) All Christians are not only Christ's servants (Rom. 1:1, 9), but also his children (Heb. 2:10), for whom it is proper to be like their parents, and to walk in their footsteps (Eph. 5:1). (5) In the conformity of our life and conversation with the life and conversation of Christ consists all the perfection of all Christians (Luke 6:40; John 13:15–16; 15:20; Matt. 5:48).

By what helps
And finally, so that, raised up by reasons, we may more easily and certainly obtain that the life of Jesus may be made manifest in us, it is necessary that: (1) by taking hold of Christ with a living faith (John 1:12), we be united with him, and he himself dwell in us (Eph. 3:17), he live in us (Gal. 2:20), his life become ours (Col. 3:4), and he communicate to us his Spirit and life, like the soul does to the body (John 1:16), so that by it we live spiritually (Gal. 2:20). That (2) of that life of Jesus, which we are zealous to be made manifest in us, we strive more and more to acquire for ourselves a distinct knowledge (2 Peter 1:2, 8; 3:18), for a person cannot successfully imitate an example if he does not have sufficient knowledge of it (John 4:10). That (3) in each of the steps of our

life and conversation, we have the eyes of our mind intent upon Christ's life and conversation, as our πρωτότυπον, prototype, ὑπογραμμός, model (1 Peter 2:21), ὑπόδειγμα, pattern (John 13:15), and that with a turning of the eyes from any others, as the apostle urges in Hebrews 12:2, ἀφορῶντες, "looking," (that is by turning) "to the author and finisher of our faith, Jesus." At the same time, (4) because there is not always in individual actions a ready example in Christ, that we also turn our eyes to those who have offered themselves as imitators of Christ (1 Cor. 11:1; 1 Thess. 1:6; 1 Cor. 4:16; Phil. 3:17), those who either had Christ present to them, or perceived his manner of living by hearing from those who were immediately present with him (Acts 1:3; Luke 1:2). Although, this is not to be done in all indiscriminately or without prudent circumspection, because all, even the holiest, are observed to be liable to their own infirmities and blemishes, from which comes the adage, "We ought to live not by examples, but by laws."[74] Even the apostle himself limits and restricts the imitation of himself among the Corinthians: "Be imitators of me, even as" (or insofar as) "I am of Christ" (1 Cor. 11:1). About this we taught more things in the dogmatic part.[75]

---

74. *non exemplis, sed legibus vivendum*
75. §XXII, above

CHAPTER TWELVE

The Death of the Mediator

Then he released Barabbas to them, but scourging Jesus, he delivered him to be crucified.... v. 35, But crucifying him.... v. 50, And Jesus, crying again with a loud voice, yielded up his spirit.

—Matthew 27:26–51

The third degree of Christ's humiliation follows.

I. Next is the third degree of humiliation, which is in the death of the Mediator, which here we do not consider so broadly that it would connote all the sufferings[1] of his entire life, in which sense we examined the sufferings of Christ in the preceding chapter; nor so strictly that it would speak of only the rending of his body and soul; but rather, that it may denote that rending with all those things preparatory and connected to it, which he sustained in the last week of his life, which some call the week of punishment, and indeed in the two days before that dissolution. As the foundation of our consideration, in our prior edition we built our exegesis upon the words of Philippians 2:8,[2] but because those words have

---

1. παθήματα

2. Up to this point in the chapter, the first and second edition are identical; cf. Petrus van Mastricht, *Theoretico-practica theologia*, 1st ed., 2 vols. (Amsterdam: Henry Boom and the Widow of Theodore Boom, 1682–1687), 2:288–89, "II. In these words [of Phil. 2:8], to these two degrees set down already, he joins the third degree of the humiliation of Christ, that which is in his death. Belonging to which he presents three things: (1) his obedience: γενόμενος ὑπήκοος, 'having become obedient,' with submission listening, and yielding to sufferings and death, according to the will of the Father, promptly, not only allowing them, but in addition undertaking them (Ps. 40:8), without which any suffering or death would have been of no use or efficacy. From which we gather in addition that in the death of Christ there was not a mere *passio*, suffering, but also an *actio*, action, of spontaneous obedience (John 10:11, 18). (2) His death: 'to the point of death,' namely that death which from the divine threat we had earned through sin in our first parents, with all those things preparatory, connected, and consequent to it (Isa. 53:4–9; 2 Cor. 5:21). (3) His cross: 'even the death of the cross,' that is, to the kind of death that was the worst and most ignominious, indeed utterly cursed (Deut. 21:23), namely so that he might become a curse for us,

already been exposited, instead of them we will expound the text of Matthew 27:26–51.

The Exegetical Part

The text is opened.

II. In it there is contained a history of the condemnation, crucifixion, and death of Christ. And in regard to it:

    A. The condemnation of Christ, in verse 26. Tertullian, according to Grotius on this passage, doubts whether the condemnation of Christ is contained in these words;[3] Lactantius denies it (*Institutes*, bk. 4, ch. 18), and so does Chrysostom in his *Second Oration on Alms*;[4] with more solid arguments Grotius affirms it, together with Ignatius, Cyprian, and others.[5] For this condemnation is proved by: (1) the place of judgment, to which Pilate went; (2) that the punishment was exacted only by Roman soldiers; (3) that the penalty of the cross was particular to the Roman legal code, for the cross was unknown in Jewish laws; (4) the title written over the punishment, which was dictated by Pilate, the body of the crucified, which was requested from Pilate, and other such circumstances. Add to these (5) that when Pilate said, "You judge him according to your law," the Jews responded that the authority of capital judgments had been taken from them. Also, (6) the shouts of the Jews at Pilate, "Let him be crucified," that is, by the sentence of Pilate. Let there be added (7) the continuous appeal of Christians and of the *Quartodecimani*[6] to the acts of Pilate, which without a doubt were extant at that time, so that they might obtain that the matter was carried out under the appearance

---

and thus redeem (ἐξαγοράσῃ) us from the curse of the law, for it is written, 'Cursed is everyone who hangs on a tree' (Gal. 3:13)."

    3. Grotius, *Annotationes in libros Evangeliorum*, 483; idem, *Opera omnia theologica*, 4 vols. (Amsterdam: Heirs of Joannes Blaeu, 1679), 2:268; idem, *Annotationes in Novum Testamentum denuo emendatius editae*, 9 vols. (Groningen: W. Zuidema, 1827), 2:354–55; cf. Tertullian, *Apologeticus adversus gentes pro Christianis*, XXI in *PL* 1:400; idem, *Apology* 21 in *ANF* 3:35.

    4. Lactantius (c. 250–c. 325), *Divinae institutiones* in *PL* 6:504; idem, *The Divine Institutes* in *ANF* 7:120. Chrysostom has at least three homilies on almsgiving: Homily 19 (on Matt. 6:1) in *NPNF1* 10:130–40; idem, Homily 3 (on Matt. 25) and Homily 10 (On Almsgiving) in *St. John Chrysostom on Repentance and Almsgiving* in *FOTC* 96:28–42, 131–49.

    5. Cf. Grotius, *Annotationes in libros Evangeliorum*, 483; idem, *Opera omnia theologica*, 2:268; Ignatius (died c. 108), *Epistolae interpolatae: ad Trallianos* in *PG* 5:789–90; idem, *The Epistle of Ignatius to the Trallians*, sect. IX in *ANF* 1:70; Cyprian (c. 210–258), *Liber de idolorum vanitate* in *PG* 4:579; idem, "Treatise VI: On the Vanity of Idols" in *ANF* 5:468.

    6. τεσσαρεσκαιδεκατῶν: "fourteenthers," called such for commemorating Christ's crucifixion on the 14th of Nisan, the date of Passover.

of a judgment. Nor without significance is (8) Barabbas's judicial release, immediately connected with Christ's judicial condemnation in verse 26, τότε ἀπέλυσεν αὐτοῖς τὸν Βαρραβᾶν, "Then he released Barabbas to them." Therefore with these arguments it is obtained that this verse contains the condemnation of Christ. Moreover, here occur:

1. The release of Barabbas: "Then he released Barabbas to them." Namely, Pilate did so, contrary to right and conscience; he released Barabbas, a notorious robber, just as he also condemned Jesus. This was done by a lawful judge, not by the uproar and sedition of the Jews, so that it would be done in the name of God (Rom. 13:1–2; Prov. 8:15–16; Dan. 4:32; John 19:11).

2. The scourging of Christ: τὸν δὲ Ἰησοῦν φραγελλώσας, "And after he had scourged Jesus." Moreover, he did this either: (1) because it was a point of Roman law that the one about to be crucified would be scourged first, as learned men observe: Jerome, Luc de Bruges, Lipsius, Lightfoot, and others.[7] Or rather (2) so that he might satisfy the cruelty of the Jews, as is gathered by comparison of Luke 23:22 with John 19:1. But he was not scourged with rods, which was a lighter punishment, but with scourges; and that not by the Jews, according to Deuteronomy 25:3, but by heathen soldiers, under whose savage scourging many died, as Ulpian teaches in the *Digesta* ("On Punishments," bk. 8), and who also customarily sharpened their lashes with bits of bone and hooks.[8] It is certain that Christ was dreadfully scourged (Ps. 35:15; Isa. 50:6).

3. The delivering of Christ for crucifixion. "He delivered him," that is, already condemned. He delivered him either to the Jews, or rather to the soldiers, as is evident from what follows. "To be crucified," for Roman laws dictate that punishment for that crime, as Paulus notes in his *Sententiae* (bk. 5, title 22;[9] cf. Philippians 2, "to death, even the

---

7. Jerome, *Commentariorum in evangelium Matthaei libri quattuor* in *PL* 26:207–8; idem, *Commentary on Matthew*, trans. Thomas P. Scheck, in *FOTC* 117:313; François Luc de Bruges (1552–1619), *In sacrosancta quatuor Jesu Christi Evangelia…commentarius* (Antwerp: Plantin, 1606), 1:516; Lipsius, *De cruce*, ch. 11–13, pp. 29–33; John Lightfoot, *Horae Hebraicae et Talmudicae in quattuor evangelistas* (Leipzig: Johannes Colerus, 1675), 490.

8. Cf. Ulpian, bk. 8 cited in *Digesta* 48.19.8.3 in *Corpus Iuris Civilis*, 1.814; cf. Luc de Bruges as, *Commentarius*, 1:516.

9. Julius Paulus (fl. 2nd & 3rd c. A. D.), *Receptarum sententiarum ad filium libri quinque* (Bonn: Adolph Marcia, 1833), 170–71.

death of the *cross*"), instead of which we read of the *furca* in the *Pandecta*; the use of this cross Constantine removed.[10]

B. The execution of the condemnatory sentence, wherein are narrated what things were done concerning Christ:

1. In the praetorium, that is, the injuries and mockeries inflicted upon him by the soldiers. Here are noted:

    a. Those injuring, namely, the soldiers, four in number (John 19:23), who among the Romans were lictors and administered punishments. These carried him away to the praetorium. For it seems that he received the condemnatory sentence outside the praetorium. Moreover, the πραιτώριον, praetorium (a term of Latin origin) was the place of judgment, perhaps so that they might place him as a king in judgment, or on a throne. To some commentators, it is Pilate's residence; elsewhere it is called the palace or hall. Although to others the judgment seat was not in the praetorium, but in a large stadium, as Josephus says, which was not far from the praetorium, an area part of which was paved with stone, for which reason in John it is called λιθόστρωτος, the Pavement (John 19:13). Not only did these four soldiers who were lictors inflict the injuries, but also the entire cohort: "Then," it says in verse 27, "the soldiers of the governor, taking Jesus into the praetorium, gathered to him the entire cohort." Τότε, "Then," that is, while the execution of the punishment was being prepared; "they gathered to him," that is, against him, the entire cohort, to be either spectators or actors in the story that would occur. "The entire cohort," that is, different from the one to whom the protection of the temple and the priests had been committed, as Grotius observes, which was called the *custodia*, the guard.[11] Σπεῖρα, "cohort," properly means a braided cord, but metaphorically, as Ennius and Appian testify,[12] a band of

---

10. *Pandecta* is another name for the *Digesta*. *Digesta*, bk. 48, titles 13.6 and 19.11, 28, 38 in *Corpus Iuris Civilis*, 1.807, 815–17. Paul Krüger et al., eds., *Collectio librorum juris antejustiniani in usum scholarum*, 3 vols. (Berlin: Weidmann, 1878), 2:128–130; Cf. Lipsius's discussion of the ancient and new forms of the *furca* in *De cruce*, 62–72, with illustrations. A Y-shaped cross found in 11th-c. architecture was known as a *furca*: cf. "forked cross" in N. Davies and E. Jokiniemi, *Dictionary of Architecture and Building Construction* (Amsterdam: Elsevier, 2008), 160. On the removal of the punishment of the furca, see *Digesta*, 48.8.3.4–5 in *Corpus Iuris Civilis*, 1.802.

11. Grotius, *Annotationes in libros Evangeliorum*, 483.

12. For a Greek-Latin text, Appian, Ῥωμαϊκῶν Ἱστοριῶν τὰ Σωζόμενα / *Romanarum historiarum quae supersunt Graece et Latine*, ed. A. F. Didot (Paris: Firmin Didot Fratrum, 1840),

soldiers, just as חבל in Hebrew properly means "rope," but figuratively "company" or "band" (1 Sam. 10:5). Moreover, a cohort was a tenth of a legion, consisting of fifty maniples, and a maniple had twenty-five soldiers or, as Vegetius says, ten.[13] They gathered such a great force of soldiers so that they might more powerfully insult Christ, and each might add his own insult to their mockery of him.

b. The injuries, in conferring upon him with mockery most of the insignia of royalty, namely: (1) a royal garment, verse 28, "Stripping him, they put on him a scarlet robe," or a crimson tunic; a purple garment, as Mark has it (15:17, 20), that is, a garment of that color which counterfeits true purple. The Hebrews call it תולע, which we commonly call crimson. There are those to whom, from this fact, scarlet and purple are the same; to Saumaise[14] they differ in color, material, and use, whereby only emperors used purple, but private citizens also used scarlet; Brodeau thinks that nonetheless they are employed as synonyms (*Miscellanies*, bk. 1, ch. 8).[15] Whatever it may be, at least the garment was a brilliant color, which some called scarlet and others purple, which are two especially choice colors in clothing. (2) A royal crown, verse 29, "And weaving a crown of thorns, they put it upon his head," that is, twisting several thin, thorny branches into a circle, they made a crown consisting of wood instead of gold, and thorns in place of gems. (3) A royal scepter, "and a reed in his right hand"—supply "they put." (4) Royal homage, "And bowing the knee before him, they mocked him, saying, "Hail, King of the Jews!" (5) Instead of royal worship and as it were royal tribute, they spat upon him (the Syriac has "in his face"), and struck his head with the reed.

---

e.g. "Romanae historiae de bellis civilibus," I.v, vi, ix, x, xiii, xvi. Quintus Ennius (239 BC–169 BC), "[Ennius] indeed so describes it as a multitude of men, when he says, *spiras legionibus nexunt*, 'They braid *spirae* with legions,'" cited in Sextus Pompeius Festus, *De verborum significatione*, ed. C. O. Mueller (Leipzig: Libraria Weidmanniana, 1839), 330.

13. Vegetius, *Epitome of Military Science* (Liverpool: Liverpool University Press), 41; Vegetius et. al., *De re militari opera*, ed. P. Scaliger (Leiden: Joannes Maire, 1583), 40.

14. Claude de Saumaise (Claudius Salmasius, 1588–1653), *Exercitationes de homonymis hyles jatricae* (Utrecht: Johann vande Water et al., 1689), 92–93, 110.

15. Jean Brodeau (1500–1563) *Miscellaneorum libri sex* (Basel: Joannes Oporinus, 1555), 14.

2. In the way, where there is narrated:

   a. His being led off to the place of punishment (v. 31), after namely: (1) they had mocked him to their satisfaction in the praetorium, (2) they had stripped his robe and clothed him in his own garments, namely so that he might be more easily recognized and mocked by anyone on the road, (3) they led him away to be crucified, that is, outside the praetorium, through the city, and outside the three camps—namely that of God, of the Levites, and of the people (Num. 15:35; 1 Kings 21:13; Acts 7:58; Heb. 13:12)—to the place of punishment.

   b. The alleviation procured for him, in Simon the Cyrenian, so called perhaps because he originated from Cyrene, a city either of the Decapolis in Syria, which Pliny, Strabo, and Mela speak of, or of the Pentapolis in Libya, which was filled with Jews (Acts 2:10; 6:9). At least he was a Jew (although Hilary and Ambrose preferred to think that he was a Gentile, so that it would be signified to the unbelieving Jews that Gentiles would carry the cross and yoke of Christ),[16] and one that favored Christ. Him they compelled, either by force or by reasons, to take up the burden of bearing the cross, either jointly with Christ or separately, so that perhaps having been exhausted in the praetorium he would not succumb to his burden, and they be deprived of the pleasing spectacle of the crucifixion, or also so that they might more easily hasten the journey and accelerate Christ's crucifixion.

3. In Golgotha, verse 33, "And arriving at the place called Golgotha." Γολγοθᾶ, Golgotha, is from the Hebrew גלגלת, that is, *calva*, scalp, or *calvaria*, skull, by an elision of the letter λ: in the Syriac and the Arabic it is read in full, as also in the Zohar.[17] Matthew translates the

---

16. Hilary of Poitiers, *Commentarius in Evangelium Matthaei*, 33.4 in *PL* 9:1073; idem, *Commentary on Matthew*, trans. D. H. Williams in *FOTC* 125:288. Ambrose of Milan, *Expositio Evangelii secundum Lucam*, 10.107 in *PL* 15:1830; idem, *Exposition of the holy Gospel according to Saint Luke with fragments on the prophecy of Isaias*, trans. T. Tomkinson, (Etna, Calif.: Center for Traditionalist Orthodox Studies, 1998), 426.

17. For the Syriac and Arabic of Matt. 27:33 with Latin translations of each, see B. Walton et al., *Biblia Sacra polyglotta*, 5 vols. (London: Roycroft, 1651–1654), 5:148–49. For גוּלְנַלְתָה (*cranium*), see Zohar, Idra Suta 2.51–57 in the Latin-Hebrew diglot, *Kabbala denudata…Liber Sohar restitutus*, trans. and ed. C. Knorr von Rosenroth, 2 vols. (Sulzbach: Abraham Lichtentahler, 1677–1684), 2:527–28; for an English translation of Knorr von Rosenroth's edition see *Kabbalah unveiled, containing the following books of the Zohar: 1. The book of concealed mystery, 2. The greater holy assembly, 3. The lesser holy assembly*, trans. and ed. S. L. MacGregor Mathers (London: George

word as κρανίου τόπος, "the place of the skull," because in that place the skulls or heads of malefactors were seen; such places at Rome were the Sestertium and Gemonian Stairs.[18] At the least, it was a place of infamy and ignominy. The actions narrated at this place are:

a. The drinking by the one to be crucified, which is different from his drinking once crucified, on which see verse 48. Concerning this there is noted:

i. The offer of the drink: they gave him ὄξος μετὰ χολῆς, "vinegar mingled with gall." For ὄξος, vinegar, Mark has wine (15:23). So also does the Ethiopic version,[19] and a certain most ancient exemplar of Beza.[20] Either way it is right, for if you should translate it by "vinegar," what is vinegar but sour wine? If by "wine," then it was acidic and sharp, especially from the mixture of gall: μετὰ χολῆς, "mingled with gall"; Mark has ἐσμυρνισμένον οἶνον, "myrrhed wine." In this place χολὴ does not mean gall precisely, but bitterness in general, whether that of gall, or of wormwood, or of myrrh: from which the Septuagint translators also render לענה, wormwood, as χολὴ in Proverbs 5:4 and Lamentations 3:15; and Psalm 69:21, from which this passage is taken, for ראש has, by the same translators, χολή, and this ראש in Deuteronomy 29:18 means, according to those same translators, πικρία, bitterness, just as in Jeremiah 23:15 they translate מי ראש by ὕδωρ πικρόν, bitter water. A drink of this sort was given to those condemned and about to die, according to Proverbs 31:6, that it might stupefy their minds, so that exhilarated by it they would think less about death, and bear it more easily.

Redway, 1887), 2:264–65. cf. on the etymology of Golgotha, Poole on Matt. 27:33, *Synopsis criticorum*, 4:673, "In the Zohar, just as also here in the Syriac and Arabic, it is read in full."

18. On the Sestertium, see Tacitus, *Annals* in *LCL* 322:310–311. Plutarch mentions a *Sessorium* in *Lives*, on Galba, *LCL* 103:270–71, which he defines as "the place where those under the condemnation of the emperors were put to death." For the *Scalae Gemoniae*, see Cassius Dio, *Roman History* in *LCL* 175:216–17, which describes the execution of the condemned and the disposal of their body by casting it down the Gemonian Stairs for public display.

19. See *Novum Testamentum Domini Nostri et Servatoris Jesu Christi Aethopice: ad codicum manuscriptorum fidem edidit Thomas Pell Platt* (London: Watts, 1830), fol. M2r. For a Latin interlinear version with the Ethiopic, see Walton, *Biblia Sacra polygotta*, 5:149.

20. So the *Codex Bezae* (MS Nn.2.41, Cambridge University), fol. 99v–100r.

ii. The rejection of the same: "And when he had tasted it, he would not drink." Mark: "He did not take it," ἔλαβε. Γευσάμενος means, "when he had lightly tasted it" only in fulfillment of the prophecy in Psalm 69:21, not so that he might drink, which is the meaning of λαμβάνειν, to take, in Mark. Matthew therefore acknowledges that he did take it, that is, that he tasted it; Mark denies that he took it, that is, that he drank it. Therefore he willed to taste it so that he might satisfy the prophecy, so that he might not appear to despise it, and so that he might show that he truly thirsted; however, he did not will to drink it, because it was given to stupefy the mind, so that he might show that he was dying peacefully, and that he was not carried headlong by impatience, or inviting further calamities upon himself, and that he did not need any drugs of this sort; although afterwards hanging on the cross, because he was exceedingly thirsty, ἔλαβε τὸ ὄξος, "He took the vinegar," that is, he drank it.

b. The crucifixion (σταυρώσαντες, "having crucified him," v. 35), which they generally describe in this way: both hands, with arms outstretched, were affixed to the transverse wood of the cross with nails (Luke 24:39; John 20:25, 27; 21:18), and both feet, standing upon a certain wooden piece jutting out from a spear, or from the upright timber of the cross, as upon a pedestal, and placed next to each other, were likewise affixed with nails. It was a kind of punishment that was agonizing, ignominious, and cursed.

c. The division of his garments, namely from the custom of the Romans wherein those who exacted the punishment claimed for themselves the spoils of the guilty. They strip him of his clothes to this end, and also so that they may expose him naked as the most vile and abject of men. But not without the divine will, so that there might be fulfilled what had been said by the prophet, namely in Psalm 22:18.[21] Beza and Grotius do not doubt that this phrase was added from John 19:24, because the best Greek exemplars do not have it, neither do any of the oldest codices, nor even many Latin ones, nor the Syriac, nor Origen, nor Jerome, though meanwhile the Vulgate, Arabic, and Hebrew edition of Matthew have it.[22]

---

21. Original, Ps. 69:22.
22. Beza, *Novum Testamentum* (1598), 1:137; Grotius, *Annotationes in libros evangeliorum* in

d. The guarding of the crucified: "And sitting down, they kept watch over him." From the Roman custom, namely so that he would in no way escape. This watchfulness of the soldiers and priests profits us, so that we may be more certain regarding the truth of his death as well as of the power of his resurrection.

e. The inscription, which had the αἰτία, the cause for punishment, and that in the language of Latin on account of the imperial dignity, Hebrew on account of the place of punishment, and Greek on account of the very great crowd of Hellenists that was present for the feast. In this ἐπιγραφή, title, Pilate calls him "the King of the Jews," certainly so that he might mock Christ, but yet also that he might vex the Jews (John 19:21–22).

f. The co-crucifixion of two thieves, one on his right and the other on his left, so that he was hung in the middle of them, as if he were the prince and leader of thieves. It was done in this way first by the counsel of God, so that satisfaction might be made to the prophecy of Isaiah 53:12 (cf. Mark 15:28), and then by the counsel of Pilate, so that he might check the baying of his conscience, as well as help his reputation, so that while he slayed the innocent, he might not appear to pardon the guilty, and also so that Christ, from the association with malefactors, might be considered a malefactor, and one similar to them, as in their penalty, so in their guilt.

g. The mockeries or insults of his enemies, and indeed those:

  i. Of the crowd, or of the people passing by, who were insulting him, partly with their gestures, verse 39, wagging their head, which was a sign of contempt and derision (as in 2 Kings 19:21; Ps. 22:7; 109:25; Isa. 37:22; Lam. 2:15), and partly with their tongue and voice, verse 40, "Ah! You who destroy the temple and rebuild it in three days, save yourself!" But Christ had said this not about the temple properly speaking, but about the temple of his body (John 2:19–21), which was just then being destroyed on the cross. "Save yourself!" But he had not come to save himself.

  ii. Of the nobles or chief men: verses 41–43, "Likewise also… they said," that is, the chief priests with the scribes, elders, and

Opera omnia (1679), 2:270. For the Vulgate, Arabic, and Syriac, see Walton, _Biblia Sacra polyglotta_, 5:138–39.

Pharisees, whose responsibility it was to restrain the uproar and insults of the crowd, said nearly the same things as the crowd. And they did so in addition by abusing the Scriptures (Ps. 22:8). But not without the divine will, because they seemed to acknowledge in this way that the Psalm spoke about him.

iii. Of the thieves: "The thieves also, which were crucified with him, cast the same in his teeth" (v. 44). "The thieves," either because both blasphemed Christ at the beginning, whereas when one had observed the miracles that happened then, and the greatest patience of Christ, he believed in him, and proceeded to rebuke his fellow who continued to reproach; or rather, only one of them blasphemed, through a syllepsis or enallage of number, which is not uncommon in the Scriptures, as in Hebrews 11:33, where what was said only of Daniel, and in verse 37 what pertained only to Jeremiah, he refers to many (so Matt. 21:2; Jonah 1:5).

h. The darkness (v. 45), concerning which are noted:

i. Its beginning: "And from the sixth hour." The sixth hour of the Jews corresponds to our twelfth hour. For the Jews began their working day from our sixth hour of the morning, then they divided the day it into four three-hour periods, and what occurred between two three-hour periods, they referred now to the first and now to the second. From this can be easily taken away the apparent contradiction[23] in which John says that Christ was condemned by Pilate in the sixth hour (John 19:14), but Mark relates that he was crucified in the third hour (Mark 15:25). And thus the crucifixion, which happened within the third and sixth hour, is referred by John to the sixth hour and by Mark to the third (cf. Grotius, Maldonado, and others).[24]

ii. Its nature: "There was darkness over all the land." Either over: (1) the whole land, namely of Judea, which here was being treated, or (2) over the whole circle of the earth, which Mornay proves in the last chapter of *The Truth of the Christian Religion*.[25]

---

23. ἐναντιοφανές

24. Grotius, *Annotationes in libros Evangeliorum* in *Opera omnia* (1679), 2:566; Juan de Maldonado, *Commentarii in quatuor evangelistas*, 1:640–43.

25. Philippe Duplessis-Mornay (1549–1623), ch. 34 of *De veritate Religionis Christianae*

Not indeed over the whole globe, for in many regions it was not then day, but night, when darkness does not happen, but simply is; so then it happened over that whole hemisphere which day occupied. This darkness also has, outside the divinely inspired Gospels, its own witnesses among the heathen astrologers and chroniclers, for example, Phlegon in the *Olympiads*, book 13, and Thallus in his *History*, book 3, cited in Africanus,[26] and indeed also the public Roman acts themselves, to which Tertullian appeals in his *Apology* (cf. Grotius).[27] However, this was an entirely miraculous darkness, since: (1) it did not happen during a new moon, at the time of which solar eclipses exclusively occur, but during a full moon. For it happened on the day of Passover, which fell on the fourteenth day of the month Nisan; but they were lunar synodic months, the first day of which always fell on a new moon, just as the fourteenth or fifteenth day on the full moon. (2) It was universal. (3) It lasted three hours. When Dionysius the Areopagite, while he was still a pagan, understood all these things (together with Apollophanes the philosopher), it is written in the Suda that he said, "Either the deity is suffering, or he is sympathizing with the one who is suffering."[28] By this darkness, God willed to bear witness to: (1) the blindness of the Jews, (2) how detestable the sin of the Jews and Romans was, which not even the sun could bear, (3) his own wrath, to which the eclipse of the sun at times bore witness (Jer. 15:9; Ezek. 32:7–8; Joel 2:10, 30–31; 3:14–16), (4) that his own Son bore his wrath on account of the sins of men.

i. The first cry of Christ (vv. 46–50), wherein is:

    i. The time of the cry: "about the ninth hour," which corresponds to our third hour of the afternoon.

---

liber: *Adversus Atheos, Epicureos, Ethnicos, Judaeos, Mahumedistas, et caeteros infideles* (Antwerp: Christopher Plantin, 1583), 774–91; idem, *De la verité de la religion chrestienne* (1581), 835–53.

26. Sextus Julius Africanus (c. 160–c. 240), *Quae supersunt ex quinque libris chronographiae* in *PG* 10:90; idem, *The Extant Writings of Julius Africanus* in *ANF* 6:136–37.

27. Tertullian, *Apologeticus* in *PL* 1:401; idem, *Apology* in *ANF* 3:35. For Grotius on Matthew 27:45, see *Annotationes in libros Evangeliorum* in *Opera omnia* (1679), 2:272–73.

28. Pseudo-Dionysius, "Letter XI, Dionysius the Areopagite to Apollophanes the Philosopher," in *The Works of Dionysius the Areopagite*, 1:182–83; *Suidas* (Geneva: Chouët, 1619), 1:265, 743, 746.

ii. The argument of the cry: *Eli, Eli, lama sabachtani*, "My God, My God, why have you forsaken me?" from Psalm 22:1, so that he appropriated that Psalm for himself. Instead of "Eli," Mark has "Eloi" (Mark 15:34), which is Syriac, with the same meaning except that the former is more Hebrew. Σαβαχθαví, "forsaken," for σαβακθαví, that is, שבקתני, instead of עזבתני in the Hebrew (Ps. 22:2). From this it is gathered that Christ employed neither ancient Hebrew nor purely Syriac speech, but rather the common dialect. שבק means the same in Syriac as עזב in Hebrew. Moreover, God forsook his Son: (1) not in grace itself, but in the sense of grace (as in Isa. 49:14); either (2) with respect to the human nature, which was exposed to the most frightful torments, in which nature he was made destitute not only of external deliverance, but also of all comfort, external or internal, of body or of soul, divine or human; or (3) because he struggled with the most sorrowful temptation of his being rejected (although without any sin), for he contended with the pains of death. He sensed that God was in some way alienated from him, and like a judge who was angry with him, and inflicting upon him the truly hellish pains due for our sins. This was his chief conflict, harder than all the others.

iii. Two false accusations:

a) The first: "Some of them," not so much the Romans, who did not know who Elijah was, as the Hellenists, who were unskilled in Hebrew, who thought that Elijah was still to come (Matt. 17:10). Unless perhaps they falsely accused him by twisting these words so that they might purposely mock Christ. Following this was the second drinking, that of vinegar, prepared, according to the custom of the Romans, so that it would be given to the crucified, either to lessen the harshness of death, or rather to prevent the loss of their mind. Instead of κάλαμος, "reed," John has ὑσσώπῳ περιθέντες, "they placed it upon hyssop," either because the rod was made of hyssop, or because crushed hyssop was mixed with the vinegar of the sponge for increasing the bitterness, so that the prophecy might be fulfilled (Ps. 69:21).

b) The second (v. 49): "The rest said, 'Let him be; let us see whether Elijah will come to rescue him.'" Thus the ἄφες,

"Let him be," would be prohibitive, "Do not offer, do not approach," because they thought that Elijah would more easily come thus to him alone; otherwise, the word could be pleonastic, attached to the following subjunctive verb, so that it would be, "Come, let us see."

j. The death of Christ (v. 50), following after a repeated cry; or rather, he cried anew, τετέλεσται, "It is finished," and likewise, "Father, into your hand I commit my spirit," as it is in Luke 23:46, after which he gave up his spirit. The centurion took this for a miracle, because he gathered that his soul was received by God, inasmuch as his death had been accelerated before his natural strength had run out. Ἀφῆκεν τὸ πνεῦμα, "He gave up his spirit," which is the same thing as גוע; in place of it Mark (15:37) and Luke (23:46) have ἐξέπνευσε, "He expired." It is a periphrasis for death, wherein the soul leaves the body.

The Dogmatic Part

The Mediator, according to the will of the Father, undertook the cursed death of the cross. It is proved by testimonies of Scripture.

III. Therefore the Mediator, according to his Father's will, undertook the cursed death of the cross for his people, which the Scriptures: (1) expressly speak of (besides the text, in Phil. 2:8; Heb. 2:9–10, 14–15; Eph. 2:15–16; 5:2, 25; Col. 1:21–22; Gal. 3:13), and signify in synonymous terms (2 Cor. 5:21; etc.); (2) predict with prophecies (Ps. 22:13, 16–17; Isa. 53:4–12; Dan. 9:26–27; Zech. 13:7); (3) prefigure, not only in Isaac (Gen. 22:2, 10 with Heb. 11:17–18), and in the bronze serpent (Num. 21:9; 2 Kings 18:4), but also in all the propitiatory sacrifices (Heb. 9:12–15, 22–23), and in the sacrifice of the Passover (1 Cor. 5:7 with Ex. 12); and finally, (4) imply, in all those passages that refer our redemption to the blood of Christ, whereby his death and entire suffering are connoted (1 John 1:7; Heb. 9:13–14; 1 Peter 1:19; Rom. 3:25; 5:9; Eph. 1:7; etc.).

And by reasons, from a manifold necessity.

IV. This death was also in many ways demanded by a strict necessity, which arose from: (1) the guilt and demerit of our sins (Gen. 2:17; Rom. 6:23; 5:12; 1 Cor. 15:22); (2) the justice or natural hatred of God against the sinner (Ps. 5:4–6; Hab. 1:13; Rom. 1:32; 2 Thess. 1:6); (3) the truthfulness of the God who threatens (Gen. 2:17; Ezek. 18:13 with Num. 23:19; Ps. 89:14); (4) the mercy and love for mankind of the Father, as well as of the Son himself, toward the lost sinner

(John 3:16; Rom. 5:8; Eph. 5:2); (5) Christ's expromission itself, whereby, in the eternal counsel of peace, he took upon himself the entire cause of the sinner liable to death (Ps. 40:6–8; Heb. 7:22) from which he is called the גּוֹאֵל, *Goel,* avenger (Job 19:25 with Isa. 59:20; Lev. 25:25), and the μεσίτης, Mediator (1 Tim. 2:5; Heb. 8:6; 9:15; 12:24 with Heb. 10:5; Isa. 53:10–11); (6) the purpose of God to manifest the glory of his mercy in the gracious redemption of the sinner (Rom. 9:23; Eph. 1:5–7).

What is the death of Christ?

V. Moreover, that death that the expromissor undertook for his people is the act of humiliation by which he undertook upon himself all that misery that was due to his people on account of sin. Therefore it is not: (1) a mere *passio,* a suffering or "undergoing," as our death is, but an *actio,* an action or "undertaking,"[29] insofar as it is said that he humbled himself, that he rendered himself obedient to the Father even to death (Phil. 2:8), that he laid down his life of his own accord (John 10:11, 18), that he gave himself as the price of redemption (Matt. 20:28; 1 Tim. 2:6; Isa. 53:10).

Is it the same death, or one equivalent to ours?

Nor (2) did he undergo a bare dissolution of body and soul, in which alone our death consists, but that entire misery which was due to his people from sin, or that same evil which burdened his people due to sin, if not in the same in kind, or rather in number, at least the same in weight and value. For he neither received to himself each and every evil that could be imposed upon us on account of sin—for example, disease, blindness, and all those evils recounted in Deuteronomy 28:15ff.—nor could he receive, for example, the deprivation of the divine image and original righteousness, the eternity of death, and other things. Yet with respect to their kinds, he did undertake those same things which were incumbent upon us to endure, which were, at the least with respect to weight and value, equivalent to our miseries. So that in this death, there was not so much a *solutio,* a payment, according to its true and proper name, wherein, according to the jurists, the *idem,* the same thing, is rendered that is in the obligation, which payment cannot be refused by the creditor, but rather a *satisfactio,* a satisfaction, wherein the *tantundem,* the same value, is rendered, and which can be rejected

---

29. Latin: *non est… mera passio, quemadmodum mors nostra; sed actio;* Dutch: *geen blote lyding, gelykerwys onze doodt; maar ene doening.*

by the creditor.[30] With this one precaution carefully observed, a great number of difficulties in the business of satisfaction will disappear.

The threefold death of Christ: 1. Natural death, the history of which is represented from the evangelists, in three periods: Preparation
VI. So then, because by our sins we contracted the guilt of a threefold death—natural, spiritual, and eternal, just as we taught above in book 4, chapter 4[31]—so also by the expromissor Jesus, a certain threefold death had to have been sustained: namely, first, natural or bodily death, the history of which all the evangelists, as if with one pen, describe through its three periods, the first of which presents the things preparatory for death, ten in number: (1) the prediction of the death that was now imminent (Matt. 16:21; Mark 14:1; Luke 22:1; John 13:1); (2) the deliberation of the Jews regarding the killing of Christ (Matt. 26:3–5); (3) the anointing made at Bethany by the woman in the house of Simeon the leper (Matt. 26:6–13; Mark 14:3; Luke 7:37–38; John 11:2; 12:3); (4) the betrayal of Judas (Matt. 26:14–16; Mark 14:10–11; Luke 22:3–6); (5) the use and abrogation of Passover (Matt. 26:17–21; Mark 14:12–18; Luke 22:7–17); (6) the establishment of the Lord's Supper (Matt. 26:26–31; Mark 14:22–27; Luke 22:19–20); (7) the washing of the feet of his disciples (John 13:3–17); (8) the detection of his traitor (Matt. 26:21–26; Mark 14:17–22; Luke 22:21–23; John 13:21–32); (9) the prediction of the offense, flight, and denial of the disciples (Matt. 26:31–35; Luke 22:31–39; Mark 14:27–32); and (10) the settling of the contention among the disciples over their prerogatives (Luke 22:24–31).

The suffering and death itself, through four acts
The second period presents the suffering and death of Christ itself, through four acts, of which: (1) the first contains what happened to him in the garden of the Mount of Olives, that is, first his agony (Matt. 26:36–46; Mark 14:32–42; Luke 22:39–46; John 18:1), then his deliverance into the hands of the Jews (Matt. 26:47–56; Mark 14:43–53; Luke 22:47–54, 63–65; John 18:3–13). (2) The

---

30. For a prominent debate at the time regarding the *idem* versus the *tantundem* of Christ's death, cf. Richard Baxter (1615–1691), *Aphorismes of Justification…wherein also is opened the nature of the covenants, satisfaction, righteousness, faith, works, etc.* (London: Francis Tyton, 1649), 44–56; and John Owen, *Of the death of Christ, the price he paid, and the purchase he made…vindicated from the exceptions and objections of Mr. Baxter* (London: Peter Cole, 1650); idem, *Works*, ed. William H. Goold (Edinburgh: T. & T. Clark, 1862), 10:437–48. Cf. Patrick Gillespie (1617–1675), *The Ark of the Covenant Opened* (London: for Thomas Parkhurst, 1677), 406, "Christ paid not the *idem*, but the *tantundem*; not the same that was due, but the value: for he suffered not the same pain, *numero* in number, but *specie* in kind."
31. 1.4.4 §§VII–XVI

second act contains what was done with him in the court of the high priest, namely: (a) his examination (Matt. 26:57, 59–63; Mark 14:53, 55–61; Luke 22:54; John 18:19–24); (b) the fall and turning of Peter (Matt. 26:58, 69ff.; Mark 14:54, 66ff.; Luke 22:55–62; John 18:15–27); (c) and his condemnation (Matt. 26:65–69; Mark 14:61–66; Luke 22:66–77). (3) The third act recounts what was done with him before Pilate, with respect to his (a) being led to Pilate (Matt. 27:1–2; Mark 15:1; Luke 23:1; John 18:28), to which was conjoined the despair and hanging of Judas (Matt. 27:3–10); (b) the accusation of the Jews and the examination of Pilate (Matt. 27:11–14; Mark 15:2–6; Luke 23:2–12; John 18:28–39); (c) the justification of Pilate (Matt. 27:15–24; Mark 15:7–14; Luke 23:4, 13–23; John 18:38–40, 19:4–15); (d) his scourging (Matt. 27:26; Mark 15:15; John 19:1); (e) his condemnation (Matt. 27:26; Mark 15:15; Luke 23:24–25; John 19:16). (4) The fourth act relates what happened around the crucifixion, among which occur: (a) his being led to Golgotha and in that, his address to the mourning women (Luke 23:26–31; Matt. 27:27–33; Mark 15:16–22; John 19:16–17); (b) his drinking of vinegar mixed with gall, and his intercession for those who crucified him (Matt. 27:33–34; Mark 15:23; Luke 23:34); (c) the title on the cross (John 19:19, 25; Matt. 27:37; Mark 15:26; Luke 23:38); (d) the care of his mother, which was entrusted to John (John 19:25–27; Matt. 27:55–56; Mark 15:40; Luke 23:49), together with the indignities inflicted upon him by every kind of person while he hung upon the cross (Matt. 27:38–45; Mark 15:27–33; Luke 23:35–37); (e) the conversion of the thief, the eclipse of the sun, and the complaint of his desertion by God (Matt. 27:44–46; Mark 15:33–34; Luke 23:39–44); (f) the complaint of his thirst, the declaration that all was finished, the committing of his spirit into his Father's hands, and his death (John 19:28–30; Matt. 27:47–50; Mark 15:35–37; Luke 23:46).

The things that followed
The third period contains the things that followed his death and crucifixion, namely: (1) the miracles which succeeded his death (Matt. 27:51–55; Mark 15:38–40; Luke 23:44–49), and (2) his burial, which we will speak about in its own place.[32]

The natural death of Christ was nearly the same as our death. With respect to its beginning: In regard to its sufferings
VII. From these periods of natural death it is certain not only that he truly and properly died, but also that he undertook a death that was well enough the same

---

32. 1.5.13 §§VI–VIII

as that which was incumbent upon us due to sin. And accordingly, just as our death has its parts, with respect to loss and with respect to sense, and also its degrees, with respect to its beginning and with respect to its consummation, and also a certain moderation mixed into them (according to that which we taught in bk. 4, ch. 4, §§XIII–XIV), so also Christ's natural death has, first, its beginning, and in this beginning, besides the mortality inborn in him, (1) weakening, brought upon him externally by various distresses, being led from place to place, the imposition of the cross, and other things (Ps. 22:1). That (2) among the disciples, he was betrayed by Judas (Matt. 26:47–50), denied by Peter (Matt. 26:69–74), deserted by all (Matt. 26:56). (3) He was declared by every kind of person, and especially by the leaders, to be a madman, demoniac, Samaritan, reveler, profane man, impostor, blasphemer, seducer, magician, rebel, and invader from another kingdom (John 19:7, 12; Matt. 26:65; Luke 23:2); he was rejected by the people, valued less than the worst sort of murderer (Matt. 27:20–25), and crucified in the middle of two thieves (John 19:18). (4) He was stripped of his clothing (Matt. 27:28–29). (5) Furthermore, when he was arrested, he was shamefully dragged from court to court, as if he were a thief (Matt. 26:50, 55–56; 27:2; Mark 14:46, 48–49; Luke 22:52–54; John 18:12). (6) He suffered the most unjust judgments, as much ecclesiastical, under the priests Ananias and Caiaphas (John 18:13–14, 19–24; Matt. 26:57, 59–66; 27:1; Mark 14:53, 55–64; Luke 22:66, 71; 23:1–2), as political, under Pilate and Herod the Tetrarch (Matt. 27:11, 26; Mark 15:2–15; Luke 23:1–25; John 18:28–40; 19:1–16). (7) He was mocked, spat upon, beaten, mangled with a thorny crown, first before Caiaphas (Matt. 26:67–68; Mark 14:65; Luke 22:63–65), then before Herod (Luke 23:11), and finally before Pilate and his officials and soldiers (Matt. 27:26–32; Mark 15:16–20). Furthermore, (8) like a villain, with his body stripped naked, in a place of infamy between two thieves, he endured a savage, shameful, and cursed kind of punishment, preceded also by a thousand insults, by a drink steeped with gall and myrrh, and by a sarcastic inscription on the placard (Matt. 27:31, 33–49; Mark 15:20, 22–36; Luke 23:25, 32–33, 35–39; John 19:16–20; Gal. 3:13). Finally, (9) he suffered in all the parts and members of his body: his ears were filled with mockeries (Matt. 27:39–40), his head battered with a reed (v. 30), and lacerated with thorns (v. 29), his body scourged (v. 26), his mouth given vinegar and gall to drink (v. 34; Mark 15:23), his face disgraced with spit (Matt. 27:30), his shoulders burdened with the wood of the cross (Luke 23:26), his side pierced (John 19:34), his arms extended over the cross, his hands and feet affixed to the cross with nails (Ps. 22:16–17; Matt. 27:35), his blood from all his veins poured out (John 19:34), his heart melted with anguish (Ps. 22:14), and so forth.

In regard to its mitigation

Meanwhile, in all these things, just as in our death, a mitigation of some sort was present: (1) in the manifestation of the divine power and majesty, in which he knocked his captors to the ground with his voice (John 18:6), and healed the ear of Malchus (Luke 22:50–51); (2) that he was strengthened by an angel (Luke 22:43); (3) multiple testimonies of his innocence, by the judge himself, and his wife (Matt. 27:18–19, 24; Mark 15:10, 14; Luke 23:4, 14, 20, 22; John 19:4, 6), indeed by his betrayer himself (Matt. 27:3–5) and by other spectators (Luke 23:47); (4) the help of Simon the Cyrenian and the compassion of the multitude (Luke 23:26–31; Matt. 27:32; Mark 15:21).

With respect to its consummation

And this was the beginning of his natural death; in addition it had, second, its consummation, through which his soul was separated from his body (Luke 23:46; Matt. 27:50; John 19:30), while at the same time the hypostatic union remained inviolate, for which reason it is said that the Lord of glory was crucified (1 Cor. 2:8), and that the Lord lay in a tomb (Matt. 28:6). Furthermore, from this consummation, this death was: (1) true, not simulated or feigned, inasmuch as it was procured by the true separation of the essential parts, of the body and the soul (Luke 23:46; Matt. 27:50); (2) certainly violent, insofar as it was inflicted by external causes; but (3) still natural, insofar as it was procured by naturally effective causes; except that (4) it can be called supernatural, and even voluntary, insofar as he laid down his life willingly (John 10:18), and delivered himself up (Eph. 5:2), and as it was supernaturally adorned with various miracles: the extraordinary darkening of the sun (Matt. 27:45; Luke 23:44–45), the rending of the veil (Matt. 27:51; Luke 23:45), the quaking of the earth, the splitting of the rocks, the opening of the graves, the resurrection of the dead (Matt. 27:51–53). So far the natural death of Christ.

2. The spiritual death of Christ: Certainly not the same as ours. But yet analogous and equivalent to ours, complete in five particulars

VIII. He had to sustain, second, spiritual death, certainly not the same in species or number as that which was incumbent upon us due to sin, but yet similar, and also the same in value and price. For since a spiritual death is incumbent upon us which includes the privation of the divine image and loss of original righteousness, conjoined with slavery to sin, the world, the devil, and the flesh (as we taught in bk. 4, ch. 4, §§VIII–XI), this spiritual death could not have fallen upon Christ, for he would have not only been unfit for the mediatorial office, but also, as the God-man, a sinner. Therefore it was some kind of spiritual sorrowful evil analogous to our spiritual death, the same in value and weight with our spiritual death. Thus by his own spiritual death, Christ: (1) was deprived of the joy and delight which his soul had been able otherwise to draw from the enjoyment of God and the fullness of grace, because having become sin for us, at the same time he had to become an object of the divine wrath (2 Cor. 5:21 with Ps. 22:1–2; Isa. 53:10). (2) Christ tasted the divine wrath, on account of our sins which he took upon himself (Rev. 19:15) and was exposed to be vexed by the power of darkness (John 12:27). And in these things properly speaking was that cup which was given to Christ by his Father to drink (Matt. 26:39; Luke 22:42). But he was presented as an object of the divine wrath, not absolutely with respect to the divine affection; for he was that Son so well-beloved of the Father (Matt. 3:17; 17:5), but with respect to his effective action,[33] that is, those penalties that were owed to the Son from our undertaken guilt. Nor was his subjection to the power of darkness properly speaking for servitude, but only for vexation, and that not forever, but only for a time, until he had crushed the serpent's head (Gen. 3:15; cf. John 14:30). From this (3) his soul received such great sorrow, horror, and terror, not only in the garden, but also beforehand (Luke 12:50; John 12:27; Matt. 26:37–38). From these things also arose (4) emphatic prayer for deliverance, displaying a confounded soul, and such a nature that shunned the harshness of death, without which he would not have sustained the punishment, all which things, however, were conjoined with the deepest submission to the divine will (John 12:27; Matt. 26:39; Mark 14:35; Luke 22:42; cf. Heb. 5:7). And also (5) bloody sweat, real indeed, and wrenched from him by the vehemence of his agony (Luke 22:44; cf. Gen. 49:11; Isa. 63:2; Rev. 19:13).

3. The eternal death of Christ: What and to what extent it was undertaken by Christ

IX. To this spiritual death was added, third, the eternal death due for our sins (as we said above in ch. 4, bk. 4, §§XV–XVI), although there was not added the eternity of death, because: (1) this eternity does not pertain to the essence of the punishment, but is added from the condition of the one punished, when he is such that in bearing the punishment, he cannot exhaust it (Matt. 18:34). (2) Sin, which wounds the infinite majesty of God, deserves a punishment that is infinite in only one way, either intensively, that is, infinite in weight, which a mere creature cannot sustain, or extensively, that is, infinite in duration. Therefore because the Savior, who is the God-man, sustained a punishment infinite in weight and value, it was not necessary that he receive a punishment infinite or eternal in duration.

---

33. *non quoad affectum divinum…sed quoad effectum*

Especially since (3) this eternity of death would render him inept for those mediatorial offices which were incumbent upon him to render after death. Therefore, he undertook eternal death, from which it is said that he was made a curse (Gal. 3:13), and as a sign of this, he willed to be hung upon a cross. But he accepted this eternal death only with respect to its essentials, and by no means with respect to those circumstantials which accompany it in the damned. And what then are the essentials of eternal death? I respond, As regards the *poena damni*, the pain of loss, it is the separation from the gracious presence, sight, and enjoyment of God as the highest good; as regards the *poena sensus*, the pain of sense, it is the intolerable torture of soul and body (Matt. 25:41; 2 Thess. 1:9).[34] Therefore if the Savior sustained both of these, he certainly sustained the essentials of eternal death. But he did sustain them: first with respect to the pain of loss, when he was forsaken by the Father, stripped for a time of all sense of spiritual consolation and joy, and compelled to lament, "My God, My God, why have you forsaken me!" (Matt. 27:46; Mark 15:34 from Ps. 22:1); then with respect to the pain of sense, when, under a curse (Gal. 3:13), he took upon himself the utmost limits of God's wrath and judgments (Rev. 19:15), experienced the sorrows of death (Acts 2:24), indeed was encompassed by the sorrows of death, and overtaken by the sorrows of hell (Ps. 18:4–6), and for all these things he laments that his soul is exceeding sorrowful, even to death (Matt. 26:38), and that his heart has become like wax that is melted in the midst of his bowels (Ps. 22:14), and he acknowledges that his soul is cast down to hell, where eternal death was usually endured (Ps. 16:10; cf. 30:3; 86:13), about which we have more to say in the next chapter.[35]

The Savior suffered not only in his body, but also in his soul.
X. Therefore from what has been said, it is clearer than the sun that the Mediator suffered not only in his body, but also in his soul, and indeed more so in his soul. For (1) not only does Scripture explicitly refer the sufferings to the soul (Ps. 22:14; Isa. 53:10; Matt. 26:38; John 12:27), but (2) also the very nature of our sins, inasmuch as they especially arise from the soul (Mark 7:19–23), demands a punishment to be inflicted upon the soul of the expromissor, if indeed he would successfully deliver his dependents from the tortures of the soul; and moreover,

---

34. On the twofold punishment or pain owed for sins, of either loss or sense, see Johannes Polyander (1568–1646), André Rivet, Antoine Thysius (1573–1639), Antonius Walaeus (1573–1639), "Disputatio XVI: De Peccato Actuali," §XXV in *Synopsis purioris theologiae*, 4th ed. (Leiden: J. & D. Elzevier, 1652), 170; idem, *Synopsis Purioris Theologiae / Synopsis of a Purer Theology: Latin Text and Commentary*, D. te Velde et al., eds., trans. R. A. Faber, 2 vols. (Leiden: Brill, 2014–2016), 1:394–95.

35. 1.5.13 §IX

by the same reason, not only in the lower part of the soul, as they say, or the sensitive part, but also the higher or rational part, since not only throughout the Scriptures by the heart (wherein the Savior laments that he suffers, Ps. 22:14) is understood the will, a faculty of the rational soul, but also our sins are said to flow from our heart (Matt. 15:18–20). Nor did the soul of Christ suffer only through sympathy, by the mediating sorrows of the body, but also immediately, which is evident from those agonies he endured in Gethsemane, when his body was not suffering yet at all, when he exclaimed, "My soul is exceeding sorrowful, even to death" (Matt. 26:38), when he began to be sorrowful, to be deeply distressed and troubled[36] (Matt. 26:37, 42; Mark 14:33, 36).

He suffered not only as man, nor only as God, but simultaneously as God and man.
XI. All these things the Mediator endured, whether in body or in soul, neither only as man, nor only as God, but as the God-man, simultaneously as God and man, just as, according to the nature of the theandric effects,[37] each nature bestowed its own part to Christ's sufferings: while the human nature alone sustained and suffered them (since passive potency does not occur in the divine nature, Mal. 3:6; James 1:17; and much less death, because the divine nature is incorruptible, Rom. 1:23; 1 Tim. 1:17; 6:16), the divine nature furnished to his sufferings an infinite weight, value, and price, so that they were God's sufferings (Acts 20:28), and the blood of the Son of God (1 John 1:7), suited to cleanse us from all sin.

The supreme cause of Christ's death was God.
XII. Christ had, as the first and chief cause of his entire death, God his own Father, the supreme Judge (Isa. 53:6, 10; Zech. 13:7; 2 Cor. 5:21; Acts 2:23; 4:28), for which reason he laments, "My God, My God, why have you forsaken me?" (Ps. 22:1). Moreover, God was involved in the sufferings and death of his Son in more than one way, namely: (1) by predetermining them (Acts 2:23; 4:28; Rom. 8:29; Luke 24:26, 46; Acts 17:3); (2) by foretelling them (Ps. 22; Isa. 53; Zech. 13:7; Dan. 9:26); (3) by sustaining him while he suffered them (Ps. 22:11, 24); (4) by permitting his enemies to do them (Acts 4:28); and (5) by limiting them (Acts 4:28; John 19:31–33); (6) by directing them to their predetermined end (2 Cor. 5:21; Isa. 53:5). God had as a moving cause, as it were: (1) his grace and mercy toward the sinner (Rom. 9:23 with 2 Cor. 5:21; Isa. 53:6; Rom. 8:32); (2) avenging justice toward the expromissor, his Son (Rom. 3:22; 8:3); and (3) the glory of both, of grace as well as justice (Rom. 3:25).

---

36. λυπεῖσθαι, ἐκθαμβεῖσθαι καὶ ἀδημονεῖν
37. ἀποτελεσμάτων θεανδρικῶν. Cf. 1.5.4 §XIII.

The second causes were people of every kind.

XIII. Moreover, the second causes were people of every kind: (1) friends (Zech. 13:6), the false, like his betrayer Judas (Matt. 26:14–16, 47–50), as well as the genuine, indeed Peter who denied him (v. 69ff.), and so forth; (2) enemies: (a) ecclesiastical enemies, the chief priests, priests, Pharisees, scribes, elders, and the Sanhedrin (Matt. 26:57–69; 27:1; etc.); (b) political enemies, as much the princes (Ps. 2:2), that is, Herod the Tetrarch, and Pilate, Caesar's legate (Acts 4:27; Matt. 27:2ff.; Luke 23:7–8), as their ministers (Luke 23:11); (c) martial enemies (Matt. 27:27; Luke 23:36; John 19:2, 23–24, 32, 34; Mark 15:16); (3) Jews as well as Gentiles (Acts 4:27); (4) the learned and unlearned; (5) men and women (Matt. 26:69, 71; 27:19, 55); (6) the entire multitude (Matt. 27:39–40). That is to say, just as he tasted death from all, so he tasted death for all (Heb. 2:9).

The fruit of Christ's death

XIV. The fruit and effect of this entire death: (1) first in general, is satisfaction for our sins, insofar as he sustained the death that was owed to our sins from the divine justice, truthfulness, and law (Isa. 53:4–10; Gal. 3:13; 2 Cor. 5:21; Rom. 8:3; etc.), which satisfaction, Lord willing, we will expressly teach in its own place;[38] from it, in specific, flowed forth (2) the universal redemption of the elect (Matt. 20:28; 1 Tim. 2:6; Matt. 1:21); from this furthermore, (3) our reconciliation with God (Rom. 5:1, 6–8; 2 Cor. 5:19, 21); in addition, (4) deliverance from the wrath of God (Rom. 5:9; 1 Thess. 5:9); also (5) from the curse of the law (Gal. 3:13; Rom. 8:3); (6) from the power of Satan (Heb. 2:14–15); (7) from death and hell (1 Cor. 15:54–57; Rom. 7:24); on the contrary, (8) the blessing of Abraham (Gal. 3:14; John 3:14–15); and (9) eternal life (John 3:16).

The double foundation of this matter

XV. The foundation of all these things is especially in these two points, that: (1) he endured all those things without any of his own guilt, being entirely innocent (Isa. 53:9; 2 Cor. 5:21; 1 Peter 2:22), and accordingly from the justice of God, he could not have sustained for himself the death which was owed only to sinners (Gen. 2:17; Rom. 5:12; 6:23); and so then, since he sustained it, he did not sustain it except for others. (2) He presented himself for us in the eternal council of peace as surety and expromissor (Heb. 7:22; Ps. 40:6–7; Isa. 53:4).

Yet he did not die for each and every person, but for all kinds,
that is, for his own people.

XVI. Yet at the same time, what he endured, he did not endure for each and

---

38. 1.5.18 §§Xff., XXVI

every sinner head by head; namely, not for those who are condemned in their own person (Rom. 8:33–34), inasmuch as when he was about to die he would not even pray for them (John 17:9), although at the same time, his death in itself could have been sufficient to deliver each and every person (from the infinite dignity of his person, it is of infinite value, 1 John 1:7; Acts 20:28), if only, from the Father's will, he had willed to destine it to all. At the same time, he destined it for all kinds without distinction (1 Tim. 2:6), namely for all who believe (John 3:14–16), for his people (Matt. 1:21), his sheep (John 10:15), his children (Heb. 2:10), his brethren (Heb. 2:17), and however many come to the Father through him with living faith (Heb. 7:25), and earnestly desire to be saved by him (Rev. 22:17; Isa. 55:1; Matt. 5:6).

The Elenctic Part

It is asked: 1. Did Christ truly suffer and die?

XVII. Concerning the sufferings and death of Christ, it is asked, first, whether Christ truly suffered and died. The Manicheans, Gnostics, Theopaschites,[39] and Aphthartodocetists,[40] ancient heretics, foolishly asserted that the Son of God suffered and died only κατὰ δόκησιν καὶ φαντασίαν, according to an appearance and apparition, as he in fact had a body which was ἄφθαρτον, incorruptible, that is, τῶν φυσικῶν καὶ ἀδιαβλήτων παθῶν ἀνεπίδεικτον,[41] that

---

39. Theopaschitism is the view that when Christ suffered and died, the divine nature suffered and died, and thus involved the entire Godhead in his suffering and death. This view was propounded by John Maxentius (John the Scythian, fl. 519–520) in his *Libellus fidei*, X.17–19. For an early rejection of this view and its formulae, see Trifolius (fl. 519), *Epistula ad beatum Faustum senatorem contra Joannem Scytham monachum*. Both of these works are in *Scriptores Illyrici Minores* (Turnhout: Brepols, 2010), CCSL 85. Pope John II (470–535) rejected the theopaschite view in *Olim Quidem*, PL 66:23, and asserts that Christ is one "of" the Holy Trinity (*unum sanctae Trinitatis*), not one "from" (*unus ex Trinitate*); cf. J. A. McGuckin, "The 'Theopaschite Confession' (Text and Historical Context): A Study in the Cyrilline Re-interpretation of Chalcedon," *Journal of Ecclesiastical History*, 35, no. 2 (April 1984): 239–55.

40. Aphthartodocetism extended the Monophysite heresy (i.e. that Christ had one nature, a divine one) to claim that the body of Christ was divine, and thus naturally impassible and incorruptible, but Christ could will to suffer and die voluntarily. This view was propounded by Julian, bishop of Halicarnassus (died c. 527) and rejected in Eastern Christianity: see *The Syriac Chronicle, Known as That of Zachariah of Mitylene*, trans. F. J. Hamilton and E. W. Brooks (London: Methuen & Co., 1899), IX.xvi, pp. 258–61. For a critical Syriac edition of British Museum Add. MS. 17202, see *Zachariae Ep. Mitylenes aliorumque scripta historica Graece plerumque deperdita*, ed. J. P. N. Land, in *Anecdota Syriaca*, 4 vols. (Leiden: Brill, 1862–1875), IX.xvi, 3:279–85.

41. Lit., "that does not display natural and not reproachable (i.e. innocent) sufferings." Cf. John of Damascus, *Expositio accurata fidei orthodoxae*, bk. 3, ch. 20 in *PL* 94:1081–82; idem, *Exposition of the Orthodox Faith* in NPNF2 9:68, "We confess, then, that [Christ] assumed all the natural and innocent passions (τὰ φυσικὰ καὶ ἀδιάβλητα πάθη) of man. For He assumed the whole man and

could not admit of physical sufferings.[42] Likewise, the Muslims want Christ to have been snatched up to the stars before his crucifixion, so that he was not crucified except in the opinion of the Jews. Otherwise, among those who profess Christ in our time there are none who do not at least profess with their mouth, and also defend, that Christ really and properly speaking died. In particular, even the Lutherans do the same, although at the same time it can hardly, and not even hardly, be reconciled with their hypotheses. For since they state that by the hypostatic union divine properties are communicated to the human nature, and among these properties in particular, omnipresence, it surely cannot be conceived how omnipresent flesh can be truly and properly separated from its soul, and thus how Christ could have died, properly speaking.

The reasons of the Reformed
The Reformed profess that he died by the true separation of his essential parts, because: (1) Scripture in countless passages teaches such a death, indeed the very rending of soul and body (Luke 23:46; Matt. 27:50; Mark 15:37; John 19:30). (2) The Old Testament Scripture quite often foretold his death (Isa. 53:10; Dan. 9:26). (3) It prefigured it by so many sacrificial victims that truly died. (4) He truly rose again from the dead (Matt. 28:6; Mark 16:6; Luke 24:6; John 20:9). (5) Otherwise he would not have really taken away the death pronounced upon and fitting for our sins (Isa. 53:4), nor accordingly would he have made satisfaction, and we would be yet in our sins (1 Cor. 15:3–4, 13–14, 16–18).

The fundamental objection
Nor is there anything, at least with any appearance, that could be objected against this fundamental truth, than this, that if he had truly died, then he would not have remained a true man, because a dead man is not a man; and consequently he also would not have been the true God-man. This knot, which has especially racked many, we think can be untied in this way: by denying that during death he was not a true man. For although a mere man when dead is not a true man, because once the separation of the parts has happened, in him there is entirely no surviving union of the essential parts, by which he could be called and be a man, yet it happens otherwise with the God-man, whose essential parts, body and soul, though when the immediate union was taken away they were rent

---

all man's attributes save sin.… For the natural and innocent passions are those which are not in our power, but which have entered into the life of man owing to the condemnation by reason of the transgression; such as hunger, thirst, weariness, labour, the tears, the corruption, the shrinking from death…."

42. *quod passiones physicas admittere non posset*

apart, yet by a mediate union remained conjoined in the divine person, for which reason it is said that God, or the divine nature, did not leave him in the grave (Acts 2:27 from Ps. 16:10).

2. By death was he reduced to a state of nonexistence?
The opinion of the Socinians
XVIII. Second, it is asked whether by his death Christ was reduced to a state of nonexistence. The Socinians, because they state that to die is nothing other than to exist no longer, insofar as by death the body is reduced to perpetual ashes, and the soul, which for them is nothing except some virtue and efficacy of God, returns to God, that is, it is reduced to God (see *A Brief Compendium of Socinianism, Refuted* by the renowned Cloppenburg, ch. 8,[43] and Smalcius, *On the Divinity of Christ*, ch. 13),[44] and that Christ, "then when he was dead, was in the same condition in which are all others have died" (as Smalcius says in the place cited),[45] at the same time state that after his death until his resurrection (which to them is nothing other than to exist again), Christ did not exist, of which God also wanted us to be persuaded by his burial and descent into hell, which according to them is likewise nothing except a state of nonexistence which all things that die go into, beasts as well as men, the pious as well as the impious, except that the pious (under the New Testament) by the resurrection will be brought back to a state of existence.

The arguments of the orthodox
On the contrary, all Christians think that, as death is in general, so also the death of Christ was nothing but a true separation of his body and soul, because the Scriptures expressly testify that: (1) throughout the three days of death his soul existed, as it had been committed into the hand of his Father (Luke 23:46; Ps. 31:6). (2) His body existed either on the cross or in the tomb (Matt. 27:59–60). (3) The entire composite did not see corruption, and much less nonexistence (Ps. 16:10; Acts 2:31; 13:35). Also (4) on the very day of his death, together with the converted thief, he existed in paradise (Luke 23:43). I would add that (5) he had life in himself (John 5:26), because he is life itself (John 14:6), and he has the power of an endless life (Heb. 7:16; 1 Cor. 15:45). I need not say that (6) by this reasoning, Christ would have emerged twice from among the

---

43. Johannes Cloppenburg, "De resurrectione mortuorum: et statu animarum: deque futuro saeculo," in *Compendiolum Socinianismi confutatum* (Franeker: Idzardus Balck, 1622), fol. O1r–R4v.
44. Smalcius, *De divinitate Jesu Christi*, 78–87.
45. Smalcius, *De divinitate Jesu Christi*, 79.

nonexistent[46]—once in the incarnation and again in the resurrection. More points of this kind will be handled in their own place, on the resurrection of the flesh.[47]

Objections of the Socinians

The arguments in favor of the Socinian views, Smalcius adduces in the passage cited: (1) that he is said to have emptied himself (Phil. 2:7). I respond, But this phrase, ἑαυτὸν ἐκένωσε, however it may be twisted, cannot be explained in any way by annihilation, unless there be acknowledged two natures in the person of Christ, one of which by a greater force reduced the other into nothing, and this greater force cannot indeed be any other than that of the divine nature,[48] or of God himself, to whom it belongs to create from nothing. However, ἐκένωσε to the apostle does not denote Christ's state when he was dead, but his grace when he was alive, by which he, while living in the flesh, presented himself as the servant of the Father, for humble obedience in life and in death. (2) That by this rationale, the resurrection is likened to generation in Acts 13:32–33, and it is said that Christ through his resurrection was begotten today (from Ps. 2:7). I respond, It is not true that Christ's resurrection is likened to generation in Acts 13:32–33, nor does it follow from the fact that after his assertion of Jesus raised up from the dead, the apostle added these words, "as it is also written in the second Psalm, 'You are my Son, today I have begotten you.'" Rather, the apostle does this to teach that on the day of Christ's resurrection, that name of Son was powerfully vindicated and asserted for him by the Father, a name more excellent than that of the angels, of which there is no true definition apart from a generation that is eternal, before every creature, for here Hebrews 1:4–5 and Romans 1:4 should be compared. (3) That the dead in the Scriptures are at times said not to exist (ὅτι οὐκ εἰσίν, "because they are not," Matt. 2:18, אֵינָם, Jer. 31:15; to which there are parallels in Ps. 104:35; Lam. 5:7). I respond, On account of this present transitory life (1 Cor. 7:29–30), those passages do not intend anything else than that the dead are no more among their communities and families, or among the living.

3. Did the Messiah have to suffer and die?

XIX. Third, it is asked whether, from the tenor of the Old Testament, the Messiah had to suffer and die. The Jews imagine for themselves two Messiahs: the

---

46. ἐξ οὐκ ὄντων
47. 1.5.15 §XV
48. τῆς θείας φύσεως

one is Messiah ben Joseph or ben Ephraim, whose name will be Nehemiah the son of Hushiel; he will be liable to various afflictions and will even be liable to death itself, as they say throughout the Talmud Masechet Sukkah,[49] and in the Aramaic paraphrase of Song of Songs 4:4, for which reason it is common among them to speak of the חבלי המשיח, pains of the Messiah.[50] The other is Messiah ben David, and they all deny that this their chief Messiah will be liable to sufferings and death. The Muslims agree with the Jews on this point, except that they acknowledge with us only one Jesus, whom they deny was truly crucified, as mentioned in a preceding section.[51]

The reasons of the Christians
Christians in agreement with the Scriptures acknowledge only one Messiah, and believe that he would be liable to sufferings and an ignominious death, not only on account of this, that: (1) Peter (1 Peter 1:11) and Paul (Acts 26:23) testify that the prophets had prophesied thus; but also (2) the prophets recount these pains of the Messiah in particular, for example, that (a) his heel would be crushed by the serpent (Gen. 3:15); (b) his hands and feet would be pierced, that is, on the cross (Ps. 22:16); (c) he would drink vinegar and gall (Ps. 69:21); (d) his face would be spat upon, and his back beaten (Isa. 50:6); (e) he would be mocked and despised (Ps. 22:6–8); (f) he would be sold for thirty pieces of silver (Zech. 11:12–13); (g) he would be pierced through (Zech. 12:10); (h) he would be stricken with a sword, or generally, he would be wounded (Zech. 13:7); (i) he would be slain (Dan. 9:26); (j) he would be wounded, beaten, snatched from the land of the living, buried (Isa. 53); and so forth. To which (3) we add, *ad hominem*,[52] if to the Jews themselves there is no inconsistency in that Messiah ben Joseph would be liable to various afflictions and even death, what inconsistency will there be in that the true Messiah is described as liable to the same things?

Objections of the Jews
They have almost nothing to object, except, first generally, that from one who is cursed, such as someone crucified (Deut. 21:23), a blessing cannot be expected.

---

49. *Massecoth sucha*: cf. in the Jerusalem Talmud, see Sukkah 52a, in the Babylonian Talmud, Sukkah 52b; *New Edition of the Babylonian Talmud*, 7:80.

50. For the Chaldean paraphrase of Song 4:4, see Walton, *Biblia Sacra polyglotta*, 3:436.

51. §XVII, above

52. This is not the more familiar abusive *ad hominem* fallacy of a personal attack "to the person," but the valid argument *ad hominem*, "according to the person," that is, using the presuppositions of an opponent to disprove his view.

I respond: (1) The text speaks of such a person who was hanged on account of his own crimes, which cannot be said of the righteous Messiah (Isa. 53:11). (2) It speaks of one hanged who is a mere man, such as the Messiah, יהוה צדקנו, "Jehovah our Righteousness," is not (Jer. 23:6). And (3) such a hanged man, who was cursed on account of the sins of others, is altogether able to procure a blessing for those who are cursed (Gal. 3:9–15). Then specifically, they take exception to those passages by which we try to prove the sufferings and death of the Messiah, saying that they do not speak of the Messiah. The antagonists of the Jews are expressly occupied with vindicating them: see Hoornbeeck, *Contra Judaeos*, bk. 6, ch. 1, and others, especially the anti-Jewish commentators.[53]

4. Did Christ suffer in his soul?

XX. It is asked, fourth, whether Christ also underwent spiritual death, or whether he also suffered in his soul, and its superior or rational part, and that immediately, and not only by sympathy with the body. The papists—so that they may more easily maintain these two things: (1) that the soul of Christ from the very first instant of his conception was blessed with the beatific vision of God, and thus with a blessedness of every sort; (2) that his descent into hell was not in the passions of the soul—deny it. The Reformed affirm it, for the reasons adduced in §VIII, to which we do not presently add anything else, other than that: (1) the division of our adversaries into the lower and higher part of the soul seems insufficiently accurate to us, and not agreeable to the simplicity of the spiritual soul. (2) From the hypothesis of our adversaries we could scarcely be solidly persuaded that Christ by his sufferings delivered us from the sufferings of the soul which threaten us due to our sins, if he did not suffer in the soul, either with respect to the *idem* or with respect to the *tantundem*.[54] For whatever things the Mediator did not take upon himself, from them he did not deliver us (from the tenor of Isa. 53:4; Gal. 3:13–14; 2 Cor. 5:21; etc.). Compare §VIII and §X, and likewise what we said on this very question in the preceding chapter, §XXXIII. There we touched on the hypotheses of our adversaries, and we also expressly dealt with the first of them in chapter 10, §XXXI; the second, Lord willing, we will examine in the following chapter.[55]

---

53. Hoornbeeck, *Pro convincendis et convertendis Judaeis*, 403–20.
54. On these terms, cf. §V, above.
55. 1.5.13 §IX, cf. §XII

5. Did he sustain the punishments of hell?

XXI. Fifth, it is asked whether he also underwent eternal death, or the punishments of hell. The Socinians deny it, lest Christ would have undertaken upon himself all the punishments owed for our sins, and by undertaking, in our place truly made satisfaction to God from the rigor of his justice. With them the Arminians collude (and among them in particular Vorstius), stating that he received no more than temporary death, and that it was considered by God in place of a full satisfaction, through acceptilation.[56] The Reformed, in the way and for the reasons expounded in §IX, affirm it, and when they have been properly pondered, satisfaction can be made without any trouble to those points that could be asserted by our adversaries to the contrary (namely, concerning the eternity of punishments, desperation, blasphemies, and other inordinate circumstances of the punishments of hell, as they are by no means required for the essence of the punishments). We will address the Arminians' acceptilation expressly in its own place, in the chapter on redemption.[57]

6. In the opinion of Calvin and the other Reformed, did Christ despair?

XXII. Sixth, it is asked whether in sustaining those punishments, in Calvin's opinion, Christ truly despaired. The papists, Lutherans, and others, through manifest devilry, strive to rub this vile blasphemy off onto Calvin and the other Reformed. No one has more successfully stopped their mouth than Calvin himself, in the *Institutes* (bk. 2, ch. 16, §12), and in the *Harmony*.[58] Nor does he say anywhere that Christ despaired, but only imagining the objection from the opinion of his adversaries, he only attributed an expression of desperation to Christ, that is, such an expression as people are commonly accustomed to make out of desperation. Moreover, the very substance of the matter speaks for itself, that he could not have despaired: for not only is it repugnant that so great a sin could befall the God-man, but also, he himself would not have been able or willing to decline those things which (from the decree of God, Acts 4:28, joined also with his expromission, well known to him) he had undertaken upon himself to be borne for us (Matt. 16:21–23; 26:51–54), nor from any promise of God could he draw hope that they would be declined, and thus through desperation he would have gone astray.

---

56. Cf. 1.5.1 §XXXVIII. On *acceptilation*, see 1.5.18 §IX.

57. 1.5.18 §XXV

58. John Calvin, *Institutes of the Christian Religion*, 2.16.12; idem, *Harmonia ex tribus evangelistis composita* (Geneva: Robertus Stephanus, 1555), 420–21; idem, *A Harmonie upon the three evangelists, Matthew, Mark and Luke with the commentarie* (London: George Bishop, 1584), 758–59, on Matt. 27:46.

7. Did he endure death as God and man simultaneously?

The difference of opinions

XXIII. Seventh, it is asked whether he endured death as the God-man. The Nestorians, because they separated the natures in Christ, stated that he endured death only as man, for which reason there was in their mouths, "Boast not, O Jew, for you have not slain God, but man." On the contrary, the Eutychians, who taught a confusion of the natures, thought that he suffered as much in the divine nature as in the human nature, because from the confusion of the two natures, they said that one nature had emerged. The papists, because they teach that he is Mediator only according to the human nature, in agreement with Francesco Stancaro, state that he only suffered as a man.[59] The Socinians agree with them, because they do not accept the Mediator's divine nature. The Lutherans, since they want the divine nature to have been communicated to the human nature through the hypostatic union, assert that God—properly and not figuratively, and thus the very divine nature—suffered for us. With them the Flemish Anabaptists agree, at least in thesis, because they think that Christ's human nature, having been drawn down from heaven or born from the divine substance, is divine.

The opinion of the Reformed

The Reformed, because they state that Christ is the Mediator according to both natures, as we have taught (bk. 5, ch. 2, §XVI; ch. 4, §IV) and vindicated (ch. 2, §§XXI–XXII), affirm that he died as the God-man, according to both natures, in the sense and by those reasons which we adduced in §XI. With respect to the hypotheses of our adversaries, those first of the Nestorians, then of the Eutychians, with whom the Lutherans collude, we have examined them in book 5, chapter 4, §VII and §XXIII, those of the papists and of Stancaro in book 5, chapter 2, §XXI, and those of the Anabaptists and Enthusiasts in chapter 10, §VI and §XIX.

8. Did the Mediator suffer in our place?

XXIV. Eighth, it is asked whether the Mediator endured all that he suffered in the place or stead of others. The Socinians, so that they may more easily take away the basis of satisfaction, do admit that he died generally for us, that is, for

---

59. See Stancaro, *De Trinitate et Mediatore*, fols. Pv recto–P[viii] verso, e.g. P[vi] recto, "The priest and sacrifice are the man-Christ, not the God-Christ, that is, Christ insofar as he is man, not insofar as he is God" (*Sacerdos et sacrificium est homo Christus, non Deus Christus, hoc est, Christus secundum hominem, non secundum Deum*).

our use and advantage, so that namely by his death he might seal the truth of his teaching, and he might confirm by his example the promise of the resurrection from the dead and of the eternal life to follow; but they deny that he died in our place and stead.

The arguments of Christians
Christians affirm that he did: (1) by all those passages in which it is explicitly said that he died for us (Rom. 5:6, 8; 2 Cor. 5:14–15; 1 Thess. 5:10), that is, in such a way in which Paul did not die for us (1 Cor. 1:13), and by such an efficacy that he takes away our condemnation (Rom. 8:34). Then (2) by those passages in which it is explicitly said that he took upon himself the punishment for our sins (Isa. 53:4), presented his soul stood as an אשם, a sacrifice for sins (v. 10), and became sin for us, that we might become righteousness before God (2 Cor. 5:21). Furthermore, (3) by those passages in which it is said that he paid the price of redemption for us (Matt. 20:28; 1 Tim. 2:6; Eph. 1:7, 14; Col. 1:14; Heb. 9:15). Also (4) by those passages in which it is said that he gave himself up for us an offering and sacrifice to God for a sweet-smelling aroma (Eph. 5:2; Heb. 7:27; 8:3; 9:22–23; 10:5–13).

Objections of the Socinians
There is almost nothing they may object, except: (1) that it is wrong to kill a just man for an unjust one (Gen. 18:23). I respond, It is certainly unjust to punish someone who is unwilling, or who does not have authority over his own life; however, it is not unjust to punish one who is willing (Ps. 40:6; Heb. 10:5–7), and who does have authority over his own life (John 10:18). (2) That it is not necessary to kill a just man for an unjust one, because God forgives sin freely (Matt. 18:32). I respond, He does freely forgive us, and that on account of Christ (Eph. 1:7; Col. 1:14; Heb. 9:22), but nowhere is he said to have forgiven Christ. (3) That it would be impossible for one man to endure death for so many countless myriads. I respond, It is impossible for one mere man to sustain it, but it is not impossible for the Son of God (1 John 1:7), God himself (Acts 20:28), the God-man, Immanuel, God with us (Isa. 7:14; Matt. 1:21) to endure it.

9. Did he have to undertake precisely death?
XXV. Ninth, it is asked whether Christ had to undertake precisely death for us. The papists, under the appearance of extolling the death of Christ, which they diminish in so many ways, affirm that only one drop of blood is sufficient for redeeming all mankind, to the end that what remains might be stored, like

a surplus, in the treasury of the church, to be disbursed through indulgences by the pope to those who offer helping hands, that is, money.

The arguments
The Reformed affirm that precisely death was necessary, because: (1) our sin, from the justice of God (Rom. 1:32), from the threat of the law (Gen. 2:17; Rom. 6:23), and from its own nature, since it injures the infinite majesty of God, demands death as a punishment. (2) From the contrary hypothesis, the death of Christ would be redundant, a drop of blood being sufficient. And so (3) God would have been cruel (forbid the blasphemy) to inflict so harsh a death upon his only begotten Son, without necessity.

Objection
Nor is there anything to what they object to us, the infinity of the value that is present in each particle of his sufferings, because: (1) from the hypothesis of those objecting, this is false, because he suffered with respect only to the human nature, and (2) from the justice and truth of God, and the nature of sin, precisely death is demanded, as we have said.

10. Was the death of Christ equivalent to all the punishments of the elect?
XXVI. Tenth, it is asked whether the death which the Mediator endured was, from the rigor of divine justice, equivalent to all the punishments which are owed to all the elect due to sin. Vorstius and the Arminians, so that they might give a sly nod to the Socinians, who deny the satisfaction of Christ properly so called, reject this and state that Christ endured something that God admitted by acceptilation, in place of an equivalent payment and compensation. The orthodox, although they certainly admit a grace by which God received for us what his Son offered, yet from the rigor of justice, they think that God could not have demanded from his Son more for our guilt than he accepted from him, because from the dignity of the person, who is the Son of God (1 John 1:7), and God himself (Acts 20:28), he accepted an infinite price, greater than which can be neither sought nor obtained, because something greater than an infinite thing cannot be conceived. The basis for the opposing opinion adheres in the denial of the eternal deity of the Mediator, and when this has been asserted (bk. 2, ch. 26, §§ VIII–XII), the equivalence of the satisfaction abides.

11. Did Christ endure death for each and every person? The difference of opinions
XXVII. Eleventh, it is asked whether Christ endured death for each and every person. The Pelagians and the Pelagianizers, as many as are outside of

the Reformed communion, affirm that Christ died for all equally, such that the application or the communion of the benefits of this death is suspended upon each person's free will. Those among the Reformed who defend universal grace think that Christ died for each and every person in this sense: under a condition, so that they could believe, if only they willed to believe, yet in such a way that he died absolutely for only the elect, that is, not only so that they could believe if they willed it, but also so that they would actually will it.

The orthodox opinion is proved.
All the Reformed agree in this, that there is such a great value and price in the death of Christ, from the infinite dignity of the person, that it could be sufficient for saving each and every person, but because neither the Father nor the Son willed that death to be destined for redeeming each and every person, it cannot be fittingly said that Christ died for each and every person, because: (1) it is restricted throughout the Scriptures to many (Matt. 20:28; Rom. 5:19; Isa. 53:11–12; Heb. 9:28), namely to the called (Heb. 9:15), believers (Rom. 3:22, 25–26), the sanctified (Heb. 10:14), the church (Acts 20:28), his sheep (John 10:14–16, 26–28), with also the world excluded, inasmuch as he would not even pray for it, and much less die for it (John 17:9). (2) It has an inseparable connection with the eternal salvation of those for whom he died (Rom. 8:34; 5:10). More things on this matter, Lord willing, will occur in the chapter on redemption.[60]

The reasons for the opinion of our adversaries are examined.
Nor is there any reason for them to allege: (1) that by his death he takes away the sins of the world (John 1:29), and God so loved the world that he gave his Son to it (John 3:16); because by "the world" is not understood anything except heathenism in distinction from Judaism (Rom. 11:12), so that the sense is, "He takes away the sins not only of Jews but also of any Gentiles." (2) That he gave himself a ransom for all (1 Tim. 2:6; Heb. 2:9; Rom. 5:18). I respond, That is, for anyone, from any rank among men (cf. Matt. 4:23; 12:31; Rom. 14:2; Rev. 5:9). In specific, (3) that he died for those who deny him (2 Peter 2:1). I respond, It is not said here that Christ died for apostates, or purchased them by the price of his blood, but that the δεσπότης, "Lord" (which word nowhere is understood of Christ), namely God, purchased (not with a price, Isa. 55:1), that is, acquired for himself by the preaching of the Word, those apostate false prophets, to the extent that by an external profession they acknowledged him as their Lord, and

---

60. 1.5.18 §XL

at the same time professed faith in Christ, which they afterwards denied. Also (4) that they crucify to themselves anew the Son of God (Heb. 6:6), and thus at least once he was crucified for them. I respond, The text does not intend anything other than that apostates of this sort have committed such a sin (that which is called the blasphemy against the Holy Spirit, Matt. 12:31) for which Christ was never crucified, so that, if they had to be delivered from this sin, Christ would have to be crucified anew for their sake. Indeed more so, (5) that he died even for the one who tramples underfoot the Son of God and the blood of the covenant, by whom he had been sanctified, who counts the blood of the covenant, *through which he had been sanctified*, a profane thing, and insults the Spirit of grace (Heb. 10:29). I respond, The text does not say that those sinners were sanctified by the blood of the covenant, but that Christ himself was sanctified in his own blood, by the interpretation of the apostle himself in Hebrews 2:10.

*Four remaining questions, which are set aside for other chapters
more proper to them*
XXVIII. There are other things that could be asked regarding the death of Christ, which will be indicated in this place, but for the sake of brevity will be set aside for other places more fitting to them. For example, twelfth, whether the death of Christ supplied a satisfaction truly and properly so called: we will set this question aside for the chapter on redemption.[61] Thirteenth, whether the reconciliation that Christ procured by his own death is μονόπλευρος, unilateral, in which he only reconciled man to God, and not vice versa: we will set this question aside for that same chapter.[62] Fourteenth, whether Christ during the three days he was dead and buried was a true man, and consequently the God-man: we will set this question aside for the chapter on the descent into hell.[63] Fifteenth, whether by the death of Christ the divine person was separated either from his body or from his soul, and thus the hypostatic union suspended: this question closely coincides with the previous, so likewise it will be set aside for the next chapter.[64]

The Practical Part

*The practice of this topic: 1. Commends to us meditation on the
suffering and death of Christ. Motives*
XXIX. The practice of the suffering and death of Christ demands, first, that we be frequently, indeed entirely, in meditation on the suffering and death of Christ,

---

61. 1.5.18 §§XXV–XXVI, XXXIII
62. 1.5.18 §XXXIV
63. 1.5.13 §XIII
64. 1.5.13 §XIII

inasmuch as: (1) it was such a great thing with Paul, that for the knowledge of it he was willing to deny all wisdom (1 Cor. 2:1), though he certainly was uncommonly supplied with it (having been educated at the feet of the great Gamaliel, Acts 22:3, and indeed caught up into the third heaven, where he saw unspeakable things which it is not lawful for man to utter, 2 Cor. 12:4), so that he could glory only in the cross of Christ (Gal. 6:14). (2) The blessed angels themselves desire to look into it (1 Peter 1:12), and long to speak of it with Christ (Luke 9:31, 35). (3) Its contents contain such wisdom that flourishes among the perfect, of which the princes of this world are ignorant, such that is the wisdom of God, and indeed the wisdom of God in a mystery, which was hidden, and destined for our glory before the world existed, which wisdom (in the world, that is) eye has not seen, nor ear heard, and which has not descended into the heart of man, which God has revealed to us by his Spirit—just as, with the greatest affection, the apostle speaks of it in 1 Corinthians 2:2–10. (4) It opens up to us all the treasures of eternal wisdom, avenging justice, grace and mercy, power, truthfulness, and so forth, about which we will soon teach a bit more particularly.[65] Compared to it (5) there is nothing more sweet, nothing more efficacious, for raising up a conscience battered by the sense of any evils, inasmuch as it represents to us, indeed it pours out into our hearts the indescribable love of God, in the sense of which we can even sweetly glory in any affliction (Rom. 5:3–12). Compared to it (6) there is also nothing more useful, for: (a) justification (Isa. 53:3–11), (b) the imitation of sanctification (1 Peter 2:21ff.), and (c) glory (Gal. 6:14; 1 Cor. 2:2, 6–8). Compared to it (7) there is nothing more necessary that we may gain Christ, be united with him, and become partakers of his righteousness (Phil. 3:7–10; cf. 1 Cor. 2:2).

Certain things should be pondered in meditating upon the suffering and death of Christ: (1) Who suffered?
Moreover, in this meditation we should reverently ponder: who suffered, namely, not some common son of man, a son of the earth, like the fictitious Messiah ben Joseph of the Jews, nor some outstanding prince or monarch, who is one worth ten thousand (2 Sam. 18:3), nor even a created angel, one of those whom the psalmist extols (Ps. 103:20), but the Messiah, the messenger of the covenant, the King of kings, the Lord of lords, the Son of God, עמנואל, Immanuel, the God-man, indeed God himself (Matt. 27:54).

---

65. §XXX, below

(2) What did he suffer?

What he suffered: not some light affliction, but the greatest of all evils, the highest affliction of all, death, and not only one kind of death, not only natural death, which we sometimes read is sought and desired by men, because it brings them deliverance from pressing evils, and an entrance into a better life (2 Cor. 5:1–2; Phil. 1:23); but in addition spiritual death, wherein deserted by God, exceeding sorrowful, even to death, he walked in darkness and saw no light (Isa. 50:10); moreover, even eternal or infernal death, which the damned experience in hell, through which he was a curse (Gal. 3:13), just as we have shown in the dogmatic part.[66]

(3) In which parts did he suffer?

In which parts he suffered, namely, not only in his body and all its members, according to those things that we delineated in the dogmatic part,[67] but also in his soul; and that not only through sympathy with the pains of his body, but through an immediate sense of spiritual horrors, according to what we adduced in the dogmatic part.[68] To which at present we add this, that from the premise of Scripture, in which his soul is said to have travailed (Isa. 53:11), it must altogether be remembered that all those things which he endured externally in his reputation, in his goods, in his body, also by analogy, he endured internally and spiritually: for example, when he was deserted externally by all his disciples, we should consider also that he was deserted by God, by his own heavenly Father; when he was delivered up bodily into the hands of the Gentiles, at the same time he was delivered up spiritually by God into the power of the hellish torturers; when he was condemned to death, first by the ecclesiastical court, then by the civil court, bodily, at the same time he was condemned spiritually, before the divine tribunal; when his head was crowned with thorns, his face defiled by spit, his body torn apart by whips, and that by men most vile, he suffered by analogy the same things in his soul spiritually; when his body was crucified naturally, his soul was also crucified spiritually. And in this way we should proceed through each and every part of his suffering, so that we may perceive and represent the weight and gravity of his suffering more distinctly.

(4) By whose initiative did he suffer?

By whose initiative he endured all those things both inwardly and outwardly, namely: (a) from enemies and friends, (b) from ecclesiastical, political, and

---

66. §§VII–IX, above
67. §X, above
68. §X, above

military enemies, (c) from masters and from servants, (d) from the educated and the ignorant; so that every kind of men, and as it were the entire world, with all its gathered strength conspired toward his torment (cf. Ps. 3:1; 22:12–14). And what by far is the most serious, (e) he endured the same things from *God*, from *his* God, from his very own *Father*, from his own *heavenly* Father, inasmuch as he is the one who not only permitted all those things to be inflicted (Acts 4:28), but he himself inflicted them (Isa. 53:6, 10; Zech. 13:7), from which the gravity of each suffering increased immensely.

(5) In what manner did he suffer?
In what manner he endured those things, namely: (a) as one entirely innocent, with respect to his person (2 Cor. 5:21). Witnesses to this of every kind are summoned by the history of his suffering: Judas (Matt. 27:4), Herod the Tetrarch (Luke 23:14–15), the wife of Pilate (Matt. 27:19), Pilate, the judge himself, when immediately after the first examination was begun, he declares him innocent (John 18:38), confirms it by the agreement of Herod (Luke 23:14–15), tries to acquit him with all his strength (Matt. 27:23; John 19:6, 12), and finally, when by all his attempts he accomplished nothing toward Christ's acquittal, after his hands were washed before the people, he protests that he is innocent of this just man's blood (Matt. 27:24). (b) He undertook upon himself the fault and guilt of others (Isa. 53:4, 10; 2 Cor. 5:21). In addition, (c) he did so knowingly and willingly (Ps. 40:8; John 13:1, 3): he frequently foretold the suffering and death, with its circumstances (Luke 18:31–32), he did not want to be freed from it (Matt. 16:22–23; 26:51–54), he went to meet death (v. 46), and he offered himself to be taken by his enemies (John 18:4, 7–8). Undoubtedly he did so for this reason, that his suffering, his death, willingly undertaken by him, though innocent, for others, might be able to result in the redemption of others.

To what end these things should be meditated upon
We ought by devout meditation to consider all these things and others, to the end that: (1) we may understand more and more the gravity and atrocity of this suffering and death (Ps. 40:12; cf. Lam. 1:12). And that we may not only understand it with our mind, but (2) we may also feel it in our heart, with the most tender compassion (Zech. 12:10). And furthermore, (3) we may successfully turn it to our uses, according to those things which we will teach below.

2. *It presents: (1) God's wisdom, (2) providence, (3) holiness, (4) avenging justice, (5) love, (6) power, and (7) truthfulness.*
XXX. Second, it presents as in the brightest mirror: (1) the depths of the divine

wisdom, by which in the suffering and death of Christ he could devise a means by which both his justice and his mercy could be satisfied (Rom. 3:25; cf. 11:33), from which Christ is called the wisdom of God (1 Cor. 1:24), that is, not only formally, insofar as he is the hypostatic wisdom of God (Prov. 8:1, 22), but also objectively, insofar as in him and his cross God made manifest his wisdom (1 Cor. 2:2, 7). (2) The hidden counsels of divine providence, by which he so carefully predetermined all those sufferings which were to be inflicted by the worst of men upon the Son the Mediator (Acts 2:23; 4:28; John 19:11). (3) The purest holiness of God, by which in predetermining, permitting, and directing those worst of evils perpetrated by the worst of men surrounding the death of his own, only begotten, most innocent Son, he nevertheless remained free from injustice and cruelty (Ps. 22:1–3; Isa. 53:5–7). (4) The rigor of divine justice, by which, so that sin would not go unpunished, he preferred to vex his own, only begotten, most beloved, most innocent Son with so many torments, and so manifold a death, in body and in soul (Isa. 53:4, 6; 2 Cor. 5:21; Rom. 8:3). (5) The treasures of inexhaustible love and mercy toward desperate sinners, by which he preferred to destroy his Son, his very own, only begotten, best, and most beloved Son, the brightness of his glory and the express image of his person (Heb. 1:3), rather than a sinner, his enemy (Rom. 5:5–10; 8:32; John 3:16). (6) The infinite power, by which, from so many and such great evils brought upon his only begotten Son, he could produce so much good for the world; from the death of the Creator, the life of the creature (1 Peter 1:18–19; 1 Cor. 6:20; cf. Rom. 11:11–12). (7) The immoveable truthfulness, by which, when the threats had been made against the sinner, he willed to show his faithfulness to fulfill them, even by the death of his own and only begotten Son (Matt. 26:53–54).

To what end does it do this?
Moreover, God in the suffering and death of his Son presents these perfections of his to us to this end, that: (1) we may acknowledge and celebrate them, as God commends his love toward us, in this, that while we were yet sinners, Christ died for us (Rom. 5:8; John 3:16). That (2) in our sufferings, by which he strives to conform us to the image of his Son (Rom. 8:29), we may analogically observe these same virtues of God—wisdom (2 Peter 2:9), providence (Matt. 10:29–30), holiness (Ps. 22:3), righteousness (Rev. 16:5, 7; 19:11), goodness (Rev. 3:19; Heb. 12:6), power (1 Peter 5:6), truthfulness (Rev. 16:7)—and in them peacefully rest (Ps. 29:10; Mic. 7:9).

3. It displays the blessedness of those who have fellowship with his sufferings.
What sort of persons are they?
XXXI. Third, in the sufferings and death of Christ, there is evident the indescribable blessedness of those to whom belongs "the fellowship of his sufferings," inasmuch as on account of it the apostle considers all things, not only the eminent things of this world, but also the prerogatives of his legal righteousness, as dung, indeed as loss (Phil. 3:7–8, 10). But to whom does this fellowship and participation in the sufferings of Christ belong? I respond: (1) To those whom God elected from eternity to be conformed to the image of his Son (Rom. 8:29); (2) to those whom he gave to his Son, to be redeemed by his suffering and death (John 17:9, 12); (3) to those for whom he gave himself up to death (Eph. 5:2), for whom he gave his soul a ransom (Matt. 20:28), for whom he died (Rom. 5:6, 8); (4) to those who give themselves up to Christ to be redeemed (2 Cor. 8:5; Song 2:16), who thirst for him (Matt. 5:6), who come to him (Rev. 22:17).

What sort of blessedness is theirs?
Moreover, what sort and how great is their blessedness? I respond: (1) They have been delivered from all that which they see that Christ endured: from every kind of death, natural, spiritual, eternal; from all that which Christ endured outwardly and inwardly, in his reputation, in his goods, in his body throughout all its parts; from all that he endured from God, from people of every kind, from the entire power of darkness itself. For all these things we would have to have endured in our own person, if not the same things in quality, at least in quantity and weight, and that for all eternity. Now, how great—O good God!—is that blessedness, to have been delivered from such a great host of evils to be sustained eternally (Ps. 32:2). (2) They have infallible proof of this deliverance in the sufferings and death of their expromissor. For since God, through his immovable justice, neither can punish an innocent man for faults of his own (Gen. 18:23, 25), nor punish anew in the debtor himself one whom he has once punished in the surety, it remains that it is impossible for him to demand anew those punishments which he demanded from the innocent expromissor, according to the rigor of his justice, from those who have the fellowship of his sufferings. So then it is said that him who knew no sin, he made to be sin for us, to the end that we might be made righteousness before him (2 Cor. 5:21). So then it is said that he has borne our diseases and carried our sorrows, that he was stricken by God, humiliated, wounded for our transgressions, crushed for our iniquities, to the end that we might have peace, and by his bruise we might be healed (Isa. 53:4–8, 10), so that they now can boast, "Who shall condemn? Christ has died" (Rom. 8:34). (3) On the other hand, they obtain the right to all the goods which are opposed

to the evils endured by their surety: namely, instead of every kind of death, bodily, spiritual, eternal, they obtain every kind of life, "that whosoever believes should not perish, but have eternal life" (John 3:16); instead of his being delivered into the hand of his enemies and torturers, they being freed from the torturers are received by God into his grace (Matt. 25:34; Heb. 2:14–15); instead of his condemnation, they are justified (Rom. 8:33–34); instead of his scourgings, they find joy; instead of his dishonor, glory; instead of his curse, blessing: and so forth throughout all parts of his suffering, by analogy with 2 Corinthians 8:9. Finally, (4) they obtain the fellowship of all the fruits of Christ's suffering and death (which we spoke of in §XIV). And how great—O good God!—is the blessedness in all these things, so that not without reason the apostle wanted to glory in the cross of Christ alone (Gal. 6:14).

By what means can the fellowship of Christ's sufferings be obtained?
Moreover, by what helps may we gain this fellowship of the sufferings of Christ? I respond, We must strive with all our effort that: (1) we may be united with Christ, that we may be found in Christ (Phil. 3:9–10), be made one plant (σύμφυτοι) with him, according to the likeness of his death (Rom. 6:5), so that we may with Paul be permitted to say, "I am crucified together with Christ" (Gal. 2:20). For union cannot but be followed by communion. To this end, (2) we should take hold of Christ by a living faith (John 3:15–16; Rom. 4:24–25). For our union with Christ, which communion follows, happens by faith (Eph. 3:17; Gal. 3:26–27). So then (3) with Christ let us enter the garden of suffering and, according to his will, suffer together with him, for in this way we will also reign with him (Rom. 8:17; 2 Tim. 2:12). Furthermore, (4) let us seriously inquire whether through faith we are united with him who was crucified, and from that union have truly obtained the fellowship of his sufferings (2 Cor. 13:5), so that if we should discover that we have not yet obtained it, afterward we can more carefully strive for it. Finally, (5) if by inquiring we have been made certain that we have obtained the fellowship of the suffering and death of Christ, we should give thanks to God (Rom. 7:24–25; 1 Cor. 15:55–57), and do so by all those duties which without any trouble can be gathered from the things that follow.

4. It shows the misery of those who are enemies of the cross of Christ.
XXXII. On the other hand, fourth, in the suffering and death of Christ, as in a mirror, the profound misery is visible of those who are enemies of the cross of Christ, whose lot the apostle deplores in Philippians 3:18, who crucify Christ to themselves anew (Heb. 6:6), and who trample underfoot the blood of the covenant, by which the Mediator was sanctified, and count it unclean (Heb. 10:29).

What sort of persons are these?

And what sort of persons then are these? I respond, They are, although in diverse degrees: (1) those who are thoroughly ignorant of the one crucified (1 Cor. 2:8; 2 Thess. 1:8), such as the chief priests, priests, elders, Pharisees, scribes, Pilate, Herod, and as many others with them who played a part in his death (Acts 3:17), in which we note all unbelievers: Jews, Gentiles, and Muslims. (2) Those who are certainly not ignorant, but with a counterfeit profession, an oral salutation, kisses, and all manner of external duties, with Judas (Matt. 26:47–50), betray him, which is done by all hypocrites (Matt. 7:21–22). (3) Those who with the disciples desert Christ, whom they received by profession, when he was about to be crucified, from fear of persecutions, and not only from weakness, like the disciples, but from hatred and malice; this the Savior attributes to those of temporary faith (Matt. 13:21), as does Paul to Demas (2 Tim. 4:10). (4) Those who in addition deny him, not only from weakness (like Peter, Matt. 26:69–75), but from malice, about whom the apostle speaks specifically in Hebrews 6:6, that they crucify to themselves the Son of God anew, and in 10:29, that they trample underfoot the Son of God, and count the blood of the covenant unclean; just like the false prophets in 2 Peter 2:1. (5) Those who, with the Jews, persecute Christ in his members (Acts 9:5), seek to slay them, capture and drag them to the courts, whether ecclesiastical or secular, falsely accuse and condemn them, mock them, spit upon them, scourge, kill, and crucify them. (6) Those who deprive him in his members of nourishment, clothing, and other necessary things, like the Jews and the soldiers, indeed who, to add affliction to the afflicted, in his anguish give him vinegar and gall to drink (Matt. 27:33–35). (7) Those who guard him, now oppressed and buried, in his members, and do not permit others to deliver them even from the tomb, who seal the tomb and guard it with soldiers, so that not even a crack of escape may be evident, just like the Jews do (Matt. 27:36, 62ff.), after the example of Pharaoh, who tortures the people of God and is unwilling to let them go (Ex. 5:1–2).

What sort and how great is their misery?

Now what sort and how great is their misery? I respond, As long as they have not attained to communion with Christ: (1) they will have to bear, if not here, at least hereafter, all that Christ endured, if not in quality, at least in quantity and weight. Therefore when they see: (a) every kind of person taking counsel and conspiring with all their strength for Christ's destruction; (b) Christ deserted and denied by the whole world, by friends as well as enemies, even by God; (c) sought to death, betrayed, taken, and bound by his enemies; (d) dragged into all sorts of courts on trumped-up charges, accused by false witnesses, and condemned; (e) vexed most sorely by the most disgraceful insults, scourgings, spittings, from the vilest sort of men; (f) condemned to death by ecclesiastics as well as statesmen; (g) placed upon the cursed cross, all his limbs outstretched, his hands, feet, and side pierced through; when they hear him (h) crying out most miserably, "My soul is exceeding sorrowful, even to death," and likewise, "My God, my God, why have you forsaken me?"; (i) from the sense of the divine fury and the horror of the cup that he would soon have to drain, perspiring drops of blood, falling to the ground, praying frequently in vain for the cup to be removed; (j) God stopping his ears to all his supplications, turning his face away from him; (k) being deprived of all necessities, in extreme thirst, having not even one cup of cold water; (l) given vinegar and gall to drink; (m) tormented by every kind of death, natural, spiritual, and eternal; and so forth—they have good reason to certainly persuade themselves that they will have to bear all these things, either bodily or spiritually, first here and then hereafter, in their own person, and that not for some short period of time, like Christ, offsetting the eternity of death with the dignity of his person, but for all eternity, until they have paid the last penny (Matt. 18:34). For whatever part of the penalties owed to their sins Christ did not undertake upon himself as the surety, remains to be paid by the debtors themselves. And this will happen (2) as certainly and unavoidably as God is just (Rom. 1:32; 2 Thess. 1:8), as he is truthful in his threats (Gen. 2:17), as he is holy, and purer in eyes than to behold sin without any punishment (Hab. 1:13), as he bears hatred of sin (Ps. 5:4–5). For if he could spare sin, he would have spared his own and only begotten Son; otherwise he would hardly avoid the reproach of cruelty. Therefore, if these things are done in the green tree, what will be done in the dry (Luke 23:31)? Thus without any hope of impunity, there no longer being any sacrifice for their sins, nothing remains for them except a certain fearful expectation of judgment, and a burning of fire to devour them (Heb. 10:26–27). And this is so (3) even more so, and more certainly, because the Son of God endured so many and such great sufferings for the sins of men, and offered to them all things freely, to be grasped by faith alone: which things, together with him who endured those sufferings, they have stubbornly rejected, after the example of the Jews (Matt. 27:17, 20–21), so that there cannot but bear down upon them that horrendous judgment which the Jews pronounced upon themselves, "His blood be on us, and on our children" (Matt. 27:25). And how unbearable all these things are, not only can they hear from the sentence of the Judge himself pronounced against the traitorous enemy, "Woe to that man, by whom the Son of Man is betrayed! It would have been better for him never to have been born" (Matt. 26:24), but also, they can see in the traitor himself, when terrified even at the thought of his sin, and of the evil looming over him from it, punished himself with hanging (Matt. 27:5).

What must they do as a remedy?
What counsel then is there in this? Must they despair with Judas? Not at all. What then must they do? They must strive: (1) to acknowledge their misery, by exclaiming, "O wretched man that I am, who shall deliver me from this body of death?" (Rom. 7:24). (2) To look upon him whom they have pierced with their sins, and mourn for him, and so forth (Zech. 12:10). In fact, (3) by the example (although not by the spirit) of Judas, they should conceive penitence (μεταμεληθείς, "having repented," Matt. 27:3). (4) They should confess their sins: "I have sinned in that I have betrayed innocent blood" (v. 4). (5) They should cast away their sins (v. 5). Meanwhile, (6) they should follow Christ into the palace with Peter, although in a different manner (Matt. 26:58). (7) They should recall to memory the word of Christ, promising the grace of forgiveness (Matt. 26:75 with 11:28). (8) They should be stirred up from their lethargy by the cock-crow of the Word, when it threatens as well as promises (Matt. 26:75). (9) They should depart from the company of the world and of sinners (Matt. 26:75). (10) They should bitterly lament their sins, and the misery resulting from them (Matt. 26:75).

5. It induces us to inquire whether he died for us. Motives
XXXIII. Fifth, it induces us to earnestly inquire whether he died for us. For since: (1) he did not die for each and everyone, but for by far the least part of mankind, according to §XVI; likewise, since (2) such great blessedness belongs to those for whom he died, according to §XXXI; since on the contrary (3) such great misery belongs to those who have no fellowship in his suffering and death, according to §XXXII; and since (4) upon a certain careful inquiry, and upon that alone, depends the determination of this matter (2 Cor. 13:5); and also (5) upon the certain knowledge of this determination depends all the tranquility, peace, comfort, and joy of every person (Gal. 6:4)—who does not see that this task of inquiry must be undertaken promptly and eagerly?

Signs
But by what marks will we come to know this certainly? I respond, Especially by these: (1) if we are his people (Matt. 1:21), that is, if by a certain covenanting, we have received him by faith as God and as our Mediator (cf. Deut. 26:16–17). (2) If we are his sheep (John 10:11, 15), that is, we know him as our shepherd (v. 14), we hear his voice, we follow him (v. 27; Luke 9:23). (3) If we belong to his

church (Eph. 5:25), that is, we are his disciples, who depend upon the mouth of him alone (Matt. 23:8, 10). (4) If he has redeemed us from all unrighteousness, and purified us for himself as his own people, zealous for good works (Titus 2:14). (5) If now we live no longer for ourselves, but for him who died for us (2 Cor. 5:15).

6. It supplies comfort in any adversities. The adverse circumstances
XXXIV. Sixth, it supplies exceptional comfort in any adversity, as much bodily as spiritual. For if: (1) plans are set in motion to eradicate us, whether they be ecclesiastical or political (Gen. 37:18–20); (2) if we are betrayed by false friends (Ps. 55:12–14); (3) if we are deserted even by true friends, even by all of them, and the best of them (Ps. 27:10; 38:11); (4) if we are delivered to the furies of our enemies (Matt. 20:17–19, 21–23); (5) if we are condemned to all of the most dreadful punishments (Dan. 3:19–22); (6) if we are afflicted by any disgrace and injury (Ps. 69:7, 9, 19–20; 79:4; Rom. 15:3; Heb. 10:30; 1 Cor. 4:9); (7) if we are deprived of our fortunes, and the necessary supports of life (2 Cor. 11:27), or any other bodily adversities befall us; if in spiritual things, (8) we are choked with fear of divine wrath (Ps. 6:1; 88:7, 16); (9) God himself seems to desert and cast us away (Ps. 88:14; 13:1–2; 42:7).

The arguments for consolation
In all these and any other circumstances, what could more effectively raise up the soul of a believing man than to consider that: (1) whatever it is, his Jesus, his master, has endured it also, and it is not fitting for a student to be in a better condition than the master (Matt. 10:24–25). (2) His Jesus suffered though in himself innocent, while each of us suffers on account of our own sins (Luke 23:41; Mic. 7:9). (3) Our sufferings, however great and whatever kind they may be (2 Cor. 4:17), cannot be compared in any way in weight with those that Christ underwent (Heb. 12:3–4). Moreover, (4) he suffered all these things for us, to deliver us (Isa. 53:4–5; 2 Cor. 5:21). And thus (5) by these his sufferings he took away the venom and sting from ours, so that we can now taunt them, "O Death, where is your sting?" (1 Cor. 15:55–57), and even glory in our afflictions (Rom. 5:3), by Paul's example (2 Cor. 11:23ff.; Gal. 6:17). Even more, (6) now all these adversities work together for our good (Rom. 8:28). I would add that (7) they result in our glory (Rom. 5:2), insofar as by them we are more and more conformed to the image of the Son of God (Rom. 8:29). From this (8) in addition, as if by a sure mark, we can gather that we have been chosen by God (Rom. 8:29).

7. It rouses us to suffer with Christ and for Christ.

XXXV. Seventh, the suffering and death of Christ most efficaciously stirs us up that, just as he suffered for us, so also we should suffer for him; just as he suffered for our sins, so also we should bravely suffer any of the worst things for his name, for his kingdom, and for his glory. Thus like his disciples, we should go with him to the Mount of Olives (Matt. 26:30) and eagerly enter the Garden of Gethsemane (v. 36), thus we should follow him, about to be crucified, to Golgotha, with Simon the Cyrenian we should bear his cross (Matt. 27:32), we should stand under his cross (John 19:25–26), suffer with him (Rom. 8:17), and willingly take up his cross, and that daily also (Luke 9:23), indeed, we should be crucified with him (Gal. 2:20).

In what circumstances
This occurs: (1) if for the sake of Christ we are compelled to experience treachery against our life, just as Christ did (Ps. 62:3–4). (2) If for the sake of Christ we suffer from the members of our household, just as Christ did from Judas and from his disciples (Matt. 10:35; Mic. 7:5–6). (3) If for the sake of Christ we suffer from the venerable chief priests, priests, scribes, and elders (Acts 24:1ff.), from the Antichrist (2 Thess. 2:4 with Rev. 12ff.), as he did for us. (4) If for the sake of Christ we are loaded with false testimonies in judgment (Ps. 27:12 with 26:1). (5) If for the sake of Christ we are overwhelmed by slanders and mockeries of every kind (1 Cor. 4:9, 13). (6) If for the sake of Christ we are stripped of resources and of any things necessary for sustaining this life (Matt. 19:27; cf. the preceding section). If for Christ's sake we are pressed by all these, and other things which could be recounted endlessly, then let us suffer them bravely.

By what motives
For (1) if our Lord and Master goes before, should his servants and disciples not follow? (2) If he suffered so much, should we not suffer so little? If he drained the cup full of God's wrath down to the dregs, should we not sip our little drops, and those not of wrath as much as of fatherly love (cf. Ps. 75:8; Rev. 14:10; 16:19 with 2 Cor. 4:17)? (3) If he, being innocent, suffered for us, so that he might deliver us, should not we, being guilty, suffer for him, so that we may in some way show ourselves but grateful to him? Especially since (4) we do not suffer alone, but with him (Matt. 26:40; Rom. 8:18). And (5) we have him continuously present with us in the garden of sufferings, with his love, with his care (Ps. 23:4; 91:15). (6) By our sufferings (however many and however great they are), we are being conformed to nothing but the image of the Son of God, our most absolute Lord and Master (Rom. 8:29), and consequently being lifted up and glorified (Phil.

1:29). (7) By suffering we prove that we are his genuine disciples (Luke 9:23); and (8) united with him, as those who are crucified with him (Gal. 2:20), and have been planted together in the likeness of his death (Rom. 6:5); indeed, that we are (9) elected from eternity (Rom. 8:29); and in the infallible persuasion of these things is fixed all of our comfort, tranquility, and joy. Let there be added that (10) if we suffer with him, we also will be crowned with him (Luke 24:26; Rom. 8:18; 2 Cor. 4:16–17). This is not to mention that (11) by suffering we in some manner supply what is lacking in the afflictions of Christ, for the sake of the body, that is, his church, in which the apostle so greatly rejoiced (Col. 1:24).

In what manner
Yet it is not sufficient to suffer with Christ, unless we also suffer as he did, that is, we should take care: (1) that we suffer with him as those who are innocent (at least with respect to men), and not as evildoers (2 Tim. 2:9); (2) freely, by taking up our cross (Luke 9:23) like Peter (excepting his rashness; Matt. 26:35; Acts 20:24); (3) forewarned well (Matt. 26:31) from the divine Word (Acts 14:22; 2 Tim. 3:12; Matt. 10:38; Luke 24:26 with John 16:2ff); (4) fortified against the offense of the cross (Matt. 26:31; John 16:1; Gal. 5:11; 1 Cor. 1:23); (5) made strong by the renewal and recollection of our covenant with God, for which purpose the Savior set the use of both sacraments, Passover and the Supper, before his sufferings (Matt. 26:17–30), so that in the midst of our afflictions we may be able to raise ourselves up by the confident cry of Christ, "My God, my God" (Matt. 27:46). (6) Let us enter the garden of sufferings (Matt. 26:36–37) led by no one but Christ (that is, by nothing except divine providence), and let us not rashly cast ourselves into dangers, like Peter did (Matt. 26:58). (7) Let us carefully beware of presumption, and confidence in our own strength, so that we may not fall with Peter (Matt. 26:33–35). Accordingly, (8) let us enter into the garden of suffering with none but Christ (Matt. 26:37), that is, not in our own strength and power, but in that of Christ (Phil. 4:13), inasmuch as without him we can do nothing (John 15:5). (9) Now that we are set in the garden of suffering, let us keep watch with Christ, so that we may not be led into temptation (Matt. 26:40–41), and while keeping watch, let us continuously fix our eyes attentively on Christ (Heb. 12:2–4). (10) Let us not only keep watch, but also pray (Matt. 26:41), by the example of Christ (vv. 39–42). At the same time, (11) let us carefully take heed that we do not, from a desire for vengeance, busy ourselves with repelling an inflicted force with force, or excessively depend upon external remedies for our deliverance, just as the disciples did (Matt. 26:51–52). (12) Let us not, on account of the fierceness of danger and persecutions, desert Christ or look out for our own safety by fleeing at an unseasonable time, as did

the disciples (Matt. 26:56), and Demas (2 Tim. 4:10). (13) Let us not busy ourselves in cunning tricks or corrupt artifices to avoid imminent evils, like Peter did (Matt. 26:58). (14) Let us not turn away from the profession of Christian truth, even under extreme afflictions, just as Christ did not (vv. 63–64), and much less deny him with Peter (v. 69ff.). Indeed rather, (15) let us peacefully commit ourselves and our cause to God (Luke 23:46; 1 Peter 2:23). And in addition, (16) let us pray for our enemies who persecute us (Luke 23:34). And (17) even in our extreme afflictions, let us be zealous to promote the eternal salvation of others, just as Christ was (Luke 23:43). At the same time, (18) let us, with the thief, acknowledge, confess, and detest our sins, by which we drew such great judgments of God upon both the Savior and ourselves (Luke 23:40–41; Zech. 12:10).

8. It rouses us to reflect the virtues evident in his suffering.
XXXVI. Eighth, it also stirs us up so that we may be, to the best of our ability, zealous to be conformed and made like the virtues of Christ evident in his suffering (1 Peter 2:21; Rom. 8:29; John 13:15–16; Matt. 11:29–30). And what virtues are these? (1) Obedience (Phil. 2:8; Ps. 40:7–8; Heb. 10:7); the same mind should be in us (Phil. 2:5). (2) Submission, and denial of our own will (Matt. 26:39, 42; John 5:30); this should also be in us (Luke 9:23; 1 Peter 4:19), and by it, even in the direst afflictions, we should remember that: (a) we are not masters but ministers; not lords but slaves, to whom it belongs not to prescribe to God our will, but to accept his will (1 Cor. 6:19; Acts 21:14; Rom. 9:19). (b) He is the Father, we are the children (Matt. 26:39, 42; Heb. 12:7, 9). Nor (c) is our will ever so holy, so wise, and so good as indeed God's will is (Rom. 12:2; Isa. 58:5, 13). (3) Patience (Isa. 53:7 with Heb. 12:1–4), through which neither the multitude of those insulting us (Ps. 3:1), nor their cruelty (Ps. 22:13–14, 20–21; 118:10), nor the long duration of the persecutions (Ps. 129:1) should move us to impatience (Mic. 7:7ff.). (4) Love (Song 8:7), toward anyone (John 15:13; Rom. 5:8), toward his disciples, even those who forsook him and fled (Matt. 26:31–32), Peter who denied him (Luke 22:61), the women lamenting for him (Luke 23:28), his own mother (John 19:26), indeed toward his enemies, the traitor Judas (Matt. 26:50), and those who crucified him (Luke 23:34); the same love should also be in us (Eph. 5:1–2; Matt. 5:44; 1 Cor. 4:12). (5) Humility, by which he emptied and humbled himself, not only for his Father, to death, even the death of the cross (Phil. 2:8), but also for men—the Jews, Pilate, Herod, and the vilest soldiers, and that to all the worst of evils; the same mind should also be in us (Phil. 2:5) when we are harassed by men. (6) Meekness and humanity toward the cruelest enemies (Matt. 26:50; Luke 22:48), which he also took care

to exercise throughout his entire life (Matt. 12:18–20 from Isa. 42:2–3); let it also be in us (1 Peter 2:21–23; Matt. 11:29). (7) Prayers, which he employed in his suffering, prayers which were: (a) so fervent (Matt. 26:39); let us also be fervent in our prayers (James 5:16); (b) frequently repeated (Matt. 26:39, 42, 44); let us also repeat ours (2 Cor. 12:8; Luke 18:1; 21:36); and (c) with profound submission and humility, cast down on his knees, indeed on his face (Matt. 26:39); so also let us (Ps. 95:6); (d) with filial confidence of being heard (Matt. 27:53: Ps. 22:2 with vv. 23–24); let us also pray with the same confidence (James 1:6; Mark 11:23–24). (8) His manner of fighting and conquering in any of the injuries brought upon him: through silence (Matt. 26:63; John 19:9–10; Isa. 53:7), through endurance (Isa. 50:6); let us also fight with these weapons (1 Peter 2:20, 24; Ps. 129:3). (9) The art of dying, by which, when all his work was completed, when he had exclaimed, "It is finished," he delivered up his spirit into the hands of his Father (John 19:30; Luke 23:46; we had more such points on preparation for death in the preceding chapter, §§XXIII, XXXIX); so also let us do the same (Ps. 31:5; Acts 7:59).

9. It commends to us the indescribable love: (1) Of the Father

XXXVII. Ninth, Christ's suffering and death also commends to us, even especially so, the indescribable love (Rom. 5:8), as much of the Father (John 3:16; Rom. 8:32), as of the Son (Eph. 5:2, 25). First, the love of the Father commends itself to us in many things: (1) insofar as: (a) he not only already created the entire world for the sake of man, and gave him all his earthly goods (Gen. 1:26; Ps. 8:5–10; 1 Cor. 3:21–22; 1 Tim. 6:17); nor (b) did he give some king or distinguished prince, such as was Moses, Joshua, David, Solomon, Hezekiah, Josiah, and so forth; nor (c) some angel (Ex. 33:2; Ps. 91:11); nor (d) some friend most tenderly beloved, such as Abraham (James 2:23) and the apostles (John 15:14–15), but his Son (Gal. 4:4); nor (e) some adopted son, even a firstborn, like Israel (Ex. 4:22; Heb. 12:23), but his own Son (Rom. 8:32); nor (f) one of many, but his only begotten (John 3:16); nor (g) a rebel, like Absalom, or hateful, but most obedient (Phil. 2:8), and therefore most beloved (Matt. 3:17; Isa. 42:1; 2 Peter 1:17). And he delivered him up (h) not so much to the end that he might command us, and we might serve him, but that he might serve, and give his soul a ransom for many (Matt. 20:28). Nor (i) only that he might serve, but that he might suffer such weighty and great things: in his goods, in his reputation, in his body, in his soul, which things we recounted in the dogmatic part. Indeed, (j) that he might suffer death of every kind—natural, spiritual, infernal—that he might be made sin and a curse. In all these things, does not the indescribable love of God appear? Especially if (2) you should consider the person offering all these things, God, who is most all-sufficient (Gen. 17:1), who, as from eternity he was most blessed without us, so to eternity could have remained and existed most blessed without us, without any such delivering up (Rom. 11:35–36; Ps. 16:2; 50:9–14). And if (3) you should proceed to those to whom he delivered up his Son in this way, what are they? Petty men, who carry their breath in their nostrils (Isa. 2:22), dust and ashes (Gen. 18:27), sinners, enemies, his foes, who had deserved all of the worst punishments—does the love of God not increase from this (Rom. 5:8)? And if to all these you should add (4) the uses for which God delivered up his own Son for men, and the benefits which he conferred upon them by his delivering him up, which we indicated in §XIV, what will you say? Will you comprehend the breadth, length, depth, and height of this love (Eph. 3:18; cf. Ps. 103:13; Isa. 49:15)? For if the love of Abraham, who delivered his son Isaac up to God, was of such value to God himself (Gen. 22:2, 16); if so for Hagar's love toward Ishmael, who was dying of thirst (Gen. 21:16); if so for Jacob's love toward Joseph (Gen 37:33–35), and all the more for David's toward Absalom, no matter how disobedient and rebellious (2 Sam. 18:32–33), what will we suppose of God's love toward his very own, only begotten, and most obedient Son? And what of his love toward us, whom he loved in his own certain way above that Son of his who was so greatly beloved, inasmuch as he even delivered him up for us, and delivered him up to such weighty and great things?

(2) Of the Son

Now if you should pass from the Father to the Son, how indescribable is his love toward us! For there is no one who has greater love than if he should lay down his life for his *friend* (John 15:13), and he laid down his life for his *enemies* (Rom. 5:10). Especially if you should consider that: (1) he delivered up not any other person, however precious and beloved to him, but himself (Eph. 5:2, 25); nor (2) just any things, his fame, his fortunes, but his soul (Matt. 20:28); nor (3) to just any ends, not just to reproaches, injuries, scourgings of every kind, but to death (Rom. 5:10); nor (4) to only one certain kind of death, bodily death, but to every kind of death—natural, spiritual, and eternal, as we have shown in the dogmatic part;[69] nor (5) unwillingly, but with the greatest promptness of will (Ps. 40:7–8); nor (6) for angels (Heb. 2:6), but for men (1 Tim. 2:5–6); nor (7) for friends, but for sinners, enemies (Rom. 5:10), for those crucifying him (Luke 23:33–34); nor (8) for any sort of advantage of his own (Matt. 20:28), but for ours: for us he was delivered into the hand of enemies (Mark 14:41) so that we might not be delivered into the hands of torturers (Matt. 18:34–35;

---

69. §§VI–IX, above

Heb. 2:14–15), in fact, on the contrary, so that we might be received by God into grace and glory (Matt. 25:34). For us, though innocent, he was accused and condemned so that we might not come into judgment, but pass through death into life (John 5:24; Rom. 8:33–34). For us he was made a curse so that we might be freed from the curse; in fact on the contrary, that he might obtain the blessing of Abraham (Gal. 3:13–14). For us he died so that we would not die, but might gain eternal life (John 3:16). And in this way we could proceed through all the parts of his suffering by the same analogy, if a fear of excessive prolixity did not restrain us.

To what end

But to what end does the suffering and death of Christ so commend the love of both the Father and the Son? Without doubt so that: (1) we would love them in return (2 Cor. 5:14–15), for there is nothing that more effectively kindles love than love (cf. 2 Cor. 12:15). (2) In pure love and genuine gratitude we would give ourselves back to God, who in pure love delivered up his Son for us, and to the Mediator, who delivered up himself for us (2 Cor. 8:5; Song 2:16; 6:3). Being prepared (3) to devote in turn ourselves and our best things—our body, mind, fortunes, reputation, and all things—to their kingdom and glory (1 Cor. 6:19–20; Phil. 1:20–21). And in addition, (4) to eagerly receive for their sake all of the worst things, in persecutions, reproaches, harassments, even to death, indeed the most ignominious death of the cross (Phil. 1:20–21; Acts 20:24). In particular, (5) even with Judas himself (Matt. 26:49), although in an entirely different spirit, we would: (a) seek Christ with an ardent desire (Isa. 55:6), even at an inopportune time of night, until we find him (Song 5:6–7); (b) embrace him with a living faith (John 1:12); (c) kiss him with love unfeigned (Ps. 2:12); (d) salute him most humanely, by a brave and noble profession of his name (Matt. 10:32; John 1:20, 26–27); (5) acknowledge his mastery and sovereignty (Matt. 23:8, 10), and that not only with our mouth, like Judas, but additionally with our deeds (Matt. 7:21–22). Moreover, (6) with the worst soldiers (Matt. 27:29), but in the best spirit: (a) we would, as much as lies in us, place upon him a crown of glory (Song 3:11), or at least cast our crown at his feet (Rev. 4:10); (b) show reverence to his purple (Song 7:5; 3:9–10); (c) shudder at his iron scepter, that is, the scepter of his fury (Ps. 2:9), but touch the golden scepter of grace held out to us (Ps. 45:6; Est. 5:2); (d) cast ourselves to our knees before him (Ps. 95:6; Phil. 2:9–10); (e) salute him with our heart and mouth, "Hail, King of the Jews!" In fact rather, (7) with Peter (yet subtracting his rashness) and Christ's other genuine disciples, and that by the grace of God, we would unflinchingly resolve even to die with Christ (Matt. 26:35; Acts 20:24; Phil. 1:20–21), nor only resolve, but also actually follow Christ all the way into the palace of suffering, yet excluding Peter's temerity (Matt. 26:58), and instead of his triple denial, we would through any dangers bravely confess his name, constantly even to death (Acts 4:28–29, 31–32). In addition, (8) with Mary, inflamed with pure love, we would devote our most precious nard for anointing his head and feet (Matt. 26:7; John 12:3), that is, we would apply all of the most precious things among our goods to reviving his members (Matt. 25:35–36, 40). Furthermore, (9) with Simon the Cyrenian, while he bears the cross, we would endeavor to the best of our ability to lighten his load (Matt. 27:32; Luke 23:26), that is, we would grieve with the pious who have been afflicted and oppressed on account of Christ, and as much as we can, strive to assist them (Heb. 13:3). Added to these things, (10) with the pious women, with Mary his mother, Mary the wife of Cleophas, and Mary Magdalene, and with the rest of his relations, we would in love be drawn to his cross, so that standing under the cross we may gaze upon his pains with eyes of living faith, so that we may minister to him (Matt. 27:55; Luke 23:49; John 19:25; Heb. 12:2–3). And indeed, (11) after his death, we would busy ourselves in rendering to him all duties of love, with Joseph of Arimathea and the women, who buried him or anointed him (Matt. 27:57–60; Luke 23:55–56). And so forth. By these and other duties of this kind, we will endeavor in some manner to repay by reciprocal charity the indescribable love of both God and the Mediator.

10. It pricks our hearts to deep repentance.
XXXVIII. Tenth, the suffering and death of Christ pricks us to deep repentance from our sins, by which we both compelled the Father, as it were, to inflict so many and such great things upon his Son, to make him sin for us (2 Cor. 5:21), and to impose our punishments upon him (Isa. 53:5–7); and we placed upon the Son, as it were, our debts (Isa. 43:24), so that it is as if we ourselves pierced him.

The motives urging this
Deep repentance of this sort: (1) is foretold by "the spirit of grace and of supplications" to be conferred one day, in New Testament times (Zech. 12:10). (2) The Savior, hanging on the cross, commends the same to the women who were already mourning (Luke 23:27–28). Calling us to it are (3) the examples of Peter (Matt. 26:75), of the Jews converted at the feast of Pentecost (Acts 2:22–23 with v. 37), of the centurion (Matt. 27:54), indeed of the traitor himself (Matt. 27:3–4), and even inanimate objects, for example, the rent veil (Matt. 27:51; cf. Joel 2:13), the dead who could not rest in their graves (v. 52), the darkened sun (Luke 23:44–45), the quaking earth, and the split rocks (Matt 27:51). Thus the whole of nature appeared as it were to be in agony because the Son of

God agonized: and will we alone not be? Indeed, (4) the matter itself urges us, if we would weigh, on one hand: (a) the quantity and quality of what he suffered, from Judas, the disciples, Peter, the Jews, Pilate, Herod, the soldiers, the mob, indeed even God himself and his Father, in his body, soul, reputation, goods, and so forth; and on the other hand, (b) that it was not only Judas, nor the Jews, Pilate, and so forth, who inflicted as it were so many wounds upon him, and upon his body and soul, but each one of us, by our sins (Zech. 12:10), since without my sins and yours, the Father would neither have inflicted all these things upon him, nor suffered them to be inflicted upon his innocent Son (Isa. 53:3–4; 2 Cor. 5:21), nor would Pilate and the others have had one whit of power over him (John 19:10–11); and especially if (c) we would add who the person was upon whom we inflicted all those things: not just any man or angel, but the Son of God himself (Matt. 27:54).

Its manner and requirements

If we devoutly pile up all those things, will they not wrench tears from us? Will they not rend our hearts? But since for this to be done on its own is not sufficient, as the one crucified himself corrects us (Luke 23:28), it must also be remembered that for this repentance is required: (1) not only a deep contrition of soul, the sort that is observed also in Judas (Matt. 27:3), by which we beat our breasts with the multitude (Luke 23:48); nor only (2) a submissive confession of sins, such as is seen even in Judas (Matt. 27:4); nor furthermore, (3) any additional sort of satisfaction of work, such as even Judas offered—in these things, good in themselves, we should not suffer ourselves to be surpassed by Judas—but also, (4) that by faith, albeit the most miniscule, we would follow Christ with Peter even to the palace of affliction (Matt. 26:58), while Judas, having betrayed him, deserted him in despair. In addition, that (5) when we have committed sins, we would with the same Peter after his triple denial nevertheless have the eyes of our mind and confidence focused on Christ, who looks upon us with eyes of grace (Luke 22:61; Zech. 12:10). Furthermore, that (6) we would recall to our memory the Word of God, first that of threatening, and then that of promise, with Peter (Matt. 26:75). Moreover, that (7) with warm tears we would lament of our sins, with the same Peter (Matt. 26:75; Zech. 12:10). Moreover, that (8) we would leave the palace, that is, we would carefully take heed of dangerous conversations and every opportunity to sin. (Matt. 26:75). Finally, that (9) we would be driven by repentance to seek out the remedies for our sins (Acts 2:37–38).

11. It frightens us away from crucifying the Son of God anew.
XXXIX. Eleventh, it frightens away from crucifying the Son of God anew for our sins (Heb. 6:6), and from, with Peter, repeating the sin of denial a second and third time (Matt. 26:72, 74). For does it not suffice to have pierced the Son of God one time, to have harassed one time our most faithful Lord, master, and brother, with so many torments, if we do not frequently repeat the same (1 Peter 4:3)?

By what sins this occurs: More generally
But by what sins is Christ crucified anew? Certainly in its full and perfect emphasis, he is only crucified anew from malice (not from weakness, as occurred in the denial of Peter, Matt. 26:33, 35, 70), effected by a denial of him and the gospel truth, or by the horrible blasphemy against the Holy Spirit, as the apostle testifies in Hebrews 6:6; but in a broader and more diminished sense, in some manner we crucify Christ anew by all our sins, by which we crucified him the one time, that is, we arose as the cause and authors of his being crucified (Isa. 43:24; 1 John 1:7); however, in the strictest sense, we do so by those sins which are delights for us, in which, not in weakness but in pleasure, with the soldiers (Matt. 27:27–32), it is a sport and pleasure to us as it were through such sins to lacerate his head with a thorny crown, and his body with scourges and beatings, and so forth, and also with the multitude and the Pharisees, when he is hanging on the cross, to wound him with insults and every kind of slander. For which reason, the apostle conjoins those ἀνασταυροῦντες, crucifying anew, the Son of God and those παραδειγματίζοντες, putting him to an open shame (Heb. 6:6), and explains it by ἑκουσίως ἁμαρτάνειν, sinning willfully (Heb. 10:26).

More specifically
But in particular, Christ is crucified anew by all those sins by which he was crucified once already, namely: (1) if with the leaders of the Jews, with the chief priests, scribes, and elders of the people, we take counsel on killing Christ in his members (Matt. 26:3–4; Acts 4:5, 15–16, 18). (2) If with Judas and the other disciples, we scoff at those who desire to anoint Christ, that is, to bless him in his members (Matt. 26:7–8; 25:42–46). (3) If due to the love of money and the love of earthly things, with Judas we as it were betray Christ (Matt. 26:14–16), or at least desert him (2 Tim. 4:10). Or (4) if we are scandalized or offended by his sufferings, death, shame, or cross (Matt. 26:31, 33; 1 Cor. 1:23; Gal. 5:11). (5) If, while he is in his agony, we sleep as it were with his disciples (Matt. 26:40, 43, 45), that is, if we do not empathize with him as he suffers in his members (Heb. 13:3), or we do not strive to the best of our ability to help them (Prov.

27:10; John 3:16). (6) If we secretly or openly seek to put Christ to death in his members, through all cruelty, as Judas did with his cohort (Matt. 26:47, 55; Acts 9:24; 2 Cor. 11:32). (7) If we deliver up Christ in his members to the tribunals of his enemies, as Judas did with his band (Matt. 26:57; 27:1–2; 10:17, 21). (8) If we condemn Christ in his members to all manner of punishments, and in accord with this condemnation carry him off to abuses and death, like the Jews and Pilate (Matt. 26:66; 27:26; Acts 12:1–2). (9) If we rage against Christ even after the crucifixion, in his members, like the Jews (Matt. 27:34–35, 39–45; Ps. 79:2). Finally, (10) if by an external profession, without the heart, or with a heart that is nothing but hypocritical, we embrace, kiss, and greet him, like Judas did (Matt. 26:48–49; 7:21–22), or we revere him through mockery, by placing a crown on him, by handing him a scepter, by clothing him in purple, and by falling before him to our knees, like the soldiers (Matt. 27:27–32).

For what reasons we must beware of this sin
In all these ways especially, Christ is crucified anew, and so that we may beware of this more than a dog or snake, we must consider: (1) how great a sin it is to have betrayed the Son of God, to have crucified the Son of God, to have betrayed him, even once! (Luke 22:48); (2) how much danger there is in it, when we are prepared little by little by these steps, and hasten with quickened step, to that horrendous re-crucifixion which the apostle declares is absolutely unforgiveable (Heb. 6:4–6); and (3) what horrendous judgments God exercises upon this sin (Luke 23:29–30; Heb. 6:7–8; 10:26–29), which he unfolded as if before our eyes in Judas the betrayer (Matt. 27:5; Acts 1:18, 25), and against the Jews who crucified him (Matt. 27:25).

By what helps we can beware of it
And so that we may be all the more free from this repeated crucifying of Christ, let us carefully take heed to ourselves: (1) of greed, love of money, and love of the world and worldly things, led by which, Judas betrayed his Lord (Matt. 26:8–9; John 12:4–6; 2 Tim. 4:10); (2) of presumption and rashness, by which we attribute too much to our own strength, through which Peter was led into such a horrendous denial of his Savior, (Matt. 26:33, 35, 70, 72, 74; Rom. 11:20; 1 Cor. 10:12); (3) of neglect of the divine Word and divine forewarnings, through which Peter fell into that horrendous denial (Matt. 26:31, 34; John 16:1–4; Gen. 2:17); (4) of audacity in seeking or undertaking dangers, by which it happened that Peter, having by an empty curiosity of seeing what would happen to Christ followed him into the palace of the priest, cast himself into danger, and into denial (Matt. 26:57–58; Gen. 3:2, 6); (5) of unprofitable business and conversation

with the impious, by which Peter was seduced into scandal and denial (Matt. 26:58, 69; Deut. 13:2); (6) of sluggishness, drowsiness, and yawning, wherein, according to the thought of Christ, we are carried away into temptation (Matt. 26:41; 25:5–6, 11–13); (7) of excessive fear of persecutions, by which the disciples were driven to flight (Matt. 26:55–56; 13:21). On the contrary, (8) it will help (with presumption and vain confidence in our own strength taken away) to have an immoveable intention, in the power of God, to endure with Christ, for by means of this Peter would without a doubt have been free from scandal and denial (Acts 14:22; 2 Tim. 3:12). To all these things (9) let there be added, devout prayers, with the Savior commending them (Matt. 26:41), as well as the apostle (Eph. 6:18), namely that he would lead us not into temptation, but deliver us from evil (Matt. 6:13). And to bring up the rear, (10) the whole armor, with which the apostle girds the Ephesians (Eph. 6:12).

12. It stirs us up to crucify sin.
XL. Twelfth, Christ's crucifixion and death stirs up whoever is his true friend, that he would crucify sin, which crucified Christ (just as the priests and elders stirred up the people to kill Christ, Matt. 27:20), that he would crucify the flesh with its affections and lusts (Gal. 5:24), that he would put to death his members which are upon the earth, fornication, and so forth (Col. 3:5), that by the power of the cross of Christ the world may be crucified to him (Gal. 6:14), that is, that by a pious desire for vengeance, and a pious cruelty, we would deal spiritually with our sins in entirely the same way in which, by the just vengeance of God on account of our sins, both Judas, and the Jews, and Pilate, and Herod, and the soldiers, and the Jewish multitude, dealt bodily with Christ.

By what actions it is crucified
Specifically, by an irreconcilable and universal hatred (Ps. 97:10; Rom. 12:9; 7:15; Jude 23), such as that by which the Jews crucified Christ (Matt. 27:18): (1) we should deny our sins (Luke 9:23) just as Peter denied Christ, "I do not know the man" (Matt. 26:72), that is, just as Christ knew no sin (2 Cor. 5:21), namely by not approving of it, "I do not know you; depart from me" (Matt. 7:23); indeed, after the example of Peter, we should deny it not only once, but frequently, and with an oath. (2) We should desert our sins and flee them, just as, driven by fear, all the disciples deserted Christ (Matt. 26:55–56; Isa. 1:16; Prov. 28:13). (3) We should deliver them up to be arrested and bound, just as Judas delivered up Christ to the Jews (Matt. 26:48), and the Jews to Pilate (Matt. 26:48; 27:2), and as Paul delivered up the incestuous man (1 Cor. 5:4–5), just as sin leads us captive (Rom. 7:23), that is, we should permit sin no liberty and

no authority (Rom. 6:12; 7:5–6). (4) We should condemn our sins to death and to the cross, just as the Jews condemned Christ (Matt. 26:66), and as the crowd demanded that he be condemned and crucified; indeed, just as God in Christ condemned sin in the flesh (Rom. 8:3), that is, we should judge and declare it to be guilty of death and destruction (Rom. 6:23). (5) We should as it were inflict blows upon sin, as upon a blasphemer, just as the Jews did upon Jesus, who had been wrongly condemned as a blasphemer (Matt. 26:67), and as Satan did upon the soul of Paul (2 Cor. 12:7), and indeed, when Christ had been condemned by Pilate, the ferocious soldiers inflicted upon him any dishonor they could (Matt. 26:27–32); that is, we should subjugate sin by every means possible (1 Cor. 9:27). (6) We should cast out sin from our hearts, just as the Jews, once Jesus was condemned and tortured, cast him out of Jerusalem (Mark 15:20), and just as Paul wants the one who is evil to be cast out of the church (1 Cor. 5:7, 13), that is, that we may remove it far from us (Eph. 4:31). (7) We should raise sin upon the cross as if in the middle of thieves, we should hang it there as unworthy of both heaven and earth, we should crucify it (just as the Jews hung Christ in the middle of thieves as if he were most evil, and crucified him, Mark 15:27–28, and just as God affixed the handwritten charge of our sins to the cross, Col. 2:14), that is, we should inflict death upon our sins, according to the example of Christ crucified, and by the power of his cross (Gal. 5:24; Col. 3:5): we should torment them as long as it takes, until they are finally dead.

By what motivating reasons
Moreover, that we should deal with sin with such pious cruelty: (1) is demanded by its very merit, for it is blasphemy, insofar as it both removes from God the supreme sovereignty over his creatures, and his lawgiving authority,[70] and it removes from creatures the glory of obedience (cf. Luke 19:27). Now from the divine law (Lev. 24:16), as well as from the sentence of the Jews' ecclesiastical court (John 19:7), blasphemy deserves death by stoning, and that to be inflicted by the whole assembly, which death was also, on account of the same blasphemy, although falsely imputed to him, inflicted upon Christ with the greatest indignation. In fact additionally, in itself it is deicide, and therefore it strives that God might be utterly destroyed (according to the nature of hatred), that he might no longer exist (Ps. 10:4; 14:1). Indeed, it also most cruelly killed the Son of God, who is God, blessed forever (Rom. 9:5), the true God, and eternal life (1 John 5:20). For what was for his enemies the cause for killing him, except the sin of hatred and cruelty? And what was for God himself the cause of his raging as it

---

70. *potestatemque* νομοθητικήν

were with just cruelty against the inmost parts of his only begotten Son, except human sin (2 Cor. 5:21; Isa. 53:6)? (2) We are also stirred up to it by a just desire for vengeance, which from retaliatory justice[71] dictates for homicide, even when perpetrated against the vilest person, homicide as the penalty (Gen. 9:6), as the murderer crucified with Christ acknowledges himself (Luke 23:41), and even more so against a king (John 19:15, "Should I crucify your king?"), and especially against the Son of God (Matt. 27:5), in fact God himself (Acts 20:28), against our king who came to us (Zech. 9:9), against our kinsman (Heb. 2:17; Eph. 5:30), our *Goel*, kinsman-redeemer (Job 19:25), indeed our brother (Heb. 2:11), for if it was lawful for the גואל הדם (whether you translate it "kinsman avenger" or "avenger of blood," that is, of blood spilled from a kinsman), exacerbated by fury for blood, to pursue and slaughter the slayer of his kinsman (Deut. 19:6), should we not pursue and slaughter sin, the murderer of our kinsman, our brother, especially since we are so naturally prone to a desire for vengeance? Besides this, (3) it is urged by the divine wrath, which kills the sinner, if the sinner does not kill sin (Ps. 7:11–13), of which a clear example is offered to us in his very own, only begotten Son, so that we should think, If this was done in a green tree, what will not be done in the dry (Luke 23:31)? If he burned with such rage against his own Son, who was so beloved by him, for our sins while they still lived, how would he not burn with rage against us, if we spare our sins? And if it were possible for him to spare sins, certainly he would have spared his Son, who so many times and with such anguish begged him that the cup of wrath might pass from him (Matt. 26:38–39, 42, 44). And if he did not spare his Son (Rom. 8:32), how will he spare the one who has spared sin? Therefore, there is reason here that we should contemplate not only the kindness of God toward those who crucify sin, but also his ἀποτομία or precipitous severity upon the rest (Rom. 11:22). (4) It also argued by the fact that there belongs to us no fellowship, no participation in the suffering and death of Christ, of any kind or amount, as long as we do not crucify sin: for as many as belong to Christ have crucified the flesh with its lusts (Gal. 5:24). And accordingly also by the fact that (5) all those things that we see that Christ endured, inwardly and outwardly, with respect to his soul, with respect to his body, we will have to bear in our own person, and that for all eternity, if we have not crucified our sins: we will be eternally denied by God (Matt. 10:33), reprobated (Matt. 7:23), handed over not to cruel soldiers, but to infernal torturers (Matt. 18:34–35; 25:41), summoned to the divine judgment (Ps. 1:5), condemned, and tortured by the most intense torments of the soul and body, without remedy (Isa. 66:24). For one of two things

---

71. *justitia talionis*

must unavoidably occur: either we crucify sin in due time, or we will be crucified by sin eternally (Rom. 8:6, 13).

13. It provides an example of the Christian art of dying.
XLI. Finally thirteenth, in the death of Christ is set forth for us the most exact example of dying well.[72] For just as we had the example of preparation for death in the preceding chapter, §XXXIX, so now follows the method of dying itself. Therefore, once the preparation has been, together with Christ, completed in its designated heads, then while health yet remains intact, when our diseases now are pressing, and death impending, the following are necessary for a person who would die blessedly: (1) a concern for his domestic affairs (Isa. 38:1), by Christ's example in committing his mother to his disciple (John 19:27); (2) the comfort of those who are anxious and worried about his death (1 Thess. 4:13–14), by Christ's example (John 16:7) in encouraging the women who were grieved by his cross (Luke 23:27–28); (3) the forewarning of his own concerning their future state after his death (Gen. 49:1), by the example of Christ while dying (Luke 23:28–31); (4) the conversion of others (Acts 7:51–53), by the example of Christ while dying, in converting the thief (Luke 23:42–43); (5) a forgiving of injuries inflicted upon him by enemies, and reconciliation with them (Gen. 50:14–22), by Christ's example while dying (Luke 23:34); (6) a reckoning of matters that must be accounted for before death (Acts 20:24; 2 Tim. 4:7), by Christ's example (John 19:28, 30). With these things set forth first, finally the chief one follows: (7) the care of the soul, that it may be reconciled to God (Luke 23:42; Rev. 14:13), and that with pious sighs it may be delivered up into God's hands (Acts 7:59; Ps. 31:5), by the example of Christ in dying (Luke 23:46). More points of this kind, Lord willing, will occur in the ascetic part.[73]

---

72. εὐθανασίας
73. 3.4.15

CHAPTER THIRTEEN

The Descent of the Mediator

My flesh also shall dwell confidently. For you will not abandon my soul in hell, nor will you let your Holy One see the pit.
—Psalm 16:9–10

The fourth and final degree of Christ's humiliation is in his descent.
I. Finally, we proceed to the fourth degree of the humiliation of Christ, to his descent in a broader sense. For (besides the glorious descent to judge the living and the dead, 2 Thess. 1:7, 10), there is enumerated in the Scriptures a threefold descent: (1) from heaven to earth, which occurred in his incarnation (John 3:13; 6:50, 58, 62; 1 Cor. 15:47); and this descent is of the divine person into human flesh; (2) from the earth into the grave, which occurred in his burial (Eph. 4:9–10; Acts 2:29, 31; cf. Isa. 38:18); and this descent is of the body; (3) as it were from heaven into hell, or from the heavenly and blessed state into the infernal and miserable state (Matt. 26:38; Ps. 88:4–7); and this descent is (at least chiefly) of the soul. With the first descent set apart in chapter 4 on the incarnation, we will cover the latter two in this chapter. We will place the basis of our consideration in the words of Psalm 16:9–10.

The Exegetical Part
The text is resolved and explained.
II. In these words is contained the Messiah's confident expectation of the goods soon to come to him, concerning which must be considered:
    A. The Messiah who expects, who is not indeed spoken of in the text, but nevertheless is hinted at, first in the pronominal suffix ʼ in *"my flesh," "my soul,"* then in the periphrasis, *"your Holy One."* Yet we will speak of him in such a way as to show that we have in these words a solid foundation for the descent of Christ into hell. There are those who want David to be speaking throughout this whole psalm about the Jewish people, and by

no means about the Messiah: thus the Jews. There are those who prefer to say that David is speaking both about himself and about the Messiah, but in more than one way: some, principally about himself, and about the Messiah only through accommodation, less principally; others, principally about the Messiah, and about David only through accommodation, that is, about himself as the type, and about the Messiah as the reality; still others, about David *a priori*, and only about the Messiah *a posteriori*. Nor are there lacking those who refer the entire Psalm only to Christ, as Piscator does, with this argument: the one who speaks in verse 10 is the one who speaks throughout the entire Psalm—which he proves from the order of the speech and the coherence of the individual thoughts, which show that the same person speaks in the entire Psalm— but the one who speaks in verse 10, as Peter testifies in Acts 2:25, and Paul in Acts 13:35, even by the "Holy One" of the Lord, is clearly understood to be Christ (Isa. 54:5; Dan. 9:24); furthermore, there is no one except Christ that did not see corruption.[1] I also am especially inclined to this opinion. Whatever may be the case, at the least the words of the text speak about the Messiah.

B. The goods expected, which concern the Messiah's:

1. Body: אף־בשרי ישכן לבטח, "My flesh also will dwell confidently." Here is:

   a. The thing secure: "my flesh." The בשר, "flesh," is polysemous, for it is taken: (1) for every animal, when there is a כל, "all," present with it (as in Gen. 6:17; 8:17); (2) for the entire person (Deut. 5:26; Ps. 56:4); (3) for the human body, which consists of flesh (Gen. 2:24; Ps. 38:3, 7), and so it is in this passage.

   b. The security of the body: ישכן לבטח, "it will dwell confidently." "It will dwell": the Septuagint translators have κατασκηνώσει, that is, he will remain in the tomb as in a tent, he will lie down, he will rest (as in Deut. 33:20; Ps. 7:6; 94:17; Isa. 26:19). לבטח, confidently, securely, safely, in hope or confidence: (1) of his preservation from rotting; (2) of his resurrection to glory, as the following points declare. Hope is attributed to the flesh figuratively, as "earnest expectation"[2] (Rom. 8:19) and hope (Rom. 8:20)

---

1. Johann Piscator, *Commentarii in omnes libros Veteris Testamenti*, 4 vols. (Herborn: Christoph Corvinus, 1643–1646), 3:132–33.

2. ἀποκαραδοκία

are attributed to the creature: the hope of the body is also taken for the thing hoped for.

2. Soul: "You will not leave my soul in hell." Here is:

a. The subject for which good is expected: the soul, נפש, ψυχή, by which can be understood: (1) the formal part of a human being, by which the composite lives (Matt. 10:28); (2) the material part of the same, that is, the body, either ensouled, that is, alive (Ps. 35:13; 107:18), or unsouled, that is, dead (Num. 5:2; 9:10; Lev. 19:28; 21:1); (3) the entire human composite, or the person (Gen. 14:21; Ps. 107:9; Prov. 25:25; 1 Peter 3:20), and thus quite commonly it signifies reciprocal pronouns: נפשה, "herself" (Isa. 5:14), נפשם, "they themselves" (Isa. 46:2); (4) the life of the person (Job 2:6; Ps. 54:3; Matt. 2:20); and (5) the will and affections (Ex. 15:9; Ps. 25:1; 41:3). In this passage, I think by "soul" must be understood the formal part of a human being (Matt. 26:38), insofar as it was in the infernal state: indeed being deprived of the beatific vision of God, or of the sense of divine grace and favor (Matt. 27:46), and in addition harassed by infernal torments, it was exceeding sorrowful to death (Matt. 26:36), that is, infernal death.

b. The place or state of the subject, in which it expects good: לשאול, to hell, or in hell. שאול, Sheol, in Greek, ᾅδης, Hades: (1) ordinarily denotes the place of the damned (Deut. 32:22; Ps. 49:14; Isa. 14:15; Matt. 11:23; Luke 16:23; Rev. 1:18; 20:13–14); (2) the tomb (Gen. 42:38; Ps. 6:5; Isa. 38:18; Acts 2:27, 31); (3) the common receptacle and state of all the dead, as much of the good as of the evil (Eccl. 9:10; Ezek. 32:21, 27; Job 14:13; 17:13); and (4) a most afflicted state (Ps. 18:5; 30:3; 28:1; 116:3). For this passage the last meaning is especially applicable, since the soul of Christ was never in the place in the damned, whatever the papists and Lutherans suppose, inasmuch as it was delivered before his death into the hands of the Father.

c. The good expected for the subject in the infernal state: "You will not abandon," that is, "You will be entirely present," not only: (1) by the presence of the nature, by which he was present after death in the personal union, both to the body—and this made it so that it would confidently, without fear of decaying, dwell as it were in the tomb for three days—and to the soul, so that, existing in the hand of God, it would remain united to the divine person;

and to the whole mediatorial person, so that by the natural presence of the divine person, he would continue even in death to be the Holy One of God, or the God-man Mediator. But also (2) by the presence of grace, through which he restored the flesh to natural life after a brief stay in the tomb; also sustained the soul in hellish extremities so that it would not fail; and freed his entire Holy One into full liberty from the power and dominion of death, which he was under for the three days of his burial.

3. The whole man, composed of body and soul: "Nor will you let your Holy One see the pit." That is, You will not permit me, your Holy One (the Holy One of Israel, Isa. 10:20, whom you sanctified to be sent as the Messiah into the world, John 10:36), to remain in the pit, under the power and dominion of death (Acts 2:24; cf. Lam. 3:53), but you will revive him. Therefore, because it ought not to be doubted from Acts 2:24–33 and 13:35–36 that the Messiah in our text prophesies about his resurrection, which presupposes his death, burial, and the state and dominion of death until the resurrection, and likewise because through this resurrection he awaits some good, distinctly: (1) for his body, namely that it would dwell securely in the tomb without any danger of rotting; (2) for his soul, that it would not be abandoned in hell; (3) to his whole person (the Holy One), that it would not see the pit, that is, not remain in the pit, or under the state and dominion of death—therefore it is evident that in the whole text is signified the burial of the body, the descent of the soul, and the dominion of death over the whole man.

The Dogmatic Part

Christ descended into hell.

III. Therefore, the Mediator sent himself down to the grave, to hell, and to the dominion and power of death for us, which three things we include in his one descent, inasmuch as by it he sent himself down into the tomb, into hell and into the dominion of death.

In the Apostles' Creed, until the time of the Athanasian Creed, the article on the descent into hell is not present.

The express mention at least of this descent occurs quite rarely in the Scriptures, for which reason, not only does Bellarmine with the papists refer it to tradition, but also the creed which they call the Apostles', and with it the Nicene Creed, make no mention of it. Also, the more ancient fathers—Irenaeus, Tertullian, Origen, Augustine, Rufinus—do not have even one whit of it in their expositions of this creed.[3] And Rufinus expressly adds, "This is not present either in the Roman Creed or in that of the eastern churches" (in Cyprian, p. 570, sect. 20, in the 1593 edition of Le Preux).[4] And this was the case until the time of Charlemagne in the eighth century. The first mention of it occurs in the creed that (incorrectly) is attributed to Athanasius, since instead of what the Apostles' Creed reads, *sepultus*, "buried," with the descent omitted, it has *descendit ad inferos*, "descended into hell." Moreover, in subsequent centuries the words "descended into hell" appeared therefore as an explanatory addition to the words of the Nicene Creed in the margin. Afterwards, they crept into the text of the Creed itself, and were recited in the same tenor with the rest, as is evident from various manuscript codices. From that time forward, they were generally recognized as received, and they are expounded by all the interpreters of the Creed, as much Protestants as papists, as a particular article of it.

It is proved by the Scriptures, and by reasons.

IV. Yet at the same time, express mention of it is not lacking in the Scriptures: for example, in Ephesians 4:9–10, "Now that he ascended, what is it but that he also descended first εἰς τὰ κατώτερα μέρη τῆς γῆς, into the lower parts of the earth? He who descended is the one who ascended"; and in Romans 10:7, "Who will descend into the abyss? For this is to bring back Christ from the dead." We add the words of the text (Ps. 16:10 with Acts 2:27). To this end they refer Psalm 88:4, 6, which many believe to be a prophetic Psalm, and in its emphasis to have been fulfilled in Christ, just as also in Psalm 18:4–5 and 116:3. Also, a type of this descent could also be in Joseph (Gen. 37:20, 22, 24, 28–29, as well as 39:20), and in Jonah (Jon. 2 with Matt. 12:40; Judg. 16:3). The reasons could be that: (1) by sins we have exalted ourselves to the greatest heights (cf. Isa. 14:13–14), indeed above God (cf. 2 Thess. 2:4), and therefore the Savior had to and willed to cast himself down to the greatest depths, all the way to hell (cf. Isa. 14:11–12; Matt. 11:23), so that with the cursed in hell, he would be made a κατάρα, curse (Gal. 3:13); (2) so that from hellish guilt, and from the pit wherein there is no

---

3. Irenaeus, *Adversus haereses* in *PG* 7:550; idem, *Against Heresies* in *ANF* 1:330; Tertullian, *Liber de praescriptionibus adversus haereticos*, 2:26–27; idem, *The Prescription Against Heretics* in *ANF* 3:249; Origen, Περὶ ἀρχῶν *libri quatuor* in *PG* 11:117–21; idem, *Origen De Principiis* in *ANF* 240–41; Augustine, *De fide et symbolo* in *PL* 40:187; idem, *A Treatise on Faith and the Creed* in *NPNF1* 3:326; Rufinus (c. 344–411), *Commentarius in symbolum apostolorum* in *PL* 21:356; idem, *A Commentary on the Apostles' Creed* in *NPNF2* 3:550.

4. Cyprian, *Opera… in tres tomos nunc primum distincta* (n.p.: Joannes Le Preux, 1593), 570.

water (of comfort), he might deliver those who were bound, through the blood of the covenant (Zech. 9:11), which was said regarding the bodily deliverance of the Jews, and is also customarily applied to Christ analogically; at the least, so that he might deliver his own from the curse of hell (Gal. 3:13); (3) so that from the deepest guilt and abyss of hell, by his descent he might lift up his own to the highest glory of the heavens (Eph. 1:3; 2:6).

What the descent of Christ is: The various opinions of the orthodox
V. But finally, what is this descent? Setting aside the opinions of the heterodox for their own place,[5] among the orthodox there are some who: (1) restrict it to his burial, so that in the Creed it is an explanation of the article on his burial: thus our Beza on Acts 2:26–27.[6] This is not satisfactory to others because: (a) not only would it introduce tautology to the most exact conciseness of the Creed, but (b) it would also endeavor to explain what is sufficiently clear by what is more obscure. Others (2) restrict it to the sufferings of Christ's soul, as does Calvin together with very many of the Reformed.[7] This is unsatisfactory to others for this twofold reason, because: (a) these sufferings of his soul concern his death, which was handled in the preceding articles of the Creed, and thus it would burden the Creed with tautology. (b) It would place the sufferings of his soul after his burial, and therefore disrupt the order of the Creed. So then, still others (3) think that neither his burial nor his soul's sorrows are meant by this descent, but rather, the state and dominion of death, to which he was subjected during the three days of his burial. Thus Sohn on the Augsburg Confession,[8] Perkins on the Creed,[9] Ames,[10] both the Shorter and Larger Catechisms of the Westminster Assembly,[11] and others.

---

5. §§XI–XII, below

6. Beza, *Novum Testamentum* (1598), 1:460.

7. Calvin, *Institutes*, 2.16.8–12; Heidelberg Catechism, Q. 44.

8. Georg Sohn, *Opera*, 3 vols. (Herborn Nassau: Christophorus Corvinus, 1591–1592), 2:257–61.

9. William Perkins (1558–1602), *Opera omnia theologica in duos tomos tributa* (Geneva: Petrus and Jacobus Chouët, 1611), 1:677–681; idem, *An exposition of the Symbole or Creed of the Apostles according to the tenour of the Scriptures, and the consent of orthodoxe Fathers of the church* ([Cambridge]: John Legatt, 1597), 422–32.

10. William Ames (1576–1633), *Christianae catecheseos sciagraphia* (Amsterdam: Joannes Jansson, 1635), 92; idem, *A Sketch of the Christian's Catechism*, trans. T. M. Rester (Grand Rapids: Reformation Heritage Books, 2009), 84.

11. Westminster Shorter Catechism, Q. 27; Larger Catechism, Q. 50.

Christ's three descents should be conjoined.

What if, for the purpose of reconciling the apparent differences of the orthodox, we conjoin them as sub- or coordinates, and enumerate a threefold descent of Christ: (1) of the body, into the grave, (2) of the soul, into the infernal state, (3) of the whole Christ, into the power and dominion of death? For (1) Scripture by the term "descent" not only customarily designates the three things, but also distinctly asserts them for Christ, as will be more clearly evident from what will follow. (2) In this way depth of his descent and humiliation will from this be all the more amplified and acknowledged. (3) The Creed itself will also be more easily vindicated from being redundant and unmethodical.[12]

1. The descent of the body into the grave

VI. Therefore, the first descent shall be that of the body, which both the text hints at in the first place, and the Creed teaches in the first place, that is, the descent into the grave. For it is more certain than certain that by שאול, Sheol, and by the descent into Sheol, in the Scriptures is frequently meant burial (Gen. 42:38; Ps. 6:5; Isa. 38:18; Acts 2:27, 31); also that the Savior, with respect to his body, was buried (Matt. 27:59–60; Mark 15:46; Luke 23:53; John 19:41); and moreover, that Christ's descent was in this burial, through a comparison of our text with Acts 2:27, 31, and 13:34–36, together with which all the ancient Creeds up to the time of the Athanasian Creed and Charlemagne manifestly agree, as we have said. This burial was once predicted, as the apostle testifies in 1 Corinthians 15:4, especially in Isaiah 53:9, where it is said that: (1) he would be killed with the wicked, or by a death worthy of criminals; (2) but he would be buried in the tomb of the rich, namely of Joseph, a rich man (Matt. 27:57), and that in a manner that was quite honorable (vv. 59–60).

The circumstances of this burial: (1) The time

VII. With respect to the circumstances of his burial, it happened: that very evening of the day of his death, with the Jewish Sabbath and its preparation[13] already impending, (Matt. 27:57), because the Sabbath (at least the Jewish one), or the seventh day from creation, contained a type of this rest in the tomb, for which reason therefore, when that rest was completed, as a shadow when the body is present, it expired (Col. 2:16–17). Calling for this also was the law (Deut. 21:23), in which it was prohibited that the corpse of a hanged man remain all night upon the tree, since the one hanged was a curse to God. From this, because

---

12. *a* ταυτολογία *et ab* ἀμεθοδία
13. παρασκευῇ. Cf. Mark 15:42; Luke 23:54.

in the death of Christ the curse would be abolished, it was fitting that his body, after death had happened and the curse had been taken away, would not be left on the tree of the curse.

(2) Its initiators

By the initiative Joseph of Arimathea, a rich man, an honored councilor,[14] secretly a disciple of Christ for fear of the Jews (John 19:38; Matt. 27:57), otherwise certainly pious, but up to this point, having weak faith, as is gathered from Mark 15:43. To him Nicodemus joined himself, who was one of the leaders of the Pharisees, and likewise of feeble, but genuine faith, which is why he came to Christ at night to be taught by him, and also was taught by him, and converted (John 3:2ff.), and from this, growing stronger in faith, he acts more freely for Christ (John 7:51). Perhaps added to them were a few upright women, Mary Magdalene, Mary the mother of Jesus, and others who had followed Christ from Galilee to serve him (Matt. 27:55).

(3) The manner

In an highly honorific manner, when: (a) Joseph wrapped his body in clean linen (Matt. 27:59); (b) Nicodemus added a mixture of myrrh and aloe, about a hundred pounds (John 19:39), according to the received custom of the Jews in the burials of more honored men (Gen. 50:2).

(4) The place

In an honorable place, not under the cross,[15] but in the garden of Joseph, not far removed from the place of crucifixion, perhaps so that he might rise again in a garden, just as we fell in a garden (Gen. 3).

(5) The tomb

And that indeed in a tomb that was: (a) new (Matt. 27:60), so that the Jews could not suspect or allege that anyone else had risen again; moreover, (b) stone (Matt. 27:60); and in addition, (c) blocked from above with quite a large stone, not only from the custom of the more honored Jews (Gen. 35:20; John 11:38), but also from divine providence, so that the Jews could not suspect a hoax. I would add, (d) sealed with Pilate's public seal, and in addition with the guards added, certainly from the depraved counsel of the Pharisees (cf. Matt. 27:60ff., cf. Ps. 41:8), but yet also not without the divine will, so that we might be rendered more certain of the true resurrection (Matt. 28:11ff.).

---

14. *Senatore*
15. *sub furca*

(6) The duration

In duration, for three days, or three days and nights,[16] according to his own prophecies (Matt. 12:40; 27:40, 63; Jonah 1:17), yet not the entirety, but in total around forty hours: from which it seems among the ancients that the forty-day fast arose, because for the same number of hours the bridegroom was taken away (Matt. 9:15).

The ends of Christ's burial

VIII. The ends of this burial were that: (1) the prophecies might be fulfilled (Ps. 16:10; 22:15; Isa. 53:9). (2) We might be persuaded by invincible arguments concerning the truth of his death, upon which our entire redemption depends (Heb. 2:14): thus Pilate was unwilling to hand him over to be buried until he had confirmed that he was certainly dead (Mark 15:42–43). (3) He might seal by his burial that the curse was taken away by his death (Deut. 21:23; Gal. 3:13). (4) He might humble himself from the height of heaven to the depths of earth (Eph. 4:9–10). (5) He might bury our sins with him, the truth of which is sealed to us in baptism (Rom. 6:4; Col. 2:12). I would add, that (6) he might abrogate, not indeed the Sabbath of the fourth commandment (which indefinitely prescribes the sanctification of that seventh day which God determined for men; for not only did this Sabbath, with all the rest of the commandments of the Decalogue, belong to moral and irrevocable law,[17] Matt. 5:17–19, but also it bore entirely no figure of Christ's rest in the grave), but precisely the Jewish Sabbath, that is, that seventh day which God numbered and prescribed to be numbered by the Jews from the seventh day of creation, when the Savior had rested on it, and thus fulfilled the type, which Sabbath, together with all the rest of the feasts of the Jews, the apostle intends in Colossians 2:16–17; and in the same stroke, that he might substitute for it the Christian Sabbath, after the travails of his humiliation (Isa. 53:11), and determine that the seventh day of the fourth commandment was to be numbered by Christians from his resurrection, for which reason that Christian Sabbath is called the Lord's Day (Rev. 1:10), which he blessed on the very day of resurrection (John 20:19); for which reason also that day is read to have been constantly observed by Christians as the Sabbath (Acts 20:7; 1 Cor. 16:2), which unless you want to refer it to condemned will-worship, you are compelled to refer it to the divine institution: from which it should accordingly be called the Lord's Day, just like the Lord's Supper (1 Cor. 11:20, 23). In addition, since the sanctification of some seventh day, from the

---

16. *tria* νυχθήμερα

17. *juris fuit moralis et inabrogabilis.* Cf. 1.8.2 §L.

fourth commandment, belongs to the moral law, and accordingly, with the Jewish Sabbath abrogated, the church could not exist even one hour without a Sabbath, that substitution must have happened soon after the resurrection. Regarding this we will say more things expressly in its own place, if the Lord wills.[18]

2. The descent of Christ's soul into the infernal state

IX. The second descent of Christ's soul shall be, not into a place, but into the infernal state, wherein he experienced infernal things, or infernal punishments, in his soul. For since שאול, Sheol, in the Scriptures not rarely designates such an infernal state, in the torments and anguishes of the soul (1 Sam. 2:6; Ps. 18:5; 116:3), from which, those undergoing hellish anguishes of this sort are said to be cast into hell (Ps. 88:4, 6), or also to be delivered from hell (Ps. 30:1, 3); and also since that infernal state is plainly attributed to Christ's soul, when it is said both that he was forsaken by God (Matt. 27:46), and that he labored under the sense of divine wrath and anger (Rev. 19:15 with Matt. 26:39, 42), and that by these things his soul was exceeding sorrowful, even to death, that is, eternal or infernal death (Matt. 26:38). By this reasoning, neither can tautology be observed in the Creed, because it had previously said entirely nothing, at least expressly, regarding the descent of the soul; nor lack of method, because by the law of method, it had to speak of the descent of the body prior to the descent of the soul. Moreover, what this descent of the soul is, or what he suffered by it, first with respect to loss, and then with respect to sense, we have explained in the preceding chapter, §VIII–XI, XX.

3. The descent of Christ's whole man into the power and dominion of death.

X. Therefore, the third descent is that of Christ's whole man into the power and dominion of death and darkness, insofar as for the three days of burial his body was dead, and his soul was bereft of its union with the body (which union was natural to it), and thus in these respects the entire composite was under death, for which reason Peter says in Acts 2:24 that at last by the resurrection he was loosed (and consequently to that point had been bound) from the sorrows of death, because it was impossible κρατεῖσθαι αὐτὸν ὑπ' αὐτοῦ, for him to be bound by it, namely θανάτου, death. From which it becomes most evident that during the three days of his death, or until the resurrection, he was ὑπὸ κράτους, "under the power" of death, as it were in its chains and prison (cf. Ps. 18:4–5; 116:3; 88:6). And this also was the hour and the power of darkness which he intimates in Luke 22:53, with "hour" taken for the whole time of his

____

18. 2.2.15

suffering and humiliation, which lasted until his resurrection (Acts. 2:24). The darkness that accompanied and followed his death also seems to have signified this (Luke 23:44–45). The goal of this descent was that he might deliver us from the power and dominion of death and of the power of darkness (Hos. 13:14; 1 Cor. 15:54–57; Col. 1:13). Nevertheless the descent of Christ's whole man should not be taken in such a way as if his soul after death suffered anything beyond the deprivation of its natural union with the body, because already when he was dying he committed his soul into the hands of the Father (Luke 23:46), and it was immediately received into paradise (Luke 23:42–43); nor as if his body experienced any pain; but rather, that during this time he was as it were under the triumph of the entire power of darkness.

The Elenctic Part

It is asked: 1. Is the descent of Christ into hell nothing but a demonstration of his nonexistence?

XI. Concerning the descent of Christ, it is asked first whether the descent of Christ to hell intends nothing other than to demonstrate that Christ certainly died just as all other men die, that is, he passed into a state of nonexistence. The Socinians affirm this (Smalcius, *On the Divinity of Jesus Christ*, ch. 13),[19] namely because they state that to die is nothing other than not to exist any longer, and that Christ from his death to the time of his resurrection did not exist. The falsity of this we have expressly demonstrated in the preceding chapter, §XVIII. Moreover, they think that the articles in the Creed regarding Christ's burial as well as his descent into hell were added so that believers, for their consolation, might be rendered more certain of this nonexistence of Christ. But the adversaries do not bring forward even one whit for this their view of the descent into hell, except the hypotheses that we have noted and demolished in the place cited. Thus it is not necessary to delay upon this question any longer, except that it altogether must be noted that from this opinion, wherein hell is nonexistence, it follows: (1) that every difference is taken away between the pious and impious who die up to the last judgment; (2) that the pious as well as the impious are cast into hell after death; (3) that by this nonexistence the immortality of souls is undone; (4) that the present state of a dying man and a dying beast is the same; (5) that no resurrection of the flesh ought to be expected for a human being more than a brute beast; (6) that hell is in fact entirely taken away; and (7) instead of Christianity, Sadduceeism is established.

---

19. Smalcius, *De divinitate Jesu Christi*, 78–87.

2. Did he descend locally to hell? The diverse opinions of those who affirm this

XII. Second, it is asked whether Christ, with respect to his soul, descended locally to hell. The papists, for the sake of their limbo of the fathers, so that from there Christ might take the believers of the Old Testament who died before his actual satisfaction into heavenly blessedness, certainly affirm that Christ did descend to hell, but not without a difference of opinions, with some thinking (1) that he descended not with respect to the essence of his soul, but with respect to its efficacy, and certain effective operations there. Thus Durandus (on bk. 3 of the *Sentences*, dist. 22, q. 3), whom Bellarmine rebuts (bk. 4, *On the Soul of Christ*, ch. 15).[20] Commonly, (2) they state that he descended locally with respect to the essence of his soul. Thus Bellarmine (*On the Soul of Christ*, bk. 4, ch. 10–16).[21] The Lutherans, motivated by I know not what, contrary to their own hypotheses, assert likewise that he descended locally so that there he might triumph over the devils. At the same time they also acknowledge a descent of his soul into the infernal state, and thus they invent for him a twofold descent. Hence, they rack themselves with various questions: whether the descent ought to be referred to the state of humiliation or of exaltation, whether it happened immediately after his burial or a while after, whether it happened in the divine or human nature, whether in the soul alone, or in the entire person.

The opinion of the Reformed, who deny this, is proved.

The Reformed deny all local descent, because: (1) he descended neither according to the divine nature (which, through its omnipresence, rejects all local motion), nor according to the human nature, as it again descended neither with respect to the body, which during that three days partly hung on the cross and partly lay in the tomb, nor with respect to the soul, inasmuch as when he was about to die he commended it into the hands of the Father, and also on that very day it ascended into paradise (Luke 23:43), just as on the very day of sin Adam was ejected from paradise (Gen. 3:23–24). (2) That local descent is entirely useless and idle: for neither did Christ descend into hell so that he might suffer for us there, for this was already finished on the cross (John 19:30), nor so that by this descent he might satisfy for our sins, for this had already been provided in his death (Heb. 2:14; 9:12; 1 Thess. 1:10), nor so that he might lead the fathers of the Old Testament out of hell, since they never were in hell, as is evident in Enoch (Heb. 11:5)

---

20. Durandus (c. 1230–1296), *In sententias theologicas Petri Lombardi commentariorum libri quatuor* (Leiden: William Rovillius, 1563), 215; Bellarmine, *De controversiis Christianae fidei in Omnia Opera* 1:284–86.

21. Bellarmine, *De controversiis Christianae fidei in Omnia opera*, 1:276–88.

and Elijah (2 Kings 2:11), nor so that he might triumph over the devils, for that had already occurred on the cross (Heb. 2:14–15; Col. 2:14–15), and afterwards also in the ascension (Eph. 4:8–12). I would add that (3) the limbo of the papists is nothing but an idle fiction, bereft of all Scripture and reason.

The arguments of our adversaries
Nevertheless, there is something for them to undertake to the contrary: namely, they allege (1) Ecclesiasticus 24:45, "I will penetrate all the lower parts of the earth and will behold all those who sleep, and I will shine upon those who hope in the Lord."[22] I respond: (a) It is an apocryphal book; (b) those words are not extant in the Greek text; nor (c) do they treat of the soul of Christ; nor (d) a local descent; nor (e) some infernal limbo; nor (f) the leading of Old Testament believers out from there. (2) Matthew 12:40, "So shall the Son of Man be three days and three nights in the heart of the earth" (cf. Eph. 4:9). I respond, His burial is understood, and not the place of the damned, much less an infernal limbo, and by "the heart," the inner regions of the earth are denoted, not precisely the center or what is closest to the center (cf. Ex. 15:8; Deut. 4:11; 2 Sam. 18:14; Prov. 23:34; 30:19; Ezek. 27:4, 25–27); nor also here is there any mention of a separated soul. (3) Acts 2:27, "You will not abandon my soul לשאול, in hell."[23] I respond: שאול, Sheol, in the Scriptures frequently designates the infernal state and infernal torments, as we already taught above in §II and §IX (4) Romans 10:7, "Who will descend into the abyss? That is, to bring up Christ again from the dead." I respond, At most nothing else is concluded from this than that the soul of Christ while dying descended into the infernal state. (5) Ephesians 4:9, "that he descended first into the lowest parts of the earth." I respond: This must be understood as either the descent from the highest heaven to the lowest parts of the world, the earth, which occurred in his incarnation (John 6:38; 1 Cor. 15:47), or the descent of the body into the grave, as we have said. (6) In 1 Peter 3:18–19 it is said that having set out by the Spirit, he preached to the spirits who are in prison. I respond, By the Spirit who was in the prophets (1 Peter 1:11), and also once in Noah, he preached to the disobedient who were still alive on earth, who are now in prison. Accordingly the apostle's discussion is not about the souls of Old Testament believers, but about the souls of the disobedient in the time of Noah. Finally, (7) they allege that before payment was made in the death of Christ, they were under guilt, and consequently could not be admitted

---

22. Cf. Ecclesiasticus 24:45 in the Vulgate and Douay-Rheims, contra the Septuagint, which lacks this verse.

23. Hebrew from Ps. 16:10

out of the infernal prison into heavenly liberty. I respond: (a) The evident example of Enoch and of Elijah refutes this (Heb. 11:5; 2 Kings 2:11). (b) They were delivered and admitted on account of the satisfaction taken from them upon himself by Christ, in the eternal absolute surety (Isa. 53:4–5; Acts 15:11 with Heb. 13:8).

3. Was Christ during the three days of his death and burial a true man?
The various opinions of various writers
XIII. Third, it is asked whether Christ during the three days of his death and burial was a man in the true and proper sense of the term. Aquinas (pt. III, q. 50, art. 4), denies this, and also judges that the contrary is heretical, because the death of Christ is of faith; yet he confesses that he was a dead man.[24] With him agrees our venerable past colleague Dr. Burman (*Synopsis*, bk. 5, ch. 18, §3): "The question arises," he says, "whether Christ was a true man during these three days of his death. Which is rightly denied by Thomas, although he can be called a man equivocally (that is, a dead man), yet not univocally. But in the manner that he ceased to be a man, he also to that extent ceased to be the God-man, although otherwise, when the bond of the body and soul was loosened, the union of both with the Word remained uninjured, and when the natural union was dissolved, the personal union still remained."[25] Hugh of St. Victor (*On the Sacraments*, bk. 2, pt. 1, ch. 11) does affirm this, but on an untrustworthy foundation, that the soul alone is man, for which reason he held that for Christ to be made man he had no necessity to be made flesh, or a partaker of flesh and blood, against which the apostle speaks (Heb. 2:14–15; John 1:1).[26] Lombard affirms the same (bk. 3 of the *Sentences*, dist. 22, §1), but likewise by a weak reason, that a union of the essential parts, body and soul, is not required for the constitution of a man, against which all wholesome philosophy protests.[27]

The opinion of the Reformed is proved.
The Reformed acknowledge that Christ truly died, and therefore the natural union of the body and soul was taken away for those three days, and hence he was also certainly a dead man, but yet he was also a man in the true and proper sense, because otherwise: (1) during those three days either he would not have been the Lord's Holy One, who having been sanctified by the Father, came into

---

24. Aquinas, *ST*, III, q. 50, a. 4.
25. Burman, *Synopsis theologiae*, 94. Burman and Mastricht both served as professors at Utrecht, 1677 to 1679.
26. Hugh of St. Victor (c. 1096–1141), *De sacramentis Christianae fidei* in *PL* 176:401–11.
27. Lombard, *Sententiarum libri quatuor* in *PL* 192:802–3.

the world (John 10:36), or he would have been destroyed, which the text of Psalm 16:10 contradicts. (2) He would not have been the eternal high priest (Ps. 110:4; Heb. 5:6; 6:20; 7:17), which the apostle opposes (Heb. 2:17). (3) During the three days he would not have been Jesus Christ. Franciscus Sylvius acknowledges this consequence (*Commentary on Thomas*, pt. 3, q. 50, art. 4): "However, there is a difficulty," he says, "whether he was the Christ during those three days. The reason for doubting is because 'Christ' means first the *suppositum* existing in the divine and the human nature, but at that time there was no human nature, for his humanity had ceased by the fact that the union of the body and the soul (which is the essence of humanity) ceased. Wherefore it seems more true to say that properly speaking he was not the Christ, except by synecdoche, in which sense, just as St. Peter is said to exist now, so it is true that at that time he was the Christ."[28] In addition the apostle confirms this consequence in 1 Timothy 2:5: "the man Christ Jesus." Also (4) during the three days he would not have been the Mediator, and thus during those three days the world would have been without a mediator, since for the constitution of the Mediator, humanity as well as deity are required, for which reason the apostle spoke in 1 Timothy 2:5 of the one Mediator, the man Christ Jesus. Nor also (5) would he properly speaking be the God-man, and thus for the two modes of subsisting heretofore commonly received, before and after the incarnation, now there will need to be enumerated three. Nor in addition (6) would that last degree of Christ's humiliation, which was in his burial and in his existence under the power and dominion of death, have been mediatorial, and undertaken on behalf of men. Indeed, (7) whether they want it or not, from this hypothesis the hypostatic union of the two natures will be dislocated. Therefore let it remain that (8) Jesus Christ, from the first moment of his incarnation to all eternity, is a true man, the God-man, the Mediator, the same yesterday, and today, and forever (Heb. 13:8).

The foundation of our adversaries' opinion is destroyed.

If they should allege to the contrary that with the union of the essential parts of the body and soul taken away, a man in the true and proper sense would not survive, then I would grant that, with all union of those parts taken away, a man in the true and proper sense would not survive, but since, in agreement with all Christians, in the incarnation a twofold union was procured by the Holy Spirit—one natural, through which he was a living man, and the other personal, through which the same person was not only God but also man—when the

---

28. Franciscus Sylvius (1581–1649), *Commentarii in tertiam partem S. Thom. Aquinatis*, 4th ed. (Douai: Gerardus Patte, 1645), 168.

former ceases, nevertheless the latter remains. So then, because the essential parts of man in death were not deprived of all union (as ordinarily occurs in the dead, who for this reason are also not men, except equivocally), but only the union that makes a living man, we conclude that he nevertheless throughout the three days of his death and burial remained a man in the true and proper sense.

The Practical Part

The descent of Christ: 1. Presents an argument for gratitude.

For what motivating reasons

XIV. The descent of Christ, or the lowest point of his humiliation, considered in general, offers us, first, an argument for the highest gratitude (1 Cor. 15:54–58; Rom. 7:24–25), because not only: (1) in the incarnation did he descend from the highest heaven into the lowest parts of the world, the earth (Eph. 4:8–9); nor only (2) from the form of God into the form of a servant (Phil. 2:6–7); nor only (3) from life, as the Prince of life, into the cursed death of the cross (Acts. 3:15); but also, (4) with respect to his body, from the earth into the grave, into the heart of the earth (Matt. 12:40), into the dwelling of corpses; (5) with respect to his soul, into the infernal state and condition (Ps. 88:4–6), wherein he was deserted by God his Father (Matt. 27:46), and tortured with the pains of death, that is, of infernal death (Matt. 26:37–38; Acts 2:24), and he was made the curse itself (Gal. 3:13); and finally, (6) with respect to his whole humanity, into the power and dominion of death, and of the entire power of darkness, such that to death and hell he was as it were a triumph and mockery (1 Cor. 15:55–56). A deeper descent than this can neither be, nor be imagined. Moreover, this occurred: (1) because we, in our sins, had raised ourselves as it were into heaven, to be as equals to God the King of heaven (Gen. 3:5; cf. Isa. 14:13), indeed above the heavens, that is, above God himself (cf. 2 Thess. 2:4; Ex. 5:2). And thus (2) we would unavoidably have had to descend into the same pit of the horrible grave, into the same infernal state, into the same dominion and mockery of the entire power of darkness, if he had not delivered us by descending (Zech. 9:11; Heb. 2:14; Hos. 13:14; cf. Jer. 38:6, 10, 12; Dan. 6:17–18, 24). And done so to the end that (3) from the abyss of infernal misery he might lift us up into heavenly glory (Eph. 2:6) and set us with himself on thrones (Rev. 3:21; 11:16). In all these things, is there not supplied for us an argument for gratitude?

By what duties

In this gratitude: (1) by the sense of our sins, let us humble ourselves before him, all the way into hell, as it were (Luke 15:21; Mic. 7:9), because we cast down the

Son of God into hell by our sins (Isa. 43:24). On the contrary, (2) him whom we have sunk down all the way into hell by our sins, let us extol all the way to heaven, indeed above the heavens, with our gratitude and praises (1 Chron. 29:11; 1 Kings 8:23, 27; Phil. 1:21). Indeed, (3) on account of his exaltation, let us humble ourselves to the lowest depths, to the worst of circumstances (John 1:27), and, if possible, let us endure being humbled to hell (1 Cor. 4:9–10, 13). And also, (4) let us willingly cast our glory, our crowns at his feet, who so deeply humbled himself for us (Rev. 4:10–11). Compare the practical section of ch. 9, on the humiliation of the Mediator.[29]

2. It provides a foundation for comfort. In what circumstances
XV. Secondly, the descent of the Mediator supplies a foundation for Christian confidence, comfort, and joy, so that with the Mediator as our head, we may sing, "Therefore my heart is glad and my glory exulted; my flesh also shall dwell in confidence" (Ps. 16:9–10, 1 Cor. 15:55–56). It provides, I say, a foundation for confidence, whenever: (1) we think upon and dread the limitless abyss of those who descend into hell, with the devil (Rev. 20:3), dreading and pleading against his descent (Luke 8:31), with the feasting rich man (Luke 16:23, 25), with Korah, Dathan, and Abiram (Num. 16), with the dragon (Rev. 12:9, 20:2), and the false prophet (Rev. 20:10); whenever we seem to hear the terrible voice of the Judge say to us, "Depart from me, you cursed, into eternal fire, which was prepared for the devil and his angels" (Matt. 25:41), and likewise the wailings and gnashings of teeth of those who have been cast into infernal darkness (Matt. 22:13); and we think about the worm that will never die and the fire that will never be quenched (Isa. 66:24)—what could be more effective to give comfort in this instance than that the Mediator descended, not for himself but for his own, into an abyss of misery so deep (Rom. 10:7), and obtained its keys (Rev. 1:18; 3:7), and upon exiting, as it were opened it and delivered his own who were bound from the pit (Zech. 9:11)? Whenever (2) the horror of the grave terrifies us, where our bodies rot, become worse smelling than the corpses of all other living things, an abomination to men, and food for worms (Job 4:19; 17:14; 21:26; Isa. 51:8; cf. Acts 12:23)—then what could raise us up more effectively than to consider that our Jesus also descended into the grave, not for himself, but for his own, and consequently made of the grave a resting place,[30] or rather a dwelling place, in which our bodies can dwell securely until the resurrection (Ps. 16:9)? Whenever (3) our souls descend into the horrors of hell, with David (Ps. 18:4–6), with

---

29. 1.5.9 §XVII
30. κοιμητήριον

Heman (Ps. 88:4, 6, 14–16), with Asaph (Ps. 77:7–9)—what then is more effective than to think that Christ also descended, and that not for himself, but for his own, and just as God did not leave him in hell, so also, on account of him, he will not abandon them? Whenever (4) the dominion of death, of the tyrant Satan (Heb. 2:14) and of darkness (Col. 1:13) torture us as they loom over us—what will be more effective to think upon than that the Lord's Holy One also descended into it, and that not for himself, but for his own, and so then we with him will never see שחת, the pit, or eternal destruction?

Under what conditions
That is, provided that: (1) we are united by true faith with Christ who descends, so that in that faith, with him we die (Rom. 6:8), are buried (Rom. 6:4), and descend into the valley of the shadow of death (Ps. 23:4). (2) In this descent of ours, that is, in all these circumstances, together with Christ who descends, God is our portion, who sustains our lot (Ps. 16:5), who when our heart fails, is our rock, and our portion forever (Ps. 73:26). (3) In our descent we continuously have before our eyes God, and also Christ who descends for us, as the one who sustains us, so that we may not be moved (Ps. 16:8), who is present by his grace to those walking in the shadow of death, and supports them (Ps. 23:4). (4) Even in our descent, with these supports, our heart endeavors to be glad and our glory to exult, together with Christ who descends (Ps. 16:9; Job 19:25–27).

3. It warns us not to lift ourselves up, even to heaven. Examples
XVI. Third, the descent of Christ to the abyss of the lowest misery most effectively warns us to earnestly take heed that we do not lift ourselves up to the heights of heaven, so that with Babylon we say in our heart, "I will ascend into heaven, and I will exalt my throne up above the stars of God (Isa. 14:13), and with Capernaum, "Let us lift ourselves up, even to the heavens" (Matt. 11:23), and like the eagle, "Let us make our nest on high" (Job 39:30).

Dissuading reasons
For is it not surely (1) most shameful for the Son of God to descend from heaven all the way to hell, and for a little manikin to ascend as it were from hell to heaven, and to place himself on God's throne, indeed to exalt himself above God (2 Thess. 2:4)? Is it not surely (2) most wicked, when we have by the depth of our misery as it were dragged into hell the Son of God, for us as it were to occupy his throne in the heavens? Is it not surely (3) most just, if we lift ourselves all the way up to heaven, when the Son of God sent himself all the way down to hell, if we have placed our throne next to God or above him, for us to be, with Babylon

(Isa. 14:11), with the men of Capernaum (Matt. 11:23), with Nebuchadnezzar (Dan. 4:25, 29–34), cast into hell, and with Herod to be devoured by worms, as if in a tomb (Acts 12:21–23)? For whoever has exalted himself will be humbled (Luke 18:14; Matt. 23:12; Prov. 29:23). Whereas on the contrary, (4) if we have before God cast ourselves down all the way into hell, he will lift us up all the way into heaven (Ps. 113:4–9). This was the more general practice of this descent; now we pass to the more specific practice, first of his burial.

4. The burial of Christ strengthens: (1) Our faith

XVII. Fourth, the descent of the body of Christ into the tomb in particular excellently strengthens: (1) our faith (1 Cor. 15:2 with v. 4), because (a) he truly and infallibly died: on which account, by divine providence, the judge Pilate was so careful in inquiring whether he was dead (Mark 15:44), and the soldiers were so certain of his death that when the legs of the thieves had been broken, they did not touch his legs. To this end also points his three-day delay in the tomb, namely that if perhaps we could suspect that he did not truly die on the cross, at least we cannot but believe that he died in the three days in the tomb. Hence, (b) he also truly made satisfaction for our sins, and took away our guilt with him into the tomb and prison, wherefore perhaps he willed to descend into the tomb of another (Matt. 27:60), and to do so bound as it were with the linen cloths of our sins (John 19:40), and upon rising to leave them in the grave (John 20:5), to signify that in the resurrection, the Judge, with all the bonds loosed by which on account of our sins he had been so long held bound (Ps. 18:4–5), released him free from the prison. For with the fullest satisfaction already rendered, it would be impossible for him to be held by death in the bonds of death and prison any longer (Acts 2:24). So that now with the disciples we can look inside his tomb, and contemplate (θεωρεῖν) the grave clothes lying there (John 20:6–7), namely for the strengthening of our faith and confidence, because now with the satisfaction offered, the bonds of our sins, by which he had lay bound in the prison of the tomb, are now loosed, and left in prison.

5. It strengthens our soul against the horror of the tomb.

Arguments for strengthening

XVIII. Fifth, it not only strengthens our faith, but also: (2) the burial of Christ strengthens our soul, whenever the tomb—which in fact for sinners is nothing but the porch and threshold of Sheol, of Hades; from which it also obtains its common name, the prison of God the most just Judge, in which he reserves those guilty of eternal death, bound by chains of darkness, until the last judgment, and meanwhile delivers them to the worms, serpents (whose seed they were), and toads to be devoured, where they will dwell with the devils themselves, who will one day be their torturers (Mark 5:3)—whenever, I say, we think of our grave in this way, what will we more effectively present to ourselves for consolation than the following? That (1) our Mediator also descended into the grave, and hence in this also we too will be conformed to him (in which a Christian's chief perfection consists), because we have been buried with him (Rom. 6:3), especially since it is unfitting for a disciple to be in a better condition than his master (Matt. 10:24–25). (2) He was buried not for himself, but for us, and therefore he drew every harm, dread, and poison from it (1 Cor. 15:55, 57). (3) We were not buried with him alive, but dead, lacking any feeling and dread. Nor (4) so that we would perish, but so that we may rest with him from our labors (Rev. 14:13). Nor (5) so that we may rot eternally, but so that we may rise again with Christ (John 11:25), as a seed is buried in a field, not so that it may rot, but so that by rotting, it may bloom again with great increase, as the apostle so emphatically teaches (1 Cor. 15:35–50). From all these things, (6) the grave is for us, as it was for our Mediator, not so much a grave as a resting place (Isa. 26:20) where with Christ, like does of the dawn, for a little while we may rest and have respite from the struggles of death and diseases, from the harassments of the world (Job 7:1–3); indeed, it is also a refuge where, secure from enemies and persecutors of every kind, spiritual and bodily, and fortified as it were by a huge stone which no one can move (Mark 16:3), and as it were by the seal of the omnipotent Judge (Matt. 27:64–66), in our flesh we may, with our head the Mediator, ישכן לבטח, dwell securely until the resurrection. And because of all these things, our heart will be glad and our glory will exult, because our flesh also will dwell securely. Moreover, (7) if either through the cruelty of enemies, or through some providence of God, we do not obtain an honorable burial, what could more effectively strengthen us against the fear of this evil, than that Christ our head was buried for us (1 Cor. 15:3–4), indeed that we have already been buried with him through baptism (Rom. 6:4; Col. 2:12)?

The requirements for those who would be strengthened
That is, provided that, as we already began to teach before in §XV: (1) we have died in the Lord (Rev. 14:13). (2) We have been buried with him (Col. 2:12), as members of the same mystical body with him (1 Cor. 12:12) and thus we have Christ, even in the grave, as if present to us (Ps. 23:4). (3) We always place before our eyes this our head, who was buried for us, so that he may be at our right hand, that we should not turn aside (Ps. 16:8). (4) In confidence, לבטח, with Mary Magdalene, at the earliest point in the morning, when it was yet dark (John 20:1), and with the disciples, we run to Christ's tomb, we endeavor to confidently

look into it by faith, and indeed to enter Christ's tomb with Peter: we will certainly discover the stone will be entirely rolled away for us; we will find, now the angels sitting in the tomb, and raising us up who were laid prostrate in dread of the tomb, and they will show the place where Jesus was laid; indeed, we will find his linen cloths, with the handkerchief in which his head had been wrapped, in which also through faith we will be able as it were to wrap our entire selves (Mark 16:1–8). Finally, (5) we take care with Christ to be laid in a new spiritual tomb, and with Joseph, that it be prepared in a timely way.

6. Christ's burial stirs us up to the spiritual burial of our sins.
By what acts and steps this is performed
XIX. Sixth, the burial of Christ most effectively stirs us up so that by virtue of it we would bury all our sins (Rom. 6:4; Col. 2:12). That is, let us earnestly endeavor that: (1) we conform ourselves more and more to Christ with respect to his burial, which occurs by different actions, namely: (a) through the contempt and despising of sin; for just as Christ once was buried by his enemies due to contempt and hatred, as an impostor (Matt. 27:63–64)—from which the throats of the ungodly are called open graves (Ps. 5:9; Rom. 3:13), because the godly fall into them, as into stinking graves—so also we should not love any of our sins (1 John 2:15), but pursue them with hatred, as the basest impostors (Jude 23; Heb. 3:13), hold them in contempt, and detest them as corpses and dead works (Heb. 6:1; 9:14; Rom. 7:24). (b) Through the denial of the same; for just as the leaders of the Jews are said to have denied the Christ who would be buried (Acts 3:14), so also we, as Christ's disciples, should deny all sins (Luke 9:23). (c) Through the mortification of the same, and that in different degrees, for just as: (i) Pontius Pilate, before he handed Christ over to be crucified and buried, first handed him over to be beaten and flogged (John 19:1), and his soldiers wounded his head with a thorny crown, so also when our sins are to be buried, we should wound and beat them; indeed, we should wound, beat, cut off (Matt. 5:29; 18:8), and torture (1 Cor. 9:27) their very head, which is found in the sins we especially love. This wounding properly occurs through the pricks and pangs of conscience for sins committed, arising from the sense of their shamefulness, and the threats of the law (Acts 2:37; Luke 15:21). Just as (ii) the Jews, before they demanded that Christ must be crucified and buried, accused, examined, and condemned him as a seducer and blasphemer (Matt. 26:59–67), so also we, with a careful examination conducted beforehand (Zeph. 2:1; Gal. 6:4), and a rigid accusation made (Rom. 2:15), should at last, without grace, together with God condemn them as seducers and blasphemers (Rom. 8:3), as guilty of death. Just as (iii) the Jews and Pilate crucified Christ who had been condemned (Matt.

27:26), so also we should crucify the sins condemned (Gal. 5:24; 2:20), that is, with the nails of the divine threats, we should as it were affix them to the cross of Christ (cf. Col. 2:14). Just as (iv) the Jews thoroughly slew the crucified Christ, raging against him even when dead, piercing his side (John 19:32–34), so also we should mortify our sins, that is, we should not desist from them until we have utterly destroyed them (Col. 3:5). Finally, (v) just as the Jews took care that Christ once crucified and dead, as an abominable and cursed spectacle, would be immediately buried before evening, and thrust from the sight of men below the earth, even setting guards and the judge's seal, so that he would not emerge (Matt 27:61ff.), so also we should thrust our sins, no matter how they have been crucified and mortified, as something cursed and abominable, in its entirety, into the grave, out of the sight of God and man (Rom. 6:4); we should assign guards to it, so that it would not break out at any time (Prov. 4:23; Job 31:1).

Likewise, by what helps

Not only should we busy ourselves, in all these and other things, to imitate the burial of Christ, but also: (2) whatever we busy ourselves to do, we should endeavor it by virtue of Christ's burial, that is: (a) through the merit of Christ's burial, insofar as it was not for himself, but for us, and loaded down with our sins, that he descended into the grave, so that there he might bury and destroy them, in token of which, he willed to enter not his own tomb, but that of another (Matt. 27:60). (b) Through the promise (Mic. 7:19), wherein the one who would one day be buried, and like Jonah cast into the abyss (Matt. 12:40), promised that he would cast our sins, and as it were bury them, in the depths of the sea, certainly not only through justification, but also through sanctification, wherein the strength is conferred to us by which we may mortify and bury sin. Especially (c) through union with Christ, in which we become unified with him in one plant, as in the likeness of his death and resurrection, so also of his burial (Rom. 6:5), and thus we are buried with him (Rom. 6:4). So then also (d) through faith, whereby we are united with Christ, we have as it were put on Christ (Gal. 3:27), and he dwells in our hearts (Eph. 3:17), and so then he as it were transplants into us his virtue, by which we bury our sins. Finally, (e) through our baptism, by the efficacious remembrance and use of which we are spiritually buried to sins with Christ, and by faith, in the power of the God who raised Christ, with our sins abandoned in the grave, we rise again to a better life (Col. 2:12; Rom. 6:4, 6).

7. It teaches us that we should bury believers in Christ, and those who died for Christ's sake. Motivating reasons

XX. Seventh, the burial of Christ teaches us that when the mystical Christ

(1 Cor. 12:12) has died in his and our members, and especially if they by the cruelty of his enemies (Ps. 79:2), and in particular of the Antichrist (whose custom this is against those whom he calls heretics, Rev. 11:9), on account of Christ not only have been unjustly deprived of life, but also of an honorable burial, we should honor him by the duty of last charity, in a honorable funeral, and wrap them as it were in our linens and perfumes: (1) by the example of Joseph, Nicodemus (John 19:38–39), and Mary Magdalene (John 12:3, 7). Because (2) we will render this to Christ himself (Matt. 25:40). (3) This offers proof to us of our union with Christ, and of the communion of the saints, through love and sympathy (1 Cor. 12:12–28). Furthermore, from this communion, (4) that which we render to other members of Christ, we render to ourselves. Chiefly because (5) they themselves also, together with us, will one day come to be raised in honor by God (1 Cor. 15:42). And also, (6) by these duties, especially in dangerous and difficult times, we will display the strength of our faith and love, with Joseph of Arimathea (Mark 15:43).

8. It provides consolation in spiritual desertions.

XXI. Eighth, the descent of the soul of Christ into the infernal state provides a most effectual comfort to those believers whom God repeatedly brings down to hell (1 Sam. 2:6), whom he leads into the valley of the shadow of death (Ps. 23:4), so that they walk in darkness and see no light (Isa. 50:10), whom he has so deserted in regard to all sense of his grace, that they are forced to cry out with Christ, "My God, my God, why have you forsaken me?" (Ps. 21:1; Matt. 27:46; Mark 15:34), whose souls he fills with so many and such great vexations, that with Christ they burst forth, "My soul is exceeding sorrowful, even unto death" (Matt. 26:37–38), to whom he so abundantly extends the cup of wrath and indignation, that day and night they lament, "Father, if it is possible, let this cup pass from me" (Matt. 26:39, 42, 44), against whose frequently repeated wailings, as against Christ, he closes his ears, from whom he has frequently for a long time utterly turned away the face of his sweetest grace (Isa. 64:7; Ps. 30:7), and whom he seems to have thoroughly removed from his memory (Ps. 13:1–2), whom he hands over to Satan for buffeting (2 Cor. 12:7). Illustrious but fearful examples are evident in Heman (Ps. 88), Asaph (Ps. 77:2–10), David (Ps. 30:8–10), Job (Job 6:2–4). And what is it to descend into the infernal state, if not this?

Comforting arguments

For all such people, there is a most efficacious comfort in this descent of Christ into hell, if they should devoutly consider that: (1) Christ also descended into hell, and it is not fitting that there should be a more prosperous state for them than for their Master (Matt. 10:24): for them, as disciples, it is sufficient if they should be equal to their Master (Matt. 10:25). Indeed, in this is the summit of their perfection (Luke 6:40): this is the supreme end of election, that we should be made to be conformed to the image of the Son of God (Rom. 8:29). (2) Christ descended into hell for them, not for his own sake, in order to deliver them forever from infernal terrors (Gal. 3:13), in order that they could one day triumph over hell (1 Cor. 15:55; Hos. 13:14; Rom. 7:24–25). (3) They do not enter alone into this Gethsemane, but are led there by Christ, with his disciples (Matt. 26:37), so then they have Christ present to them in this state (Matt. 26:36) and bearing the most tender care for them (Matt. 26:41; Ps. 23:4; 91:15; Rom. 8:31). (4) They, in this state, were abandoned by God, together with Christ, not with respect to grace itself, like the reprobate (e.g. Saul, 1 Sam. 16:14), but only with respect to the sense of grace (Ps. 22:9; Isa. 49:14–16). (5) They, with Christ, will not be under this miserable state forever, but hardly for three days, like Christ was (Matt. 12:40), indeed for two days (Hos. 6:1–2), indeed for an hour (Luke 22:53; Rev. 3:10), in fact for a brief moment (Isa. 54:7), until the definite hour of grace (Isa. 49:8 with John 2:4). (6) Meanwhile their soul, just as also that of Christ, will not be abandoned by God in this hell (Ps. 16:10; Heb. 13:5; Deut. 31:6, 8; Isa. 54:6–12; Jer. 31:16–21), but will be supported by the hidden rod and staff of gracious divine providence (Ps. 23:4). (7) The more bitter their misery has been, the more sweet to them their deliverance will be (Ps. 30:7–12; 116:3, 7), when God will wipe away all their tears (Rev. 7:17), when, instead of a moment of dereliction, they will receive eternal grace (Isa. 54:7–8). Indeed, the deeper their descent has been, the higher their ascent will be, when God has raised them together with Christ, and set them with him in the heavenly places (Eph. 2:6).

The laws that must be observed here

That is, provided that: (1) in their infernal state, they have continuously fixed the eyes of their mind on Christ descending to hell (Heb. 12:2–3), just as Christ while descending placed Jehovah before his eyes, that he would be at his right hand (Ps. 16:8). (2) In their infernal state, they preserve some sort of confidence in God (Isa. 50:10), just as Christ not only when he was about to descend to hell (Ps. 16:10, "You will not leave"), but also when he was in his hell (Ps. 22:4), in crying out, "My Father" (Matt. 26:39, 42), "My God, my God" (Matt. 27:46). And if there is not supplied to them the faith of evidence, such as there was to Job (Job 19:25), they should at least foster and stir up the faith of adherence (Ps. 63:9), like Job (Job 13:15) and Asaph (Ps. 73:25). (3) By this confidence of some sort, they ceaselessly with groanings make solicitation before God for their deliverance, just as Christ (Matt. 26:39, 42; Ps. 22:2), Asaph (Ps. 77:1–2), and Paul (2 Cor. 12:8). Meanwhile, (4) they peacefully submit their entire lot to the divine will, just as Christ (Matt. 26:39, 42) and Asaph (Ps. 77:10). (5) They circumspectly employ the consolatory helps which are supplied to them through the providence of God, as Christ did with the angel (Luke 22:43), and with the disciples (Matt. 26:37, 40). (6) Under all these helps, they patiently look for the hour of deliverance (Ps. 27:13–14; 130:5–7).

9. The descent of the Mediator into the power and dominion of death calls us to a fourfold duty.

XXII. Finally, ninth, that Christ during his three days of burial came under the power and dominion of death, not so that he might succumb to it and to see שׁחת, the pit, but so that by his death he might take the power from him who has the power of death, that is, Satan, and deliver as many as through fear of death were all their lifetime subject to bondage, as the apostle says (Heb. 2:14)—this, I say: (1) offers an infallible sign to us that he is that Holy One of the Lord, as he is called in Psalm 16:10, whom the Father set apart and sent into the world as the Messiah (John 10:36), that true seed of the woman, which by the crushing of his heel, done by the serpent, he crushed the serpent's head, according to the promise (Gen. 3:15), on whom accordingly we ought to lean in faith (Isa. 10:20). This (2) most effectively moves us to gratitude, because he willed to pass under the power and authority of death during the three days, so that he might deliver us from the fear of death, and from all manner of spiritual slavery (Col. 1:12–13), and restore us to the liberty of the children of God (Rom. 8:21; cf. Jer. 38:11). This (3) summons us, that having been redeemed (by his descent into the power of death) from the power of our spiritual enemies, we might serve him without fear, in holiness and righteousness in his sight, for all the days of our life (Luke 1:74–75). And (4) that we might bravely contend for the spiritual liberty that had to be acquired and preserved by such a great descent of the Mediator, against his and our spiritual enemies—Satan, the world, and sins (Eph. 6:12ff.).

CHAPTER FOURTEEN

The Exaltation of the Mediator

Wherefore God also has exalted him to the greatest height, and given him a name which is above every name, that at the name of Jesus every knee should bow, of those in heaven, and on earth, and under the earth, and that every tongue should confess that Jesus Christ is Lord, to the glory of the Father.
—Philippians 2:9–11

Following the humiliation is the exaltation, and its more general contemplation.
I. Up to this point we have contemplated the Mediator's humiliation; we now continue to his exaltation. And just as we were engaged in thinking about the former, first generally, then specifically, through its individual degrees, so we will be engaged about the latter, first in general, then in specific, with respect to its individual degrees. The former will be the argument of this chapter, with the apostle leading us by the hand in Philippians 2:9–11.

The Exegetical Part

II. In these words are presented what follows the humiliation, the exaltation of the Mediator, with respect to:

A. The foundation which undergirds the exaltation: "Wherefore," διό. The preceding profound humiliation of the Mediator and his submissive obedience is understood, either as the meritorious cause of the exaltation, as pleases the papists, and even many orthodox when taken in a proper sense, or as the necessary and natural antecedent, without which the exaltation must not and cannot follow. I think both can easily be united, such that the humiliation is both the antecedent of the glorification (Luke 24:26), and also the cause, and that strictly meritorious, not only from the eternal covenant between the Father and the Son, who appointed to him glorification as the reward of humiliation and obedience (Isa. 53:8, 10–12), and moreover from the nature of the law, promising glorification to the obedient as a reward, but also from the nature of the humiliation and obedience itself, which was of infinite value, whereby both for himself and for us he was able to merit glorification, as we will teach in the dogmatic part.[1] Compare chapter 18, §XX.

B. The exaltation built upon the foundation of the humiliation, regarding which are noted:

1. The exalting cause: "God," first considered theologically, the entire most holy Trinity because the exaltation is an operation *ad extra*; then economically and by appropriation, the Father (John 17:1), inasmuch as he is the one to whom he had submitted himself (Phil. 2:8), whom he had glorified (John 17:4), and who additionally in the whole business of redemption, must be considered, according to the economy, as the Judge who appoints to each his own, and as the Lord who distributes that which is his.

2. The one exalted: "him," namely the Mediator in his entirety, according to both natures, although in different ways, as we will teach in the dogmatic part.[2]

3. The exaltation, with respect to two acts:

   a. The general act: ὑπερύψωσε, he "has highly exalted," "raised to the greatest height," by raising him: (1) above the grave, through the resurrection; (2) above the earth, through the ascension; (3) above heaven or heavenly things, angels as well as men who died in faith, through his session at the right hand.

   b. The specific act: he has "given him a name which is above every name," concerning which two things are noted:

      i. The height conferred: "a name which is above every name." Here by "name" is understood not so much: (1) that name *Jesus*, inasmuch as, before the exaltation, it already obtained from the time of his circumcision (Matt. 1:21); nor only (2) fame, which throughout both Testaments is signified by "name" (Gen. 6:4; Mark 6:14); but also (3) glory, as much internal glory, which consists in those perfections from which someone merits glory—for example, wisdom, power, illustrious actions—as external glory, which consists in the acknowledgment and

_____

1. §VII, below
2. §VI, below

public testimony of internal glory; however, chiefly (4) author-ity, power, and dominion over others and other things. In all these things, Christ, above all who are in heaven and on earth, is said to have a name that is above every name.

ii. The conferral of the height: he has "given," ἐχαρίσατο, that is, he has conferred by grace, so that it is signified that this name was conferred upon him according to the human nature, not so much by merit, at least strictly so called (since thus he is a crea-ture that cannot merit anything from his Creator, Rom. 11:36), unless tempered by grace, just as our first parents, by their own obedience, from the grace of the promise would have merited for themselves eternal life; although at the same time, accord-ing to both natures, as the God-man Mediator, by the strictest right, on account of the infinite value of his obedience, and thus from condignity, he altogether merited glorification for himself.

4. The twofold end of exaltation, namely the glorification:

a. Of the Mediator, the proximate end, namely:

i. The subjection of the heart: "that at the name of Jesus…." Here is noted:

a) The authority to which the subjection is to be rendered: "at the name of Jesus." This is not understood to mean the uttering of the name of Jesus, at which the knee should be bowed or the head uncovered; but Jesus himself, endowed with authority and dominion. The name stands for the one named, by metonymy of the sign for the thing signified.

b) The subjection to be rendered to the authority: the "knee should bow" that is, should honor, obey, subject itself to him. Whether it is done freely and frankly, or unwillingly and through hypocrisy. For no other bowing of the knee can be rendered by spirits to Christ.

c) The persons to render the subjection to the authority: "of those who are in heaven," that is, the angels and souls of the blessed in heaven; those who exist "on earth," that is, people who live on earth, whether they are pious or impious; and those who dwell "under the earth," that is, demons and the impious.

ii. The confession of the mouth: "and every tongue confess that

Jesus Christ is Lord," that is, that one to whom all power has been conferred in heaven and on earth (Matt. 28:18; Eph. 1:21–22; Heb. 2:7–9). Moreover, here is understood not only the mediatorial dominion (through the passages cited), but also the divine dominion, which belongs to him as Jehovah, God, the Creator (Heb. 1:5, 8, 10).

b. Of God: "to the glory of God the Father." This glory is the ultimate end, to which all the glorification of the Son finally redounds (John 5:22–23; 1 Cor. 15:23–29).

The Dogmatic Part

Christ was elevated to the highest glory. It is proved by the Scriptures.

III. Therefore from what has been said, it is evident that the Son of God, just as he sent himself down to the lowest misery, was elevated by God to the highest glory. This exaltation of the Mediator was: (1) predicted (Ps. 8:5 with Heb. 2:7; Isa. 52:13; Zech. 6:12; Ps. 110:7; 89:19). (2) Prefigured, in Joseph (Gen. 41:14 with v. 37; 42:6); in David, who when he had bravely waged the wars of the Lord (1 Sam. 25:28), and then subjugated and triumphed over his enemies (2 Sam. 22; Ps. 18:37–38), grew very great in glory (2 Sam 5:10), and obtained a name like the name of the great men who are on the earth (2 Sam. 7:9). In exactly the same manner, the Savior, when he had bravely waged the wars of the Lord against the entire power of darkness (Luke 22:53), and gloriously conquered all, triumphed (Col. 2:13–15; Eph. 4:8; John 16:11, 33), and gained a name above every name (Phil. 2:9). In addition, this exaltation of the Mediator was prefigured in Solomon: for just as Solomon gained rest from all his enemies that surrounded him (1 Chron. 22:9), and possessed a kingdom that was most wealthy (2 Chron. 2:15; 9:22), most glorious, above all who were kings either before or after him (2 Chron. 9; Eccl. 2), the most wide (Ps. 72:8–11; 2 Chron. 9:24, 26), in exactly the same way Christ, now that his enemies have been subjugated, has a kingdom that is, at least spiritually, peaceful (Isa. 11:6), most rich, with respect to spiritual things (Eph. 3:8; John 16:15; Col. 1:17), most glorious (Heb. 1:3; Rev. 19:11–17), most wide, extending to the uttermost parts of the earth (Ps. 2:8; 72:8). (3) Fulfilled (Phil. 2:9–10; Heb. 2:7–9; 1 Peter 1:11; Eph. 1:19–21; 4:9–10).

And by reasons

IV. And it also had to be fulfilled (Luke 24:26), not only: (1) so that satisfaction would be made to the divine truthfulness of the promises and types, but also

(2) because it was thus fitting that such a great humiliation would be compensated with such a great exaltation. And also because (3) this so closely regarded the glorification of God (Phil. 2:11), that the Father might be glorified in the Son (John 5:22), and because the glorification of God is the universal and final end of the entirety of redemption (Eph. 1:6; Rom. 9:22–23). (4) The Son glorified the Father, and thus it was fitting that in turn he would be glorified by the Father (John 17:4–5). (5) Our redemption demanded that he would not only procure redemption for us by his humiliation, but also apply it once procured, by his exaltation, by appearing for us in heaven at the right hand of God before the Father (Rom. 8:34; John 17:20; Heb. 9:11–12), by sending down his Spirit (John 16:7), that he might vivify us (John 3:5; Titus 3:5) and create faith in us (2 Cor. 4:13). (6) In the eternal covenant of grace, God the Father promised exaltation to his Son as a reward, if he completed the work of redemption, as we have demonstrated in chapter 1 of this book.[3]

What the exaltation is
V. Moreover, for us this exaltation is nothing except that glorious and most blessed state of his, into which he entered after he had completed the business of redemption under his humiliation. The term "exaltation" is indeed at times taken for that virtual glorification which he experienced in his deepest humiliation itself, or in the crucifixion (John 3:14; 12:32), but the glorification which belongs to this topic followed his emptying.

Its components
The components of it are in general the following: (1) he set aside, not the form of a servant, or the human nature, but the servile form of the human nature (Ps. 8:5; Heb. 2:9). (2) He gloriously triumphed over his and our enemies (Ps. 110:1; Col. 2:15): over death, by enduring it bravely (Heb. 12:2; 1 Cor. 15:55); over sin, by most fully satisfying for it, when he was made sin for us, so that we might be made righteousness before God (2 Cor. 5:21; Rom. 7:24–25); over Satan, by crushing his head (Gen. 3:15), by stripping him of his authority (Heb. 2:14; Col. 2:15; Eph. 4:8). The perfection and revelation of this victory is in the exaltation: for although the virtual and meritorious triumph was on the cross and in his death, wherein therefore he is said to be lifted up (John 3:14; 12:32), not only in position and place, but also in virtue and merit; nonetheless, the actual triumph, with respect to state, was not in the humiliation, but in the exaltation. He certainly triumphed on the cross, as in the field of victory; but in the exaltation

---

3. 1.5.1 §VI

he did so as on the throne, in the palace, and in the triumphal chariot. (3) The manifestation[4] of the form of God, through which he was equal to God,[5] which because he assumed the form of a servant and the fashion of a common man, and finally through so many reproaches of his adversaries, had been hidden to an outstanding degree (Phil. 2:7–8), and did not shine forth, except from time to time more obscurely, through certain small rays, when he performed miracles in his earthly life (John 2:11; 1:14). It was a most illustrious revelation (John 17:1–2; Matt. 26:64); and also as it were a releasing, or most full use of the divine power and authority, (Ps. 2:9, 12; Eph. 1:22; Heb. 2:8–9), which during the period of humiliation had as it were held itself back (John 19:11; Matt. 26:53–54). (4) The conferring to the human nature of all the perfection which can occur in a creature (Ps. 68:18 with Eph. 4:8–9, 13, where it is said that he received gifts to pour out upon men, by which he would fill all things in the church, "to the measure of the stature of the fullness of Christ."[6] For in his soul thrived every sort of fullness of wisdom and grace, not only with respect to its principle and habit (for in this sense he had already obtained it from the hypostatic union, John 1:14; 3:34; Isa. 11:1–2), but also with respect to its activity and exercise (Col. 2:2–3, 9–10). And likewise his body was adorned with the highest purity and splendor (Phil. 3:21). (5) The abundance of glory, from the acknowledgment and celebration of that whole perfection which under this state was either conferred upon him or manifested and illustrated in him (Luke 24:26; Ps. 8:5; Heb. 2:9). And in this is the name which is above every name (Phil. 2:9), on account of which every tongue will acknowledge and profess that Jesus Christ is the Lord (Phil. 2:11). Finally, (6) the most absolute authority and dominion, certainly over the church, as his kingdom and body (Eph. 1:20–23; Ps. 2:6; Acts 2:36), and with respect to the church, over all things (Matt. 28:18)—heavenly, earthly, and subterranean— from which authority it is said that at his name all things that are in heaven, and on earth, and under the earth, will bow the knee (Phil. 2:10, to which end also point Ps. 8:6–8 and Heb. 2:7–8).

How Christ was exalted according to the whole person and both natures
VI. Now from what has been said, with no great difficulty it can be settled that the whole Christ was exalted, not only he who is the God-man, which is hinted at throughout in concrete expressions designating his whole person, for example, "Wherefore God has exalted *him*" (Phil. 2:9; Eph. 1:20; Acts 2:36),

---

4. *manifestatio*; Dutch: *Openbaring*
5. ἴσος θεῷ. Cf. Phil. 2:6.
6. εἰς μέτρον ἡλικίας τοῦ πληρώματος τοῦ χριστοῦ

and, "All authority is given *to me*" (Matt. 28:18); but also as he is such, or with respect to both of his natures, although in different ways: (1) with respect to the divine nature, certainly not in the conferral of new perfections, which his one infinite perfection rejects, but with respect to the manifestation of that hidden perfection (in which sense also it is frequently said that God himself is exalted by us, Ps. 46:10; 145:1; Isa. 5:16; Luke 1:46), and with respect to the awakening and use of the authority that as it were lay dormant under the humiliation. Moreover, (2) with respect to the human nature, not through the full use of the divine properties communicated to it from the hypostatic union with the divine person—because those properties neither were ever communicated to a finite nature, nor could be, as we have taught and will teach elsewhere[7]—but because all that created perfection which can occur in a creature was communicated to it, as we have just shown. Therefore, he was exalted (3) with respect to the whole person, as regards: (a) the laying aside the servile form; (b) the triumph over all his enemies; (c) glory; (d) and the mediatorial authority and dominion.

The cause of this exaltation: The meritorious cause
VII. As to what relates to the causes of this exaltation: first, the meritorious cause could be described easily enough as the Mediator Christ himself, insofar as by his abasement and obedience he merited glory from the double promise: (1) that of the covenant of works, "Do this and you will live" (Lev. 18:5; Ezek. 20:11; Gal. 3:12; Rom. 10:5). For although when the covenant of works was first established, he was not reckoned in Adam, yet afterwards he came under the conditions of the law for us (Gal. 4:4; Rom. 8:3), and also received its promises and rewards. (2) That of the covenant of grace, insofar as in the eternal counsel of peace between the Father and the Son, when the Son undertook humiliation and obedience for his own, the Father on the other hand appointed to him a recompense (Isa. 53:10–11). The meritorious cause was Christ, insofar as, I say, from this double promise he merited his exaltation. Add to these that (3) from the condignity and infinite value of his humiliation and obedience, he merited infinite glory both for himself and for us. For which reason after his humiliation and obedience, it is said significantly, διό καί, "Wherefore God also ὑπερύψωσε, has highly exalted him" (Phil. 2:9); "we see Jesus, on account of the suffering of death, crowned with glory and honor" (Heb. 2:9), and, "For the joy set before him, he endured the cross" (Heb. 12:2). Nor is it any hindrance here that he merited glory for us, for he could merit it both for himself and for us: for himself as a man, for us as the God-man Mediator, who was not bound by the divine law to obedience.

---

7. 1.5.4 §XII, XXIV; 1.5.17 §XVII

The conferring cause

The conferring cause is noted to be God (Phil. 2:9), certainly theologically, with respect to the individual persons of the Trinity, from which it is distinctly referred to the Father, as the one glorifying (John 17:1), to the Son, as the one rising again, ascending, and sitting at the right hand of God (in which things his glorification consists, as we will speak of in their own place),[8] and to the Holy Spirit, as the one announcing (John 16:13–14). However, economically and by appropriation (as we taught in the exegetical part), the Father is considered the cause of the exaltation.

The acknowledging and celebrating causes

Men are also causes of the exaltation, in acknowledging and celebrating the height conferred on him, and in submitting themselves to his authority, either freely and willingly (Phil. 1:23) or unwillingly (Ps. 110:1); indeed, so also are angels, as much the good (Heb. 1:6; Matt. 4:11) as the evil (Mark 3:11–12): from which it is said in the text that at the name of Jesus every knee will bow, of those who are in heaven, on the earth, and under the earth, and every tongue confess that Jesus Christ is Lord.

The degrees of exaltation

VIII. The degrees by which he ascended to the greatest height are enumerated in various ways by different persons. There are those who enumerate four, and that in different ways: there are those who locate the first in his descent into hell, and then they subjoin to it the resurrection, ascension, and session at the right hand, about which we will speak in their own place; others constitute the first degree in the resurrection and the last in the return to judge the living and the dead. Still others admit, as for his humiliation, so for his exaltation, only three degrees: the resurrection, opposed to his passion and death; the ascension, opposed to his descent into the grave; and the session at the right hand of God, opposed to his descent into hell. For ourselves, just as we spoke of four degrees of his humiliation—his incarnation, life, death, and descent—so also we will oppose to them four degrees of his exaltation: the resurrection from the dead, in which he was exalted above the grave; the ascension into heaven, in which he was elevated above the earth; the session at the right hand of God, in which he was exalted above all creatures; and his return to judge the living and the dead, in which he will be elevated as the Judge above all those to be judged. The three

---

8. 1.5.15–17

prior degrees we will contemplate successively in subsequent chapters, but the last we will lay aside for a place more appropriate to it.[9]

The Elenctic Part

It is asked: 1. Through the exaltation, is Christ's flesh of the same essence and power with his deity? The difference of opinions
IX. Belonging to the elenctic part of this chapter, it is asked first whether Christ's flesh in the state of glory according to its substance is of the same essence and power with his deity. Eutyches once taught concerning the incarnation of Christ that this sort of confusion of the natures occurred. The modern enthusiasts—Schwenckfeld, Weigel, and others—state that this confusion occurred at last in the exaltation.[10] The Lutherans, whether they intend it or not, approach closer to Eutyches, when in the incarnation they want the divine subsistence, essence, and properties to have been communicated to the human nature, although he put aside as it were the full manifestation and use of those properties until his exaltation.

The reasons of the party denying
Christians assert that during the exaltation the human nature nevertheless remained distinct in its essence and properties, just as the divine nature did, because: (1) Scripture makes entirely no mention of this confusion. Moreover, (2) on the contrary, it expressly mentions throughout the truth of the nature, and its distinct qualities[11] (Luke 24:15, 30, 39, 43; John 20:20, 27; Rev. 1:7). I need not mention that (3) by this confusion a double deity is introduced: the one eternal, the other temporal; and that (4) the difference between deity and humanity is well enough taken away. Finally, (5) it implies an open contradiction for the flesh of Christ to become of the same essence with the Father, and yet not be destroyed.

The objections of the party affirming
I do not see what could be objected with even the least appearance of truth, other than: (1) that it is said that the Word became flesh (John 1:1). For (a) this would

---

9. 1.8.4 §IVff.

10. E.g. Caspar Schwenckfeld (1489–1561), *Vom Fleische Christi* (1584), fol. Oii recto; idem, *Vom Fleische Christi* in *Corpus Schwenckfeldianorum*, 19 vols. (vols. 1–14, Leipzig: Breitkopf & Härtel, 1907–1913; vols. 9–19, Pennsburg, Penn.: Board of Publication of the Schwenckfelder Church, 1928–1961), 7:338; Valentin Weigel (1533–1588), *Of the Life of Christ* (London: for Giles Calvert, 1648), 2–3, "But to be short, Christ God and Man, the whole person, is of Heaven, his bloud and Flesh is of the holy Spirit…."

11. *affectionum*

argue with a greater appearance of truth that the divine nature was changed into the human nature than that the human nature was confused with the divine. Then (b) that phrase does not argue anything other than that the divine person assumed the human nature (Phil. 2:7–8; Heb. 2:16), or that God was manifested in the flesh (1 Tim. 3:16). (2) That divine things seem to be attributed to the human nature, for example, divine authority and omnipresence (Matt. 28:18, 20; 18:20). But these and similar passages are not speaking of the flesh or human nature in the abstract, but of the whole person of Christ in the concrete.

2. Does the exaltation consist in this, that by it the human nature received the full use of the divine properties?

X. Second, it is asked whether the exaltation consists in this, that by it the human nature received the manifestation and full use of those divine properties, the communion of which it received through the hypostatic union. The Lutherans, because in favor of the omnipresence of the flesh of Christ they had taught that through the hypostatic union the proper qualities[12] of the divine person were communicated to it, such as omniscience, omnipotence, omnipresence, and others, so that they can rescue themselves, at least with some appearance of the truth, from so many and such great difficulties which that opinion urges, distinguish with respect to κτῆσις and to χρῆσις, that is, with respect to possession and to use, such that, although he had the divine properties communicated to him through the hypostatic union with respect to their κτῆσις or possession and οὐσία, being, yet he did not have them, until his exaltation, with respect to their χρῆσις or use and ἐξουσία, authority. The Reformed, although they acknowledge that the μορφή θεοῦ, the form of God or the divine nature in the Mediator, through the μορφή δούλου, the form of a servant, or the human nature and its σχῆμα ἀνθρώπινον, human form, was greatly hidden, that it as it were restrained itself until the exaltation, and that at last through the exaltation it was plainly revealed to the world, and as it were unfolded itself through its attributes, at least those by which it customarily operates outside itself, nevertheless deny that this manifestation and use of the divine properties occurred in the human nature, inasmuch as it never had those properties communicated to it, just as we expressly demonstrated in chapter 4 of this book.[13] So that at least here there remains nothing left to be done except for the Lutherans to demonstrate that through the personal union the human nature of Christ under the state of humiliation had the divine power, glory, and properties, at least with

---

12. *idiomata*

13. 1.5.4 §§XXIII–XXIV

respect to possession: which the passages of Scripture they adduce do not teach (Matt. 11:27; John 3:34; Acts 10:38; Matt. 9:6; John 2:24–25), because none of these passages speak about the human nature in the abstract, but about the whole person, although sometimes denominated by the human nature, and even much less do any teach that the human nature had divine properties.

3. Was Christ also exalted according to the divine nature?

XI. From this, third, it is asked whether Christ was also exalted with respect to the divine nature. The Lutherans, so that they may obtain more easily that the divine properties were exalted in the human nature of Christ by their manifestation and full use, deny that he was exalted with respect to the divine nature. The Reformed, although they grant that by this exaltation the divine nature received nothing as regards intrinsic perfection, nevertheless teach that it was exalted in the same way (as even the Lutherans confess) that the deity, outside of a consideration of the personal union, is exalted, as taught throughout both Testaments: namely, through its manifestation and operation, as we have shown in the dogmatic part.[14] With these points carefully observed, a response can be made without any trouble to whatever will be objected. For the testimonies of Scripture which are objected or could be objected (e.g. Acts 2:32ff.), either do not speak about the human nature abstractly, but about the entire person of the God-man, although it is denominated from the human nature more than the divine, or, if they do speak about the human nature, yet they do not speak exclusively about it alone having been exalted: that alone is what is in question.

Objections

Moreover their reasons—for example, (1) that the exaltation introduces a change, (2) that it presupposes a defect and a lack, (3) that it introduces an elevation or improvement—are only binding upon Christ's exaltation insofar as it concerns the human nature. If otherwise, all those things mistakenly introduced will most effectually strike down the adversaries themselves by their own hypotheses, for they teach: (1) that the divine properties were communicated to the human nature in the personal union. They teach (2) that these properties were hidden in Christ by the servile form and lacked their full exercise. (3) That by the exaltation those same properties set aside the humble form of a servant and fully unfolded themselves in their exercise and operation. Now if the exaltation should introduce a change, if it should presuppose a defect and a lack, if it should introduce an elevation and improvement, will these things not apply to

---

14. §VI, above

the divine properties that were communicated to the human nature through the hypostatic union?

4. Through the exaltation, were only finite gifts communicated to the human nature?
XII. Fourth, it is asked whether through the exaltation only finite gifts were communicated to the human nature. The Reformed uphold the affirmative, because: (1) the finite cannot contain the infinite.[15] (2) Infinite gifts involve a manifest contradiction. (3) The things which we spoke about in §V as the components of the exaltation—the laying aside of the servile form, the triumph over his enemies, and so forth—speak of nothing except finite things. (4) The adversaries themselves locate the exaltation partly in the laying aside of the servile form, and partly in the full use of the divine properties communicated to the human nature through the union, in which things there is certainly not any new communication of infinite good. Yet at the same time, the Lutherans censure the Reformed for asserting that nothing but finite gifts were conferred to the human nature through the exaltation; but they do so without any reason.

5. Is the first degree of the exaltation the descent into hell?
XIII. Fifth, it is asked whether the first degree of the exaltation is in the descent into hell. The papists, because they state that Christ descended locally into hell, so that he might from there take with him to heaven the fathers of the Old Testament who died in faith, affirm this. The Lutherans, although with the papists they accept a local descent (with this difference, not so that he might lead Old Testament believers out of hell, but so that he might triumph over it), notwithstanding separate into factions, with some referring it to the state of humiliation, others to the state of exaltation, and some refer to a certain middle state, such that inchoatively, or with respect to the beginning, it pertains to the humiliation, but terminatively to the state of exaltation. Nor also are there lacking among them those who suspend their judgment entirely, and allow each to enjoy his own opinion: thus the *Book of Concord*.[16] The Reformed, according to the preceding chapter, think in agreement with the Scriptures that the last degree of the humiliation was in Christ's descent into hell.

---

15. *finitum infiniti non sit capax*
16. *Formula of Concord*, ch. 9, in both the *Epitome* and *Solid Declaration*.

The Practical Part

In Christ's exaltation: 1. An inseparable connection is evident between humiliation and exaltation. The foundation of this connection

XIV. In the exaltation of the Mediator, first for comfort, an inseparable connection is evident between humiliation and exaltation, because after Christ had emptied himself, after he had assumed the form of a servant, after he had become obedient to his Father to the point of death, even the death of the cross, God the Father exalted him and gave to him a name above every name, and made subject to him all things which are in the heavens, on the earth, and under the earth, and did so on account of that very humiliation of himself: "Wherefore...." This connection is signified also elsewhere, and indeed throughout the Scriptures, not only in the Mediator (Luke 24:26; Heb. 2:6–7; Ps. 8:4–6; Isa. 53:10; Heb. 12:2; 1 Peter 1:11), but also in all of his members, or those who are truly believers (Luke 18:14; 1 Peter 5:6; Rom. 8:17–18; 2 Cor. 4:16–17), who in addition are said to have been crucified with Christ, and to live with Christ (Gal. 2:20), to become one plant with him in the likeness of his death, so that they may also become one in the likeness of his resurrection (Rom. 6:5), and that they who were dead in sin, being made alive together with him, may also be set in heaven in Christ Jesus (Eph. 2:5–6; cf. 1 Cor. 15:42–44). The foundation of this connection is also: (1) in God's eternal establishment (Rom. 8:29); (2) in our union with Christ, as that of the members with the head (1 Cor. 12:13), from which it is said that we are his σύμφυτοι, those planted together with him, as much in his death as in his resurrection (Rom. 6:5), that we are crucified together with him (Gal. 2:20), and also that we rise again with him (Col. 3:1); (3) in the immovable promise of Christ (Matt. 16:25; 19:28–30); (4) in the very congruence of this connection, for although in our humiliation we could not (as Christ could) merit anything from God (Rom. 8:18; 11:36) and our goodness does not extend to him (Ps. 16:2), yet it is congruent and agreeable to equity that those who are humbled on his account, would also with him be exalted (Rom. 8:17–18; Heb. 6:10).

The use of this comfort. In what circumstances

Accordingly, if: (1) the world empties us, if it counts us as nothing, on account of God and Christ (1 Cor. 1:28), and if we with Christ have emptied or denied ourselves (Luke 9:23). If (2) we bear in the world the form of a servant, or even more than a servant (1 Cor. 4:13), or if we bear ourselves as bondservants in our conduct (Luke 22:25; John 13:13–14), and not as masters (1 Peter 5:3; Matt. 20:21). If (3) we are compelled through the hostilities of enemies to be obedient to our heavenly Father to the point of death, indeed any death of the most shameful sort, even the death of the cross (Acts 20:24; Heb. 11:35–37; 10:32–33; Phil. 1:20–21).

By what consolatory arguments
Then in these and similar circumstances, what would be more effectively conducive than to earnestly consider the following? (1) This indissoluble connection between present humiliation and future exaltation. And accordingly, that (2) if here we have been emptied with Christ, and have emptied ourselves, we will also with him more certainly than certain be exalted (Luke 18:14; 1 Peter 5:6). (3) If for Christ and with Christ we have borne the most vile and abject form of a servant here, we will with Christ gain a truly new, or excellent, name (Rev. 3:12; Luke 10:20), we will hereafter reign with him (Rom. 8:18; Rev. 3:21). (4) If with Christ we have been obedient to the Father to the point of death, even the most shameful death of the cross, we will be with Christ so far exalted by God, that every servile form will be taken from us, as it was from Christ, and we will be conformed to the glorious body of Christ (Phil. 3:21). So much so that (5) we will triumph with him over all our enemies (1 Cor. 15:55–56; Rom. 8:37). That in addition (6) that illustrious nature of God in us (2 Peter 1:4), as it were hidden here by so many miseries, as it was in Christ (Isa. 53:3), will be manifested to the eyes of all (Matt. 13:43). And furthermore that (7) with him we will be adorned with all the most splendid gifts (Eph. 5:27). That also (8) with him we will be crowned with eternal honor and glory (Ps. 8:5; 2 Tim. 4:8). That finally (9) in some way all things will be subjected to us (Ps. 8:6), and we with Christ will judge the whole world (1 Cor. 6:2).

2. It rebukes those who bring down the one exalted. Those to be rebuked
XV. Second, Christ's exaltation marks as most evil those who strive to bring down the one exalted by God, who tread underfoot the Son of God and regard the blood of the covenant as profane (Heb. 10:29), who crucify to themselves the Son of God afresh, and expose him to mockery (Heb. 6:6). And who then are these? I respond: (1) in different degrees they do this who, in spite of the fact that God highly exalted him, strive to diminish him as much as possible. Those who do this are: (a) first open and express unbelievers—pagans, Muslims, Jews (1 Cor. 12:3)—who, with their ancestors, with the papists, with the Pharisees and scribes, harass Christ in the worst way, shackle him in chains, condemn, crucify, and mock him. Those who (b) more covertly, indeed with an external profession, busy themselves to subjugate his kingdom, to weaken his followers by the most dreadful persecutions, indeed to eradicate them (Ps. 2:1–2; Acts 2:23; 4:26–27), which especially is characteristic of the Antichrist and his followers,

of the apocalyptic beast, of the scarlet whore drunk with the blood of the martyrs (Rev. 17:6). Those who (c) exalt themselves above Christ, like the Antichrist (2 Thess. 2:4), heretics and any other false Christians, and every high thing that exalts itself against the knowledge of God (2 Cor. 10:5). (2) Those who misrepresent and profane his name, which by God's establishment is above every name, either: (a) by transferring the honor that belongs to the one named, through superstition, to the name, which is common among the papists and Lutherans, whom we already noted in chapter 3, §XX; or (b) by falsely naming Christ, when by a conversation that is insufficiently Christian, they bring injury and insult upon him (2 Tim. 2:19; Rom. 2:23–24); or (c) by resting in only a confession of the name of Christ (Matt. 7:21–22; Rom. 2:17, 28–29). (3) Those who do admit to him a name which is above every name, and even add the most abundant titles, but do not bow their knee to him, except perhaps: (a) by mockery, with the soldiers who crucified him (Matt. 27:29); or (b) by superstition, with the papists and Lutherans, bowing the knee of the body, not of the heart; or at least (c) they do not receive his authority and lordship over them (Job 21:14; Jer. 44:16), indeed they oppose it with all their might (Luke 19:14, 27; Ps. 2:1–3). (4) Those who: (a) do not confess that Jesus Christ is Lord, just like the unbelievers that we already mentioned, or (b) do not confess that he is their Lord, as Thomas did (John 20:28), or they do so only with their tongue (Matt. 7:21–22), like Judas (Matt. 26:49).

The rebuking arguments
Now, (1) what could be imagined that is more shameful or intolerable to God, than to diminish or to oppose this one whom God exalted, and exalted to such a degree (ὑπερύψωσε, highly exalted), to whom he gave a name which is above every name, under whose feet he placed all things which are in heaven, on earth, and under the earth, whom he wills to be acknowledged and declared by all as Lord, and that for his own glory? (2) Will God by any means ever exalt such persons? Unless perhaps like Pharaoh's baker was exalted (Gen. 40:19). Will he not surely cast him from all his height, even into hell (Matt. 11:23)? (3) Will he not utterly blot their name out of the book of life, however famous and distinguished it was among men (Ps. 69:28)? (4) Will he not set them as a footstool for his feet (Ps. 110:1)? Will he not with his iron scepter dash them in pieces like a potter's vessel (Ps. 2:9)? Will he not cause them to perish in his fury (Ps. 2:12), and take care that they be slain before his sight (Luke 19:27)? (5) Will he not one day deny before his heavenly Father those who would not confess with their tongue that he is Lord (Matt. 10:33)?

3. It provides a foundation for: Trust

XVI. Third, Christ's exaltation provides a support and basis for: (1) trust, because they have a Savior, not only who was humble, who was fully man, who bore the form of a servant, who was in his appearance just like any common man, who was not only crucified (in which consists a scandal to the Jews, 1 Cor. 1:18, 23, and to all unbelievers), but one who in addition was in the form of God, equal to God, who had been exalted by God, and highly exalted, to whom God gave a name which is above every name, to whom every knee must bow, as much the heavenly as the terrestrial and the subterranean, and whom every tongue must confess to be Lord. Therefore, will we not surely rest secure by faith upon this one, who is so great and such a Mediator (Heb. 1:4–14; Isa. 10:20)? Through so great and such a Mediator, will we not hasten with boldness to the throne of grace in every circumstance (Heb. 4:14 with v. 16)? Will so great and such a Mediator not be sufficient for us for all things? The one in whom is all fullness (Col. 1:19; 2:9), from whom accordingly we can draw grace for grace (John 1:14, 16), in whom alone we can be complete (Col. 2:10). Compare the practice of chapter 2, on the Mediator.[17]

Boasting

Next, (2) it provides a foundation for Christian boasting (Phil. 1:26; 3:3). While entirely nothing is supplied for Christians in which they may boast, all things are supplied in their Mediator, who has been exalted by God, who has from him a name that is above every name, to whom all things that are in heaven, on earth, and under the earth must bow the knee, whom every tongue must confess to be Lord, who is the Lord of glory (1 Cor. 2:8), King of kings, Lord of lords (Rev. 19:16).

Worship

Finally, (3) it provides a foundation for all religious worship. For we do not worship idols that have no eyes to see (Ps. 115:5–8), as the Gentiles do; nor do we worship angels, our fellow servants (Rev. 19:10; 22:8), nor do we worship Abraham, Isaac, Jacob, the blessed Virgin, and other saints in heaven (Isa. 63:16), as the papists, nor a mere man,[18] as the Socinians, but we worship the one whom God has highly exalted, to whom he has given a name which is above every name, under whom he has put all things, to whom all things in heaven, on earth, and under the earth must bow their knee, whom every tongue must confess to be Lord, to the glory of the Father.

---

17. 1.5.2 §XXXIII

18. ψιλὸν ἄνϑρωπον

4. It provides an argument for humiliation. Motives

XVII. Fourth, Christ's exaltation provides us with an argument for the most profound humiliation, that the more God exalted him, the more we should humble ourselves before him, and the more readily we should bow our knee to him. For if: (1) when he was still in the state of humiliation, in the form of a servant, in appearance like any common man, at certain lighter evidences of his divine excellence, making a comparison between his excellence and his own baseness, Peter fell to his knees before Jesus saying, "Depart from me, Lord, for I am a sinful man!" (Luke 5:8), as did Mary (John 11:32), and Jairus (Mark 5:22), and the woman with an issue of blood (Luke 8:47), and the Syrophoenician Gentile woman (Mark 7:25). If (2) at his glorification to a certain extent on the mount, the disciples who were present fell humble to the ground before him on their face, and feared greatly (Matt. 17:6). Indeed, if (3) when he was not yet glorified, the devils themselves, in those they had possessed, when they first saw him fell down before him, crying out, "You are the Son of God" (Mark 3:11), then what would we not do before him now so solemnly glorified? Especially if (4) we should ponder the appropriateness and equity of the matter: for if God has exalted him above us all, is it not most equitable that we should cast ourselves down before him? If (5) God has given him a name which is above every name, that is, a glory which is above every glory, should we not say with the psalmist in Psalm 115:1, "Not to us, O Lord, not to us, but to your name give glory"? Should not we, with the elders in Revelation, cast our crowns at his feet (Rev. 4:10)? If (6) he has given all authority to him in heaven and on earth (Matt. 28:18), if he has put all things under his feet (Ps. 8:5–6), if he wills that every knee, the heavenly, the earthly, and the subterranean, must be bowed to him—in all these things is there not cause for us to most deeply humble ourselves before him? If (7) from God's commandment, every tongue must confess that he is Lord, is it not our part, as servants, to submit ourselves to him (cf. Mal. 1:6)?

The components of this humiliation

Adduced by these and similar motives, let us humble ourselves before Christ, inwardly as well as outwardly, and certainly first inwardly, with respect to: (1) our intellect, with humility or humiliation of mind,[19] wherein we with reverent attention compare our baseness with Christ's highness, and when we have acknowledged our immeasurable distance from him, we think of ourselves most humbly, as Agur says to Ithiel and Uchal,[20] that is, "God with me" and "I will pre-

---

19. ταπεινοφροσύνῃ *seu* ταπεινώσει τῆς φρενός
20. אִתִיאֵל וְאֻכָל. Cf. 1.5.4 §XI.

vail" (by which Christ is designated, cf. Isa. 7:14), "Surely, I am more foolish than any man, and there is not in me the understanding of a man" (Prov. 30:1–3; Job 42:5–6; Gen. 18:27, 31). (2) With respect to our will, wherein we are humble in heart[21] (Matt. 11:29), we readily subject our will to his (2 Cor. 10:5), we will that which he wills (Rev. 2:6), as the Savior himself did (Matt. 26:39; Phil. 2:7–8), and we set his glorification before us as our highest end (Phil. 1:20; Ps. 115:1), being to this end prepared to be least in the world (John 1:27), to undergo all the most dreadful things for his glory (Acts 20:24). Yet we should humble ourselves before Christ not only inwardly, but second, also outwardly, by most willingly offering all the outward signs of inward humility and reverence, for example, by bowing the knee, and so forth (Phil. 2:10; etc.).

5. It invites us to render the duties suited to his exaltation:
The exaltation of the heart
XVIII. Fifth, the exaltation invites us to faithfully render to the exalted one the duties suited to his exaltation. And what then are they? I respond: (1) the exaltation of the heart, wherein, in our esteem and love, the one whom God exalted we also should exalt (Phil. 1:20), and just as God exalted him above all things, ὑπερύψωσε, so also we should raise him up above father and mother, that is, above our most beloved things (Matt. 10:37), above ourselves, and also our own life (Matt. 10:39; Mark 8:36; 1 John 5:4), even above the heavens themselves (Ps. 73:25), to such a degree that in relation to him we count all other things as nothing, as dung, as loss (Phil. 3:7–9), that passing by all others, we rest in him alone (Ps. 16:5–6), that he should be for us one worth them all, in whom alone we are complete (Col. 2:10).

The glorification of the mouth
(2) The glorification of the mouth, wherein, to the one whom God gave a name which is above every name, we also should freely give ourselves, by celebrating him (Rev. 4:8–11): (a) from the excellence of his divine nature (Rom. 9:5), from which all things apply to him which we spoke of concerning God's majesty and glory in book 2, chapter 22; (b) from the dignity of the person of the God-man, as he is Immanuel (Isa. 7:14) and Ithiel (Prov. 30:1), the child and the son (Isa. 9:5), absorbing the perfections of both natures; (c) from the excellence of the mediatorial office (1 Tim. 2:5; Heb. 8:6; 9:15; 12:24), and its prophetic (Deut. 18:15, 18–20), high-priestly (Ps. 110:4; Heb. 7:26–27; 8:1, 3), and kingly dignity (Ps. 2:6); (d) from the incarnation (1 Tim. 3:16), which the angels themselves

---

21. ταπεινοὶ τῇ καρδίᾳ

celebrate (Luke 2:13–14); (e) from his virtues, which he displayed throughout his whole life, as an example (Isa. 11:1–2); (f) from his miracles, which he performed throughout his entire life, and in every kind of creature (Luke 24:19; Acts 2:22); and thus furthermore, (g) from his gracious actions, the resurrection, ascension, session at the right hand, return to judge the living and the dead, and so forth.

The submission of the whole person. The confession of the tongue.
(3) The submission of the entire human composite, wherein we should reverently and devoutly bow our knee to him, we should kiss him (Ps. 2:12), we should willingly subject and make captive to him the inner workings of our thoughts and reasonings (2 Cor. 10:5), which occurs: (a) by obedience most precisely rendered to his decisions and laws (Heb. 5:9; 2 Thess. 1:8); (b) by receiving and bearing his rebukes and chastisements peacefully and patiently (Rev. 3:10, 19; 2:3, 10), and that in a manner neither feigned (Eph. 6:5; Col. 3:22–23) nor forced (1 Peter 5:2), the manner in which hypocrites and also unclean spirits, willing or not, bow their knees to him (Mark 3:11). (4) The confession of the tongue, wherein we should fearlessly confess his name, that is, the gospel truth which professes that Jesus Christ is Lord (Rev. 3:8; Matt. 10:33; Mark 8:35, 38; 1 Peter 3:15).

Motives
By these duties therefore we should exalt Christ, because: (1) God has exalted him, and commanded that we must exalt him (Phil. 2:9–10). (2) He deserves to be exalted: "Wherefore God has highly exalted him"; "You, O Lord, are worthy to receive glory and honor and power" (Rev. 4:11). (3) In his exaltation, our exaltation is accomplished, insofar as he is our head, and we his members (Eph. 1:22–23). (4) If we have exalted him, then he in turn will exalt us, by the law of retribution[22] (1 Sam. 2:30, 1, 8; Phil. 3:21; John 12:32; 17:24). On the contrary, (5) if we have not exalted him in our duties, God will exalt him in our downfall and destruction (Ps. 110:1; 2:2–3 with vv. 5, 9). Compare book 2, chapter 22, on God's majesty and glory; likewise book 5, chapter 3 with respect to the practice of the name "our Lord"; likewise chapter 8 on the Mediator as a king; and below in the chapter on his session at the right hand; and finally, the practice of each degree of his exaltation, namely his resurrection, ascension, session, and so forth.[23]

---

22. *jure talionis*

23. 1.2.22 §XVI; 1.5.3 §XLI; 1.5.8 §XX; 1.5.15 §§XXII–XXIII; 1.5.16 §XIX; 1.5.17 §XXII; 1.5.18 §§XLV–XLVI

CHAPTER FIFTEEN

The Resurrection of the Mediator

Now when Jesus had risen in the morning on the first day of the week, he appeared first to Mary Magdalene....

—Mark 16:9

The first degree of exaltation is the resurrection.
I. Now we progress to a discussion of each degree of exaltation separately, beginning from the first, through which the Savior was exalted above death and the grave, that is, by the resurrection from the dead.

The Exegetical Part

The text is opened.
II. Mark concludes the history of the resurrection with a certain summary[1] (16:9), in which three things are prominent:

    A. The resurrection: "when Jesus had risen." In this, observe:

        1. The person rising: "Jesus," the God-man. The same one who had fallen in death was the same one who had risen again, according to the preceding verses. Therefore, he had not passed by death into a state of nonexistence, for that which does not exist, does not rise again. "Jesus," with respect to both natures, the divine as well as the human, about which we will say more in its own place in the dogmatic part.[2]

        2. The act of rising: "when he had risen," ἀναστάς. This denotes the person who rose, not the time, as if he had appeared to Mary Magdalene immediately after the resurrection. Those who do not heed this have expunged this clause, with the same recklessness with which some have expunged this whole chapter, and again others the entire

---

1. ἀνακεφαλαιώσει
2. §§III, VII, below

first part of this chapter, because they judged that in it was an irreconcilable conflict with Matthew's narrative (Matt. 18:1–9). He "rose," that is, by a reunion of the essential parts of the body and soul, and by leaving the tomb, about which we likewise will say more in the dogmatic part.[3]

B.	The time of the resurrection, which is twofold:

1.	In a narrower sense: "in the morning," πρωΐ. In Matthew 28:1, ὀψὲ δὲ σαββάτων, ἐπιφωσκούσῃ εἰς μίαν σαββάτων, "and on the evening of the Sabbath, with the sun dawning toward the first day of the week." In Luke 24:1, τῇ δὲ μιᾷ τῶν σαββάτων, ὄρθρου βαθέος, "Now on the first day of the week, at early dawn," they came. In John 20:1, "Mary Magdalene comes early in the morning, while it was still dark." From these words, Maldonado, on Matthew 28:1, concludes that his passage, a parallel of ours, is in the judgment of all most difficult, because not only does it seem to contradict itself, insofar as it places ὀψέ, "evening," with ἐπιφωσκούσῃ, "with it dawning" (namely, the sun), but also it seems to disagree with the remaining Gospels, and others for this reason have expunged the whole of the chapter of our passage in Mark, or at least up to our verse.[4] Grotius more correctly says on the same passage that if there may be something obscure or apparently contradictory[5] here, it comes from the error, not of the writers, but of the readers; indeed, he does not see in these narratives that there is such a great amount of difficulty.[6] Different people endeavor to reconcile the texts in different ways. There are those who think that the ὀψὲ must be taken more broadly for the entire night that followed the Sabbath, even when it was then receding, so that they make space here for daybreak; and in support of this they adduce a passage in Gellius (bk. 7, ch. 21): "When two periods of time are opposed to each other, and yet are so closely connected that the end of one coincides with the beginning of the other, it makes no difference whether the exact point of their meeting is designated by the end of the first period or the beginning of the second."[7] So then therefore,

---

3. §V, below

4. Maldonado, *Commentarii in quatuor evangelistas*, 1:661–64.

5. ἐναντιοφανές

6. Grotius, *Annotationes in libros evangeliorum* in *Opera omnia theologica*, 2-1:279–80.

7. In early modern editions, this citation of bk. 7, ch. 21 is correct, e.g. Aulus Gellius, *Noctes Atticae* (Cologne, 1576), 170; but in modern editions, see bk. 6, ch. 21, e.g. idem, *Attic Nights* in *LCL* 200:85.

Matthew calls ὀψέ, the evening, ἡ ἐπιφώσκουσα, the dawning day. To this some add that to the Hellenists[8] the night is sometimes called ὀψία, as the Hebrews use ערב (Gen. 1:5, 8, etc.; Ex. 16:6), and thus here ὀψὲ is "at night." Others distinguish a sacred from a civil ὀψία, so that what was an evening in relation to the sacred, in relation to the civil was night until daybreak. Still others distinguish among the women who hurried to the grave, such that some set out toward evening, and others toward dawn, or the same women twice, both toward evening and toward dawn. Most satisfying to me is Grotius: "Without doubt," he says, "the women had risen at first daybreak; while some wait for others, while they prepare the spices, while they go through the city, and then out of the city to the tomb, enough time easily passed so that upon arrival at the tomb, a bit of the sun had already appeared."[9] To this view, Dr. Lodewijk de Dieu seems to incline: "In our estimation," he says, "the women, in the very evening of the Sabbath, when from the custom of the Jews the first day of the week took its beginning, readied themselves for a trip to the tomb, on that trip bought spices, went out of the city, spent the whole night in the suburbs, and in the early morning, before the gates of the city were opened and they could be seen by anyone, hastened to the tomb. From that point, Mary ran ahead σκοτίας ἔτι οὔσης, 'while it was still dark' (John 20:1), then the rest came to the tomb ὄρθρου βαθέος, 'at early dawn' (Luke 24:1)."[10] And in this way there will be no opposition among the evangelists. Therefore it seems that he rose after the evening of the Jewish Sabbath ended, when day was already dawning, that is, when the first day of the week was beginning, between the evening of the Sabbath and daybreak of the first weekday; and moreover, that the women reached the tomb after he had already risen.

2. In a broader sense: "on the first day of the week," πρώτῃ σαββάτου, "on the first of the Sabbath"; in Luke 24:1, τῇ δὲ μίᾳ τῶν σαββάτων, "Now on the first of the Sabbath"; and thus in John 20:1, "On the first

---

8. Greek-speaking Jews. Cf. LXX Gen. 1:5.

9. Grotius, *Annotationes in Novum Testamentum* in *Opera omnia theologica*, 2-1:327.

10. For a comparative commentary on editions of the Gospels in Syriac, Arabic, Hebrew, and Latin, see Lodewijk de Dieu (1590–1642), *Animadversiones sive commentarius in quatuor evangelia, in quo collatis, Syri inprimis, Arabis, Evangelii Hebraei, Vulgati, Erasmi et Bezae versionibus, difficiliora quaeque loca illustrantur, et variae lectiones conferuntur; accessit appendix in Matthaeum, in quo cum praetermissa quaedam, tum Aethiopicae versionis nonnulla adduntur et expenduntur* (Leiden: Bonaventure and Abraham Elsevir, 1631), 148.

of the Sabbath," that is, on the first day after the Sabbath, namely the first day of the week. For "Sabbath" is employed for the week by a synecdoche of a member of it, because it is the last day of the week, on which it is completed. So also the teachers of the Jews everywhere called the weekdays the first, the second, the third of the Sabbath. Hence the statement in Leviticus 23:15, "You shall count seven whole שבתות, Sabbaths." The Hellenists, and likewise the Aramaic, Rabbi Saadia, and the Spanish Jews, translate it as "whole weeks,"[11] as they also do in Leviticus 25:8. And so from this common way of speaking, even the Gentiles in their weekly order called each day a "sabbatical day," that is, a weekday, as Selden notes.[12] Therefore, Christ rose again around the time that the evening of the Sabbath ended, that is, on the first of the week, nearing daybreak. After, that is, he had remained for three days in the tomb and under the dominion of death, according to the Scriptures. Thus from this he prescribed that day for Christians as their Sabbath. Moreover, he appeared to the women at first daybreak.

C. The first appearance: "He appeared to Mary Magdalene." Regarding this first appearance one will be able to see a more lengthy account in John 20:14–17.

The Dogmatic Part

Christ rose again on the third day. It is proved by the Scriptures.

III. Therefore it is more certain than certain that Christ rose again on the third day after his death. This is: (1) frequently read to have been predicted (1 Cor. 15:4), not only under the Old Testament (Ps. 16:10 with Acts 2:27, 31; Isa. 55:3 with Acts 13:34; Ps. 68:18 with Eph. 4:8; Ps. 110:7; Isa. 53:8–10; Dan. 9:26; Hos. 6:2; 11:11; 13:14; cf. Mic. 2:13), but also under the New Testament, by the very one who would rise again (John 2:19; Matt. 12:38–40; 16:1, 4; 17:12, 23; Luke 18:33). Likewise, (2) prefigured, in Adam, when he awoke (Gen. 2:21), Isaac (Gen. 22:11; Heb. 11:18–19), Joseph, who was imprisoned for three years but afterward established as the lord of the entirety of Egypt (Gen. 37:28 with 41:41), Jonah (Jonah 1:17 with Matt. 12:40). Compare the bush that was burning yet not consumed (Ex. 3:2), Aaron's rod that was dry yet became green again

---

11. *hebdomadas integras*

12. Mastricht's sources here are found in John Selden (1584–1654), *De anno civili et calendario veteris ecclesiae seu reipublicae Judaicae* (London: Richard Bishop, 1644), 30–31; idem, *Opera omnia*, 3 vols. (London: William Bowyer, 1726), 1:15.

(Num. 17:8 with Isa. 11:1), Samson breaking through the gate at night (Judg. 16:3), Daniel delivered from the lions' den (Dan. 6:17–18, 24). Add the flesh of the thanksgiving sacrifice, which had to be eaten before the third day (Lev. 7:16–18). (3) Fulfilled, according to the history of the New Testament and its whole series of events, in which the body came forth from a new, stone tomb (Luke 23:53; John 19:41); and that it was not removed by theft is easily established from the fearfulness of the disciples, and the watch of soldiers posted at the tomb. (4) Witnessed, by the statements: (a) of the angels, who published it at the tomb itself, indeed and demonstrated it to the women with a rebuke (Luke 24:5; Matt. 28:7); (b) of the tomb itself, "Behold the place where he lay" (Mark 16:6); add, (c) of Jesus himself (Mark 16:9; 1 Cor. 15:6); (d) of the women (John 20:18; Matt. 28:9); (e) of the apostles (John 20:20, 25; Acts 10:41); and (f) of the soldiers (Matt. 28:11–13). (5) Demonstrated, by very frequent appearances, of which at least ten are noted by learned men. Indeed, (6) confirmed, by the testimony of the very senses themselves, insofar as he very frequently presented himself to be seen, heard, and touched.

And by reasons
IV. Not only did he more certainly than certain rise again, but he also necessarily had to rise again (Acts 2:24). The foundation of this necessity adheres in: (1) the eternal decree of God, whereby the things that regard his resurrection were determined just as much as those that concern his death (Acts 2:23–24); (2) the predictions of Scripture (1 Cor. 15:4), already reviewed; (3) the very person of the Christ who rises, whereby he was not only the Lord's Holy One (Ps. 16:10), but also bore a human nature which had been united with the divine person, and hence could not be consumed; (4) his glorification, into which he necessarily had to enter (Luke 24:26); (5) his mediatorial office, whereby he had to conquer death, and free us from death (Hos. 13:14; 1 Cor. 15:54–57); (6) the eternity of the mediatorial kingdom (Luke 1:33); (7) the necessity of the entrance into the heavenly sanctuary (Heb. 9:24), of sending the Holy Spirit from there (John 16:7), of putting away sins (Heb. 9:26); (8) in his prerogatives, by which he had to be a life-giving spirit (1 Cor. 15:21, 45); (9) the last judgment of the living and the dead, which is destined for him (John 5:27). From all these points, it is most clear that he necessarily had to rise from the dead.

The nature and components of this resurrection
V. This resurrection of the Savior, wherein from the state and place of the dead he was exalted into glorious life, generally includes these three components: (1) revivification, through which the essential parts of human nature, body and

soul, though united in their own way in the divine person, yet separated from each other through death, were restored and reunited anew. (2) Glorious transmutation, by which first the soul, if it was not endowed with new perfections, as pleases some, at least was recalled from the state preternatural to it, that of the separation from the body, to the state native to it; and the body obtained incorruptibility and glory (Phil. 3:21; Acts 13:34; Rom. 6:9–10; Heb. 2:9, 14; Matt. 26:29), that of spiritual and heavenly bodies (on which see 1 Cor. 15:42–43, 53). Yet in such a way that he by no means set aside the nature of the human body, its finitude, locality, and palpability; nor could he have set these aside without the destruction of the human nature. (3) Departure from the tomb, whereby with the linen cloths left there, by which he had been as it were shackled under the dominion of death, he came forth to the living (Matt. 28:6).

In what sort of body he rose
VI. Yet we must discuss a little more distinctly the sort of body in which he rose: namely, one that was: (1) true (Luke 24:39; 1 John 1:1); (2) his own (Luke 24:39; John 20:20, 27); (3) immortal (Rom. 6:9; Rev. 1:18); (4) glorified, no longer liable to any infirmities, to weariness, hunger, thirst, sorrows, and other things. Although this glory of his body was especially visible only after the ascension (2 Cor. 13:4; Rev. 1:14; Phil. 3:21).

The causes of the resurrection: The principal cause
VII. The causes of the resurrection he experienced in two kinds: (1) the principal cause, the entire most holy Trinity: the Father (Acts 2:32; Eph. 1:20); himself (John 2:19, 21; 10:17), so that for this reason it is said that he was powerfully demonstrated to be the Son of God, according to the Spirit of sanctification, from the resurrection from the dead (Rom. 1:4), namely by virtue of his divine nature, and not of some divine power communicated to his human nature through the personal union; and the Holy Spirit (Rom. 8:11; 1 Peter 3:18). The foundation of this cooperation is certainly in the unity of the strength which is common to the three persons, from which all the operations *ad extra* are procured, but nevertheless with there being observed, on account of each person's different mode of subsisting, also their different order of operating, such that the Father through the Son and the Spirit of sanctification (Rom. 1:4) raised the human nature of the Son.

The ministerial cause
(2) The cause of his departure from the grave which was in its own way ministerial, was the angel who rolled back the stone from the opening of the tomb (Matt.

28:2), who was employed certainly not from any lack in the divine nature—just as neither was the angel who strengthened him in his agony employed for this reason (Luke 22:43)—but from choice, to increase the majesty of this resurrection.

The time of the resurrection: 1. The third day

VIII. The time of this resurrection was: (1) the third day from his death or descent (1 Cor. 15:4), because: (a) so it seemed good to God in the eternal counsel of the decree, by which all things that concern his death as well as his resurrection were predetermined (Acts 2:23). (b) So the Old Testament prophecies had it, namely, that he would not see corruption (Ps. 16:10), as the corpse of Lazarus did after three days shut up in the tomb (John 11:39). (c) So it was prefigured in Jonah (Matt. 12:40). (d) So the one who would rise foretold it (Matt. 12:40; 16:21; 17:23; Mark 8:31). Moreover, the counting of these three days should be made this way: on the day of preparation, which coincides with our Friday, he was laid in the grave (John 19:42); for the entire Jewish Sabbath he rested in the tomb (Matt. 27:62); on the day just after, which was the *primus* σαββάτων, first day of the week, at first daybreak, he rose again (Mark 16:9). And thus it must be observed that in the Scriptures whole days and nights not infrequently stand for parts of them (e.g. 1 Sam. 30:12 with v. 13; Est. 4:16 with 5:1). With this presupposed, some begin these three days from the first moment of his crucifixion, in which, although he was not yet dead and buried, yet he was under the state and power of death and darkness. Others, a little more strictly, begin them from his death, which occurred around midday (Matt. 17:23 with Luke 24:21; John 2:19). Others, most strictly, begin them from the time of his burial (Matt. 12:30). Others, most broadly, by these three days understand the entire time of humiliation which proceeded from the Last Supper until the first evening on which he showed himself alive to his disciples, which makes three whole days. There are also several who assert that the calculation can be made from the Roman reckoning, which begins the day from midnight. Whatever may be, you will speak of the three days correctly if by synecdoche, under these three days and their parts, you should include the nights, which was most often done among the Jews and in Scripture, as we have already taught (cf. Gen. 1:5; etc.). Moreover, for what reasons he willed to stay in the grave for precisely three days, there is no reason for us to anxiously investigate. Nevertheless, these causes can be observed: that he willed not to stay longer in the tomb, seems to have been partly so that his body would not experience putrefaction (Ps. 16:10), and partly so that he would not suspend the hope of believers for too long (Luke 24:21). That he willed not to come out sooner, seems to have been partly so that he would render his death more certain, and partly so that he would have an occasion for sanctifying the Lord's Day as the Sabbath for Christians, about which we will speak presently.

2. The first day of the week

IX. The time of the resurrection (2) was ἡ μία σαββάτων, the first day of the week, because when the Jewish Sabbath, a figure and type of his rest in the grave (as we showed in ch. 13, §VIII), ceased, he willed to substitute for it the Christian Sabbath, for which reason this day is called the Lord's Day (Rev. 1:10), namely after the Lord and founder of the Sabbath (Matt. 12:8), just as the Supper, after the same Lord, is celebrated as the Lord's Supper (1 Cor. 11:20, 23). Also, to this end he stood on that very day among the disciples who had gathered together in his name, and bestowed a sabbatical blessing (John 20:19). And who would determine that Christ, immediately after his resurrection, either in the first meeting with the disciples, or at least during his conversation with the disciples during the forty days, when he spoke about matters which pertain to the kingdom of God (Acts 1:3), did not determine this day to be the New Testament Sabbath? Whatever may be, at the least this day was in use in the apostolic church (1 Cor. 16:1–2; Acts 20:7), before any ecclesiastical constitutions, distinct from apostolic constitutions, had been received into the church. Thus certain persons, serving their own hypotheses, wrongly refer it to the constitutions of the primitive church that followed the apostolic church; about which we will speak more fully, if God should will, in its own place.[13]

3. The early morning of that day

X. Finally, the most defined time of this resurrection (3) was the early morning, πρωΐ. Namely, after he had fulfilled both the prophecies, and the figures, and his work, he did not will to remain long idle in the grave, but at the first beginning of the morning he girded himself anew for labor, and also willed by his own example to determine that the beginning of the Christian Sabbath was to be taken from daybreak. So then the resurrection of Christ by no means fell on the evening of the Sabbath (that is, while the Sabbath still remained), as pleased many of the ancients, and in particular, the Syriac version, because in Matthew 28:1 is said, ὀψὲ δὲ σαββάτων, "Now on the evening of the Sabbath"; nor precisely at midnight, as pleased Cyril, Ambrose, and Jerome; but during the evening of the Sabbath, as it began and was dawning toward the first of the week: this is what

13. 2.2.15

Matthew intends by ὀψὲ τῶν σαββάτων, ἐπιφωσκούσῃ εἰς μίαν σαββάτων (Matt. 28:1), as we have observed in the exegetical part.[14]

The four properties of the resurrection
XI. The manner of the resurrection, whereby it differs from every resurrection of others, is evident in these properties and circumstances: that it was (1) most powerful, insofar as it was procured not by the strength of another, but by his very own, for which reason he is not only said to have been raised, by another, but also to have risen, by his own strength (Matt. 28:6; John 2:19; 10:18), so much so that by his own resurrection he had declared himself to be the Son of God in power (Rom. 1:4). Accordingly, (2) plainly miraculous, conjoined with an earthquake, and under the ministry of angels, who not only rolled back the stone so that it would be more convenient for him to leave the tomb, but also who declared to people the resurrection after it occurred (Matt. 28:2ff.). Hence, (3) also exceedingly glorious, insofar as he not only came forth attended by a band of angels, but he also all but tormented the enemy guards with fear and trembling (Matt. 28:4), and as a victorious conqueror over the devil, death, hell, and the entire power of darkness (1 Cor. 15:55–56), showed himself to be the one who carries in his power the keys of the infernal pit, and all its inhabitants (Rev. 1:18). Finally, (4) springing forth with the sweetest comfort, from which the angels say to the trembling women, "Fear not," and he himself, by frequently appearing to his own, stirred up and confirmed their faith and trust, when they were assembled in one place for fear of their enemies, pronounced to them peace, and supplied them other things that made for their comfort and tranquility, as the evangelists witness (Matt. 28; Luke 24; John 20).

The use of the resurrection concerns: 1. Christ himself
XII. The end and use of the resurrection, first, concerns Christ, the very one who rises, insofar as by it was demonstrated: (1) his holiness, indeed that he was the Holy One of Israel (Isa. 10:20), whom, as the promised Messiah, the Father sanctified and sent into the world (John 10:36), which is evident from the resurrection (Ps. 16:10; Acts 2:31). Also (2) his eternal deity (Rom. 1:4), insofar as he rose by his own strength (John 10:18). In addition, (3) his infinite power, by which he was able to crush the head of the infernal serpent (Gen. 3:17), like the strong man Samson to break open the gates, even of hell (Judg. 16:3), to take away the sting from death, the venom from hell (1 Cor. 15:55–56), and the power from the devil (Heb. 2:14), and thus show that he is Lord both

---

14. §II.B.1, above

of the living and the dead (Rom. 14:9). Finally, (4) his heavenly glory, which he necessarily had to enter into through his resurrection (Luke 24:26), and obtain that name which is above every name (Phil. 2:9–10), and thus be crowned with glory and honor (Heb. 2:7).

2. Christians

Second, the use of the resurrection concerns Christians, inasmuch as to them this resurrection: (1) seals the fullest victory over death and the entire power of darkness (1 Cor. 15:57; Col. 2:15). (2) It makes indubitable that most exact satisfaction which was supplied for their sins (Rom. 4:25; 1 Cor. 15:17), because the surety and expromissor is not released from prison before he has exhausted the guilt (cf. Matt. 5:26; 18:34). (3) It opens the way for the benefits which are customarily dispensed through the remaining degrees of exaltation, the ascension into heaven and session at the right hand of God: for example, for his unceasing intercession for us (Rom. 8:34; Heb. 7:16–17 with vv. 24–25), for the sending of the Holy Spirit (John 16:7), the begetting of faith through the gift of the spirit of faith to us (2 Cor. 4:13), and others which we will speak of more specifically in the subsequent degrees of exaltation. (4) It supplies to them the ground,[15] exemplar, and beginning of a blessed resurrection, as much spiritual as corporal, insofar as: (a) he makes alive those who are by nature dead in sins (Eph. 2:5–6); (b) he supplies to them an example to which they may compose themselves in their spiritual resurrection (Rom. 6:5); (c) and an indubitable foreshadowing of the blessed natural resurrection that will one day follow, because they have been united, as members with their head (Rom. 6:5).

The conversation of Christ with the apostles after the resurrection, through the forty days until the ascension

XIII. It remains for us to briefly touch upon Christ's life and deeds from the resurrection to his ascension, through forty days in all (Acts 1:3). First, he presents himself to be seen by Mary Magdalene, and after a few words, also to be recognized (Mark 16:9), from which the certainty of the resurrection began to spread to the disciples (John 20:14–18). Second, he appeared again to the women as they returned from the tomb (Matt. 28:9–10). Third, he presents himself as a companion to the two disciples traveling to Emmaus, he instructs them from Scripture of the necessity of the humiliation and exaltation of the Messiah, and at last in the breaking and distribution of the bread he presents himself to be recognized (Luke 24:13–31; Mark 16:12). Then also he appears to Peter (Luke

---

15. *hypostasin*

24:34), and to the rest of the apostles, although Thomas is absent, and he presents himself to them to be handled, he eats bread with them, certainly not by necessity, but by usefulness for conversation and movement, so that he might deprive them of all potential to doubt his resurrection (John 20:24–25; 21:4–6). Fourth, again after eight days, when Thomas is there, he is present with his own, and to Thomas he presents his hands and side to be examined (John 20:26). Furthermore, in Galilee he appears to his disciples while they are fishing on the Sea of Tiberias, he searches out Peter as to the sincerity of his love toward him, repeatedly commits the pastoral office to him, and teaches other things (John 21). Again, he appears to the apostles on a mountain in Galilee (Matt. 28:16ff.), at some point also to five hundred and more brethren at once, then again to James (1 Cor. 15:6–7). Finally, when all the apostles have been led to the Mount of Olives near Bethany, and he is about to ascend to heaven, he speaks about matters that concern the kingdom of God (Acts 1:4–9, 12). That is, he without doubt deals with the proclamation of the gospel, the formation of the churches, the dispensation of the sacraments, church discipline, the sanctification of the Lord's Day as the Christian Sabbath, and other things that are not so distinctly expressed in the sacred text, and he promises to them the presence of his grace, even to the end of the ages (Matt. 28:16ff.; Mark 16:14–19; John 21:44ff.; 1 Cor. 11:23). So that it is entirely agreeable to reason that the apostles drew from these last words of Christ the majority of those things which they constituted in the churches in regard to church government and order,[16] the observance of the Lord's Day, and other rituals.

The Elenctic Part

It is asked: 1. Did Jesus truly rise again?
XIV. Regarding the resurrection, it is disputed, first, whether Christ truly rose again from the dead. There are not any among Christians who deny it, except perhaps those who falsely allege that he died by an illusion.[17] The Jews once tenaciously denied it, and deny it even still; when they were gathered in a most full festal assembly, Peter in a single sermon convicted them so powerfully that on one day about three thousand were added to them (Acts 2:40–41). And so that we also may convict the Jews of our day—if not with the same success, at least with some—it will help in conversation with them to observe this method, that: (1) by the examples of Peter (Acts 2:24–33) and Paul (Acts 13:32–38), above all we demonstrate that the once promised Messiah had both to die and

---

16. εὐταξίαν
17. *per phantasma*

to rise again (Luke 24:25), to which end the prophecies and figures aim which were adduced in §III. Then (2) we should compare their fulfillment, from the history of the evangelists, and other testimonies of the New Testament. And so that these things may bind them more strongly, it will help (3) to have arguments ready by which both the universal truth of the New Testament and its divine authority can be demonstrated, which we have furnished in book 1, chapter 2.[18] Finally, (4) all those arguments can be added by which we demonstrate that our Jesus is the promised Messiah. For if the Messiah had to rise from the dead according to the Scriptures, and our Jesus is the Messiah, who could doubt that he rose again? Therefore, with these things successfully supplied, I do not see what, at least with any appearance of truth, the Jews could undertake against the resurrection of Christ.

2. Is the resurrection nothing other than to exist again after not existing?

XV. Second, it is asked whether the resurrection of Christ is nothing other than to exist again after not existing. The Socinians affirm it in express words (thus Smalcius in *On the Divinity of Christ*, ch. 13),[19] namely, as to them to die is to no longer exist, so to them to rise again is to exist again, and the descent of Christ to hell is to them nothing other than a certification of the state of nonexistence into which the Savior descended, by the truth of his death. Christians, on the contrary, in agreement with the Scriptures, think that a resurrection is nothing other than a reunion of the essential parts of body and soul, which are indeed separated by death, but still existing. We expressly destroyed the foundations of the Socinian opinion in chapter 12, §XVIII and chapter 13, §XI, and we do not add anything here, except that the Socinian opinion in fact takes away: (1) the resurrection of Christ, to which they want to seem to attribute so much, indeed even more, than to his death, since such a resurrection is not anything but a new creation of a new body. (2) All resurrection of the flesh altogether, for the very definition of the term demands that the *cadaver* of a human being (which is derived from *cadendum*, "falling," in Hebrew, Greek, and Latin) be raised up and awakened from its fall by which it was laid low, so that there may be a true ἀνάστασις, as John of Damascus elegantly interpreted the term: δευτέρα τοῦ πεπτωκότος στάσις, "a second standing of that which had fallen."[20]

---

18. 1.1.2, §§XXXI–XXXII

19. Smalcius, *De divinitate Jesu Christi*, 79.

20. John of Damascus, *Expositio accurata fidei orthodoxae* in *PG* 94:1220; idem, *Exposition of the Orthodox Faith* in *NPNF2* 8:99a.

Objections

Meanwhile the Socinians allege for their own opinion, besides what we adduced in the cited place in chapter 12: (1) that from this second existence of the resurrection he is called the firstborn from the dead (Col. 1:18; Rev. 1:5). I respond: (a) This is false, for by this reasoning Christ would have been begotten two or three times, namely first from eternity (Ps. 2:7), next from the blessed Virgin, and finally through the resurrection. Rather, (b) he is so called by right and authority of primogeniture, by which he is Lord of the living and the dead (Rom. 14:9), which belongs to him from his eternal generation, from which he is called the firstborn over all creation (Col. 1:15). (2) That he is called the firstfruits of those who have fallen asleep (1 Cor. 15:20). I respond, Certainly not from any new existence received through the resurrection, but from that blessing by which through the resurrection of Christ the whole mass of believers rising again was sanctified, according to Romans 11:16, "If the firstfruits are holy, so also is the mass." (3) That he is thus called the Father of eternity, אבי עד (Isa. 9:6), because from such a resurrection of his, a beginning was made of living an eternal life, just as from Adam a beginning was made of living a perishable life, as Smalcius says (*On the Divinity of Christ*, ch. 13).[21] I respond: (a) Such a resurrection of Christ is nothing but a chimera. (b) He could not by his resurrection be the Father and author of eternity for his own, if he did not have eternal life in himself (John 5:26), as one who was himself true God (1 John 5:20).

3. Did he rise again by his own power, that of his divine nature alone?
XVI. Third, it is asked whether he rose again by his own strength, that of his divine nature alone. The Socinians, because they deny the divine nature of Christ, are forced to deny the debated point.[22] The Lutherans, serving their own hypotheses, in which through the hypostatic union divine attributes were communicated to the human nature (and among them, divine power), do acknowledge that he was raised by the power of the divine nature, but they add that he was also raised by the human nature, by the strength of the divine power communicated to it. So then they state that Christ raised himself in three ways: (1) substantially,[23] by the strength proper to his divine nature; (2) hypostatically,[24] by the power communicated to him by the Father through eternal generation; (3) by communication,[25] according to the human nature through the personal union.

---

21. Smalcius, *De divinitate Jesu Christi*, 78–87, especially 80.

22. κρινόμενον

23. οὐσιωδῶς

24. ὑποστατικῶς

25. *per* συγκοινώνησιν

It is affirmed against the Socinians
The Reformed, first against the Socinians, affirm that Christ rose by his own strength, because: (1) this is said expressly (John 2:19; 10:18; 1 Cor. 15:45; Zech. 6:12; John 5:26; Acts 1:3). (2) It has already been demonstrated (bk. 2, ch. 26)[26] that he is true and eternal God, consubstantial with his Father, and that he assumed the human nature into the unity of the person.

Objections
To these things they wrongly oppose: (1) that he is said throughout to have been raised by the Father (Acts 2:24; Eph. 1:19–20). I respond, Things subordinate are not opposed here, for just as the Father is said to have delivered up the Son (Rom. 8:32), and the Son to have delivered up himself (Gal. 2:20; Eph. 5:2, 25); as the Father set the Son at his right hand (Eph. 1:20), and the Son himself sat down (Mark 16:19); as the Father subjected his enemies to him (Ps. 110:2), and he to himself (1 Cor. 15:25)—so also the Father raised him, and he raised himself, because there is one essential power of both persons. (2) They state that it is ridiculous for anyone to call himself back to life. I respond, It is not ridiculous to him who acknowledges with Scripture that there are two natures in Christ, such that the divine nature could raise the human nature. (3) That he demanded his resurrection from his Father (Ps. 16:8–10; Acts 2:26–27). I respond, It is not said in those passages that he demanded his resurrection from the Father; rather, he only relates the certainty of his future resurrection. Nor if it were said would it follow that he did not rise by his own strength. For Christ also could have raised Lazarus by his own strength (John 5:21), and nevertheless, in his prayers he referred to it as acceptable to the Father (John 11:42).

And also against the Lutherans
Then second, the Reformed maintain against the Lutherans that Christ by no means raised himself by the strength of the divine power communicated to the human nature through the hypostatic union, not only because the hypothesis of the divine power communicated through the hypostatic union to the human nature is a fiction, as we have expressly demonstrated in chapter 4,[27] but also because by this reasoning the human nature would have raised itself, which is absurd.

---

26. 1.2.26 §§VIII–XII, XVIII
27. 1.5.4 §XXIV

4. Did the body of Christ as it rose penetrate through the stone, and the shut door?
XVII. Fourth, it is asked whether the body of Christ as it rose penetrated through the stone rolled to the opening of the tomb, and the shut door. The Lutherans, so that they may more easily defend the presence of the flesh of Christ in the eucharistic bread, notwithstanding the penetration of dimensions, affirm both. The Reformed deny them, because: (1) Scripture has not even one whit of it. In fact, (2) all the evangelists expressly testify to the contrary, when they mention that there was an earthquake, and that the angel came from heaven to roll the stone away (Matt. 28:2; Mark 16:4; Luke 24:2; John 20:1). (3) A penetration of dimensions implies a most manifest contradiction, and takes away the very nature of a body; from which Christ would no longer be the God-man, or like us in all things, except for sin. I would add that (4) it contradicts the very hypotheses of our adversaries. For if the flesh of Christ possessed omnipresence from the personal union with respect to κτῆσις, possession, and from glorification with respect to χρῆσις, use, in what way could he change place by penetrating?

Objections
There is not anything that they may oppose, except: (1) that the angel rolled back the stone after the resurrection had already happened. I respond, It is denied; let them prove it. He moved it away, they insist, so that he might show to the women who were coming that it had happened, for which reason the angel, as it were with his index finger pointing toward the tomb, employs the address, "He is risen; he is not here: see the place where he lay." I respond, Things subordinate are not opposed: the angel removed the stone when Christ was about to leave it, then at last when the women came the angel showed them the place where the Savior had lain. (2) If he could raise himself, he could also rise while the tomb was shut by the stone. I respond, (a) It is not valid to argue from what can be to what is. (b) It is a dissimilar reckoning, because a penetration of dimensions implies a contradiction, and destroys the truth of the human body. (3) He declared powerfully by his resurrection that he is the Son of God (Rom. 1:4): now what sort of argument would it be if he needed the help of someone else to open the tomb? I respond: (a) It is not from need that he employed the angel's ministry, but from the abundance of his authority, inasmuch as it extends even over angels (Heb. 1:14), just as for the sake of revealing his resurrection he made use of the ministry of angels, not from need, but from the abundance of his authority. Then also (b) notwithstanding this angelic ministry in removing the stone, by his resurrection he most powerfully demonstrated that he is the Son of God, insofar as he made himself alive by his own power. (4) John 20:19, "And when it was evening, on that day, the first of the week, and the doors were shut

where the disciples were assembled for fear of the Jews, Jesus came and stood in the midst": therefore, he penetrated through shut doors. I respond, It does not say, διὰ τῶν θυρῶν κεκλεισμένων, "through the shut doors," which is the only thing disputed here; rather, only the time is designated when he came to them, namely evening, when the doors had been shut.

5. Did he rise with a glorified body?

XVIII. Fifth, it is asked whether he rose with a glorified body. The Socinians deny that the body which he possessed in the resurrection was glorified, but say that it received glorification only after the ascension. The Reformed, as they confess the splendor of the glorified body was more apparent and recognized after the ascension, so they think that it possessed this glorification immediately after the resurrection, for the reasons noted in the dogmatic part, §V, through which it cannot be imagined that believers in their resurrection receive immortality and incorruptibility, indeed even glory, as Paul witnesses (1 Cor. 15:52–54), and Christ did not receive it.

The objections of the Socinians
Meanwhile, our adversaries urge: (1) that he ate and drank (Luke 24:42–43). I respond: He did so adduced not by necessity, but by his will: not by hunger, but so that he might prove to his disciples that he was not a spirit or a specter. (2) That he displayed the stripes and scars of the wounds on his hands and feet (Job 20:25). I respond, He certainly did not show them due to weakness, but so that he might make them more certain that it was he, the one who died, as Thomas urges (John 20:25, 27). (3) That the place of glorification is in heaven. I respond, Certainly that is the ordinary place, but it is not repugnant to this for glorification to occur also extraordinarily on earth, as is evident in Moses and Elijah, who were glorified with Christ (Matt. 17). (4) That he asks to be glorified, certainly through the ascension and session at the right hand of God (John 17:24). I respond, Indeed, but this is no hindrance from his having been glorified also previously, and in the resurrection (John 12:28; 1:14).

6. Is there more importance in the resurrection than in the death of Christ?

The opinion of the Socinians
XIX. Sixth, it is asked whether there is more importance for Christianity in the resurrection than in the death of Christ. The Socinians, so that they may more powerfully eliminate satisfaction and merit from the death of Christ, state that Christ, to those who believe him and obey his gospel (which is to them nothing except the law of Moses as it was corrected and augmented by Christ), promised

remission of sins, and through the resurrection, in addition eternal life. And so that they might believe this more securely and submit more readily, he willed to die so that he could rise, ascend, and sit in glory, that in this way by his own example he might attest to the resurrection and eternal life. So then the resurrection is the goal of his death, and consequently there is more importance in the resurrection than in his death. Moreover, they misrepresent the Reformed, saying that they detract from the resurrection and glorification, when they refer remission of sins, strength for new obedience, and all blessings and eternal salvation, to the death and humiliation of Christ.

The opinion of the Reformed
The Reformed, as in agreement with the Scriptures they refer the impetration[28] of salvation and every good to the death and humiliation of Christ, so they refer its application to his resurrection and exaltation; and just as the application is impossible without the impetration, so also the impetration is vain and useless without the application. Hence they consider humiliation and exaltation, death and resurrection, as things coordinate, not subordinate, things which accordingly are equal to each other in their own species, and that in agreement with Scripture (Rom. 4:25). To examine the hypotheses of the Socinian opinion belongs in part to chapter 2 on the Mediator, and in part to chapter 18 on redemption.[29]

7. Ought a special feast be prescribed for the church in memory of the resurrection?
XX. Seventh, it is asked whether some special feast ought to be prescribed for the church in memory of the resurrection of Christ. The papists, so that they might fight more effectively in favor of traditions and the legislative authority of the pope, tenaciously affirm it (after the example of Victor the Roman bishop, who already at the end of the second century excluded from the communion of the church the parishes of all of Asia Minor, together with others bordering it, as they differed from him in the matter of celebrating Easter, as Eusebius testifies in *Ecclesiastical History*, bk. 5, the Latin edition, ch. 22–24).[30] The Lutherans, for reasons I do not know, contrary to their own hypotheses and the perfection of Scripture, in agreement with the papists affirm it, and heap up more veneration on that feast than on the Lord's Day itself. The Reformed, although they grant that some time can be devoted to the remembrance of God's singular benefits

---

28. The term *impetration* here refers to the accomplishing, procuring, and obtaining of salvation by Christ's work of redemption.

29. 1.5.2 §XVII; 1.5.18 §XXIV

30. Eusebius, *Ecclesiasticae historiae libri decem* in PG 20:489–508; idem, *Ecclesiastical History* in NPNF2 1:240–44.

(the sort displayed to us in Christ's resurrection), nonetheless deny that some special feast ought to be prescribed for the entire church, because: (1) Scripture clearly knows nothing of this sort of feast. (2) It is not read that Christ gave to the church the authority to appoint new feasts. (3) He abrogated all the feasts of the Jews (Col. 2:16–17; Gal. 4:10–11). (4) The Lord's Day, which was in fact instituted in memory of the resurrection, is sufficient. It will suffice to have touched on these things, at least for now, as they will be treated expressly elsewhere.[31]

The Practical Part

Christ's resurrection: 1. Provides a support for our faith. In how many ways
XXI. Christ's resurrection, first, provides an outstanding support for our faith: "If Christ is not risen…your faith is vain" (1 Cor. 15:14). Thus: (1) God in his providence was so concerned that once the resurrection had happened it would be revealed to men as soon as possible, indeed, that it would be shown to people by invincible proofs on that very day, at earliest daybreak (Matt. 28:1; Mark 16:2, 9). So (2) he employed as its first revealers not men of any sort, but angels, and those shining with such great majesty (Matt. 28:3), and not just one certain angel, but two, so that in the mouth of two witnesses, and such great witnesses, every truth might be established (Deut. 17:6). And that they testified to that resurrection is said not once, but four times (Matt. 28:2ff.; Luke 24:4ff.; John 20:12ff.; Mark 16:5ff.). Nor only did they testify, but they most painstakingly demonstrated it in many ways: (a) by refuting the vain attempts of the women, whereby they sought the living among the dead (Luke 24:5); (b) by denying that he was in the grave (Luke 24:6); (c) by expressly affirming the resurrection, "for he is risen" (Luke 24:6); (d) by reminding them of the prediction of Christ himself, "Remember how he spoke to you when he was still in Galilee" (Luke 24:6–7); (e) by showing the place where he had lain (Matt. 28:6; Mark 16:6); (f) by ordering that the women communicate also to the disciples the resurrection revealed to them (Mark 16:7), and that they do it quickly (Matt. 28:8). Thus (3) the Savior himself soon after the resurrection appeared to his disciples so many times, most familiarly conversed, ate, drank, and spoke with them for forty days in all, as we have shown in the dogmatic part.[32] Accordingly, (4) Paul so extensively and carefully impresses Christ's resurrection upon the Corinthians (1 Cor. 15:3–21) as a chief part of his whole gospel, by telling of his various appearances, and by explaining its eminent importance for faith, for hope, for eternal

---

31. 2.2.15
32. §XIII, above

salvation. For on the resurrection depend: (a) faith in the eternal deity of Christ (Rom. 1:4); (b) the truth of the mediatorial office, that he is the Messiah, who had to rise again, according to the Scriptures (Acts 13:32–37); (c) the most exact certainty of satisfaction, and of our justification (Rom. 4:25); (d) the immovable success of our blessed resurrection (1 Cor. 15:18–20); I would say in a word, (e) the whole ground[33] of the Christian religion. For if Christ did not rise again, either we have no Messiah, or one that died, which is certainly no Messiah.

To what end

Therefore, there is reason that we should strive with every effort that: (1) we would be immovably convinced regarding the infallibility of Christ's resurrection, for to this end the apostle waxed so great (1 Cor. 15:3–21); that (2) we would perceive its nature more and more (Phil. 3:10); that (3) we would carry the memory of it everywhere (2 Tim. 2:8; Luke 24:6–8); that (4) we would fearlessly confess it (Rom. 10:9).

2. It provides an argument for divine glorification.

XXII. Second, Christ's resurrection offers us an argument for divine glorification. For the glory of God is the highest end, as of the whole work of redemption, so also of this resurrection: "that just as he was raised to the glory of the Father" (Rom. 6:4; Phil. 2:11). In it is evident: (1) the glory of the divine truthfulness and faithfulness, in keeping the promises once made to the Mediator the Son (Isa. 53:10). (2) The glory of distributive justice, by which God provided the glory due to Christ for his freely undertaken humiliation and obedience (Phil. 2:7–9). (3) The glory of power, which he put forth in the raising of the Son (Eph. 1:19–20). (4) The glory of wisdom, by which from so profound a humiliation and emptying he could call forth so sublime an exaltation, wherein the Mediator could triumph over all things, death, hell, and the whole power of darkness (Phil. 2:7–9; Col. 2:15). (5) The glory of grace and mercy, by which he not only called forth from life to death our Mediator, king, Lord, head, brother, surety, and that for our sake, but also made us alive and raised us in and with him (Eph. 2:4–5, 7).

In what manner

In glorifying all these and other such glorious perfections of God that are obvious in the resurrection of Christ: (1) let us acknowledge them with our mind, (2) celebrate them with our mouth, (3) and repay them with our work, so that

---

33. *universa* ὑπόστασις

just as Christ was raised up to the glory of the Father, even so we also should walk in newness of life (Rom. 6:4).

3. It stirs us up that we may rejoice in the one who rises again.

XXIII. Third, Christ's resurrection stirs us up that we may rejoice from the heart in Christ who rises again from the dead and gloriously triumphs over death, hell, and all his and our enemies, and that we may gladly sing to him a song of victory,[34] with the apostle: "Death is swallowed up in victory. O death, where is your victory? O hell, where is your sting?... Thanks be to God, who has given us the victory through our Lord Jesus Christ" (1 Cor. 15:54–57 from Isa. 25:8; Hos. 13:14).

Arguments

For if Moses with his people sang to God a song of victory when God slew their enemies the Egyptians in the Red Sea (Ex. 15:1–22); if the Israelites rejoiced in David that their enemy Goliath was struck down (1 Sam. 18:6–7); if the four apocalyptic beasts, if the twenty-four elders, if the myriads of myriads of angels, if all the creatures which are in heaven, and on earth, and under the earth, and in the sea, and which are contained in all of them, rejoiced in him who lives forever, for his honor, glory and power (Rev. 4:9–11; 5:11ff.), will we not also surely rejoice, since he rose not so much for himself as for us? Will we not surely rejoice for: (1) deliverance from such a deep abyss of humiliation and misery (Phil. 2:7–9; Acts 2:24); (2) such a glorious life recovered after so many and such disgraceful deaths (Ps. 16:9–10; Acts 2:27–28; Ps. 110:7); (3) triumph over all enemies, as much his as ours (1 Cor. 15:55–57; Col. 2:15); (4) indescribable glory acquired for him (Heb. 2:6–10 from Ps. 8:4–6, 9); and (5) righteousness restored to us (Rom. 4:25)?

Manner

Therefore, let us rejoice: (1) by being glad, with the disciples, "They were glad when they saw the Lord" (John 20:20); (2) by wishing him prosperity (Ps. 118:22, 25–26); (3) by celebrating him who rose again (Ps. 118:22–26); (4) by giving thanks (1 Cor. 15:57; Rom. 7:24–25) for all those benefits which he acquired for us by his resurrection, according to §XII.

---

34. ἐπινίκιον

4. It provides a most effective comfort. In what cases

XXIV. Fourth, Christ's resurrection provides outstanding comfort: (1) by driving away fear (Matt. 28:5); (2) by raising up living hope (1 Peter 1:3; 3:21); (3) by stirring up joy (John 20:20); (4) by procuring peace (John 20:19); (5) by wiping away tears (John 20:13). In this way it provides a most effective comfort in the case: (1) of sin, if it should bear down and distress us, for he was raised for our righteousness (Rom. 4:25; 1 Cor. 15:17); (2) of divine wrath, kindled by our sin, for his resurrection convinces us that he reconciled the Father to us (Rom. 5:10); (3) of Satan who tempts us, because in his resurrection he conquered Satan and triumphed over him (Col. 2:15; Ps. 110:1); (4) of earthly enemies, because when he rose he tormented the enemy guards with terror and put them to flight (Matt. 28:4); (5) of any of the soul's disturbances, because when the disciples were afraid of their enemies' persecutions, the Mediator stood in their midst and pronounced upon them peace (John 20:19–20), and when they were exceedingly troubled (σκυθρωποί) by their teacher's death, he was present, though unrecognized, as their comforter (Luke 24:17); (6) of hell which terrifies, because the one rising was neither himself abandoned in hell, nor will he abandon his own there (Ps. 16:10), and he will take away hell's victory (1 Cor. 15:55, 57); (7) of death, because in rising he conquered death and took away its sting (1 Cor. 15:55): he is the resurrection and the life itself (John 11:25).

By what comforting arguments

All these will raise us up more effectively if we have paid attention to a good many of the circumstances of the resurrection, namely: (1) the one rising, that he is the same one that died so that he might free us from the fear of death (Heb. 2:14), and save us by his life (Rom. 5:10). (2) The working[35] of the resurrection, since it provides evidence that he most fully satisfied for us, that he is more powerful than death, the devil, and hell, that he lives forever and so can save us to the uttermost (Heb. 7:24–25), and that he bears the keys of death and hell (Rev. 1:18). (3) Heaven, by his resurrection, was opened so that his soul was reunited with his body, the angels descended, who cast out fear from the trembling women (Matt. 28:5), and as it were, a certain ladder reaching from earth to heaven was erected in the place where this heavenly Jacob had lain and slept (Gen. 28:12), by which we henceforth can ascend with him to his God and our God (John 20:17). (4) The white garments, in which the angels announced the resurrection, provided as it were a pledge of the white garments in which the bride of Christ (Rev. 19:8) and every one of his people (Rev. 6:11), when

---

35. ἐνέργειαν

they rise again from the promise of Christ, will be clothed (Rev. 3:5), so that in them they may shine like the sun (Matt. 13:43) and be equal to the angels[36] (Matt. 22:30). (5) The angels, the heralds of his resurrection, show that they now have become our friends, because the Christ who rose again has become our friend: they now have become to us ministering spirits (Heb. 1:14), and our fellow servants (Rev. 19:10), ready to deal familiarly with us, as with the women (Mark 16:6), inasmuch as with them we will one day be gathered into a most blessed festal assembly (Heb. 12:22–23). (6) The horrendous enemies, greatly alarmed when the resurrection happened, signified by their flight that we also have been delivered from all enemies, to serve God without fear all the days of our life (Luke 1:74). (7) The one who himself rose again, when he was scarcely raised, being anxious as it were for the comforting of his sorrowful disciples, took care that his resurrection be announced to them (Matt. 28:10), came to them when they were assembled together for fear, greeted them most kindly, and bestowed upon them peace (John 20:19), and then commanded that the gospel of this resurrection should be spread throughout the whole world (Matt. 28:18; Mark 16:15). Finally, (8) he declared that he by no means rose to the end that he might abandon his own people, but so that by his grace and his Spirit he would be present with them, even to the consummation of the ages (Matt. 28:20), would protect them, and would bless them forevermore, inasmuch as he now lives forever (Heb. 7:25). Oh good God, how great and how indescribable a comfort there is in all these things!

5. Christ's resurrection strikes his enemies with terror. Who those enemies are
XXV. On the contrary, fifth, Christ's resurrection strikes his enemies with terror and trembling (Matt. 28:4). And who then are these enemies? (1) Those who slay Christ, and attempt to destroy him from their midst, if not in himself, then at least in his members, as did the Jews, the priests, the Pharisees (Matt. 27:22), who even after his death persecute his disciples (John 20:19). Those who (2) are afraid of his resurrection, such as the chief priests and Pharisees (Matt. 27:62–63), and who do not desire his appearing (2 Tim. 4:8).[37] Those who (3) attempt to impede the same appearing by calling for help upon the secular arm, as those same men did (Matt. 27:64). Those who (4) resist it with an armed band of soldiers, and by other means, such as the sealing of the tomb, just as Pilate did, together with those same men (Matt. 27:65–66). Those who (5) lend their effort in some way to the end that Christ might not rise or live, as the soldiers on

---

36. ἰσάγγελοι, from Luke 20:36
37. ἐπιφάνειαν

guard did (Matt. 28:4). Those who, (6) although convicted in their conscience of the truth of the resurrection, hold it down in unrighteousness (Rom. 1:18), just like the chief priests and Pharisees, who to this end struck an agreement with the soldiers on guard (Matt. 28:11–14). Those who (7) with joint counsels and violence, by lies, by deceit, by money, by promises of security, cause others to suppress and oppose the truth, just as the Jewish Sanhedrin did (Matt. 28:12–14). Those who (8) from love of money, suffer their mouths to be stopped so that they may not profess the truth, indeed so that they may suppress it with lies, as the soldiers on guard did (Matt. 28:15). Those who (9) lend open ears to the lies by which the truth of Christ is suppressed, and while knowing the truth, do not want to acknowledge and profess it, just as the Jews, who greedily received the widespread lies of the soldiers on guard (Matt. 28:15). Those who (10) most cruelly persecute Christ's disciples on account of their profession of the truth (John 20:19; Acts 4:16–18; 5:17–18, 28, 40).

Why Christ's resurrection is a terror to them
To all these, just as to the soldiers on guard, Christ's resurrection will be a terror, even to the point that, stricken with fear, they become like dead men (Matt. 28:4), because: (1) they will one day experience the angels—who were sent to the disciples to deliver them from their fear—as avengers of the hatred, murder, and hostility exercised against Christ and his people, armed with majesty, strength, and flaming swords (Gen. 3:24), whom after his resurrection the Son of Man will send so that they may destroy every scandal, and every worker of unrighteousness from their midst (Matt. 13:41), so that with him, they may in flames of fire take vengeance on them (2 Thess. 1:7). (2) That very Jesus whom they crucified, whose resurrection they attempted to prevent with all their might, and to snuff out his glory, they see alive, returning with such majesty, so that he may take vengeance (2 Thess. 1:7–9). How much trembling will these things cause! So much that they will cry out, "O mountains and rocks, fall on us, and hide us from the sight of him who sits upon the throne" (Rev. 6:16). (3) They experience the wrath of God revealed from heaven upon their impiety and unrighteousness, by which they held down the truth in unrighteousness (Rom. 1:18). (4) They sense their very conscience accusing and condemning them (Rom. 2:14), because they crucified the Lord of glory (1 Cor. 2:8; Acts 2:36), and tried to deprive him of the glory of his resurrection. And so forth.

6. It demands that we examine whether he rose for us.
XXVI. Accordingly, sixth, Christ's resurrection should compel everyone to carefully examine himself, whether or not Christ rose for him, since: (1) he did not

rise for each and every person, not for the chief priests, the Pharisees, the Jews, Pilate, Herod, the soldiers who crucified him, not for the guards who obstructed and snuffed out his resurrection; since (2) so great are the benefits, so great the comforts of this resurrection, as we have said; since (3) so great a terror, so great a misery remains upon all those for whose sake he did not rise—is it not surely worth the effort to painstakingly investigate whether he also rose for us?

Marks
But by what marks then should we certainly attain this knowledge? I respond, He rose: (1) for all those, and for those alone, for whom he died (Rom. 4:25; Rom. 6:5), so then we can be persuaded that he rose for us by all those marks by which we are made certain that he died for us, which we will set forth in their own place in the chapter on redemption.[38] He rose (2) for his disciples, to whom he wills his resurrection be announced (Matt. 28:10). However, those who are his genuine disciples, he designates in Luke 9:23 and elsewhere. He rose (3) for those who have died and been crucified with him (Gal. 2:20; Rom. 6:5). He rose (4) for those who, even when he is dead, sincerely love him, take care for his burial, anoint him, seek him in the early morning, grieve when he is taken from them, rejoice when he by the resurrection is restored to them, just as did Joseph of Arimathea, Nicodemus, the women, Mary Magdalene, Peter, John, and all his disciples, as is evident from the history of the resurrection. He rose (5) for those who believe, who have confidence in the angels when they announce the resurrection, who with Thomas are no longer unbelieving, but believing (John 20:27), who believe in their heart that God has raised him from the dead (Rom. 10:9), that is, those who with true faith apprehend the one who died and rose again (John 1:12). He rose (6) for those who are united with him by living faith, so that they rise with him (Col. 3:1; Eph. 2:5–6). He rose (7) for those who, together with the one who rose, walk in newness of life (Rom. 6:4). He rose (8) for those who live no longer for themselves, but for him (Rom. 14:7–9; 2 Cor. 5:15). He rose (9) for these who love and desire his appearing (2 Tim. 4:8), unlike the chief priests and soldiers.

7. It kindles a desire to experience the power of Christ's resurrection.
With respect to spiritual awakening
XXVII. Seventh, Christ's resurrection kindles a desire and zeal to experience the power of his resurrection (Phil. 3:10–11), that by it, first, we may be raised with Christ from spiritual death (Eph. 2:5–6), and then being raised, obtain

---

38. 1.5.18 §XLIX

communion in the fruits of Christ's resurrection. The Savior himself provides an illustrious example of the former, immediately after his own resurrection, in the conversion of the two disciples traveling to Emmaus (Luke 24:13–36), such that in it, as in a kind of mirror (1 Tim. 1:16), he might present by what method and what turns God is ordinarily accustomed to bring a person from the state of sin into a state of grace, and thus apply the power of his death and resurrection. This method consists in the preparation for conversion, the conversion itself, and its results. Each of these are visible in these travelers. They certainly were disciples, that is, Christians by profession, but yet ἀνόητοι καὶ βραδεῖς τῇ καρδίᾳ τοῦ πιστεύειν, "fools and slow of heart to believe" (v. 25), and they represent the natural condition of us all, as long as we are in the state of sin. For we are, with them: (1) in our mind and intellect, ἀνόητοι, fools (1 Cor. 2:14; Eph. 4:18; Gal. 3:1); (2) in our heart or will, slow, βραδεῖς, devoid of all propensity toward spiritual good (Eph. 4:18–19, 22); (3) prone to ἀπιστία, unbelief, lacking faith by which we should believe God and the Scriptures (John 20:25). And from all these things we are dead in sins (Eph. 2:1, 5).

The preparation for conversion, consisting in four degrees
Intending to convert these men as an example, and in them to display the power of the resurrection: (1) he prepares them immediately by his providence through four steps, which are represented in the departure of the disciples from the city of Jerusalem to the village of Emmaus. The first of these steps is in God's immediate vivification and awakening (Eph. 2:5). For to these disciples, perhaps leaving on a walk by chance, and not even thinking one whit about their conversion, who despite so many sermons of Christ himself, so many of his miracles, such familiar conversation with him, and thus so many and such effective means of grace, could not, in this spiritual death, be freed by them from their folly, σκληροκαρδία or hardness of heart, and unbelief—to these disciples, I say, God is present in their travels by his vivifying grace (on which see Eph. 1:19–20), and begins the business of conversion. Thus, he allows himself to be found by those who were not seeking him (Isa. 65:1–2; Rom. 10:20), just as God suddenly apprehended Peter and Andrew when they were occupied in fishing (Matt. 4:18–19), Matthew when he was sitting in the tax booth (Matt. 9:9), Paul when he was traveling and even raging against Christians (Acts 9), the jailer (Acts 16:27–35) and others, and made them alive when they were previously dead in sins.

The second degree is in contrition, humiliation, and a certain saving despair. For what drove these disciples on this walk, except profound grief (v. 17), since their master was just crucified in Jerusalem, in whom all their hope was fixed (v. 21), which grief and despair they try to assuage in some measure by this short walk. So God, when he has vivified those who will be converted, reduces them to a profound sorrow from a sense of sins, and of pressing guilt and misery, withdraws from them every hope of a remedy, either in themselves or in any other besides Christ, and consequently confers "the spirit of slavery to fear" (Rom. 8:15), and likewise πνεῦμα δειλίας, the spirit of timidity (2 Tim. 1:7), as in the example of the Israelites at Pentecost (Acts 2:37), the jailer (Acts 16:27), Paul (Acts 9:3–6), and others.

The third degree is in aversion to the world and worldly things, inasmuch as by them, as it were, Christ was crucified. For what else drove the disciples from Jerusalem, the darling of the whole world, except aversion, because their master was crucified there? What demanded them to prefer Emmaus, an obscure and very poor hamlet, except aversion? So God, in those to be converted, customarily excites contempt for and aversion toward all the pride and pomp of the world (1 John 2:15–17), so that they leave it (Heb. 13:13; cf. Gen. 12:1; Ps. 45:10–11).

The fourth degree of preparation is in the desire for conversation with the godly, and in the sort of discussions that can promote spiritual things. For the disciples, now made alive, filled with grief and sadness, after they had left Jerusalem, what conversation do they seek, except with each other? And what discussions, except about their crucified master (v. 14)? So also in those to be converted and those who have been converted, God stirs up a love and desire for godly conversation (Ps. 16:3; 42:4).

Conversion itself, through various ways and acts
With these steps laid down first in preparation, (2) the Savior himself immediately after his resurrection approaches the business of conversion with his disciples, through various ways: (a) he is present with them in their afflictions, although unknown to them; so to those soon to be converted, who are sorrowful and contrite, he is present by his grace (Ps. 34:18; 51:17; 91:15), although their eyes are kept from recognizing that he is present with them. (b) He examines them so that they come to a knowledge of themselves (v. 17), as those to be converted customarily examine themselves (Lam. 3:40; 2 Cor. 13:5; Zeph. 2:1; Gal. 6:4). (c) He wrenches from them the manifestation of their spiritual state, through a frank confession (vv. 17, 25); so God deals with our first parents when they were to be converted (Gen. 3:8–14), and so also Nathan deals with David (2 Sam. 12:1–8), (d) wrenching from the disciples, after their reproving him (v. 18), a confession of their faith, concerning: (i) the person of Jesus, "Jesus of Nazareth" (v. 19);

(ii) his office, only the prophetic, "who was a prophet mighty in word and deed" (v. 19); (iii) his state of humiliation and death (v. 20); (iv) his state of exaltation, in the resurrection (vv. 22–24); and (v) their faith and hope in him, "But we hoped" (v. 21). By this confession, they represent the common, natural state of all those still to be converted, with respect to: (i) blindness of the mind, whereby their eyes are kept from recognizing God, Christ, or themselves (v. 16), while Satan pours into their mind the smoke of wealth, glory, and worldly pleasures (2 Cor. 4:4); (ii) rebelliousness of the will, whereby they growl at those laboring for their conversion (v. 18, "Do you alone…?"), they cry out against and oppose the motions of the Holy Spirit and his ministers (Acts 7:51; Isa. 63:10; Ps. 95:7ff..; 81:11–13; 78:8); (iii) some sort of speculative knowledge of divine things, whereby they can put forth a confession that is attractive enough, but yet it is maimed in the chief points (vv. 19–24; cf. Matt. 7:21–22; Rom. 2:18–21; 1 Cor. 1:20); (iv) some sort of love, faith, and hope in God, in Christ, but lacking a solid foundation, "We certainly hoped that he would deliver Israel" (v. 21), namely from the violence of the Romans. This sort is also frequently observed in others who are not converted (Heb. 6:4–5; Matt. 13:20). After the disciples had by this confession betrayed the bad disposition,[39] of their spiritual state, the Savior (e) sharply pricks them and rebukes their foolishness with respect to their mind, "O fools"; their hardheartedness with respect to their will, "slow of heart"; and their unbelief with respect to both faculties of their soul (v. 25), namely so that he might confer to those to be converted not only a knowledge of their bad spiritual disposition, but also a sense of their spiritual misery, whereby they exclaim, "O wretched man that I am! Who shall deliver me?" (Rom. 7:24), "Men and brethren, what shall we do to be saved?" (Acts 2:37; 16:27, 30). Thus convicted, humbled, and reduced to a knowledge and sense of their spiritual bad disposition and misery, the Savior (f) carefully informs them about himself: (i) as Christ, whom they had not up to this point recognized except as some sort of eminent prophet, and as Jesus of Nazareth, "Ought not Christ…?" (v. 26); (ii) about his suffering, death, and humiliation, "Ought not Christ to have suffered…?" (v. 26); (iii) about his exaltation, "and to enter into his glory?" (v. 26). He did this to indicate that a person is only in a state to hear Christ announced to him when at length, from the recognition and sense of his sins and misery, being sufficiently contrite and humbled, he has been driven to a saving despair about himself and all others besides Christ (Matt. 11:28; 5:6; Isa. 55:1; Rev. 22:17). Therefore with these things laid down first, at last (g) he kindles the flame. of saving faith (about which the disciples speak in v. 32, "Did not our hearts burn within us?"), and its subsequent acts: in

---

39. καχεξίαν

which they love Christ, they pant after his communion (v. 29, "They constrained him, saying, 'Abide with us...'"). And this is the last act of conversion, whereby a sinner is in actuality established in a state of grace, and in truth made a partaker of the resurrection of Christ. Therefore with this accomplished, Christ attempts to go on and leave them.

The results of conversion

There now remain the results of this conversion, whereby conversion is brought to its climax. In them the first is union with Christ: for after being urged, he goes in with them, soon to be with them and in them: this union is the proximate end of saving faith (Rev. 3:20; Eph. 3:17; Phil. 3:9). The second, flowing from union, is communion with Christ, insofar as he not only goes in, but also reclines with them, takes bread, blesses it, breaks it, and gives it to them (v. 30). In this communion he communicates to his own all his riches: justification, adoption, sanctification, preservation, and glorification (1 Cor. 1:30; Phil. 3:9; Rom. 8:32). This union and communion are followed by the third result, a more distinct and spiritual knowledge of God, Christ, and spiritual things (v. 31, "And their eyes were opened, so that they knew him"), so that those who previously did not know Jesus except as some traveler accompanying them on their journey, or as a gardener, now from union and communion, from the breaking of the bread, know him as their own teacher, their own Lord. From this also arises the fourth result of conversion, a more intense love toward God and toward Christ, so that their heart burns toward God and toward Christ (v. 31, "Did not our heart burn within us?"; 2 Cor. 5:14). And hence furthermore comes the fifth result of conversion and vivification: zeal, and fervent desire for good works, through which their love, and faith in Christ, are no longer idle (2 Peter 1:8), but at work through love (Gal. 5:6), which the disciples, being made alive and converted, show forth, when immediately, at that very hour, they rise up (v. 33), notwithstanding their fatigue arising from their recent journey, notwithstanding their supper and fellowship, notwithstanding the fearful night. There is also added a sixth result, love, namely toward their neighbor, and a desire to share their joy and spiritual goods with their brethren; for the disciples return to Jerusalem, find the eleven disciples gathered together, and declare to them what had happened to them on their journey (vv. 33–35; cf. Luke 22:32). From this also springs a seventh result, a reciprocal strengthening of faith and increase of spiritual joy. For when they tell the others what they experienced, and in the telling strengthen their joy, the others in turn tell them, and in the telling strengthen their faith and increase their joy (v. 34, "They say to them, 'The Lord is risen indeed, and has appeared to Simon'"). And in this way, as if by reflecting off them both, their joy increases by degrees until finally it comes forth complete (John 15:11). And finally in this way there follows the eighth result, the climax of faith and joy, when Christ himself is present to all, and removes all hesitation by his presence, prays his peace upon them, and communicates it to them (v. 36, "And while they were speaking about these things, Jesus stood in the midst of them and said, 'Peace be to you'"). Therefore in these turns he shows forth in his disciples the first efficacy of the resurrection, by making them alive, by spiritually raising them, and by converting them. The additional second efficacy of the same is in the communication of the fruits of his resurrection, which we already reviewed in §XII, and out of desire for brevity will not recount anew here.

The motivating reasons

Now, what else will be incumbent upon us to do here, except that we should strive with our entire strength that we may also in ourselves experience this double efficacy of Christ's resurrection? For otherwise, would we not surely (1) as much as it is in us, at least as regards ourselves, enervate the resurrection of Christ, and render it vain and idle, thus committing unspeakable evil? Would we not surely (2) in turn deprive ourselves of the fruits of this resurrection, so many and so splendid? Would we not surely (3) deprive ourselves of all the comfort and joy that redounds from the resurrection of Christ to those who experience its efficacy, as we spoke of in §XXIV? Would not, on the contrary, (4) the resurrection of Christ surely be for us an eternal terror and horror, as we taught in §XXV?

The manner of acting

What therefore will we do here? (1) Above all things we must strive, from what has been said, that we may more and more perceive the method and turns by which Christ customarily confers the power of his resurrection for spiritual awakening. To the end that (2) we may not resist him as he endeavors to confer that power to us, and by it to enliven and awaken us. Indeed rather that (3) we may eagerly turn toward and accommodate ourselves to him, that he may proceed more easily. And especially, (4) we must strive to embrace with living faith the Mediator who rose from the dead, and in embracing him, be united with him (Col. 2:6–7), to the end that we may be raised in and with him (Eph. 2:5–6), and with him rise again (Col. 3:1). And so forth.

*8. It teaches us that we should strive to be more and more conformed
to the resurrection of Christ.* In what particulars

XXVIII. Eighth, it teaches us that by the efficacy of Christ's resurrection, we who have already been enlivened and awakened should arise with him, that is, we should be conformed more and more to his resurrection (Rom. 6:5; Col. 3:1; Eph. 2:6). And that generally in these particulars: just as (1) Christ's natural resurrection followed his death; so also we should first die to our sins (Rom. 6:5), by conscientiously abstaining from them (Ps. 34:13; Isa. 1:16–17; 1 Peter 3:11). Just as (2) Christ's resurrection (and one day our own natural resurrection) was nothing except a movement from death to life; so also our spiritual resurrection is a movement or passing from spiritual death to spiritual life (John 5:25), so that we who were by nature dead in sins (Eph. 2:5), and buried in sins, should be raised up (Eph. 2:5), and walk in newness of life (Rom. 6:4), and in the Spirit (Gal. 5:16–17). Just as (3) Christ arose in his entirety, and brought up all his members from the grave, leaving behind only the linen cloths; so also we should spiritually arise in our entirety (1 Thess. 5:23), so that in our intellect there comes forth a new and spiritual light (Eph. 4:23), in the will new motions toward spiritual things (Col. 3:1), the members of our body become weapons of righteousness (Rom. 6:13), and the whole person becomes a new creature (2 Cor. 5:17). Just as (4) the resurrection of Christ was a work of the utmost difficulty, inasmuch as it was procured by the exceeding greatness of the power of God; so also our resurrection, being in itself of the utmost difficulty, should proceed from an equal power of God (Eph. 1:19–20). Just as (5) in the dead body of Christ, in the same way as in our dead bodies, there was no disposition, no preparation for the resurrection; so also for our spiritual resurrection, we should not imagine in ourselves any disposition, power, or preparation at all for spiritual resurrection (Rom. 5:6; 8:3; 2 Cor. 3:5), but indeed on the contrary, a total aversion to it (Acts 7:51). Just as (6) Christ in his resurrection (and we one day in our natural resurrection) had as causes, first the principal cause, God who raised him (Eph. 1:19–20), then the ministerial cause, the angel who removed the stone from the entrance to the tomb, and the preceding earthquake (Matt. 28:2); so also we should endeavor to arise by the power of the God who raises (Rom. 4:17), and that by the ministry of ecclesiastical angels (Rev. 2:1; etc.), and the blast of the gospel trumpet (cf. 1 Thess. 4:16), whereby they stir up a kind of earthquake (σεισμός) in our hearts (Acts 2:37; 2 Cor. 7:8). Just as (7) Christ rose to an entirely other sort of life, differently than what happened in all who ever rose again to natural life (1 Kings 17:22; 2 Kings 4:34–35; 13:21; John 11:43; Acts 9:40), namely the same life that they had led before; we with Christ should rise to another life (Rom. 6:4), namely a spiritual life, about which we will have more to say in its own place.[40] Finally, (8) just as Christ rose again to the glory of the Father (Rom. 6:4); so also we should rise again and live to the glory of God (1 Cor. 10:31), about which we will speak expressly a little further on.[41]

By what motivating reasons

Moreover, so that we may strive more willingly toward this spiritual resurrection, let us consider: (1) the command of the Holy Spirit, "Awake, you who sleep, arise from the dead, and Christ shall give you light" (Eph. 5:14; 1 Cor. 15:34, ἐκνήψατε, "Awake," that is, from your sins, like those buried in sleep and wine; cf. Gen. 9:24; Joel 1:5). Let us consider (2) that each of us is spiritually addressed by Christ, "Rise up, Lazarus!" (John 11:43; cf. Acts 9:40). Let us consider (3) that because we will all rise naturally (2 Cor. 5:10), if we have not risen here spiritually, it would be more profitable for us if we did not rise again at all (cf. Matt. 18:6; Mark 14:21), because then we would arise to eternal condemnation (Dan. 12:2). Let us consider (4) that if we have been partakers of this first resurrection, that is, the spiritual, we will be blessed and holy, and that then the second death will have no power over us, but that we will be priests of God and Christ, and will reign with him a thousand years, that is, eternally (Rev. 20:6). Let us consider (5) that if we have arisen spiritually with Christ, we will also be set with him in the heavens (Eph. 2:4–5).

By what means

But what is incumbent upon us to do that we may rise spiritually with Christ? Presupposing God's immediate vivification and awakening (Rom. 4:17), regarding which we spoke in the preceding section, (1) we must receive the loud shout of God's Son who would rouse us (John 5:28–29). For just as Lazarus, in receiving Christ's omnipotent voice, arose from natural death (John 11:43), so also he who has heard the voice of the Son of God will live (John 5:25). And just as we are roused from natural sleep by receiving shouts, so also we are roused from spiritual sleep (Eph. 5:14). Therefore, we must receive: (a) the voice of the law, that by it a kind of earthquake our hearts may be roused, not only as happened around the time of Christ's resurrection (Matt. 28:2), but also as, by the voice of the Mediator promulgating the law at Sinai, the earth was shaken (Heb. 12:26), as were the mountains (Ex. 19:18), and Moses himself (Heb. 12:21), and those who rose from their tombs around the time of the death of Christ experienced a prior quaking of the earth (Matt. 27:51–52). So also, by the voice of the law,

---

40. §XXIX, below
41. §XXIX, below

a quaking must occur in the hearts of those rising again: one of compunction (Acts 2:37), of contrition (Ps. 2:19), of the spirit of slavery to fear (Rom. 8:15), of saving despair, whereby we exclaim, "Who shall deliver me?" (Rom. 7:24), "What must I do to be saved?" (Acts 16:30). (b) The voice of the gospel (Matt. 11:28; cf. 1 Kings 19:11–12). (2) We must receive the life-giving Spirit of God. For just as by his work a natural resurrection was procured for Christ (1 Peter 3:18), so also must a spiritual resurrection be procured for us (Rom. 8:11). And just as a natural resurrection does not occur except by the return of the spirit into its body (Luke 8:55; Ezek. 37:13–14), so neither does a spiritual resurrection. From which he is called the Spirit of life (Rom. 8:2), and likewise the πνεῦμα ζωοποιοῦν, life-giving Spirit (1 Cor. 15:45), inasmuch as he must make our intellect alive by illuminating it, and by instilling into it new light (Heb. 6:4; 1 Cor. 2:11–15), and in addition, our will, by stirring up in it a new propensity toward spiritual good, and also new motions (Rom. 8:13–14). (3) We must receive the very life of Christ that we may spiritually rise again; for which reason he is called the resurrection and the life (John 11:25), the way, the truth, and the life (John 14:6), our life (Col. 3:3–4). From this Paul says, "I am crucified with Christ, and I live: no longer I, but Christ lives in me" (Gal. 2:20). There is required (4) living faith, through which we may be united with Christ (Gal. 2:20), that together with him we may be crucified, may live, and may arise with him (Col. 3:1), that we may be rendered one plant with him, in conformity to his death as well as to his resurrection (Rom. 6:5). It is required (5) that we carefully attend upon those means by which God customarily awakens us, after the example of that bedridden man in John 5:4–5: for instance, the hearing of the word (Ezek. 37:4; Acts 10:15), inasmuch as it is like the trumpet by which he customarily wakes up the dead (1 Cor. 15:52). And finally, (6) we must take heed to ourselves regarding three things: first, that when Christ calls, whether externally or internally, we would not cry out against him (Heb. 3:7 from Psalm 95:7–8; Acts 7:51), not quench the motions of the Spirit when he would awaken us (1 Thess. 5:19). Let us take heed (7) second, of procrastination in regard to spiritual resurrection, such as is observed in the Jews who were to raise the temple (Hab. 1:2), and in the lazy (Prov. 6:9), such that the work of resurrection or conversion, which is by far most difficult, we put off until the time of old age, which is most unsuited to it (cf. John 11:39; Gen. 18:12), when our strength has been debilitated by senility: for it is uncertain whether it will be that God grant us senility, or in senility, the will or strength to rise again (cf. Matt. 26:45; Prov. 1:21ff.). Let us take heed (8) third, of despair, whereby we think it is too late, that we have stuck too long in sin, grown old in it, and now the matter is hopeless. This sort of despair is shown by Martha in the case of the raising of her dead brother (John 11:39), and Christ corrects her (v. 40). On the contrary, let us think here, "Never late, if genuine,"[42] and although it is more difficult for spiritual resurrection to come upon us in our old age, when our strength is worn out, yet it is not more difficult for God to raise a sinner even when he is a centenarian (Isa. 65:20), just as he raised up the thief in the extremity of life (Luke 23:42–43).

9. It teaches us that we must pass into new life with Christ. In what particulars XXIX. Ninth, the resurrection of Christ teaches us that we must pass with him into new life, that just as Christ was raised to the glory of the Father, even so we also should walk in newness of life (Rom. 6:4). But what kind of life did Christ pass into and walk in after his resurrection? I respond, it was a life: (1) entirely different, by a whole species, utterly differently than how it happened with the "twice-dead," those who were restored from natural life to natural life, since Christ by his resurrection passed from natural life into spiritual life. We therefore should walk rather with Christ, in newness of life (Rom. 6:4), with respect to: (a) new principles of living, not according to the flesh, but according to the spirit (Rom. 8:1; Eph. 2:3), according to the Spirit of holiness (Rom. 1:4 with 8:11; 2 Tim. 1:14; Gal. 5:25); (b) a new rule of living, not according to the customs of this world (Rom. 12:2), according to the course of the world (Eph. 2:2), disorderly (2 Thess. 3:11), but according to the rule of regeneration (Gal. 6:16), according to the will of God (Ps. 119:133, 9); (c) a new goal of living, by which we should live not for ourselves (Rom. 14:7–8), not for the world, not for wealth, glory, or pleasures (1 John 2:15–17), but for God (Rom. 6:11), for God's glory (1 Cor. 10:31); (d) a new method of living, not according to the vain way of life (1 Peter 1:18) which proceeds from vanity of mind (Eph. 4:17), and tends toward vanity (Hab. 2:13; Rom. 6:21; Eph. 2:3), but according to such a way of life as becomes the gospel (Phil. 1:27), that is good (James 3:13), honorable (1 Peter 2:12), profitable (Philemon 11–12), holy (1 Peter 1:15), heavenly (Phil. 3:20), genuine (Ps. 37:14). (2) The life of Christ was immortal, that is, a life which: (a) was not sustained by natural supports, like others who rose again (Luke 8:55). Indeed, after his resurrection, it is read that he ate fish and honeycomb with the disciples (Luke 24:42), yet he did not do this out of necessity, but for the purpose of strengthening the faith of the disciples. So also we, while we are in this natural life, should not so much enjoy the things of this life, as use them (1 Cor. 7:30–31) being otherwise content in God alone (Ps. 119:57); we should feed upon the body and blood of Christ (John 6:35). A life which (b) was unceasing (Rom. 6:9–10). So also we should live for God unceasingly

---

42. *nunquam sero, modo vere*

(John 11:25–26): about such a life the Savior himself speaks (John 11:25–16; cf. 2 Cor. 4:16; Rev. 20:6). (3) The life of Christ, after the resurrection, was for the glory of the Father (Rom. 6:4), as much (a) actively, so that he might glorify the Father (John 17:4; Phil. 2:11), as (b) passively, so that he might be glorified by the Father (John 17:4; Phil. 2:11). So also we in our own life should both glorify God (1 Cor. 10:31; 6:20; Matt. 5:16), and wait to be glorified by him (2 Peter 1:3). Hence sanctification is included under our glorification (Rom. 8:30). (4) The life of Christ, which he lived after the resurrection, was eternal (Rom. 6:9). We also in our own life should strive toward a blessed eternity (Matt. 25:46; Luke 20:35–36; 1 Cor. 15:53; cf. Isa. 66:24). And moreover, so that we may, being raised, walk in this newness of life, it is also necessary (5) that Christ himself live in us (Gal. 2:20), that (a) his sinlessness (1 Peter 2:22; Heb. 7:26) live in us (Matt. 10:16; Acts 20:26); (b) his longsuffering (Zech. 9:9; Matt. 21:5; 2 Cor. 10:1) live in us (Matt. 11:29; James 3:13; 1 Peter 2:1); (c) his patience (1 Peter 2:23; Isa. 53:7) live in us (Rev. 1:9; 13:10; 14:12); (d) his humility (Matt. 11:29; Phil. 2:6–7) live in us (Phil. 2:5 with vv. 7–8; Isa. 57:15; James 4:16); (e) his obedience (Phil. 2:7; John 5:30) live in us (Isa. 1:19); (f) his love toward his own (Eph. 5:2, 25; John 15:13; Rom. 5:8) live in us, toward God (Matt. 22:37, 39), toward Christ (Eph. 6:24), toward the saints (Eph. 1:15), toward enemies (Matt. 5:44); (g) his contempt of the world (John 18:36; 6:15; Matt. 4:8) live in us (1 John 2:15–17; Rom. 12:2); (h) his heavenly conversation (John 3:13) live in us (Phil. 3:20; Col. 3:1–2). Compare the practice of chapter 11, on the life of the Mediator.[43]

10. It commands us to await our blessed resurrection.
XXX. Tenth, Christ's resurrection commands us to await our blessed natural resurrection. "For if we have been made one plant together with him in the likeness of his death, we shall be also in the likeness of his resurrection" (Rom. 6:5).

The foundation of this expectation: (1) Christ's resurrection is the exemplar of our resurrection
For of this blessed resurrection of ours, Christ's resurrection is: (1) the prototype or exemplar, for just as (a) Christ's resurrection was true, and a resurrection properly so called (John 2:19; Luke 24:39–40; John 20:27), so also ours will be true, a resurrection whereby the same thing that fell, will rise (Job 19:25–27; 1 Cor. 15:53; 2 Cor. 5:10). Just as (b) Christ's resurrection was to life (Rom. 6:9), so believers, different from unbelievers on this point, will rise to life (John 5:29);

---

43. 1.5.11 §XLII

they for this reason are called the children of the resurrection (Luke 20:36), because they obtain a better resurrection (Heb. 11:35), and their resurrection is not only an ἀνάστασις, rising again, but also an ἀναβίωσις, living again, or the ἀνάστασις ζωῆς, resurrection of life (John 5:29), and likewise the resurrection of the just (Luke 14:14), whereas the resurrection of the others will be the ἀνάστασις κρίσεως, resurrection of judgment (John 5:29) or of condemnation (Matt. 25:46). Just as (c) Christ rose to a spiritual life, which was not sustained by natural things, as we have said, so also we will rise to a spiritual life, with our very bodies, for this purpose, made in their own way spiritual (1 Cor. 15:44; Matt. 22:30). Just as (d) Christ rose to a glorious life, the prelude of which he sensed in his transfiguration (Matt. 17:2ff.), and which he in fact experienced (Luke 24:26), so also ours will be glorious (1 Cor. 15:43; Phil. 3:20; Col. 3:4). Just as (e) Christ rose to eternal life (Rom. 6:9), so also we will rise to eternal and immortal life (1 Cor. 15:53; Matt. 25:46; Luke 20:35–36).

(2) The source
For of this blessed resurrection of ours, Christ's resurrection is (2) the source, since ours, through union with him (whereby we are planted together with him, Rom. 6:5), flows forth from his resurrection, as from its cause, as much the meritorious cause (just as in Adam as the meritorious cause, we all die, so in Christ as the meritorious cause, all believers rise, 1 Cor. 15:21), as the efficient cause (John 5:28–29), according to his working (Phil. 3:21), and the power that goes out from him (Mark 5:30).

(3) The pledge and beginning
For it is in addition (3) the ground, pledge, and beginning of our blessed resurrection (1 Cor. 15:20–21, 23) since with him we have been united into one mystical body (1 Cor. 12:12), of which he is the head, and we the members. From which it happens that we are said to have already risen in Christ (1 Cor. 15:20), and to have been raised with him (Eph. 2:6), and that he is the firstfruits of those who have fallen asleep (1 Cor. 15:20), in the order of nature, the first one to rise (1 Cor. 15:23); and thus he is called the firstborn from the dead (Col. 1:18), about which we will say more things in its own place, in the chapter on the resurrection of the dead.[44]

---

44. 1.8.4 §VI

The manner of awaiting our resurrection

Therefore given these foundations, it is our part, from the glorious resurrection of Christ: (1) to await our own with patience and trust, until the hour of this blessed resurrection has arrived (2 Cor. 5:1, 4; 1 John 3:2; Rom. 8:23, 25; 1 Cor. 1:7; Job 14:14; 1 Peter 1:13), just as also Christ, after his resurrection, willed for forty days to dwell on earth and to await his glorious reception;[45] meanwhile, (2) to rise spiritually more and more from sins, to go "from troop to troop," that is, from strength to strength, until we appear before God in Zion (Ps. 84:7), so that while our outward man wastes away, our inward man grows strong from day to day (2 Cor. 4:16). That is, just as daily we must die, with Paul (1 Cor. 15:31), so also daily we must rise again; just as even a righteous man falls seven times each day (Prov. 24:16), so also every day he rises, even seven times. In addition, also (3) to give thanks to God, who has already made us partakers of the first resurrection, through the exceeding riches of his grace (Eph. 2:7), and through the exceeding greatness of his power (Eph. 1:19), and has by the first resurrection provided a pledge of the second glorious resurrection (Rev. 20:6). Furthermore, (4) let us beware, more than we would a dog or snake, that we never return to the grave of sin, just as Lazarus did naturally, and the other twice-dead, but like Christ, who after he rose once, now no longer dies (Rom. 6:9), so let us also do the same (John 11:26). Finally, (5) let us gradually prepare ourselves for this our blessed resurrection, by opportunely finishing our work which is incumbent on us to do here (2 Tim. 4:8), just as the Savior for the forty days till his ascension was entirely devoted to unfolding those things that concerned his kingdom (Acts 1:3; Matt. 28:18–19).

---

45. ἀνάληψις. Cf. 1.5.16 §II.B.1.a

CHAPTER SIXTEEN

The Ascension of the Mediator

This Jesus, who is taken up from you into heaven, shall so come in the same manner as you have seen him departing into heaven.

—Acts 1:11

The second degree of exaltation

I. The second degree of exaltation follows: the ascension into heaven, to which two angels bear testimony, in the form of two men clothed in white garments, standing by the apostles while, as Jesus was departing to heaven, they followed him with their eyes and affections (Acts 1:11).

The Exegetical Part

The text is opened and explained.

II. By this testimony, the angels present and describe to the Galilean men, who, as Christ was departing toward heaven, were following him with their eyes and affections, the reason for this departure, for their consolation. And in it they make known:

A. The one departing: οὗτος Ἰησοῦς, "This Jesus." They had rebuked the disciples, not so much because they followed him with an intent gaze as he ascended, as because they followed him with such a heart, that is, with excessive sorrow, mixed with a kind of unbelief, namely that their Jesus, whom they had complained was snatched from them by death, and whom they had hardly rejoiced was restored to them by the resurrection, by whose sweetest conversation they had been encouraged for such a brief time, that is, forty days, they now saw being taken away from them forever. Against this unbelieving sorrow, so that they might comfort them more effectively, they said, οὗτος Ἰησοῦς, "This Jesus," as if to say, "That very Redeemer whom you lost through death, whom you received back through the resurrection, whom you had for forty days, who now has departed from you toward heaven—that very one will more certainly than certain be restored to you again one day.

B. The departure, in which is included:

1. The going away, or the ascension into heaven: "who is taken from you into heaven." In it is described:

a. The motion of going away or ascending: "who is taken," ὁ ἀναληφθείς, who in verse 10 is described as πορευόμενος, departing. Ἀναλαμβάνομαι is a word composed from ἀνά, up, and λαμβάνομαι, I am taken. To many it has a forensic meaning, taken from fathers, by whom, if at some point their sons were away from home for a long time, they are received back into the family. So the heavenly Father, when satisfaction had been made, received as if back into his favor the Son whom on account of our sins he had as it were renounced and denied as degenerate, and recalled and received again the Son who had been dismissed. To others, it means to take again, speaking as it were of something that you had lost or cast off, as the father received his lost son in Luke 15. To yet others, it means to be taken up, as if from ἄνω, up, and λαμβάνεσθαι, to be taken, because the Father took up his Son, whom he had sent down εἰς τὰ κατώτερα μέρη τῆς γῆς, into the lower parts of the earth (Eph. 4:9), into highest parts of the world, into heaven. Ἀναληφθείς, being passive in meaning, designates that he was taken up by the power of another person, that is, his Father, just as he ascended by the power of his own essence, namely by the one identical with the essence of his Father, for which reason he is described as πορευόμενος, departing. From these things, both Scripture (Mark 16:19; 1 Tim. 3:16), and the primitive Greek church customarily called the ascension of Christ into heaven the ἀνάληψις, the taking up (Eusebius, *Ecclesiastical History*, bk. 2, ch. 1–2, and elsewhere).[1]

b. The two termini of the motion:

i. The terminus *a quo*: "from you," ἀφ' ὑμῶν. From the earth, from the Mount of Olives, where he had entered into his utmost humiliation, so that he might teach his disciples that the passion and ascension look to the same end, and are connected

---

1. Eusebius, *Ecclesiastica historia* in *PG* 20:136–140; idem, *Ecclesiastical History* in *NPNF2* 1:103–6.

(Luke 24:26; Rom. 8:17). "From you," not from just anyone, not from unbelievers, the wicked, and hypocrites, to whom he had never been given, who did not have him (Eph. 2:12), but from his apostles and disciples. From which it remains that as Christ was ascending, with respect to his body he truly left both his people and the earth.

ii. The terminus *ad quem*: εἰς τὸν οὐρανόν, "into heaven," with the article, such that it means a definite place opposed to the earth (John 16:28). "Into heaven," not only through the airy heaven, nor only through the starry heaven (as the more recent Lutherans want it, so that they may hold that he was taken by a local motion up to the clouds, because he had omnipresence of the flesh, at least with respect to possession, but he did not want to use it until the ascension, from the time of which his flesh became omnipresent: about this we will speak in the elenctic part),[2] but into the third, empyrean heaven, which preeminently is called heaven in the Scriptures, otherwise known as the house of God, in which there are many mansions, from which he promises his disciples that he will return (John 14:2–3).

2. The return, in which are noted:

a. The motion: ἐλεύσεται, he "shall come." The word ἔρχομαι in the New Testament is employed with a singular emphasis, sometimes (1) regarding the coming of the incarnation (John 3:2; 16:28; and throughout John); sometimes (2) regarding the coming of his humiliation (Matt. 20:28); sometimes (3) regarding the coming of grace or sanctification, which occurs through the Word and sacraments (Matt. 9:13; John 1:5, 7, 9; 3:19; 12:46–47; 18:37); but in this passage (4) regarding the coming of glory (as also in Matt. 25:31; 1 Cor. 11:26). The angels speak this way so that they might more effectively encourage the hearts of the disciples, who were unduly dejected over the departure of their teacher, saying, "He is departing, but he will return," just as the Savior himself said in John 14:3, "I will return, so that I may receive you to myself."

b. The way of moving. Here there is:

i. The idea of seeing: ὃν τρόπον ἐθεάσασθε, "in the same way as you have seen." Therefore, the ὃν τρόπον refers to the nearest

---

2. §XIII, below

word following, ἐθεάσασθε, and not to the thing seen. For Christ will return somewhat differently than he departed (Matt. 25:31–32; 2 Thess. 1:7–8). Therefore, the indubitable certainty of the return is noted, that with their own eyes they will one day see him returning, just as they now see him going away, and as they do not doubt his departure, so they must not doubt his return. The verb θεᾶσθαι means more than ὁρᾶν, for the latter simply denotes seeing, even through a lattice, but the former means contemplating something long and hard, inside and out, as a new thing, and a marvelous spectacle. It is referred to the eyes, both of the body and of the heart (1 John 1:1; John 1:14). Thus we read in the preceding verse, ὡς ἀτενίζοντες ἦσαν εἰς τὸν οὐρανόν, πορευομένου αὐτοῦ, "while they looked steadfastly toward heaven as he departed." For ἀτενίζειν means to look with eyes fixed, unmoved, and intent.

ii. The thing seen: αὐτὸν πορευόμενον εἰς τὸν οὐρανόν, "him departing into heaven," Πορεύομαι means "I go away," "I make a journey." It is used regarding the departure of Christ to death (Luke 13:33), but it includes his resurrection, ascension, and session at the right hand of the Father (John 14:2, 3, 12, 28; 16:7, 28), though here among these it means only his ascension, as is evident in the connected phrase "into heaven," about which we spoke in the preceding points. By this whole clause is signified his return to judge the living and the dead, which is the fourth and final degree of glorification, which will happen visibly, just as his departure occurred visibly. About this return we will philosophize expressly in its own place, if God wills.[3]

The Dogmatic Part

Christ locally and visibly ascended to heaven. It is proved by the Scriptures.
III. Therefore with the two angels as witnesses, the same Jesus who rose from the dead ascended locally and visibly into heaven, according to: (1) prophecies, as much of the Old Testament (Ps. 68:17–18; 110:1; cf. Acts 2:34; Ps. 47:5; Mic. 2:13) as of the New (Matt. 26:64; John 16:28; 20:17); (2) types and figures, for example, the high priest, who entered into the holy of holies once every year, and that indeed after the beginning of a new year (Lev. 16 with Heb.

---

3. 1.6.4 §IVff.

9:23–24), Enoch (Gen. 5:24), Elijah (2 Kings 2:11; cf. Gen. 28:12 with John 1:52); (3) history (Mark 16:19; Luke 24:51; Acts 1:9–11); (4) witnesses, the angels (Acts 1:11), the eleven apostles, who were witnesses with their own eyes and ears (Acts 1:9); (5) testimonies (Eph. 1:20–21; 2:6; 4:8, 10; Rom. 10:6; Heb. 1:3; cf. Luke 19:12).

And by reasons
IV. Not only did he ascend, but he also necessarily had to ascend. And that not only: (1) on account of the Scriptures, so that the prophecies and types already designated might be satisfied; but also (2) on account of the righteousness of his merits, which demanded heavenly glorification as a reward (Luke 24:26; Heb. 12:2; Phil. 2:8–9); in addition, (3) from the mediatorial office that he had undertaken, whereby he had to enter into the heavenly sanctuary, that he might appear there on our behalf before the Father (Heb. 9:24), the necessity of which was so great that if he were now still on earth, he would not be a priest (Heb. 8:4); (4) on account of the benefits for his own people, "It is good for you that I go away" (John 16:7), about which benefits we will say more things in due course.[4]

What is the ascension?
V. This ascension, with respect to its denomination, is designated in different ways in the sacred page: "he was taken up" (Acts 1:9); "when he had ascended" (Eph. 4:8); "made higher than the heavens" (Heb. 7:26); "he entered into the sanctuary" (Heb. 9:12); "I go to the Father";[5] to "my Father's house" (John 14:2); "I go away" (John 16:7); "I leave the world, and go to the Father" (John 16:28). With respect to its substance, it is nothing other than the second degree of exaltation, whereby having left the earth with respect to his body, he passed locally into heaven.

Here there is distinctly represented: 1. The one ascending
VI. Concerning this degree, the following things should be considered. First, the one ascending, or the one moved, "This Jesus," or his whole person, on account of the mediatorial operations, and with respect also to both natures, although in different ways: with respect to the divine nature, in no way but actively, only by elevating the human nature, because the divine nature is omnipresent; with respect to the human nature, properly by ascending, and that according to both of its essential parts, such that the same soul as well as the same body ascended,

---

4. §X, below
5. John 16:16–17

and the angels rightly said, "This Jesus…will so come in the same manner as you have seen him departing."

2. The components of the ascension

VII. Second, the ascension, which includes: (1) the termini: (a) The terminus *a quo*, from earth, from the Mount of Olives, eight stadia distant from Jerusalem (Acts 1:12), which was in the region of Bethany, about fifteen stadia away from Jerusalem (John 11:18); the ancients teach that on this mountain the ascending Savior imprinted his footsteps (which is very unlikely). This mountain was the place where he entered into his utmost humiliation (Luke 22:39), and therefore since he wanted to hasten into his glory from there, this seems to teach that his humiliation and exaltation look toward the same end (Luke 24:26; Rom. 8:17). (b) The terminus *ad quem*, into heaven, a higher place (Ps. 68:18), not only the airy heaven, such that he disappeared in the clouds, but into the empyrean heaven, whereby he was made higher than the lower heavens (Heb. 4:14; 7:26), above all heavens (Eph. 4:10), where we will one day be after our blessed dissolution[6] (John 14:2; Phil. 3:20; 1 Thess. 4:16; Heb. 12:23). (2) The motion, in which he in fact left the terminus *a quo*, at least with respect to the body (John 16:28), and occupied the terminus *ad quem* (Acts 3:21). (3) The mover, certainly the Father, by whom he is said to have been taken up (Acts 1:11; 1 Tim. 3:16), as well as his own power, that whereby he had raised himself (John 10:18), from which he is said to have ascended (Luke 24:51; John 20:17; 3:13), and likewise to depart (Acts 1:11; John 14:2), which was in addition aided by the glorified condition of his body, which after the manner of a spirit, is carried up and down with the same ease.

3. The properties of the ascension

VIII. Third, the properties, through which he ascended: (1) truly, not by an illusion,[7] nor with doubting, as the ecstatic ascension of Paul was (2 Cor. 12:2), nor only in soul and thought, in which manner it is incumbent also upon us day by day to ascend spiritually into heaven (Phil. 3:20; Col. 3:1), but by his total assumption, such that the Lord was taken up into heaven (Mark 16:19); (2) visibly (Acts 1:9, 11); (3) locally, insofar as he is said to have been taken up (Acts 1:9); taken up by a cloud, he departed from the disciples (Luke 24:51); he went away and will come again (John 14:28; Acts 1:11); he left the world (John 16:28); he passed into the heavens (Heb. 4:14); (4) suddenly and unexpectedly,

---

6. ἀνάλυσιν

7. *per* φάντασμα

while he was speaking with the disciples (Acts. 1:9); (5) quickly, not suspended long between heaven and earth; he soon passed out of the disciples' view (Acts 1:9–10); (6) gloriously, that is, as one triumphant (Col. 2:15; Ps. 68:18), conveyed upon a certain shining cloud, like a triumphal chariot (Acts 1:9), having left behind the two angels after him as heralds (Acts 1:10); (7) with the eleven apostles watching (Acts 1:8), among whom were present those whom he had previously had as spectators, first of his agony (Matt. 26:37), then of his transfiguration or preliminary glorification on the mountain (Mark 9:2ff.), so that he might have the same men as witnesses as much of his glorification as of his emptying (Acts 1:8; John 19:35).

4. The time of the ascension

IX. Fourth, the time, that is, the fortieth day from the resurrection (Acts 1:3), which number is perceived to be fairly common, first in the case of Moses, Elijah, and others, and then particularly also in the case of Christ, according to different degrees of excellence (Luke 2:22; Matt. 4:2; Acts 1:3). However, it is not for us to meticulously investigate the reasons why he willed to ascend neither earlier nor later, when in place of reasons could be that it was simply the will of the one who ascended (Acts 1:7). Yet there is something here we may consider probable: on the one hand, not earlier, so that he could not only prove to his disciples the truth of his resurrection, but also inform them sufficiently regarding the matters of his kingdom to be maintained and observed after his departure (Acts 1:3); and on the other hand, not later, not only so that he might supply the promised outpouring of the Holy Spirit precisely on the feast of Pentecost, but also so that he might remove from the disciples the suspicion and thought of an earthly kingdom (Acts 1:6).

5. The ends and fruits of the ascension

X. Fifth, the ends and fruits, namely (1) that he might place the human nature, already glorified in part in the resurrection, on the throne of glory (Eph. 1:20), and show himself to be the Lord from heaven (1 Cor. 15:47–49; John 6:58, 61–62), and that he might gloriously triumph over his enemies (Eph. 4:8; Ps. 68:18; Col. 2:14–15), and thereby seal his full victory over them (1 Cor. 15:57). (2) That he might in heaven gloriously discharge those things he had to perform there for the salvation of his people by his intercession and power: (a) that he might open heaven to them (Heb. 10:19–20),[8] (b) prepare mansions for them in heaven (John 14:2–3; Rom. 8:34); (c) appear in heaven before the Father

---

8. Original, Heb. 9:1

as the advocate for his people (Heb. 9:24); (d) and also send to them another advocate (John 16:7); (e) and from there distribute to his own all saving gifts (Ps. 68:18; Eph. 4:8–11). (3) That he might, in the name of his people, take possession of the heavenly kingdom, and occupy a place for them in the heavens (John 14:2–3); that he might set our flesh in heaven as a pledge of our future ascension, and also provide an indubitable argument of this future ascension (Eph. 2:6; 1 Cor. 15:49; John 12:26; 17:24; Rev. 3:21); (4) that he might call our mind and heart upward, that is, our thoughts, desires, and exertions (Col. 3:1; Phil. 3:20); and so forth.

The Elenctic Part

It is asked: 1. Did Christ truly ascend?

XI. It is asked here, first, whether Christ truly ascended to heaven. The Docetists and Phantastici (who arose immediately upon the departure of the apostles, and with whom later the Manichaeans, Marcionites, and Cerdonians associated themselves), just as they deny the truth of his human nature, so also deny the truth of his death and resurrection, and accordingly of his ascension, as Augustine witnesses (*On Heresies*, ch. 21).[9] We refuted their primary falsehood in chapter 4, §XVIII. The Carpocratians in the first century wanted him to have ascended only in his soul. Apelles or the Apellites stated that the ascension was a διάλυσις, dissolution, of the body into the four elements. The Seleucians and Hermians said that the body of Christ was bound to the stars, but especially to the orb of the sun. The Muslims only hold this, that Christ escaped the hand of his Jewish enemies and came to the elemental heaven,[10] and there before his Creator shines among the stars. As these errors are already obsolete, it is of no use to address them anew. The Jews, just as they deny that our Jesus truly rose again, so also tenaciously deny that he ascended.

The grounds of the affirming side

Christians affirm it with one voice, on these grounds: (1) because the Messiah once promised by prophecies and figures necessarily had to ascend, as was demonstrated in §III. (2) Our Jesus truly is that once-promised Messiah, according to chapter 2, §XIX. (3) By the mouth of the two angels, as well as of eleven witnesses at minimum, all without exception adults, and who undertook death for

---

9. Augustine, *De haeresibus ad Quodvultdeum* in *PL* 42:29; idem, *Arianism and Other Heresies* in *The Works of St. Augustine*, 44 vols. (Hyde Park, New York: New City Press, 2001–2021), 1-18:37.

10. Latin: *ad coelum elementare*; Dutch: *tot den hoofdstoffelyken (elementairen) hemel*

their testimony, it is certain that he ascended. And so then, if the Jews rightfully accept the testimony of the one man Elisha for the ascension of Elijah, will we reject the testimonies borne by two angels and at minimum eleven witnesses? And (4) the New Testament, upon the trustworthiness of which we teach this, is just as much of universal truth and divine authority as is the Old Testament, which we expressly demonstrated in book 1, chapter 2.[11]

Objections
They do not have anything to oppose against this except their own rancid hypotheses: (1) that our Jesus is not the Messiah, which we have opposed in chapter 2, §XIX; (2) that he did not rise again, that which we demonstrated in the previous chapter;[12] (3) that the New Testament is not of universal truth, which we resist in the place already cited. Therefore, with these things taken away, there is no exception for them to make.

2. Did he ascend to heaven in the same body in which he was born
and rose again? The opinion of the Socinians
XII. Second, it is asked whether he ascended in the same body in which he lived, in which he died, and in which he rose again. The Socinians, because they state that man is reduced by death to a state of nonexistence, and accordingly upon rising again receives a new existence and a new body, namely a certain spiritual body, because flesh and blood cannot enter into the kingdom of Christ, think that Christ likewise by no means brought into heaven the body in which he lived here on earth, but received another body, and that a spiritual one.

The opinion and arguments of Christians
On the contrary, Christians think that Christ passed into heaven in the same body in which he lived and in which he rose again, because: (1) the angels expressly say that the same Jesus whom the disciples saw ascending would also return in the same manner in which he departed (Acts 1:11). (2) A body of flesh and bone is ascribed to him after the resurrection (Luke 24:39), in which body he also ascended (Acts 1:11). (3) It is said that he will appear as such in the future (Zech. 12:10; Rev. 1:7). (4) His flesh did not experience corruption (Ps. 16:10). (5) From the contrary hypothesis, Christ in heaven would consist in a double or triple spirit, namely the eternal spirit of deity (Heb. 9:14), the spirit of the soul (Luke 23:46), and the spirit assumed in the ascension. (6) If he did not

---

11. 1.1.2 §XXXI
12. 1.5.15 §§III–IV, XIV

have a human body in heaven, neither would he be a true man there, and since from the opinion of the Socinians, neither is he true God, nor an angel, what will he be? Nothing. At the least (7) if he did not have the same body in heaven, he would not be the same man who was on earth. And (8) if he did not have the same body in heaven that he had on earth, when John the Baptist said, "Behold the Lamb of God!" (John 1:36), he could not be so called now after the ascension; yet this is said about him while he is in heaven (Rev. 5:9). (9) In his first ascension (from our adversaries' hypotheses), he ascended into heaven in his own body that he had received from the blessed Virgin, during his forty day fast.

The hypotheses of the Socinians
The hypotheses of our adversaries (1) regarding the nonexistence of the dead, we have handled elsewhere,[13] and if it seems good to God, we will handle it further in its own place, in the chapter on the resurrection of our flesh.[14] (2) Regarding flesh and blood not entering into the kingdom of God (from 1 Cor. 15:50), this hypothesis is vain, since that passage should be understood to be not about the very substance of our flesh, but about its moral corruption (as in Gal. 1:16; John 3:6), or at least about its weakness and corruptibility. (3) He is the Lord from heaven, and heavenly (1 Cor. 15:47). I respond, He is, insofar as with respect to the divine nature he descended from heaven (John 6:33, 38), that is, he was manifested in the flesh (1 Tim. 3:16), just as God is read to have descended (Gen. 18:21). (4) "The belly for food, and food for the belly; God will destroy them both" (1 Cor. 6:13). I respond, He will destroy them, with respect to the use that they have here; not simply, nor with respect to every use, even that which they will have in the future.

3. Is the heaven into which Christ ascended some definite place?
The opinion of the Lutherans
XIII. Third, it is asked whether the heaven into which the body of Christ ascended after being locally elevated up to the clouds, is some determinate and definite place. The Lutheran Ubiquitists, so that they may have the body of Christ essentially present in the symbols of the Holy Supper, state that the body, from the personal union with the divine person, did receive the attribute of omnipresence with respect to possession, but with respect to use, he did not will to employ it until after he was elevated above the clouds, when he arrived at that heaven in which God is, which is everywhere. Hence, so that they may

---

13. 1.5.12 §XVIII; 1.5.13 §XI
14. 1.8.4 §XII

satisfy the history of the ascension in some way, they certainly deny that the ascension of Christ was a bare invisibility and disappearance, and confess that it was a local transition,[15] but they add that: (1) this visible and local ascension did not happen from the necessary condition of Christ's body, but from a most free dispensation. Then (2) they distinguish between the beginning of the ascension, from earth up to the clouds, during which he ascended visibly and locally, and the completion of the same, after he was taken up by a cloud. Then they deny that Christ locally and successively, from the clouds, through the orbs of the planets and the *primum mobile*,[16] entered into the empyrean heaven, because that heaven is where God is, that is, everywhere.

The opinion of the Reformed with their reasons
The Reformed, with the Scriptures, know nothing of all these avoidance tactics and hidden things of dishonesty, because: (1) Scripture always speaks about heaven as some definite place (Deut. 26:15; Ps. 2:4; 33:14; Isa. 66:1; etc.), which is clearly distinguished from earth and other places. (2) The heaven into which Christ ascends is denoted as a determinate place, which Christ had to occupy: Acts 3:21, "whom heaven must receive," for which reason he is said to have ascended up far above all heavens (Eph. 4:10), likewise to have been made higher than the heavens (Heb. 7:26), that is, the lower heavens, and again to have passed into the heavens (Heb. 4:14). (3) That same heaven of Christ is designated with such synonyms which cannot but denote a certain specific place distinct from the rest: for example, that it is called the Father's house (John 14:2), the highest heaven (Heb. 1:3), the heaven of heavens (1 Kings 8:27), the third heaven (2 Cor. 12:2), the heavenly Jerusalem (Gal. 4:26), paradise (Luke 23:43), the place of the angels (Matt. 6:9–10), from where we look for Christ (Phil. 3:20). (4) The hypotheses upon which the error of our adversaries is either built or wants to be supported, namely, the essential presence of the flesh of Christ in the symbols of the Holy Supper, the omnipresence conferred through the communication of attributes to the human nature, and so forth, have been refuted elsewhere, or will be.[17] In particular, (5) the distinction between the possession and use of omnipresence, whereby he could, according to his own choice, be present and not be present, is absurd, because in this way, God also, according

---

15. *negant quidem, ascensionem Christi, fuisse nudam* ἀορασίαν *et* ἀφανισμόν; *et fatentur fuisse* μετάβασιν τοπικήν.

16. In the Ptolemaic system, the *primum mobile*, "the first movable thing," is the outermost sphere rotating around the earth and causing the motion of the inner spheres. Cf. Dante Alighieri, *Divine Comedy*: Paradise, canto 28.

17. 1.2.10 §XIII; 1.5.4 §§XXIV, XXVI; 1.7.5 §§XXI, XXV

to his will, can be present or not present, since the omnipresence of God and Christ is the same. I would add that (6) Scripture nowhere teaches that Christ only ascended visibly and locally up to the clouds; in fact, it expressly testifies to the contrary, in all those passages which we already adduced for the second and third reason.

The objections of the Lutherans
The Lutherans do not have anything to allege for themselves, except: (1) that in many Scripture passages—"above the heavens," "in the heavens," and so forth—is denoted God's incomprehensible power and glory (Ps. 8:1; 108:4; Job 11:8; 22:12). I respond: (a) Is it said in these passages that heaven is not a definite place, because God displays his incomprehensible power and glory there? By the same reasoning, will not also the earth not be a definite place? (b) Is there any Scripture passage evident in which ascending into heaven means departing into an indefinite place? They allege (2) that in that way Christ could not have completed his ascent except by a long space of time; several determine more than fifty years. Whereas: (a) the Savior expressly says that *today* the thief will be with him in paradise (Luke 23:43). (b) They do not consider either the infinite power of God, or in nature itself, the swiftest motion of the stars. They allege (3) that on the last day, the heavens will pass away, while Christ will remain in heaven for eternity. I respond: (a) Not all the heavens will pass away, not the empyrean, for then where would the blessed in heaven abide (2 Cor. 5:1–2)? (b) Nor will they pass away with respect to substance, but with respect to vanity (Rom. 8:21), so that a new heaven and a new earth will come forth (Rev. 21:1). They allege, (4) Stephen saw Christ, or beheld him, standing at the right hand of God (Acts. 7:56), as did Paul (Acts 9:27). I respond: (a) And therefore the heaven where they saw Christ was not a definite place? (b) What if God elevated their ability so that they might see him in the empyrean heaven? Rather, (c) they saw Christ in an ecstasy, in a vision, not in his substance, as Paul declares (2 Cor. 12:2–4). They allege, (5) He did not properly and locally descend to earth in the incarnation; therefore, he also did not so ascend into heaven. I respond: (a) He descended into a definite place, the earth (Eph. 4:9, "into the lower parts of the earth"). (b) He descended with respect to the divine nature, he was manifested in the flesh (1 Tim. 3:16), but he ascended with respect to the human nature.

4. After his ascension is he still on earth?
The opinion of the Lutherans and the papists
XIV. Fourth, it is asked whether after his ascension, with respect to his human nature, Christ is still on earth. The Lutherans and papists, in favor of an oral

eating in the Holy Supper, answer in the affirmative, yet in such a way that the Lutherans guard his omnipresence, whereby he is always on earth and everywhere, whereas the papists only want him present in the Mass.

The opinion of the Reformed with their reasons
The Reformed, with the Scriptures, teach that after the resurrection until the final return he exists in his human nature only in heaven, because: (1) it is expressly stated that he left earth in his ascension (John 14:3; 16:5, 7, 28; 17:11–13; Matt. 26:11; Luke 24:51; Acts 1:9, 11). (2) By ascending he occupied the highest heaven, which is opposed to the earth (Mark 16:19; Acts 3:21; John 16:28). (3) On the premise of his bodily absence, he warns against seductions (Matt. 24:26), and exhorts to duties (Col. 3:1–2; 2 Cor. 5:6, 8; Phil. 1:23; Heb. 8:4). (4) It is said that he will return to earth from heaven (Acts 1:11; Matt. 24:27, 30, 44; 25:31–32; 26:64; 1 Cor. 11:26; 2 Thess. 1:7). (5) Our adversaries' παντοπία, presence in all places, and πολυτοπία, presence in many places, are repugnant to the nature of a true body, and import an open contradiction. (6) It is repugnant to the Holy Supper itself, inasmuch as it was instituted in memory of him till he come (1 Cor. 11:25–26). Compare what we said above in chapter 4 against divine properties being communicated to the human nature, and in particular omnipresence.[18]

Objections
They do not have anything that they may oppose to these things, except: (1) that after the ascension it is read that he was seen often: by Stephen (Acts 7:55–56), by Paul (Acts 9:4, 17; 22:6; 26:19), by John (Rev. 1:10, 12–13). I respond: (a) It is not said that he was seen existing on the earth, but that he was seen from earth in heaven (Acts 7:55–56); (b) those were ecstatic visions, in an internal vision (Acts 18:9; 1 Cor. 9:1; 2 Cor. 12:2), or they were emblematic, such as befell John in Revelation, the sort of visions which do not at all imply any true presence of the thing seen. (2) That it is said that he will be present with his own even to the end of the age (Matt. 28:20). I respond, By the presence of grace (about which see 2 Cor. 13:14). Likewise, (3) that he fills all things (Eph. 4:10). I respond, With his gifts (Ps. 68:18). Furthermore, (4) that he is eaten in the Holy Supper (Matt. 26:26, 28). I respond, Sacramentally, not orally, because it is done in remembrance of the one who is to come. (5) That otherwise his two natures would be divided. I respond, By no means, since his human nature is nowhere the divine person is not present united to it. (6) That through the personal union,

---

18. 1.5.4 §§XXIV, XXVI

divine properties are communicated to the human nature, and among them also omnipresence. I respond, We have expressly refuted those things in chapter 4.[19]

5. Did he ascend alone into heaven? The opinion of the papists
XV. Fifth, it is asked whether he ascended alone. There are those who think that when he was ascending he led with him into heaven those who had arisen at his death (Matt. 27:53), but they rest on no grounds at all in Scripture. The papists, so that they may more easily safeguard their limbo of the fathers, just as they state that before the actual satisfaction, that is, before Christ's death, no believers had been admitted into heaven, so they want him to have descended into hell to the end that he might lead those believers existing there out of it; and to have ascended so that he might convey them to heaven with him.

The opinion of the Reformed with their reasons
The Reformed believe that he ascended alone, because: (1) Scripture makes no mention of any company (Acts 1:9, 11). (2) Under the Old Testament, those who died in faith, by virtue of the satisfaction promised by absolute surety,[20] were received into heaven, as evidenced by Enoch (Heb. 11:5), Elijah (2 Kings 2:11; cf. Heb. 11:16), and Abraham (Luke 16:22). (3) His death is extended to Old Testament believers (Rom. 3:25; Heb. 9:15), and by virtue of it, they were able to pass into heaven. (4) Old Testament believers also were members of his body, flesh of his flesh (Eph. 5:30), and thus while existing on earth, they just as much had a pledge of their ascension in the future ascension of Christ, as we have in his past ascension (cf. Rom. 9:5; Gal. 3:16; Ps. 68:18).

An objection
Nor could they object anything more plausible than that before the Messiah was shown forth, the way into the heavenly holy place was not yet made manifest, while the first tabernacle was yet standing (Heb. 9:8). I respond, There is not anything understood by "the way" except Christ (John 14:6), the Son of God, who was manifested in the flesh in his incarnation (1 Tim. 3:16), who notwith-standing, by virtue of the satisfaction promised by absolute surety in the eternal counsel of peace, accepted believers in the Old Testament as well as the New Testament, just as we have said.

---

19. 1.5.4 §§XXIV, XXVI
20. *virtute satisfactionis expromissae.* Cf. 1.5.1 §XXXIV

6. Did he ascend into heaven so that he might become a priest?
XVI. Sixth, it is asked whether Christ ascended into heaven so that he might become a priest there. The Socinians, so that they might more easily defend their view that by his death, which happened on earth, he did not make satisfaction, state that he was not a priest on earth, but only became one by ascending and presenting himself before the Father on our behalf. The Reformed observe that there are two chief acts of a priest, the offering of a sacrifice, and intercession. The Savior performed both in his priesthood while still on earth: certainly by offering (Eph. 5:2 with 1 Peter 2:24), and by intercession (John 17; Luke 22:31–32), and thus he was a perfect priest, even while he existed on earth; although now that the offering has ceased, he continues his intercession in heaven (Rom. 8:34; Heb. 7:25). We have examined this controversy in both parts in chapter 7, §XVI.

7. Did Christ ascend more than once?
XVII. Seventh, it is asked whether this was the first and only ascension of Christ. The Lutherans and papists, in favor of his bodily presence in the eucharistic symbols, distinguish between a visible and an invisible ascension of Christ. They acknowledge that the former happened only once, but they state that the latter happens continuously. The Socinians also (due to their hatred of his eternal deity) state that he ascended once after his baptism at the time of his forty-day fast, so that he might learn about the mysteries of the gospel more perfectly there, and then that he ascended a second time after his resurrection. The Reformed, with the Scriptures, acknowledge none other than the one ascension of Christ (Heb. 9:12; Acts 1:9, 11; John 20:17). We have expressly examined the opinion of the Socinians in chapter 6, §XIV.

The Practical Part
The practice of the ascension demands from us:
1. That we contemplate his ascension.
XVIII. The practice of the ascension of Christ demands from us, first, that with the disciples of Christ, having been taken by Christ (Luke 24:50), we leave Jerusalem for the Mount of Olives to contemplate his glorious ascension, and guided there in our mind, we have our eyes intent upon him (Acts 1:9–10, ἀτενίζοντες, "gazing intently"). This occurs by considering frequently and devotedly, and carrying around in our memory, this glorious ascension, until we see him return, just as we have observed him ascending (v. 11).

Motives

For to this end (1) he took with him his disciples, not others, that is, he commanded that they leave with him. So also (2) our faith will be more and more strengthened regarding the truth, first of the resurrection, then of the ascension (Acts 1:3). So (3) he will inwardly speak also to us, and instruct us regarding the things of his kingdom (v. 3). So (4) we also will receive the promise of the Father, and be baptized with the Holy Spirit (vv. 4–5). So (5) we also will be able to speak with him about those things that pertain to the restoration of the kingdom of Israel, that is, of the church (v. 6). So (6) we also will be able to be witnesses of his resurrection and ascension to all sorts of people (v. 8). So (7) he will lift his hands over us and bless us (Luke 24:50) with every spiritual blessing (Eph. 1:3). So (8) also for us and for our sake, he will be taken up (Acts 1:9). So (9) also for us, he will leave behind him his *angeli*, messengers, to instruct us in the truth (vv. 10–11). So (10) we also will adore him with greater confidence (Luke 24:52). So (11) we also will return to Jerusalem, that is, to the church, with great joy (Luke 24:52). So (12) we also will worship God in the temple with greater courage, and give thanks to him (v. 53). Indeed additionally, (13) for this purpose he impressed his footsteps on the Mount of Olives (Zech. 14:4), certainly not natural footsteps (as many of the ancients wrongly gathered from this passage), but spiritual footsteps: (a) of love toward his disciples, whom he led out of Jerusalem to the Mount of Olives for this purpose, so that he might ascend for them, in the same place instruct them, bless them, make them partakers of a spiritual joy; footsteps (b) of suffering joined with glorification, when from the same place of Olivet, where he had begun his passions, he willed to ascend to his glory; footsteps (c) of gracious care and providence toward his disciples, when he lifted there his hands over them, and perhaps even placed them upon them; footsteps (d) of blessing to be poured out upon his own from heaven (Ps. 68:19; Eph. 1:3); footsteps (e) of saving promises, namely of the Holy Spirit and of strengthening through this Spirit (Acts 1:4–5, 8); footsteps (f) of spiritual desertion, when in the midst of the sweetness of conversation he is taken away from the disciples, and vanishes as it were from their eyes (v. 9; cf. Ps. 30:6–7); footsteps (g) of the new Comforter who is substituted for him in these desertions, and of new comfort, in the angels who encourage the disciples in the hope and promise of the return of Christ (Acts 1:10–11); footsteps (h) of contempt and desertion of this world, insofar as when he had finished with his business among the disciples during a brief space of forty days, he immediately left the world (v. 9; John 16:28); footsteps (i) of desire for heavenly conversation, since when he left the world, he hastened straight into heaven to his Father (cf. Col. 3:1; Phil. 3:20; Prov. 15:24).

2. That we rejoice and exult in the one ascending.

XIX. Second, Christ's ascension demands that we sincerely rejoice in the one ascending, for his triumph: (1) according to the example of the disciples, who due to his ascension are glad, celebrate, and give thanks (Luke 24:52–53), in which are included most of the elements of a song of rejoicing. For to this (2) we are called (Ps. 47:5–7). This (3) is demanded from us by the very glory of the triumph (Ps. 68:17–19; Col. 2:14–15). For just as: (a) among the Romans (to whose triumphs there is a clear allusion, at least in the last text cited) the generals did not triumph except after a victory, and one not common, but outstanding, so our Jesus also does not triumph except after a victory (Rev. 6:2), and indeed one gained over the most powerful things in this world, death, hell (1 Cor. 15:55–56), the infernal dragon (Rev. 12:11), principalities and powers, even the entire power of darkness (Col. 2:15; 1:13; Heb. 2:14). Just as (b) Roman triumphers were borne on a brilliant triumphal chariot, so also our Jesus is borne on a shining cloud (Acts 1:9 cf. 2 Kings 2:11). Just as (c) triumphers displayed their trophies, spoils, and enemies in chains, so also does our Jesus (Col. 2:14–15; Ps. 68:19; Eph. 4:8). Just as (d) triumphers lavished money upon the people, so our triumpher Jesus received gifts to distribute to men (Ps. 68:18; Eph. 4:8). Just as (e) Roman triumphers in the triumphal chariot directed their course to the Capitoline hill, so also our Jesus, into heaven itself (1 Peter 3:22). Accordingly, if the Romans, effusive with joy, acclaimed their own triumphers with the most glorious titles, gave thanks to them, and prayed upon them all the most favorable things, should not we, with the apostles returning to Jerusalem after the ascension of our so great and excellent triumpher, with indescribable joy also acclaim him, and earnestly desire all favorable things upon him? Compare here, with necessary changes made, the things we said in the preceding chapter, §XXIII.

3. The ascension supplies comfort. Its general grounds

XX. Third, Christ's ascension supplies a most effective comfort to true believers in any adverse circumstances, for which reason when he was about to go away he declared to the disciples who were grieved at his departure, "It is good for you that I go away" (John 16:6–7), regarding which comfort these are at least its chief grounds, that: (1) from the ascension, they now have in heaven an advocate with the Father that is perfect in every way (1 John 2:1). For whatever you could desire in an advocate, you will discover in Christ: for example, in an advocate it is desired (a) that he would be righteous; such is our Jesus (1 John 2:1; Isa. 42:1); (b) that he would be endowed with the ability to speak; such is ours (Isa. 50:4; Ps. 45:2; Luke 4:21); (c) one that regularly triumphs in court; ours always triumphs (Rev. 6:2), and obtains from the Father all that we desire (John 16:23);

(d) that he would be kind and accessible toward his clients; such is ours (Matt. 11:28); (e) that he would be pleasing to the judge; such is ours (Isa. 42:1; Matt. 17:5); (f) that he would be skilled in law and equity; such is ours (Prov. 8:6, 12; Isa. 11:2); (g) that he would not rely upon troublesome shouting, but peacefully conduct his case with reasons before the tribunal; so ours does (Isa. 42:2; Matt. 12:19); (h) that he would conduct himself as an expert, or one taught by experience; so ours does (Heb. 4:15; 5:8); (i) that he would be inclined to help the oppressed; so also ours is (Heb. 2:17; Isa. 61:2); (j) that he would not deny his services to any oppressed person; such is ours (Isa. 61:2; Matt. 11:28; John 6:37). Therefore just as in such an advocate is a most effective comfort for the oppressed and afflicted in this world, so also for believers in this their advocate, whom they have in heaven because of the ascension, is there not the most effective support for comfort? This is the first point. (2) From the ascension they obtain the Holy Spirit as the Comforter (John 16:7–8), who helps (συναντιλαμβάνεται) our infirmities, so that when we know not what to pray for as we ought, the Spirit himself makes intercession (ὑπερεντυγχάνει) for us with groanings which cannot be uttered (ἀλαλήτοις, Rom. 8:26). In this, is there not an indescribable foundation for comfort? Furthermore, (3) he promises that even after his departure he will not abandon his own, but will be present with them by his grace, even to the consummation of the ages (Matt. 28:20). In addition, (4) from his ascension, he received gifts to be poured out upon his own (Ps. 68:18; Eph. 4:8). Finally, (5) he promised more certainly than certain that he would return in his own time (John 14:3, 18), and take his own up with him (John 14:3; 17:24). I should add that (6) for this purpose he ascended into heaven, that he might prepare a place there for his own (John 14:2).

Adverse circumstances

Now, if: (1) Satan (the accuser of the brethren, Rev. 12:10), sins, or conscience should reproach true believers, what would be a more effective help than to have one who pleads on their behalf in heaven, and indeed such a great one (cf. Rom. 8:33–34)? If (2) they should especially lack necessities, in body or in soul, things that must be obtained from heaven alone, what could be more comforting than to have such an intercessor in heaven who always prevails with the Father (John 16:23)? If (3) any intolerable fate should bear down upon them on earth, through diseases, poverty, and other such things, and in it there is none to comfort them, what will raise them up more effectively than to have promised to them, from the ascension of Christ, the Holy Spirit himself as their Comforter? If (4) in the world we should be deserted by anyone, by our best friends, even our father and mother (Ps. 27:10), what will comfort us more effectively than that Jesus, when he was about to ascend, promised that he would be present with his people with his grace, even to the end of the ages? If (5) they should sense that they are destitute of the gifts necessary for salvation, what will raise them up more than that Christ when he ascended received gifts to be poured out upon his own? If (6) they should suspect that they have been deserted by God and Christ (Hos. 9:12), what will raise them up more effectively than that when he was departing, he promised that he would return (Isa. 54:7–8) and take his own with him to heaven? If (7) they must depart either from their country or from the world, what will raise them up more effectively than to consider that in heaven there are many μοναί, mansions, and that their own brother, who rose again for them, ascended to prepare a place for them there. And thus through any other adverse circumstances, if you should seek comfort, it will be supplied from Christ's ascension. Compare, with necessary changes made, the preceding chapter, §XXIV.

4. It teaches us to carefully inquire whether he ascended also for us.
XXI. Fourth, Christ's ascension also teaches to carefully inquire whether Christ ascended also for us, for since (1) the comfort of the preceding section does not apply to each and every person; since (2) he did not lead all men from Jerusalem to the Mount of Olives, to make them participants in his ascension; nor (3) does he serve as advocate with the Father for all; nor (4) prepare mansions in heaven for all, then it is certainly necessary that we would be concerned whether he ascended also for us; especially since (5) for the vast majority, he sits in heaven as their enemy, he sets them as his footstool for his feet (Ps. 110:1), and triumphs over them in heaven (Col. 2:15); and (6) the whole certainty of this distinction depends upon a careful investigation, upon which certainty rests all our genuine tranquility, peace, joy, and comfort.

Marks
But by what marks will we be rendered more certain of our participation in this? I respond: (1) By the same marks by which we have shown in the previous chapters that he died for us and that he rose for us,[21] because the ascension has an indivisible connection with these (Rom. 6:3–5, 8; Eph. 2:5–6; Gal. 2:20). If (2) we have been united by living faith with Christ, as members with the head, for thus in and with him we will be accounted as those set with him in the heavens (Eph. 2:6), and it will be said that by ascending he departed to his God and our God, to his Father and our Father (John 20:17). If (3) we are of the number

---

21. 1.5.12 §XXXIII; 1.5.15 §XXVI

of his disciples, whom he describes in Luke 9:23, about whom he expressly declares, "It is expedient *for you* that I should depart" (John 16:7; 14:2–3; and so forth). If (4) with his disciples, he has also led us out of Jerusalem (Luke 24:50), that is, out of the world (Heb. 13:13; 1 John 2:15–16). If (5) having been led out with him and his disciples, we have ascended to the Mount of Olives and to Bethany (Acts 1:12; Luke 24:50), that is, to the house of affliction, and the place of his sufferings, so that from there we might not only look up to see him ascending, but also from sufferings pass as it were with him into participation in glory (Luke 24:26; Rom. 8:17). If (6) as he conversed corporally with the disciples for forty days (Acts 1:3), so also he has conversed spiritually with us, and thus we have contracted friendship and familiarity with him, just as Enoch was not taken up by God except after continual conversation with him (Heb. 11:5 with Gen. 5:24). If (7) by that conversation Christ has revealed himself to us by many certain marks, so much that we not only have heard, but also seen him (Acts 1:3). If (8) we have been sufficiently taught by him regarding those things which pertain to the kingdom of God (v. 3). If (9) we have shown faith in his promises and obedience to his precepts (v. 4). If (10) we should ask him (yet without curiosity) about those things which concern the restoration of his spiritual kingdom in us (v. 6). If (11) we have experienced the power of the Spirit who sanctifies and converts (v. 8). If (12) by the same power of the Spirit we have presented ourselves as faithful witnesses of Christ (v. 8). If (13) we have the eyes of our mind intent toward heaven and Christ, so that we would look with fervent affection for him to return from heaven, just as by faith we saw him ascending into heaven (v. 9). If finally, (14) from the command of Christ, we have returned to Jerusalem, awaiting for the Holy Spirit, in his saving gifts, to be poured out more and more upon us, according to his promise when he was ascending (v. 10 with v. 4).

5. It rouses us to endeavor to experience the power of the ascension of Christ.
What this power is
XXII. Fifth, Christ's ascension urges us to endeavor by every means to experience more and more the power of this ascension. For his ascension, as well as his death and resurrection, has its own power, and is different in this respect from the ascension of Enoch and Elijah, who only ascended for themselves. Moreover, this power is: (1) in the confirmation of our faith (Acts 1:3); (2) in intercession for us (Rom. 8:34; Heb. 9:24); (3) in the sending of the Holy Spirit (John 16:6); (4) in the communication of those gifts that are necessary for the application of the redemption acquired for us (Eph. 4:8, 10); (5) in the subjugation of our spiritual captivity (v. 8); (6) in the spiritual attraction (John 12:32) by which we have the eyes of our mind continuously intent (ἀτενίζοντες) toward heaven,

and we lift up our hearts and affections, so that we may seek those things which are above, where Christ is, seated at the right hand of God (Col. 3:1–2); (7) in the preparation and occupation of the place where after this life we may dwell eternally (John 14:2–3).

By what motives it must be taken hold of

Now we must strive with all our gathered strength to experience this manifold power of Christ's ascension. For otherwise (1) we will, as much as lies in us, or at least with respect to ourselves, thoroughly enervate that most glorious ascension of Christ, and in fact deny it, thus committing a horrendous evil. (2) We will most cruelly abuse ourselves and our wretched souls, by depriving ourselves of all those benefits which redound to true believers from Christ's ascension and its efficacy. On the contrary, (3) we will arm Christ, who from his ascension now sits most glorious at the right hand of the Father, against us, such that, even on account of this neglect, this contempt for his most glorious ascension, he sets us, as his enemies, as a footstool for his feet (Ps. 110:1), and leads us despoiled publicly in his triumphal train, together with the infernal powers and authorities (Col. 2:15).

In what manner we must strive

Moreover, the manner of striving is occupied chiefly with these two things: (1) those means by which we strive toward union with Christ and communion in the benefits of Christ, namely faith and the Spirit, which two are as it were the bonds of our union with Christ. For while we are united with Christ, all his benefits, just as of his death and resurrection, so also of his ascension and intercession, are ours. (2) The use of the means, through which these benefits of union are dispersed to us in actuality, in which use the chief means is: (a) a confident approach[22] through prayers to the Father (Rom. 5:2; Eph. 2:18; 3:12). Yet in this (b) it is necessary that we deliver up our prayers as it were into the hands of Christ, who has been made through the ascension our only intercessor in heaven (1 John 2:1–2), such that, with the disciples (Luke 24:50) we do not go to the Father except as those taken up and led to him, and we do not ask for anything except in his name (John 16:26). And also (c) such that we approach with a heart purified from an evil conscience (Heb. 10:22), because sins separate us from God (Isa. 59:1–2), and God does not hear sinners (Prov. 15:29).

---

22. *fiducialis* προσαγωγή

6. Christ's ascension urges us to leave the world. What it is to leave the world
XXIII. Sixth, it urges us, with the ascending Christ, to leave the world (John 16:28). But we do not understand by *world* here the earth itself, in which sense Christ in ascending left the world, and we in dying will at some point leave the same world, but rather: (1) worldly and earthly things, wealth, honors, and worldly pleasures (1 John 2:15; James 4:9; John 8:23); and (2) a worldly manner of living (Rom. 12:2). And for us, leaving the world here does not mean simply not having the world and worldly things, or not having them in plenty. For you may also see that those who most fervently pursued heaven and heavenly things had worldly goods, and that in plenty, indeed in abundance, for example, Abraham, Isaac, Jacob, about whom the apostle testifies notwithstanding that they sought a city that has foundations, whose builder is God (Heb. 11:8–10); so also for Paul (Phil. 4:12). Rather, leaving the world is for us at present nothing except: (1) not loving the world immoderately (1 John 2:15), that is, (a) not esteeming it excessively (Phil. 3:7–8); (b) not excessively desiring, seeking, or panting after it (Col. 3:1–2; Matt. 6:33); (c) not rejoicing and delighting excessively in the possession and use of worldly things (Ps. 4:7; 62:10); (d) not being excessively troubled over the loss of earthly things (Heb. 10:34); (e) not loving the world and worldly things above God (2 Tim. 3:4), above Christ (Matt. 10:37), above heaven or heavenly and spiritual things (Col. 3:1–2; Matt. 6:33). Then (2) leaving the world is nothing but not abusing the world (1 Cor. 7:29–31), which happens: (a) by possessing the world as if without God (Ps. 10:3–4); (b) by elevating it above God (2 Tim. 3:4), such that it is for us as if in the place of God (Phil. 3:19); (c) by placing it in our heart next to God, as a strange god (Ex. 20:3); (d) by opposing God, and by our wealth and rank, fighting against God (Acts 23:9). Furthermore, (3) leaving the world is nothing but not conforming ourselves to it, or to its morals and manner of life (Rom. 12:2). Finally, (4) it is nothing but promptly renouncing the world and all worldly things, either on account of God and of Christ (Mark 10:28; Matt. 19:27, 29; 16:25–26), or through natural death, and a desire for a heavenly life (Phil. 1:20–21, 23; 2 Cor. 5:1–2).

By what motives the world ought to be left behind
Now, that we would leave the world in this way, is urged by the following: (1) because otherwise we cannot spiritually ascend into heaven, for just as Christ could not naturally ascend into heaven except by leaving the world, so neither can we do so spiritually (Col. 3:1–2). Then (2) because the world entirely deserves to be left by us, for it is: (a) vain (Eccl. 11:8; 1 Cor. 7:31; Ps. 39:6; Prov. 23:5), while heaven, to which we tend with Christ by leaving the world, is a

city which has foundations (Heb. 11:10). It is (b) passing and transient (1 John 2:17): so for honor (Jer. 22:22), wealth (Prov. 23:5), the most expansive edifices of men (Matt. 24:2), and pleasures (Heb. 11:25), whereas heaven, toward which we strive with Christ by leaving the world, is a kingdom which cannot be moved (Heb. 12:28). It is (c) vile and abject, thick clay (Hab. 2:6), dung (Phil. 3:7–8), whereas heaven (the holy Jerusalem, Rev. 21:10), which we seek with Christ by leaving the world, has goods that eye has not seen, ear has not heard, and the heart of man has never perceived (1 Cor. 2:9). It is (d) deceitful, with its specious promises (Job 15:31), just as its god is (Matt. 4:8–9), whereas Jesus, with whom we leave the world, is trustworthy in fulfilling his promises made to those who leave the world (Matt. 19:27–28; John 14:2). It is (e) useless for true blessedness (Prov. 11:4; Ps. 49:7–8), whereas heaven, which we seek by leaving the world with Christ, is most necessary (Matt. 16:26). It is (f) also at times harmful, by impeding true blessedness (Matt. 13:22; 19:23), and obstructing the road to heaven (1 Tim. 6:9; James 4:4), whereas Jesus, with whom we leave the world, prepares a new and living way (Heb. 10:19–20), indeed, he is the way itself (John 14:6), and puts us who are leaving the world into heaven (Eph. 2:6). (3) Because nothing more absurd and incongruous could be thought of than if a Christian should be dying with love for the world, which Christ left. Indeed also, (4) nothing is more foolish than to be unwilling to leave what you have to leave shortly (Luke 12:19–20), and likewise to prefer to leave heaven rather than earth.

7. It rouses us to strive together with Christ for heaven, which occurs by:
(1) Ascending
XXIV. Seventh, the ascension of Christ rouses us to strive spiritually for heaven, together with the Christ who ascends, just as the disciples, taken up by the one about to ascend, had their eyes, their thoughts, and undoubtedly also their hearts intent toward heaven ("And they were looking steadfastly toward heaven as he went up," Acts 1:10). That is, let us ascend with him spiritually, with the bride (Song 3:6), which happens by striving that our heart, and affections, and desires, would be in heaven, where Christ is, seated at the right hand of God (Col. 3:1; Eph. 2:6; Joh. 17:24; Heb. 11:10, 14–15; Phil. 1:23), so that, not only with our bodies and external things, but with our very soul and internal things, we may be near God and Christ (Matt. 15:8 from Isa. 29:13).

(2) Abiding
Let us dwell constantly with Christ in heaven, as in our mansion (John 14:2), as in our homeland (Heb. 11:14), as in our city, whose citizens we are (Eph. 2:19; Heb. 11:10; Phil. 3:20). Just as the apostles desired when they were with

the glorified Christ on the mountain (Matt. 17:4), and as David did (Ps. 27:4; 84:1–2, 4; 15:1), as those who are pilgrims on the earth (Ps. 39:12; 119:19; Heb. 11:13; 1 Peter 2:11).

(3) Living

Let us live as in heaven, in a heavenly manner, such that we have our πολίτευμα, citizenship,[23] in heaven (Phil. 3:20), that is, let us have: (a) a heavenly mind, that savors heavenly or spiritual things (Rom. 8:6–7), that is endowed with a heavenly and divine character (2 Peter 1:4). Let us have (b) a heavenly goal, to which the heavenly calling points (Phil. 3:14), which those who are in heaven pursue together with Christ (Rom. 14:17), whereby we live not for ourselves, but for God and Christ (Rom. 14:7–8; 2 Cor. 5:15). (c) Let us be engaged in heavenly occupations, as much in our intellect, by thinking, by meditating (Rom. 8:6), as in our will, by seeking, by pursuing those things in which those who dwell in heaven are occupied: for example, seeing God (Matt. 18:10; 1 Cor. 13:12), glorifying him (Isa. 6:3; Rev. 4:8), and so forth. (d) Let us set for ourselves a heavenly norm of behavior (Matt. 6:10), whereby we behave not according to the flesh or the custom of this world, but according to the Spirit (Rom. 8:1; 12:2). (e) Let us seek heavenly company (Ps. 16:3), in which we will someday rejoice in heaven (Heb. 12:22–24; Matt. 8:11). (f) Let us apply ourselves to heavenly studies (Matt. 6:10), so that we may opportunely learn on earth those things the knowledge of which continues in heaven (John 17:3), so that we may be spiritual and heavenly not only in our spiritual pursuits (Rev. 1:10), but also in our temporal ones, for example, while eating and drinking (Luke 14:15; John 6:26–27), in gathering wealth (Matt. 6:19–20), and so forth.

(4) Conducting business

Let us nurture commerce with heaven, like heavenly merchants (Matt. 13:45): (a) let us seek the merchandise of the kingdom of heaven (Matt. 6:33), the prize of the high calling (Phil. 3:14), heaven's pearl of great price (Matt. 13:45–46); (b) for the sake of heavenly things, let us sell all other things, and despise them (Matt. 13:45–46; 19:27–28); (c) let us conscientiously lay hold of heavenly market days, that is, of all opportunities to acquire heavenly things (2 Cor. 6:2; Gal. 6:10; Rev. 10:6); (d) let us equip ourselves with skill in heavenly trade, and in opportunities for heavenly merchandise (Matt. 13:45, 52; 16:3).

---

23. Dutch: *burgerschap*

The motivating reasons

The following things altogether urge us that we should therefore strive in this way toward heaven: (1) the example of our forerunner (Heb. 6:20, "where the forerunner has entered for us, even Jesus"), our head, our king, our brother, our bridegroom, who ascended into heaven and there sits at the right hand of God (Col. 3:1). That (2) there is nothing besides and beyond heaven worthy for a Christian to strive for, insofar as he is a Christian: he may strive for other things insofar as he is a man, and an earthly and fleshly man (Ps. 17:14), but insofar as he is a Christian, there is nothing for which he may rightfully strive except heaven, where his all is. For this reason, Chrysostom (on Phil. 3, homily 13) says, "Our all is in heaven, both our Savior and our city, and anything that anyone can name."[24] There is our Father (Matt. 6:9), our mother (Gal. 4:26; Heb. 12:22), our brother (Heb. 2:10–11), our head (Eph. 1:22), our homeland (Heb. 11:16), our inheritance (1 Peter 1:4), our mansion (John 14:2; 2 Cor. 5:1), our substance (Heb. 10:34), our hope (Col. 1:5). Would we not surely therefore strive upward, and lift up the gates of our heart (Ps. 24:7, 9)? (3) This our spiritual ascension, through which we seek the things above, offers us an infallible mark of our union and communion with Christ, through which we have died and risen with him (Col. 3:1–2), upon which all tranquility of heart depends. For if we do not ascend with Christ, then we have not risen with him, and consequently neither have we died with him; accordingly, neither have we been united with him (cf. Rom. 6:5; Gal. 2:20). Finally, (4) this our spiritual ascension with Christ supplies to us a certain argument of our future natural ascension (Phil. 3:20; Eph. 2:5–6). We have said more things of this kind above in book 3, chapter 6, §§XLII–XLIII.

Means

Now, so that we may be more inclined and suitable to strive spiritually for heaven in this way, it will help: (1) to wean our heart more and more from the world, for which reason the apostle desired to be dissolved, so that he might be with Christ (Phil. 1:23); nor can we pant after a heavenly home before the earthly house of this tabernacle (at least in our affections) be destroyed (2 Cor. 5:1–2, 4), and to signify this, when Christ was about to ascend, he led his disciples from Jerusalem to Olivet (Luke 24:50; cf. Ps. 131:2; 2 Tim. 2:4). It will help (2) to opportunely heap up treasures in heaven; for where our treasure is, there will our heart be (Matt. 6:20–21), just as on the contrary, those whose treasure is on earth, their

---

24. πάντα ἡμῶν ἐν οὐρανοῖς, καὶ σωτὴρ, καὶ πόλις, καὶ ὁ, τι ἂν εἴποι τίς. Chrysostom, *In epistolam ad Philippenses commentarius* in *PG* 62:280; idem, Chrysostom, *Homilies on Philippians*, Homily 13 on Phil. 3:18–21 in *NPNF1* 13:244.

heart also is stuck to it. It will help (3) to have a mind that is heavenly, spiritual, and subtle, which strives upward (Ps. 25:1), just as crass and earthly things tend downward. Let us have a fiery heart, which ascends like a flame, or a column of smoke (Song 3:6). It will also help (4) to be accustomed more and more to heaven and heavenly things (cf. Dan. 6:11), to take any opportunities by which our heart could be raised upward, such as are found in exercises of divine worship, discourses, meditations, heavenly conversations (Luke 24:32), and so forth.

8. It condemns those who do not want to follow Christ to heaven.
Who those people are
XXV. Eighth, the ascension of Christ condemns those who, although they profess that they are Christians, that is, the sort who follow Christ (Luke 9:23), and although they acknowledge that Christ ascended into heaven, yet refuse to follow him there that they may dwell with him in heaven. And who then are these people? They are: (1) those whose conversation is so far from heaven that it is in hell itself, so far from Christ that it is with Satan himself, namely those who are accustomed to hellish and satanic vices, hatreds, curses, lies, blasphemies, jealousies; or whoever are openly ungodly (John 8:44), under which name Judas is said to have departed into his own place (Acts 1:25). They are (2) those whose conversation is at least on earth and earthly (John 3:31), who pay attention only to earthly and worldly things, wealth, honors, pleasures, who are earthly-minded (Phil. 3:19, 1 John 2:15–16). They are (3) those whose conversation is neither in heaven nor thoroughly in hell, but as it were in the middle, that is, who are neither truly godly nor openly ungodly, who participate to some extent in both: with respect to outward duties of piety, they appear godly, but with respect to inward and spiritual duties, they are thoroughly ungodly, such as hypocrites (2 Tim. 3:5; Matt. 7:22; 23:23–27). They are (4) those whose conversation is at least not with God, with Christ, with the inhabitants of heaven, or with heavenly things, that is, those who do not delight in heavenly exercises such as the knowledge, worship, and enjoyment of God, those who do not endeavor to do the will of God on earth as it is done in heaven (Matt. 6:10; Job 21:14–15).

What kind of misery they have
All these, (1) as they are strangers to heaven and heavenly things (Eph. 2:12), so they exhibit a worldly, hellish, and diabolical character (John 8:44) inasmuch as in them the god of this age works (Eph. 2:2). They are (2) shut out from union with Christ, inasmuch as the Spirit of Christ is not in them (Rom. 8:9, 14), and Christ does not live in them (Gal. 2:20). Accordingly, (3) they do not have communion with Christ and his benefits: with his death, inasmuch as they are its

enemies (Phil 3:18), with his resurrection (Col. 3:1), with his ascension (Eph. 2:5–6). Finally, (4) just as they do not delight in heaven and heavenly things, but in fact attend to hell and hellish things, so by God's just judgment they will be eternally cut off from heaven and heavenly things, and will be cast with Judas into a place analogous to their character, to their desires, that is, into hell (Acts 1:25; Matt. 11:23).

The causes of the evil

So that we may effectively remedy such evils, these sorts of causes must be sought out and removed: (1) blindness of mind, which does not know heavenly, divine, and spiritual things as they are in themselves, and indeed considers them foolishness (1 Cor. 2:14; 1:23); (2) aversion of the heart from heavenly and spiritual things, and a contrary propensity toward earthly and carnal things (Rom. 8:5–7; Phil. 3:19); (3) excessive care and anxiety for earthly things, whereby the heart is weighed and pressed down (Luke 21:34), and all heavenly and spiritual things are choked out (Matt. 13:22); (4) unbelief, whereby they do not sufficiently believe those things that are declared in the Scriptures regarding heaven, God, Christ, spiritual matters, and the weight of heavenly glory (Heb. 3:12); (5) perverse examples of this world, which most effectually entice them from heavenly to earthly things (1 John 5:19; Rom. 12:2).

9. *It supplies a pledge of our future ascension.* In how many ways

XXVI. Ninth, the ascension of Christ supplies us with an infallible pledge of our future natural ascension, insofar as: (1) it is his immovable will that where he is, there we may also be, that we may behold his glory (John 17:24). (2) By his intercession, which is never ineffective (John 11:22), he entreated this from the Father on our behalf (John 17:24). (3) For this very purpose he ascended into heaven, that he might prepare a mansion for us there (John 14:2). (4) He added his infallible promise that he would return and take us (John 14:2), and indeed all people (John 12:32). (5) He entered into heaven for us, or in our stead (Heb. 6:20). (6) He ascended that he might open the way for us (Heb. 9:8; 10:19–20), in fact that he himself might supply the way through which we may come to the Father (John 14:6). (7) Through the ascension of Christ we now have our very head (Eph. 1:22–23) and our flesh (Eph. 5:30) present in heaven.

And to what persons he supplies this pledge

Nevertheless, Christ's ascension does not supply such a pledge to each and every person, but: (1) only to those who are his disciples, that is, who are truly Christians; for to these only did he promise (John 14:2) and entreat (John 17:24); who

(2) have spiritually died with him, been made alive, and risen with him (Eph. 2:5–6); who (3) with him have already left the world, for he does not pray for the world and the worldly (John 17:9), nor does he seek their presence (v. 24); who (4) have already spiritually ascended with him (Col. 3:1), and already have their conversation in heaven (Phil. 3:20); who (5) tread the way of life, which leads the wise upward (Prov. 15:24), that living and new way (Heb. 10:20); who (6) look with longing for his return, or his appearing, and in the meantime fight a noble fight to the end, and keep faith and a good conscience undiminished (2 Tim. 4:7–8).

CHAPTER SEVENTEEN

The Session of the Mediator
at the Right Hand of God

And he set him at his own right hand in the heavens, far above all rule, and authority, and power, and dominion, and every name that is named,[1] not only in this age, but also in the one to come, and has put all things under his feet, and established him the head over all things to the church itself.
—Ephesians 1:20–22

The third degree of exaltation is the session at the right hand.

I. And so we ascend to the third degree of the exaltation of Christ, which is in his session at the right hand of God, which the apostle presents in Ephesians 1:20–22.

The Exegetical Part

The text is explained.

II. In these words, the elevation of Christ to the right hand of his Father:

A. Is set forth in verse 20, where there is noted:

1. The one elevating, implied in the copulative "and." Here is signified the God of our Lord Jesus Christ, the Father of glory, inasmuch as it was fitting for him to confer the glory of session at his own right hand to his own Son, the Lord of glory (1 Cor. 2:8), through the Spirit of glory (1 Peter 4:14). So then, although this elevation, first theologically considered, belongs to the whole Trinity inasmuch as it is a work *ad extra*, yet economically it belongs first to the Father, who set the Son in this glory, just as the Son sat down in the same glory.

2. The elevation: ἐκάθισεν, "he set." Καθίζω, although it not uncommonly denotes, intransitively, to sit (just as יָשַׁב in Hebrew means to

---

1. The phrases "and dominion" and "that is named" are not in the Latin, but were supplied from Mastricht's exegesis below, and also appear in the 1749–1753 Dutch translation.

remain, to dwell, to sit with tranquility), as in Hebrews 1:3, ἐκάθισεν ἐν δεξιᾷ, he sat down at the right hand, yet in this passage it denotes, transitively, "I make to sit" (as also in Matt. 21:7; 1 Cor. 6:4), namely, as judges and lords customarily do, and God also does (2 Thess. 2:4). Although Stephen saw Jesus also standing at the right hand of God (Acts 7:55), so that sitting seems to denote the lordship itself, and standing the exercise of that lordship. But whereas he is said to have been set at the right hand, it is hinted that he was elevated by the power of another, and hence he did not sit at the right hand of God simply as the Son of God, or only with respect to his divine nature, inasmuch as it cannot be elevated, but also with respect to his human nature, or rather, as the God-man Mediator, with respect to both natures simultaneously, as "God manifested in the flesh…received into glory" (1 Tim. 3:16).

3. The one elevated, namely Christ, whom according to the preceding half-verse, God raised from the dead by his infinite power: "him," αὐτόν, as the manuscript codex of Camerarius has it: καὶ καθίσας αὐτόν, "and having set him."[2] Therefore he was elevated in the concrete with respect to his person, not just with respect to his human nature, to which divine glory, omnipresence, and omnipotence had been communicated, as the Ubiquitists want it. But he was elevated to the right hand of God with respect to both natures, as we will explain in its own place.[3]

4. The terminus of elevation: ἐν δεξιᾷ αὐτοῦ, "at his right hand" or "on his right hand." It is also frequently ἐν δεξιῶν, in a plural sense (Heb. 1:13), perhaps so that it may be signified that God does not properly have a right hand, in an anthropomorphic sense, but not that the right hand of God denotes a place, such that with the Ubiquitists you would conclude from the plural that the human nature of Christ, since it sits at the right hand of God, is by that fact omnipresent. But it denotes the glory of God in an improper sense, because one human being does not have but one right hand, and to sit at someone's right hand is nothing except to attain a glory proximate to him, for which

---

2. Joachim Camerarius (1500–1574) in *Commentarius in Novum Foedus*, 72 in *Novum Testamentum…Bezae…accessit etiam Joachimi Camerarii in Novum Foedus commentarius* (Cambridge: Roger Daniel, 1642).

3. §§XIV, XVIII, below

reason to sit at Christ's left denotes glory as well as at his right (Matt. 20:21; cf. Ps. 45:9).

5. The place of elevation: ἐν ἐπουρανίοις, "in the heavenly," or "in the higher-than-heavenly"[4] (supply "places"); in the highest and glorious heaven, the seat of God and of the blessed (John 3:12; 1 Cor. 15:40, 48–49; Phil. 2:10; 2 Tim. 4:18). So that the place is designated where he obtains the glory of the right hand of God. For although the right hand of God is not a place, yet "the higher-than-heavenlies" designates the place of glory, and thus after his resurrection, Christ ascended into heaven so that he might gain glory there.

B. Is expounded, in verse 21, with respect to things belonging to this session:

1. Glory, wherein it surpasses everything. Ὑπεράνω, not simply ἄνω, above, but "exceedingly above," supplying "he was exalted" or "he sits at the right hand of God"; not only in the location of his body ἐν ὑπερουρανίοις, in the higher-than-heavenly places, as we have said, but also, and much more, with a surpassing excellence of glory. Ἀρχῆς, ἐξουσίας, καὶ δυνάμεως, καὶ κυριότητος, exceedingly above "principality, authority, power, and dominion": some refer the origin and difference of these terms (1) to earthly rulers, such that ἀρχαὶ are kings, ἐξουσίαι are any other lesser magistrates, δυνάμεις are authorities, even tyrannical ones, κυριότητες are any kind of lords, even private ones, in the commonwealth, the church, and elsewhere, that is, from the idea of the Persian empire, under which the Hebrews once were, where ἀρχαὶ are רברבנוהי (Dan. 5:2), δυνάμεις are שריו (Est. 2:18), ἐξουσίαι are שלטנין from שלט, which in Aramaic means ἐξουσιάζω, I exercise authority. Thus, ἀρχαὶ or ἄρχοντες are ראשון (Job 12:24; 39:25; and in Ezekiel and Ezra), and κυριότητες or κυριείαι are ממשל (Dan. 11:3–4).[5] Moreover, it is common for all eastern peoples to use abstract concepts for concrete things. Thus Grotius thinks on Romans 8:38.[6] Others (2) refer it to the angels and their classes, orders, and companies, whose names these are, which names are frequent among the Hebrews. This is apparent, first, from the phrase "in the supercelestial places," and then

---

4. *in coelestibus, aut supercoelestibus*; below, "supercelestial"
5. Cf. *loc. cit.* in Montano, *Biblia sacra Hebraice, Chaldaice, Graece et Latine.*
6. Grotius, *Annotationes in Nouum Testamentum* in *Opera omnia theologica,* 2-2:725.

from the comparison of Romans 8:38, 1 Corinthians 15:24, Ephesians 3:10, and Colossians 1:16. It is as if you should call them (if you should derive their names from the Roman Empire) prefects, praetors, vicars, presidents, and overseers. Thrones (θρόνοι) are added in Colossians 1:16, meaning kings, such as some who were under the great monarch of the Persians, who for that reason was called "the king of kings." A similar distinction of orders is also observed in the kingdom of Satan (Eph. 6:12). Christ therefore is proclaimed superior to all those, even the most excellent spirits, as King of kings and Lord of lords (Rev. 17:14). Still others (3) think that these are said of both the earthly and the heavenly, as much the wicked as the good, as is evident from the goal of the apostle, whereby he endeavors to demonstrate that Christ was exalted above all creatures (likewise from Matt. 28:18; cf. Col. 1:15–17; 1 Peter 3:22). The apostle adds, καὶ παντὸς ὀνόματος ὀνομαζομένου οὐ μόνον ἐν τῷ αἰῶνι τούτῳ, ἀλλὰ καὶ ἐν τῷ μέλλοντι, "and every name that is named, not only in this age, but also in that which is to come." Here he takes ὄνομα, "name," either: (1) for what is named, or for an existing thing, so that the sense is, whatever exists in the nature of things, for everything that exists has a name; or (2) for any excellent person, whether he be human or angelic, who, by reason of some sort of excellence, deserves to be named with fame, for שֵׁם to the Hebrews often signifies a dignity, for which they designate honored men as "men of name," just as the Greeks call the same ὀνομαστοί, "named men." "Name" stands for a celebrated thing, and being named for being celebrated. Ὀνομαζομένου, "that is named," a present participle, by syllepsis also connotes that which is to come. The succeeding clause can be referred either: (1) to the entire complex of the preceding statement, or to those words, "He is seated at the right hand," so that it teaches that Christ not only is already seated there—that is, reigning over all things "in this age"—but also will reign "in that which is to come," and thus his reign is eternal, and includes the age which is to come, without any exception, which age he calls "to come" not because it does not already exist, but because it is to come with reference to us; or, (2) to the word most closely preceding, "is named," so that the sense is that Christ is not only above the aforementioned orders of angels, but also, if there are any others more exalted, or any things more outstanding, which in this age at least cannot be named, but will be known in another, if there are still more august terms for angels than those names, such angels as were thought by the Hebrews to be obscurely designed in Ezekiel by the name חיות, "living creatures," (Ezek. 1:14–15, 19), whom the ancient heretics of the Christians named aeons (as also did Tatian), whose names and offices will be known in the future age—also over these will Christ have command, with no nature excepted, besides the Father (1 Cor. 15:27). Compare what we considered about the orders of angels above, in book 3, chapter 7.[7]

2. Authority of ruling, which is twofold:

   a. Common authority over all things: καὶ πάντα ὑπέταξεν ὑπὸ τοὺς πόδας αὐτοῦ, "and he has put all things under his feet." Πάντα, all things, that is, as much angels as men, both good and evil, and all creatures (as is evident from a comparison of the preceding words with Phil. 2:10; Matt. 28:18), even his and the church's enemies (Ps. 110:1). All these things "he has put under his feet," that is, in perfect subjection, such as belongs to us over those things and those people that we have under our feet, that we trample underfoot and crush (cf. Josh. 10:24). To the first Adam he had subjected livestock, cattle, and all earthly things (Gen. 1:26), and to the second he also subjected the heavenly hosts, and hell itself, and death (1 Cor. 15:27; Phil. 3:21).

   b. Particular authority, over his own church: καὶ αὐτὸν ἔδωκε κεφαλὴν ὑπὲρ πάντα τῇ ἐκκλησίᾳ, "and he gave him to be head over all the church," that is, the church of both Gentiles and Jews, of angels and men, militant and triumphant. Or, "and he gave him who is over all things to be head to the church," or, "he gave him" (supply, "who was set") "over all things to the church to be its head, namely, for the great good and solace of the church, and thus in these words there is a transposition. To others, it seems here must be supplied, ὥστε εἶναι αὐτὸν ὑπὲρ πάντα κεφαλὴν τῇ ἐκκλησίᾳ, that is, so that he might be the highest and omnipotent head of the church, or even, the sole and only head of the church. Ἔδωκε, he "gave," through a Hebraism, for κατέστησε, he constituted (as in Gen. 41:43), unless it first connotes a singular grace of the one constituting. He gave him to be not only the βασιλεύς, king, to whom it belongs only to govern his subjects,

---

7. 1.3.7 §§XIX, XXX

and not to influence them by his immediate power over them, but the κεφαλή, head, just as he makes clear in the following verse 23. That is, not only by reason of rank, as the chief member, such as the head is in our body, but also, through union with his members, he communicates to each one his power, spirit, and grace, and sustains, governs, and directs them in all spiritual things (1 Cor. 12:12). Furthermore, he more distinctly represents this church in verse 23, but we put this aside for the chapter on the church.[8]

The Dogmatic Part

Christ sits at the right hand of the Father. It is proved by the Scriptures.

III. Therefore, Christ not only ascended into heaven, just as others also did, but has also been elevated there by the Father to his right hand. For this was: (1) predicted in the Old Testament, and promised to him (Psalm 110:1), and in the New Testament by Christ himself (Matt. 26:64). It was (2) prefigured in the ark of the covenant, insofar as with the tabernacle, after various wendings and windings, it was at last brought most magnificently into the glorious temple of Solomon, so that it might gloriously rest in the seat of glory (cf. Ps. 24:7–8). Hence also (3) it is read to have been most exactly fulfilled (Acts 2:34–35; Rom. 8:34; Col. 3:1; Heb. 1:3; 8:1; Mark 14:62; Heb. 12:2), as Stephen testifies (Acts 7:56).

And by reasons

And indeed, it also necessarily had to be fulfilled: (1) not only due to the truthfulness and faithfulness of the one predicting and promising; but (2) also due to his righteousness, insofar as by his utmost humiliation and obedience he had merited this apex of exaltation (Phil. 2:7–9; 1 Peter 1:11); also because (3) the standing to govern, enlarge, and protect the church required this apex of power and might (Eph. 1:21–22; Matt. 28:18–20); and finally, because (4) the more glorious discharging of the prophetic, priestly, and kingly office required it (Heb. 8:1–4).

What the phrase means, to sit at the right hand

IV. Now, so that we may more properly ascertain the nature of this session, it must be presupposed that from the infinite simplicity of God, a right and left hand do not belong to him properly, but in a human way,[9] by way of a metaphor

---

8. 1.7.1

9. ἀνθρωποπαθῶς

taken from kings, who set those who are to be granted singular glory at their right hand (as is evident in the case of Nero setting Juba the king of Armenia at his right hand, according to Suetonius;[10] and in the case of Bathsheba, set at the right hand of Solomon, 1 Kings 2:19; cf. Ps. 45:9), and that it signifies the power, authority, and glory of God (cf. Isa. 48:13; Ps. 118:14–16; Hab. 2:16). For this reason, Christ in Hebrews 1:3 is said to have been set ἐν δεξιᾷ τῆς μεγαλοσύνης ἐν ὑψηλοῖς, "on the right hand of the Majesty on high" (cf. Luke 22:69), and is said to be sitting, according to the manner of judges, who customarily do not stand before the tribunal, but sit, unless perhaps he is said to be sitting in order to distinguish him from the Old Testament high priest, who did enter into the holy place, but stood, not sat. Although also, for the reason explained in the exegetical part, he is said to be standing in Acts 7:56. But here is the chief difficulty, that Christ in this session at the right hand appears to be exalted above his Father, inasmuch as the Father sits at his left hand. Some try to remove this difficulty by stating that the left hand is more dignified, adducing on this point certain comments of heathen writers; to whom are added some of the papists, who, since they had observed on certain episcopal seals that Paul held a position at the right hand of Peter, so that on this account the primacy of Peter would not lose anything, think that the left hand is more preeminent than the right. Against this cry countless testimonies of approved authors, and also Scripture in several places (e.g. Gen. 48:17–19; Matt. 25:33–34). Others prefer to say that Christ sits at the right hand of the Father in a comparative way, with respect to others who sit on his left: so Maldonado on Matthew 16:18–19.[11] And again, others want this to be said with relation to the sitting on the left, such that sitting on the right is more prestigious. But the apostle takes away this difficulty in 1 Corinthians 15:27, when he certainly says that God has put all things under his Son Christ, but still he adds that he must be excepted who put all things under him; with which the usage of Scripture agrees, in the case of Bathsheba, who sat at the right hand of King Solomon (1 Kings 2:19), and of the church, which sits at Christ's right hand (Ps. 45:9), and most of all, in the fact that the Father is said to be at the right hand of the Son in Psalm 110:5 and also in Psalm 16:8. Therefore it seems that an allusion is being made to the session of the highest Jewish court, wherein the אב דין, the father of judgment, or the אב בית דין, the father of the house of judgment, occupied the right hand of the נשיא, the president of the

---

10. Suetonius, *Lives of the Twelve Caesars*, Nero, 13.
11. Maldonado, *Commentarii in quattour evangelistas*, 1:332–43.

Sanhedrin, who delivered the judgments for execution. Compare the Targum on Song 7:4 (cf. John 5:22).[12]

What it is to sit at the right hand of God
V. Hence, to sit at the right hand of God, in the case of Christ, denotes supreme authority, power, and glory (Eph. 1:20–21; Heb. 1:3; Phil. 2:9; Heb. 2:9): not indeed the essential authority and glory, which belongs to him by the divine nature, and which is entirely equal to that which belongs to the Father and to the Holy Spirit; but rather, the mediatorial authority and glory communicated to him by the Father (Matt. 28:18).

The particulars of this session: 1. Majesty and glory
VI. Therefore this session of the Mediator at the right hand consists, first, in majesty and glory, which is not quite infinite, yet is as great as can apply to the God-man Mediator. By it he displays that he is king, sole monarch (Ps. 2:6), and supreme head of his church (Eph. 1:20–22), to whom belongs all authority in heaven and on earth (Matt. 28:18; Ps. 8:5–6; Heb. 2:6–10). And indeed it consists also in power, to which all things in heaven, on earth, and under the earth, whether willing or unwilling, must submit (Phil. 2:9–10). If I should say it in a word, it is a majesty and glory by which he is closest to God the Father.

2. The consummation of the mediatorial work
VII. Second, it presupposes an exact discharging and completing of the mediatorial task that he was to accomplish on earth, for which reason the apostle in Hebrews 1:3 says, "after he had by himself accomplished the cleansing of our sins, he sat down at the right hand of God" (cf. 10:12). Hence even the Savior himself, does not request his own glorification before the Father except when the glorification of God has been accomplished through the completion of the mediatorial task (John 17:4–5), and the apostle attests that he was exalted after he had emptied himself, and become obedient to the Father to death (Phil. 2:8–9). Moreover, it also had to happen this way necessarily, as the Savior himself acknowledges (Luke 24:26, 46), because the repose of sitting is not appropriate except after the work is finished (Heb. 4:10), nor is reigning, except for him who has suffered (Rom. 8:17), nor is triumphing, except for him who has conquered (2 Tim. 2:5).

---

12. Cf. Montano, *Biblia sacra Hebraice, Chaldaice, Graece et Latine*, 3:674–75.

3. *The administration of kingly power*

VIII. Third, it implies the actual administration of kingly power. So then the apostle explains the session at the right hand, which is promised in Psalm 110:1, in 1 Corinthians 15:25, by saying, "he must reign" (cf. Rom. 14:9). This includes: (1) νομοθεσία, lawgiving, or rather the promulgation of the gospel, for which reason the mighty scepter that will be sent out of Zion (Ps. 110:2) is explained by the prophets through the law and Word that will go out from Jerusalem (Isa. 2:3; Mic. 4:2). By it he sends out workers into his harvest, to promulgate the gospel to men, and be promoters of their faith and repentance, and he breathes upon their labors with his efficacy and blessing, that his church may be gathered in, preserved, and grown. (2) Subjugation of enemies, which occurs in the powerful conversion of sinners (Acts 16:14), procured first through the preaching of the Word (Rom. 10:14–15), and then through the illumination and renewal of the Holy Spirit (Rom. 15:18–19), whereby they cross from Satan into the camp of Christ. (3) Governance, whereby those brought by conversion into his kingdom he by his Word and Spirit powerfully directs, stirs up, and supplies with everything necessary for spiritual life and godliness (Isa. 2:2–3; 1 Cor. 1:4, 8; Isa. 30:21; 1 Peter 1:1). (4) Preservation and strengthening against the attacks of Satan, the world, the flesh, and so forth, so that they would not faint or fail (Acts 23:11; John 16:33; 1 Cor. 10:13; 2 Cor. 1:5; Phil. 4:7, 19). (5) Confounding of enemies, with respect to their efforts, treacheries, persecutions, as well as their persons (Ps. 2:3–5, 9; 110:1), from which Stephen saw him standing in heaven at the right hand of God (Acts 7:56).

4. *The extraordinary outpouring of the Holy Spirit*

IX. Fourth, it supplied the extraordinary outpouring of the Holy Spirit, so splendidly promised, not only under the Old Testament (Joel 2:27–28 with John 14:26; Zech. 12:10; Isa. 44:3), but also under the New Testament, by Christ himself (John 16:7; Acts 1:4–5).

The time of the outpouring

This outpouring was supplied: (1) with respect to the time, on the fiftieth day after the resurrection, and on the tenth after the ascension, on that very day wherein the Mediator (Acts 7:35, 38 with Gal. 3:19) at one time handed down from heaven the Jewish religion, complete in the moral law and the gospel (which was in the ceremonial law), to be promulgated only to the Israelites, namely on the day of Pentecost (Acts 2), so that on that same day, the same Mediator might hand down most fully through the Holy Spirit to the apostles the Christian religion, which was to be published to all the nations of the whole world, and which was published to many (Acts 2:9–11), with such great emphasis that on that very day about three thousand souls (v. 41), being as it were the firstfruits of the future harvest to be sanctified from all nations, crossed into the camp of Christ.

The manner of outpouring
Then (2) with respect to the manner, this outpouring was supplied with various and outstanding symbols to represent the efficacy of the outpouring of the Spirit, for example: (a) with a sound (v. 2), which the apostles drew in, that it might be echoed in the promulgation of the gospel (Ps. 19:4; Matt. 28:19; Rom. 10:18; cf. Isa. 58:1); (b) with a *heavenly* sound or a sound *from heaven* (Acts 2:2), to prefigure the heavenly gifts of the Holy Spirit (Eph. 1:3), namely illumination and sanctification, and to stir up heavenly motions, first in the apostles, and then in their hearers; (c) with a sound of some kind of *wind* (Acts 2:2), that is, a penetrating (Heb. 4:12–13), purging (Ps. 66:10; Zech. 13:9), refreshing (John 16:7), and driving wind (Rom. 8:14), to signify the Spirit's operations; (d) of a *mighty* wind, or one that knocks down (Job 1:19; Matt. 7:27 with Acts 2:37), and also scatters (Ps. 1:4; 35:5); (e) with tongues (Acts 2:3), inasmuch as they would be equipped with them by the Holy Spirit in order to proclaim the gospel (Isa. 50:4; Ps. 45:1; 1 Cor. 13:1); (f) with *divided* or variegated tongues, namely so that the apostles would be equipped to proclaim the gospel to all nations (Acts 2:3, 6 with Matt. 28:19); (g) with *fiery* tongues (Acts 2:3), so that they would render the apostles fiery, that is, fervent and effective, that they might speak with great boldness (v. 14, 4:18ff.; Eph. 6:19), and also in their hearers they might stir up fervor and zeal (Rom. 12:11): (i) in faith (Matt. 15:28; Rom. 4:20); (ii) in confession of the truth (Ps. 116:10; 119:46), (iii) in godliness (Ps. 119:138–39), and (iv) in prayers (Rom. 8:27).

The efficacy of the outpouring
(3) With respect to its efficacy and effects, it: (a) occupied the entire house (Acts 2:2), as a sign of occupying and filling the entire church (1 Cor. 3:16 with Eph. 4:9–10); (b) rested upon each and every person who was in the house (Acts 2:3); (c) in such a way that all were filled with the Holy Spirit (v. 4; 7:55; 6:8), and in relation to all their faculties (1 Thess. 5:23); such that (d) they began to speak with other tongues (Acts 2:4), that is, to become other people (Eph. 4:22–24), new creatures (2 Cor. 5:17), who spoke, thought, and behaved in a way different than before (Rom. 12:2; cf. 1 Cor. 3:12); such that (e) they spoke of the wonderful works of God (Acts 2:11); and that (f) to the amazement of their hearers (vv. 7, 12); and (g) the conversion of many (v. 41).

*5. The ordinary outpouring of the Holy Spirit in fuller measure than under
the Old Testament, in three particulars: (1) With respect to the manner*
X. Fifth, it supplies even now the ordinary outpouring of the Holy Spirit, which
consists in the communication of spiritual gifts, whereby the one sitting at the
right hand of God fills all things (Eph. 4:10 from Ps. 68:18; Eph. 1:3), in a much
fuller measure than once occurred under the Old Testament. This is especially
evident in these three things: (1) in the manner of communicating his gifts:
whereas once under the Old Testament he communicated a sufficient knowledge of divine things through dreams and visions, through figures and shadows,
now under the New Testament he confers knowledge through the demonstration and evidence of the Spirit (1 Cor. 2:4–5), from which he is called the Spirit
of wisdom and revelation (Eph. 1:17), inasmuch as by him, according to the gift
of the grace of God, there are revealed to us through the gospel the unsearchable
riches of Christ, and the mystery hidden from the ages in God, in which is the
manifold wisdom of God (Eph. 3:7–10). This also seems to have been signified when, under the figures of a powerful wind, fire, divided tongues, and an
earthquake, the Spirit is communicated under the New Testament (Acts 2:2–3;
4:31), whereas once under the Old Testament the Lord was in a still small voice
(1 Kings 19:11–12).

(2) With respect to the object. (3) With respect to the abundance of gifts
(2) In the object and its fullness: whereas at one time the Spirit was poured out
only on the Jews, now he is poured out on all flesh (Joel 2:28; John 4:21, 23; Acts
10:34–35). (3) In the very abundance and measure of the spiritual gifts, whereby,
while at one time he was poured out just by drops, in the manner of a dew (Deut.
33:28), now he thoroughly inundates, in the manner of a river (Isa. 44:3), from
which it is said that the whole earth will be full of the knowledge of God, as the
waters cover the sea (Isa. 11:9; Jer. 31:34; John 16:12–13).

6. His glorious intercession
XI. Sixth, it supplies his intercession (Rom. 8:34), whereby he pleads the cause
of his people, not with a humble oration, as he interceded while he lived on earth
(Luke 22:32), but in an altogether glorious way, by presenting his satisfaction
and merits for his people to the Father, by purposing for them, and so forth
(John 17:24). This intercession, because it pertains to his priestly function, we
have already treated expressly in its own place, in chapter 7.[13]

---

13. 1.5.7 §VIII

7. The establishment of the ecclesiastical ministry

XII. Seventh, it also brought forth, and does daily bring forth, the establishment of the ecclesiastical ministry, as much the extraordinary as the ordinary (Eph. 4:4–13), as well as its being made fruitful, and its protection, through the presence of his grace until the consummation of the ages (Matt. 28:18–20). On this we will say more elsewhere.[14]

8. The authority to judge the living and the dead

XIII. And finally, eighth, it will present to us his authority to judge the living and the dead (John 5:22), when he will one day, at the end of time, summon all before his judgment seat (2 Cor. 5:10), and lift his own up to the highest glory (Matt. 25:34), and lay low his enemies, and subjugate them as a footstool for his feet (Ps. 110:1; Matt. 25:41). On this we will say more in its own place.[15]

Christ as God and man sits at the right hand of God.

XIV. Moreover, the Savior sits at the right hand of God as the God-man, according to both his natures, the human as well as the divine, although in an altogether different way: with respect to the divine, not indeed by the acquisition of some new majesty or glory, or of any perfection, whether *de jure* or *de facto*, but (1) by the glorious manifestation of the divine glory which he possessed in the Father's presence, indeed together with the Father, from eternity (John 17:5), and which during his humiliation he had as it were restricted and hidden; (2) by the irresistible use and exercise of the divine power and authority in the gathering, preservation, government, and protection of the church. But with respect to the human nature, by the reception of a new majesty, authority, and power given to him (from which he is more properly said to have been set by God at his right hand, Eph. 1:20), and by the use and exercise of it once received.

The circumstances, of: 1. Place. 2. Time

XV. With respect to the circumstances, as much of: (1) place, he sits at the right hand of God in heaven (Eph. 1:20), in the highest heaven (Heb. 1:3), the throne of divine majesty (Heb. 8:1), to where it is said that he was elevated by his ascension (Mark 16:19; Eph. 4:8); as of (2) time: (a) first as God, if you understand his essential glory, he has sat from all eternity (John 17:5); (b) as the promised Mediator, not yet present in the flesh, he was designated as the one who would sit in his own time at the right hand of God (Ps. 110:1), and thus, in his own

---

14. 1.7.2 §VI
15. 1.8.4 §VII

way, he also sat in potency, and as it were *de jure* (Ps. 2:6; Isa. 9:5); (c) as man, he began at last to sit at the right hand of God after his humiliation (Heb. 1:3; Phil. 2:8–9) and ascension into heaven (Mark 16:19); finally, (d) as the God-man, he was also elevated after the ascension, insofar as the glory of the divine person was made more illustrious, and exerted itself more efficaciously; but in his human nature, having received new glory, authority, and power in its full emphasis, he began to conduct himself as the head of his church (Eph. 1:20–21). And just as he sat after the ascension, so to all eternity he will sit at the right hand of God (Heb. 10:12).

The Elenctic Part

It is asked: 1. Is the Mediator called the Son of God at least in part from this session?

XVI. We previously dealt with most of the controversies of this topic in chapter 8 on the Mediator as a king, and in chapter 14 on the exaltation of the Mediator,[16] so that here we need not make more than a certain gleaning. Therefore it is asked, first, whether the Mediator is called the Son of God, if not entirely, at least in part from this session at the right hand of God.

The opinion of the Socinians, Remonstrants, and Reformed

The Socinians, due to their hatred of the coeternal and consubstantial deity of Christ,[17] state that he is called the Son of God, first (1) from his conception from the Holy Spirit, then (2) from the divine miracles he performed, then (3) from his resurrection from the dead, then (4) from his session at the right hand of God, through which the Father so devolved to him the whole kingdom of the church that he himself no longer reigns, but has committed all authority of ruling to his vicar, who also from this, in his own certain way, is superior to the Father. The Remonstrants collude with the Socinians, at least to the extent that they state that there are plural causes of this sonship, and do so out of pure and unadulterated love for the Socinians. The Reformed, as they do acknowledge that there are plural causes by means of which he is acknowledged by us as the Son of God, such as the conception by the Holy Spirit (Luke 1:35), miracles (John 5:19ff., 36), the resurrection (Rom. 1:4; Acts 13:32–37), to which could be adjoined (although Scripture nowhere adduces it for this end, as far as I know) his session at the right hand. Nevertheless, they do not read of any other constitutive cause of this sonship than his eternal generation from the Father

---

16. 1.5.8 §§XVI, XVII, XIX; 1.5.14 §§IX–XII
17. συναϊδίου καὶ ὁμοουσίου *deitatis Christi*

(Ps. 2:7), from which he is called God's very own Son (Rom. 8:32), the only begotten (John 3:16), whose goings forth are from of old, from the days of eternity (Mic. 5:2). Just as they also grant that the mediatorial authority whereby he rejoices in sitting at the right hand of God was delegated to him (Ps. 2:6; Matt. 28:18; Eph. 1:20–23; Phil. 2:9–10; Ps. 110:1). Yet they do not admit: (1) that the Father when he delegated it stripped himself of his kingdom; (2) that the delegated authority excludes the essential authority of the divine person. Rather, it presupposes it, from the fact that the one sitting at the right hand of God could not powerfully gather, grow, govern, and defend the church except by the strength of his divine person. For which reason, when he sends out his apostles to gather the church, after he had impressed upon them that all authority was given to him, he promises that he will be with them, even to the end of the ages (Matt. 28:18–20).

The grounds of both opinions are displayed.

The ground of the orthodox opinion is in his deity, which is eternal and consubstantial with the Father, and also in his eternal generation, which we have expressly demonstrated in book 2, chapter 26.[18] The ground of our opponents' case is in this, that the sonship of the Mediator is referred to different reasons in the Scriptures. Just as we have already acknowledged that those reasons are referred to as causes of manifestation, so we also deny that they are referred to as constitutive causes of sonship, on which matter our opponents adduce not even one whit, nor can they adduce anything beyond their own hypothesis, namely their denial of the eternal deity of Christ.

2. Does sitting at the right hand of God mean using in a plenary way the divine attributes communicated to him?

XVII. Second, it is asked whether the session of Christ at the right hand of God consists in this, that his human nature employs in a plenary way the divine attributes communicated to it through the personal union: power, omnipresence, omniscience. The Lutherans, so that they may hold that in the Holy Supper the flesh of Christ is present to be eaten with the mouth, state that divine properties were communicated to him through the hypostatic union, but only with respect to possession and substance; however, with respect to use and authority, that is, with respect to the full use of the same properties, he only received them in his exaltation, and especially in his session at the right hand of God. The Reformed, just as they deny that any divine properties were communicated to the human

____

18. 1.2.26 §§ VII–XII, XVI

nature through the hypostatic union, so also deny that the human nature had use of those divine properties, although they do grant that the person of the Mediator, sitting at the right hand of God, uses the properties of both natures in a plenary way. The grounds of both opinions we have examined in chapter 14, §X.

3. Does he also sit at the right hand of God according to the divine nature?
XVIII. From this, third, it is asked whether he also sits at the right hand of God according to the divine nature. The Socinians, because they do not acknowledge the divine nature in the Mediator, are compelled to deny it. The Lutherans, because (per the preceding section) they constitute the nature of the session at the right hand of God in the full use of the divine properties conferred upon the human nature, also deny it. The Reformed, because they state that the entire person of the Mediator according to both natures sits at the right hand of God, in the way which we explained in the dogmatic part,[19] affirm it. The grounds of both parties we examined in chapter 14, §XI.

4. Through the session at the right hand, is he alone the head of the church?
XIX. Fourth, it is asked whether through the session at the right hand of God, the Mediator alone is the monarch and head of the church. Just as the Socinians make Christ the vicar of God from the session at the right hand, so the papists, from the ascension of Christ and his session at the right hand, state first that Peter was his vicar on earth, and then also Peter's successors, the Roman pontiffs. But we have examined this opinion with its supports in chapter 8, on the Mediator as a king, §XV.

5. From the session at the right hand, ought he to be worshiped as a man,
or as the Mediator?
XX. Fifth, it is asked whether, from the session at the right hand, Christ ought to be worshiped as a man, or also as the Mediator. The Socinians, because they do not recognize him as God from eternity, affirm it. The Lutherans, because they teach that the human nature in the session at the right hand obtained the full use of the divine properties communicated to it, think that it must be entirely affirmed. The papists, so that they can more easily confer the honor of adoration upon saints in heaven, likewise affirm it. Some of the Reformed, because they do not distinguish carefully enough the concept of pure deity from the concept of the Mediator, likewise affirm it. The common opinion of the Reformed denies it. We have noted this controversy in book 5, chapter 2, §XXVI.

---

19. §XIV, above

6. Is Christ, sitting at the right hand of God, present in body in heaven only?

XXI. Sixth, it is asked whether Christ, sitting at the right hand of God, is present in his body in heaven only. The papists, in favor of transubstantiation and their Mass, and all Lutherans, in favor of consubstantiation, so that his body may be orally eaten in the Holy Supper by communicants, state that his body, even as he is now sitting at the right hand of God, is present both in the symbols and in the communicants. To this the Ubiquitists also add that it is everywhere, and endeavor to prove it (among other things) from his session, because, of course, the right hand of God is everywhere, and consequently the human nature of Christ, sitting at the right hand of God, is everywhere. We have already been occupied with this question more than once (e.g. bk. 2, ch. 10; bk. 5, ch. 4), and we will be occupied with it in book 7, chapter 5.[20]

The Practical Part

The practice of this topic presents to us: 1. An argument for glorification.

XXII. With respect to the practice, because the majesty that belongs to the Mediator through his session at the right hand of God is properly and formerly kingly, nearly the entire practice which we discussed in book 5, chapter 8 with regard to the Mediator as a king, with the necessary changes made, and some things more distinctly accommodated to the present argument, can be transferred here without any trouble, so that it is not incumbent upon us here to make more than a certain gleaning. Therefore, first, the session of our Mediator at the right hand of God presents us a most effective argument for glorification, after the example of the four beasts and twenty-four elders in Revelation, who bring glory and honor and thanksgiving to him who sits on the throne (Rev. 4:9–11).

The motives

For in his glorification: (1) the Father made his glory, the glory of his strength and power, so illustrious and marvelous (Eph. 1:19–20). (2) He so glorified him that he set him at his own right hand, that is, he made him to be next to him, and as it were a partner, in majesty, authority, and power (v. 20; Zech. 13:7). (3) He elevated him far above all principality, authority, power, and dominion (Eph. 1:21). (4) He gave him a name above every name that is named, not only in this age, but also in that which is to come (Eph. 1:21; Phil. 2:10). (5) Under his feet he put all things (Eph. 1:22; Heb. 2:7–8). (6) To him he willed every knee to bow, of those who are in heaven, on earth, and under the earth (Phil. 2:10). (7) He willed him to be worshiped by all the angels (Heb. 1:6). (8) He constituted

---

20. 1.2.10 §XIII; 1.5.4 §XXVI; 1.7.5 §XXI

him head or king of the church, whose members we ourselves are, by his grace (Eph. 1:22), so that (9) he would be over all things (Eph. 1:22). (10) He fills all in all, by his grace, with his gifts (Eph. 1:23; 4:8, 10; John 1:16). In addition, (11) he is worthy of all glory (Rev. 4:11), and he merited it by his humiliation and obedience (Phil. 2:7–10). And hence, (12) by his own right, he seeks glorification from his very own Father (John 17:1, 5). (13) We are bound to thank and glorify him for so many benefits (Rev. 5:8–9). (14) In his glory and glorification consists our very own glory (Phil. 1:26). This one therefore whom the Father so greatly glorified, who by himself merited all glory, and from whom all glory awaits us—this one, I say, why would we ourselves not glorify with all zeal?

In what manner he ought to be glorified
But in what way shall we glorify him? I answer, We will do so when (1) him whom God exalted far above all the most excellent things of the whole world (Eph. 1:21), we exalt in our hearts and affections above the whole world and all things in it that could be precious to us (Phil. 3:7–8; Matt. 10:37). When (2) with our mouth, with the beasts in Revelation, we claim majesty, glory, and thanksgiving for him who sits on the throne of the divine right hand (Rev. 4:9). When (3) we prostrate ourselves, with the twenty four elders in Revelation, before him who sits on the throne of the divine right hand (v. 10), and bow our knees submissively to him (Phil. 2:9–10). When (4) with them we worship him who lives for ever and ever on the throne of God's right hand (Rev. 4:10; Heb. 1:6; Ps. 95:6). When (5) with the same elders, we cast our crowns before his throne (Rev. 4:9), that is, for his glory, we hold all our own glory to be insignificant (Ps. 115:1), indeed we promptly expend all our glory, authority, power, and whatever we are or can be, for his glorification (Phil. 1:20–21). When finally, (6) we glory in him alone (Phil. 1:26; 3:3; Jer. 9:24), because we have our head occupying the right hand of God. Compare what we have said above in chapter 8, §XX.

2. It supplies the sweetest comfort. In what cases
XXIII. Second, the session of Christ at the right hand of God supplies the sweetest comfort, with the apostle commending the contemplation of it for this use in Hebrews 12:2, "Looking to the author of our faith, who for the joy that was set before him, endured the cross: when he had despised its shame, he sat down at the right hand of the throne of God." It supplies comfort: (1) in any affliction, and however great, whether it be spiritual or bodily, that we have a Lord, indeed a head, most near to God, who is seated at the right hand of the power of God (Luke 24:49), whereby he can regard our lot (Isa. 66:1), and change it with only a nod (Ps. 77:10). Particularly, (2) in the case of persecutions, when enemies

threaten us with their abundance, strength, and frauds (Ps. 3:1), that we have a head sitting at the right hand of God, far above all principality, authority, power and dominion (Eph. 1:20–21), who will set all his and our enemies as a footstool for his feet (Ps. 110:1; 118:15). (3) In the case of any insults, that our head, after he had despised insults, was set at the right hand of the throne of God (Heb. 12:2), and that in the same manner we shall be set there with him (Rev. 3:21). (4) In the case of infirmity, wherein we are no match for sustaining so many and such great bouts of afflictions, that the excellent greatness of his power, whereby he set Christ at his right hand, is also at work in us who believe (Eph. 1:19–20), and that we can do all things through Christ who strengthens us (Phil. 4:13). (5) In the case of death and agony, if with Stephen, we focus the eyes of our mind and faith upon heaven, so that we may see Jesus standing at the right hand of God, ready to receive our spirit (Acts 7:55, 60).

3. His session at the right hand brings horror to his enemies.
XXIV. Third, the session of Christ at the right hand of God brings horror and trembling to all his enemies, such that with the kings of the earth, the great men, the rich men, and so forth, they hide themselves in the dens and rocks of the mountains, and cry out, "Fall on us, and hide us from the sight of him who sits on the throne" (Rev. 6:15–16).

Who those enemies are
But who then are these enemies of Christ? They are: (1) the openly ungodly, who publicly clamor against his majesty and rule which he obtains at the right hand of God (Job 21:14; Luke 19:14, 27; Ps. 2:1–3). They are (2) secret hypocrites, who in external matters, which are of lesser import, flatter him (Matt. 7:21–22), but in internal matters, which are of utmost import, show themselves to be enemies of the cross of Christ (Phil. 3:19; 2 Tim. 3:5). They are (3) those who publicly attack his kingdom, or his church, with the kings and peoples of the earth (Ps. 2:1–3; Acts 4:26–27; with Saul in Acts 9:1–2) and especially the Antichrist, that false prophet, the scarlet whore, for whom it is common, with the red dragon, to declare open war upon our Michael and his angels (Rev. 12:7–8; 19:19).

The terrifying arguments
These things strike terror in them: (1) the majesty of the one sitting on the throne of the majesty on high, at which, when it was presented to him in a certain vision, even John himself, his friend, was horrified (Rev. 1:13–18); (2) his iron rod, whereby he will shatter those his enemies like potter's vessels (Ps. 2:9); (3) the promise of the Father, who will more certainly than certain set those enemies as a footstool for the feet of his Son who sits at his right hand (Ps. 110:1);

and (4) his horrendous judgments themselves, when they are exercised against his enemies (Rev. 19:20; 16:10).

4. It supplies a motive to fight, with him, against spiritual enemies. Who they are
XXV. Fourth, it adds a most effective spur for bravely fighting against Christ's spiritual enemies and ours: (1) Satan, that red dragon, who strives with all his strength to drown the woman (the church) with her son (Rev. 12:4, 12, 17; 1 Peter 5:8; Eph. 6:12); (2) the flesh and its lusts (1 Peter 2:11; Gal. 5:16–17); (3) the world and worldly things (James 4:4; 1 John 2:15–16; Rom. 12:2).

By what motives
Against those enemies we must bravely fight, because: (1) we have a captain who sits at the right hand of the power of God (Luke 24:49), far above all magistrates, authorities, and dominions (Eph. 1:21), who has already powerfully subjugated those enemies (John 14:30; 16:11), who spoiled principalities and powers by his own power (Col. 2:15), and will crush them shortly (Rom. 16:20), who in like manner was tempted in all things as we were, so that he would be merciful, and be able and willing to sympathize with us when we are attacked (Heb. 2:17; 4:15). Because (2) if we do not, with Christ who sits at the right hand of God upon his throne, fight faithfully (2 Tim. 2:5; Rev. 3:21; 2 Tim. 4:7–8), we will not be exalted like Christ, who was not elevated to his throne at the right hand in heaven before he had fought and conquered (Rev. 3:21). Because (3) by bravely fighting, with Christ, in the power of God, with him we will set his enemies and ours, in their own way, as a footstool for our feet (Ps. 110:1; 1 John 2:13; 4:4).

5. It teaches that we should render our just duties to our head. What they are
XXVI. Fifth, it teaches that as his members, we should render our just duties to our head who sits at God's right hand. And what are these? (1) him whom God, by placing him at his right hand, established as head of his church (Eph. 1:22–23), and him alone (Heb. 1:13), let us acknowledge, as the Israelites did David (2 Sam. 19:42–43). (2) With him, just as members with their head, let us be united as closely as possible, so that we may be rendered one spirit with him (1 Cor. 6:17), rooted in him and strengthened (Col. 2:7); let us hold fast (κρατῶμεν) to the head, from which the whole body by joints and ligaments being supplied and knit together, increases with the increase of God (Col. 2:19). Also (3) let us nurture communion with him, as members with their head, and subjects with their prince (1 John 1:3; 1 Cor. 1:9). In addition, (4) let us render love to him, as members to their head, and subjects to their prince: this love he required of them before his death (John 14:21), this love Peter called to witness after the resurrection (John 21:17), this love Paul prescribes under penalty of an anathema

(1 Cor. 16:22), and Peter commends in believers (1 Peter 1:8). Furthermore, (5) let us extol him as our head, with all honor and all glory, inasmuch as to this end he is said to be crowned with glory and honor (Heb. 2:7), and the Father highly exalted him, and gave to him a name which is above every name (Phil. 2:9–10; Eph. 1:21), and in keeping with these things, every creature in heaven honors him (Rev. 5:13). In addition, (6) under him, as under our head and the author of our salvation (Heb. 12:2), let us fight bravely against his and our enemies, as soldiers of Christ (2 Tim. 2:3), as he with his angels fights against the dragon (Rev. 12:7), about which we said more in the preceding section. Also (7) let us freely and sincerely bow our knees to him as our head (Phil. 2:9–10), and render ourselves to him obedient in all things (Heb. 5:9; 1 John 2:4), and with our eyes turned to him as our head, let us walk in all things even as he walked (1 John 2:6; 3:3), just as Saul, when Christ was speaking to him from heaven, immediately offered himself compliant to him, "Lord, what will you have me to do?" (Acts 9:6). Finally, (8) let us in every circumstance confidently place our trust in him, as in our head that sits at the right hand of God (Acts 18:10; Heb. 13:6; Rev. 2:10).

For what motivating reasons

Moreover, so that we may render these and other duties to our head more promptly, we must ponder that: (1) he requires them of us (John 15:17). (2) From the nature of the matter, they belong to him, for he has been exalted by God to his right hand, far above all principalities, and so forth (Eph. 1:21), obtains a name above every name (Phil. 2:9–10), and is the Lord from heaven (1 Cor. 15:47). (3) He is the holy (Isa. 10:20) and righteous head (Acts 3:14; 7:52), whose commands are holy and righteous (Rom. 12:2), who came as the righteous one (Zech. 9:9), who suffered as the righteous one (1 Peter 3:18), who departed into heaven as the righteous one (1 John 2:1), and reigns in righteousness (Heb. 7:2; Ps. 9:9). (4) He is the meek (Matt. 11:28–29), merciful head (Heb. 2:17), inclined to sympathy (Heb. 4:15), kind and ready to grant access to the throne of grace (Heb. 4:16). (5) He is the head everywhere present with his members, dwelling in their midst (Matt. 18:20; 28:20). (6) He is the head watching over all things from heaven with his flaming eyes (Rev. 2:18), and John saw him as such in heaven (Rev. 1:14), who examines hearts and reins (Rev. 2:23), who knows most exactly all that belongs to us (v. 2). Finally, (7) he is the powerful, indeed omnipotent head (Rev. 1:8), armed with a rod of strength (Ps. 110:2), with an iron rod to dash his enemies in pieces (Ps. 2:9), and a golden rod as well, like Ahasuerus had (Est. 5:2), to show favor to his own; indeed, the head which has all authority in heaven and on earth (Matt. 28:18).

CHAPTER EIGHTEEN
The Mediator's Redemption Itself

The Son of Man came not to be served, but to serve, and to give his soul as the price of redemption for many.

—Matthew 20:28

Following the Redeemer is redemption, considered on its own.

I. In this book we have contemplated, regarding the state of grace, its foundation and norm, according to which all grace and salvation is dispensed to the sinner, that is, the covenant of grace. We have considered the procurer of all grace and salvation, the Mediator Jesus Christ. Now it remains to pass on to the procurement of grace, regarding which there come four points to be examined, namely redemption, whereby the Mediator impetrated[1] grace for the sinner; then the application of the grace impetrated; next, the object of both, the church; and finally, the various ways that the covenant of grace is dispensed. The first point we will handle in this chapter, the second throughout the whole of book 6, the third throughout book 7, and the last throughout book 8. The procurer of grace himself will present to us the nature of this redemption in a quite suitable way, in Matthew 20:28.

The Exegetical Part
The text is explained.

II. In these words, the Savior, after he had rebuked and rejected the vain and proud petition of the mother of the sons of Zebedee, and called the disciples together, urges them to humility and ταπεινοφροσύνη, lowliness, after other reasons, by the example of his coming to procure redemption for sinners. Regarding this there is noted:

---

1. On *impetration*, see the note on 1.5.15 §XIX.

A. The one coming to redeem: "The Son of Man," the Redeemer himself who is speaking, who according to his two natures is sometimes designated the Son of God (Ps. 2:7; Matt. 16:16; and elsewhere), and sometimes the Son of Man (Matt. 16:13; Ps. 8:4; cf. Heb. 2:6–8; 1 Cor. 15:27; Ps. 80:17; Dan. 7:13; and throughout the Gospels, e.g. Matt. 9:6; Mark 2:10; Luke 5:24; John 1:51; Acts 7:56; Rev. 1:13). Moreover, אדם and בן אדם, man and son of man, for the Hebrews most frequently is a person of a despicable condition (Ps. 82:7). So the ancient Hebrews interpret בנות אדם, daughters of men (Gen. 6:2), and oppose to them the בני האלהים, sons of God, likewise בני האיתנים, sons of the mighty, of heroes, and likewise in Psalm 49:2, בני איש, sons of a great man, such that בני אדם are γηγενεῖς, sons of earth. So Ezekiel, Daniel, and Zechariah, when they converse with angels, are reminded of their frailty when addressed as sons of men. Christ, for the most part, if not always, also speaks of himself in this way, whereas he scarcely, and not even scarcely, is so named by another person. He does so for this purpose: (1) that he might point to the truth of his human nature; (2) that he might distinguish himself from the other divine persons, inasmuch as he alone among them is man; (3) that from the many descriptions that are read to have been given to the Messiah, he might choose the most modest one, and signify his κένωσις, emptying (on which see Phil. 2:7), to which end also points the fact that he is named בר איש, the Son of Man, in Daniel 7:13, in the same sense that he is said to be נבזה וחדל אישים, "despised and rejected by men" in Isaiah 53:3, one who does not have his own home where he may lay his head when tired, which is most appositely fitting in this passage where he strives to shape his disciples toward modesty and a disdain for human arrogance. As if he should say, "I who am your Lord and teacher, whom you are certainly not greater than, I who am the Son of God, I call myself the Son of Man: I have given you an example, for I did nothing from reasons of my own benefit, and I did not behave as a king in splendor or pleasure, but I endured every kind of trouble for the sake of my people, and furthermore, I will endure greater, even the most ignominious death, that is, contrary to what happens in earthly kingdoms, where subjects die for the glory and greatness of their kings: so you also," and so forth.

B. The coming to redeem: οὐκ ἦλθε, he "came not," that is, in the flesh, so that this coming may be distinguished from his coming for glory, to judge the living and the dead, which will be with the greatest glory

(Matt. 25:31; 2 Thess. 1:7). At the same time is signified his existence before this coming, for no one comes who does not exist. Moreover, this his coming of the incarnation is not but a preparation for humiliation, death, and redemption.

C. The goal of coming, which is twofold, namely:

1. The rejected goal: "not to be served," as earthly kings usually are. Διακονηθῆναι, "to be served," that is, ἵνα διακονηθῇ, "in order that he might be served" or "that he might suffer being served." The Greek phrase is the kind found in Matthew 2:18, 1 Timothy 1:11, and Hebrews 7:11. Διακονέω is "I minister", "I serve", "I have another for my master, I submit myself to him, I seek his glory and gain." Therefore, he denies that this was the first and immediate goal of his first coming, namely that he might be exalted, but rather, that he might be humbled, empty himself, and take on the form of a servant (Phil. 2:6–7), although at the same time the mediate goal of his first coming, and also of the second, altogether was his glorification (Luke 24:26; Phil. 2:8–10).

2. The admitted and asserted goal, likewise twofold:

a. The more general goal: ἀλλὰ διακονῆσαι, "but to serve," that is, not only God, whose servant he had become through the eternal surety (Isa. 53:11; cf. Isa. 42:1; 52:13; Zech. 3:8), a servant whom God subjected to himself and to his law (Gal. 4:4), and who was obedient to him to the point of death, even of the cross (Phil. 2:7); but also men (John 13:5, 12–14ff.). By this διακονία, service, is signified the whole state of his humiliation.

b. The more specific goal, namely redemption: "to give his life as the price of redemption for many," in which words are expressed:

i. The price of redemption: τὴν ψυχὴν αὐτοῦ, "his soul." Not anything lesser or cheaper, but that which is most excellent, his very soul: ψυχή, נֶפֶשׁ, the significance of which we handled in the exegetical part of chapter 13.[2] Here, if it denotes the nobler part of man, then it will mean that Christ did not expend for us only a bodily death, but in addition a spiritual death. If it denotes a lifeless body, then it will indicate on the other hand that he offered a redemption price that was not only spiritual,

―――――――――――――

2. 1.5.13 §II.B.2.a

but also bodily. If it denotes the man, then it will say that Christ gave himself as the redemption price not only as man, but in addition as God (Acts 20:28; 1 John 1:7), and so as a price that was altogether infinite, and hence one so great than none greater than it can either exist or be imagined, and one suitable in every respect to those to be redeemed. Finally, if it denotes life, then it will signify that he offered all the life that he had, natural, spiritual, and eternal, as a redemption price.

ii. The payment of this price: δοῦναι λύτρον ἀντί, "to give the price of redemption for…." Here λύτρον means a ransom, or that price which must be paid to liberate captive soldiers. It is derived from λύω, "I set free" or "I pay," either because through that ransom those bound or captive are set free, or because payment is made for the deliverance of captives. Thus it means that the deliverance from our spiritual captivity is accomplished not by mere forgiveness, but by the payment of a price or ransom (1 Cor. 6:20; 1 Peter 1:18–19), from which it is designated throughout Scripture as an ἀπολύτρωσις, redemption (Rom. 3:24; Eph. 1:7, 14; Col. 1:14; Heb. 9:15). The particle ἀντί, if used concerning persons, whenever it does not denote opposition, indicates substitution (Matt. 17:27), as Hugo Grotius testifies (*On the Satisfaction of Christ*).[3] And δοῦναι, "to give," denotes the very act of payment, insofar as it is performed willingly and freely by him who has authority over life and death from his divine nature (John 10:18).

iii. The debtors, the persons for whom he paid the price: ἀντὶ πολλῶν, "for many." Not for a few, although comparatively to the rest who are not redeemed, this also is said (v. 16; Matt. 7:14), yet not for all (Matt. 7:21–22; John 17:9), but for people of some certain order, who elsewhere are called his people (Matt. 1:21); elsewhere, his sheep (John 10:11, 15); elsewhere, his church (Acts 20:28); and so forth. And for each and every person in this order, who, considered at least absolutely, are not a few, but many, as the sand of the sea (Gen. 13:16; 22:17), as

---

3. Hugo Grotius, *Defensio fidei catholicae de satisfactione Christi adversus Faustum Socinum* (Leiden: Joannes Patius, 1617), 73–90; on ἀντὶ in Matt. 20:28, see idem, *Annotationes in libros evangeliorum* in *Opera omnia* (1679), 2:194–5, on Matt. 17:27, idem, *Opera omnia* (1679), 2:171.

the stars of heaven (Gen. 15:5; 22:17), although comparatively they are also few (Matt. 20:16; 7:14).

The Dogmatic Part

The Mediator, having been substituted for his own, by paying the price delivered them from slavery into spiritual freedom. It is proved by the Scriptures.

III. Therefore, the Mediator whom we have presented so far, having been substituted for his own, by laying down his life as the price of redemption he delivered them from the state of spiritual slavery into a state of freedom. For this was: (1) once predicted under the Old Testament (e.g. Hos. 1:7; Ps. 130:8; Hos. 13:14 with 1 Cor. 15:55; Isa. 25:8; Ps. 49:15). This was (2) prefigured in Moses, leading the Israelites out of Egyptian slavery; in Joshua leading them into Canaan; in the Judges freeing the Israelites from the slavery of their enemies, who from this are sometimes called redeemers (Judg. 3:9; 2 Kings 13:5); in the high priest and Levitical priests, when they substituted lives, or the death of the sacrifices, for sinners to be freed from guilt (Lev. 1:5ff. 3:2ff. with John 10:17–18; 18:4–6; Heb. 9:22–23, 26). This was (3) fulfilled under the New Testament, by all those passages wherein he is said to redeem, λυτροῦσθαι (Matt. 20:28; Mark 10:45), ἀντιλυτροῦσθαι (1 Tim. 2:5–6), ἀπολυτροῦσθαι (Eph. 1:7; Col. 1:14; Rom. 3:24; Heb. 9:12; Titus 2:14; 1 Peter 1:18); to buy, ἀγοράζειν (1 Cor. 6:20; Rev. 5:9), ἐξαγοράζειν (Gal. 3:13); to give himself for us an offering to God, παραδοῦναι ἑαυτὸν ὑπὲρ ἡμῶν, προσφοράν τῷ θεῷ (Eph. 5:2; Heb. 9:14); to save his people, σώζειν τὸν λαὸν αὐτοῦ (Matt. 1:21; Luke 19:10). From this (4) he is called throughout Scripture Redeemer, גּוֹאֵל, *goel* (Isa. 59:20; Job 19:25); Deliverer, ῥυόμενος, (Rom. 11:26); Jesus (Matt. 1:21), Savior, σωτήρ (Titus 2:13); salvation, σωτήριον (Luke 2:30; 3:6), יְשׁוּעָה (Gen. 49:18; Isa. 49:6; Acts 13:47); and so forth.

The foundations of redemption

IV. The foundation of this redemption is: (1) in the φιλανθρωπία, love for mankind, and the most tender mercy of God toward the ruined sinner (Ezek. 16:3–7; John 3:16; Rom. 5:8; 3:24); then (2) in his immovable justice (Gen. 18:25 with Hab. 1:13; Rom. 1:32; 2 Thess. 1:6), which did not will for sin to be dismissed unpunished (Ps. 5:5; Zech. 8:17; Isa. 1:13–14); furthermore, (3) in his immutable truthfulness (Matt. 5:18), which had pronounced death upon the sinner (Gen. 2:17; Ex. 32:33); and especially (4) in the absolute surety (Heb. 7:22; Jer. 31:22), whereby in the eternal counsel of peace (Zech. 6:13), he took upon himself the entire cause of the elect sinner (Ps. 40:6–8 with Heb.

10:5; Isa. 53:10). Compare chapter 7, §V, and what we will say a little further on from here in favor of the necessity of Christ's satisfaction.[4]

What redemption is: With respect to the term
V. Redemption, with respect to the term (λύτρωσις, Luke 1:68; 2:38; Heb. 9:12; ἀπολύτρωσις, Rom. 3:24; 8:23; Eph. 1:7, 14; Col. 1:14; Heb. 9:15), properly denotes a deliverance that occurs by a payment of a set price, the kind by which captive soldiers are set free, and although perhaps, now and again in the Scriptures it may denote a deliverance procured without the payment of a price (Act 7:35), yet that happens improperly, and cannot be extended to that deliverance for which the price itself is expressly noted. Also concerning the word it must not be neglected that sometimes it may signal a future deliverance that is more actual and perfect (Luke 21:28; Rom. 8:23; Eph. 4:31; Heb. 11:35), and sometimes a present deliverance that is more virtual and imperfect (e.g. 1 Cor. 1:30; Eph. 1:7; Heb. 9; etc.).

With respect to the substance
With regard to the substance, redemption is nothing but a deliverance of the sinner from spiritual slavery into the freedom of grace. In it: (1) the terminus *a quo* is spiritual slavery (Heb. 2:14; Luke 1:71, 74), with all the host of miseries which are contained in this slavery: for example, the enmity and wrath of God, eternal condemnation, and other things, about which we will say more as we progress. (2) The terminus *ad quem* is spiritual liberty (Gal. 5:1), with all its adjuncts and dependents: the grace of God, and the fullness of all goods (Eph. 1:3), about which we will speak more distinctly in its own place.[5] (3) The action is the virtual deliverance or liberation, to be conferred by application. (4) The means is not prayer, nor power, which also have their own use in application, but it is the payment of the just price.

The first cause of redemption is God alone.
VI. The cause of this redemption is not every man for himself, by his own sufferings and actions (Matt. 16:26), nor just any man, by vicarious sufferings and actions (Ps. 49:7), nor an angel, nor any mere creature, because in it there is an infinite guilt to be borne and an infinite good to be recovered. Rather, its first and chief cause is God himself (Ps. 34:23; 35:3; Isa. 41:10; Rom. 8:3; 2 Cor. 5:18–19), and certainly a less principal or impelling cause, first outwardly, was

---

4. §§XIX, XXXV, below
5. See book 6, *passim*; on Christian liberty, 1.6.7 §XVI.

our misery (Ezek. 16:3–6). Inwardly, however, at least in part, was: (1) mercy (Rom. 11:32), whereby because from the violation of a legal covenant we were liable to condemnation (Rom. 3:19–20), he willed to substitute the covenant of grace (Heb. 10:14–17), to give us his Son as a surety and Mediator (John 3:16; Rom. 8:3, 32), and to accept his λύτρον, ransom, for us (1 Tim. 2:3–6); and in part, (2) justice (Rom. 3:25–26), whereby he delivered up the surety to death on account of our sins (Rom. 3:25 with 8:32).

How God should be considered in the business of redemption
Moreover, in the business of this redemption, God, insofar as he redeems or delivers on account of a satisfaction-making compensation, must be considered, not as: (1) the party injured by the sinner to be redeemed, for as such, he could not punish the injuring party, since for this, judicial dignity[6] is required; nor (2) as an absolute lord, for in this way he could set free the injuring party without any compensation, because an absolute lord can decide regarding his property according to his preference (Matt. 20:15), and there would have been an argument from generosity and clemency to not accept any compensation (Matt. 18:27), if he had had to act here according to an absolute lordship; but (3) he must be considered as a ruler, who is responsible to inflict punishments, and to free from punishment someone whom he could punish rigorously, to guard law and justice, as justice personified,[7] and that for the benefit of the whole.

The act of God that punishes the expromissor for the guilty: what kind is it?
VII. Consequently, the act of God, whereby on account of the punished expromissor, he freed the guilty, was not the act of an absolute lord, but a judicial act, or an act of jurisdiction, to which belongs prescribing the norm of law, sanctioning laws, investigating and judging cases, and committing judgments to execution. Nor by punishing one for another did he: (1) abrogate his own law, and thus deprive it of obligatory force, since unbelievers still remain liable to its threatening sanction (John 3:36; 1 Thess. 2:16); indeed, it is not abrogated even by faith, but rather, is established (Rom. 3:31), not to mention that the law, at least the moral law, inasmuch as it is for the most part of natural right, cannot be abrogated by either God or man (Matt. 5:18). Nor did he (2) dispense with the obligation of the law by excepting this or that person or case from its obligatory force, since in regard to natural law, there is no dispensation; nor when it is violated can the natural obligation to punishment be taken away; nor was it

---

6. ὑπεροχὴ *judicialis*
7. δίκαιον ἔμψυχον. Aristotle, *Nicomachean Ethics*, 5.4, 1132a21.

taken away in our redemption, but only transferred from us to our expromissor. Rather, he only (3) declared that the intention of the law is not that precisely the one sinning be punished, but it is sufficient if the penalty pronounced upon the sin be borne either by the sinner himself or by his expromissor; and thus the choice is left to the lawgiver.

The second cause of redemption is the Mediator. Those to be redeemed
are the impelling causes.
VIII. Besides God, the secondary cause, as it were, of redemption is the Mediator, insofar as he is such, who by offering the redemption price for us, became the meritorious cause of redemption itself (Isa. 53:7, 10, 12; Ps. 40:6–8 with Heb. 9:5–10). The impelling cause of his offering was: (1) our extreme, eternal and absolutely unavoidable misery (Eph. 2:1, 3, 5; Ezek. 16:4, 6); then (2) his compassion (Ezek. 16:5; Jer. 31:20); then (3) the fittingness of him alone for accomplishing the matter of redemption, whereby he alone was able to redeem miserable people without his own destruction, because he alone possesses all the requirements of the Redeemer: he is God, he is man, he is a righteous man, he is God and man in one person; without which things no one can be sufficient for the matter of redemption, as we have taught expressly in its own place.[8] From these things he is said to be the one Mediator (1 Tim. 2:5), the one name in which there is salvation (Acts 4:12), the way, the truth, and the life, without whom no one comes to the Father (John 14:6), who by God is made to us wisdom, righteousness, sanctification, and redemption (1 Cor. 1:30).

The two acts of redemption: 1. Deliverance from the guilt of sins
IX. Moreover, the Mediator redeemed by two means: (1) by delivering us from the guilt[9] of sins, from which all spiritual slavery, all our misery, and all evil flows, so that once it is taken away, all our evil ceases; and (2) by acquiring the right to all good. With respect to the first, guilt can be taken away either: (a) by mere pardon, when nothing at all is demanded or offered in compensation for the guilt, either by the guilty himself, or by his surety; this sort of pardon conflicts with the wisdom, righteousness, and truthfulness of the Ruler (Gen. 18:25; Rom. 1:32 with 2 Thess. 1:6) and with the public good (1 Cor. 5:6–7; Ps. 101:8), wherefore in our matter of redemption it cannot have any place. (b) By acceptilation, most similar to pardon, whereby something is demanded and offered for the guilt, but it is far below equivalence to the guilt, for example, if a creditor should receive

---

8. 1.5.2 §IV
9. *a reatu*. In financial law *reatus* is a debtor's liability, but in criminal law a criminal's guilt.

one penny for a debt of a thousand gold florins; it hardly differs at all from pardon, and hence for the same reasons, in this matter it cannot be admitted.[10] (c) By payment, properly so called (Matt. 18:26), whereby what is offered is exactly what is in the obligation, wherein the creditor is bound to acquiesce and the one liable is by that very fact freed from liability, apart from any grace. This also in the present matter of our redemption cannot have any place, because: (i) payment only takes away civil liability, whereas our guilt is criminal; because (ii) in a payment, the same thing is offered that is in the obligation, whereas the Mediator did not undergo all penalties both bodily and spiritual, for example, not deafness, pestilence, and other things mentioned in Deuteronomy 28:15ff., nor our spiritual death, nor the eternity of infernal punishment, and its other inordinate corollaries; because (iii) in these things that the Mediator offered for us, God was not obligated through his justice to acquiesce, and because he could have rejected them through his absolute authority, according to what appears in Exodus 33:19 and Ezekiel 18:4, 20; hence because (iv) those things which the Mediator offered for us did not exclude all grace, as much that of admission and acceptation, with respect to the Mediator himself who offered it, as that of pardon with respect to us for whom he offered it (Rom. 3:24–25), although at the same time, in a broader and less proper sense, as our sins are called debts, so also that on account of which they are taken away can be called a payment.

Through satisfaction

Finally, (d) guilt is taken away by satisfaction, whereby not precisely *idem*, the same thing which is in the obligation, is rendered to the creditor, but *tantundem*, or an equivalent,[11] which the creditor is still not obligated through justice to accept. Thus in satisfaction is required some ἐπιείκεια, equity, or grace, wherein strict justice is not urged. Such a satisfaction is either offered for one's own guilt or for that of another. And it is at last this latter satisfaction, on account of which our guilt is taken away, that belongs to our present consideration.

What satisfaction is. With respect to the term. With respect to the substance
X. Therefore, with regard to the term, satisfaction does not occur in the Scriptures in express words, perhaps because it is forensic, and in the times of Scripture was not so commonly received that it could be transferred to the ecclesiastical state;[12]

---

10. The term *acceptilation* means release from debt without its full payment. See the note on 1.2.1 §XXIV (2:18n15).

11. On *idem* and *tantundem*, cf. 1.5.12 §V.

12. *ad civitatem ecclesiasticam*

nor does τὸ ἱκανὸν ποιεῖν ("to satisfy," Mark 15:15), represent its force sufficiently, because it connotes no substitution or compensation. Yet there is in the Scriptures, especially in our present matter, an abundant supply of equivalent terms, for example, λύτρωσις, ἀπολύτρωσις, ἀγόρασις, ἐξαγόρασις, and so forth. With regard to its substance, satisfaction in the present argument does not denote to us anything other than the mediatorial act of Christ whereby, having been substituted for elect sinners, by offering to God a ransom, equivalent to their guilt, he reconciled them to God.

Its components are: (1) Innocence

XI. So then the following are included in its nature, and exhaust it: first, the innocence of the one satisfying, whereby he is free from all his own guilt. Thus it is said that he who knew no sin was made sin for us (2 Cor. 5:21), that he is ὅσιος, ἄκακος, ἀμίαντος, holy, harmless, undefiled (Heb. 7:26), and in the judgment of everyone—his betrayer, his judge, and the thief crucified with him—is righteous, as we taught above regarding his death.[13] For the one who is under the guilt of any of his own sin cannot discharge the guilt of others, and also much less can he offer a spotless sacrifice, the sort that our Redeemer offered for us, and had to offer (Heb. 9:14 with Lev. 10:17). But here we understand not the righteousness of merit, which is included in the ransom or redemption price itself, as a part of it, but rather, the righteousness of the person, which, from the causes already delineated, is presupposed in the one who would make satisfaction, so that he may be suitable to render the satisfaction.

(2) Substitution

XII. Second, substitution, whereby he accepted, not his own punishments, but the vicarious punishments of others: either freely undertaken (Matt. 20:28; Eph. 5:2; 1 Tim. 2:6; John 1:29), or imposed and imputed to him by God, on account of his eternal promise of absolute surety (Isa. 53:6; 2 Cor. 5:21). That substitution (once prefigured in all the sacrifices, but especially in the scapegoat,[14] Lev. 16:20) is customarily designated in various ways in the Scriptures: when, for example, (1) he is expressly called a surety (Heb. 7:22), one who, by the consent of all, is substituted for the principal debtor before the creditor (Philemon 18–19); so also Christ in the eternal counsel of peace substituted himself for us, so that for us he might be made אשם, or guilt (Isa. 53:10; cf. Ps. 40:6–8). When (2) it is said that God, without a doubt from this surety, made him to be sin, that

---

13. 1.5.12 §XV
14. *In hirco Hasaël*

is, a sacrifice for sin (2 Cor. 5:21), made our depravity fall upon him (Isa. 53:6), made him a curse for us (Gal. 3:13 with Deut. 21:23). When (3) it is said that he gave himself a λύτρον, ransom for many (Matt. 20:28), an ἀντίλυτρον, ransom, for all (1 Tim. 2:6), that he bore our diseases and carried our sorrows (Isa. 53:4; John 1:29), that he laid down his life for his sheep (John 10:15, 17–18). When (4) it is said that he suffered and died for us: he suffered and died, the just for the unjust (1 Peter 3:18). The New Testament abounds with phrases of this sort (e.g. Mark 10:45; John 11:50; Heb. 2:9; 5:21; 1 Cor. 15:3; 2 Cor. 5:14–15). According to them he died not only ὑπὲρ ἡμῶν, on our behalf (Rom. 5:8), and that in an entirely different way than Paul (Col. 1:24 with 1 Cor. 1:13), but also ἀντὶ πολλῶν, in place of many (Matt. 20:28), which particle, whenever it does not mean opposition, denotes substitution, as we have already taught in the exegesis[15] (cf. 1 Peter 3:9; Matt. 5:38). When (5) it is said that he himself bore our sins in his own body on the tree (1 Peter 2:23–24), and was delivered up for our sins (Rom. 4:25; Gal. 1:4). When (6) it is said that he offered a sacrifice for our sins, once (Heb. 10:12; Eph. 5:2; cf. Lev. 10:17; 17:11).

(3) A redemption price

XIII. Third, a redemption price or ransom, which likewise is attributed to Christ in more than one way in the Scriptures: when (1) there is asserted for him, in exact terms, a ransom, a λύτρον and ἀντίλυτρον (Matt. 20:28; 1 Tim. 2:6), and the redemption procured by it, the ἀπολύτρωσις (Eph. 1:7, 14; 1 Cor. 1:30; Col. 1:14; Heb. 9:15). When (2) it is said that he bought with a price (1 Cor. 6:20; Rev. 5:9), that he perfectly redeemed, ἐξηγόρασε (Gal. 3:13; 4:5). When (3) that redemption price is expressly said to be Christ's precious blood (1 Peter 1:18–19; Rom. 3:25) and death (Heb. 9:15).

What that redemption price was

XIV. But this ransom was not provided either by (1) the essential righteousness and holiness of his divine nature, since (a) that nature could neither be offered to God for our guilt, nor be accepted by him, because he had it from eternity; however, it is constantly declared by the Scriptures that the ransom was offered to him in time, in all those passages which we already brought forward in the preceding sections; nor (b) could it on any account become ours, unless we should become God himself, and be united with God, either naturally, as the divine persons of the Trinity are one amongst themselves, or personally, as in the person of the Mediator the divine and human nature are united; and also, (c) if,

---

15. §II.C.2.b.ii, above

through an impossibility, it were to become ours in some way, it would utterly take away all necessity and use of the righteousness of Christ procured through his death and obedience, because, since it is infinite, it alone would be entirely sufficient; I would add, (d) that divine righteousness cannot pertain to the compensation of the divine majesty and law wounded by our sins.[16] Nor also (2) is this ransom provided by the original righteousness of the human nature, because that was a necessary prerequisite for the qualification of the Mediator who would make satisfaction, insofar the priest who would make an offering for us necessarily had to be holy, harmless, undefiled, and separate from sinners (Heb. 7:26), who knew no sin (2 Cor. 5:21). Therefore, this is more correctly described as the righteousness of the person than the righteousness of merit. Rather, by (3) the procured righteousness of the God-man Mediator, which is supplied by: (a) his sufferings, death, and blood (Rev. 5:9; 1 Peter 1:18–19), inasmuch as by them he redeemed us from the curse of the law, and was made a curse for us (Gal. 3:13), for this righteousness by its nature concerns the compensation of that death the guilt of which we contracted by our sins; (b) the obedience of his life and conversation, whereby he fulfilled the divine law we violated, on the exact observance of which God had suspended the merit of eternal life (Lev. 18:5; Ezek. 20:11, 13; Rom. 10:5; Gal. 3:12). Therefore, from this active righteousness, it is said that by the obedience of one righteous man, many are made righteous (Rom. 5:19), and by the righteousness of one, the justification of life flowed to all men (v. 18; 10:4; Gal. 4:4–5; Matt. 3:15; 5:17); from this righteousness, it is said that the Mediator became for us δικαιοσύνη, righteousness (1 Cor. 1:30), and יהוה צדקנו, Jehovah our Righteousness (Jer. 23:6). This twofold righteousness, passive and active, must by no means be divided in the one making satisfaction, because both are necessary for us for participation in redemption, and both are required for the compensation of the injury inflicted upon God, which is not taken away more fittingly in any other way than by suffering penalties and by offering obedience to the law; indeed if you should divide them, you would do injury to both, by depriving them both of the dignity of making satisfaction, or of meriting. Indeed, neither in this matter should that twofold righteousness be excessively distinguished out of curiosity, such that the prior alone delivered us from guilt and made satisfaction, and the latter alone obtained for us and merited the right of eternal life. For in so doing, you would deprive the passive righteousness of the dignity of meriting, and the active righteousness of the dignity of making satisfaction. Especially because in the matter

---

16. *laesae…majestatis et legis divinae*: i.e. *crimen laesae majestatis*, a form of treason against a king or state

before us, satisfaction and merit do not differ in substance, whereas he who by satisfaction is delivered from the guilt of eternal condemnation, at the same time, to him is restored the right of eternal life; rather, they differ only in reasoning, for that twofold righteousness, insofar as it concerns God, is called satisfaction; insofar as it concerns man, it is called merit. About this we will perhaps say more in its own place.[17] Wherefore it must be concluded that both kinds of Christ's righteousness, the passive and the active, are included as so many parts in the constitution of the one ransom by means of which satisfaction is made for our guilt, and at the same time the right to eternal life is obtained for us. So then (c) it is said that he delivered up himself, ἑαυτόν, speaking indefinitely, as a ransom for us (1 Tim. 2:6; Gal. 1:4; 2:20; Eph. 5:2, 25; Titus 2:14; Heb. 9:14–15), insofar as he expended for us his entire self, in all that he is, although in a diverse manner: first with respect to original righteousness, for the qualification of the person of the Mediator; with respect to both kinds of procured righteousness, as much active as passive, for the qualification of the ransom or the redemption; with respect to the examples of his life, and to his miracles, for the benefit of men, for the confirmation of our faith, and for imitation in our life; with respect to his priestly intercession, and likewise his entire exaltation—the resurrection, ascension, session at the right hand—for the application of redemption to us.

He offered a redemption price exactly equivalent to the guilt
of those to be redeemed.

XV. Therefore, this redemption price was exactly equivalent to the guilt of all those to be redeemed, such that from the rigor of his justice God could neither demand nor receive more from the Mediator. For since the guilt of all those to be redeemed is nothing but infinite (because to think that an infinite can be greater than infinite, or that something can be added to an infinite, is to think of an infinite that is not infinite), then whereas he offered a ransom that was infinite in merit and value, he surely rendered, for infinite guilt, an equivalent infinite price of redemption. Moreover, he supplied an infinite ransom because he supplied his precious blood, worth more than all gold and silver (1 Peter 1:18–19; 1 Cor. 6:20), the blood of the Son of God himself (1 John 1:7), indeed, the blood of God himself (Acts 20:28), offering himself, the God-man (1 Tim. 2:6), and that in the most perfect manner of offering, wherein you could not desire one bit more; indeed, not even God could (Heb. 9:14), because the manner was divine, from the person who offered, which was God himself and man (Acts 20:28). Accordingly, although a manifold grace of God is evident in this

---

17. §XXXVII, below

matter, for example, the grace whereby he gave his own Son for us as a surety; whereby he accepted the surety offered and the ransom provided in accord with it; whereby he restricted what was provided to redeem these persons or those, with others excluded; nevertheless, we do not read that any grace was given to the ransom itself, or to the Mediator offering it, by which it could be said that God received it by acceptilation. Moreover, just as through this equivalence he offered no less than our guilt demanded, so he offered no more, because the guilt of those to be redeemed is infinite in value. And just as furthermore, although the guilt of each one to be redeemed is infinite, and yet the guilt of all, considered collectively, does not become greater, because an infinite consists in something indivisible, and is not capable of increase or decrease, so also, although the Mediator expends an infinite ransom for each one to be redeemed, yet by the same reckoning of infinity, he was not able and did not have to expend a greater price at the same time for all of those to be redeemed.

To whom he delivered up the redemption price, and in what way
XVI. The Mediator had to deliver up the redemption price not to the devil, although he had the power of death over those to be redeemed (Heb. 2:14), because in court one does not make satisfaction to the warden or the executioner, but to God as the Judge, for which reason throughout Scripture it is said that he offered himself to God (Heb. 9:14; Rev. 5:9). Yet it must not be understood that he delivered up the price to God as if God had accepted something from him by which he would become more perfect, because not only can nothing be added to the one infinite perfection of God, but also, according to the jurists, a punishment does not have a creditor, and so does not require such a delivering up; rather, he is said to have delivered it up, insofar as he destined and devoted the redemption price of both kinds of his righteousness, active and passive, to placating the wrathful Judge, and healing the injury inflicted upon God, according to his demand. And so satisfaction includes the payment of an equivalent redemption price.

(4) Reconciliation with God
XVII. Fourth and finally, the same satisfaction includes propitiation, and the reconciliation of those to be redeemed with God, whereby, through the provided equivalent ransom, the enmity arising from sin between God and those to be redeemed (Isa. 59:2; Eph. 2:3)—that is, given faith and repentance, at least with respect to the intention to abandon sins—thoroughly ceases (Rom. 5:10), and perfect peace and friendship follows it (Rom. 5:1–2). Scripture frequently ascribes this reconciliation to the redemption price of the death of Christ (2 Cor.

5:18–21; Eph. 2:16; Col. 1:20–22). Moreover, 2 Corinthians 5:18ff. points to a twin reconciliation: one meritorious and virtual, whereby God, who due to sin is averse to those that are to be redeemed (Isa. 1:15; 59:2), is placated toward man, from which Christ is called the propitiation (*propitiatio*, ἱλασμός) for our sins (1 John 2:2; 4:10), and the means of propitiation (*propitiatorium*, ἱλαστήριον) by faith in his blood (Rom. 3:25); the other ministerial and actual, whereby the soul of man, averse to God, is placated toward him through conversion, by the work of the Holy Spirit and the gospel ministry: "and has committed to us the word of reconciliation...be reconciled with God" (2 Cor. 5:19). This latter reconciliation is a fruit and consequence of the prior, which (the prior) belongs especially to our present consideration, inasmuch as to obtain it, the payment of the ransom was most necessary.

The truth of Christ's satisfaction

XVIII. And these four components, because they exhaust the nature of a proper and perfect satisfaction offered for another, supply beyond contradiction an invincible argument for the truth of Christ's satisfaction: for that to which, in the opinion of Scripture, all the components of a true and perfect satisfaction belong, to the same cannot but belong the reckoning of a true and perfect satisfaction; and that to which these four things belong, to the same all the components belong. Other arguments on this matter, more particular to it, perhaps will follow in the elenctic part.[18]

The necessity of the same

XIX. Not only is this satisfaction of the Mediator true, but also entirely necessary. And that from more than just one head: (1) from the immutability of the divine purpose and decree of not forgiving sin without just punishment, by which he does not will to hold the guilty as innocent (Ex. 34:7; Ps. 50:20–21). From (2) the immovable truthfulness of the divine threatening (Gen. 2:17), which pronounced the punishment of death and of the curse upon the sinner (Deut. 27:26; Gal. 3:10). From (3) the holiness and righteousness native to God, whereby he cannot but hate sin (Ps. 5:4–6; Hab. 1:13; Isa. 1:15), which hatred does not denote an affection in God, but an effective action, or the will of punishing. From (4) the intrinsic demerit of sin, from which the perpetrators are worthy of death (Rom. 1:32), to which accordingly God, as the just Judge of the earth, cannot but give its just desert (Gen. 18:25), from which it is said that it is a righteous thing with God to recompense evils with evil (2 Thess. 1:6). From

---

18. §XXIII, XXVI, below

(5) the nature of law, since it is nothing except the prescription of duty, under the threat of punishment either expressed or tacitly understood (insofar as by this, law differs from counsel or simple direction, such as is, for example, in the prescriptions of doctors, or in the opinions of counselors), and since God cannot but prescribe a law to rational creatures, he cannot but demand the execution of the punishment pronounced upon its violators. From (6) the wisdom and prudence of God, as the Ruler, inasmuch as it does not suffer laws justly made for the public good to be violated with impunity, to the public detriment (cf. Ps. 101:2, 8). Finally, from (7) the consideration of the Son of God, who himself was punished, for if God could, without loss to his glory, have dispensed with the punishments of sinners, certainly he would have spared his Son, his own and only begotten, most beloved Son (Rom. 8:32), and, if there were no necessity for him to punish him, it certainly would have been (let no blasphemy be said) an evidence of inglorious cruelty, not simply to punish him on account of others, but also to punish him to such a degree on account of others. All these things, at least in my judgment, to demonstrate the necessity of this satisfaction, are better joined into one argument, and are more strongly binding against the adversary denying it, because their force becomes stronger when united than if we should argue from this or that topic alone, for example, from the justice natural to God, that through it, setting aside his will, decree and threat, he cannot but punish the sinner, even through his absolute power.

2. The acquisition of a right to good

XX. The first means of redemption was deliverance from the guilt of sins through satisfaction. The second follows, the impetration of the right to good through merit, insofar as the redemption price rendered is ordered not only to removing from us the guilt of all evil, but also to acquiring the right of all good. Namely, "That as sin has reigned to death, so also might grace reign through righteousness to eternal life through Jesus Christ our Lord" (Rom. 5:21). However, the dignity of meriting belongs to the redemption price of Christ: (1) from the very nature of satisfaction itself, insofar as in delivering us from the guilt of death and every sort of curse, at the same time he restored us to the right of life and every sort of blessing (Gal. 3:13–14). Hence, (2) from the promise of the law, insofar as by supplying the δικαίωμα τοῦ νόμου, the righteousness of the law (Rom. 8:3–4), not only by bearing the punishments pronounced upon disobedience, but also by supplying most exactly the duties prescribed by the law, he acquired the right to the reward that the law promised the obedient (Lev. 18:5; Ezek. 20:11, 13; Rom. 10:5; Matt. 19:17; Rom. 2:6–10). Furthermore, (3) from the condignity of the redemption price supplied, insofar as it is of infinite value due to the person of the one supplying it, as we have already shown, and therefore it merits that we would not only by its efficacy be delivered from evil, but also obtain good. Also, from this we perceive that Christ's merit does not originate: either (a) by mere covenant agreement,[19] as the merit of our first parents would have, if they had kept the law exactly; or (b) from any sort of congruency, from which, without any debt or promise, he at times confers some external reward to the good works of the unregenerate (Ex. 1:19–20); but rather, (c) from the condignity of the obedience, insofar as not only did he obey as a divine person, being in the form of God, equal with God (Phil. 2:6–9), but also the obedience itself, as it came from the God-man, was not owed, and was superabundant, because the law binds not the God-man to obedience, but only men. I should add that he also rendered more than what the law demands of men, namely, so many miracles, so many extraordinary benefits provided to men, from all of which his obedience came forth with infinite value.

The object of redemption. Not each and every person, but his own people
XXI. We have considered the nature of redemption, its causes, and its means; now follows its object, which is supplied not by the angels, either the good, who do not need it, or the evil, bound in everlasting chains of darkness, set outside of any hope of redemption (2 Peter 2:4; Jude 6; Rev. 20:2), but by men, and of these, neither a few, speaking absolutely, nor each and every one, but many (Matt. 20:28). For although the ransom of redemption that was supplied is of infinite value, such that by means of it each and every person could have been easily redeemed (from which some say that Christ died sufficiently, though not effectually, for each and every person), nevertheless, because its efficacy depends not only on its value, but also upon the determination of the Father,[20] and on the intention of the one redeeming (John 17:19), hence we say with the Scriptures that he did not redeem each and every person; specifically, he did not offer his ransom for these who had been damned prior to his death (1 Peter 3:19–20), nor for those that were to be damned after his death (Rom. 8:34), but (1) for his church (Eph. 5:23, 25–27; Acts 20:28; Rev. 5:9; 1:5; Titus 2:13–14); (2) for his sheep (John 10:11, 15; Heb. 13:2), with the goats excluded (Matt. 25:32ff.); (3) for his people (Matt. 1:21; Titus 2:14); (4) for his brothers (Heb. 2:11ff.); for his children and seed (Heb. 2:13–15; Isa. 53:10; Ps. 22:30); (6) for the children or people of God (John 11:50–52); and finally, (7) for those whom the Father gave to him to be redeemed (John 17:1–2, 9; cf. John 6:50–51, 35–54 with 17:24).

---

19. *ex puro puto pacto*
20. *a destinatione Patris*

The fruits of redemption

XXII. There remain the fruits and products of redemption, death, and satisfaction, namely: (1) the sanctioning and confirmation of the covenant of grace, and of all its benefits (Matt. 26:28; Heb. 9:15–16), insofar as that covenant, according to the reckoning of a testament, is confirmed upon the death of the testator (Heb. 9:16–17), nor can any benefit of the covenant of grace, at least any saving benefit, pass to us unless sin has been taken away by a redemption price (Isa. 59:2), from which only in Christ are all the promises of this covenant said to be yes and amen (2 Cor. 1:20). (2) Our reconciliation with God, given faith, whereby on the one hand, all our enmity with God has been taken away (Col. 1:20; Eph. 2:16; Rom. 5:10; 2 Cor. 5:18–21), for when the cause of all hatred and enmity has been taken away through the redemption price supplied, necessarily every effective action of hatred ceases; and on the other hand, peace with God has been restored to us, from which Christ is called our peace (Eph. 2:14), our propitiation (1 John 2:1–2), and means of propitiation (Rom. 3:25), insofar as when the cause of enmity has been taken away by the redemption price, God's peace and good will cannot but follow (Luke 2:14). (3) Deliverance from every truly evil thing (Rev. 14:4; Matt. 6:13; Titus 2:14); specifically, (a) from original and actual sin (Heb. 1:3; 1 John 3:8; 1 Peter 1:18); (b) from the wrath to come (1 Thess. 1:10); (c) from the curse of the law (Gal. 3:13–14); (d) from the wages of sin, death (Heb. 2:14–15); (e) from the dominion and tyranny of Satan, and of all our spiritual enemies (Heb. 2:14–15; Luke 1:74); (f) from the present evil age (Gal. 1:4; Rev. 14:3, 5). (4) Conferral of the blessing of Abraham, and in that, of the Holy Spirit (Gal. 3:13–14). (5) Adoption and reception into the family of God (Gal. 4:4–6). (6) Justification and forgiveness of sins (Eph. 1:7; Col. 1:14; Rom. 5:19; 2 Cor. 5:20–21; Rev. 1:5; Rom. 5:9; Heb. 10:16–18). (7) Sanctification (1 Cor. 6:11; 1:30; Titus 2:14). (8) Spiritual liberty (Gal. 5:1). (9) Boldness, and access to the throne of grace in any necessity (Heb. 10:19–20). Yet, all these things, with respect to possession, presuppose the prerequisite conditions, that is, faith and repentance.

The Elenctic Part

It is asked: 1. Is there a true redemption through Christ?

XXIII. In this chapter there is as it were a seedbed of controversies. It could be asked, first, whether there is a true redemption through Christ. Denying it are all open unbelievers, pagans, Muslims, and Jews. Affirming it are as many as profess Christ, even only with their mouth, and accept the truth of the New Testament. In order for unbelievers, if possible, to be successfully convinced, it will be useful to follow in the footsteps of Paul, who treats upon this issue with the pagans, for example, with the Athenians (Acts 17:22ff.), with Felix and Drusilla (24:25), and with the Romans, in his epistle to them. Specifically, if we are dealing with pagans, we should endeavor to convince them from the principles of right reason, and if with Jews and Muslims, then in addition from the writings they receive, of the unavoidable necessity of either the eternal destruction of the whole human race, or of some kind of redemption.

The hypotheses to be demonstrated here
This can be done, through these hypotheses, solidly demonstrated: (1) that there exists a God, upon whom all things, according to each one's own nature, depend and are governed; a God who accordingly (2) cannot but prescribe laws for his rational creatures, whereby they may be governed in a moral way, suitable to their nature; (3) these divine laws by their own nature imply threats of punishment analogous to the violation of the law; wherefore, (4) since by any violation of the law, the infinite majesty of the lawgiver is violated, an infinite guilt is contracted by any sin; which guilt, (5) by the lawgiver's natural holiness, righteousness, and hatred of sin and the sinner, the Judge and lawgiver cannot pass by without a condign punishment; wherefore (6) it is necessary that either the sinner himself perish eternally, or another intercede to undertake that punishment for him, and in undertaking it, redeem him; and because (7) the sinner himself, being finite, cannot sustain an infinite punishment except eternally, then it is necessary that some person infinite in worth come forward to bear the punishment infinite in value; and because (8) God, by justice, does not will to punish the sin of man except in man, it was also necessary that the one who would endure and take away that punishment at the same time be a true man, and thus God and man simultaneously; and because (9) there is no God-man except our Jesus, who being in himself innocent, endured all the most dreadful things; it remains (10) that he alone is the Redeemer of man, who by fulfilling the righteousness of the law, freed man the sinner from the guilt of eternal death, and in its place recovered the right to eternal life; or if (11) our Jesus is not this Redeemer, it is necessary that our adversary designate some other one, whom it will be an easy business for us to refute, through the requirements necessary for the Redeemer, such as a divine and a human nature, and being in himself innocent, which requirements are lacking in theirs; and because (12) this is such a thing that human reason could not find out, it is necessary that this be revealed by God; and thus (13) this writing by means of which this is revealed to us, is of divine origin and authority; and finally, (14) a response must be made to anything that our adversary can allege to the contrary.

2. Does the redemption of Christ consist in this alone, that he promised forgiveness and eternal life to those observing the Mosaic law, as corrected and augmented by him, and so forth? The opinion of Christians

XXIV. Second, it is asked whether the redemption of Christ consists in only these points: that having been sent by God, he announced to sinners the promises of God regarding the forgiveness of sins and eternal life, under condition of obedience rendered to the Mosaic law, as it was corrected and augmented by him; furthermore, that he lit the way in this obedience by his own example; that by his death and resurrection he confirmed the promises made, and after his ascension pleads the cause of sinners in heaven before his Father, and in the last judgment after the resurrection will confer the promised eternal life upon them. The Socinians, due to their hatred, first of the eternal deity, and then consequently of the equivalent satisfaction of Christ, limit the matter of redemption to the aforementioned components. Christians on the contrary, just as they grant that Christ was sent by God, declared the way of salvation, lit the way by his own example, confirmed the truth of his teaching by his death, and since his resurrection and ascension, pleads our cause in heaven, and also will confer the crown of righteousness on the last day, so they deny: (1) that Christ was the first to announce the promises of forgiveness of sins and eternal life; (2) that he corrected and augmented the Mosaic law; (3) that he suspended the forgiveness of sins and eternal life upon obedience rendered to any law; but they affirm that (4) it depends upon an equivalent satisfaction that was certainly provided by him, but which we must lay hold of by a living faith. Regarding the perverse hypotheses of the Socinians: (1) that Christ was the first to make known the spiritual promises about the forgiveness of sins and eternal life, an almost infinite number of testimonies of the Old Testament refute (first on forgiveness, Lev. 4:20, 31, 35; 2 Chron. 7:14; Jer. 31:34; 33:8; Zeph. 3:17; Ps. 32:1; 65:3; 103:3; on eternal life, Lev. 18:5; Ezek. 20:11 with Rom. 10:5; Matt. 19:16–17; Gal. 3:12; etc.); (2) that Christ corrected and augmented the law of Moses, we refuted in book 5, chapter 6, §XVII and we will expressly refute it in its own place;[21] (3) that he suspended the forgiveness of sins and eternal life upon obedience to be supplied to some law, or upon good works, we will confound in its own place, in the chapter on justification;[22] and moreover, (4) that Christ redeemed us with an equivalent satisfaction, we have already demonstrated in the dogmatic part, and will vindicate in subsequent sections.[23]

---

21. 1.8.2 §XLVIII; cf. 1.8.3 §XLVI
22. 1.6.6 §XXII
23. §§XXXIII, XXXV, below

3. Did Christ satisfy through a mere acceptilation of God?

XXV. Third, it is asked whether, if any satisfaction must be admitted in the matter of redemption, it is nothing other than that which rests upon a mere acceptilation of God. The Socinians, so that they may, if not utterly remove the odium of their denial of the satisfaction of Christ, then at least soften it, and so that they can more easily hide among Christians, affirm that Christ can be said to have satisfied, insofar as he most exactly rendered everything that God had imposed upon him, without any substitution or price. Approaching Socinus, though in a subtler way, are the Socinianizing Arminians, such as Courcelles in his *Dissertation on Trinitarian Terms* (§XXX), Episcopius in his *Apology* (ch. 8, folio 94), and others.[24] And among these, Conrad Vorstius, so that he would not jeopardize his call to the professorship at Leiden by denying the satisfaction of Christ in express terms, did admit a kind of substitution of Christ, and even a price, but one that on its own was not equivalent to our guilt, but was sufficient only by God's acceptilation, in which way one satisfies who renders to the receiving creditor one gold imperial instead of a thousand. Christians indeed grant that he most exactly rendered what the Father willed, but they add that the Father willed that Christ would substitute himself for elect sinners, and that he would render an equivalent price of redemption (Ps. 40:6–8 with Heb. 10:5–11; Isa. 53:10). These two points controverted here we will distinctly vindicate in the following controversies.[25]

4. Was Christ substituted for us in his satisfaction? The opinion of the adversaries, and of the Reformed

XXVI. Fourth, it is asked, whether in satisfying Christ was substituted for his own in such a way that their sins and their entire guilt was imputed to him. The Socinians, out of hatred for an equivalent satisfaction, do admit that Christ died for us, that is, for our good, just as Paul also did (Col. 1:24), and specifically so that: (1) he might for our sake seal the new covenant, and by his death confirm its new and spiritual promises of forgiveness of sins and eternal life, which were to be rendered to those obeying him; so that (2) he might more powerfully draw people to embrace the condition of that new covenant, namely obedience to his commands; so that (3) having by his sufferings and death been

---

24. Etienne de Courcelles (1586–1659), "Prima dissertatio theologica: de vocibus Trinitatis, ὑποστάσεως, personae, essentiae, ὁμοουσίου, et similibus" in *Quaternio dissertationum theologicarum adversus Samuelem Maresium* (Amsterdam: Henry Dendrin, 1659), 44–47; idem, *Opera theologica* (Amsterdam: Daniel Elsevir, 1675), 1:811–83; Episcopius, *Apologia pro confessione*, fols. 94r–95r.

25. §§XXVI, XXXIII, below

thoroughly taught mercy, and obtained supreme authority, he might be better able to intercede for us. The papists, although to some extent they confess that the satisfaction of Christ was for us, even so deny that Christ's obedience and righteousness is imputed to us, to the end that they may be able to more easily substitute their own righteousness for the righteousness of Christ imputed to us, that by means of it they may merit eternal life. The Reformed teach that Christ in satisfying was substituted for us in such a way that our sins and entire guilt were imputed to him, and thus he suffered and died in our place. The foundations of the orthodox opinion, we have demonstrated in §XII. We do not add anything here except that: (1) the Socinian opinion does not attribute anything more to the suffering and death of Christ than to the sufferings of any of the martyrs (Col. 1:24 with 2 Tim. 2:10), against which the apostle himself cries out (1 Cor. 1:13). (2) From the Socinian opinion, the fruit of Christ's death could not extend to believers in the Old Testament, which Paul expressly argues against (Heb. 9:15). (3) Scripture nowhere teaches that Christ suffered and died as a prophet or martyr, but in the most express words, as a testator (Heb. 9:15–17; Gal. 3:17). (4) From the hypothesis of Socinus, Christ's suffering and death would not make for the demonstration of God's righteousness, against which the apostle cries out (Rom. 3:25). (5) From the same opinion, Christ could not be said to have been made a curse for us (Gal. 3:13 with Deut. 21:23).

Objections of the Socinians

They do not have anything to allege except: (1) one or another testimony of Scripture that seems to reject this substitution (Ex. 32:33; Ezek. 18:17–18, 26). I respond, But those passages do not reject all substitution, but only that whereby Moses would be substituted for the Israelites, or some father for his son, and on the contrary some son for his father, or a mere man for another man. They do not, however, reject the extraordinary substitution whereby from the covenant of the Father and the Son, he was substituted for his elect. (2) That in capital offenses, substitution is not permitted (Deut. 24:16; 2 Kings 14:6). I respond, True, but (a) although God prohibited it for others, yet he did not deprive himself of the authority to substitute; because (b) no creature has authority over the life of an innocent person, hence neither can a judge accept the life of one for the life of another, nor can one justly offer to the judge his own life for another. But, both because the supreme Judge has the most absolute right of life and death, and because Christ, as God, claims for himself that right (John 10:18), it appears here that the reasoning is most dissimilar. (3) That it is unjust to punish the innocent for the guilty, and in addition cruel to punish an innocent son for the guilty. I respond: (a) It is unjust to punish the innocent for the guilty if he is unwilling. However, it is not unjust to punish him if he is willing, if he is in possession of his own right, for there is no injustice done to the willing. (b) Neither is it unjust or cruel if the Father should punish the Son who is willing, when it can be accomplished with the greatest profit and advantage, as well as without the destruction of the Son. (c) It would be equally unjust and cruel to afflict the innocent Son to the advantage of the guilty (which Socinians acknowledge was done in Christ), as to punish the innocent in the place of the guilty.

5. *By substitution, did he undertake our sins only with respect to their guilt, or also with respect to their stain? What the Reformed grant, and for what reasons* XXVII. It is asked, fifth, whether the sins of the elect, not only with respect to their guilt, but also with respect to their stain, were placed upon and undertaken by Christ. In full agreement, all the Reformed acknowledge that the sins of the elect, by this substitution, in the eternal counsel of peace were placed by the Father upon Christ, and undertaken by him, because: (1) if our sins had not been undertaken by him, their punishment could not have justly been required of him, for he who in no way possesses sin, cannot be justly punished on account of it. Hence, (2) Scripture says throughout that Jehovah made to fall upon him the punishment of us all, ויהוה הפגיע בו את עון כלנו (Isa. 53:6); "and he shall bear their iniquities," ועונתם הוא יסבל (v. 11); "and he bore the sins of many," והוא חטא־רבים נשא (v. 12), and in 1 Peter 2:24, "Who himself bore our sins, ἁμαρτίας ἡμῶν, in his own body." Thus it is said that God made him who knew no sin to be sin for us (2 Cor. 5:21). From this, foolishness is attributed to him (Ps. 69:5–6); in Psalm 40:12, "My iniquities, עונותי, have surrounded me." (3) We read this prefigured in the placing of hands and of sins upon a beast destined for sacrifice, from which the sacrifice was called sin and guilt, חטאה and אשם (Lev. 16:26, 28; Num. 19:7–8). But the question remains, whether the sin of the elect was placed upon him only with respect to its guilt, or in addition with respect to its stain. That it was placed upon him with respect to its guilt, all the Reformed confess with one voice. But that it was placed upon him with respect to its stain also, the Antinomians teach, to the end that they may hold that the elect from this substitution and undertaking are as pure, as just, and as holy as Christ himself—indeed, in some respect even more pure than Christ, inasmuch as he drew the stain of their sins from them onto himself—and in addition that they may hold that repentance and holiness, by which they take hold of the prior redemption of Christ, are not necessary in the elect, because Christ drew all their sins onto himself not only with respect to their guilt but also with respect to their stain.

What they deny

The Reformed deny that the sins of the elect were placed upon Christ with respect to their stain; rather, they say that the sins were only imputed to him, with respect to their guilt, insofar as he was dealt with by God in such a way as if he had the stain of their sins. For otherwise: (1) he would have been a sinner inherently, if not through commission, at least through imposition; for to him upon whom the stain of sin has been placed, it inheres. Otherwise, (2) from the stain of drunkenness and incest undertaken from Lot, of lying from Abraham and Isaac, of theft from the thief, he would have inherently been a drunkard, incestuous, a liar, a thief, which breathes of open blasphemy; we will speak more fully on this point in due time.[26] Otherwise, (3) there would be an error in the divine mind, by which he thought either that the sins committed by the elect were perpetrated by Christ, or that the corruption of sin was propagated to Christ, or at least placed upon him; however, all of these are impossible. Furthermore, (4) the imposition of the stain of our sins would have been vain and useless, because the undertaking of our sins in Christ does not look to any other end than that he would satisfy for them, and in satisfying take them away, and deliver from their guilt; to this it would not confer anything for him to undertake the stain and shamefulness of sins. In addition, (5) the one who took such careful heed that his body would not see corruption, without a doubt took heed all the more that his soul would not see the pollution of sin. Moreover, (6) he could not be said to be ὅσιος, ἄκακος, ἀμίαντος, κεχωρισμένος ἀπὸ τῶν ἁμαρτωλῶν, "holy, free from malice, undefiled, separate from sinners" (Heb. 7:26), if he had put upon him the stains of so many elect. Indeed, (7) in this way he would have been unsuited to satisfy for the sins of the elect. For that person who bears the stain and shamefulness of so many sins cannot even satisfy for himself, and much less for others. Thus the apostle says in Hebrews 7:26, "For such a high priest was fitting for us, who is holy," and so forth. And in a satisfaction, a just man must be substituted for the unjust, as in 1 Peter 3:18, "the just for the unjust, that he might bring us to God." For this purpose, the sacrifices of the Old Testament had to be pure, ἄμωμα, blameless, from which Christ is also said to have by the Holy Spirit offered himself ἄμωμον, without spot (Heb. 9:14). Nor does it help to take exception that he had to be immune from his own sin, or sin committed by him, for that stain of our sins which was placed upon him, is in the same place as that which would have been from him originally. Finally, (8) if he had transferred the stain of our sins from us to himself in such a way that he

---

26. §XXVIII, below

had thoroughly delivered us from it, such that the sins were no longer ours, but Christ's, then he would have satisfied not for us, but for his own sins.

The foundations of the opposing opinion
I do not see what could be said for the opposing view, except that our sins were imputed, which we mentioned previously, through which it does not follow that the stain of our sins was placed upon him, but only that through imputation he was held and punished by God as if he himself had perpetrated the same sins. Therefore, our adversaries seem to sin, in that: (1) they consider sins as something positive, which can be placed upon someone by a physical transfer, whereas in fact they cannot be placed upon someone except with respect to guilt, through imputation. (2) Since, they say, from a civil obligation, the one who is to pay is considered as the debtor, so also from a criminal obligation he is rendered an idolater or a blasphemer, and thus has not only the guilt, but also the sin itself; whereas Christ, when he paid our debts, was the satisfier or criminal payor, who does not render anything except the punishment of the guilt, and does not undertake the stain, since it is clear that if anyone undertakes the monetary punishment, for example for theft, that one does not automatically become a thief.

6. Did Christ by this substitution become a sinner, a drunkard, a liar, and so forth? The difference of opinions. The negative with its reasons
XXVIII. From this, it is asked, sixth, whether Christ from the undertaking of our sins through substitution became a sinner, a drunkard, a liar, a blasphemer, and what not, and in fact ought to be called a sinner more than we, indeed, the greatest sinner, because he transferred our sins to himself, and delivered us from them. The Antinomians, because (per the preceding controversy) they state that our sins were transferred to him not only with respect to their guilt, but also with respect to their stain and shamefulness, are forced to affirm it. There are not lacking among the fathers those who speak this way, although with a different intent: for example, Chrysostom (homily 11 on 2 Cor.), and Oecumenius (on Heb. 9); and even also among the Reformed: for example, Calvin (on Gal. 3:13), and Jacob Alting (*Two Heptads of Academic Dissertations*, theological diss. 1, §§4–8).[27] Yet neither the fathers, nor the Reformed, nor indeed all Christians

---

27. Chrysostom, Homilia XI in *In secundam ad Corinthios epistolam commentarius* in *PG* 61:477–80; idem, Homily XI in *Homilies…on the second epistle…to the Corinthians* in *NPNF1* 12:334–35; Oecumenius (c. 550–c. 600), *In epistolam divi Pauli ad Hebraeos…commentaria* in *In omnes S. Pauli epistolas absolutissimi commentarii* (Basel, 1552), 596–97; Calvin, *Opera omnia*, 9 vols. (Amsterdam: Jan Jacob Schipper, 1667), 7:295–96; idem, *Commentaries on the Epistles of Paul to the Galatians and Ephesians* (Edinburgh: Calvin Translation Society, 1854), 91–93; idem,

together in common, speak or think in this way, because: (1) per the preceding question, Christ undertook the sins of the elect not with respect to their stain, but with respect to their guilt and punishment only. (2) Scripture nowhere teaches that Christ became a sinner, a liar, a drunkard, a blasphemer, and so forth. (3) It breathes of blasphemy and exposes Christian truth to the mockeries and calumnies of its enemies, to say that our Savior is a sinner, blasphemer, and so forth.

The affirmative with its objections
Neither (1) is it true what they lay for a foundation of this horrendous opinion, that Christ undertook our sins, not only with respect to their guilt, but also with respect to their stain, as we have taught in the preceding question. Nor (2) does it pertain to this that he is said to have been made sin for us (2 Cor. 5:21), and that *sin* there says even more than *sinner*, because *sin* to the apostle has the same force as אשם, the victim and sacrifice for sin (Isa. 53:10), which being without blemish or fault was substituted for sinners so that, as a type, it took away the guilt contracted from their sins, and thereby reconciled the sinner to God, but not so that it might make the sacrificial victim a sinner, or the sinner not a sinner. Nor (3) that he is said to have been numbered with sinners (Isa. 53:12), because this, from the continuous tenor of this chapter, is said only about the punishments laid upon him for our sins, whereby he was treated by God in such a way as if he were a sinner. Unless you prefer to say that he was numbered with sinners by his enemies, when they put him on the cross as a thief, seducer, blasphemer, and rebel, in the middle between the worst thieves, by which very thing they brought fulfillment to this prophecy. Nor (4) that in this substitution of Christ in the place of sinners, a certain exchange of persons happened, whereby Christ became a sinner and sinners became righteous. The Reformed gladly acknowledge that a certain kind of exchange of persons with Christ was made, but not an exchange of every kind, not such whereby the Savior became a sinner, and sinners in turn became saviors; nor in this exchange did the stain of sin itself transfer to Christ as the expromissor, but only the guilt. Nor (5) that he was substituted for us in such a way that he had no comeliness, no glory, indeed was despised (Isa. 53:2–3), for he had this only before men (Isa. 53:2–3), who considered him as some kind of flagrant sinner, from so many and such great punishments that

---

Commentaires…sur les Epistres de l'Apostre S. Paul ([Geneva]: Conrad Badius, 1562), 211–12; Jacob Alting, *Academicarum dissertationum heptades duae. Prior theologicarum, posterior philologicarum. Accessit heptas orationum* (Groningen: Aemilius Spinniker, 1671), 6–7; see in addition, theological diss. 1, §IX.

the Father laid upon him on account of our sins, as the context of that chapter teaches, not however because he bore the stain of sins. Nor (6) that he was also abominable to the Father, and was rejected and deserted by him, which would certainly not have obtained if he had not been a sinner; since we read nowhere that he himself was abominable to God, nor also that he was rejected by him as a degenerate son, although he was deserted by him, not because he was a sinner, but because this was the punishment for our sins, which was due to him from the fact that he took upon himself the guilt of our sins.

7. Ought the actual transfer of our sins begin at the crucifixion of Christ and terminate in his resurrection? The difference of opinions
XXIX. It is asked, seventh, when and how long Christ bore the sins of the elect, whether the transfer of sins to Christ and the bearing of them by Christ ought to begin from his crucifixion and terminate in his resurrection. With respect to the obligation to sustain, at the established time, not the stain of our sins, but their punishments, at least to all the Reformed it is beyond doubt that Christ undertook them from eternity, namely in the counsel of peace between the Father and the Son, when the Father demanded and the Son undertook to satisfy for our sins; although in the manner of undertaking them, it has begun to be controverted recently whether, he undertook them on certain terms, as a *fidejussor*, a conditional surety, such that elect sinners nonetheless remained under guilt until the actual payment, or absolutely, as an *expromissor*, an absolute surety, such that he drew all guilt from elect sinners onto himself once and for all, and in this regard delivered all elect sinners from guilt, even in the Old Testament. We have examined this question above in book 5, chapter 1.[28] However, with respect to its execution, there is not lacking one who states that Christ began and ended our punishments in the space of the three hours of the crucifixion. And this question we determined in book 5, chapter 11, §XXXIV. The Antinomians in England want Christ to have begun to bear our sins when he was affixed to the cross, and to have ended with his resurrection.

The opinion of the Reformed with their reasons
The Reformed think that Christ bore the punishments of our sins from the beginning of his incarnation, although eminently on the cross and in his death, and that he ended it in death when he exclaimed, "It is finished" (John 19:30), unless you prefer to add the three days of his burial, insofar as in them he certainly did not suffer anything for sins, but was under the state and dominion

---

28. 1.5.1 §XXXIV

of death (Acts 2:24). Moreover, they state it in this way because: (1) the very assumption of the human nature was a recognition of the debt undertaken for our sins (Ps. 40:7 with Heb. 10:5, 7, 9), and by the blood of circumcision, it was as if the handwritten record of our sins was sealed. (2) The form of a servant, and the ὁμοίωμα σαρκὸς ἁμαρτίας, likeness of sinful flesh, which endured from the beginning of his life until death, is an argument that sin was transferred to him (Phil. 2:7–8). (3) The death which God pronounced upon our first parents if they were to sin, included in its compass all the miseries to which the sinner is liable throughout his whole life, and hence it was fitting that Christ also, for the payment of the undertaken debt, would lead a life liable to many vicissitudes of miseries. (4) All those sorrows which Christ bore through his entire life looked to the satisfaction for our sins (Isa. 53:3–5). (5) There will scarcely be found among Christians one who would dare to say that the most humble birth of Christ, whereby he was made lower than the angels, his poverty, temptation, stoning, beatings, agony in Gethsemane, bloody sweat, condemnation in both courts, ecclesiastical and political, his thorny crown, so many mockings, and six hundred other things, did not pertain to his bearing of our punishments. Especially since (6) the apostle expressly declares that he became poor that he might make us rich (2 Cor. 8:9).

Objections of our adversaries

Nor is there any substance to what they may allege to the contrary: (1) that Paul frequently refers the reconciliation of our sins to the cross of Christ (Col. 1:20; Eph. 2:16), and Christ is said to have reconciled us when the handwriting of our sins was blotted out and taken away on the cross (Col. 2:14). For we do not deny that the chief part of the payment occurred on the cross; indeed, without the death of the cross, all the rest of his sufferings would not have had value, because death had been threatened as the punishment of sin (Gen. 2:16; Rom. 6:23), nor does remission occur without the shedding of blood (Heb. 9:7); we only deny that this was accomplished in the sufferings on the cross alone. (2) That throughout the time preceding the cross he quite often experienced the favor of the Father toward him. I respond, Just as God employs much deferral of wrath toward sinners, and tempers the bitter sorrows of this life with some sweetness of patience until the day of wrath and just retribution comes, when he will heap up the entire weight of the curse upon the sinner (Rom. 2:4–6), so Christ also was not always so pressed down in his servile condition throughout his whole life by the weight of the sins bearing down upon him, that he was not occasionally refreshed by a notable sense of divine grace, until the hour and power of darkness arrived, when he was called to judgment, and experienced the direst trials.

8. Did only the imposition of our guilt on the cross immediately free the elect from all punishment? The difference of opinions
XXX. It is asked, eighth, whether in this substitution only the imposition of our guilt that Christ sustained on the cross immediately freed the elect sinner from all guilt and punishment of his sins. The Antinomians in England affirm this. The Reformed certainly acknowledge that: (1) Christ supplied a full satisfaction on the cross; (2) and it more certainly than certain will be applied to the elect in its own time for the actual remission of sins, as its effect. (3) We by that satisfaction, insofar as it was supplied on the cross, to that extent have been delivered from all our sins, so that God cannot now demand for them a satisfaction from us or any other person, if only it has been applied to us by faith. (4) Once the punishments had been borne by Christ on the cross, satisfaction was so thoroughly made to the divine law and the wounded majesty of God, that sins do not hinder God from offering and promising the forgiveness of sins and eternal salvation. (5) Sins, when they are already forgiven, do not acknowledge anything except the satisfaction of Christ alone as the meritorious cause of forgiveness; and the things that are required in advance from sinners, such as faith and repentance, do not supply anything except conditions, without which God does not will to apply to us the satisfaction of Christ. (f) The satisfaction of Christ is the only way to the forgiveness of sins, which we apprehend by faith. But they deny that the very laying of our sins upon Christ on the cross is the absolution of the elect from all their sins.

The reasons of the negative party
They deny this because: (1) it was not the will or purpose of either God or Christ that by this imposition alone the elect would be immediately absolved (John 3:16; 6:40; 1 Peter 1:2; Acts 10:43), to which end those passages point which require in advance, for obtaining the forgiveness of sins, faith and repentance, and declare to unbelievers and the impenitent that their sins are retained (e.g. Prov. 28:13; Isa. 1:16–18; Mark 1:4–5; Matt. 6; etc.). Accordingly, (2) by the contrary reasoning, that most wise counsel of God is overturned, wherein he determined for the fruits of Christ's death not to be imparted except under the condition of faith and repentance, to be conferred through the exaltation of Christ (Acts 5:31), and through the influence of the Holy Spirit in the application of Christ's death for the remission of sins (1 Cor. 6:11; Acts 26:18). (3) If through the opposed error, the elect had been absolved, it would be just as if

Christ had never even risen from the dead, for if only the imposition of our guilt upon Christ were sufficient, then if Christ had never risen again, we would still have been delivered from the guilt of our sins, insofar as they ceased to be ours due only to this imposition, since this imposition occurred before the resurrection of Christ; and thus the continuation of Christ's death would have been a most certain reason for our deliverance, the contrary of which is obvious in the Scriptures (1 Peter 1:3; 3:21). In fact, (4) if the imposition of our sins alone had been our deliverance, then our deliverance would have been before the death of Christ, inasmuch as our sins were laid upon Christ before his death, and thus removed from the elect; from which it would follow that the elect were exonerated before the death of Christ, and thus were delivered, even though Christ had not taken those sins away in his death. (5) The contrary opinion presupposes that the covenant of grace, from the tenor of which all benefits are dispensed, is absolute in every way, the contrary of which we have demonstrated expressly elsewhere (bk. 5, ch. 1, §§XX–XXII, XXXVII). For although on the part of God and Christ, that covenant was not suspended upon any condition moving God to establish the covenant, nevertheless from this several of the benefits of this covenant—justification, adoption, glorification—were suspended upon certain conditions people are to supply. Finally, (6) from the contrary hypothesis, elect persons before their birth, before faith, before repentance, would have had full forgiveness, because before these things their sins would have been laid on Christ and borne by him, and therefore removed from them, which is contrary to all of Scripture.

Objections

Nor is there substance to what they may object: (1) that God laid upon his own Son the sins of all the elect absolutely, and that Christ undertook the same absolutely. I respond, It is true that God laid those sins on Christ absolutely, and Christ drew them onto himself not suspended upon any condition that must be supplied by creatures; but this does not hinder him from having suspended the application and actual possession of all the fruits of this imposition upon certain conditions that must be supplied by elect creatures, just as in predestination, he certainly elected absolutely, but still suspended salvation upon means and conditions, faith and repentance, that must be supplied by the elect. (2) That the covenant of grace is absolute, free from all conditions that must be supplied by the elect. I respond, The extent to which the covenant of grace is absolute, and also conditioned, we have declared elsewhere:[29] namely, with respect to the ben-

---

29. 1.5.1, §§XX, XXXVII

efits of the covenant of grace which are accounted as means, such as regeneration, conversion, and so forth, the covenant of grace is absolute; but with respect to those that are accounted as an end, namely justification (under which is comprehended actual remission of sins), adoption, and glorification, it is conditioned, insofar as God did not want these to be obtained apart from faith and repentance. (3) That the apostle teaches that God reconciled the world to himself by making Christ, who knew no sin, to be sin for us, so that we might be made righteousness before him (2 Cor. 5:19–21). I respond, But it adds, "He committed to us the word of reconciliation…be reconciled to God," namely, by believing and repenting. Therefore, reconciliation through Christ has been impetrated absolutely, but nonetheless is still to be applied, by supplying the conditions of faith and repentance. Otherwise, to what purpose would he say, "Be reconciled to God"? To what purpose would someone who has been reconciled absolutely still be reconciled? (4) That Christ obtained for himself a right over all the elect, which also the Father gladly and worthily grants him: Psalm 2:8, "Ask of me, and I will give you the nations for your inheritance." This is the reward of his work before God his Father, that not only would he restore the captives in Israel, but that he may be God's salvation to the ends of the earth (Isa. 49:6), and that from the covenant: "If his soul shall make itself a sacrifice for guilt, he shall see his seed" (Isa. 53:10). I respond: (a) He altogether did obtain for himself a right over all the elect, but at the same time the right to distribute his benefits to his own according to his choice, and in the order, and upon the terms, which he settled in the counsel of peace, namely, God so gave him that whosoever believes should not perish, but have eternal life (John 3:16). Then (b) he also makes such absolute use of his right obtained over all the elect, that not even one of these is lost to him (John 17:12), but with the conditions of faith and repentance intervening. (5) That Christ impetrated for the elect not only the possibility of the forgiveness of sins, but forgiveness itself (Matt. 26:28; Eph. 1:7), and grace so that they may believe. I respond, It is so, namely that they do more certainly obtain that very forgiveness, but with faith and repentance intervening as prior conditions, which he also will more certainly than certain confer upon them by his Spirit.

9. Are the elect, from the substitution and satisfaction of Christ,
never not justified, and so forth?

XXXI. From the preceding controversies, ninth, it is asked whether the elect—first from the eternal decree, then from substitution, whereby the Father laid their guilt upon the Son, and then the Son, from the will of the Father, undertook and in time paid it—are never not justified, not adopted, never children of wrath and liable to condemnation, even at the time when they are still under the dominion of sin, when they wallow in all wickedness, when they are still devoid of saving faith and sincere repentance. The Antinomians, by the hypotheses already outlined in the preceding controversies, affirm it. The Reformed state that even the elect for whom Christ satisfied, before they have been effectually called, or before they have been regenerated, converted, and have come to faith and repentance, as long as they live in sin, are under the wrath of God, under condemnation, and if, through an impossibility, they should thus die, they are eternally condemned.

The state of the controversy

At the same time, so that we may touch the state of the question with a pin, it must be recognized that we are not asking: (1) whether God decreed from eternity that certain persons chosen by him would more certainly than certain at some point be justified and adopted, and thus obtain forgiveness of sins and be eternally saved; nor (2) whether the elect are an object of love and benevolence even while they are yet sinners; nor (3) whether God continues his gracious purpose of blessing them, in the manner determined by him, their sins notwithstanding; nor (4) whether Christ rendered for them a perfect satisfaction, and merited for them eternal life, that they may gain it in the time and manner designated by him, and thus there is nothing incumbent upon them to do that they may satisfy for their sins or merit life; nor (5) whether there is the greatest difference between elect sinners and others, by reason of what they will one day be in time. All these are beyond controversy on both sides, but the question remains, whether elect sinners, before their regeneration, faith, and repentance, are justified and children of God in actuality; or likewise whether the elect, while still dead in their sins and still unbelieving, are children of wrath, and not justified by the divine promise. The Antinomians affirm these things, while the Reformed deny them.

The opinion of the Reformed with their reasons

The Reformed deny them because: (1) Scripture constantly affirms that the elect, before their conversion, before their faith, are children of wrath (Eph. 2:1–3), enemies (Col. 1:21), not the people of God, and not beloved (Rom. 9:25). (2) The gospel removes all unbelievers and impenitent from actual forgiveness of sins, declares to them the continuation of condemnation, and restricts its benefits to believers only: "He who believes not is condemned already" (John 3:18); "The wrath of God abides on him" (v. 36); "If anyone loves not the Lord Jesus, he is anathema, Maranatha" (1 Cor. 16:22); and it adds, "Such were some of you, but you have been washed" (1 Cor. 6:11). (3) From the opposed hypotheses, neither the Spirit nor the Word of God would have any of the efficacy and influence to save the sinner which Scripture so often testifies that the Spirit and the Word of God have. For it is certain that all efficacy of the Spirit and the Word of God to convert a sinner presupposes that he is still in the estate of sin, outside the estate of salvation (Titus 3:5; John 5:34; 2 Thess. 2:10; James 1:21). Now the lack of the Spirit and the Word would not create any loss for the elect, if before faith and before repentance they are already children of God and heirs of eternal life, and are delivered from the wrath of God. (4) The benefits of the gospel presuppose and imply that there is a time wherein we are actually guilty and wretched; but now, one cannot be delivered from the guilt of his sins who is not previously under guilt (Rom. 4:7). (5) You could just as well infer that a person was sanctified and glorified in his mother's womb, because God elected him to this from eternity, laid his sins upon the Son in the counsel of peace, and Christ satisfied for his sins, as you could infer that he has already been justified and adopted. (6) Scripture says that an elect person is justified in actuality after he has been effectually called (Rom. 8:30), and that there is so much joy in heaven upon the conversion of a sinner (Luke 15:7, 10). But how will this be so if the sinner before his conversion should already be in a state of grace and salvation? Not to add that (7) Scripture speaks about sinners before their conversion as wounded, wretched, and lost (Ezek. 33:11; Acts 26:18; 2 Tim. 2:25–26), all which things would be said quite harshly and crudely if before their conversion these things had already been thoroughly dealt with.

Objections

There is nothing substantive to what they may object: (1) that Jacob is said to have been loved by God in his mother's womb before he had done any good, before he had repented, and so forth (Rom. 9:10–11). I respond, Certainly he was loved with the love of benevolence, whereby God willed in his own time to confer upon him regeneration, faith, and repentance, but he was not loved with the love of complacency, whereby it would have pleased God for him to have forgiveness of sins in actuality, before he was regenerate, converted, and truly believing. (2) That a son, even still being in his mother's womb, is an heir. I respond, He is so potentially, not actually; he will be, but is not. For the prerequisites are the death of the parents, and that he have the requirements of legitimate heirs. And Scripture expressly requires for gaining the ἐξουσία υἱοθεσίας, right of adoption, that we receive Christ by faith (John 1:12; Gal. 3:26). (3) That God, by an eternal and immutable decree, appointed forgiveness of sins and a heavenly inheritance to the elect. I respond, He did, that is, he determined that in his own time it would be conferred on certain terms—"Scripture foreseeing that

God would justify the Gentiles by faith" (Gal. 3:8)—however, he did not actually confer it by the decree, for the decree of God is an internal and immanent action that produces nothing outside of God; it only predetermines the certain and infallible futurity or outcome of the thing decreed. (4) That God removed all the sins of the elect from sinners and transferred them once and for all to the Son. I respond, Certainly the Father placed the sins of the elect on the Son, and the Son bore them, so that he might impetrate the full and sole δικαίωμα, righteousness, on account of which the elect sinner would be justified and obtain pardon for his sins, provided that he apply it to himself by faith, and so forth, just as we presented more fully in the preceding controversies.[30]

10. Is an elect sinner, from Christ's substitution and bearing of his sins,
no longer a sinner? The state of the controversy
XXXII. Therefore, tenth, from the preceding controversies, it is asked whether through the substitution of Christ that was made in the eternal counsel of peace, and the satisfaction offered in time on the cross, the sins of the elect are not their sins, but Christ's, so that Christ is an adulterer, murderer, drunkard, liar, and so forth, and not the elect themselves. The Antinomians, from the hypotheses they laid down already in the preceding controversies, affirm it. The Reformed on the contrary, from their tearing down of those hypotheses, deny this. It must be observed: (1) as regards the stain or lawlessness[31] of sins, with respect to it, according to the degrees of their innocence and holiness, they are more or less sinners. (2) As regards the guilt of sins, which concerns the threatening sanction of the law, sinners are more or less sinners, insofar as those sins have been forgiven or not. (3) As regards the obligation of a sinful deed, and with respect to it, neither before nor after sin is taken away by forgiveness or sanctification is the transgressor of the law so delivered that after transgression, the perpetration of sin does not remain his doing. And so from the doing or commission of sin, a man is properly denominated a sinner, just as from forgiveness and sanctification, he is denominated a sinner who will not be punished. The Antinomians, according to their own hypotheses, think that an elect person as elect ceases to be a sinner, and thus when they speak about a believer, they do not want to say that before his faith he is a sinner, but rather, that from that time when Christ undertook and bore his sins, he is not a sinner, but Christ is in his place. On the contrary, the Reformed state that from the imposition of his sins on Christ, and the bearing of them, he is and remains a sinner with respect to the stain until his

---

30. §§XXV–XXVI, above
31. ἀνομίαν

sanctification, although he is immune to the curse with respect to guilt, from forgiveness, and he will be purged from the shamefulness or stain after his perfect sanctification; and although Christ bore the punishments of sins, nevertheless those sins are not Christ's stains, but those of the elect. Accordingly, it is not asked: (1) whether the sinner after forgiveness is delivered from condemnation; nor (2) whether God no longer deals with a justified sinner as with a sinner; nor (3) whether forgiveness takes away all of his obligation to punishment; nor (4) whether the satisfaction of Christ applied to the sinner removes from him all guilt, and in addition purges him from every stain—but rather, whether from this imposition, the transgressor is no longer a sinner, but Christ is in his place; likewise whether the sins of the elect are actually forgiven at the time when Christ bore them on the cross; and finally whether when the elect sin they are not transgressors, and the sins that they commit are not their sins.

The arguments of the Reformed

The Reformed affirm the opposite, because (1) no one can doubt whether someone transgressing the law is a sinner, nor whether the one perpetrating a sinful act is its agent, nor whether the sin belongs to the one who perpetrates it. (2) Christ commands believers themselves to pray for the forgiveness of sins, insofar as they are their sins (Luke 11:4). (3) Saints in the Scriptures considered the sins they perpetrated as their own sins (Jer. 14:7; Isa. 59:12; Job 7:21; Ps. 25:11). Were they not Peter's sins, over which he wept bitterly (Matt. 26:75)? (4) God accounts the sins, even of believers, as their sins, and he forgives them as their sins (1 John 2:12; Jer. 33:8; Rev. 2:20; 3:19; 2 Tim. 4:16). By this reasoning (5) the sins of the elect would not be under any just censures of the church; no true Christian would have to be punished on account of his perverse deeds, because the things wrongly perpetrated are not his own, but Christ's sins; and six hundred other absurdities of this sort could be justly drawn from it. I need not add that the contrary opinion colludes with the errors of the papists, who state that justification takes away not only the guilt, but also the very stain of sin. (6) God observes the sins even of his believing ones, and visits them with his most severe judgments, and in addition imposes a necessity upon them of acquiring for themselves by faith and repentance the forgiveness of sins.

The foundations of the Antinomians

The foundations of the opposing opinion were already destroyed in the preceding sections, namely: (1) that Christ transferred to himself not only the guilt but also the stain of all sins that are in the elect. We expressly dispatched this error in §XXVII. (2) That Christ, because he undertook the sins of the elect and bore them on the cross, became a sinner in the place of the elect; which we refuted in §XXVIII. Hence, (3) that because God removes sins from the elect through forgiveness, by delivering them from the deserved punishments, so the sins of the elect cease to be their sins; which is most false, by the preceding arguments. Furthermore, (4) that because the justified sinner has been delivered from condemnation and guilt, so the title of *sinner* does not apply to him from his violation of the divine law; which likewise is most false, as is abundantly clear from what has been set forth previously. Finally, (5) that because Christ satisfied for the sins of the elect, so no stain of sin can inhere to elect transgressors, nor can they be said to be sinners and transgressors; which things, from the preceding arguments, are overthrown by their own absurdity. It seemed good to present this controversy, with the preceding five concerning Antinomianism, in a more free and developed manner, not only because, just as Antinomianism once disturbed Germany, by the influence of Johann Agricola of Eisleben, then New England, by John Cotton, and then England, by Dr. Crisp, so under the name of "the Hebrews," it has by certain obscure men crept into our Netherlands; but also because it is apt to enervate all practice of godliness and Christianity.[32]

11. Did he redeem us by an equivalent price? The opinions of our adversaries
XXXIII. Eleventh, it is asked whether Christ redeemed his own by an equivalent price. The Socinians, in hatred of an equivalent satisfaction, deny that any price

---

32. Johann Agricola (1494–1566), *In Evangelium Lucae Annotationes* (1525), 142ff.; idem, *Predig auff das Euagelion vom Phariseer und zolner, Luce xviii* (1526); idem, *De Duplici Legis Discrimine M. Joannis Agricolae Isleben Sententia* (1539); cf. T. J. Wengert, *Law and Gospel: Philip Melanchthon's Debate with John Agricola of Eisleben over "Poenitentia"* (Grand Rapids: Baker Academic, 1997). Agricola came to disagree with Luther's views on the role of the law and the point that Christians are *simul justus et peccator*, stating that a Christian was no longer a sinner, and that the law belonged in the city hall, not in the church: cf. Martin Luther, *Wider die Antinomer* (Wittemberg: Klug, 1539); idem, "Against Antinomianism" (1539) in *Luther's Works* (Minneapolis: Fortress Press, 1971), 47:109–15; John Cotton (1585–1652), *Sixteene questions of serious and necessary consequence propounded unto Mr. John Cotton of Boston in New England together with his answer to each question* (London: E. P. for Edward Blackmore, 1644); cf. John Cotton, "Rejoynder" in *The Antinomian Controversy 1636–1638: A Documentary History*, ed. David D. Hall, 2nd ed. (Durham: Duke University Press, 1990), 78–151; Tobias Crisp (1600–1643), *Christ Alone Exalted, in the perfection and encouragement of the saints, notwithstanding sins and trials, being the complete works of Tobias Crisp*, ed. John Gill, 7th ed., 2 vols. (London: John Bennet, 1832); idem, *Christ Made Sin: II Cor. V. XXI Evinc't from Scripture*, ed. Samuel Crisp (London, 1691). On the antinomian debates from a contemporary of Mastricht, see Herman Witsius, *Animadversiones irenicae ad controversias quae, sub infaustis antinomorum et neonomorum nominibus in Britannia nunc agitantur* (Utrecht: Guilielmus vande Water, 1696); idem, *Conciliatory, or Irenical Animadversions on the Controversies agitated in Britain under the unhappy names of Antinomians and Neonomians*, trans. T. Bell (Glasgow: W. Lang, 1807).

was offered for our guilt. Vorstius acknowledges that some price was offered, but denies that it was equivalent to our guilt, and asserts that through God's acceptilation alone was it valid and sufficient. With him the Socinianizing Arminians collude, by stating that Christ paid this price by his temporal death alone, without any punishments of hell, and that temporal death alone was received by God in place of a full satisfaction. The papists on the contrary, so that they may make space for their indulgences, state that he rendered a superabundant price, and that only one drop of his blood was sufficient to take away all our sins; we will specifically refute them in their own place, if God wills.[33]

The foundation of the Reformed

The Reformed teach that he rendered an exactly equivalent price, on this foundation, that not even the guilt of all those to be redeemed could be greater than infinite, for something greater than infinite cannot be thought of; and Christ rendered an infinite price. We have expressly demonstrated this in §XV, and also specifically taught in chapter 12, on the death of the Mediator, §§VIII–X, XX–XXI, that he endured more than a temporal death.

The objections of the Socinians

The Socinians allege to the contrary: (1) that a price is something external and adventitious, such as silver or gold. I respond, The price is understood as everything required and rendered to take away guilt, and thus according to the diversity of liability, whether civil and monetary, or criminal and capital, the price varies, such that for a civil liability, it is a thing or action to be rendered, whereas for criminal liability it is a punishment to be sustained, inasmuch as by these the guilt or debt is taken away. (2) That a price must be paid to someone, whereas in death, nothing was paid by Christ to anyone. I respond, The price, the λύτρον and ἀντίλυτρον, ransom, is said in Scripture to be everything that is supplied to take away our guilt and restore freedom, and when to this end Christ is said to have offered himself to the Father (Heb. 9:14; Eph. 5:2), it is indicated well enough that, and to whom, he paid it. (3) That God pardons and forgives our sins through grace, and hence also does not accept a price. But he does not freely pardon our expromissor. Nor is the insistence valid that a price, even supplied by another, takes away the grace of forgiveness. It certainly takes it away when a guilty person has constituted an expromissor, or has substituted and delegated the one paying for him. However, it does not take it away when the expromissor

---

33. §XXXVIII, below

immediately offers himself to the creditor, and renders payment without being asked by the debtor.

12. Did Christ reconcile only man to God, or also God to man?
The Socinian opinion
XXXIV. Twelfth, it is asked whether the reconciliation procured by the redemption of Christ is μονόπλευρος, unilateral, that is, of such a kind that by it he only placated toward God the heart of a sinner which was averse to him, or δίπλευρος, bilateral, that is, such as by which he in addition, and indeed more so, placated toward the sinner the heart of God which was averse to him. The Socinians, so that they may more easily safeguard their view that Christ redeemed us without any payment of a redemption price, and thus without any satisfaction properly termed such, state that God, when he gave the Son to the world, was already placated and reconciled to it, and accordingly did not send the Son so that he might placate him toward the world, but so that he might reconcile the world to him, by offering conditions to it, so that when they are supplied, it could obtain forgiveness and life.

The Reformed opinion, with their foundations
The Reformed on the contrary teach that Christ by redeeming reconciled us to his Father, who was angered due to sins, by the arguments that we brought forward in the dogmatic part, §XVII. To them at present we add that: (1) before the expromissor was given for us and an equivalent satisfaction was made for us, we were under God's wrath (Eph. 2:3; Rom. 1:18), under his hatred (Ps. 5:4–6; Isa. 59:2), under his enmity (Rom. 5:8–10). (2) When the redemption price was rendered, he made expiation for us (Rom. 3:25), he cleansed us from our sins (1 John 1:7). (3) For our reconciliation, he made his Son to be sin for us (2 Cor. 5:21), indeed a curse (Gal. 3:13).

An objection
It is no hindrance that he loved his own from eternity, and led by love, gave his Son as their Redeemer (John 3:16). For that love of benevolence looked to supplying the redemption (2 Cor. 5:19, 21). Nor does this love necessarily imply that the reconciliation is accomplished, as is evident in the case of Absalom, whom David most tenderly loved in earnest, yet was not by that fact reconciled to him (2 Sam. 13:30 with 14:1–24, 32–33).

13. Is satisfaction necessary for redemption? The divergent opinions
XXXV.[34] Thirteenth, it is asked whether satisfaction procured by substitution and an equivalent redemption price, was necessary for redemption. The Socinians, because they deny the very reality of this satisfaction, by the same stroke deny its necessity. Durandus and other Scholastics, although they admit the reality of the satisfaction, yet deny its necessity.[35] All of the Reformed recognize that satisfaction is necessary, but not in one and the same way. For there are some who state that it is necessary only from God's will, and from the threat made, whereby God does not will to forgive sins simply, without a punishment or its equivalent satisfaction, though if it had seemed good to him, through his absolute authority he could have done otherwise. Others again, from his natural holiness and avenging justice, and its outworking, think that God, even apart from the will and threat, could not let existing sin go unpunished, or forgive the sinner and receive him back into grace, without an equivalent compensation for his wounded majesty.

Its necessity is proved.
We already have taught in §XIX that its necessity is more easily and effectively demonstrated from many topics gathered together. Nor do we add anything to the reasons adduced there, except that: (1) it is said that he certainly punishes, or will punish, indeed that he will not hold the guilty as innocent (Ex. 34:7), namely lest he seem like them (Ps. 50:20–21), but now, it must not be believed that he does this freely, led purely by choice (Ezek. 33:11; Ps. 81:13–14), because in punishment by itself, there is nothing good or desirable; hence it is from some necessity. (2) Not only the right to punish, which arises from sin, but also the exercise of punishment, is referred to the justice of God (2 Thess. 1:6), so that not punishing appears to look toward injustice. Indeed, (3) it is said that he is purer in eyes than to behold evil, that is, without punishment (Heb. 1:13).

Objections of the Socinians
It does not help the Socinians: (1) that he is said to forgive graciously (Ex. 34:6–7, 9), without compensation (Matt. 18:26–27). I respond, For he forgives graciously, not the expromissor Christ, but us, insofar as he neither accepts one whit in compensation from us, nor from Christ as one delegated by us, but Christ as he was graciously given to us by God. (2) As anyone can, so all the

---

34. The duplicated section numbering of the original has been corrected, and the following sections renumbered accordingly.

35. Durandus, *In Sententias theologicas…commentariorum libri quatuor*, 212–13.

more can the supreme Lord forgive of his own right. I respond, God, although he is the supreme Lord, yet in this matter must not be considered as a lord, but as a judge and ruler (Gen. 18:25), who punishes not so much for himself, but for the public. (3) The supreme Judge can also renounce his right. I respond, He certainly can (a) as one injured, but not as a judge; (b) if even as a judge, yet not *de jure*, but only *de facto*; and (c) if he may renounce it *de facto*, he does not do so without a violation of his own law, which is blasphemy to think about God. (4) Anyone can pardon without compensation, and thus all the more can the omnipotent God. I respond: (a) It is not repugnant to the natural purity and justice of man, from the permission and prescription of the highest legislator, to pardon without compensation, as it is repugnant to the purity, holiness, and justice natural to God; also (b) not everything man can do, can God also do, because man can abdicate his own dominion and even deny himself, which God nevertheless cannot do (2 Tim. 2:13).

14. Are we redeemed by the righteousness of the divine person of Christ?
XXXVI. Fourteenth, it is asked whether the Savior as the God-man redeems us by the essential righteousness of the divine nature. Andreas Osiander, so that he might more strongly obtain that Christ is our Mediator only according to the divine nature, stated that we are justified through the essential righteousness of the divine person of Christ, to which we are united either naturally or personally by faith. We have examined this opinion above in chapter 2, §XXII.

15. Did Christ redeem us only by his passive righteousness?
The difference of opinions
XXXVII. Fifteenth, it is asked whether Christ redeemed us only by his passive righteousness, or in addition also his active righteousness. Johannes Piscator, otherwise an outstanding theologian, together with several others, because they thought that the necessity of passive righteousness and death would be abolished if it were stated that in our place he most exactly kept the divine law, because one who kept the law exactly could not be punished with death, chose the prior. Protestants commonly prefer the latter, and certainly correctly, but not all in one way. Some divide the passive and active righteousness of Christ in such a way that only by his passive righteousness did he satisfy in our place for the law that was not observed, and by it delivered us only from the guilt of punishment, and likewise, only by his active righteousness did he keep the law perfectly in our place, and by keeping it, acquire for us the right of eternal life. Others, with that more subtle division laid aside, prefer to state that Christ devoted both these kinds of righteousness to us, to the end that he might satisfy for the divine law

that was not observed by us, and by satisfying, also merit for us the right of life, in such a way that by this satisfaction he at the same time delivered us from every evil and gained the right of every good.

The difficulties raised by Piscator are removed

We have adduced the reasons for this view in §XX:[36] with them presupposed, it is not so difficult to respond to the difficulties raised by Piscator. For if (1) it should be alleged that the law demands nothing but one or the other, either obedience or punishment, we will respond that the law, first from man in his integrity, demands only obedience under threat of punishment, but from the sinner, it demands punishment for past sin and obedience in the future, because punishment cannot deliver from the obedience owed to God. Wherefore the Redeemer had to supply both. If (2) it should be alleged that the necessity and use of the death and passive righteousness are removed when he has most fully kept the law on our behalf, we will respond that it is by no means removed, because both kinds of righteousness were necessary for him to satisfy for the injury we inflicted upon the divine majesty and his law, and in satisfying, to merit for us the right of eternal life. If (3) it should be alleged that Scripture refers the consummation of our salvation to his one and only sacrifice accomplished on the cross, we will respond that by that sacrifice is understood by synecdoche his entire satisfaction, the outstanding part of which his death on the cross supplied, just as by the same synecdoche, the blood of Christ designates the same satisfaction (1 John 1:7; Acts 20:28). If one should proceed (4) to allege that obedience was necessary for his own self as a man, and thus could not be expended for us, we will respond that (a) the obedience, insofar as it resulted from the God-man, was not necessary for him, because the law obligates not the God-man to obedience, but a mere man; (b) that obedience of the God-man is of infinite value, whereby it was able to suffice both for himself and for us, because an obedience greater than infinite could not be demanded or supplied for him, or at the same time for us.

16. Did Christ offer more than was necessary for our redemption?

The opinion of the papists

XXXVIII. Sixteenth, it is asked whether Christ offered more than was necessary for our redemption. The papists are completely perverse on this topic, and cherish hypotheses that contradict themselves, for now they state, in favor of their indulgences, that even one drop of blood is sufficient for all those that will

---

36. Cf. §XIV.

be redeemed, and therefore what he offered over and above that was superabundant, and thus has been conveyed into the treasury of the church, together with the supererogatory sufferings and works of the saints, to be indulged to those laboring in purgatory; and now again they state that he satisfied only for sins before baptism, only for mortal sins, for the guilt of fault but not the guilt of punishment, for the eternal punishment of sins yet not for their temporal punishments, all to the end that there may be space for human satisfactions, about which we will speak just below.

The opinion of the Reformed

The Reformed think that the entire satisfaction of Christ was of infinite value (from the infinite dignity of the one satisfying, of the price offered for satisfaction, and from the manner of offering it), such that a greater could not be conceived of or exist, and that it was also necessary to take away the infinite guilt of each of the elect, and to obtain for them the right of infinite good. And accordingly, if he had supplied less (at least with respect to the substance of the thing) than he did supply, it would not have been a sufficient satisfaction. Thus, it is superstitious and impious to teach that a drop of Christ's blood was sufficient.

Their reasons

This is so because (1) it was necessary for the sufficiency of the satisfaction that the punishment be endured which the guilt of the wounded infinite majesty, the demerit of sin, and the threat of the lawgiver had prescribed, which was not a drop of blood, but death (Gen. 2:17; Rom. 6:23). (2) In the shedding of a drop of blood, God would not have sufficiently revealed his natural hatred toward sin (Ps. 5:4–6). (3) In a drop of blood, God would not have been adequately sanctified for the violated law and the wounded majesty. I would add that (4) it seems to rub off the blasphemy of cruelty upon the Father, to say that he torments his own and only begotten Son, for a drop of blood, with a cursed death.

An objection

Nor is there anything to what they object, that a drop of the blood of Christ is of infinite value. For if: (1) it is of infinite value, certainly nothing could be added to it, and thus with the shedding of such a great abundance of blood, it would have to be said that he supplied a price greater than infinite, which is an open contradiction. (2) If whatever he endured beyond a drop of blood is supererogatory, to be conveyed to the treasury of the church, then there would be more in the treasury of the church than was offered to the Father, and thus more than in God's treasury. And so it is more solidly said that (3) all that he spent for his satisfaction confers to it one infinite value, to which nothing could be added or subtracted.

17. Does the satisfaction of Christ take away all sin, and all its guilt?
The opinion of the papists
XXXIX. Seventeenth, it is asked whether the satisfaction of Christ is so great that it alone takes away all the guilt of all of the elect. The papists, so that they may make a place for human satisfactions, purgatory, and indulgences, so useful for filling the papal larder, distinguish between sins committed before baptism and afterwards, between mortal and venial sins, between the guilt of fault and of punishment, between temporal and eternal punishment, and then they restrict Christ's satisfaction to pre-baptismal, mortal sins, the guilt of punishment, and eternal punishment, so that it is incumbent upon men themselves to make satisfaction for sins committed after baptism, for venial sins, for the guilt of punishment, and for temporal punishments, whether that happens in this life through penal works, fasts, sackcloth, macerations, flagellations, pilgrimages, processions, and so forth, or after this life through purgatory, the punishments of which indulgences and Masses succor.

The opinion of the Reformed with their reasons
The Reformed state that the satisfaction of Christ takes away all our guilt, because: (1) not only is it of infinite value, to which entirely nothing could be added by anyone, without a contradiction; but also (2) it is of such kind that it cleanses us from all sin (1 John 1:7); (3) he is said to have been made to be sin for us, that we might be rendered righteousness in him (2 Cor. 5:21); in such a way that (4) on account of his satisfaction, there now remains no condemnation upon us any longer (Rom. 8:1); and that (5) any other satisfaction detracts from the fullness of Christ's satisfaction; and thus (6) excludes us from participation in Christ's satisfaction (Rom. 10:3; Gal. 5:3–4); especially since (7) every sin, from the infinite wounded majesty of God, is mortal (Gal. 3:10 from Deut. 27:26; James 2:10; cf. bk. 4, ch. 3, §XXII); the distinction between the guilt of fault and the guilt of punishment is empty and without a difference, as we have taught elsewhere (bk. 4, ch. 4, §XXIII); in the Scriptures temporal punishments are nowhere separated from eternal ones (see bk. 4, ch. 4, §XXIV); and purgatory, indulgences, and Masses are not but figments, as we will demonstrate in its own place.[37]

---

37. 1.6.9 §XXII; 1.8.4 §XVII; 1.7.6 §XVI; 1.7.5 §XXIV

Foundations of the papal opinion

Nor is there anything that could be brought forward to the contrary, at least with any appearance of truth, except: (1) that temporal evils are frequently mentioned in the Scriptures that were inflicted upon true believers in this life. But these do not argue that punishments properly so called were pronounced upon them, from justice, by God as Judge, in some kind of compensation. Rather, they are only fatherly chastisements, inflicted out of love, for their correction, on the occasion of committed sin (Heb. 12:6–7; Rev. 3:19; cf. Aquinas, *Summa Theologiae*, II^a II^{ae}, q. 17, art. 7).[38] And (2) that the term of human satisfaction frequently occurs among the fathers. But they do not understand satisfactions to be rendered to God, but only canonical satisfactions, in reparation for a scandal given, to be rendered to the church.

18. Did he satisfy for others than the elect? The difference of opinions

XL. Eighteenth, it is asked whether he satisfied or acquired some right for others than the elect. There is in this question a kind of seedbed of contentions: (1) the Remonstrants think that Christ by his satisfaction acquired for God himself the right, that with his justice preserved, he can now deal with sinners, and dictate to them new laws to gain salvation, according to his choice. The same Remonstrants add (2) that Christ by his satisfaction acquired for himself the right not only to save believers, but also to damn unbelievers. (3) Once Origen with his followers thought that Christ also satisfied for the devils, and they, after a sufficient time of punishment, would be saved at some point. (4) The Socinians, state that Christ, without any substitution or payment of a redemption price, died for the good of each and every person. (5) The Arminians, acknowledging some kind of substitution of Christ and payment of a redemption price, state that he satisfied or died for each and every person, and although he impetrated redemption for them, he does not apply it to them unless they be truly believers, in such a way that the impetration, from the intention of the Father and Christ, was made for each and every person, and its application depends on each person's choice. And they state this by various hypotheses: (a) that God predestined his Son to death and satisfaction before he had predestined anyone to salvation. (b) That redemption in itself is indeterminate, and accordingly the death of Christ pertains to all. (c) That God did not intend to apply that satisfaction of death to anyone, but achieved his goal in the very death and satisfaction of the Son, so that by his

---

38. Latin: *Aquin. 2. 2^{dae}. quaest. XVII. Art. VII:* This does not appear to be the correct citation since it addresses Heb. 11:6, on the nature of guilt and satisfaction, cf. Aquinas, *ST* III, q. 49, art. 3; cf. Aquinas (via R. da Piperno), *Supplementum*, q. 12.

satisfaction eternal life was not appointed for anyone, but only the way to the new covenant was laid open, wherein from the precept of Christ, everyone is able to gain eternal life. And so (d) the impetration of salvation, procured by his satisfaction and death, in their opinion is in this, that God, with his justice intact, can save a sinner, either through faith or through works; from which they also fabricate another certain subsequent decree. Thence, (e) they maintain that Christ died in such an indeterminate and vague way that he died neither for believers or unbelievers (both considered as such), but for all, from which afterwards some would be believers and some unbelievers, according to their pleasure. And (f) whatever happens next in application, after the requisite condition is supplied by man, it is not conferred as the goal intended by satisfaction, but as a prize or reward, and thus it pertains to justice rather than to grace. Nor are there lacking (g) among them those who say not only that a universal impetration was intended by the satisfaction and death of Christ, but also a universal application, insofar as to each and every person, grace as well as sufficient strength are conferred whereby they can, if they will, supply the stipulated conditions. With these, with respect to universality, albeit in different degrees, the Anabaptists, papists, and even Lutherans collude. (6) From among the Reformed, those who uphold a universal objective grace think that Christ satisfied for each and every person under a condition, if they should will to take hold of him with living faith, but for the elect alone absolutely, so that they should will it; and thus he certainly died for the good of all, but in place of the elect only.

The common opinion of the Reformed with their reasons
The common opinion of the Reformed is that Christ by his satisfaction neither acquired any right for God, because he already had every right over everything, from the preeminence of his deity; nor obtained anything for himself, except immunity from expromissorial liability (Col. 2:14) and the glory of exaltation (Phil. 2:7–9); nor for the angels, as we taught in chapter 2, §XXIV; nor for each and every person; but only for the elect, who were given to him by the Father to redeem (John 17:6–7), as we said in §XXI. To which we add that: (1) nowhere in the sacred page is it said that he satisfied or died for each and every person, which is the proper point of debate on this topic. (2) He did not satisfy for those who before his death were in prison (1 Peter 3:19–20). Nor (3) for these who sin against the Holy Spirit (Matt. 12:31–32 with 1 John 5:16), nor for Judas (John 6:70; 13:11; 17:12). (4) He did not will to pray for each and every person, much less to satisfy for them by dying. (5) The inseparable results of his death and satisfaction—(a) deliverance from condemnation (Rom. 8:34), (b) actual reconciliation with God (Rom. 5:10), (c) calling to participation

in the acquired redemption (Eph. 1:13), (d) remission of sins (Matt. 26:28), (e) sanctification (John 17:19), (f) the love of God (John 15:13 with 1 John 3:16), (g) participation in eternal life (Heb. 9:15)—these inseparable results, I say, or accompaniments of satisfaction do not happen for each and every person, which our adversaries themselves, together with experience, will witness. (6) At least from the hypotheses of certain adversaries, he did not satisfy for those who die in infancy, because in their opinion they do not have original sin, nor for those adults who take heed to themselves regarding every actual sin, which they think has been put in their power through the strength of their free choice.

Objections
They allege to the contrary: (1) that he is in various passages said to have died for all (2 Cor. 5:15; Heb. 2:9; 1 Tim. 2:6; Rom. 5:18). I respond: (a) Nowhere is he said to have died for each and every one, which alone is what is in question. (b) The mark of universality, "all" or "everyone," frequently in the Scriptures excludes only διαστολή, or distinction, but not exception: "Scripture says, Everyone who believes in him will not be put to shame, for there is no διαστολή, distinction, between the Jew and the Greek" (Rom. 10:11–12; cf. Gal. 3:26–28; Col. 1:20, 28); he "has shut up all" (that is, Jews as much as Gentiles) "under disobedience, so that he might have mercy upon all" (Rom. 11:32). So the word "all" here intends nothing but to remove the division between Jews and Gentiles (Eph. 2:14–16; Rom. 3:29), and it alludes to the promise once made to Abraham, "In you shall all the families of the earth be blessed" (Gen. 22:18; 12:3; 28:14), from which promise he is described as the heir of the world (Rom. 4:13; Gal. 3:8), which even so is expressly restricted (Gen. 21:12; Rom. 9:6). (c) "All" does not always denote individuals of classes, but frequently classes of individuals, as they say in the schools (Matt. 4:23; 12:31; Rom. 14:2; Rev. 5:9; etc.). (2) That he is frequently said to have died for the world (John 1:29; 2 Cor. 5:19; John 3:16), and for the whole world (1 John 2:2). I respond, With the necessary changes made, the second response to the preceding objection can easily be applied to this matter: namely, by "world" is quite frequently understood whatever is distinguished from the Jewish church, that is, the Gentiles (Rom. 11:12; 4:13), so that the sense is that Christ died not only for Jews, but also for Gentiles. (3) That he is said to have died for those who are destroyed (Rom. 14:15, 20; 1 Cor. 8:11). I respond, That is, those who are offended by the abuse of things indifferent[39] (e.g. food or drink), or for whom an occasion is offered to sin, and thus, if it were possible, to perish (Matt. 24:24), as is evident from the whole con-

____

39. *rerum adiaphorarum*

text of the objected passages. (4) That he is said to have died for false prophets who deny him (2 Peter 2:1). I respond, This is false, for the text is not speaking about Christ, who never is called δεσπότης ("Lord"), but about God (Luke 2:29; Jude 4); nor does the verb ἀγοράζειν, to buy, mean to acquire by the price of blood (as happens in 1 Cor. 6:20; 1 Peter 1:19), but simply to acquire for oneself (Isa. 55:1), so that the sense of the passage is: God led those false prophets, by the proclamation of the truth, into the external communion of the church, wherein they acknowledged and professed him as their δεσπότης, their Lord. (5) That he is said to have died for him "who has trodden underfoot the Son of God, and has counted the blood of the covenant, by which he was sanctified, a profane thing, and has insulted the Spirit of grace" (Heb. 10:29). I respond, The matter itself speaks: he is not sanctified who treads underfoot the Son of God, counts the blood of the covenant a profane thing, and commits horrendous blasphemy against the Holy Spirit (John 17:19); rather, the apostle says that by the blood of the covenant the Son of God himself was sanctified, with the apostle himself as the interpreter in Hebrews 2:11. (6) That all are obligated to believe that Christ died for them, and consequently he also died for all, unless they were bound to believe what is false. I respond, All to whom the gospel is announced (something that does not happen to each and every person, Ps. 147:19–20; Acts 16:6), are obligated to believe in Christ, that is, to receive him with a living faith (John 1:12) and only after that is done, and not before, are they obligated to conclude from it that Christ died for them.

19. Did Christ merit anything for his people?
XLI. Nineteenth, it is asked whether Christ truly and properly merited any good for his own. Since merit does not differ from satisfaction except by reason, and hence because it implies, with satisfaction, a substitution and a payment of a redemption price, the Socinians, since they deny satisfaction, substitution, and a redemption price, are compelled at the same time also to deny merit.

The affirmative reasons of the Protestants
Protestants on the contrary, as they accept satisfaction, so they also accept the merit of Christ, generally for these reasons: (1) because he was subjected to the law for us (Gal. 4:4; Matt. 5:17), and by obeying and suffering, most exactly rendered its righteousness (Rom. 8:1–4), so he also was a partaker of the promised reward of the law (Lev. 18:5; Matt. 19:17; Rom. 10:5). (2) He is the second Adam, and so then, just as the first by his disobedience merited the guilt of death for himself and his own, so the second by his obedience merited the right of life, with the apostle clearly explaining this analogy (Rom. 5:14, 18–21; 1 Cor.

15:21–22, 45). (3) Because by supplying for us, with both kinds of obedience, passive and active, an infinite price, while he satisfied from the rigor of divine justice, and thus delivered from the guilt of death, he at the same time acquired for us the right of life from the dignity of the ransom, just as we have demonstrated in the dogmatic part.[40]

The negative objections of the Socinians
Socinus objects in *On the Savior* (pt. 3, ch. 5): (1) Neither as God nor as man could he merit, because a man cannot merit life even for himself, and God also cannot merit.[41] I respond, There is a third option, as the God-man. (2) Christ, as a rational creature, owed all obedience to God for himself, therefore he could not merit anything thereby for others. I respond, Christ as a man did owe all obedience to God, for himself, but as the God-man, he did not owe it, because the law does not bind the God-man, but a mere man. (3) From certain hypotheses of yours, he merited mediatorial glory for himself, and therefore not for others. I respond, From the fullness of the infinite price rendered, he merited both for himself and for us, insofar as to obtain glory for both there is neither required, nor can there be rendered, a more than infinite price.

20. Did he merit regeneration and faith for his people?
The reasons of the affirmative opinion
XLII. Twentieth, it is asked whether he merited for his own, not only eternal life, but also the things necessary for obtaining it, such as regeneration, faith, and so forth. The Remonstrants, so that they may more easily suspend faith and repentance upon the free choice of every person, deny it. The Reformed affirm it, because: (1) it is expressly said that he gave and sanctified himself for us, so that he might sanctify us in the truth (John 17:19; Eph. 5:25–26; Heb. 2:10–11). (2) God, in Christ and on account of Christ, is said to give us not only life, but all things that are necessary for life and for godliness (2 Peter 1:1, 3; Eph. 1:3–4), and in particular, repentance (Acts 5:31; 11:18; 2 Tim. 2:25) and faith (Phil. 1:29). (3) Regeneration and faith are conferred upon us from the promise of the covenant of grace (Jer. 31:33–34; Ezek. 36:25–27 with Heb. 8:8–12; 10:16), the basis and ratification of which is in the blood of Christ alone (Matt. 26:28; Heb. 9:15–18), as that which cleanses us from all sin (1 John 1:7). (4) Also, the seals of the covenant of grace, the sacraments, seal the grace of regeneration to us (Titus 3:5; Rom. 6:3; 1 Cor. 12:13), but they do not seal it except in Christ, in whom all

---

40. §§XIV, XX, above
41. Faustus Socinus, *De Jesu Christo Servatore*, 277–81.

the promises of God are yes and amen (2 Cor. 1:20), in whom he confers upon us every spiritual blessing (Eph. 1:3). Compare the disputation of the celebrated Voetius on this very question.[42]

Objections of the negative opinion
They urge to the contrary: (1) that faith and repentance are a condition of the covenant of grace, which is prerequisite for the conferral of the blessings of the same covenant. I respond, In what manner faith and repentance supply both a condition and a benefit of the covenant of grace, we have expressly taught above in chapter 1, §§XX–XXII, and also vindicated in §§XXXVII, XXXIX. (2) That in this way the Father, from the force of that merit, would have been obligated to confer faith upon us, and to effect in us all that he prescribes to us under the threat of death. I respond, Indeed, from that gracious covenant which was established between the Father and the Son, the Father was obligated to provide that, after the Son had offered his soul as the price of redemption, he would see his spiritual seed (Isa. 53:10), which, without the conferral of faith and repentance, could not have happened.

21. Did Christ alone merit the right of eternal life for his own?
The opinion of the papists
XLIII. Twenty-first, it is asked whether Christ alone merited the right of eternal life for his own. The papists, just as they have given the dignity of satisfying to human sufferings, so also confer to their good actions a twofold dignity of meriting: one from congruence, whereby to the good works of the unregenerate, not from debt, but from superabundant generosity, God repays certain benefits, because this is congruent; the other from condignity, whereby to the good works of the regenerate, from justice, God repays eternal life, on account of condignity, because they are works produced by the Holy Spirit, and Christ merited so that our good works could merit.

The opinion of the Reformed with their supports
The Reformed leave all dignity of meriting to Christ alone, because: (1) for an infinite reward, such as is in eternal life (2 Cor. 4:17; Rom. 8:18), is prerequisite, from condignity, an infinite price, such as only Christ, who is God blessed over all (Rom. 9:5), could and did supply. (2) For merit properly so called is required

---

42. Gisbertus Voetius (1589–1676), "Quaestio: An Christus electis et salvandis specialem gratiam regenerationis et fidei sit meritus?" in *Selectae disputationes*, 5 vols. (Utrecht: Anthony Smytegelt, 1648–1669), 5:270–77.

a work that is not owed (Luke 17:10), the kind that only the God-man, who in himself was subjected to no law, could supply. (3) The one who would merit has to supply what is his own, and not what belongs to the one from whom he intends to merit, but only Christ could supply to the Father what was his own, whereas we all supply nothing but what are God's gifts (James 1:17; 1 Cor. 4:7). (4) A good work that would merit eternal life from condignity has to be absolutely perfect, for which no pardon of imperfection is necessary; however, such a work only Christ could and did supply.

Objections of the papists

There is nothing to what they allege: (1) that the good works of the reborn are works of the Holy Spirit, at least efficiently, and so then are of infinite value, and thus are meritorious from condignity. I respond, Indeed they are not meritorious even on that very account, because God or the Holy Spirit cannot merit. (2) That Christ, by his own merit, merited the dignity of meriting for the good works of the reborn. I respond: (a) Then he would have merited the dignity of meriting for the works of the Holy Spirit, which are of infinite value in themselves. (b) Scripture nowhere teaches that Christ by his own merit merited the dignity of meriting for our good works. The remaining points about the merit of good works we will lay aside for the chapter on justification.[43]

The Practical Part

Christ's redemption: 1. Commends the excellence of the Reformed religion above any other.

XLIV. The practice of Christ's redemption commends to us, first, the truth, divinity, and excellence of the Reformed religion above any other. For while some: (1) are thoroughly ignorant of any redemption of the sinner, such as the heathen; others (2) spurn the redemption that is procured through Jesus Christ, such as Muslims and Jews; others (3) fashion a redemption that happens without any substitution of Christ the Mediator, or payment of an equivalent price, by mere pardon or acceptilation, such as the Socinians, Socinianizing Remonstrants, and Anabaptists; others (4) do claim redemption from Christ, and his satisfaction and merit, but only on the one hand, yet on the other hand from human satisfactions, merits, purgatory, indulgences, Masses, and the merits of good works, such as the papists; or at least (5) from the observance of the Mosaic law, as it has been corrected and augmented by Christ, such as the Socinians; others (6) search

---

43. 1.6.6 §§XX, XXII

for redemption from some kind of conditioned satisfaction, all the efficacy of which depends upon the free choice of every person, as, with the Pelagians, the Remonstrants and Jesuits do; others (7) do acknowledge a redemption procured by the satisfaction and merit of Christ, but still such a kind with which you can perish eternally, with which most by far are eternally damned, indeed which for most results in the aggravation of their eternal condemnation, such as the Lutherans. Whereas the Reformed alone teach such a redemption whereby the Mediator, having been substituted for his own, rendered an equivalent price for them, whereby more certainly than certain all those given to him are saved. And thus, they teach the redemption: (1) which God himself manifested in his Word; which (2) is most fitting for God, and best makes the glory of his (a) avenging righteousness, (b) love toward man, and mercy, (c) wisdom, (d) independence of every kind, and so forth, to be illustrious and evident, as we will distinctly demonstrate in the following section; which (3) most effectually leads a person to eternal blessedness, presses him down to profound humility and dependence upon God and his pure, unadulterated grace; which (4) supplies the immovable blessedness of the redeemed, and most precisely shapes him to gratitude and a holy manner of life, as will be evident through the following sections.

2. It commends the immeasurable glory of God.
XLV. Second, this incomparable and indescribable act of redemption commends the immeasurable glory of God. This is the ultimate goal of the entirety of this so illustrious undertaking, from the beginning, eternal election (Eph. 1:5–6; Rom. 9:22–23) through the middle, deliverance in time (Titus 2:14), to the end, eternal beatification (Titus 3:7). For resplendent in redemption is the glory: (1) of holiness, hatred against sin, and avenging justice, whereby that he might not let sin go unpunished, he substituted his Son, his very own and only begotten Son, for the sinner, laid on him the entire guilt of the elect sinner, and for him made him to be sin, indeed, a curse (Isa. 53:4–6, 10; 2 Cor. 5:21; Gal. 3:13). What is more, in this one act of vengeance taken up by his own Son, a greater rigor of divine justice is evident than if he had condemned the whole world. The glory (2) of love for mankind, grace, and mercy, which God extols (Rom. 5:7–8), and the Redeemer himself marvels at (John 3:16), and the apostles celebrate—Paul (Eph. 2:4–5; Titus 3:4–5), John (1 John 3:1)—which certainly is most illustrious in this, that for a wretched sinner, guilty of having wounded his infinite majesty, he did not merely pardon the offense, but furnished his very own and only begotten Son, to be made sin and a curse for him. The glory (3) of infinite wisdom, the manifold wisdom of God, which deserves to be revealed to the heavenly principalities and powers themselves (Eph. 3:10), for which reason the

apostle deservedly cries out, "O the depth of the riches both of the wisdom and knowledge of God! How unsearchable are his judgments, and his ways past finding out!" (Rom. 11:33–34). And what could be more amazing to think of than that he exercises infinite avenging justice and infinite mercy at the same time in the same thing?

For what reasons God preferred to bless man through redemption from sin, rather than through preservation from sin

We will recognize this wisdom yet more clearly if, with a comparison made between the beatification of man according to the tenor of the covenant of works, through preservation from sin, and the beatification of the sinner according to the tenor of the covenant of grace, through redemption, we should weigh the reasons whereby the divine wisdom was adduced to prefer redemption to preservation. For it could hardly be out of place for you to wonder, since God undoubtedly could have preserved man with no trouble from the fall, just as he preserved the blessed angels, what cause there was for God to permit sin, a thing so base and so detestable to him, and which could not be removed without the substitution of his very own and only begotten Son, and without a death inflicted upon him so strictly. But if you should weigh the matter devoutly, you will grasp that the path of redemption pleased God more than the path of preservation, because in many ways a richer glory arises for him from the latter than from the former method of beatifying. For if: (1) he had beatified man by preservation from sins, like the good angels, or if he had condemned him by strict rejection of him, like the evil angels, he would not have supplied so glorious a specimen of wisdom, power, and mercy, because he was able also to beatify a sinner. He had supplied a specimen of grace in preserving the good angels from sin, and in confirming them in an immovable state of perfection; he likewise had supplied a specimen of justice and rigor in the eternal rejection of the evil angels (2 Peter 2:4; Jude 6); there was still yet for him to supply a specimen of wisdom, power, and mercy, whereby he could save and beatify a sinner; from which Christ is called the wisdom and power of God (1 Cor. 1:24; Eph. 1:19). If (2) he had beatified man through preservation from sin, so that he needed no mediator, then he would have been deprived of that entire glory with which he now shines in his Son the Mediator, who is so glorious, and in every way perfect (John 13:31, 32), from which splendor we read of the gospel of the glory of Christ, who is the image of the invisible God, and of the knowledge of the glory of God in the face of Jesus Christ (2 Cor. 4:4, 6), and the Savior himself is said to be the brightness of the Father's glory, and the express image of his person, who, once the purging of our sins was completed, was set upon the right hand of the throne of the majesty on high (Heb. 1:3). And this glorification of the Father in the Son as Mediator is frequently made known as the supreme goal of the entirety of redemption (Phil. 2:9–11; Rom. 6:4), and from it the Son is said to have glorified and to glorify the Father (John 17:4). If (3) he had beatified man by preservation, then the Son of God would have lacked, so to speak, his entire mediatorial glory which arose to him from the glorious task of redemption (on which see Eph. 1:20–22; Phil. 2:9–10), which, after his own glorification, God primarily intended through the entire work of redemption (John 5:22–23). So much so that although Christ, in all that he is, in many ways exists for us (Eph. 5:2), yet on the other hand, we in more ways exist for him: namely, just as Christ supplies to God the means of our beatification, so also we, and even more, supply to God the means of his Son's glorification (Phil. 2:10–11). If (4) he had beatified man by preservation, he certainly would not have had the opportunity of manifesting in the sinner the glory of such great goodness, love, and mercy, as now shines through redemption (John 3:16; 1 John 3:1; Titus 3:4; Eph. 3:18–19). If (5) he had beatified man by preservation, he would not have been "manifested in the flesh…seen by angels" (1 Tim. 3:16), and thus the immeasurable deity, invisible and inaccessible to us, would as it were have remained hidden eternally in itself (1 Tim. 1:17; 6:16; Ex. 33:20), whereas now it is visible in the Son, the God-Man Mediator (John 14:9–10; Job 19:27). If (6) he had beatified man by preservation, God would not have been made so near to man (Deut. 4:7), as now he is in the incarnate Son (Prov. 8:30–31), nor would it have been right for man to draw near with such great boldness to God as is certainly now granted to him in the incarnate Son (Heb. 4:16; Eph. 3:12). If (7) he had beatified man by preservation, then there would not be such a great dependence of man upon God, nor such frequent access to God through faith and prayers, as now there is that sin exists, and a greater need and necessity (1 Peter 3:18; Rom. 5:2; Eph. 3:12). If (8) he had beatified man by preservation, then neither would the foulness and horror of sin, inasmuch as it would be nonexistent, nor the beauty and grace of holiness, from opposition, be as illustrious as they are now that sin exists (Isa. 1:15–16; Ps. 5:4–6). Nor (9) would the obligation of man to offer every duty to God have been so great, from only creation and the promise of the covenant of works, as it certainly is now, from redemption and new creation, which are superadded to the prior (1 Cor. 6:20; Titus 2:12–14). Nor (10) for man in his integrity would such great humiliation and denial of himself have been necessary, as now is from sin (Luke 14:11; Rom. 7:24; Luke 5:8). Nor (11) would the estate of blessed immortality, if sin or redemption did not exist, have been so clearly explained to man, and presented in Scripture, as it certainly stands explained now (2 Tim. 1:10; 3:16). Nor (12) would eternal salvation stand on so firm and immovable a footing in the native strength of a fallible will, as it certainly now does, supported by the merits and intercession of the God-man Mediator (1 Tim. 1:12; John 17:2; 6:39; 10:26–29). From these points (which seemed good to present a little more distinctly, as they are more rarely observed and inculcated) and others, is evident the manifold wisdom of God, shining forth in the matter of redemption, to the glory of God.

To what end these must be meditated upon
Now it is our task: (1) by meditating on the indescribable act of redemption, to studiously trace out the arguments of this glorification, with the prophets, indeed with the blessed angels themselves (1 Peter 1:10–12); (2) according to its dignity, to celebrate it, and exalt it with praises among others, with the heavenly host of angels (Luke 2:9–10, 13–14; Eph. 3:9–11; 1 Peter 2:9); and finally, (3) in our whole manner of life, to promptly and freely refer to God such great glory for this redemption, especially by glorifying him in his Son, such a glorious Mediator (Luke 1:68–69, 71–72), about which we will say more in what follows.

3. It commends the glory of the Redeemer.
XLVI. Third, at the same time redemption commends the Redeemer and his glory, indeed that glory which God primarily intended through this whole business of redemption (John 5:23; 12:23), which glory even the Redeemer himself seeks from the Father as the reward of redemption (John 17:1, 4), which glory the Father repays to him with such great magnificence as the reward of the redemption, obtained by his most profound humiliation (Phil. 2:8–10; Eph. 1:19–22; Heb. 1:3), which glory the heavenly host, the apocalyptic beasts, the elders, and the myriads of myriads so magnificently pour out to him, from this very head of redemption (Rev. 5:8–12), which glory the apostle strives after with such great ardor, whether by life or by death (Phil. 1:20). It commends, I say, the glory: (1) not only of the mediatorial dignity, which we spoke about above in chapter 2; nor only (2) the glory of so many most glorious names and titles, which we spoke about in chapter 3; nor only (3) the glory of the person of the God-man, which we observed in chapter 4; nor only (4) the glory of the threefold function, prophetic, high-priestly, and kingly, which we noted in chapters 6–8; nor only (5) the glory of the most profound four-part humiliation, which we expounded in chapters 9–13; nor only (6) the glory of the triple exaltation, which we presented in chapters 14–17, which glory, so manifold and so great, of the Redeemer entirely unburdens itself in this one head of redemption; but specifically, (7) the glory of redemption itself, whereby, in utterly astounding kindness toward mankind (φιλανθρωπία, Titus 3:4), and love (Eph. 5:2), he expends not only what he has, but himself, in all that he is (Eph. 5:2); not for the righteous,

but for sinners, rebels, those guilty of high treason, and enemies of his Father (Rom. 5:6–8); nor does he expend himself simply, but in such a way that he substituted himself for them, and took upon himself every punishment applicable to them; and that not only to the end that he might free them from all ill (Gal. 3:13; 2 Cor. 5:21), but also that he might acquire the right to every good (2 Cor. 1:20; Eph. 1:3; 1 Cor. 3:22–23), to such a point that, since even God's infinite goodness itself, although naturally communicative of itself, could not unfold itself to them, given the obstacles of the violation of the covenant of works, the demerit of sin, the threats of the law, and the clamors of avenging justice, now with all obstacles removed through this redemption, the divine goodness unloads and pours itself upon them, with every blessing (Eph. 1:3)—of justification, of adoption, of sanctification, of glorification—so that now with redemption supplied, they have access with confidence (Eph. 3:12; 2:18), they can draw from his fullness grace for grace (John 1:16), they are complete in him (Col. 2:10), and for them he is all in all (Col. 3:11).

To what end it commends it

Redemption thus commends this glory of the Redeemer, so that: (1) we may be frequent, indeed assiduous, in devout contemplation of this glorious redemption (Eph. 3:17–19); that (2) we may glorify the Redeemer on this account, in our body and spirit (1 Cor. 6:20); that (3) we may exalt the Redeemer above all things, and on account of him count everything as of no consequence, as loss, as dung, that we may gain him alone (Phil. 3:7–9; Heb. 11:24–26).

4. It commends the most blessed lot of the redeemed, from five heads.

XLVII. Fourth, redemption commends to us the most blessed lot of the redeemed, in which the blessed angels rejoice with them (Luke 2:10–11; 15:7), as indeed does God himself (Luke 15:23–24, 32). For if they should weigh: (1) the lot from which they have been delivered by this redemption, the evils so many and so great: (a) wrath, hatred, and enmity with God, against which David so anxiously pleaded (Ps. 6:1; 38:1); (b) spiritual slavery, worse than that of Egypt (Ex. 1:11–14; 2:23; 5:13–14 with Luke 1:68–69, 71); (c) death, hell, and the eternal curse (1 Cor. 15:55–56; Gal. 3:13); (d) that whole body of death, about which the apostle so complains in Romans 7:24, "O wretched man that I am! Who will deliver me from this body of death?"; (e) the torments of hell (Ps. 18:4–6; 116:3), that cup that was so bitter for the Redeemer himself (Matt. 26:37–39); indeed, (f) that eternal separation from the highest good, indeed from all good, with the resulting intolerable torments (Matt. 25:41, 46; Isa. 66:24; Mark 9:44). If on the contrary they should weigh (2) the goods so many and so great, the right to which was acquired for them by this redemption, for example: (a) reconciliation and peace with God (2 Cor. 5:19, 21; Rom. 5:1), his love, grace, and benevolence (Rom. 5:5; Luke 2:14), friendship and familiarity with him (John 15:15); (b) the freedom to come to God with confidence in any necessity (Rom. 5:2; Eph. 2:18; 3:12; Heb. 10:22); (c) the communication of every blessing (Gal. 3:13–14; Eph. 1:3; 2 Peter 1:3; Col. 2:9–10; John 1:16); (d) peace and tranquility of heart, comfort in all adversities, unspeakable joy (Matt. 11:28–29; Rom. 5:1–3; 1 Peter 1:8); (e) eternal life itself (John 3:16; Acts 4:12; John 14:6); (f) and its immovable certainty (John 10:27–28; Rom. 8:32, 38–39; 1 Peter 1:2–5). If (3) they should weigh the manner of acquiring it, in which they have not been redeemed through mere power, nor through prayers only, or by entreaty, but through the substitution of God's very own and only begotten Son (Rom. 8:32; Eph. 5:2, 25), whereby he endured the entirety of those things that were incumbent upon them due to sin, even to the curse (Gal. 3:13; 2 Cor. 5:21; Isa. 53:4, 10). So that now this redemption applies to them not from the mere grace of the Father, but also from justice, on account of the satisfaction and merit of the Son of God (Rom. 8:33–34). If (4) they should weigh the cause and font of this redemption, the superlative and plainly amazing love of the Father (John 3:16; Rom. 5:8; 1 John 3:1), and of the Son (Eph. 5:2, 25), specifically toward them. If (5) they should weigh that this redemption was procured not for angels (Heb. 2:15–16; 2 Peter 2:4; Jude 6; Rev. 20:2), nor for each and every person (John 17:9), but for them exclusively, whom the Father gave to the Son to be redeemed (John 17:6, 9). Compare, with the necessary changes made, what we have said on this matter in chapter 12, §XXXI.

5. *It presents the misery of the unredeemed.* What their misery is
XLVIII. Fifth, it presents on the contrary the indescribable misery of the unredeemed (Eph. 2:1–3, 11–12; Heb. 3:3 with vv. 10–11, 17–18), through which (1) not only are they liable to all those evils from which the redeemed were delivered, as we mentioned in the previous section; but (2) they are also deprived of all those benefits, so many and so great, which the redeemed rejoice in and enjoy (per the preceding section). Indeed in addition, (3) from the redemption of the Mediator itself, to what a frightful extent their misery grows! For since: (a) God, led by pure love, gave the Redeemer to the world (John 3:16), and gave as the Redeemer his very Son, his own Son (Rom. 8:32), his only begotten Son (John 3:16), his most beloved Son (Eph. 1:6; Matt. 3:17); since (b) he substituted him for sinners, and cast all their guilt upon him (Isa. 53), made him to be sin for us, that we might be made righteousness before him (2 Cor. 5:21), and indeed a curse (Gal. 3:13); since (c) he indiscriminately offers him to be received by faith

(John 3:16), indeed invites them with the most excellent inducements and promises to receive him (Isa. 55:1–2); since (d) the Redeemer himself is so inclined to bestow his redemption, so liberally offers it, and insists with such great effort that we would receive him (Matt. 11:28–30; John 7:37–38; Rev. 3:20; 22:17; Song 5:2); since (e) nothing stands in the way of their becoming partakers of such a great redemption, except their pure rebellion and intransigence (Matt. 22:3–5; 23:37; John 5:40)—will not the misery of the unredeemed increase immeasurably from all these things (Heb. 3:3 with vv. 10–11, 17–18)?

Who the miserable are
But who are these unredeemed? (1) Those who do not at all profess either a redeemer or redemption, such as the heathen, Muslims, and Jews, unless perhaps only a temporal one, such as the Jews. (2) Those who do profess with their mouth, but in reality deny him, and profess such a redeemer who did not redeem, but only announced redemption, such as the Socinians, who utterly deny the substitution or vicarious punishments of the Redeemer, and the equivalence of Christ's death with our guilt. (3) Those who do profess a redeemer, but only partly, one who delivered only from eternal punishments, but not from temporal ones, and who obtained for us the right of meriting, rather than in fact meriting for us the right to eternal life, such as the papists. (4) Those who have themselves, if not totally, at least partially, as their redeemers, when they seek their salvation in the strength of their free choice, in their own satisfactions, in the merits of their own good works, or in others besides Christ, in the intercessions and supererogatory merits of the angels, of the blessed Virgin, of other inhabitants of heaven, or at least in obedience to the commandments of Christ, such as, although in different degrees, the Socinians, Anabaptists, Arminians, and others. (5) Those who do acknowledge and profess Christ alone as the all-sufficient Redeemer, but yet do not seek redemption from him, such as those who at least profess the Reformed faith, but do not live it.

What the causes of the misery are
And what are the causes of this evil? (1) There is gross ignorance, in open unbelievers (Rom. 10:3; Ps. 79:6); (2) heresy, in the Socinians, papists, Arminians, and others, who seek redemption either totally or partially outside of the only Redeemer, Jesus (Acts 4:12; John 14:6; 1 Tim. 2:5; Gal. 5:4; Rom. 10:3); (3) negligence, whereby even those who profess Christ as the only Redeemer, do not know themselves (2 Cor. 13:5), and do not feel their own misery (Rev. 3:17; Matt. 19:20); (4) hopelessness, whereby they sense more sin in themselves than either mercy in God or sufficiency in the Redeemer (Gen. 4:13; Matt. 27:3–5); (5) timidity, whereby from consciousness of their own foulness, although they

accept the sufficiency of the Redeemer, yet they do not dare to take themselves to him with confidence (Luke 18:13; 5:8; Isa. 33:14; Ezek. 33:11). Which causes, in the healing of this misery, must be carefully removed with the analogous remedies. One may consult, with the appropriate changes made, chapter 12, §XXXII.

6. It commands us to inquire whether he also redeemed us. Motives
XLIX. Sixth, redemption commands us to earnestly inquire whether Christ also redeemed us. For since: (1) he did not redeem each and every person (per §§XXI, XXIV); since (2) so great is the blessedness of the redeemed (per §XLVII); since (3) so great is the misery of the unredeemed (per §XLVIII); since (4) upon a devout exploration of ourselves depends, if not redemption itself, at least its certainty (2 Cor. 13:5), and all the sweetest results of this certainty—peace and tranquility of conscience, comfort, joy, and the undoubted persuasion of eternal life itself—there is altogether reason why we should earnestly inquire whether he also redeemed us.

Signs
But by what marks will we certainly attain to this? I respond, The first mark is available from the object, to which we demonstrated redemption has been restricted (§XXI), if namely we be living members of the Redeemer's church, belonging to the sheep, not the goats, belonging to his people, and so forth. Second, from the means by which the Redeemer, with his redemption, is ours, that is, living faith (John 3:16; 1:12), by which we are united with the Redeemer (Gal. 2:20; Eph. 3:17), and we obtain the communion of his righteousness (Phil. 3:9). Third, from its chief result, namely reconciliation, whereby the Redeemer not only placated God toward us, but also us in turn toward God, from which it follows that if we feel our heart in us placated toward God, casting away all acts and arms of hostility, namely sins, and bearing itself as a friend of God (Titus 3:3–4; Acts 5:39; 23:9), we have been certainly redeemed. Fourth, from its chief fruit, fleeing ungodliness, carnal desires, and empty conversation, and the opposite zeal for godliness, righteousness, and temperance (Titus 2:12–14; 1 Peter 1:18). Compare, with necessary changes made, chapter 12, §XXXIII.

7. It raises us up so that we may strive for the communion of redemption.
Motivating reasons
L. Seventh, it raises us up so that we may strive with all zeal for the communion of this redemption, with the apostle persuading us (2 Cor. 5:19–20) and lighting the way by his own example (Rom. 7:24, "O wretched man that I am! Who shall deliver me?"), and with him in addition, Peter's audience at Pentecost (Acts

2:37), and the jailer (Acts 16:30), and the publican (Luke 18:13); and also with the following persuading us: (1) the very nature of the thing. For if God, adduced neither by necessity, nor by hope of profit or gain, but rather by pure love toward man (John 3:16; Rom. 5:8; 1 John 3:1), sought out a method of redemption, prepared it, substituted his Son, his very own Son, his only begotten and most beloved Son, for sinners to be redeemed, and laid on him their entire guilt, and if the Son of God gave himself up that they might be redeemed, then what kind of madness would it be to neglect so great a redemption, procured at so great a price (1 Cor. 6:20; 1 Peter 1:19)? To count it as of no consequence (Matt. 22:2–5)? (2) Such great abundance of such great evils, from which redemption delivers us, according to §XLVIII. (3) Such great weight and abundance of indescribable benefits (2 Cor. 4:17–18), which we spoke about in §XLVII. (4) So generous an offering he made, so effectual an invitation, by the enticements of so many and such great promises (Isa. 55:1–2; Matt. 11:28–29; 22:2–3). (5) The easiness of the stipulated condition to partake of redemption (Matt. 11:30; 1 John 5:3; cf. Mic. 6:6–7), insofar as for accepting redemption, God does not stipulate anything but that we take hold of the Redeemer and redemption with true faith (John 1:12; 3:16). Finally, (6) the harsh and unavoidable necessity, insofar as we must either be redeemed, or eternally perish (John 3:16, 36)

Means
But, what is necessary for us to do that we may be made partakers of this redemption? (1) We must be on guard against: (a) all perverse means of redemption, whereby (b) we promise ourselves redemption, either within ourselves, whether from the strength of our own choice, or from our own satisfactions by sufferings, or from virtues and the merits of our good works; or outside ourselves, from blessed inhabitants of heaven, or the intercessions of the living; or anywhere outside of Christ alone (Phil. 3:7–9; Gal. 6:14; 1 Cor. 2:2; Rom. 10:3–4; Gal. 5:2, 4). Next, we must also be on guard against (c) the prejudices of the common crowd, whereby we promise ourselves redemption from the pure mercy of God, without any satisfaction of Christ, through the mere pardoning of our sins, or through some kind of universal redemption. We must be on guard against (d) vain imaginations, whereby we promise ourselves redemption either from the intercessions of the godly (Ex. 8:8; 28; 1 Sam. 2:25), or from our own groans at the moment of death, "God be merciful to me," and so forth. Rather, (2) we must strive to gain in time a sufficient knowledge of the nature of our redemption through the satisfaction and merit of the Redeemer (Acts 4:12; John 14:6; 1 Tim. 2:5), and that so that we would not be led astray. Hence, (3) we must do this so that we may have (a) a practical and experimental knowledge of sin (Luke

15:21, "Father, I have sinned"; Ps. 51:3); (b) a sense of unavoidable misery from sin (Rom. 7:24), so that from both we may grow in the acknowledgment of the redemption we need (Rom. 7:24, "Who shall deliver me?"); (c) a saving despair of our own and anyone else's sufficiency for our redemption (Rom. 7:24; Ps. 49:7–8; 130:3; 143:2); (d) an acknowledgment of the sufficiency and fullness which is in Christ Jesus for redemption (Phil. 3:8–9; John 1:14, 16; Eph. 3:8; Ps. 73:25); (e) a departure to Christ alone (Phil. 3:8–9; John 6:67–68; Matt. 11:28); (f) an agreement to any of the conditions stipulated of us by him for participation in redemption (Luke 9:23; Gal. 5:24); (g) a confident laying hold upon him (John 1:12), and resting in him alone (Isa. 10:20; Ps. 73:25). About these things we will speak more specifically in their own place.[44]

8. It supplies the most effective comfort to the redeemed. Arguments for comfort
LI. Eighth, it supplies the most effective comfort to the redeemed, and a panacea as it were against any ill in life and in death, because: (1) they have a Redeemer (Job 19:25); (2) such a one who is God Most High (Ps. 78:35; Isa. 44:6, 24 with Rom. 9:5), and hence can and did deliver; who likewise is man, in all points tempted like they are, so that he is able and willing to sympathize with them (Heb. 4:15; 2:17); and thus who is the God-man. (3) They have such a Redeemer who, although he knew no sin, substituted himself for all their guilt, who was made to be sin for them (2 Cor. 5:21), indeed a curse (Gal. 3:13), so that he might take away everything accursed from them (Rom. 8:1). (4) They have such a Redeemer who offered for their guilt a redemption price exactly equivalent from the rigor of divine justice, indeed a price altogether infinite, to which then redemption is owed from the immovable justice of God itself. Therefore, (5) in him is supplied to them a certain redemption (1 Cor. 1:30), a manifold redemption, indeed a redemption of every sort (Ps. 130:7–8), so that outside of him there is no redemption (Acts 4:12); (6) such a redemption that by his own precious blood (1 Peter 1:18–19; Acts 20:28) he acquired them for himself as his own possession (Titus 2:14; 1 Cor. 6:19–20); (7) such a redemption that he has a care of them that is as exact as that of his own self (Ps. 105:15; Acts 9:4; Matt. 10:40), and he preserves them, even to the hair on their head (Matt. 10:29–31), and also directs adversities of any kind to their advantage (Rom. 8:28).

Cases in which redemption provides comfort
Hence: (1) if a disease presses in, their Redeemer took upon himself and carried all their diseases (Isa. 53:4), and heals all their infirmities (Ps. 103:3; Matt.

---

44. e.g. 1.6.2 §§XXIV–XXV

8:17). If (2) want of any necessities, he himself, though he was rich, for our sakes became poor (2 Cor. 8:9; Matt. 8:20). If (3) contempt and debasement, he freely accepted every kind of insult on behalf of his own (Ps. 69:7–9; Isa. 50:5). If (4) the most atrocious persecutions, he also suffered them on behalf of his own (Ps. 69:26; 22:16). If (5) sin, he was made to be sin for his own, so that they might be made righteousness before God (2 Cor. 5:21). If (6) death, he died for his own (Rom. 5:6, 8). If (7) eternal condemnation, he was made a curse for his own (Gal. 3:13). If (8) anguish of soul and spiritual desertions, his soul was exceeding sorrowful for his own, even to death (Matt. 26:37–38); abandoned by his Father for his own, he cried out, "My God, my God, why have you forsaken me?" (Ps. 22:1; Matt. 27:46). And all these things the Redeemer accepted for this purpose, that he might deliver his own from them all (Isa. 53:5). What great redemption—O good God—is in these things! What great comfort is in this redemption! If only by certain marks they be persuaded that the Redeemer is *theirs*, so that they may say with Job, "I know that my Redeemer lives" (Job 19:25), and with Paul, "who loved *me*, and gave himself for *me*" (Gal. 2:20).

9. It inculcates the duties that must be observed after redemption.
LII. Ninth, it inculcates in us, that now having been made partakers of redemption, we should conduct ourselves as those redeemed (Luke 1:74), that is, that we should model the ends of redemption throughout our whole life, which will be done: if (1) even after redemption we cultivate a knowledge and sense of sin, as most foul and detestable (Rom. 7:24; Ps. 51:3), inasmuch as from it none but the very Son of God himself was able to redeem us, and indeed having been substituted for our guilt, and bearing all we had to bear. If (2) due to our redemption, we also attend both to God, who procures for us by his indescribable love and grace the Redeemer and redemption (John 3:16), and to the redeeming Mediator, with great esteem and affection (Luke 7:47; Phil. 3:7–9; 1 Peter 2:4, 6–7). If (3) redemption, procured for us with such difficulty and at such great price, through the satisfaction and merit of the Son of God, shapes us to profound humility (Gen. 32:10). If (4) it makes us dependent in all things upon God, and upon the Savior and his grace (1 Cor. 15:10; 2 Cor. 3:5–6), upon whom we safely lean (Song 8:5; Isa. 10:20). If (5) it strikes us with a godly amazement at the purest holiness of God (Hab. 1:13), his despising of sin (Ps. 5:4–6), and his severest justice toward the sinner (Lev. 10:2–3), which in the business of redemption he has rendered by far most illustrious (Rom. 8:32). If (6) it daily places before our eyes, to be pondered and marveled at, the kindness of God toward man (Titus 3:4), his incomprehensible love (John 3:16), his most tender mercy toward miserable man (Ps. 8:4; Heb. 2:6–7), which, if they shine anywhere, it is certainly in

the matter of redemption (Rom. 5:8; 1 John 3:1). If (7) it effectively lifts us up to a reciprocal love, and to a zeal for gratitude, for a redemption obtained for us at such a great price (Rom. 7:24; 12:1–2; 1 Cor. 15:54–58; Luke 1:68–69). If (8) it provokes us, in gratitude, to an earnest zeal for holiness and righteousness (Luke 1:74; Titus 2:11–14; 1 Cor. 6:19–20).

10. It stirs up everyone, and especially preachers, to strive to make others partakers of this redemption. Motives

LIII. Tenth, the example of the Redeemer and the redemption of Christ should stir up everyone, and especially preachers,[45] according to their office or by reason of their gifts, to strive with all zeal to make others partakers of this redemption. The basis of this practice is laid in 2 Corinthians 5:18–21. And so that they may do this more promptly and courageously, they should think: (1) with how much fervor the best and greatest God, from the eternal counsel of peace up to this present time, has done, is doing, and will do until the end of the world, for this business of redemption (John 3:16; Rom. 5:8). They should think (2) at what great price the only begotten Son of God obtained that redemption for miserable sinners (1 Cor. 6:19–20; 1 Peter 1:18–19; Acts 20:28). They should think (3) that this business of redemption, the διακονία τῆς καταλλαγῆς, ministry of reconciliation, has been laid upon them by God (2 Cor. 5:18; 1 Cor. 9:16). They should think (4) that they in this manner have become συνεργοί, fellow laborers, with God (1 Cor. 3:9); indeed, (5) in their own way, saviors of men, with Christ (1 Tim. 4:16; Acts 26:18; 2 Tim. 2:25–26). They should think (6) of the brilliant promises, and fullest rewards of this work (Dan. 12:3; 1 Thess. 2:19; 1 Cor. 9:17, 24–26).

Means

But in what way will they spread the redemption of Christ, and save others? (1) By proclaiming the Word of reconciliation that God has placed in them, and that with all affection and fervor (2 Cor. 5:19–20; 2 Tim. 4:2); (2) by lighting the way everywhere with their examples (1 Tim. 4:15–16; 1 Cor. 9:20–22); (3) by bearing any adversities for this redemption of others, that after the example of Christ who redeemed by suffering, they also in their own way should suffer for those that will be redeemed, and by suffering, fill up as it were the ὑστερήματα τῶν θλίψεων τοῦ Χριστοῦ, things lacking in Christ's afflictions, for the sake of his body, which is the church (Col. 1:24).

---

45. *Ecclesiastas*

Scripture Index

Exodus (*continued*)

32:9	370
32:33	62, 130, 587, 604
33:2	442
33:3	370
33:19	591
33:20	635
34:6	50
34:6–7	213, 621
34:7	597, 621
34:9	621
34:10	22
35:19	235
35:21	235
40:35	294

Leviticus

1:5	587
3:1	313
3:2	587
4:3	99
4:4	230
4:5	235
4:15	230
4:20	602
4:20–21	175
4:24	214, 230
4:28	230
4:29	230
4:31	602
4:33	230
4:35	602
5:11	222
6:18	191
6:22	191
6:23	226
7:16–18	503
8	235
8:10–11	213
10:2–3	163, 643
10:10–11	234
10:11	207
10:17	592, 593
11:25	235
11:43	369

12:2	310
12:2–4	348
12:6–8	348
12:7	313
14:4–7	34
16	214, 538
16:2	212
16:2–4	213
16:11–12	215
16:15–16	215
16:20	592
16:26	605
16:28	605
17:11	593
18:5	32, 193, 485, 594, 598, 602
19:18	369, 370
19:22	228
19:28	455
20:11–12	266
20:14	266
20:17	266
20:19–25	266
21:1	455
21:10–15	213
21:12	212
21:13	337
21:18–21	235
22:22	235
23:15	502
24:16	450
25:8	502
25:25	64, 408
26:14–40	378
26:19	287
27:32	234

Numbers

2:19	407
3:13	348
4:47	351
5:2	455
6:23	207, 216, 217, 225, 228
6:23–24	214
8:16	302

Deuteronomy (*continued*)

28:57	3, 8, 309
29:1–2	25
29:4	25
29:9	52, 53
29:10–11	25
29:12	26, 53
29:14	26
29:14–15	25
29:18	401
29:19–21	52
29:24	24
29:25	52
29:25–27	52
30:1–9	24
30:6	347
30:15	40
31:6	476
31:8	476
31:20	52
32:6–7	53
32:10	119
32:11	293
32:12	108
32:15	113
32:22	455
32:35	193
33:10	234
33:20	454
33:28	573
34:9	176n10
34:10	175, 176, 182, 195, 373n49

Joshua

1:17	196
7:21	272
10:24	567
23:26	52
24	265
24:14–26	53
24:15	382
24:15–16	22
24:21–22	22
24:25	22

Judges

2:1	26
3:9	587
6:13	390
6:37	300, 302, 311
7:14	89
9:7	353
13:18	196, 296
14:6	293
16:3	457, 503, 507
16:7	274
16:11	274
17:10	234
18:7	265
18:19	234

Ruth

1:20	298
2:20	64
3:9	337
3:12–13	131

1 Samuel

1:10	340
1:11	382
1:22	382
1:24	382
1:25	382
2:1	497
2:6	240, 462, 475
2:8	497
2:13	234
2:18	384
2:25	641
2:30	497
2:34	311
3:10	288
6:19	164
8:7	266
8:15	6
10:2–3	311
10:5	399
10:6	201
10:10–13	201
12:12	266

Psalms (*continued*)

17:6	495
17:9	356
17:10	406
17:10–12	368
17:12	70, 502
17:18	354
17:21	363, 391
17:22–23	360
17:23	502, 505
17:27	354, 359, 586
18:1–9	500
18:5	160, 196
18:5–6	334
18:6	529
18:7	197
18:8	473
18:10	65, 558
18:15–19	359
18:15–22	244
18:18	249
18:19	359
18:19–20	86
18:20	156, 167, 198, 251, 333, 488, 582
18:25	84
18:26	591
18:26–27	621
18:27	79, 589
18:32	425
18:34	413, 436, 508
18:34–35	84, 443, 451
18:35	79
19:2	354
19:3	370
19:8–9	370
19:13–14	382
19:16–17	602
19:17	598, 629
19:20	639
19:22	370
19:23	557
19:27	52, 334, 385, 439, 556
19:27–28	557, 558
19:27–29	263
19:28	260, 290

19:28–30	491
19:29	385, 556
20:1	262
20:2	262
20:4	262
20:15	589
20:16	25, 31, 33, 58, 199, 233, 587
20:17–19	438
20:18	360
20:20–21	334
20:20–24	333
20:21	246, 491, 565
20:21–22	122
20:21–23	438
20:23	75
20:25–26	122
20:28	65, 75, 80, 90, 103, 122, 143, 147, 158, 159, 199, 212, 213, 214, 248, 304, 346, 378, 408, 416, 425, 427, 433, 442, 443, 537, 583–87, 587, 592, 593, 599
20:34	122, 354, 359
21:2	404
21:2–3	358
21:3	266
21:4–5	253
21:5	532
21:7	564
21:7–8	266
21:9	297
21:12	359
21:12–13	359
21:14	354, 355
21:18	357
21:19	354, 355
21:25	188
21:25–26	250
21:27	188
21:28	199
21:37	172
21:45	199
21:45–46	353

Mark (*continued*)

8:1	354
8:3	121
8:8–9	354
8:25	354
8:26	356
8:31	360, 505
8:34	393
8:35	497
8:36	496
8:38	159, 497
9:2	541
9:35	354
9:31	277, 360
9:37	160, 196
9:41	198
9:44	637
10:13–14	382
10:14	301
10:24	197
10:26	197
10:33–34	277
10:33	360
10:45	65, 587, 593
11:13	137, 327
11:23–24	442
13:22–23	197
13:32	137, 138, 147, 155, 327, 375
14:1	409
14:3	409
14:10–11	409
14:12–18	409
14:17–22	409
14:21	529
14:22–27	409
14:24	347
14:27–32	409
14:32–42	409
14:33	415
14:33–34	357
14:35	215, 413
14:36	415
14:41	443
14:43–53	409
14:46	411
14:48–49	411
14:49	200
14:53	410, 411
14:54	410
14:55–61	410
14:55–64	411
14:61–66	410
14:62	568
14:65	357, 411
14:66	410
14:67	350
15:1	410
15:2–6	410
15:2–15	411
15:7–14	410
15:10	412
15:14	412
15:15	410, 591
15:16	416
15:16–20	411
15:16–22	410
15:17	357, 399
15:19	357
15:20	399, 411, 450
15:21	412
15:22–36	411
15:23	401, 410, 411
15:24–25	357
15:25	404
15:26	410
15:27–28	450
15:27–33	410
15:28	403
15:33	354
15:33–34	410
15:34	406, 414, 475
15:35–37	410
15:37	407, 418
15:38–40	410
15:40	410
15:42	459n13
15:42–43	461
15:43	460, 475
15:44	471

John (*continued*)

16:5	547
16:6	554
16:6–7	551
16:7	214, 216, 231, 323, 452, 483, 503, 508, 538, 539, 542, 547, 554, 571, 572
16:7–8	552
16:7–16	244
16:8–11	21
16:9–11	85
16:11	482, 581
16:12–13	573
16:13	201
16:13–14	187, 486
16:15	482
16:16–17	539n5
16:20	197
16:21	302, 339
16:23	82, 178, 197, 232, 551, 552
16:23–24	216, 224
16:26	216, 555
16:26–27	231
16:28	156, 190, 537, 538, 539, 540, 547, 550
16:33	267, 482, 571
17	224, 360, 378, 389, 549
17:1	88, 215, 290, 480, 486, 579, 636
17:1–2	484, 599
17:2	19, 215, 636
17:3	83, 87, 92, 110, 558
17:4	359, 480, 532, 635, 636
17:4–5	17, 483, 570
17:5	112, 154, 253, 278, 281, 290, 574, 579
17:6	110, 638
17:6–7	627
17:8	187
17:9	19, 61, 75, 81, 103, 215, 216, 219, 233, 234, 332, 417, 427, 433, 562, 586, 599, 638
17:9–10	215
17:11	17, 61, 156
17:11–13	547
17:12	82, 433, 613, 627
17:13	347
17:15	82, 231
17:17	17
17:19	599, 628, 629, 630
17:20	215, 216, 483
17:20–21	234
17:21	134, 166, 231
17:24	17, 19, 61, 167, 215, 230, 231, 245, 259, 497, 514, 542, 552, 557, 561, 562, 573, 599
17:26	110
18:1	409
18:4	431
18:4–6	587
18:6	412
18:7–8	431
18:12	411
18:13–14	411
18:15–27	410
18:19–24	410, 411
18:22	369
18:24	357
18:28	410
18:28–39	410
18:28–40	411
18:33–38	242, 243
18:33	66, 173, 246
18:36	66, 121, 173, 221, 238, 240, 242, 245, 246, 248, 267, 360, 532
18:37	253, 359, 537
18:38	431
18:38–40	410
19:1	357, 397, 410, 473
19:1–16	411
19:2	357, 416
19:4	412
19:4–15	410
19:6	413, 431
19:7	411, 450
19:9–10	442
19:10	244

Revelation (*continued*)

17:14	121, 173, 242, 267, 290, 566
18:7	287
19:8	519
19:10	321, 494, 520
19:11	86, 432
19:11–17	482
19:13	125, 413
19:15	16, 266, 413, 414
19:16	121, 174, 242, 248, 263, 266, 290, 334, 494
19:19	244, 266, 580
19:20	581
20	258
20:1–3	244
20:1–8	257
20:2	5, 242, 469, 599, 638
20:3	258, 469
20:6	102, 118, 529, 531, 534
20:7–9	244
20:10	245, 469
20:13–14	455
20:14–15	245
21:1	245, 256, 546
21:1–4	244
21:2	245
21:5	245
21:7	267
21:10	557
22:3	263
22:5	245
22:8	321, 494
22:14	117
22:16	305
22:17	49, 63, 82, 86, 117, 123, 179, 216, 417, 433, 639
22:18–19	187
22:20	179
22:23	88